About the editors

SIDNEY RATNER, Professor of History at Rutgers, The State University, has been an authority on Dewey's philosophy since 1940 when he edited *The Philosopher of the Common Man: Essays in Honor of John Dewey.* He has written numerous essays on pragmatism, evolutionary naturalism, and the philosophy of history. He has also written on Bentley's life work and edited in 1954 Bentley's *Inquiry into Inquiries.* In 1956-57 he was a member of the Institute for Advanced Study at Princeton and in 1959-60 served as chairman of the national John Dewey Centennial Committee.

Jules Altman, field examiner for the National Labor Relations Board, studied philosophy at New York University and the New School for Social Research. He was closely associated with Bentley and helped him see *Knowing and the Known* and *Inquiry into Inquiries* through the press.

James E. Wheeler, Chairman of the Department of Social and Philosophical Foundations in Education at Rutgers, The State University, did a doctoral thesis at Yale University on certain aspects of Dewey's philosophy. He has published various essays on Dewey's thought in journals of educational philosophy.

D1261116

JOHN DEWEY and ARTHUR F. BENTLEY

A Philosophical Correspondence, 1932-1951

JOHN DEWEY *and* ARTHUR F. BENTLEY

A Philosophical Correspondence, 1932-1951

Selected and edited by
SIDNEY RATNER *and* JULES ALTMAN

with JAMES E. WHEELER *as Associate Editor*

With an Introduction by SIDNEY RATNER

Rutgers University Press

New Brunswick   *New Jersey*

ACKNOWLEDGMENTS

We thank Mrs. Arthur F. Bentley and Mrs. John Dewey for their permission to publish the philosophical correspondence selected from their husbands' letters, and certain related essays. To the Arthur F. Bentley Publication Fund, established by Mrs. Bentley, we are indebted for underwriting a major part of the cost of publication of this volume. The Rutgers University Research Council has also contributed support. We are deeply grateful to Professor Sidney Hook of New York University for critically reading the Introduction to this volume and offering valuable suggestions on various important points. We are obligated to M. Halsey Thomas of Princeton University for encouragement and for his indispensable, comprehensive volume, *John Dewey: A Centennial Bibliography* (Chicago, 1962). Charles Madison of Holt, Rinehart & Winston carefully examined the original selections and proposed certain additions that we adopted. Professor Louise M. Rosenblatt of New York University offered much constructive criticism and sound advice. Dr. Rudolf Clemen of Princeton kindly read an early draft of the Introduction. From the beginning of this project, the Rutgers University Press staff have demonstrated their concern and interest. The major part of this manuscript has been cheerfully typed by Carolyn Kappes and Dania Smith. Charlotte Cohn and Lillian Vitello gave helpful secretarial assistance.

Spelling, punctuation, and grammatical slips have been corrected without comment. We have added a Bibliographical Appendix and a Biographical Appendix for the benefit of the general reader and of students of philosophy and American history, to whom many of the persons mentioned in the letters may not be familiar. Following recent precedents, we have given the English translation of nearly all the foreign titles cited in the Bibliographical Appendix.

We appreciate the extensive help received from the librarians at the Indiana University Library Manuscript Division, the Rutgers University Library, the Princeton University Library, the Princeton Theological Seminary Library, and the New York Public Library. The Antioch Press has kindly given permission to utilize some material in the essay on A. F. Bentley by Sidney Ratner in *Life, Language, Law*, Richard W. Taylor, ed. (Yellow Springs, 1957). The editors of *Social Research* have granted permission to draw on the essays by Sidney Ratner on John Dewey in *Social Research*, XVIII (Dec., 1951), 435–48 and XX (Summer, 1953), 127–54. We are indebted, of course, to all those who have previously worked on the life and thought of Dewey and Bentley.

S. R., J. A., J. E. W.

CONTENTS

JOHN DEWEY and ARTHUR F. BENTLEY

A Philosophical Correspondence, 1932-1951

Introduction

Sidney Ratner

The intimate exchange of letters between John Dewey and Arthur F. Bentley gives us the opportunity to gain insight into the creative processes of two great thinkers. We are fortunate in having about two thousand communications—letters, drafts of essays, and postcards—that contain searching inquiries into the nature of scientific knowledge and into modern theories of knowledge. From these my editorial associates and I have sought to select the philosophically most important. These form a series of fascinating dialogues between the internationally most famous American philosopher since William James and a great American theorist in political science, sociology, psychology, and scientific method.

The letters, as a continuous series, began May 22, 1935, after Ernest Nagel suggested to Dewey that he might look into Bentley's writings, and ended in 1951, shortly before Dewey's death. Dewey found two of Bentley's books, *Linguistic Analysis of Mathematics* (1932) and *Behavior, Knowledge, Fact* (1935) so stimulating that he acknowledged a special sense of indebtedness to Bentley in the preface to his *Logic: The Theory of Inquiry* (1938). Within the next few years, Dewey and Bentley very gradually established an unusual intellectual partnership. Their letters contain a lively, frank, and free interchange of ideas on a wide variety of philosophical problems. They give Dewey's and Bentley's solutions to these questions, and explain why Dewey and Bentley rejected various solutions that had been proposed by such leading contemporary philosophers as Rudolf Carnap, Morris R. Cohen, G. E. Moore, and Bertrand Russell.

As their friendship ripened, Dewey and Bentley encouraged and advised each other on essays and books they were preparing. Then they decided to collaborate, at Dewey's suggestion in a letter dated June 25, 1943, on a project to clarify and to reformulate the "leading words" used in logic and the theory of knowledge. This co-authorship began when Dewey was eighty-three years and Bentley seventy-two years old. In addition to various other essays, these two old but intellectually vigorous men published between January 4, 1945, and May 26, 1949, eight articles jointly signed, three articles signed by Bentley alone, and two articles under Dewey's signature. These were revised and appeared in 1949 in book form as *Knowing and the Known*. This was an appropriate celebration of Dewey's ninetieth birthday and Bentley's seventy-ninth, and an important event in the history of American philosophy.

Dewey's name had appeared as co-author on several previous publications, notably in 1895 with James A. McLellan on *The Psychology of*

3

Number and in 1908 with James H. Tufts on *Ethics*. These collaborations do not seem to have been as extensive and close as with Bentley. In the case of *Knowing and the Known* Dewey contributed, through important criticisms and suggestions, to every chapter, even though many of them were originally drafted by Bentley and signed by his name in the book. Similarly, Bentley made extensive valuable comments and proposals on the essays that ultimately appeared under Dewey's signature. In response to these mutual criticisms, each essay went through numerous drafts, ranging usually from five to ten. In addition to these drafts (deposited in the manuscript division of the Indiana University Library at Bloomington, Indiana), Dewey and Bentley wrote challenging discussions of the key philosophical and scientific issues involved in each essay. The present collection permits the reader to participate with Dewey and Bentley in the process of challenge and clarification.

The Dewey-Bentley *Philosophical Correspondence* is the most extensive correspondence of any *two* contemporary philosophers published in America or Europe. This interchange constitutes a rare example of genuinely shared, cooperative thinking. Though Bentley did a larger share of the essay writing, no word was printed without Dewey's stamp of approval or without the benefit of his painstaking evaluations and proposals for revision. With the publication of this material, Dewey's share in writing *Knowing and the Known* must be given its proper weight and seen as the final phase of his philosophical career and development.

Dewey and Bentley wrote with impassioned intensity on philosophic themes. They were consumed with the desire to sweep away linguistic confusions and fictions in philosophy. They sought to work out scientifically justifiable formulations for every important word they thought needed clarification or correction. Some of these words were "action," "behavior," "experience," "knowledge," "mind," "nature," "reality," "sign," "space-time," "substance," and "truth." In the letters can be studied the evolution of ideas from the stage when Dewey or Bentley first expressed sharp dissatisfaction with some fashionable formulation of a problem and went on to experiment with a new approach, to the final stage of agreement on the question.

Contrary to the assertions of some of Dewey's recent critics, Dewey and Bentley scrutinized past and current linguistic usage of philosophic terms and phrases as scrupulously as the English and American devotees of "linguistic analysis." Dewey in this correspondence brilliantly characterized the classic figures in philosophy: e.g., Plato, Aristotle, Descartes, Bacon, Berkeley, Hume, Locke, and Kant. Dewey and Bentley both made incisive and valuable judgments on the work of such recent thinkers as William James, Charles Sanders Peirce, Henri Bergson, Alfred

4

North Whitehead, George Herbert Mead, Frederick J. E. Woodbridge, George Santayana, and Morris R. Cohen. These compact and penetrating thumbnail sketches of philosophic personalities and doctrines provide long-range perspectives on contemporary problems and fresh evaluations of past great thinkers.

To give the reader a sense of the process of innovation and critical revision behind each finished published essay, this volume includes two drafts by Dewey and two by Bentley of essays later printed in final form in *Knowing and the Known*. We have also included two hitherto unpublished essays by Dewey, "Means and Consequences" and "Importance, Significance and Meaning." These carry to completion certain themes and ideas that grew out of the epistolary discussions between Dewey and Bentley. Dewey sent copies of these essays to Bentley, and would have published them if his health had not failed in the last few months before his death. Also included are two brief essays by Bentley on "Dewey's Logic Compactly Presented" and "Dewey's Development," dated October 5 and November 21, 1945, respectively, which sum up incisively Bentley's analyses of basic positions and trends in Dewey's work.

John Dewey: Experimental Naturalist

The philosophical correspondence of Dewey and Bentley should be seen against the background of the separate, yet confluent, intellectual developments of these two strikingly different men. Dewey was born on October 20, 1859, in Burlington, Vermont, on the eve of the Civil War. His father, a grocer, served for four years as a quartermaster with the First Vermont Cavalry. John spent the last winter of the war with his parents and two brothers in northern Virginia, where the privations suffered by the people of the devastated region made a deep impression on the young boys. Upon returning to Burlington, John resumed the life of a typical middle-class Yankee schoolboy and eventually went on to study at the University of Vermont (1875–79). There he first acquired an interest in Darwinian evolution. From T. H. Huxley's impressive textbook on physiology he came to appreciate the unity of the living creature. His reading of Auguste Comte's writings stimulated a concern for political and social philosophy, especially the interaction between social conditions and the development of thought in science and philosophy. But the greatest influence on Dewey's future career came from the philosophical teaching of Professor H. A. P. Torrey. Dewey learned about Scotch Common Sense, German Intuitionist and a priori philosophy (mainly Kant) in Torrey's undergraduate classes. Some three years after graduation from college, he received special tutoring from Torrey in German philosophy. Torrey encouraged Dewey to make philosophy and college teaching his life vocation.

Dewey was an outstanding graduate student in philosophy at Johns Hopkins University from 1882 to 1884. There he read the writings of T. H. Green, John and Edward Caird, and other neo-Hegelians, and under the inspiration of the learned George Sylvester Morris he became converted to neo-Hegelianism. Dewey also studied psychology with G. Stanley Hall, a pioneer in experimental psychology. Dewey studied logic with Charles Sanders Peirce, the founder of pragmatism, but unfortunately only some ten to twenty years later did he reach a full appreciation of Peirce's stress on the mathematical approach to logic and the methods of the physical sciences. In the 1930's, the long-delayed publication of Peirce's *Collected Papers* aided Dewey in perfecting his own great treatise on logic.

The impact of George Sylvester Morris on Dewey's philosophic outlook was twofold. Morris's neo-Hegelian logic and metaphysics appealed to Dewey because it overcame the oppressive dualisms that he had acquired in New England at college and at home; the divisions of one's self from the world, of soul from body, of nature from God. Hegel's synthesis of subject and object, matter and spirit, the divine and the human, gave Dewey an immense emotional and intellectual liberation from the frustrating Kantian dichotomy between the world of phenomenal existents and events in space and time, and the "supersensible," "noumenal," or "intelligible" world of entities which are neither in space nor time. Hegel's treatment of human culture as molding the ideas, beliefs, and intellectual attitudes of individuals led Dewey to reject the widespread theory that isolated, individual minds respond to the physical world, each from his own center. To Dewey the only possible psychology was a social psychology. Here his thinking was to anticipate and to influence that of anthropologists like Ruth Benedict in her classic study, *Patterns of Culture* (1934).

Despite the fact that during the fifteen years after he won his doctorate in philosophy at Johns Hopkins, he gradually lost confidence in Hegel's dialectic, Dewey felt he owed to Hegel his emphasis on the principle of continuity and the important role of conflict in human affairs and in nature. C. S. Peirce at this period expressed an appreciation of Hegel's insight into these themes, although Peirce rendered his own thoughts on these subjects in a more precise, mathematical form. Bertrand Russell, champion of logical atomism, in 1939 emphasized Dewey's Hegelian synthetic background as against his own British analytic background, but when Russell was a student and a fellow at Cambridge University in the mid-1890's, he was an enthusiastic adherent of Hegelianism in the form made palatable to him by F. H. Bradley and John McTaggart.

Dewey was also permanently affected by Morris's transmission (from his early Scotch philosophical training) of a common-sense belief in the existence of the external world. He used "to make merry" as Dewey put it, over those who thought the *existence* of this world and of matter needed to be proved by philosophers. The only philosophical question he saw was: "What is the *meaning* of this existence?" Here G. S. Morris and Dewey were at one with the no-nonsense position about common-sense matters of fact expounded with such force by G. E. Moore in "A Defence of Commonsense" (1925) and "Proof of an External World" (1939). But British admirers of Moore have not mentioned the fact that in 1915 Dewey, in "The Existence of the World as a Logical Problem," powerfully attacked Bertrand Russell's doubts about the basis for our belief in an external world. In this essay, reprinted in his *Essays in Experimental Logic* (1916), Dewey demonstrated that there is no problem of an external world, logically speaking, because the very attempt to state the problem involves a self-contradiction.

Dewey remained a confirmed neo-Hegelian during the first four years of his teaching at the University of Michigan (1884–88) where G. S. Morris and James B. Angell, president of the university, gave him his first chance at college teaching. After a year at the University of Minnesota, Dewey returned to Michigan as chairman of the philosophy department (1889–94). At this time, he developed a view of ideas as plans or working hypotheses that induced him to characterize his philosophy as "experimental idealism." During his stay at Michigan, Dewey's philosophical and social interests expanded and deepened. After his marriage in 1886 to (Harriet) Alice Chipman (1859–1927), he became more aware of the need for action in social affairs and in education. Dewey also enjoyed the stimulating friendship of such colleagues as Henry Carter Adams, an economist with strong views on the need for trade unions and government curbs on business exploitation of labor; George Herbert Mead, "a seminal mind of the first order," who pioneered in bringing biological and sociological theory to bear upon psychology; Arthur H. Lloyd, an original exponent of Dynamic Idealism, who supported Dewey's experimentalism, but went beyond Dewey in advocating a panpsychic cosmology; and James H. Tufts, an authority on ethics.

During this Michigan-Minnesota period Dewey published almost a volume a year: a *Psychology* in 1887, *Leibniz's New Essays Concerning the Human Understanding* in 1888, and his first book on education, *Applied Psychology: An Introduction to the Principles and Practice of Education* (with James A. McLellan) in 1889. None of these books revealed any notable Darwinian outlook on man in nature. The first book tried to harmonize the universal mind of absolute idealism with the contemporary findings of psychological research on the human mind. The *Leibniz* revealed Dewey's sympathy for Leibniz's view that the world forms an organic unity, with continuity and interdependence prevailing throughout. Dewey praised Leibniz for seeing mind as an active process, but deplored his devotion to formal logic and failure to anticipate Hegel's logic of organicism and process. The *Applied Psychology* offered a scientific basis for the thesis that education should be based on the interests, activities, and ideas of the children taught. In this work, Dewey made two important points: first, there is a basic distinction between "having" a sensation or feeling and "knowing" or understanding something, e.g., the meaning of any words uttered and heard. Second, all knowledge is "mediate," that is, it is based on the interpretation of signs as representative of sensations; this is achieved through the individual mind's extracting the ideal elements already existing in a Hegelian-conceived "universal mind." Dewey was still far from a naturalistic philosophy in these early writings.

In 1891 Dewey in his *Outlines of a Critical Theory of Ethics* broke through to a tentative Darwinian concern with desire and intelligence functioning in direct control of human action. Three years later in his *Study of Ethics* he presented the kernel of "instrumental" pragmatism in the thesis that intelligence is the "mediation" of native impulses in the light of reflection on the consequences of satisfying these impulses. In this work Dewey introduced the special philosophical idioms and turns of phrase that were to characterize the writings for which he is best known, e.g., "experiment," "ideas as plans of action," "instruments," "practice," and "conflict." Here he briefly enunciated a theme to be developed in later books: An antithesis between science and art is not tenable. "Science does not *teach* us to know; it is the knowing; art does not *teach* us to do, it is the doing." Knowing is one form of art or doing.

The liberation of Dewey from neo-Hegelian idealism was due in large part to the impact of William James's *The Principles of Psychology* in 1890 on Dewey's whole way of thinking and his bedrock presuppositions. Reading James was intellectually as revolutionary an experience to Dewey as reading Charles Renouvier's essay on free will had been to James twenty years before. The chapters in James's *Principles* dealing with conception, discrimination, comparison, and reasoning served as a better introduction to a pragmatic theory of knowledge for students, Dewey thought, than James's later book on *Pragmatism*. Dewey found especially congenial that strain in the *Psychology* which emphasized the objective approach to psychology, based upon a biological characterization of the *psyche*, as against the more subjective view of psychology as a theory of "consciousness," even when James presented it as a "stream of consciousness." This behavior-centered psychological approach worked its way more and more into Dewey's ideas and transformed his basic philosophic beliefs.

8

Another influence was Franklin Ford, an obscure economic journalist from New York, who led Dewey in 1891–92 to see that freedom of inquiry and effective public education on social issues were hindered by business and other pressure groups. Ford persuaded Dewey of the need for a newspaper that would make inquiry and the reporting of the truth its business, and that would so organize and socialize public intelligence as to make enlightened social action feasible. Nothing ever came of their project for a periodical to be called "Thought News," but Dewey was led to abandon his idealistic belief that the world was "logical through and through." He came to believe instead that the world needed to be transformed through the application of intelligence to social affairs.

A highly important influence on Dewey's development as a pragmatist was the rearing of his six children; three of them were born in Michigan. This increase in his family stimulated his interest in the theory and practice of education. Few philosophers have taken education with sufficient seriousness to consider, as Dewey did, that "philosophizing should focus about education as the supreme human interest in which, moreover, other problems, cosmological, moral, logical, come to a head." His observation of his own children and the insights he had derived from James about the importance of children's native impulses and interests led Dewey to base education upon the interests, ideas, and activities of children. He stressed the view that ideas should center on possible action and that action should always grow out of ideas. The basic principle of Dewey's: "Learn to Do by Knowing and to Know by Doing" was not original with him; it had been advanced by many progressive educational theorists during the nineteenth century and can be traced back to Giambattista Vico, the great Italian Renaissance philosopher of history. Dewey's distinction was that he worked out in detail the psychological basis and implications of these new ideas and assisted in giving them some scientific support. This he did in such influential books as *The Psychology of Number*, with McLellan (1895), *School and Society* (1899), *The Child and the Curriculum*, and *The Educational Situation* (both 1902).

In the fall of 1894, just as he was turning thirty-five, Dewey became Professor of Philosophy and Chairman of the Department of Philosophy, Psychology, and Education at the University of Chicago. There he was to achieve national and international recognition as the leader of what William James and others were to call the "Chicago School" of American philosophy. The ten years he spent at Chicago were decisive in his philosophical development from experimental idealism to instrumentalism, the special variety of pragmatism that he fashioned in contradistinction to the pragmatism of William James and the "pragmaticism" of

Charles Sanders Peirce. Dewey hammered out his own logical and cosmological theory as the most articulate, powerful, and productive member of a gifted philosophical group. George Herbert Mead was his chief stimulus in logic and psychology, James Hayden Tufts his main co-explorer in theoretical and applied ethics, and Addison W. Moore the most able champion of Dewey's "experimental logic" among the younger philosophers. (Tufts and Mead had been at Michigan with Dewey.) James R. Angell, a former student of Dewey's at Michigan and of James's and Royce's at Harvard, became one of the most important figures in *functional* psychology. This laid stress on the role "mental" phenomena play in satisfying the needs and aims of the organism, as against the *analytic* psychology of Edward B. Titchener at Cornell, with its emphasis on describing and analyzing the facts of experience from a static rather than a dynamic point of view. Dewey himself felt that the functional psychology movement (which stemmed from James originally) contributed to the development of his instrumental logic and served as a bridge from his logical to his moral theory.

The University of Chicago, started only a few years before, had notable figures in every discipline: Franz Boas in anthropology; Albert Michelson in physics; Jacques Loeb in biochemistry; Thorstein Veblen in economics; W. I. Thomas in sociology; William Vaughn Moody and Robert Herrick in English literature. In education Dewey had high esteem for Francis W. Parker, head of a Chicago Teachers Training School, and Ella Flagg Young, a district superintendent of the Chicago City Schools. Dewey attributed to her and to his wife the greatest influence on his educational theories and activities during the period 1894–1904. With their aid he started an experimental school in 1896. He attempted to combine psychological principles of learning with the principle of cooperative learning and living. "The Laboratory School" or the "Dewey School," as it was popularly known during the seven-and-a-half years of its existence, tested the educational, philosophic, and psychological theories of Dewey and his departmental colleagues. Dewey also found great satisfaction in his association with Hull House, a noted Chicago social settlement. Its remarkable founder and director, Jane Addams, taught various groups of the poor and the more fortunate how to live together and to help one another.

In the spring of 1904 Dewey and the President of the University of Chicago, Dr. William Rainey Harper, came into sharp conflict about the administration of the recently united Laboratory School and University Elementary School (established by F. W. Parker), especially on a moot point concerning Mrs. Dewey's tenure as school principal. Dewey resigned from both his directorship of the School of Education and his professorship of philosophy, much to the regret of Dr. Harper and

Dewey's colleagues. Columbia University came to his aid by offering him a professorship in philosophy, which he accepted.

From 1904 to 1930 Dewey taught students from all over the world at Columbia; from 1930 to 1939 he held a special position as Professor Emeritus in residence; after that he continued with unabated activity to write until a few months before his death on June 1, 1952, at the age of ninety-two. During the years at Columbia Dewey brought to fruition many ideas in ethics, education, and logic that he had initiated at Chicago. But he also developed new insights and approaches from his associations at Columbia and his meditations on philosophic and public problems. These developed in reaction to, or parallel to, such new philosophies as the New Realism, Critical Realism, Logical Positivism, and Linguistic Analysis. He also responded to national and international affairs as he lived through the turbulent years of the Progressive Movement, World War I, the rise of Soviet communism, of fascism and Naziism, the New Deal of Franklin D. Roosevelt, and World War II.

At Columbia Dewey found himself part of a vigorous, varied, and imaginative philosophical group. Frederick J. E. Woodbridge was a powerful exponent of a naturalistic metaphysics, who convinced Dewey that metaphysics need not rest upon non-empirical principles. William Pepperell Montague was a forcible spokesman for the New Realism and an original form of panpsychism. He did not win Dewey over to his views, but stimulated Dewey by his ingenious dialectic and his interest in modern science. In education, William H. Kilpatrick and John L. Childs, after Dewey's temporary loss of influence in education in the early 1900's, were instrumental in making Dewey's educational theories widely influential again. Kilpatrick developed certain doctrines in education that deviated from Dewey's in some important respects. Sidney Hook, Joseph Ratner, Herbert Schneider, John H. Randall, Jr., Ernest Nagel, and Irwin Edman, brilliant graduate students of Dewey's in the 1910's or 1920's, soon established themselves as thinkers in their own right and contributed to Dewey's development of his system by their suggestions, essays, and books. Dr. Albert Barnes of Merion, Pennsylvania, a great art collector and connoisseur, encouraged and helped inspire Dewey to publish his *Art as Experience* (1934).

Friends of Dewey's at The New School for Social Research, founded after World War I with Dewey's cooperation, included Charles A. Beard and James Harvey Robinson, the chief exponents of the New History; Thorstein Veblen, the economic iconoclast; Horace Kallen, distinguished cultural pluralist and pragmatist of the Jamesian variety; and Alvin S. Johnson, the wide-ranging social scientist. Most of them wrote, along with Dewey, for *The New Republic*. Dewey benefited from the challenges of such independent, highly critical philosophers as Arthur O.

11

Lovejoy, author of *The Revolt Against Dualism* (1930), and Morris R. Cohen, a champion of rationalistic naturalism, as well as from pragmatists of diverse views like William James and C. I. Lewis at Harvard; F. C. S. Schiller at Oxford; and C. S. Peirce in Milford, Pennsylvania.

Philosophic currents abroad also had some effect on Dewey's thinking, often negatively, sometimes positively. He reacted against the absolute idealism of F. H. Bradley, the realism of G. E. Moore, the logical atomism of Bertrand Russell, the oversimplified positions of Logical Positivism, and the dogmatisms of the neo-Thomists and neo-Marxists. On the other hand, Dewey was sympathetic to the focus on process, time, culture, and human experience in Bergson, Croce, Cassirer and in the early philosophical writings of Alfred North Whitehead. Dewey did not, however, approve of their metaphysical and epistemological doctrines. The early Wittgenstein of the *Tractatus Logico-Philosophicus* (1922) repelled Dewey, yet there is much in the later Wittgenstein of the *Philosophical Investigations* (1953) and in the work of such English linguistic analysts as John Austin, Gilbert Ryle, P. F. Strawson, and Stephen Toulmin that can be harmonized with Dewey's philosophy.

The output of Dewey is so great that it is impossible in brief compass to do justice to the variety, complexity, and richness of his thought. Only a bald outline of the salient features of his philosophy as it evolved from 1894 to 1938 is possible here. Dewey developed a naturalistic ethics by putting men's moral acts and choices in their biological and social setting. In 1898 he asserted that the ethical progress of society was a part of the cosmic process of evolution. This phase of evolution required replacing ruthless competition with social cooperation if men were to survive and develop their full potentialities in civilization. He agreed with George Santayana's statement in *The Life of Reason* (1904–5) that everything ideal has a natural basis, and everything natural a possible ideal development.

Dewey disagreed with the "transcendental" view of G. E. Moore in *Principia Ethica* (1903) that goodness and other ethical qualities, although objective and real, independent of any mind, are indefinable in terms of any descriptive, psychological predicates unless one commits the "naturalistic fallacy." To Dewey this doctrine reinstated the transcendental eternal values of idealism under a new guise. He also took issue with the alternative "empirical" view of Ralph Barton Perry, author of the *General Theory of Value* (1926), that anything has value if it is the object of an interest held by some person or persons. See Dewey and J. H. Tufts, *Ethics*; Dewey, *Human Nature and Conduct* (1922), and *The Quest for Certainty* (1929), especially Chapter X: "The Construction of the Good."

Dewey's solution was to distinguish between immediate goods, the

12

desired; and reasonable goods, the desirable. He asserted that an object desired by a human being is rightly considered valuable or desirable only when analysis leads one to believe that the consequences of satisfying the desire yield, or are likely to yield, more benefit than harm. In brief, he proposed that the experimental method be applied to judgments on moral values as well as to hypotheses about physical objects and processes.*

Dewey applied his experimental theory of ethics to the theory and practice of education. His educational philosophy had widespread repercussions in the United States and in other countries, such as Mexico, China, Japan, Turkey, and Soviet Russia. A series of powerful essays and books published between 1896 and 1916 established Dewey as the world's leading philosopher of education in the twentieth century. His essay, "Interest as Related to Will" (1896) and his early books culminated in his outstanding contribution to this field, *Democracy and Education* (1916). Dewey persuaded many leading educators throughout the world that students' interest in different subjects should be elicited, that "doing" should be an integral part of their learning, and that these processes should lead to self-discipline. He inspired the practice of student cooperation in daily school activities and urged that students be given the opportunity to explore a variety of subjects ranging from the arts and crafts to the sciences.

Strong criticisms of Dewey's educational philosophy have come over the past seven decades from adherents of classical traditionalism and champions of "tough" scientific discipline, as well as from supporters of reactionary business enterprise, uncritical supernaturalism, and communist, fascist, and nazi totalitarianism. However, educators who were classical scholars, like Alvin S. Johnson, knew that Dewey was a modern Socrates, close to the ancient Greeks in his concern for *Paideia*, the education of the whole individual's character and intellect. Such contemporary philosophers of science as Russell in his *Education and the Good Life* (1926) and Whitehead in *The Aims of Education* (1929) took positions in harmony with much in Dewey's educational philosophy. The loudest criticisms of Dewey usually came from those who had not read—or read carefully—his writings. They castigated Dewey for the sins of others, especially those who went to extremes about the child-centered school. Dewey's *Experience and Education* (1938) is especially relevant on this point.

* For criticism of Dewey's position, see Morton G. White, *Social Thought in America* (2nd ed., 1957), pp. 203–19; for a defense, see Sidney Hook, ed., *John Dewey, Philosopher of Science and Freedom* (1950), pp. 194–216; Israel Scheffler, "Is the Dewey-like Notion of Desirability Absurd?" *Journal of Philosophy*, LI, (Sept. 30, 1954), 577–82; and Charles L. Stevenson, *Facts and Values* (1963), pp. 94–116.

In the last few years Dewey's educational theories have been under especially fierce attack. After the Soviet Union launched *Sputnik*, the criticism of Dewey became even more intensified. A spirited reply to most of these charges, based upon a re-examination of Dewey's philosophy of education, was made by Sidney Hook in his *Education for Modern Man* (second ed., 1962).

In politics, economics, and law Dewey fought for the fullest utilization of free, experimental intelligence in establishing and maintaining the conditions for political, economic, and social democracy. During most of his long life Dewey supported the programs of such liberal and progressive reformers as Henry George, William Jennings Bryan in 1896 and 1900, Theodore Roosevelt in 1912, and Robert LaFollette in 1924. In 1919 Dewey lectured in Japan and China; in 1924 he undertook an educational survey for Turkey, in 1926 for Mexico, and in 1928 for Soviet Russia.

He was sympathetic to that social program which seemed best adapted to the special conditions of each country. In Japan, for example, he approved efforts to adapt Confucian standards to modern economic conditions and thereby to by-pass the Marxian type of social evolution. On the other hand, he was favorably enough impressed by what he saw of the voluntary cooperative movement and the educational experiments then allowed in Soviet Russia to write articles, later made into a book, *Impressions of Soviet Russia* (1929) that led newspapers hostile even to evolutionary socialism to brand him a "Bolshevik" and a "red." Dewey himself by the early 1930's came to believe in democratic socialism, with the emphasis on the *democratic*.

This deep-grained commitment to democracy and fair play led Dewey to take an anti-Stalinist and anti-Trotskyite stand in his essay, "Why I Am Not a Communist" in *The Modern Monthly*, April, 1934. In 1937 and 1938 he served as chairman of the Commission of Inquiry into the Charges Made Against Leon Trotsky at the Moscow Trials. The verdict he and his associates handed down of "Not Guilty" aroused the fury of the American communist press. But Dewey's logical acumen and moral courage were vindicated to the full after his death when Khrushchev revealed in a famous speech some of the methods and the tortures Stalin had ordered the G. P. U. to use to obtain the confessions of those falsely accused of crimes they had not committed.

Dewey, as a result of his key role in the Trotsky inquiry, was led to study at first hand the writings of Lenin and other revolutionary leaders. This confirmed him in his belief that the method of violent revolution and dictatorship used by the Communists was ineffective for the ends sought and was an unintended, but nonetheless powerful, factor in bringing about fascism. "As an unalterable opponent of Fascism in every form," he said in the April, 1934, article, "I cannot be a Communist." In his judgment, "to be asked to choose between Bolshevism and Fascism is to be asked to choose between the G. P. U. and the Gestapo." In 1937 he anticipated the 1939–41 Nazi-Soviet alliance that pro-Soviet liberals had thought impossible. Dewey also foresaw the post-1945 drive by Soviet Russia to penetrate and to master the non-Soviet world.

In 1938 Leon Trotsky published a pamphlet entitled *Their Morals and Ours* that was essentially a reply to John Dewey and other critics of Bolshevik Leninism. To this Dewey made a masterly rejoinder in his article, "Means and Ends," in *The New International*, August, 1938. In it Dewey showed how the allegedly scientific and naturalistic morality of orthodox Marxism betrayed its empirical pretensions by using an alleged "law of the class struggle" to rationalize decisions taken by those leaders who wished to remain in power independently of whether or not the consequences of such decision *in fact* both increased man's power over nature and decreased man's power over man. The so-called "laws of history," which presumably justified attempts to make the inevitable come to pass a little sooner, turn out to be arbitrary readings of historical possibilities, realized by the daring and will of a revolutionary minority, not responsible to the masses in whose name a dictatorship based on force is ruthlessly imposed on society.

In *Freedom and Culture* (1939) Dewey set down an even more impressive critique of both the Stalinist and Trotskyist forms of Marxism. This book was a worthy successor to such earlier path-breaking works as his *The Public and Its Problems* (1927), *Individualism, Old and New* (1930), and *Liberalism and Social Action* (1935). Dewey's reward for his insights and courageous exposure of the dangers of communist dictatorship has been condemnation by Soviet and pro-Soviet American writers as "an ideologist of American imperialism, a violent enemy of the U.S.S.R." whose philosophy is "the philosophy of war and fascism." This verdict in the article on Dewey in the 1952 edition of the *Great Soviet Encyclopedia* seems to have inspired Harry K. Wells's much more extended attack on Dewey in his book, *Pragmatism: Philosophy of Imperialism* (1954). The Hungarian Revolt of 1956 opened the eyes of many devoted European Communists and fellow-travelers to the naked force behind Soviet imperialism. Dewey's ideas on freedom and democracy continue to have relevance, as Milovan Djilas's *The New Class* (1957) and the continuing Soviet restraints on intellectuals have demonstrated.

Dewey's "pragmatic" method, but not his specific economic doctrines, had an impact upon domestic politics and economics within the United States through the activities of Rexford Tugwell, A. A. Berle, Jr., and other members of Franklin D. Roosevelt's successive Brain Trusts as

15

they applied their own interpretation of Dewey's experimental method to the problems of New Deal relief, recovery, and reform. Dewey himself, largely influenced by his student and close friend Sidney Hook, espoused a version of socialism that had an appeal among intellectuals and certain trade-unionists, like Walter Reuther and David Dubinsky in the early 1930's. But by the late 1930's most trade-unionists abandoned socialism and supported the New Deal. Among scholars, Wesley C. Mitchell, John R. Commons, and Walton H. Hamilton did much to bring realism into the study of economic institutions and experimentalism into governmental policy-making. In political science Dewey's ideas on group interests and the need for community-centered reforms were applied most fruitfully by Arthur F. Bentley, Charles E. Merriam, and T. V. Smith. In law, Roscoe Pound, Jerome Frank, and Walton H. Hamilton shared with Dewey a concern for judging the value of decisions by their consequences to specific human beings. To this sociological jurisprudence and legal realism the Supreme Court since the mid-1930's has become increasingly committed. The Court's decisions in defense of civil liberties and civil rights are in accord, in general, with Dewey's ideals as set forth as early as the 1890's.

The importance of Dewey's work in ethics, education, and social philosophy is paralleled by the significance of his work in logic, conceived as the theory of scientific inquiry. Dewey naturalized logic by stressing the relation of thought to human conduct and by explicating the role of intelligence in biologic evolution. He thus freed logic from being a "ballet of bloodless categories," the study of a Platonic universe of pure forms independent of all human origins and functions. In his pioneering *Studies in Logical Theory* (1903), and in *Essays in Experimental Logic, Creative Intelligence* (1917), and *The Quest for Certainty,* Dewey presented forcibly the thesis that human thinking arises out of specific needs and frustrations. When it is successful, it represents a control, an alteration of the environment as the result of an analysis of the original complex situations leading to the proposal of an experiment or plan of action. Ideas are used as working hypotheses for achieving the solution of the problem that initiated the active inquiry. Dewey calls the "meaning" of an idea, in its simplest terms, the plan of action it sets forth as a solution to a problem. This "operational" or "experimental" characterization of meaning is an extension of C. S. Peirce's pragmatic maxim that the meaning of a statement is the sum of its verifiable consequences.

The widespread and long-enduring fallacy of ancient and of most modern theories of knowledge has been the assumption that the norm of knowledge is some antecedent existence or reality. The rationalism of Idealists like Kant, Bradley, and Royce held that human logic was simply the reading off or coming to consciousness of the inherently rational structure already possessed by the universe. The new rationalism expounded most impressively in Bertrand Russell's *The Principles of Mathematics* (1903) taught that the terms and types of order constituting formal logic and pure mathematics have a "reality" or realm of being of their own, and are at most led up to and discovered by human thinking. A few years later Russell developed his theory of descriptions which enabled him to treat of mathematical and logical meanings in such a way that their affirmation or denial did not require the assumption that they were non-existential *entities* inhabiting some realm of Platonic or ghostly subsistence. But certain eminent mathematical logicians like Kurt Gödel and Alonzo Church still adhere to this belief. The sensationalistic, empirical logic of John Stuart Mill asserted that only particular facts are self-supporting and that sensory qualities, as merely given, are the antecedent models with which sound or true ideas must agree. The "New Realism" expounded in England by G. E. Moore and his Cambridge disciples, and in America by Edwin B. Holt, W. P. Montague, and R. B. Perry *inter alios,* in the early 1900's, maintained that the existence and nature of things are independent of, and prior in time to, the fact they are sometimes known by human beings.

In answer to the neo-Realists, Dewey stated that he agreed that things existed before being known, but he denied things had or enjoyed in direct personal experience are identical with the objects of knowledge as objects of either common sense or scientific knowledge. Antecedent existences or "realities," he pointed out, are the subject-matter or materials *for* knowledge, but are not, properly speaking, the *objects* of knowledge until the scientist has transformed them through the processes of scientific inquiry into such "objects of knowledge." A logic which rules out knowledge-getting through modern scientific observation and experimentation, yet bases itself exclusively upon the traits of known objects, is self-contradictory. We cannot know with any degree of assurance what are the traits of scientifically "known" objects as distinct from objects of speculation, opinion, or uncritical "common sense" until *after* we have tested our hypotheses by controlled investigation into, and interaction with, antecedent existences or materials.

Dewey took sharp issue with the spectator theory of knowledge and argued, on the basis of experimentation in the natural sciences, that action is at the heart of ideas and that conclusions about nature and society are affected by the acts of observation and experimentation involved in achieving knowledge about specific situations. To Dewey, as to Peirce, the categories and valid forms of logic are the discoveries of men concerned with formulating the most trustworthy processes of inquiry into specific problems. The laws of logic and mathematics thus

17

have their origin, existence, and functioning within the framework of scientific inquiry.

These revolutionary positions of Dewey's inspired sharp attacks by opponents like Morris R. Cohen, William E. Hocking, Arthur O. Lovejoy, and Bertrand Russell, but did not disturb what one critic called the "godlike calm" of Dewey under fire. Decade after decade, he defended himself in quiet, masterly replies to his critics. These rejoinders dispelled most of the misinterpretations and invalid criticisms, but many of his philosophic foes failed to read them or to absorb their points, and persisted in presenting a caricature of his views. Dewey, for example, never doubted or denied that every science makes some a priori statements, assumptions, or postulates. He acknowledged the nature of a genuine hypothesis to be prospective and thus *temporarily* a priori, but he refused to call any hypothetical or postulated statement a "truth" until it resolved the problematic situation in which it arose.

Dewey's experimental theory of truth recognized that truth cannot be attributed to any theory when several alternative theories may equally, or almost equally, well explain the same event. He stressed the practice of scientists in calling that theory true which has been confirmed in a comprehensive variety of empirical situations and has been most fertile in leading to new discoveries and new evidence. Dewey realized that the stability or eternity of "truth" of any hypothesis cannot be guaranteed; like Peirce, he regarded such stability as an ideal limit and wisely objected to converting this ideal limit into an inherent and antecedent property of ideas. Similarly, he denied that there were any immediately perceivable truths: Every argument presents ideas that may seem self-evident and perfectly clear; but logically they are only *claims* to truth, and each can be asserted as a warranted statement only as the outcome of a scientific inquiry.

Although Dewey stressed verifiability as the test of each warranted assertion, he called attention to the importance of new theories that might lead to new discoveries and evidence. He appreciated the fact that individuals are the only source for new ideas, but he stressed the fact that the testing and establishment of hypotheses as warranted assertions of fact has to be a public, social process if individual prejudice, error, and whim are to be avoided.

Foes of pragmatism have charged Dewey with opposition to art, science, and philosophy as ends in themselves, but his most careful writings on what he means by practical and useful, e.g., his *Art as Experience* and *Logic: The Theory of Inquiry*, show that he appreciated the immediate joys and satisfactions of human experience. At the same time he was aware that all human activities or achievements have another dimension; namely, that of being means or instruments for other persons or for the same person in a different stage of his life.

Those who have deprecated his emphasis on the role of action or experiment in human thinking have themselves relied on examples drawn from individuals writing symbols on paper, gazing at tables, neighbors, or scenery, or observing through telescopes or microscopes objects they cannot touch or change. Actually, all philosophical, mathematical thinking involves "ideal experimentation": the creation and manipulation of diagrams, signs, and symbols that represent either actual or ideal entities or situations. We cannot observe mountains, stars, and microscopic life without moving our eyes and bodies and, in many such cases, creating and using specially designed instruments. We do not change physically the mountain, star, or microscopic form of life we study; we *do* change the situation—or position and/or instruments—by means of which we carry on our observations. In short, the "object" we come to know is never known immediately or by intuition, but is known always as the result of a specific inquiry.

This position on the logical status of "objects" follows rigorously from the basic pragmatic theory that meanings connote action, truth connotes prediction, and that both truth and meanings are always to be tested. The limitation of meaning to what makes a verifiable difference, and of truth to what can be objectively tested, leads to the recognition that abstractions are at the heart of thought and are necessary means to the control and enrichment of concrete human experience. In this way Dewey avoided "immediatism," or the presentation-theory of knowledge, namely, that empirical knowledge—or *some* empirical knowledge—is immediately given. At the same time Dewey avoided the tendency to erect abstractions into complete, self-subsistent things or into a realm of superior Being.

On the subject of the relation of logic to existence, Dewey took the position that logical characters and "method must in some sense reflect or refract orders of things that are knowable orders" and that "there must be a connection between logic and metaphysics." But he denied that nature embodied man's logic directly. Although he acknowledged that he had a metaphysics in the sense of attributing certain generic characters to nature as existent, he maintained that there was a ground or criterion for distinguishing between logical and ontological characters. The distinction between the two is made on the ground of experience. Reflective inquiries by human beings occur in nature and are *had* in direct experience. Their distinctive properties can then be ascertained. Dewey denied that logical properties exist prior to human reflection, although physical and biologic factors *condition* logical inquiry and discourse. Just as certain things in nature are edible, but not eaten until

19

acted upon by biological organisms, so all of nature, apart from thinking, is "logic*ible*," but not "logic*ized*." Through human action, qualities and relations previously only potential in nature become actualized. Thus Dewey made clear the human contribution to logic as he had in earlier discussions on the nature of man's experience of secondary and tertiary qualities in nature. (Cf. Dewey, "The Applicability of Logic to Existence," *Journal of Philosophy*, March 27, 1930.)

Dewey's views on metaphysics went through various phases. From the 1890's to 1915 he repudiated metaphysics in the positivistic tradition of Comte and Ernst Mach. But Dewey gradually came to the conclusion that his advocacy of experimental or instrumental logic did not preclude his developing a descriptive or naturalistic metaphysics. He sketched his program for such a metaphysics as early as 1915 in an essay, "The Subject-matter of Metaphysical Inquiry," *Journal of Philosophy*, June 25, 1915. Like Kant, and unlike C. S. Peirce in the speculative cosmology of his later years, Dewey forswore any metaphysics that sought the ultimate origins and ends of man or the universe. But he regarded as proper and valuable a descriptive and analytical metaphysics that would study certain irreducible traits found in any and every scientific inquiry. Then years later, at the age of sixty-six, he published a fully rounded treatise, *Experience and Nature* (1925, rev. ed., 1929), that ranks among the most important contributions to metaphysics of the past century.

Nature, for Dewey, is the infinite number and variety of events or existences that human experience, especially scientific inquiry, cumulatively reveals under specific bio-cultural and spatio-temporal conditions. The prevailing views of scientists on the nature and structure of the universe have varied and will vary as new methods, instruments, and hypotheses are developed and tested. Dewey's high valuation of the best authenticated canons of scientific observation and verification led him to reject all forms of idealistic spiritualism, supernaturalism, and dualism. He also repudiated such appeals to transcendental a priori entities or principles *above* nature and *beyond* experience as Whitehead's "eternal objects," Santayana's "essences," and Russell's Platonic realm of mathematical entities.

Dewey's experimental naturalism placed man within nature, instead of outside and over against it. While he believed nature has a mechanism, he did not accept its *reduction* to a mechanism. Although he held that human life and experience are dependent upon physical conditions, he refused to use the term "materialism" to describe his philosophy and would have rejected the Vienna Circle's fashionable term "physicalism." He considered that the traditional view of matter and mind or spirit as two antithetical, separate things or substances rested on questionable premises and faulty analysis. To him events are primary; matter and

20

mind are special phases of events. Matter expresses the sequential order of natural events; mind the order of their meanings in their logical connections and consequences.

Against Hegel's picture of a "block universe" and Russell's atomistic view of the world as a congeries of relatively isolated things, individuals, and events, Dewey saw the universe as composed of closely related fields of interconnected events, things, and individuals. In this concatenation of Dewey's, three levels are distinguished: the physical, the biological, and the sociocultural (that arising out of human association, communication, participation). Each of these three levels has its own special traits and its own descriptive categories. Nature or "reality," among other things, is characterized by growth processes in which these different levels may succeed one another as phases of a continuity in which each earlier and simpler level makes it possible for a later and more complex level to come into existence. For Dewey, both the earlier phases in a historic process and the latter phases are equally important to an understanding of this process. "The reality is the growth process itself . . . the real existence is the history in its entirety."

Dewey shared with C. S. Peirce the view that every human being, subhuman biologic organism, and inanimate physical object possesses certain unique qualities and relations that give it individuality. The history or temporal seriality of an individual is inseparable from his "essence" or "nature." This position challenges the theory that every development is an unfolding of what was previously latent or implicit. Dewey advanced a new view of potentialities: that they are unactualized powers or capacities in objects and persons which become realized and known as a result of the interactions of these objects and persons. Lincoln's changing personality, for example, was created by the way in which he responded to different crises with which he was presented at successive stages of his career.

This approach to individuality as a temporal development grew out of Dewey's belief that both nature and science have basic elements of contingency, indeterminacy, uncertainty, or unpredictability. Though statistical laws of nature can aid in calculating frequencies or probabilities, certain unpredictable situations occur because genuine individuality exists and is pregnant with new developments. He saw evolution as the collective name for the varied processes of unceasing change in which individual things and organisms develop. The universe that science revealed to him is an open universe in which all known limits, beginnings, forces, and goals evolve and are what they are, as special phases of the long-range processes of change.

In this theory of nature Dewey emphasized the crucial role of human experience as a means of disclosing the "realities" of nature. Everyday gross experience discovers the nature of events through the immediately felt qualities of things. Scientific inquiry adds a new dimension to experience by theory, controlled observation, and experiment. Each form of experience supplements the other; everyday experience is the starting point and the testing ground for the scientist's theoretical constructs. "Experience" in nineteenth- and twentieth-century philosophy has been identified as a subjective-knowledge-affair, centered on the past, the "given," the particular, and the non-theoretical elements in life. Dewey formulated a new interpretation of "experience," based in part on sixteenth- and seventeenth-century English usage, as the interactions of a living creature, a member of some human culture, with its world, physical and social. As Dewey pointed out, "experience," like "life" and "history," is a double-barreled word in that "it recognizes in its primary integrity no division between act and material, subject and object, but contains both of them in an unanalyzed totality." This "new empiricism" gives full weight to the role in human experience of experiment, anticipation of the future, awareness of the connections between specific things and persons, and the thinking that precedes, accompanies, or follows human actions. Hence, Dewey's philosophy could grapple with problems in the philosophy of logic and science without the handicaps of either the old, sensationalistic empiricism of J. S. Mill or the over-intellectualized rationalism of Russell and some of his admirers. On the "new empiricism," see Dewey, ed., *Creative Intelligence, Experience and Nature,* and "Nature in Experience," *Philosophical Review,* March, 1940.

After Dewey set forth his naturalistic metaphysics in *Experience and Nature,* he moved forward to his attack on *The Quest for Certainty;* to his critique of the American economy in *Individualism, Old and New* (1930), and *Liberalism and Social Action* (1935); to his analysis of *Art as Experience;* and to his interpretation of the religious experience in *A Common Faith* (1934). In 1935 he turned his major energies to writing in final form a great treatise, *Logic: The Theory of Inquiry.* At this time certain writings of Arthur F. Bentley helped him to solve some problems blocking the completion of this book.

As we pointed out at the beginning of this essay, Bentley was to become Dewey's closest philosophical co-worker from the later 1930's to 1951. It is difficult to imagine two thinkers of such sharply contrasting personalities and careers. Dewey at seventy-five was the most world-celebrated American philosopher of the previous three decades, a power in the academic world as the leading professor of philosophy, first at Chicago, then at Columbia; an author of so many books and articles as to be almost a household word for most college and university students and the general public from New York to Moscow, Peking, Tokyo, and

22

Mexico City. Bentley, at sixty-five, on the other hand, was unknown to the great American reading public. His name was familiar to the leading figures in law, political science, and sociology as one of the great political and social theorists of the twentieth century. No large group of college or graduate students and teachers, however, knew his work. Similarly, a few students of mathematical philosophy were aware that Bentley had done a pioneering critique of the conflicting theories on the foundations of mathematics in 1932. His book was more favorably reviewed and discussed in Europe than in the United States. Bentley suffered the fate of two other innovators in thought, C. S. Peirce and Thorstein Veblen, who received limited recognition throughout most of their lives. Bentley, furthermore, never held any academic post of importance. After 1935, and especially after 1945, however, he had the satisfaction of having his work both in political science and in philosophy recognized on a wider scale.

In temperament the two men were at opposite poles. Dewey was a person of remarkable insight and energy who had a genius for presenting his own highly original views to audiences brought up in conflicting philosophic traditions. He would meet them halfway and win them over gradually to his own radically different position. He believed that by encouragement or persuasion he could help students to develop their abilities, and opponents to transcend positions he thought erroneous. Bentley, in contrast, was uncompromising in adhering to the most technically exact or precise formulation of his ideas. He believed in challenging his opponents in the most straightforward manner. He did not attempt to conciliate those with whom he differed, and delighted in a no-holds-barred attack on philosophic positions he deemed unsound. But he also had a capacity for winning affection and lifelong loyalty from his peers, and a generous compassion for the unfortunate.

Dewey and Bentley took pleasure from the stimulation each gave the other. They arrived at new positions from different backgrounds and viewpoints derived from training in, and mastery of, overlapping disciplines. Dewey was both the originator of "experimental logic" and a great authority in the techniques and history of philosophy. He also had a rich background in the social and natural sciences. Bentley had a technically expert knowledge of certain developments in diverse branches of mathematics, mathematical logic, and contemporary physics. Moreover, he had a deep interest in and command of the main trends in biology, psychology, and the social sciences, that supplemented and confirmed Dewey's own wide knowledge in these fields. The two were able to form an unusually close friendship and philosophical partnership.

From 1935 to 1952, each showed he had a rare capacity for self-renewal and self-development. They were as intellectually original and powerful in meeting and solving problems in the last two decades of their lives as they had been in their most productive earlier years. Each could revise or reject an old position ruthlessly and formulate a new position if such a change seemed justified in the light of new analyses and evidence.

Arthur F. Bentley: Behavioral Scientist

Arthur F. Bentley was born on October 16, 1870, in Freeport, Illinois, eleven years after John Dewey. Charles Sanders Peirce and William James were then entering into their thirties. The United States was going through the throes of the reconstruction period and was becoming transformed from a predominantly rural society toward a predominantly urban, industrial society.

Arthur Bentley went to public school in Freeport, Illinois, and was graduated from high school in Grand Island, Nebraska, at fourteen years of age. In 1885–86 he studied at York College, a small nearby college in Nebraska for one year, and at the University of Denver for part of the next year. He left Denver for reasons of health and worked for some three years in his father's bank in Grand Island. In 1890, at the age of twenty, he entered the Johns Hopkins University, mainly because he was attracted by the prospect of doing work in economics, especially labor relations, with Richard T. Ely.

Since Bentley was conscious of being a few years older than his classmates, he undertook to do the three-year college program in two years. He received an A.B. in 1892, graduating fourth in his class. Although Ely left for the University of Wisconsin after Bentley's first year, Bentley's interest in economics continued, and he received considerable stimulation from two leading economists of that period, John Bates Clark of Smith College and Simon Nelson Patten of Pennsylvania, who came down from their universities to lecture at Hopkins. Bentley had the advantage of personal meetings and discussions with them, but he seems to have profited most from his own wide readings in the British classical and neo-classical economists, especially Alfred Marshall, and from the original German writings of Carl Menger, one of the founders of marginal utility economics. Menger's theories interested him, but he was most concerned with finding out for himself what empirically verifiable materials Menger had been using or should have used in his theoretical constructions.

The regular professors at Hopkins do not seem to have made any great impact upon Bentley at this time. Herbert B. Adams, though famous for his pioneering seminars in institutional history, did not inspire Bentley, nor did Professor Griffin in philosophy. Unfortunately, C. S. Peirce, with whom Dewey had studied in the mid-1880's, had not obtained per-

24

manent tenure at Hopkins and hence was not there to influence Bentley. James Mark Baldwin came to grace the psychology department later. Bentley found Edwin A. Ross, then a graduate student who had come back from Germany to take his doctor's degree, vivid and interesting in conversation.

After taking his A.B. degree, Bentley wrote an essay, "The Condition of the Western Farmer as Illustrated by the History of a Western Nebraska Town." Published in 1893 in the *Johns Hopkins University Studies in Historical and Political Science,* this essay stands out as an example of objectivity and compact style.

The next year, 1892–93, Bentley did graduate work in economics and sociology at Johns Hopkins. In 1893–94 he went to Germany to study at the universities of Berlin and Freiburg im Breisgau. This German experience was crucially important in his intellectual and emotional development. On the way over to Germany he became acquainted with, and a lifelong friend of, Hutchins Hapgood, who afterward acquired a reputation as a brilliant journalist and writer on labor and other social problems. Hapgood, in his intriguing autobiography, *A Victorian in the Modern World,* recaptured the excitement that he and Bentley felt as young Americans discovering both the beauties and the social problems of Europe twenty years before the catastrophic breakdown of European society ushered in by the First World War. The interchanges between Hapgood and Bentley on art and philosophy were richly stimulating to both, as shown by the letters reprinted in *The Story of an American Family* (n.d.), edited by Neith Boyce and Hutchins Hapgood.

At Berlin Bentley gained entirely different views of political economy and the social sciences in general from those he had received in America. He learned from Adolf Wagner and Gustav Schmoller that German economists were in favor of supporting state measures for social and economic reform. Wagner stressed the importance of historical relativity through his famous distinction between the "historico-legal" and the "economic" categories of institutions, forms of behavior, and processes. But Bentley became disappointed by Wagner's emphasis upon classificatory schematism. Bentley found that Schmoller, whom he had not esteemed as highly as Wagner before he came to Germany, was admirable for his broadness of view and fair-mindedness. Although Bentley was sympathetic to Schmoller's idea of developing economics on an inductive basis from detailed historical, descriptive studies instead of following the English and Austrian a priori hypothetical-deductive model, Bentley eventually felt that Schmoller overemphasized the historical details and did not adequately develop or supply theoretical economic insights.

Bentley found intellectual stimulation in the lectures of Wilhelm Dilthey, a leader of the revolt in German philosophy and the social sciences against the attempts of the positivists to apply the methods of the natural sciences to the general study of man. But Georg Simmel was the teacher who gave the greatest impetus to Bentley's development. Bentley later characterized Simmel as "the keenest and most searching investigator society has yet had." Bentley was especially impressed by Simmel's analysis of the groups which cross one another in a thousand directions in the social mass, and at whose intersections "personality" and individuality are to be found. Simmel contributed also the idea that two groups cannot have a conflict except with common ground to stand on (culturally as well as physically). Bentley derived much later from Simmel's *Sociologie,* the great treatise on sociology published in 1908, the insight that in the *Geisteswissenschaften,* the "philosophical foundations" are usually much weaker than the scientific structure supposedly built on them.

In June, 1894, Bentley won a $500 fellowship in Economics from Johns Hopkins and decided to return to America because the depression of 1893 had hit his father hard, and Bentley felt he had to support himself. That summer he visited France and England before returning to America. He admired Paris and London, but he was horrified by the slums of London.

Upon his return to Hopkins in 1894–95 as a graduate fellow in Economics, Bentley worked hard and performed all his obligations as a candidate for the doctorate. The faculty at Hopkins in the field of social sciences at this time was competent, but could not compare with that of Berlin, except for John Bates Clark, who was a visiting Professor in Economics from Amherst. Bentley took work with H. B. Adams, J. B. Clark, Sidney Sherwood, and J. B. Hollander. The last three professors gave courses as varied as the History of Economic Theory and the Economics of Competition and Monopoly.

While at Hopkins, Bentley seems to have worked mainly on his own, reading widely everything he could find on economics and sociology in English, French, and German. He recalled being primarily interested in the problem: What will the components of economic theory be made of? He was dissatisfied with the explanations then offered by all the schools of economics, but was never able to complete a general theory of economic behavior that would be centered on social processes.

In Sherwood's Economic Conference course, Bentley wrote an essay, "Units of Investigation in the Social Sciences," which was accepted as a doctoral thesis. In this essay Bentley stressed the human mind as a central point in the study of all social phenomena. His work reflected the mentalistic formulations then prevalent of such writers as Simon

26

Patten, J. M. Baldwin, Lester F. Ward, Albion Small, and F. H. Giddings. Bentley soon came to disregard the assumptions and framework he had presented in this thesis, and he later found it difficult to understand how he had ever come to hold any of these earlier positions.

In June, 1895, Bentley received the Ph.D. degree at Johns Hopkins for his work in economics, philosophy, and jurisprudence. That same month he had the satisfaction of having his thesis appear in the *Publications of the American Academy of Political and Social Science.* He obtained a position as a docent or lecturer in Sociology at the University of Chicago for the academic year 1895–96 and made an attempt at discussing French and German systems of sociology with about five students. Owing to the ambitiousness and difficulty of the subjects proposed by Bentley for study by the group, they and Bentley quietly agreed to discontinue their meetings after some five sessions. Bentley at this stage of his career had become a superb research scholar, but simply was not gifted or trained as a teacher. Nevertheless, his position at the University of Chicago gave him a chance to extend his readings in French and German sociology and in the fields of logic and the philosophy of science. Durkheim's early work was especially influential in Bentley's thinking at this time.

An even greater influence on Bentley was John Dewey. As we have pointed out above, Dewey was then formulating the experimental logic and evolutionary naturalism for which he later became famous. Dewey gave a seminar in the Theory of Logic and another in the Logic of Ethics, both of which Bentley attended. The classes were so large that Bentley did not come into intimate contact with Dewey at this time. If he had, it can be conjectured, Dewey might have helped Bentley find a place in the academic world. Bentley might have become the brilliant collaborator with Dewey then rather than fifty years later. In the seminar on the Theory of Logic, Bentley was especially struck by Dewey's statement that the individual mind or self *is not* an existing thing by itself. Bentley later put this idea as follows: The "individual" formulation can be developed out of the "social" formulation much more vividly and completely than the purportedly "social" can be developed out of the "individual."

We are fortunate in having Bentley's manuscript notes on Dewey's Seminar on Logic. As Bentley's theories underwent a revolutionary change in this period, owing in large part to the influence of Dewey, some of the most significant passages from these notes are worth quoting. I have expanded Bentley's telegraphic notes as follows: "Dewey urged students to ignore the whole question of subject and object, and to ask instead, 'What is the act of knowing itself?' This for two reasons: first that subject and object are constructions of the primitive acts of knowledge; the second that logical judgment is a form of action, a form of conduct. . . . Various phases of Judgment and the categories into which it resolves itself are due to phases in which conduct finds itself."

The rest of the notes deal with a careful explication of the logical doctrines of Bacon, Hobbes, Descartes, and Locke. The key questions Dewey treated were: 1. What is the object, purpose, or function of knowledge? 2. What is the definition or essence of knowledge? 3. What is the method of knowledge for; what distinction is there between truth and error? What is the nature of each? Dewey questioned the sufficiency of the clearness and distinctness of ideas as validating their truth.

Dewey criticized Descartes for taking his data readymade from within his self-consciousness, and opposed Descartes' ontological proof of God. Dewey denied that a concept necessarily involves existence. He pointed out that Hobbes's reliance upon general names in reasoning presupposed abstraction and that abstraction meant taking or perceiving a thing from a particular point of view. These analyses took root in Bentley's thinking and helped him to develop his own original ideas.

It is unfortunate that Bentley at this time did not become acquainted with such other members of the Chicago Philosophy Department as James H. Tufts, George Herbert Mead, and Addison W. Moore. Bentley did meet and talk with William I. Thomas, the sociologist now perhaps best known for his work on the *Polish Peasant in Europe and America*. Bentley also found two friends in Richard Philip Baker, an able English mathematician, eventually a professor at the University of Iowa, and Michael A. Lane, a brilliant physiologist, later professor at the University of South Dakota.

After a year at the University of Chicago, Bentley left the academic world to go into journalism. He worked first as a reporter, then as an editorial writer (after 1903) on the Chicago *Times Herald* and the *Record-Herald*. This work was the best thing that could have happened to a young intellectual like Bentley. He was brought up against the harsh facts of life as revealed in the political, social, and economic activities of that turbulent industrial transportation center, with all its contrasts in wealth, poverty, virtue, and iniquity. Labor leaders like Eugene Debs and public officials like John P. Altgeld battled for the rights of working men and the middle classes against millionaires, who represented the world of economic power.

While carrying on his work as newspaper reporter and editorial writer, Bentley did the research, thinking, and writing that resulted in the publication of his first magnum opus, *The Process of Government*, in 1908. He was able to accomplish this herculean feat because his job left him a great deal of free time and because he had available a first-class

28

library in politics and economics at the Crerar Library in downtown Chicago. He worked out his ideas alone, except for an occasional discussion with Michael Lane, who in 1902 had published a book, *The Level of Social Motion.* But Bentley disagreed with Lane's thesis that sex and food desires are the primary forces in life. Bentley probably also got some stimulation from friends like Victor Yarros, a writer for the Chicago *Post,* Richard P. Baker, a mathematician, Hutchins Hapgood, his old friend from Germany, then a newspaper man, and Hapgood's brilliant, charming wife, Neith Boyce. In 1899 Bentley married one of the pioneer women doctors, Anna Harrison, whom he had known as a schoolgirl in Nebraska. She died in 1924. Six years later he married Susan Chipman; their marriage lasted until her death in 1942.

From 1896 to 1908 Bentley was absorbed in analyzing the stream of facts, mainly political, that constantly came across his newspaper desk. These facts were about "man-acting." The rich raw material that he accumulated concerning the play of specific interest groups in the Chicago City Council and in the Illinois State Legislature on various important issues stimulated him into developing his more generalized study of social pressures for all phases of government in the United States and the rest of the world. The first sketch and outline for this volume in 1905–6 has an inscription to: "Ludwig Gumplowicz, John Dewey, Georg Simmel, Walt Whitman, and the many other joint makers of this book." The Finis reads: "To Any Reader—I am no more the slave of this book than are you."

In the last two decades *The Process of Government* has come to be recognized as one of the outstanding classics in political science. But when it was first published, and for almost thirty years thereafter, it was not widely appreciated. Only a few astute critics like Charles A. Beard and Morris R. Cohen recognized its value until Bentley's work was rediscovered in the 1930's and 1940's by people in various fields, like Karl Llewellyn, Bertram Gross, David Truman, and the present writer. *The Process of Government* has a one-line preface: "This book is an attempt to fashion a tool." Bentley sought a method for understanding the processes of social life, with the processes of government as the main focus or starting point. The first part of this book is devoted to demonstrating that feelings and faculties, ideas and ideals, including the "social-will" are not definite "things" in or behind society, working upon it as causes. Bentley did not deny the existence of the feeling, thinking, ideal-following phenomena to which eminent writers like Herbert Spencer, Rudolph von Jhering, and Albert V. Dicey referred. But Bentley rejected the separation of feelings and ideas from social institutions and social activity as a legitimate procedure in the scientific investigation of society. To him, feelings and ideas could not be located apart from the

29

activities they are called on to explain. Once the specific social activities and situations are described, the feelings and ideas "vanish" into the activities or are seen as phases in the social situation or situations.

Bentley's own positive advance over the "dead political science" of his time is to be found in the last two-thirds of his book. The raw materials of government, he asserted, cannot be found in the law books; in the proceedings of constitutional conventions; in the addresses and essays on tyranny or democracy; or in the "character of the people," in their specific "feelings" or "thoughts," in their "hearts" or "minds." "The raw material can be found only in the actually performed legislating-administrating-adjudicating activities of the nation, and the streams and kinds of activity that gather among the people and rush into these spheres."

After developing his theory of group interests and activities, Bentley examined some cardinal problems of political science: public opinion and leadership, individual endowment and race type, government, law, classifications of governments, and the separation of government agencies. Each subject received incisive analysis and illuminating illustrations. A few of the distinctive contributions made by Bentley in this volume are the following:

1. The repudiation of any simple and rigid classification of social groups. Bentley rejected Marx and Engel's theory of the class struggle and historical materialism, as well as other oversimplified group theories of contemporary German sociologists.

2. The "instrumental approach" to the classification of the elements of a population into groups. Bentley was free of the prevalent tendency to regard groups as fixed entities or classes, given in nature and society.

3. The "functional" approach to groups, group activity, and group interests: "A thing is what it does." To Bentley a group is "a way of action in which many people participate." "Group," "group activity," and "group interest" are "conjoined phases of one process."

4. Social Behaviorism: centering the attention of political and social science upon socially observable human behavior. Bentley set as his objectives the description of the "manifest, or evident, or palpable activity" of human beings, not in the purely physical or psychological aspect, but in the social context, situation, or frame of reference. Those forms of social conduct which are not palpable or evident in their early stages, Bentley called "tendencies of activity."

5. The "transactional" approach to individuals and groups. Bentley and Dewey forty years later in their volume, *Knowing and the Known* used and developed the meaning of the term "transaction." But some of the basic materials for their point of view are to be found in *The*

Process of Government. One example is Bentley's plea for considering the physical and social environments as phases of the activities of
men (pp. 193–96). Another is his proof that the distinctions between
subjective and objective, mind and matter, wants and the men who
want, the external acts of men and the institutions or things done by
them, are very crude statements that can best be treated as different
phases of a process. Similarly, he minimized the distinctions between
the conscious and the unconscious, the individual and the social contribution to policy-making, invention and discovery (pp. 196–97).

Despite the magnitude of Bentley's achievement, he modestly refused
to claim any special merit for having developed the theory and method
expounded in this great work. His intellectual pioneering was based,
he maintained, on his sensitivity to the prior insights and empirical
findings of such social scientists as Gumplowicz, Simmel, Ratzenhofer,
Marx, and Durkheim in Europe. Among Americans he received some
inspiration from the writings of Simon N. Patten, Dean Bigelow, and
Brooks Adams, not to mention his great debt to Dewey. Actually, Bentley's selective synthesis and improvement upon the seminal ideas of
these thinkers constitutes a major and distinctive contribution to the
social sciences.

After the publication of his book, Bentley took a rest from his newspaper work to recuperate from the strain of completing so massive a
work in some three years, and to readjust his and his family's affairs after
his father's death in July, 1908. Although he returned to his newspaper
work and stayed in Chicago until 1911, he had new relapses into muscular overstrain, and decided to quit Chicago and the newspaper world.
From then on he made Paoli, Indiana, the center of his life-activities.
He started and managed an apple orchard for many years; after improving in health, he resumed his scientific researches and writing. During the First World War he helped to organize the state of Indiana for
the American Red Cross, raised money effectively, and emerged at the
end of the war as Associate Director of Indiana for the "Lake Division"
and chairman of the Indiana State Executive Committee.

After 1918 Bentley became interested in the cooperative work of the
Non-Partisan League in North Dakota and made an intensive personal
investigation of their activites. He then wrote a book of some 100,000
words or more on the American business and political scene, entitled
Makers, Users and Masters in America. Unfortunately, the volume was
turned down by several publishers, and Bentley allowed the manuscript
to remain unpublished. The book, however, is valuable for revealing
Bentley's critique of profiteering and the concentration of economic
power in America at that time. He proposed that the economic position of small farmers, small businessmen, and industrial workers be

31

improved through the organization of these groups into pressure groups that would be able to bargain effectively with big business interests. Although Bentley admired many of Thorstein Veblen's insights, Bentley's own practical proposals were closer to those of middle-class reformers like Louis Brandeis and Robert LaFollette. In 1924 Bentley became a member of the national Progressive Party committee and chairman of the Indiana state committee in charge of the campaign for Robert LaFollette as President.

During the early 1920's Bentley reformulated his ideas on the science of society. Some time before the outbreak of the First World War he had tried to develop a technical terminology for the kinds of social phenomena he treated in *The Process of Government*. After Einstein's theory of relativity was first confirmed in 1919, Bentley regarded his early attempt at recasting social theory as antiquated. By 1924 he had written a volume, *Relativity in Man and Society* (1926) that did not thoroughly reconstruct his social theory, but carried out the critical preliminaries.

Relativity in Man and Society is not so important in its presentation of Bentley's ideas as his earlier and later published works, yet it occupies an important place in the development of his theory of the social sciences. He took the position that Einstein's experimental procedures and theoretical constructions affected social inquiries. Bentley urged that sociologists discard the old Newtonian space-and-time frame of reference and use instead Einstein's method of viewing space and time as integral phases of the events with which they were dealing. Bentley extended the operational logic employed in relativity physics to problems in the study of society. First he reviewed the social constructions of such great European sociologists as Durkheim, Ratzenhofer, Simmel, Vierkandt, and von Wiese. Then Bentley presented his own alternative frame of reference for sociological investigation. He suggested a new term "man-society" to designate the subject-matter of sociology, and insisted that this should be regarded as one field. Every social fact was to be considered as a cross-section of activity occurring across a group of human beings.

Bentley argued that for handling social facts, sociological frames of reference can be established comparable to those now used in physics. Formulations can be made in such a way as to indicate the particular social position of each investigator. Exact meanings can then be conveyed from one social investigator to another. But it is important to point out that even without the analogy with Einsteinian physics, these positions of Bentley's concerning social inquiry are sound.

In 1932 Bentley saw the publication of his challenging inquiry, *Linguistic Analysis of Mathematics*. This was the fruit of years of intensive study and grew out of his desire to develop an adequate theory of

32

scientific method, with particular reference to mathematics and its application to such problems of social science as the relation of the individual to society. The great success of the nineteenth-century mathematicians in fostering increasingly rigorous formulation of postulates led to a crisis around 1900 in the foundations of mathematics. During the following three decades programs for solving these difficulties were advanced by noted thinkers.

The logistic established by Alfred North Whitehead and Bertrand Russell in their *Principia Mathematica* (1910–13) was centered on deducing pure mathematics from logic. The formalism or meta-mathematics of David Hilbert sought a mathematics free from contradiction by an interpretation of mathematics as exclusively the study of strings of symbols or marks on paper, and their interrelations, without any reference to "external things or realities." His great objective was the establishment of mathematical consistency in its own right. The mathematical intuitionism of L. E. J. Brouwer asserted the supremacy of the individual's intuition as to what are natural numbers and the general rules for constructing mathematical entities. It attempted to avoid certain paradoxes encountered by Whitehead and Russell by formally denying the application of Aristotle's law of excluded middle to infinite aggregates. Brouwer also asserted that mathematics was basically independent of ordinary language or any symbolic languages, except for communication purposes.

Impressed by Hilbert's achievements, Bentley sought to establish a firm construction for the linguistic materials with which mathematical signs and symbols are developed, communicated, and interpreted. He proposed to push Hilbert's work one stage further so as to cover the full system of linguistic materials used in the research for mathematical consistency as well as a system of specifically mathematical "zeichen" (signs or symbols). Bentley suggested eradicating the inferior forms of expression through a fully clarified postulation. He refused to interpret any mathematical system or element of such a system as "manifest," "intuitive," "true," or "necessary." His sole criterion was the complete consistency of the signs, symbols, and statements adopted for investigation. He called this procedure "semantic" postulation; the current usage now would be "syntactic." He contrasted this with "realistic" postulation, in which the elements are assumed to represent external reality; today the adjective used would be "semantic."

Bentley also presented a new terminology which he hoped would be free from the ambiguities of conventional language. He had come to the conclusion that many problems which vexed the philosophers concerning the foundations of mathematics were due to linguistic obsessions. He proposed that these be resolved by clarifying the relation of "ordinary language" to the mathematical subject-matter under investigation. He also stressed the importance of observing the distinctions among "things," "relations," and "operations" in postulate theory.

Bentley's analysis of the nature of mathematics was part of the increasingly intense and exact study of the foundations and structure of mathematics that occurred in the 1920's. Bentley's book appeared just when a new phase had been initiated by the publication in 1931 of Kurt Gödel's two incompleteness theories. This was followed in 1933 by Alfred Tarski's work on the concept of truth in formalized language; in 1934 by the Herbrand-Gödel notion of "general recursive function"; and in 1936 by Alonzo Church's thesis concerning this function. The most important recent study in this field is Raymond M. Smullyan, *Theory of Formal Systems* (Revised ed. 1961). These new studies show that the hope for presenting the whole of mathematics as a complete, consistent formal system is an impossibility, although it is possible to organize certain parts of mathematics as formal systems. We now know that no "mechanical" method exists capable of deciding which sentences are provable in which mathematical systems. Hence, certain theses in Bentley's *Linguistic Analysis of Mathematics* are no longer in the center of attention of mathematical logicians. Yet the volume is in accord with various *avant-garde* positions advanced by Ludwig Wittgenstein in his *Philosophical Investigations* and *Remarks on the Foundations of Mathematics* (1956).

Bentley's book on mathematics may be taken as an attempt to join Hilbert's mathematical formalism to Dewey's experimental method and Bridgman's operational logic. Bentley acknowledged Dewey's influence in a paper, "Knowledge and Society" as early as October, 1910 (first published in *Inquiry into Inquiries,* Sidney Ratner, ed., 1954). Bentley stated explicitly in his *Linguistic Analysis of Mathematics* (p. 43) that his approach to the problems of logic and language was "in the broadest and most general sympathy" with that of John Dewey, as he had developed it especially in his *Essays in Experimental Logic.* Bentley also praised P. W. Bridgman's *The Logic of Modern Physics* for breaking with the verbalisms of formal logic. Bentley insisted upon taking mathematical and logical entities and relations as processes, procedures, events. He recognized the validity of logical operations, but insisted that logic had to be seen as an integral part of scientific inquiry and had to have its assumptions and primary terms clearly related to their empirical sources. His chapter "Reconstructions of Logic," lent considerable support to Dewey's experimental logic.

The impact of Bentley's work in mathematics on Dewey's thought is important. In the letters to Bentley included in this volume, Dewey wrote that the *Linguistic Analysis of Mathematics* had helped him greatly in analyzing the procedures of mathematics. The book had also strengthened his contention that both the new mathematical logic and the old Aristotelian logic imposed on scientific inquiry meanings not derived from any specific scientific inquiries. Bentley's work aided Dewey in making more precise his demonstration that modern logicians often uncritically assume obsolete psychological conceptions.

In 1935 Bentley published *Behavior, Knowledge, Fact,* the fullest presentation of his ideas on techniques for studying human behavior. He had started work on this volume as early as 1931, intending to collaborate with the psychologist J. R. Kantor at the University of Indiana, but they diverged on basic points. Bentley proceeded to write this volume on his own, while Kantor went on to publish his *An Objective Psychology of Grammar* (1935). Bentley's major goal was the construction of a language in terms of which a science of human behavior, comparable in accuracy and verifiability to the physical and biological sciences, could be developed. He criticized most of the current systems of psychology for isolating the individual from the environment and for concentrating their attention upon the internal and reciprocal behaviors of isolated organisms. Only a few psychologists, such as Dewey and Kantor, stressed an approach to events as the matrix out of which bodies and behaviors emerge as the products of analysis. But even their theories did not yet provide a satisfactory framework for the observation and description of such basic behavioral phenomena as the communication of meaning.

Bentley's analysis of the procedures called "knowing" and "being known" led him to the conclusion that Language, Knowledge, Experience, and Fact are equally important phases of the knowing-known processes. He proceeded to set up as the criterion of social fact the rigorous requirement of direct observability in space-time. Social facts had to be "specifically 'behavioral' as distinct from either 'physical' or 'vital' in the same manner that these two last are specifically and scientifically distinct from each other." In contrast to the mechanistic "space-time" of Watsonian behaviorism, Bentley proposed the construction and use of a "behavioral space-time," in which the whole social situation with its aspect of "meaning" or "reference," could find an observable place. He also provided a new set of terms to bring out the primacy of communication in human behavior. The participating individuals and the objects of perception and of communication were presented as distinguishable but inseparable aspects of the behavioral whole. All behavioral events and social problems, in his judgment, had to be studied by a combination of psychological and sociological techniques; psychology and sociology divided the labor between them in terms of selective emphasis rather than levels of complexity. Bentley's own psychology was one in which organism and object combined in the perceptional processes. In his system the phenomena of society appeared without any arbitrary severance of individuals from social groups, or of social groups from physical nature.

Dewey, who had come to know Bentley in May, 1935, was interested enough in the volume to read it for Bentley in galley proofs. Dewey was so impressed that he called the volume "a landmark in the development of psychology." He went on to say: ". . . it has been a long time since I got so many *ideas* as I have from yours."

A Revolution in Logic

In 1938 Dewey crowned a lifetime of work on experimental logic with his great work, *Logic: The Theory of Inquiry.* In contrast with Morris R. Cohen and Bertrand Russell, who drew a sharp line between logic and scientific method, Dewey expressly identified logic with the theory of effective practical and scientific inquiry. He provided the basis for a fully empirical account of the logical process. Dewey undertook to show that the formal distinctions of logic arise within "the matrix of inquiry" and have no significance except as elements in that matrix. Logical principles, according to him, have evolved as science has developed increasingly complex methods of inquiry.

The traditional formal logic, in Dewey's eyes, had developed from the Platonic and Aristotelian view of science as a means of intuiting relations between essences. The syllogism represents that process of inquiry in which, according to Aristotle, species are brought under genera. But modern science does not rely upon essences. The relations to which it points cannot be appropriately brought within the formal pattern of species-genus organization. Contemporary formal logic has added relational propositions and inferences to the ancient and scholastic list of subject-predicate propositions and syllogistic inferences. But Dewey contended that this addition has confused instead of clarifying the situation. Modern logic has added new forms when it should have radically reconstructed the whole subject.

Modern logic also has stressed the "merely formal" character of logical patterns when abstracted from the context of inquiry. What modern science requires, however, is a new logical inquiry, in which the sharp distinction of Greek science between the formal and the material will be out of place. The principles of logic actually "state habits operative in every inference that tends to yield conclusions that are stable and productive in further inquiries" (p. 13). The modern need is for "a unified theory of inquiry through which the authentic pattern of experimental and operational inquiry of science shall become available for the

36

regulation of the habitual methods by which inquiries in the field of common sense are carried on" (p. 98).

When we discover various recurrent logical forms in the course of our inquiry into inquiry, we must not assume that these forms have any absolute ontological or metaphysical status. As Dewey pointed out, the "logical forms accrue to subject-matter in virtue of subjection of the latter in inquiry to the conditions determined by its end—institution of a warranted conclusion" (p. 372). A normative in logic is based upon an analysis of those generic traits of scientific procedures which have operated successfully in specific inquiries. *Logical* validity is grounded on *natural* fact. The implications of logic are discovered in the objective behavior-procedures that we follow in obtaining knowledge.

Dewey's characterization of logic is a carefully worked out alternative to both an empiricistic logic (for which logical traits are mental entities and hence have only a psychological existence), and a logical realism (for which the laws of logic are formulations of the invariant relations among all possible entities in nature). Logical forms are not mentalistic, yet they are modes of behavior only when things are caught up in reflective inquiry and are subjected to the conditions required for inference. Dewey avoided both Platonic realism and the linguistic conventionalism which makes the laws of logic in some sense laws of language. He held an objective view of logical relations as coming into existence in the process of inquiry during various human beings' attempts to solve problem-situations through hypotheses and experimentation. The logical relations have their locus or existence in the process of scientific inquiry, not of one single individual, but of the whole human community as it has acquired education and the ability to deal with these problems. In short, following a suggestion by Bentley to P. W. Bridgman in an unpublished letter dated February 26, 1950, we may take "the three great characteristics of the Dewey *Logic*" to be the pursuit of warranted assertions within situations; the treatment of the "proposition" as throughout instrumental, and the description of "object" as an outgrowth of inquiry in a situation at a relatively settled stage.

The pattern of inquiry is the controlled or directed transformation of an indeterminate situation into a determinately unified one. In the process of transformation of the indeterminate situation, *discourse* through the use of symbols is employed as one means. In received logical terminology, propositions or terms and the relations between them, are intrinsically involved. A judgment is the provisional and existential settlement of an inquiry; a proposition is conceptual instrument or intermediary. A logical subject is something pointed *out*, not merely pointed *at*; a logical predicate is a definite conceptual means of possible

37

further determination of its subject. The copula stands for operations in a process of temporal existential reconstitution.

Dewey distinguishes between two basic types of general propositions: the generic and the universal. Generic (existential) propositions locate and circumscribe the problem set by an indeterminate situation and provide the evidence (the perceptual material) which tests solutions that have been suggested and proposed. Universal propositions express necessary relations between possibilities that may be non-existent. They represent possible solutions of the problems in hand and prescribe operations which when performed yield new data tending in the direction of a solution. Universal propositions are definitory in character and are expressed in hypothetical "if-then" form. A judgment or warranted assertion is the outcome of a competent inquiry, but it may be employed as a *means* in a subsequent inquiry and become a proposition in that inquiry.

In the last part of his *Logic*, Dewey asserted that form and matter are joined as "form-of-matter" and that scientific method "both constitutes and discloses the nature of logical forms." In discourse, especially in mathematical discourse, there is an immense formulation and transformation (through symbols) of non-existential possibilities; in fact, a most extensive development of transformability in the abstract. He declared that language "is intrinsically free from the necessity of existential reference" because "the subject-matter or *content* of discourse consists of *possibilities*" (pp. 394–95). He distinguished between possibilities and potentialities. Potentialities "are existential powers that are actualized under given conditions of existential interaction"; they are the stuff of which indeterminate situations are made (p. 289). On the other hand, possibility is "a matter of an operation as such—is operability" (p. 289). Since the metaphysical status of possibilities is to be non-existential, "they require full relation in symbols" (p. 395). To Dewey it was clear that the use of existential and universal propositions makes possible the resolution of an indeterminate situation into a determinate one, one that is structured and known. Language, therefore, enables us to see the potentialities in a situation and to start them on a process of actualization. Putting both the possibilities and potentialities of a situation in linguistic form enables us to act in inquiry through deliberate operations.

Various writers on Dewey's *Logic* have misinterpreted Dewey's position on the status of scientific laws. Hence, it is important to clarify his position. Dewey states (p. 354) that one meaning of the word "law" is to designate the content of physical generalizations when a specified conjunction of traits has been observed and confirmed without an exception. It is then called a general fact and is existential in reference. The second meaning of the term "law" is that it designates a relation as one member of a system of interrelated universal propositions. The latter meaning is definitely non-existential in reference. In other words, for Dewey, empirical laws are determined inductively and are therefore only probable. In subsequent investigations they may be utilized as means and may function in that capacity as universal propositions.

In the final chapter of his *Logic*, "The Logic of Inquiry and Philosophies of Knowledge," Dewey argued persuasively that each of the main types of epistemological theory which mark the course of philosophy "represents a selective extraction of some conditions and factors out of the actual pattern of controlled inquiry." He showed that this borrowing is what gave or gives plausibility and appeal to sensationalistic empiricism, logical atomism, materialism, positivism, direct and representative (critical) realism, and perceptual, rationalistic, and absolute idealism. Their arbitrary isolation of the elements selected from the inquiry-context in which they function invalidates their sweeping claims. These philosophies do not violate *all* conditions of inquiry as means of attaining knowledge, but their selection is so one-sided "as to ignore and thereby virtually deny any other conditions which give those that are selected their cognitive force and which also prescribe the limits under which the selected elements validly apply" (p. 514). The error of these philosophies is in extracting the material from their context and making that material "structural instead of functional, ontological instead of logical" (p. 534).

Dewey's *Logic: The Theory of Inquiry* has been widely appreciated as an epoch-making work by philosophers sympathetic in whole or in part to Dewey's challenging program and argument, e.g., Sidney Hook, Felix Kaufmann, C. I. Lewis, Joseph Ratner, Paul Weiss, and Ernest Nagel (who, however, uncovered some important difficulties in Dewey's distinction between "generic" and "universal propositions"). Some writers have pointed out that Dewey's book was a climax to the movement to replace formal logic with a theory of inquiry which dates back to Descartes and Locke in the seventeenth century. Others have likened Dewey to a post-Darwinian John Stuart Mill desirous of developing logic as "the science of evidence" in close connection with all the sciences, but without Mill's narrow empiricism. But a number of formal logicians, notably Bertrand Russell, have been critical of Dewey's work. They have pointed out the link between his "instrumental" logic and the logic of Hegel and of such post-Hegelian logicians as F. H. Bradley and Bernard Bosanquet. To them what is striking in Dewey's *Logic* is that Dewey replaced the conception of a static Reality by the idea of systematic inquiry and showed a greater sympathy for Hegel's "Spirit" than for Bradley's "Absolute." They have taken issue with Dewey's theory of truth, with his

39

attempt to replace formal logical validity by such an idea as effectiveness of means, and with his thesis that the development of modern science has brought changes in the character of logic.

Some critics have failed to come to grips with Dewey's view that truth is to be understood in terms of knowledge and that knowledge cannot intelligibly be assumed in terms of an absolute and eternal truth—outside the context of the methods by which assertions are warranted. For Dewey all meaningful assertions of truth are interpreted as assertions warranted ultimately by experiment and evidence. Consequently they can never be final. Truths are *working* truths. The awkward feature of this theory is that on the basis of evidence at any specific time, conclusions may be warranted which at a later date we discover are false. We "know" something subject always to the possibility of discovering confirming or conflicting evidence. When we discard what was warranted at one time, according to Dewey, it is only because in a wider and more inclusive context we have better grounds. This is the pattern of scientific discovery, and corresponds to the way in which scientists use the term "true" to characterize hypotheses which are confirmed. The only alternative to this theory of truth is the view that an assertion is true or false independently of the evidence for it or of the methods by which it is reached. Since, however, no one can reasonably assert truth or falsity without reference to evidence (guessing is not knowing), the consequence of the absolutist theory of truth is complete skepticism. One would then have to believe that there are absolute truths—timeless, tenseless, unrelated to man and inquiry, but that we are never warranted in asserting them since the warrant is a function of evidence which may change. This alternative is unintelligible. Dewey's view is only terminologically awkward because the term "true" has been invested with the overtones of the classical theory of eternal truths which Dewey's experimental naturalism rejects.

There have been a number of strictures against Dewey's logic on matters of detail, most of which seem to center around his attempt to do justice to the "non-existential" aspect of logical forms or universals. Nevertheless, since the publication of his logic there has been an increasing body of evidence that various leading figures in mathematics, logic, and the philosophy of science have come to support some basic positions of Dewey's, sometimes from an independent line of reasoning and background, but in all cases confirming these crucial points. Four citations may serve to document this statement. John von Neumann pointed out in 1947 in a brilliant essay on "The Mathematician," in *The Works of the Mind* (1947), pp. 180–96, that much of the best mathematical inspiration has come from experience and it is hardly possible to believe in the existence of an absolute, immutable concept of mathematical rigor, dissociated from all human experience. Von Neumann cited three episodes during his own lifetime during which his own views concerning absolute mathematical truth had changed. In another essay on "Probabilistic Logics" he asserted that error had to be viewed "not as an extraneous and misdirected or misdirecting accident, but as an essential part" of logic and of automata-synthesis. The implications of his theory of error were not fully worked out by von Neumann in relation to the foundations of mathematics and of logic. But one can see that if error is an essential part of scientific inquiry, its correction leads to the establishment of new logical systems as our knowledge of different subject-matters leads us to new insights concerning the structure of knowledge. See *Automata Studies*, C. E. Shannon and J. McCarthy, eds. (1956), pp. 43–98.

Hermann Weyl, a colleague of von Neumann's at the Institute for Advanced Study, took the revolutionary stand in his *Philosophy of Mathematics and Natural Science* (rev. English ed., 1949), p. 235, that a truly realistic mathematics has to be conceived in line with the modern physics of relativity theory and quantum mechanics, as "a branch of the theoretical construction of the one real world." With this view Haskell B. Curry concurred in *Foundations of Mathematical Logic* (1963), p. 26, when he expressed the belief that mathematics does not need absolute certainty or consistency any more than does physics. As in physics, all theories are hypothetical; we adopt a theory so long as it makes useful deductions and abandon it or modify it as soon as it ceases to be useful.

In confirmation of Curry's and Weyl's point, Stephen E. Toulmin in his important, provocative book, *The Uses of Argument*, (1958) independently stated:

But not only will logic have to become more empirical; it will inevitably tend to be more historical. To think up new and better methods of arguing in any field is to make a major advance, not just in logic, but in the substantive field itself: great logical innovations are part and parcel of great scientific, moral, political, or legal innovations. In the natural sciences, for instance, men such as Kepler, Newton, Lavoisier, Darwin and Freud have transformed not only our beliefs, but also our ways of arguing and our standards of relevance and proof: they have accordingly enriched the logic as well as the contents of natural science. Grotius and Bentham, Euclid and Gauss, have performed the same double feat for us in other fields.

Finally, we cite Hilary Putnam, who wrote in his essay "It Ain't Necessarily So," *Journal of Philosophy*, LIX (October 25, 1962), pp. 670–71: "The distinction between statements necessary relative to a body of knowledge and statements contingent relative to that body of knowledge is an important methodological distinction and should not be jettisoned. But the traditional philosophical distinction between statements necessary in some eternal sense and statements contingent in some external sense is not workable." In quantum mechanics, for example, we may have a choice between accepting a physical theory based upon a non-standard logic, on the one hand, and retaining standard logic and postulating given variables, on the other. This difference is of logical significance. It supports Dewey's evolutionary and historical view of the development of logical principles.

When Dewey's *Logic* was published, he was greatly pleased by the enthusiastic response of Arthur Bentley to its radical theses. Dewey valued the forthright criticisms and proposals for revision of certain formulations that Bentley offered as a means of making its basic framework and theme more secure against criticism. (Two important essays of Bentley's on this subject, as we pointed out earlier, are: "Dewey's Logic Compactly Presented," and "Dewey's Development.")

Dewey and Bentley's Philosophic Partnership

It is interesting to trace the way in which Dewey's and Bentley's philosophical activities developed from 1938 on, first separately, then, from the early 1940's with increasing cooperation. In 1938 Dewey was the chief sponsor of *Not Guilty:* Report of the Commission of Inquiry into the Charges Made against Leon Trotsky in the Moscow Trials, the chairmanship of which he had courageously assumed in 1937 and the duties of which he had carried out with integrity and wisdom. (The fascinating story of Dewey's role in this inquiry is given by James Farrell's essay in *John Dewey: Philosopher of Science and Freedom.*) In 1939 Dewey celebrated his eightieth birthday by publishing a critique of totalitarianism and a defense of democracy, *Freedom and Culture*, an analysis of the *Theory of Valuation*, and "Experience, Knowledge and Value," a powerful reply to his critics in *The Philosophy of John Dewey*, Paul A. Schilpp, ed. During the next few years Dewey wrote essays on logic, ethics, education, democracy, William James, and public affairs, many of which were published in his volume, *Problems of Men* (1946). Two of the philosophically most noteworthy were "Nature in Experience," *Philosophical Review*, March, 1940, a reply to criticisms of his work by Morris R. Cohen and William E. Hocking, and "Propositions, Warranted Assertability, and Truth," *Journal of Philosophy*, March 27, 1941, a magisterial rejoinder to an attack upon his *Logic* by Bertrand Russell in *An Inquiry into Meaning and Truth* (1940). A third essay of importance by Dewey was "Peirce's Theory of Linguistic Signs, Thought and Meaning," *Journal of Philosophy*, February 14, 1946.

During these years Bentley published articles on such themes as situational versus psychological theories of behavior, behavioral space-time,

42

the locus of human behavior, and an incisive reply to some critics of Dewey's *Logic*. These essays were reprinted later with some earlier and later essays of Bentley's in *Inquiry into Inquiries*. Among other things Bentley demonstrated the importance of localizing seeing, talking, thinking, and all other human behaviors in organic-environmental situations rather than in organisms viewed in isolation. These conclusions, although independently arrived at, were in harmony with the positions developed by John Dewey in his *Logic: The Theory of Inquiry*.

Dewey applauded the way in which Bentley broke down the sharp distinctions between the "knower" and the "known" and the manner in which he presented the knowing activity as a transaction involving the human organism and its environment. In 1941 the Columbia University Philosophy Department invited Bentley to be a visiting lecturer for the academic year 1941–42. Bentley gave some talks on a "Program of Research into Language," which won high praise for its arraignment of those formal logicians and semanticists who thought that language can best be studied in isolation from the context of its use and users.

Bentley continued to work on an adequate theory of language and on the relation of "knowing" to the "known." He also worked intensively on the nature of the visual image and came to question the factual basis of several accepted doctrines. In June, 1943, Dewey's suggestion to Bentley that they do a joint language-study led, as we know, to the unusually rich philosophical correspondence to which this volume bears witness, and to the publication in 1949 of *Knowing and the Known*.

It is relevant to mention that both men remarried in 1946. In May, Bentley married Imogene Shaw of Indianapolis. In December, Dewey married Roberta (Lowitz) Grant of New York City. Thus Dewey and Bentley were given the support and companionship of their wives during the major period of their correspondence and co-authorship, and until their deaths—Dewey on June 1, 1952, at the age of ninety-two, and Bentley on May 1, 1957, at the age of eighty-six.

The first half of *Knowing and the Known* exposed with verve and wit various errors and weaknesses, especially inconsistencies in usage, in widely accepted "mentalistic," "realistic," and "positivistic" theories of logic and scientific knowledge. The constructive portions of the book centered on two objectives: first, an attempt to "secure a set of leading words capable of firm use in the discussion of 'knowings' and 'existings' in that specialized region of research called the theory of knowledge"; second, a presentation of the transactional approach deemed necessary by the authors for obtaining reliable namings in that field. Almost one-fourth of the book (pp. 47–102, 287–306) was devoted to developing a trial group of names that would promote cooperation and lessen misunderstanding among philosophers. Dewey and Bentley attacked with gusto and vigor the job of getting others to see "language, with all its speakings and writings, as man-himself-in-action-dealing-with-things." They rejected the still fashionable isolation of "real" objects from "mind," of "words" from the speaker, of "knowings" from the "knowns."

Dewey and Bentley gave a forceful and persuasive analysis of the advantages of viewing physical nature and human society from the transactional as against the interactional or self-actional point of view (pp. 103–69, 270–86). The three levels of the organization and presentation of inquiry they most compactly characterized and contrasted as follows: "Self-action: where things are viewed as acting under their own powers. Inter-action: where thing is balanced against thing in causal interconnection. Trans-action: where systems of description and naming are employed to deal with aspects and phases of action, without final attribution to 'elements' or other presumptively detachable or independent 'entities,' 'essences,' or 'realities,' and without isolation of presumptively detachable 'relations' from such detachable 'elements'" (p. 108).

Knowing and the Known provided the stimulus or reinforcement for important creative research in several significant fields. The transactional approach, for example, has been put to use in biology, physics, political science, psychology, and sociology. Leaders in this work have been Adelbert Ames, Jr., Ludwig von Bertalanffy, P. W. Bridgman, Hadley Cantril, Bertram Gross, and George Lundberg.

Dewey's *Logic* served as the basis upon which the theoretical structure of *Knowing and the Known* was built, with supplementary support coming from Bentley's *Linguistic Analysis of Mathematics*, his *Behavior, Knowledge, Fact,* and his essays of the late 1930's and early 1940's. Dewey's earlier thought and language underwent some major changes in *Knowing and the Known*. "Experience" is dropped in favor of the "knowing-known" transaction. "Transaction" replaces most of the previous uses by Dewey of "interaction." The continuity between the investigator and his field of investigation, the "subject" and the "object," the "knower" and the "known" is conveyed by abandoning the word "knowledge" and using the phrase "knowing-known." In the knowing-known process the "namings-named" occupy a central place. "Designation" is used as the most general name for the naming phases of the process, and "existence" as the most general name for the named phases.

"Definition" is rejected in favor of "symbolization" for non-empirical fields of investigation, e.g., pure mathematics. In empirical fields of inquiry, "definition" is replaced by "specification." "Concept" as a mentalistic entity is banned; but the word is tolerated as a current phrasing for subject-matters designed to be held under steady inspection in inquiry. "Consciousness," "mind," and "meaning" are given up as reified entities that can be replaced by more direct expressions, usually verbs. A "be-

44

havior" is never taken as *of* the organism alone or *of* the environment alone, but always as *of* the organic-environmental situation, with organisms and environmental objects taken as equally its aspects. "Individual" is supplanted by "organism" as an aspect of "behavior." "Names" are treated as forms of knowing, with empirical reference, and are distinguished from "symbols" that have no specific empirical reference functions.

The new formulations that Dewey and Bentley jointly agreed to adopt in *Knowing and the Known* were intended to strengthen the fundamental insights and positions embodied in Dewey's *Logic*. Certain formulations in the *Logic* were taken over without change in *Knowing and the Known*. One is "inquiry," a word that Bentley later appropriated for the title to his volume, *Inquiry into Inquiries*. Another is "object," which is specifically said to emerge "as a definite constituent of a resolved situation, and is confirmed in the continuum of inquiry." Others include "connection," "postulation," "reference," "relation," "situation," and "truth."

Admirers of Dewey's and Bentley's pioneering work may dissent from some of their conclusions or emphases in *Knowing and the Known*. One example is their equating of "Fact" with "the cosmos in course of being known through namings by organisms, themselves among its phases." Another is their advising abandonment of the word "individual" and all substitutes for it wherever positive general *theory* of language is undertaken or planned (pp. 294–95). Valuable as the transactional approach is, when the need arises to stress the moral value or historic significance of individual choice and action, a non-transactional phrasing is justifiable. Too rigid an adherence to the "transaction" formulation could liquidate the special qualities of individuality. Although some readers have inferred that the transactional approach must be mechanistically applied, or interpreted, this was not the intention of Dewey and Bentley, as I understand their writings.

In some respects retention of the "interaction" form guards against this type of misinterpretation and conduces to the development of a theory of the self that Dewey and Bentley never worked out adequately. One may also feel that important as improvements in language are for increasing accurate specification and exact symbolization, the authors of *Knowing and the Known* might well have elaborated on the fact that a *general* theory of relativity in language, as in physics, makes possible the translation of ideas from one language system or perspective to another. Their correspondence reveals their awareness of this point, but they failed to get it into their book.

Both Dewey and Bentley continued publishing independently after 1949. They also continued to exchange ideas through 1951. Among the most important essays that Dewey wrote in his last years are two

45

that he sent Bentley, but did not publish: "Means and Consequences," and "Importance, Significance and Meaning." We feel privileged to publish them for the first time as Parts VIII and IX of this volume. Bentley agreed with most of the theses advanced by Dewey in these essays, but differed on some turns of phrase involving Dewey's use of "meaning." Bentley himself published his *Inquiry into Inquiries,* which included significant essays on language, logic, logical behavior, and kennetic inquiry. These essays of Dewey's and Bentley's represent the furthest stretch of their thought on problems that continue to hold the attention of philosophers.

The Dewey-Bentley Legacy

New advances have been made in philosophy since these writings, e.g., the brilliant attack on the dichotomy between analytic (a priori) and synthetic (a posteriori or empirical) statements by Willard Van Orman Quine in *From a Logical Point of View* (1953) and Morton G. White in *John Dewey: Philosopher of Science and Freedom.* But it is amazing to discover how certain ideas of Dewey and Bentley, as well as of Peirce and James, are at work in transforming the character of contemporary philosophy, notably in, and outside, America. Dewey and Bentley did not believe that philosophers, any more than scientists, should refrain from departing from "ordinary language" in order to secure a more adequate expression for new ideas or approaches. Nevertheless, English "ordinary language" philosophy, as exemplified by the articles and books of Gilbert Ryle, Ludwig Wittgenstein, P. F. Strawson, Stephen Toulmin, and Stuart Hampshire, among others, agrees with Dewey and Bentley that language is an instrument, that thought is inseparable from linguistic formulation, that the use of a word clarifies its meaning, and that one's mind is best seen as a function of one's body and as geared to decision-making and action. The major trend in England is in revolt against the Platonic status of meanings that Russell and G. E. Moore had celebrated in their earlier writings. It is also in revolt against the excessive claims of formal logic and the creation of logical calculi that are presented as being completely adequate for all the subtleties of philosophical analysis. Although English philosophers have been more familiar with the writings of James, Peirce, and C. I. Lewis, than with those of Dewey and Bentley, it is reassuring to have the insights of Dewey and Bentley confirmed by the converging analyses of their British contemporaries. It is to be hoped that the adherents of philosophic schools previously opposed to pragmatism will enlarge their horizons and benefit from the pioneering work of Dewey and Bentley.

This overview of the major works and ideas of each of these men and of the book which resulted from their collaboration will, it is hoped, provide a frame within which to place the correspondence that follows. As against their definitive publications, the correspondence reveals Dewey and Bentley at work in their shirtsleeves. Here they are seen starting projects, trying out ideas, rejecting some, clashing about others, reaching common agreements about many, then repeatedly revising. Here they can be observed formulating bold new hypotheses, and criticizing accepted doctrines. Often verbal sparks are struck in these letters that deserve to be remembered, but were not used in final print. Both writers explain with great candor why and how they came to make decisions on the important philosophical questions which have been outlined here. Sometimes fierce differences of opinion are disclosed which after a time get settled through discussion, e.g., on the validity of "concept." Usually there is a remarkable harmony of attitude toward the approach to be used in settling problems, as well as in the final conclusions.

The reader will perceive the first glimmerings of ideas later made central in Dewey's and Bentley's published writings. He will undoubtedly be startled by the authors' amazing flexibility and courage in abandoning doctrines or phrasings with which their names had been associated for decades. Whatever the reader's philosophic stand, he will be impressed by Dewey's and Bentley's passion for clarity, respect for evidence, and concern for communication with their fellow men. This correspondence enables us to share the thinking, and to come to know intimately the intellectual temper, of two great contemporary thinkers.

Part I

Letters: November 15, 1932–June 25, 1943

My Dear Professor Dewey:

While you were at Chicago, I had a place at the outer edge of one of your courses, where I secured a certain manner of vision which, so far as I can appraise such things, I have long regarded as one of the three or four most valuable aids I have received. I have at length found a region of investigation in which some tentative results can be secured, and I am permitting myself to send you a copy of the resulting book, *Linguistic Analysis of Mathematics*.

I do this, I may add, entirely for my own satisfaction by way of making acknowledgment.

With the strongest wishes for success in your present political work.

Sincerely yours, *Arthur F. Bentley*

New York, May 22, 1935

Dear Mr. Bentley:

Some time ago I received a copy of your *Linguistic Analysis of Mathematics*. I fear I didn't acknowledge it. At all events as I was occupied with other matters, I didn't read it. Recently I have read it, and am still re-reading it. It has given me more enlightenment and intellectual help than any book I have read for a very long time. I have been engaged during this year in trying to get my ideas on logical theory into systematic shape for publication, and I cannot put into words how much your book has meant to me in this process. Besides the great specific help it has given me in attacking the special theme of the procedure of mathematics, in which I am rather deplorably ignorant, it has greatly encouraged and strengthened me in my general position. While my terminology differs from your "realistic" and "semantic" [terminology], your treatment of that subject enabled me to clarify and make more precise a distinction I had made between control of inquiry from within and externally, and I have already rewritten some pages I had set down on that point to the effect that recent "mathematical logic" as well as the traditional Aristotelian logic assumes control by meanings fixed outside the operations of inquiry. I had also written that contemporary logicians who profess to make the sharpest division between logic and psychology nevertheless assume without examination certain conceptions taken over from a psychology that is already outmoded. Here too your treatment

51

has helped make my ideas much more definite. These are but two points of the many in which your book has been invaluable to me.

Sincerely yours, *John Dewey*

Paoli, Indiana, May 28, 1935

Dear Mr. Dewey:

It was a very great pleasure indeed to me to know that you find my book [*Linguistic Analysis of Mathematics*] of use. I have not exactly been overfertilized with praise, and your comments, combined with [Karl N.] Llewellyn's somewhat emphatic endorsement (["The Constitution as an Institution"] in the *Columbia Law Review*) of my earlier work [*The Process of Government*], make a red-letter week.

I am especially glad to hear from you at this time, because I am about to send to the press a book, completed about six months ago, *Behavior, Knowledge, Fact,* and I have long wished that I could secure your verification or amendment of two passages about your work—in chapters II and XI. . . . I am very anxious to know whether I miscarry in any way in the point at which I descend for criticism of your special psychological position in the second passage. . . .

Your remark on logicians who rest on outmoded psychology will be illustrated in my text by a brief account of C. K. Ogden (who is introduced solely to show how *not* to use language). I am unkind enough to describe his "double-language hypothesis" as a specialized duplicity for the specialized psychological problem and as a resurrection of the very "verbal magic" which he had once thrown out.

Perhaps when my book finally appears, you may be interested in my attempt to show how far [Edward Bradford] Titchener had come over towards the position which you, and I also, occupy. I know nothing whatever about Titchener personally, nor about the last ten years of his life, but the impression I get is that he had got hold of something [which] he was powerless to handle, and which nevertheless turned all his earlier work inside out, leaving him practically paralyzed. Certain it is, the editor of his posthumous book [*Systematic Psychology*] could not even read the text accurately. . . .

Sincerely yours, A. F. Bentley

Paoli, Indiana, May 29, 1935

Dear Professor Dewey:

I meant to say to you, in writing yesterday, that I am not to be trusted in the detail of my mathematical statements—the probabilities of error on any particular item are high. It is a risk I had to take in order to do anything at all.

The situation is this. I have been working most of my life with a view to a generalized economic theory—one that will have the "makings" of a construction for any particular population or era. Six or eight years ago I concluded that if the type of attack made by [Bertrand] Russell and other mathematical logicians was sound, my entire procedure was unsound. I was forced to go into the issue as thoroughly as I could. I published the results, not for any precision value they had, but to get the whole matter out of my system once and for all.

Sincerely yours, *A. F. Bentley*

Hubbards, Nova Scotia, July 20, 1935

Dear Mr. Bentley:

. . . I am pretty callous to criticism myself, except as far as it is intelligent and I learn from it. I do not pretend to be a psychologist anyway, and what I've written on that subject has been mostly for the sake of clearing up my own mind about something in either ethics or logic: consequently I'm aware that it is not systematic and probably not even self-consistent. Making something subsidiary to something else is not a good way to get at the roots. . . .

Sincerely yours, *John Dewey*

Hubbards, Nova Scotia, July 26, 1935

Dear Mr. Bentley:

I haven't absorbed the material [in *Behavior, Knowledge, Fact*] as yet, but can see that it is characterized by the same penetrating and thorough consistency that marks your mathematical book; if it receives the attention it deserves, it will be a landmark in the development of psychology.

Naturally I have so far given most attention to what you say about me. I certainly have no ground of complaint. On the contrary, I am much honored by the attention you give my writings, especially as . . . for years they have been incidental to other pursuits as far as psychology is concerned, and it is many years since I have attempted to keep up with the writings on the subject.

Your special point is well taken; it was [bad] thinking and writing to reduce "life-careers" to acts and attitudes; just what would have happened if I had sense enough to use a more general term than "acts," such as activities, and say dispositions for "attitudes," I haven't thought out yet. I have the feeling that there is something to be said for the position that the centering or focussing of the whole spatial-durational scene so as to constitute the life histories of individuals—the kind of individual needing, of course, to be adequately specified— . . . [differentiates] the peculiar subject-matter of psychology. But there is no defense for the break to which you call attention.

It happens that in the last few weeks I have had occasion to write an introduction to [Myrtle B.] McGraw's report on the development of infants [*Growth*], a study incidentally that ought in my opinion to revolutionize work in that field. In it I had occasion to criticize the "whole child" method on the ground that an individual child could not be investigated until general principles of development had been determined. If I had had this point in mind when I wrote the article ["Conduct and Experience"], I might not have reached a satisfactory conclusion, but I think I would have avoided the particular break you have indicated.

Sincerely yours, John Dewey

Paoli, Indiana, August 3, 1935

Dear Mr. Dewey:

. . . The situation, as I may have remarked before, is peculiarly difficult. I have the greatest admiration for your work on two or three different lines, and some day I may be in a position to express it; on the other hand, the only way I can indicate the direction further work should go is by critical analysis. I do not personally see the breakage I have stressed as a flaw in the work, but rather as the overlapping of two trends of development which extend through you and the other workers of the generation. . . .

Sincerely yours, A. F. Bentley

Hubbards, Nova Scotia, August 15, 1935

Dear Mr. Bentley:

. . . I am far from having read it [*Behavior, Knowledge, Fact*] through, but am most enthusiastic about it, as far as I have got, and will now add that the book ought to be a landmark in more than psychology. I get suggestions from most of the books I read, but it has been a long time since I got as many *ideas* as I have from yours. I expect to get many more when I come to the logic of science, natural and mathematical; so far I have been working, as far as writing is concerned, on what I call the logic of the common-sense world of "empirical" things.

But there are two fundamental points in which I am greatly indebted to you, points that were, I think, implicitly involved in my own position, but which are greatly cleared up by the help you have given in making them explicit. One is the conception of logic as autonomous and as heteronomous which springs very directly from your distinction of "semantic" and "realistic." It has become much clearer to me that a basic defect of present theory is due to the fact that "premises" of most constructions of logical doctrine are not themselves derived from analysis of inquiry, but imported from outside, psychological, epistemological, metaphysical, thus compromising the autonomy of logic. You will readily see how this is a restatement of your point. The other point is your emphasis upon the indefinite spatio-temporal background of every specified determination. I had made this point in connection with the perceptual *field* as over against the theory of *an* object as the [subject-]matter of perception, but had failed to carry it over adequately into treatment of other matters. . . .

Sincerely yours, John Dewey

Paoli, Indiana, September 20, 1935

Dear Mr. Dewey:
 . . . You mention "the perceptual field as over against the theory of *an* object as the [subject-]matter of perception." I recognize the extent to which you cover this in the essay in *Psychologies of 1930* ["Conduct and Experience"] which I criticised. But I wonder whether in one of your later works which I have not read, you go more specifically into the matter. Is there some discussion to which I can make further reference?

The point is this: I am closely (though in late years not directly) affiliated with your work. It is a case of that flowing thought which I briefly indicated in chapter XXIX [*Behavior, Knowledge, Fact*]. It is of advantage to me to bring this out. What is of much more importance, it is of great advantage to our construction, as it stands before the world. My unfortunate position is that in both the coming book and the preceding one, the margins of similarity and dissimilarity have interfered with any positive expression. It was largely because of this that I was anxious to have you check what I had written about you. . . .

Sincerely yours, A. F. Bentley

New York, September 23, 1935

Dear Mr. Bentley:
 . . . I don't think I've written anything explicitly along [the] line you mention though I developed the point more or less when I was lecturing. I thought perhaps I had done something of the kind in my *Quest for Certainty*, but looking over it this morning, I couldn't find anything explicit. It is perhaps implicit in the discussion from [pp.] 235–240, but as my purpose there was something else, the particular point is only

implicit. In my lectures and now in writing on logic, I distinguish between the perceptual field and the object of *observation*, the latter being selective and analytic within an indefinite field.

Sincerely yours, *John Dewey*

[P.S.] I am wrestling now with mathematics. When I get things in better shape, I'd like to impose a ms. on you. I'm enough of a specialist myself to know how easy it is for a layman to make breaks in a technical field. I'm in this quandary: that while I feel confident of my general direction, I'm over my depth technically, and it will be easy for me to make breaks which would discredit the whole thing in the eyes of the technically expert, when, I feel sure, a correct technical statement would only strengthen the argument. . . .

New York, November 14, 1935

Dear Mr. Bentley:

I am reading your book [*Behavior, Knowledge, Fact*] more consecutively and with more care than when I read the page proofs. In the course of this reading, I have, of course, taken in what you say about my article ["Conduct and Experience"]. I want to take the opportunity to suggest what I might have written because of not having thought [through] the meaning of some things I wrote, where I "acted" mechanically rather than reflectively. [This amounts] to an explanation, but not, I hope, to a defence of what I would have meant by "life-career" if I had thought out what was vaguely, and more or less automatically in mind—if it can [be called] mind—when I wrote about its connection with psychology. . . .

I may begin by saying that the main purpose was putting psychology in the context of reference to experiencing, not in that of experience, as illustrated by treating sensory qualities and things remembered, things loved and hated, etc.—as so much of psychology used, at least, to do— as somehow themselves "mental," trying to place them in the larger temporal-spatial and social context [which] you so generously give me credit for. Then I pointed out that, for certain problems, it is legitimate and indeed humanly necessary to "abstract" experiencing—just as for his problems the physicist or the historian selects from the whole experienced world certain aspects—and [I] identified the subjectmatter of psychology with these selected aspects, as illustrated by sensing (not sensations), perceiving, remembering, hating, reflecting, and so on. I should not of course [have] called them acts, but modal patterns of acting, i.e., behaving. And when I said "specific," I should have said "specified" (as, I believe, I did in one instance) and "specifiable," i.e., capable of observable discrimination with respect to identification and description.

56

Then I should either have stopped, saying nothing about "life-career," or have gone on to state the meaning of the latter word in its connection with these and other specifiable modes of experiencing. . . . I [did] go on and shirked and jumped the responsibility imposed.

But I should have meant two things: First, that there is a connection between the designated modes of experiencing and an individual organic self or individual, using those terms for the nonce in a purely denotative way, you, me and the other person. This, of course, is a selected aspect having no isolated being. Second, that sensing, perceiving, remembering, hating, etc., cannot be adequately studied by themselves, but only in connection, finally, with the whole durational spread of particular creatures born at designable times and after an interval dying. . . .

The final point would be that finding out about the process and "laws" of, say, perception, while an indispensable condition of the required knowledge of individuals, is still material to serve, and not full psychological science or information and understanding. It is, of course, possible that that wouldn't be psychology as such, but only a selected section of it that happens to be particularly interesting to me because I have been, in the course of my own "life-career," especially impressed with how damn little we know about the behavior of *individuals* and consequently make such a terrible mess of our relations to one another. Yet I can't get away from the hunch that after all the other sciences had covered the ground, there would be something left until we got at individuals as individuals. If I were asked to *define* "individual," I should use the reply you make—that is what we are trying to find out, and any definition made prior to the study having gone much further than it has, is only a way of rough staking out of certain problems for inquiry. . . .

I don't know exactly why I have written this to you, certainly not by way of justifying myself against your just criticism, but I suppose because I feel this particular problem so [deeply] as being basic to all improvement of human relations that I want to get a statement off my chest.

Sincerely yours, *John Dewey*

[P.S.] Anyway, it is one sign of the stirring of the waters [that] I'm getting from reading your book.

Paoli, Indiana, November 18, 1935

Dear Mr. Dewey:

I think your description of your own position fully justifies whatever I said about you [in *Behavior, Knowledge, Fact*] that was not criticism (in the Preface, for example). I made a snapshot of your action at a bad moment (throughout my text, you remember, I keep insisting that it is not "men" or "systems," but specified situations with which I deal). I needed that snapshot. I am ruthless, irresponsible, willing to seem absurd, where necessary: I probably would not spare my best friend, if his slaughter seemed important for what I was trying to do. In your case, I could not honestly let the matter stand without an indication of the broader position, more especially since something of the same kind of acknowledgment was needed in my preceding book [*Linguistic Analysis of Mathematics*]. . . .

It seems to me that your broad theoretical position permits the development I made; and probably requires something of the kind. Not that I took any of my later development from your later development; I am not interested in issues of that kind; your work is "there," and that is all there is to it. You, however, have a range of practical interests and activities which I forfeit. You switched your attention from one to the other without the qualifying clauses, and that gave me an opening. I go out and get my head cracked now and then by way of exercise; but in my writing I try to content myself with the belief that if I can contribute to welfare in the future (via knowledge), it is just as important as contributing to welfare today—which maybe will be the reverse of welfare, when all is said and done, just because of present ignorance.

Incidentally, have you ever looked at two books by E[lijah] Jordan (Butler University, 1928 [actually 1927] and 1930), *Forms of Individuality*, and *Theory of Legislation?* . . . I have just read them. He uses a linguistic technique of "mind" and "will," regarding mind as "objective," as "the order of related fact," or something of that kind. Despite this polar difference of approach, he seems to me to be *factually* almost equated with me in his development, so far as we touch similar fields. I am going to check up with him this winter, and see if my impression is correct. It will be amusing, if true.

What I would be very glad to hear from you some time in the future, when you can look back on the situation, is where you think my development goes wrong, or is specially defective. I do not refer to the last two or three chapters, which are dribblings anticipatory of further work, but to the main positions. Primarily there is the "dicaud" as itself direct fact. Secondarily there is the assertion of observability and the construction for it. This last is main force, and awkwardness also, as the saying goes. But maybe it is sound, for all of that. I couldn't know. . . .

Sincerely yours, *A. F. Bentley*

58

Dear Mr. Dewey:

When I wrote you a few days ago, I made some remarks about the "dicaud" and about "visibility." I intended to put on a postscript to get the stresses right, but forgot it. So I want to add it.

In preparing my book [*Behavior, Knowledge, Fact*], the first thing written was the chapter on Language and Knowledge, which is included in substantially its original form. Alongside it I had a correlated, cumbersome paper (out of which came the remarks in chapter XIX); a paper on the visibility of social fact (which I had long been intending to do); and several short papers or sketches growing out of the mathematical language work (one of them, I think, attempting to show that when the mathematical-logician did his denumerability work, he was controlled by some underlying visual patterns). This last group I dropped as irrelevant.

Now the "visibility of the social" paper simply would not come out right. I think I wrote it fifteen or twenty times, and it remained full of holes. It forced me to do two things; on the one side to develop the "dicaud" and companion phenomena; on the other to justify the method of observation. This last job in its turn forced me to run over the current psychologies—a procedure I have gone through every five or six years, but which [up to] this time had been repeatedly deferred.

I feel pretty confident that the direct observation of the "dicaud" and of other social phenomena (perhaps all social phenomena) in comparable forms, ought to be basic for construction in social sciences. . . . As for the general postulation, it is postulation and nothing more, and has as good a right to promenade as any. But the particular manner of justifying observation in "selective" forms is something not at all so substantial, especially as regards the stress on visibility. All I could do was publish it the way I got at it, with the possibility open that a vastly better job could be done in ways I did not find, and also that my own way might have some serious positive flaws.

It will be a couple of years before I can do any more work on the social side; and I did not mean to ask you to force out any comment at present; only to say that I would be glad to hear any criticism you had, at some convenient future time.

Sincerely yours, *A. F. Bentley*

New York, November 21, 1935

Dear Mr. Bentley:

. . . I could not have read as much of your book as I have without seeing that you treat the authors you criticize by holding them up to a strictly mathematical level of coherency. The proceeding is perhaps ruthless, but it is much needed, especially, as you suggest, for getting a clear-cut conception of the various positions instead of the fuzzy ones that most of us now have.

I am afraid that your strict application of mathematical standards will limit your reading audience in the present state of psychological and social thinking. But I am sure from my own experience that it will prove most illuminating to those who have enough intellectual backbone to stand up to it.

I have a copy of Jordan's book on *Forms of Individuality,* but have only glanced at its contents. However, even this has led me to believe that he is a worth-while writer. . . . The other book I have never seen. . . .

Sincerely yours, John Dewey

Paoli, Indiana, October 27, 1938

Dear Mr. Dewey:

Thank you for sending me your *Logic*[: *The Theory of Inquiry*], which all of us have been awaiting with so much interest. I am deeply appreciative of your reference to my work, as I could not possibly have anticipated anything of the kind; I am only too well aware of the chaos in which my formulation still stands. . . .

Sincerely yours, A. F. Bentley

New Orleans, Louisiana, January 24, 1939

Dear Mr. Dewey:

. . . I have finally been able to read the *Logic.* Needless to say, I have taken the greatest pleasure in it. My sympathy with your approach is complete, and there is not a single important positive feature with which I would want to quarrel. This testifies, I imagine, very heavily to the impress you made on me a long time ago, even though I have developed along a different line. I have, it is true, a number of notes about terms made as I went along—terms which did not straighten out satisfactorily for me—but none of these seems to me of any special importance.

The difference between my present status and yours, I take it, is something as follows: You have taken the "biological"—or, more broadly, the "naturalistic"—position, given it well-rounded form, and developed the logical process out of it. To my mind you have done this triumphantly as against everything I know of in the way of the older logic, symbolic logic, or mathematical foundation theory. You have protected your work with practically everything in the way of postulatory background that seems to me of importance. . . .

60

You nevertheless retain and continuously employ a number of words belonging to the old power-mind terminology, most conspicuous among them being the group containing "concept," "conceive," "conceptual." My rough list for further inspection has between three and four hundred instances from the "concept" group. This form of speech is, I assume, forced on you if you are to make your points so that they reach the ears of the older logicians whose work you are causing to disintegrate. Nevertheless, so long as the symbolic *relations* of this word remain chaotic, and so long as I cannot establish for myself any existential *reference* for it, I cannot help regarding your heavy use of it as a flaw in your exposition (though not in your program). Both under your postulation and under my own, "concept" specifies something within the range of language-symbol behaviors. Personally I regard the word as in this way comparable with such words as "noun" or "verb" on one side, and with "theory" or "construction" on the other side. It must indicate something that is describable, and in its way observable, within language behaviors, but the problem is just "*what* observable." This is still very obscure to me, though I have a considerable number of experimental specifications filed away among older materials.

My development, instead of being made biologically, was primarily made among law-language problems, and I came out of it with a strong bias in favor of direct observations and primary descriptions *across* sets of men. This should be correlated with (and not contrasted with) your observation and description *across* the cells and organs of the organism and the environmental response situations. My feeling, however, is that the language-reasoning-symbolization-concept construction will only get itself efficiently formulated when it is worked out in a naturalistically social rather than in a naturalistically organic form. I won't bother you with an account of the troubles I have had while adventuring in this field, but I will say that in your uses of the words I noted none of the positive abuses I have found practically everywhere else, but I did feel considerable vagueness and imperfection. This, however, is nothing more (I take it) than what you yourself said when you insisted that "a general theory of language" is still required.

About a year and a half ago I drafted an essay, approaching book size, under the provisional title: "The Concept: A Study of Talking and Thinking as Forms of Doing." I made considerable use of the development from [Thomas] Reid to [G. J.] Romanes, aimed to bring [I. P.] Pavlov into organization, and planned an evolutionary percept-to-concept, sign-to-symbol discussion. But I got into most serious trouble over the "skin," since the anatomical skin of the organism had to be kept from dominating the interactional behavioral event, and a proper "superfice" for the latter had to be provided. I had been assuming that when I needed a "psychology" in the narrower sense I could adapt it from [J. R.] Kantor,

61

or perhaps even from [Kurt] Lewin, but here I was entirely wrong. All I got was that which, I believe, are called "repercussions." Adolf Meyer's "attitude," your present development, and (in a narrow range) Pavlov's "signalization" come nearer to what I need than anything I have found. I talked chaotically about this matter at a meeting in New York last spring, and it has taken me ever since to straighten it out. . . . I sent the *Journal of Philosophy* (though hardly anticipating publication) a paper ["Situational vs. Psychological Theories of Behavior"] in three sections, sketching (1) the direct use of "sights-seen"—in [Frederick J. E.] Woodbridge's phrasing—as observables of inquiry, (2) the ways in which Pavlov, [H.] Klüver, A. Meyer, Kantor and Lewin have made interactional constructions, all of them incompletely, and (3) a set of postulates for such attempts.

I should be able in a couple of months now to take up the old ms. again, and develop my form of "a general theory of language" as an outstanding form of behavior among behaviors, all of them interactional, or as my last essays term it, "situational." It looks to me now as though, in doing this, I could throw away all my old introductory work and build directly upon your *Logic*. Of course I do not know how this would come out in the end: I only know it looks to me like an excellent opening. It would (1) save me a great deal of labor in my present clumsy approaches, (2) sharpen my formulation of the issues for the use of possible readers, and (3)—though of this I cannot yet be as sure as of the other two points—enable me to take over as it stands the general pattern of organization [that] you provide for "relations" and "references" (or for "sign" to "symbol," or for "perceptual" to "linguistic" behaviors), modifying it only to correspond with the terminology of the language scheme [that] I build up (a terminology which cannot possibly include both "word" and "concept" alongside one another—whatever it may need in the way of sharpened substitutes for either or both).

Now comes the point of this letter. I would not want to take such a step unless you thought it was at least a fairly reasonable way to proceed. Or, to put it the other way around, I would not want to do it, if it should seem that it would tend to throw obscurity around either your development or mine, or otherwise injure either. This, of course, is one of those cases in which either (1) I can assume certain common factors as belonging to our general situation of knowledge, and proceed by elaborating a contrast with your development of special feature within that situation, or (2) I can stress most heavily the common features of our approaches in common contrast with the older situations, and let my own development be more in the way of giving heavier stress than you do to one of the features of the situation, and thereby introducing modifications in the methods of statement or formulation employed. My bias is always in favor of the latter attitude, and in the present case I would think the former would be extremely unfortunate. . . .

Sincerely yours, *A. F. Bentley*

Key West, Florida, February 5, 1939

Dear Mr. Bentley:

. . . If I didn't think I had come out of it pretty well, I should be ashamed to admit how backhanded my intellectual course has been. I started with other men's ideas—those of philosophers—rather than with direct observations, and got ahead, as far as I did, by criticizing their ideas; all that saved me, aside from fortunate personal contacts, was a disposition sufficiently sceptical to be critical. As I look back, it took a rather unconscionably long time before the results of the examination of other men's ideas coalesced in a fruitful way with my own observations, so that I could use the distinctively "philosophical" ideas to direct and interpret observations.

If there is an over-use of "conception and conceptual," it is probably due to what I have just indicated. I regret now that I nowhere, as far as I recall (I haven't the book [*Logic*] with me), attempted a formal definition, stating just how I was using the word. If the word "idea" is permissible—in its idiomatic sense, not, of course, as a mental state—I think an observable meaning can be assigned to "conception," along the line of an "idea" that has become first in use and then in formulation a standardized rule of operations for ordering perceived materials. Such ideas or principles or whatever name be given them . . . are characteristically decisive in settling judicial disputes. However, as far as usage is concerned, I realize that the word is likely to be understood by many readers in the objectionable sense that has become traditional, so that it would have been better to have used the word much less frequently, and then with qualifying explanations.

More specifically I agree with [you] fully about the necessity of such a definite language symbol-behavior that, if the word is used, there will be no doubt as to what it designates, so that also the behavioral language could be employed for the most part in order to avoid misconceptions. One thing that I imagine influenced me more than it should have done is the fact that a number of writers who are influential at present have identified "words" and "language" generally with mere marks independently of anything they referentially stand for. In consequence I was solicitous to show that apart from *meanings*, these marks are not words at all. In consequence—this is more or less ex post facto reconstruction—in order to make explicit the presence of "meanings," I employed the word "conceptions" when, after making the point about words clear, I should have stuck simply to the word "word" as a behavior

63

symbol. Then the interactional, situational aspect would have stood out more than it does now, where it is left too implicit.

Now as to the special question you raise, I hardly need say that if you find anything in my formulations usable, along with such critical modifications as you would need to make, I should be immensely gratified—and not just personally, though I should be honored in that respect, but as a matter of the development of a point of view, which I am confident is the proper one, whatever my own shortcomings with regard to it. As you work along, it will become clear to you whether the attempt you mention would obscure your own development or not, by involving, for example, attempts at accommodation that would blunt your points. I think you can see from my earlier paragraphs (which is one reason I put them in) that whatever you do, I shall have no ground for objecting to the critical modifications you find it advisable or necessary to introduce. My satisfaction will come in any case through others finding what I have written usable, as long as it [is] used in a certain direction, and anything that will make that direction clearer is all to the good. In short I agree with you that the second approach you mention is most likely to be helpful, stressing anything in my presentation only as it agrees with yours *in contrast with certain older situations,* and not in any way restricting or changing your own independent mode of approach. . . .

As to "non-existential," there are times when I qualify the expression by saying "in direct reference" or something of that kind—it is also quite possible that, in order to find some point of contact with the mathematical formalists, I leaned too far backward from the requirements of my own position. I think I could make out a case for my use of "possibility," as distinct from "potentiality," but I agree as to the need of more analysis.

I shall [be] very glad to get any material you send me.

Very sincerely yours, *John Dewey*

[P.S.] I am sending under separate cover an article ["Fight for Clarity: Logical Empiricism"] by a young Columbia man [Ernest Nagel] of great natural ability and an adept in mathematical formal symbolism. I don't think he has precipitated yet, and I doubt if he is aware of how much he is adapting and changing "logical empiricism" of the [Rudolf] Carnap type. He is the author of the *Probability* monograph [*Principles of the Theory of Probability*] in the *Chicago* [*International*] *Encyclopedia* [*of Unified Science*]. . . . Nagel is acquainted with some, at least, of your writings, and I know was much impressed by them. He was brought up philosophically by Morris [R.] Cohen, who gave an ontological, "realistic," interpretation to all basic logical ideas, and I think reaction from that has carried him further toward formalism than he will stand by in further development.

Dear Mr. Dewey:

. . . It is clearer all the time (though without venturing predictions too far ahead) that my work in view expands directly out of yours. Consider, for instance, the "double-barreled" words I refer to [in "Situational vs. Psychological Theories of Behavior"]. . . . In that paper I have set up the "duplicity" of a series of such words, "concept," "percept," even of late "operation"—the incurable, historical, duplicity—as one of the strongest indications of the need of a thorough interactional theory of behaviors. You apply exactly the same test to the rejection of the particular word that comes most strongly into the field you develop, and retain only words of that type when their use is incidentally communicational. . . .

I want to tell you at length exactly how I got this sort of an approach, since I know so little about Woodbridge that I doubt if I would have identified his name before I read the paper referred to ["The Problem of Consciousness Again"]. I saw a reference by some[one] else to his paper, read it, marked the words "sights-seen," etc., and then tried occasionally to mention them—one time was in New York last spring. Each time I bungled them, which made me think they were pretty powerful in holding subjects and objects together in one presentation. . . . I began with the postulates in practically the form I now have them; followed this with a discussion of Kantor, Lewin, Meyer, Pavlov, etc., and then with some remarks on application and development. I found, however, that the postulates stuck in front were bumptious—like a chip on the shoulder —and that the following discussion looked too much as if I . . . [were] trying to drag all the other people in as subordinate support. Those defects were bad enough, but worse than that, I was unable to get firm statement anywhere as I went along. Then I found out by a deliberate and careful review of every piece of work I had ever done that what was wrong was that I was omitting the proper emphasis on the preliminary requirement of direct observation, and that the introduction of this as the third in a set of five postulates was not enough. That meant that the paper on observation had to come first, and it meant that a situational or interactional psychology had to be expressly presented. Here is where I found, as I wrote you before, that the existing specimens defaulted entirely. . . .

When I came to the preparation of a new paper starting with stress on direct observation, the Woodbridge phrasing, "sights-seen," impressed me more and more as successfully *saying* exactly what I have long held, but never myself successfully said, that when "I see a tree," there is present an interactional immediacy (Woodbridge calls it "consciousness"), and that the "I" and the "see" and the "tree" are all linguistically engineered, "remote-control" (in your characterization) presentations

—the linguistic to cover a mess of symbol-sign stuff not yet fully differentiated.

I then prepared the paper . . . and associated with Woodbridge in parallel, so to speak, a position [that] a man named [Virgil C.] Aldrich took in *Journal of Philosophy* last year ["What We See With"], in which he said the "organ of vision" included the rays that "touched" the seen-object. The Aldrich thing was pretty feeble, in particular because it treated light-rays in the form of opticians' fictions, as "things" that had "an end" at the edge of an object. . . .

Still and all, I now have some qualms about the use of Woodbridge. . . . What he has given us, it seems to me, is in the nature of a literary by-product, and I have made it the head of the corner, which seems hardly fair to those who have borne the burden and heat of the day (I love to mix metaphors and allusions, when the privacy is sufficient). Still, again, it seems to me to be exactly what I say of it—the finest verbal tool I have ever got my hands on [in] this region; and a good verbal tool, such as a minus sign, or a sign of differentiation, is something pretty important in holding unwilling heads to a theoretical grindstone. At any rate, I can infer that Woodbridge will not disavow my use of him. And after all, putting prominently at the front a worker as remote from this field as Woodbridge seems to have been, may be a good thing in the end for the "cause." . . .

Sincerely yours, *A. F. Bentley*

Key West, Florida, February 14, 1939

Dear Bentley:

. . . I am sure you are justified in using the citation from Woodbridge as you do—in fact I think you are doing a real service in taking it out of the particular theoretical context in which he uses it and employing it as just the linguistic tool which enables one to get rid of a lot of hampering impedimenta—including, it is possible, some that Woodbridge himself carries along. . . .

Although I have been associated with Woodbridge many years, and during the earlier years had many conversations with him and learned a lot from him, I have never been sure of whether I had hold of his actual ideas or not. He bases himself largely upon Aristotle—fundamentally so; he obtained from that source an organ of eliminating and criticizing the "subjectivism" of modern philosophy, and acquired the belief in a direct approach—which he calls "realism," leaving out the complex epistemological machinery built up by Locke, Kant, the Mills, etc. So far the passage cited means just what you take it to mean. But I have to confess that I had never seen its immense simplifying value as a linguistic tool till you pointed it out, and I think the reason is that I was too conscious of the philosophical context in which I think—without being sure—it was used, to take it at its face value. Woodbridge was educated among other things for a clergyman in the Episcopal Church, though he never took orders. I mention that because I think the Aristotelian theology is involved in what I have called the context. He identifies "mind," "intellect," with what I have called the signifying or evidential relation of things to one another—which is o.к. in a way; only he gives it a "realistic"-ontological interpretation. "Language as a living communication with nature" is, I believe, a reflection of the idea that objects in nature are related to one another just as words are related to one another in intelligible discourse. What I have said in the last chapter of my *Logic* about a "realistic" interpretation of Berkeley is directed at a view which I believe is very similar to that of Woodbridge. . . .

Sincerely yours, John Dewey

Key West, Florida, February 24, 1939

Dear Mr. Bentley:

I can't express very well the help I've got from your papers ["Situational vs. Psychological Theories of Behavior"]. I can understand what you said in your earlier letters about the struggle you went through. Our language is so loaded and so treacherous that it is an achievement of mark to have come out as clear and concise as you have in these papers—it is too condensed in spots for easy understanding, but it shares that property with algebraic formulae that are fertile in development. . . .

I haven't read much psychology of recent years, but as far as I am acquainted with it, your second paper seems to me both just and clarifying. Your treatment of Pavlov was a definite aid to me; I could understand his experimental work on dogs, etc., and his conclusions, but the word [term] "conditioned reflex" has been used in such a comprehensive and vague way that I had taken a strong prejudice against it, without knowing why. Lewin struck me as having something, but as pretentious; Adolf Meyer I have always admired greatly—as a man who carries his integrity into his work.

The only sentence at which I hesitated was your remark about John R. Commons; I think you disposed of him rather too summarily on the strength of his use of a single word—and a word which, after all, is open to interpretation in a way that is quite consistent with the fact that the only behaviors observable are those of individual organisms. I wouldn't say that he always uses the word in the latter sense, but upon the whole he seems to me to have done more direct observing of the economic scene—and also of the history of its theory—than any other economist. . . .

Sincerely, *John Dewey*

New Orleans, Louisiana, February 28, 1939

Dear Mr. Dewey:

. . . I will examine Commons more fully before publishing. I did not mean to criticise his work—only to exhibit this phrasing. I admire the man and his accomplishment, but not his formulation.

The problem I have faced for many years is not whether the consolidated organism-object activity is basic observation and fact (this will take care of itself in time), but how to describe the possibility of such observation in such a way that other people will directly experiment with it a little. The point is that everybody uses some of this observation, that very few people will generalize the possibility, that each man stops short at a stage that suits his own work, that I find all these short-stop positions inconsistent, that I assume I still have stoppages in my own generalization, and that I believe that nothing but whole-hog *postulation* gives safe ground for procedure. . . .

Accidentally I read a review ["An Effective Logic"] of your *Logic* by Paul Weiss in the *New Republic*. One paragraph gives you the highest praise, and hands you the future; the next points out a fatal flaw; this is repeated three times perhaps. . . .

Sincerely yours, *A. F. Bentley*

Key West, Florida, March 5, 1939

Dear Mr. Bentley:

. . . Perhaps it's one of the advantages of age, but anyway I don't mind adverse criticism provided I learn something from it. A review that is laudatory on the whole like that of Paul Weiss' you mention does irritate me some. The criticism is not explicit [or] as pertinent to any particular passage or idea. . . .

Nagel['s "Fight for Clarity: Logical Empiricism"] set me thinking as to why a person like him (he is able and has for a philosopher a wide scientific, including mathematical, knowledge) should be taken with logical positivism. I came to the conclusion that it is because, on the one hand, of the professed eschewing of metaphysics and the claim to be empirically scientific, while on the other hand, the profession seems to absolve them . . . [from the] responsibility for examining their own basic postulates—or finding out what they are. The reference to Commons wasn't very important—if I had found serious matters to object to, I wouldn't have mentioned it. My objection was chiefly, I think, to the idea that implied that action couldn't take place through individuals and still be in some sense "collective"—it's the same problem as with the word "social," I think.

Your paragraph about the problem of thoroughgoing linguistic description of observational material is very helpful to me—I think it would help others if you made the point in writing sometime—it's a tough job.

Yours, *John Dewey*

Key West, Florida, April 7, 1939

Dear Mr. Bentley:

. . . My theory about [Charles W.] Morris is that after being influenced by [George Herbert] Mead and the latter's type of "pragmatism," he was impressed by the symbolic formalists and decided the weakness of pragmatism was its failure to do justice to the formal-mathematical element—so he set out to remedy the defect—and did it by distributive pigeon-holing . . . [in] the paper [*Foundations of the Theory of Signs*] you refer to. If the "pragmatic" has any place at all, I can't see that it means anything on his own statement [other] than a certain kind of *behavior*, that of scientific inquirers. Well, you have covered the ground in your *Fact, Knowledge and Language* [*sic*], and I don't need to argue with you about contradictions that will arise when one tries to put the three in separate pigeon-holes. The attempt to make a mechanical union of Mead and Carnap is doomed. If Morris gave up his pragmatism entirely, he could at least be more consistent. . . .

I am more and more impressed as far as most of the logical positivists are concerned by their practically total lack of any historic, cultural interest or sense. The idea that there is a linguistic short-cut to dismissing metaphysics as meaningless is an example.

In cultural anthropology the appearance of metaphysics of different sorts is a highly instructive, evidential phenomenon—and I don't see the possibility of complete genuine eradication without putting it in its genetic-functional context.

Sincerely yours, *John Dewey*

[P.S.] Along the line of the memory-image business (foot of p. 176) ["Situational vs. Psychological Theories of Behavior"], some epistemologist is going sooner or later to think he can impale you on the existence of errors.

Paoli, Indiana, April 20, 1939

Dear Mr. Dewey:

Your letter of the 7th had double stimulation. First about Morris and Mead.

I doubt if Morris ever got a grasp of Mead's *problem,* and this defect seems to be present in others of Mead's editors. For this Mead (in his unfinished presentation) may be partly responsible. Mead stated his problem as that of "self," and when he had got his interpretation, he stated his conclusions in terms of what is presumably the very "self" he began with. His followers seem to regard the problem-posing and the interpreting as merely quaint and interesting by-play of a type which it is real snooty for them to profess, but which they do not have to *do* anything about. I think the interpreting's the thing, that Mead did a splendid job, but that the outcome is that "self" must be presented *within* the interpretative frame, and no longer be used the way it was before Mead's work on it began. I wish I had known of Mead's work long ago, and could have built on it. I criticize his followers for not "carrying on." You say in your prefatory remarks to *The Philosophy of the Present* that Mead set a problem that others did not see, that he never had the specious clarity based on familiarity, but that he was moving toward a much better expression when he died. A slick and specious clarity is all I can see in anything Morris has done. . . .

I am considerably concerned about Mead. . . . Except for two of his early essays, I apparently knew nothing of his work (so far as my notes indicate) until a year and a half ago when I examined *Mind, Self, and Society.* Two or three weeks ago I got together all four of the post-humous volumes, and I have been running over them. My 1937 notes on *Mind, Self, and Society* indicate that I recognized an immense amount of development that I needed and should have known of; but I was repelled by his continual recurrence to "self"; by his failure to connect his work with other comparable inquiries of which I knew; by my feeling that in orienting to "self," he took away from, rather than added to, the significance of his own work in comparison to the other work; and per-haps above all by the dumbness of editors, in their introduction, in their footnotes, in some phrasings they used, and in their total lack of any sense of durations as applied to Mead's work, thus omitting in applica-tion to Mead one of the best qualities of his own position as applied to others. . . . But last week I got a sharp jolt from the *Philosophy of the Present.* I have had on hand for several years a paper I cannot yet finish, called in its present draft "Skin and Psychology" [published as "The Human Skin: Philosophy's Last Line of Defense"], containing an argument that affects somewhat the phrasing of the papers now appearing. Sharp in Mead's text appeared the statement that the great difficulty in his inquiry was "cutting off life and consciousness at the boundaries of the organism." In other words, not vaguely and generally, but precisely with pointing finger, he marked the issue of "anatomical skin with refer-ence to behavior," or better, of the locus of a "behavioral skin," if any. I have found two other expressions approximately the same. This is

70

the stuff that counts with me. (Incidentally it does *not* count with his editors. In the Introduction to *Philosophy of the Act*, they allege the opposite, saying that for Mead the boundary of the organism is *terminus a quo* for response.) I am now beginning to understand why you could mention my work along with that of [Charles Sanders] Peirce and Mead and your own. Peirce had four great insights (that I know of), those of practicality, continuity, precision, and (more striking to me than any other) that of his early assertion that all thought has duration and hence all thought is in signs ("more striking" means to me for pending work— not in any wider sense). But Peirce lacked materials for his progress. You took one job, Mead another, and I (a bit indirectly) seem to have taken another. Each of us seems to have stuck like the devil to his purpose. And the jobs seem to fit in the end.

The other stimulation from your letter concerns images, epistemologists and error, with reference to my p. 176 ["Situational vs. Psychological Theories of Behavior"]. Until I meet some authoritative right, I can't see how any issue of wrong is basic, and hence I doubt if I have ever said a word about error. (Even B. Russell once got a hunch that the real was just a select grade of dream—but he could not stick it.) . . . But your point is not what my view is, but how [to] answer the objector. I just don't think . . . [he] can be answered. It is like getting one shoulder set lower than the other when young. In middle age, one just does not bring them back to a level. One might as well forget it. However, I have listed a dozen or so lines of argument that are lying around, and I will try to find opportunity to see if I can put a corporal in charge and train them to the goose-step. . . .

Sincerely yours, A. F. Bentley

Paoli, Indiana, April 24, 1939

Dear Mr. Dewey:

. . . It may be proper to say that Peirce very early coupled durational thinking with sign-process; that he was not in a position to develop on the first line, but went clear over to static schematism with his signs; that you and Mead have both developed in the durational form; and that Mead's followers are seemingly untouched by it, and remain on the level of Peirce's handicap. . . . While away, I read Morris' paper ["Peirce, Mead and Pragmatism"] . . . in a recent *Philosophical Review*, and it is a much more competent job than I have ever known him to do, except for his conclusion that Carnap belongs to the same family.

Sincerely yours, A. F. Bentley

[P.S.] It is maddening in the Mead volumes not to be able to get any hint at his earlier or later forms of expression, especially when conflicting phrasings are before one.

New York, May 8, 1939

Dear Bentley:

. . . Mead was an immensely stimulating person with an original approach—with great difficulty in finding his right linguistic expression. Moreover, he was never satisfied and kept working this over and over— which was why, I suppose, the essays found posthumous publication. You are right, then, about the importance of knowing the date of a given statement of his. I owe an immense amount to him personally, and yet have never been sure at a given time that I "got" him—his ideas were in transitional development, and he was the most conscious struggler I've ever known personally; if it hadn't been so genuine a struggle in and with himself, the "analysts" might say he had a "perfection complex."

You are probably right about what Morris is constitutionally—as a student and later colleague of Mead's, his relation to Mead is probably one of a kind of academic piety rather than grasp.

Of course my remark about "error" was an implicit criticism of the attitude of your probable critics. They have the problem because of their premise that knowledge is a relation between consciousness or the mental and the nonmental. To take amiss is, in behavioral terms, a natural enough occurrence.

Sincerely yours, *John Dewey*

Paoli, Indiana, June 14, 1939

Dear Mr. Dewey:

. . . I have had one of the excitements of my life reading Peirce the last six weeks or so. I knew I had been "nourished on fragments"—in somebody's phrase about [William] James and [Josiah] Royce—perhaps; and I knew his 1868 papers had seemed incredibly rich when I read them; but I had never gone into his work. I quickly found I had to order his six volumes so as to be sure to have them all at hand. I have about 150 pages now closely packed with classified citations. I can see how he chose his own special line of development (the symbolic logic), and what blocked him at every turn (the thingy-thought, factually maintaining itself in his work despite his frequent wider visions) and thus shunted him to categories and varied metaphysics. I can see how parts of him developed in James, Royce, [Henri] Bergson, Russell, [Alfred North] Whitehead, [P. W.] Bridgman (even [John B.] Watson), [F. W. E.] Schroeder, of course, and in Mead and in you (perhaps [Richard] Dedekind and [Georg] Cantor)—I think there are more, but I am not looking them up. These all either go just a step or two (as, I would now say, James and Bridgman), or popularize (like Royce and Bergson and Whitehead), or demonstrate their own imperfection (like Russell). The big thing seems to me the "durational" behavioral phenomenon, represented in Peirce's own development mainly by the pragmatic "principle," carried on by you in the *Logic* much further than by anyone else (so far as I know), participated in by Mead and by me, and (I think) bound now to go ahead in rapid development. The "degenerate" case—to use one of Peirce's favorite phrases—is Logical Positivism and Morris' "signs." Everything that Carnap ever hollered is fully stated by Peirce, with, in addition, the "vital spark" that Carnap's crew lack—a vehement assertion that he (Peirce) was not making a calculating machine to give the answers, but was doing his best to sketch the living behavior of sign-using men in a long-time world. I am not done with this inquiry, and I cannot be done till I have hammered it down into a paper; and when that time arrives, I am hoping you will give me your opinion as to the accuracy of my observation. That may, however, be some time yet, as various matters interfere.

Sincerely yours, A. F. Bentley

Paoli, Indiana, December 6, 1939

Dear Mr. Dewey:

Your *Theory of Valuation* came while I was away last summer, and since my return the ordinary follies of living have used up most of my time, so that I have not made acknowledgment. Your point of approach, your audience, and consequently your stresses in expression, are so different from mine that I get distracted and have to sneak back again in roundabout ways, but I always find myself fully in accord with what I take to be the essentials, except in the minor matter of the courtesy you show where my habit is discourteous.

I expect some time in the future to build directly on your terms, "connection," "reference," and "relation" [*Logic*, p. 55]. They are more "factual," they have better "reference," they are freer from distorting tendencies than any I know. The fact that I have repeatedly gone on record that the word "relation" is unusable makes no difference. It *is* usable here. They look to me like words which it will be possible to *establish*. I want to do what I can from time to time to establish them. I am using them in a paper ["Observable Behaviors"] I have about finished in which I restate the material of the *Journal of Philosophy* papers ["Situational vs. Psychological Theories of Behavior"], giving a better background in modern science, a better fitting into the development of psychology, and a slight approximation to a placement of language-knowledge "situationally" with respect to perceiving behaviors and culture behaviors. . . .

Sincerely yours, A. F. Bentley

Dear Bentley: New York, December 11, 1939

I was glad to send you my pamphlet [*Theory of Valuation*], but I didn't mean to impose on you the task of trying to translate—I know from experience how difficult that is in some cases, and often the outcome doesn't pay for the trouble taken. Although my piece was in the rather miscalled *Unity of Science* series, my main object was to criticize the point of view of the "logical positivists" regarding value, to point out its sources, and to point out the dualistic consequences. . . .

Sincerely yours, *John Dewey*

Dear Mr. Dewey: Paoli, Indiana, March 16, 1940

I think I spoke to you about Felix Kaufmann, refugee dozent from Vienna, now at the New School [for Social Research]. I do not recall your saying that you had met. At any rate here is an extract from another letter from him:

I almost envy you for your having been able to spend some time with John Dewey. Did I write you how strongly I was impressed by his *Logic* and by his personality when he spoke at a symposium during the meeting of the American Philosophical Association last December? I have now a seminar on pragmatism and shall have next year two seminars concerned with Dewey's *Logic*.

I am sending you this in the hope that some time when the opportunity comes you will talk with him. . . . I am inclined to say of Kaufmann that I know of no one who is a better prospect to carry on your torch. He had gone quite a way along your line under his own power before he came to this country. . . .

Sincerely yours, [*A. F. Bentley*]

Dear Bentley: Key West, Florida, March 20, 1940

. . . I'm glad to know about Kaufmann—not just personally either. But so many of the Germans in the New School were so bound up with their "idealisms" as to be more or less out of step with American life. He can't but have a healthy influence there. . . .

I wish I knew more physics. This damn individual-social business must be linked with the discrete-continuity. As far as I can get is that, no matter how extensive the field, observation is so centered that a certain discreteness or "nuclear" quality belongs to its material. While reasoning (discourse that is ordered) is like radiation or continuous wave motion.

Maybe this is a crazy notion. . . .

John Dewey

Paoli, Indiana, April 14, 1940

Dear Mr. Dewey:

We just touched on individual-social in talk [at Key West, 1939], and I was sorry we had no chance to go further with it. My general suspicion here would be—as is very seldom the case—the opposite of yours in one respect at least. I suspect that discrete-continuity will learn more from individual-social in the long run than the other way round. However, re-reading your phrases, that may be your view too, and you just put the physics thing at the front as an entry cue. My experience is that three or four years ago I put in several months on the physical radiation situation. My "climbing-tool" here was the hypothesis that radiation should be stated, not as a thing definable in terms of space and time, but as the thing out of which space and time are derivative or, more definitely said, as the thing with respect to which our human language in space- and time-forms represents snapshot views. The physicists, however, began to throw new "physicules" (how's this for a word? animalcules, homunculus?) at us faster than I could handle them, and the whole thing took "concept" form. So I started out to find what the concept—not the old universal animal, but the modern physical or social specification—is, or how it is to be stated, in terms of non-spiritist behavior. Of course, I will never get back to the physical examination (which is all the better, considering the odds against me), but the by-pass runs around into the discarded language construction.

In your "Reflex Arc" essay you spoke of little sensations sitting on a ridge between Platonic inners and outers . . . and in your last December address ["Nature in Experience"] . . . you speak of the "breach of continuity" between nature and man just at the moment being thrust at you. Mead in his last lectures [*The Philosophy of the Act*] spoke of our greatest difficulty being on the "boundary." I have been obsessed with "skin" for three years. . . .

Now my guess is that if we can state "an event" across the skin-line, perceptionally, linguistically, socially, the individual-social dilemma disappears. The "reality-assertion" is all gone, and the alternative squint takes its place. In the "Reflex Arc" paper you made stimulus and response phases rather than factors (where "factors" are *solus*, causally connected, in the terminology of ["Observable Behaviors"] . . . and "phases" are in or of one system). My assertion would follow you up, by saying, not as general attitude, but as direct working observation, that *if* stimulus and response are phases, then *the* event includes them both, and we must train ourselves habitually to see *the* single event so, and work with it so. Similarly, *an* event socially is in, across, two or more individuals, not as individual-*solus*, but viewed as phases, possibly where needed, and perhaps not even that. . . . I would similarly take up your argument and apply it in direct observation. It occurs to me that mathematics and physics accomplish this *direct observation* procedure by their devices of imaginaries, infinites, continuities. They go ahead and use these devices, and get the practical advantage, even while all hell and the devil could not drag out of them the admission of the *directness* of their treatment. This remark is a flash, adopting the ever-extending newspaper and radio word, and I do not know whether it will flash the same way again. But I suspect what I have been trying to do is to acquire in the social field, where the mathematical formulation is unavailable, the advantage of this *direct* statement which the physicists secure mathematically, even while they say Fie! Fie! My guess would be that my *Process of Government* tried something of this kind in a crude way though I can't verify it.

Personally I cannot use a contrast of observation and reasoning any more than one of discrete-continuous, or one of individual-social. If I ever get the language set-up, it will go back to the 1868 Peirce remark that all thought is in duration and in signs [*Collected Papers* (5.251) V, 151]. It will similarly say all observation is in duration and in signs. It will then run the durational-sign scheme up across the whole field without any skin-gap, and without any gap between observing and reasoning. This "signing" process will be the technically behavioral process, as characteristically distinct from the technically physiological process. I have a sort of a cue-name for it, but I don't dare use it for fear of distortion. . . . I can say, however, it is not "semiotic." . . .

Sincerely, *A. F. Bentley*

New York, April 19, 1940

Dear Bentley:

. . . I agree with you that the individual-social will throw more light on the discrete-continuous in physics than the other way around. . . . In general I think it is much safer to go from the more obvious, that written in large letters, to the microscopic, written in very small letters, than the opposite, and the discrete-continuous is a case in point.

Your "flash" about the direct method in contrast with that *nominally* used by physicists and covering up their actually direct method is enlightening—and shouldn't be allowed to flash *out*.

I ought in all logical consistency to be the last person to draw a sharp line between observation and reasoning. As phases of the same thing, they seem to me to present a distinction in em-phasis, of which so-called *sense*-perception is one limit and "abstract"—or mathematical—reasoning the other limit—the red and violet of the spectrum, coming together in the purples of actual experience. This is a flash also, and likely one that doesn't give much light. But it indicates where I am at present in the *problem* [of] individual-social, expressing limits in a spectrum, which spectrum can be called a *continuum* only at the risk of ignoring the qualitative diversifications of the rainbow. There is, of course, continuity within an observed field, but it is also centered in a way [that is] lacking in the "rational discourse," which compensates [for] the limitation of the special centering by linking up the material of observations with one another. After all, we animals work only by coordination of antagonistic systems.

I think if I knew enough, I could develop this in a way consistent with what you are saying—at least I hope so. I don't get as yet the full force of the language element in your knowledge-fact-language trinity, but am getting a glimmering through seeing its significance as a member, and can realize, as I didn't at first, the radical import of the point. I've got to the point of seeing that a lot of questions can't even be stated properly until the place and connection of language-construction is worked out.

Going back to the macroscopic and microscopic, I was much impressed with what Peirce says about philosophy starting with and building on "those observations which every person can make in every hour of his waking life . . . the study of obvious phenomena."

Sincerely yours, *John Dewey*

[P.S.] . . . When I see you in New York, I want to ask if you have the same objection to the words "human environment" that you have to "social environment"—or some word to designate the environing conditions that are the products of human contrivance, tools, machines, legal rules, works of art, language itself, as distinct from conditions that are as yet raw and unmodified—say, to take an extreme, an earthquake—or more moderately, the raw materials out of [which] the things used in the arts are finally developed.

Paoli, Indiana, April 22, 1940

Dear Mr. Dewey:

. . . As to my "language" as a component, I am doubtless too far out on the end of the branch in what I wrote. I notice that all sorts of people—for example even [W. S.] Hunter and [K. S.] Lashley—wake up sometimes in the middle of the night and howl "It's all language." Then they get scared stiff and take it all back, and apologize. Look at it this way: It is an old commonplace of psychology that in anything "conscious," some way or other, one process has to get outside of another process enough to look it over and size it up. The point about "language" is probably that in the more elaborate cases (and we need not at once formulate statements about transition cases) this "looking-over" is operated by language-communication behavior. . . .

I would rather try to answer your question about "human environment" on a piece of paper than in conversation. I would simply lighten the stress on "environment" and throw the stress heavily on "human." In other words, a "tool" is only significantly a tool *in* human use; and if human usings (doings) are our study, that is the way to stress it.

It is always proper to say that "to *this* organism (here at this instant) *that* tool (there, at this instant) is environment." The only question is: how significantly can a general statement be constructed on that basis? You can study ways of getting boy and hatchet organized at kindling pile, but (in my view) will never get a significant statement about a kindling-cutting form of living on that basis. In other words, the simply cultural statement is to me much more significant than any matching of such a phenomenon as boy-not-a-tool over against tool-not-a-boy. . . .

Sincerely yours, *A. F. Bentley*

Paoli, Indiana, May 15, 1940

Dear Mr. Dewey:

. . . You said something about using some passage from our correspondence and crediting it to me. Nobody can trace very exactly how the words got themselves together, and certainly I have no special claim to my half-contribution to any passage between us. . . .

Sincerely yours, *A. F. Bentley*

New York, May 24, 1940

Dear Bentley:

I just ran across a passage from the writings of my old student and colleague A. W. Moore, *Pragmatism and Its Critics*, 1910, p. 275.

"My" consciousness is a function of a social process in which my body or brain or mind is only one factor. . . . "My" thinking and feeling may be as truly a function of "your" brain or mind as of my own. My thinking of sending for you as a physician to treat my headache is as truly a function of your medically trained brain as of my own aching one.

I don't know how I got so much switched off from following out this line. Partly lack of nerve, partly moving from Chicago to Columbia and getting into a new set of problems that interrupted, I guess. . . .

Yours, *John Dewey*

Paoli, Indiana, May 27, 1940

Dear Mr. Dewey:

. . . Moore makes a strong statement, the world gets little result except from the long, slow process of exploration and specific formulation.

78

What you have done is to force the "reasoning" work back into place in a "natural" form (which I doubt Moore would have on a show-down) and with plenty of reservation for such a position as Moore takes. I appraise your job as complete (regardless of how well anyone follows it at the moment). That job could not be done, I believe, except in terms of the personal formulation. What I am trying to do now is to state "a fact" in the framework such as Moore suggests. What I tried to do in . . . [*The Process of Government*] was . . . to get a glimpse of the process across several people at once. . . . (Probably a very short inspection would show you what I was trying to do. There is a little interest in it now in law schools and even among political scientists, but only in side issues. I have never seen any reference, or developed any recognition in conversation of the kind of "tool" I professed to be seeking.)

I am afraid I must retreat quite a way back about Kaufmann. He has sent me his notice ["On Dewey's *Logic*"] about your *Logic* in *Social Research*. When he says your "naturalism" has presuppositions which cannot be defined in naturalistic terms, I feel very bad. To apply a narrow "natural" as a touchstone seems like a failure to recognize the big "natural" as the issue. I have asked him as cautiously as I could in what sense he would combine a natural and a not-natural in one system, or rather, I have indicated the question. I really prefer him not to answer. . . .

Sincerely yours, A. F. Bentley

Paoli, Indiana, June 5, 1940

Dear Mr. Dewey:

. . . Concerning your citation from Moore, I got my squint on this business from you, just as Moore no doubt did. Where James was pleasantly descriptive about a "me," you fixated "me" definitely. That was at some course at Chicago in 1895–96. I can still remember [a] vivid denunciation by some young woman who teetotally denied that it was possible for me to hold any such view as I alleged I accepted. I think I associate the syllables "Amy Tanner" with the phenomenon, but they may be imaginary.

It's all your stuff, even though you have worked considerably with a different medium.

Sincerely, A. F. Bentley

New York, June 6, 1940

Dear Bentley:

. . . I want first to thank you for your two notes and also to say how much I got out of your article ["Observable Behaviors"]. I got it better in print than when I read it in Key West. It's a classic—nothing can be clearer or more complete.

The point that students of psychology had [could have] anticipated the space-time of present physics if they had only known what they were about is like a revelation from on high.

Yours sincerely, *John Dewey*

New York, June 7, 1940

[To Bentley:]

Yes, that's wonderful—there was an Amy Tanner graduate student in '95–'96.

But I fear I can't claim credit for your developments—even though it would make me happy to.

Yours, *J. Dewey*

New York, July 25, 1940

Dear Bentley:

. . . I may be moved to try to put together some ideas about the "personal" on a behavioral basis which have been stirring in my head because of interaction with that part of the environment constituted by Arthur Bentley—I have a feeling that it may be possible to give a sensible account of the meaning of the words "personal" and "person."

I also think I could give an intelligible signification to "conception," provided my use of the word "*idea*" to stand for a possibility through the medium of a symbol for an operation that is projected to actualize the possibility, would pass muster. I have found that you are right in saying that the word [conception] is useless at least $\frac{4}{5}$ of the time—my own writings included—and it may be safer to avoid its use entirely. But there are ideas which become a kind of standardized rule of operation, and a word may be needed to mark off such ideas from others that are so to speak more casual. . . .

Sincerely yours, *John Dewey*

[P.S.] As I wrote you once before, the point about the bearing of the non-Newtonian space-time scheme upon the psychological theory of behavior is at once so important and, as far as I know, so new that I hope you will develop it in full in a special article. I doubt if half a dozen persons . . . have seen just how the new physical scheme undercuts the grounds that under the Newtonian scheme gave color to the "inner-outer" dualism. . . .

Dear Mr. Dewey:

If you can give an account of "person" and "personal" that suits you better than what you have given in the past, it will be fine. If I have been part of the stimulus, it will be on the basis of the well-known man who sneezes in China. As to the person, my attitude is less and less, not more and more—I don't mean "attitude"—I mean "contact" with the problem. But as to "conception," I have a strong positive desire to see your development. I am quite certain that there is a very important process (whether described as language or as idea) that needs some such name. But I never can be satisfied with a word like "idea," which to most people stands for a bird-in-hand, when used to apply to bird-in-flight. The difficulty is purely communicational, so far as I am concerned. Possibility-actualization process as a form of behavior, with adequate durational-span for its "existence," can be made that which the word "idea" stands for—providing the reader does not transform it into "an idea is," thus implying the presence, here and now, of what has presence to me only in the form of "here-into-hereafter." . . .

Let me ask you straight-out: Would you suggest throwing out this whole figure of speech of "skin"? . . .

Finally as to social space-time, I have been "taking for granted," and have sagged away. I probably need to have the course pointed. I first developed this in the *Relativity in [Man and] Society* book, 1926. In 1927 or 1928 I wrote four papers [" 'Individual' and 'Social' in Recent American Studies," "Time and the Environment in Recent Sociology," "The Data of Sociology Examined with Respect to Time and Space," "Space, Time, Environment and Society"] examining the way "space," "time," "environment," and "society" . . . were used in sociology. All four received the usual rejection from the journals. Then I covered part of the field in *Revue Internationale de Sociologie* ["L'Individual et le social: Les Termes et les faits"], and I had three papers in *Sociological Review* (Brailsford's) ["New Ways and Old to Talk about Men," and "Sociology and Mathematics I and II"] . . . which most certainly . . . dealt with space-issues in the main. I think it was there I suggested the topological device for formulating individual-social problems, though I have not checked it up. Since then I have just gone ahead assuming that the space and time of social-psychological events was whatever the description of the facts required: that what happened to an instant, or a spot to an ear or eye had nothing much to do with the case (except for local performance); that is to say, in unbossed effort at observation. . . .

Sincerely yours, *A. F. Bentley*

Dear Mr. Dewey:

Perhaps now I can get my status with respect to your *Logic* and the way I should proceed, brought into the clear.

As I have told you several times, I definitely intend to build a language-knowledge system on the immediate structure of your work by the technical device of my behavioral area (within superfice).

Probably I have not directly stated it, but I am pretty sure that in sending you manuscripts, what I want to know is whether I attribute positions to you that you would be inclined to disclaim or qualify significantly in answer to some man . . . who comes close enough to you to *ask* questions, but still is far enough over towards the waste land of logical positivism to make it uncertain how he will *grasp* your answers. In the use of the "Reflex Arc" paper in . . . ["The Human Skin"], I can't be wrong. The presence of the paper at a critical fork in inquiry is a bit of history. But in many regions where we "feel after meanings," it is not so certain—I make too many errors all the time to be confident.

To that question I want now to add this: Am I practically wise at this stage, in reaching out as I have been repeatedly doing lately to connect my work with yours, and involve you in it? Here again all sorts of distorted views are possible. . . . Perhaps you can answer me bluntly. It looks like the proclamation of banns, or whatever stage it is at which one has to "forever after hold your peace." . . .

My "reason" more or less for direct interest is that I find nobody taking literally my attitude in this matter, except you. I have been beginning to suspect that your central view is under similar insulation. . . . There is [Jerome] Nathanson's review ["Dewey's Vivisection of the Logical Process"], which seems to me by far the best I have anywhere seen of the *Logic,* and even he, as I read him (though I have not gone back to verify), seemed to me at the end to fall away from the center. . . . It is literally true that not one single person except you has made a *significant* remark about the "Observable Behaviors" paper now out three months. . . . This is not of the nature of hollering; I long ago replaced weeps with winks. But it is a *problem.* It is a problem in the sense that I see a stream—Darwin's base spreading through [Chauncey] Wright to Peirce, appearing in three general attitudes in him, running out a by-path in Mead (who ought to be included in the not-literally-taken list), rising to a full development for knowledge in your work, undertaking a specialized technical procedure in mine, and as yet nowhere near a standardized formulation which will hold for any great length, but pretty certain to get such a formulation in a generation or so. . . .

Sincerely yours, *A. F. Bentley*

New York, August 6, 1940

Dear Bentley:

. . . I confess I was somewhat shocked when I did read it [E. O. Sisson, "Relation in Reality and Symbolism"], not so much about his conclusion as to the universality of relations . . . as [by] the method by which he reaches his conclusion. I shouldn't have been surprised, much less shocked, if he hadn't professed in the past a certain agreement with my views—which as you point out is still assumed in this paper. But, p. 345, the offhand identification of "meaning" with "the inner and private," "the invisible and inaccessible *meaning*," p. 350, "incurably evasive and enigmatic, since it resides in the private minds of the communicants," seems to [be] as nearly the exact opposite of the state of things and of what I have tried to say as anything could well be. Even if I believed in the existence of a private and mentalistic mind, I think I should still say that the miracle of communication or language is that it marks an escape in[to] the public and common—or that the most obvious characteristic of "meaning" is that it just *isn't* what Sisson says it is. There is a certain sense in which the noise or mark as a part of a *word* is less public and common than meaning, though to say this would be an awkward way of phrasing what Sisson acknowledges—the conventional or "contractual" elements in words of different languages. That practically there *is* a krypton and hazard of error in all communication only means, as I see it, that genuine communication is an extremely difficult process since it is the climax of all inquiry, of all scientific method, to achieve meanings. Sisson seems to take the obstacle to be overcome in communication as if it were the intrinsic definition of communication.

I've read Nathanson also—I agree it's the best notice I've seen. Perhaps it doesn't cover the whole ground or point out the central postulate. But I didn't find in a hurried reading anything off in it. On p. 121, the word "individual" is used where the word "human being" would have been better. But while his point in that paragraph is too briefly stated to be entirely clear, I fancy he has a real point—though, of course, I thought I had pointed out that the development of a new common sense or *seeing things* differently requires a change in social conditions—economic, political, educational—as a condition of scientific method doing what it is capable of doing.

Well, I haven't said anything about your paper ["Decrassifying Dewey"]; it would sound like kind words of a high exponent if I said what I think. I don't see a word to change, and I'm deeply indebted to you for making the points, and especially *the* point, so clear and precise. Sisson's article is [more] than worth-while in bringing out such a rejoinder. I couldn't have got outside of myself enough to begin to do such a good job.

Sincerely yours, *John Dewey*

[P.S.] There was Nagel's paper ["Dewey's Reconstruction of Logical Theory"] on my *Logic* at the meeting of the Conference on Methods held in connection with my birthday, now printed in the volume *The Philosopher of the Common Man* [Sidney Ratner, ed.], but I don't think there was one at the main birthday show. . . .

Paoli, Indiana, August 10, 1940

Dear Mr. Dewey:

. . . Another thing that has me excited: Last week's *Science* (Aug. 2, p. 110) has a report [G. A. Schumacher, "Uniformity of the Pain Threshold in Man"] from Russell Sage Institute [of] Psychiatry on the pain threshold by a new technique eliminating reaction or opinion. It shows variations of plus-or-minus 30 around a mean of 206, in energy units necessary to give a pain-stab on the forehead, for 150 subjects— all kinds. *No correlation whatever* with either subjects' reactions or subjects' estimates. What this means is that pain is as definitely organic and technically physiological as a cancer or a broken leg (I mean: what it means to me, if verified). I have gone on that supposition for ten years but [have] not known how to say it. It goes a long way to open up "situational" treatment of behaviors. It makes "person" in the usual sense a mess of pain (which is organic, not behavioral) falsely hypothe-sized out of the grammatical "I." It is exciting, but I am having the dickens of a time trying to fit a reference to it slickly into the "Skin" paper. . . .

Sincerely yours, *A. F. Bentley*

New York, August 15, 1940

Dear Bentley:

. . . I am not going to ask you to read anything about "mind" even in a letter. But I had enough curiosity to look up the passage [cited by E. O. Sisson] in *Experience and Nature*. "Mind" is said to be a system of beliefs; the view that endows a self, whether body [bodily] or spiritual being immaterial, with mind is criticized. The question discussed is simply that of how the systems of belief socially current (traditional and customary) get changed through the desires and inventions of individ-uals—by every Tom, Dick, and Harry, who question custom and try to introduce innovations.

Doubtless the wording could be improved—but the idea of [mind as an] "agency of novel reconstruction of a pre-existing order" is ex-pressly stated.

Yours, *John Dewey*

Dear Mr. Dewey: Paoli, Indiana, February 8, 1941

This may amuse you.

Clearing out old rubbish heaps . . . we ran across the first outline and sketch (about 1905) of . . . [*The Process of Government*]. It carried an "inscription":

To

Ludwig Gumplowicz

John Dewey

Walt Whitman

and

Georg Simmel—

the real writers of this book.

That is possibly an accurate statement. I occasionally wish I had let myself run free instead of compressing myself so severely in an academic pattern.

Regards, *A. F. Bentley*

Key West, Florida, February 12, 1941

Dear Bentley:

. . . I was in damn good company in that inscription, even including the Germans—whom in general I would draw the line at—even before the wars and Nazism. Am just reading [Jan Valtin's] *Out of the Night*— hard to check for authenticity, but it has the psychological earmarks of genuineness. In any case, it is a wonderful picture of the uprooted people who, in connection with genuine idealists—of whom they get the better as time goes by—produce revolutions of both the Bolshevist and Nazi types. Its most evident moral won't be drawn though—the completely disturbing consequences of war under modern conditions of industry and social organization.

. . . It seemed best for me to write a reply ["Propositions, Warranted Assertibility, and Truth"] to Russell's account of some of my views given in his last book [*An Inquiry into Meaning and Truth*]. The best thing in my reply is a reference in a footnote to what you say about physical extrapolation and behavioral space-time in *Behavior, Knowledge, Fact*.

I doubt if that particular kind of controversy is worth-while, but it helped me clear up my own beliefs on some points—and made me see more clearly a weakness in the subject-object position which Russell has brought out in his own attempt to give a simpler statement of it than have others who hold it—in spite of the fact that he adopts the revised view, it is as near a *reductio ad absurdum* of it as could well be. . . .

Yours, *John Dewey*

Dear Bentley:

. . . The first light that dawned on me was the joint product of having lived in darkness a long time and your paper ["The Factual Space and Time of Behavior"]. It's simple enough now that I see it, but I was looking for something more complicated; maybe that is the reason I "eased away"; I don't know. The point I didn't see before is that space-time in the new physics doesn't of itself determine what behavioral space-time must be, any more than Newtonian space-time ever did. But it does free the observer of behavioral events to construct behavioral space-time in terms of what he observes, and doesn't stand in the way of that construction as the separate space and separate time of Newtonian physics did. I could easily condemn myself for stupidity for not seeing all the time such was the case. But I don't, at least not harshly, because light, in my case, comes in pulses and not in radiant waves.

The generalized use of "adaptation" in the present paper strikes me as something new, though maybe you've done it before. The consistent and thoroughgoing statement of the organism-environment connection in terms of varieties of adaptations strikes me as opening a promising lead. . . .

Sincerely, *John Dewey*

Paoli, Indiana, May 18, 1941

Dear Mr. Dewey:

. . . Recently he [Kaufmann] has written much ["Truth and Logic," "Strata of Experience"] about "rule," using "rule" closely in Carnap's manner.

No matter what question I ask, he ignores it in his letters, though he will write all around the issue copiously. The question I ask, but he ignores, is something as follows:

> If you establish "rules" to establish "fact" in a natural world;
> If your procedure is within a "system"—one system;
> Then what sort of fact is a "rule"?
> If you use two correlated systems, say so.
> If it is all one system, answer me.

I have not sharpened the question quite this far to him, but I have asked it in many forms. I have no answer, and no recognition whatever. . . .

Sincerely yours, *A. F. Bentley*

New York, May 20, 1941

Dear Bentley:

. . . Kaufmann has sent me some reprints, but . . . [they] are all on phenomenology, and I never followed [Edmund] Husserl; I got the impression that he was trying to say things that should be said empirically, in some circuitous language that would keep up some connection with the Teutonic tradition in philosophy. But I've nothing in the way of knowledge to go on.

I can't tell you how glad I am you are to be here next fall; it's a fine thing for Columbia and the department, and I think you will get some fun and other satisfactions out of it. I don't know what the quality of graduate students is just now, but there should be some men or women that will react.

I believe that you will find the effect of your writings is definite, though cumulative and slow. In a few years you may expect to see some parts of your ideas appearing in other men's writings, with little or no recognition—not deliberate ignoring, but they will have absorbed something so gradually they won't quite know the source themselves. . . .

Sincerely yours, *John Dewey*

Paoli, Indiana, May 30, 1941

Dear Mr. Dewey:

. . . A day or two ago I examined Kaufmann's last two papers, one in the Phenomenology journal ["Strata of Experience"], the other in *Journal of Philosophy* ["Structure of Science"], and "coincidentally" . . . I had written Kaufmann in effect withdrawing my question about "rule" and "fact" on the ground that when he said "natural," he only meant an interesting limitation, while when I said "natural," I meant an organism-environment base within which such words as "rule" should be placed. So there is agreement. His positivistic interest was only a tinge, and I was fooled as often before. . . .

Sincerely, *Bentley*

Greencastle, Missouri, November 1, 1941

Dear Bentley:

. . . It seems to me it is the first time a full statement has been made ["Memorandum on a Program of Research into Language"] that at once completely shatters the formalistic idea that language can be analyzed in isolation from a context (save on the old-fashioned grammatical text book level) . . . and also gives an empirically verifiable context.

Yours, *Dewey*

Dear Dewey:

The seminar is over. I never knew how come I was asked to attend, but might guess you suggested that the procedure might be good for me, them, or it. It *was* good for me, but otherwise it wound up in a great outburst of failure. So I make a report in a way.

My formal participation covered the last three sessions. I remember telling you of the first one of these—just before Christmas. I offered a 3-dimensional diagram. The result was a chaos of irrelevant remarks. I never got to tell what simple language event the diagram outlined, nor the connection of its parts, nor the fact that it was primarily designed to separate three types, or universes, of discourse (really there are four) that clashed with one another, and could not offhand be made into one stew—specialized "manners of talk about language itself" is what I mean. The chaos was so great, and the irrelevances so unanimous that I suggested to Nagel that I quit, and listen to someone else for a while.

However, the next session proceeded with a set of 30 numbered paragraphs, including certain emphasized "Observations" and "theses." The questions, now, for the first time since I have been here, began to be pertinent. Nothing came out sharply, however. So I went on once more.

The final session, last Monday, I concentrated on whether language was a process or event in time, using three questions brought by members. One was a charge that I had omitted a fixed definition of language and a demand for such a definition. Another was a question as to a possible precedence in time of "thinking" or "meaning" as before utterance in speech or writing. The last was a question . . . put to me after the session: Why bother with time or space forms at all? As to the first, of course, if the fact is an event, you cannot give it a timeless rating, and any man really after knowledge ought to know today that the subtleties are best handled after you know something rather than before one starts. As to the "priorities" between thinking and talking, I diagrammed them four cases, full precedence, partial precedence, full concomitance, and full fusion as event. This certainly brought them to earth—or rather nearer to earth, but not near enough to get their feet on it. . . .

Best regards, *Bentley*

Key West, Florida, January 20, 1942

Dear Bentley:

. . . Thanks for your interesting report—it doesn't bear out in fact what you said about the outburst of failure. But, with respect to failures, my experience in teaching has been that it takes a very long time for a new point of view to be taken—the "instinct" of most persons is to resist. But very often something breaks through the crust, and ideas come out after a time quite changed. You'd have to wait a year or two to judge of actual effects. . . .

I'm sorry to say I had nothing to do with your being invited to Columbia—I should be glad to have been an instrument. I heard Nagel, years ago, speak highly of your mathematics book. . . .

I guess you got something out of the discussions, and that is the main thing in teaching I discovered. Woodbridge prided himself on being an Aristotelian "metaphysician," and [John Herman] Randall [,Jr.] was greatly influenced by both Aristotle and Woodbridge. "Metaphysics" in their case sometimes means simply getting beyond thinking in terms of "Mental States"—on that score you *are* "metaphysical." What else it means to them, I never really found out; only it doesn't mean necessarily anything "transcendental." . . .

Yours, Dewey

Key West, Florida, February 19, 1942

Dear Bentley:

. . . Does he [Kaufmann] suppose any sane person will deny there are such things as "beliefs"; there are political platforms and the 39 Articles and the Nicene Creed anyway, and lots of people do what is called "holding" them; allegiance, loyalty, devotion are also familiar facts of behavior—also treachery. And on p. 7 of the *Logic*, which he professed admiring, the ambiguity of the word is expressly pointed out, and the idea that "belief" is "merely a mental or psychical state" is expressly repudiated. I hope [that] in the long run the influx of German refugees will contribute something, but meantime a lot of them are committed to advertising the goods they brought over with them . . . and those who have "phenomenology"—whatever this is—to sell seem the worst.

. . . I hope you got enough out of the contacts to have made it worth while. It's always a help in the end to see how many different ways there [are] of misunderstanding. At least I've found it a help in clearing up my own formulations to see how other people took them. The effect of communication on the need for being understood, and the reflex effect of this need in compelling a man to become articulate will make an interesting chapter sometime. . . .

Yours, John Dewey

Paoli, Indiana, February 26, 1942

Dear Dewey:

. . . Now I have long had a feeling that James's development and yours could be put together in positive form. You set that up, of course, in your paper on James ["The Vanishing Subject in the Psychology of James"] last fall. Incidentally, I do not think I have remarked to you—though I have to others—what an astonishing output of extremely significant papers you have produced in the last year or so. Did you not tell me a couple [of] years ago you were tired and sluggish, and not doing much? What I would do would be to take the James "immediate experience," including his later factual report on the immediacy of relation as well as of thing—then strip off the passing thought and the consciousness, as he did—then let "languaging" enter to cover the full range he covered with the word "cognition" (incidentally, he remarked that in his own case all the cognizing he could find was verbal), thus socializing the whole business. Then I would introduce James's immediate acceptance of your logical essays [*Studies in Logical Theory*] in their earliest form as right along his line. Also I would develop the situational and social and language phases of your work. You have the whole thing there, except the direct, flat statement that the basic business is the direct pre-subject and pre-object event. Then I would argue something like this: James did not develop in terms of language, and [did] not [develop] in terms of the directly social, but went a-glittering with philosophizing lectures. You have had a weather eye in your expositions on the great range of philosophical systems, organizing your arguments with reference to them very largely; also you have steadily allowed for the imperfections of your hearers and tried to use phrasings that would not shock them. The result is that nobody bothers with the positive James observation. . . . Also nobody is willing to think that you really mean it when you say you do not need a spirit to operate things. You can be credited with basing everything on a "conative unity," as in the current paper I referred to above.

What I would most like to see is a straight, direct paper from you stating emphatically that you do not need some of these things [that] young philosophers insist you must use just because they have never themselves been without them. If I were to make a guess as to why they are free to misread you, it would be that, personally, you do not give a damn about "real objects," but you usually feel your probable audience is so deeply concerned with them that it is necessary to introduce them into the discussion, or each side will put you in the camp with the other side, and you do not want to be in either. The only thing I feel certain of is that whatever guess I made would be mostly wrong —the present state of philosophical public opinion being too intricate.

90

Another thing I could be certain of is that I have no right to an opinion, since I have never succeeded myself in getting anybody to believe that I really mean what I say—or rather, if anyone does think I believe it, he quits my neighborhood for good. Still a further thing is that success will not come until the statement about the mental-thing can be made positively, instead of negatively. I am putting my own bet on the possibility of making "languaging" cover the full range (as direct behavior in mind-body fusion) of the cognitive and knowledge-about; and making sign-processes of a sub-verbal form cover the full perceptive and sub-perceptional activities in one behavioral system, and base the whole thing on a fusion of you and James with a throw-back to Peirce. The main trouble with my scheme is that I have never been able to state it so that anybody knew what I said—which is some considerable defect. . . .

With best regards, Bentley

Paoli, Indiana, March 2, 1942

Dear Dewey:
. . . I have a grandiose scheme—maybe delusions of grandeur. Having broken the ice about my old inclination to unite you and James at a special point . . . I believe I will proceed to ask a question.

Introductory. I do not take—or rather I try not to take—I sometimes succeed in not taking—people as right or wrong, but as making statements oriented to settings—primarily, . . . then other verbal set-ups current around them—then other cultural formulations. Thus:

Peirce I see as having observation after observation that he could not develop in the terminologies of his time.

James ran his direct thing-experience up to a direct relation-experience, and on a parallel track reduced the "conscious" more and more, but reacted toward philosophizings, popular lectures, etc. (somebody once told me he needed the money), and never got back (as you have shown) into the factual statement.

Mead got the "self" stripped down to where it vanished, but having around him a large fringe which would have fainted if the self did vanish, never succeeded in dropping the word after he had wiped out the pseudo-fact.

Myself, by not presenting my work in construction out of the materials I was using, but instead by opposing other constructions, and not allowing for the under-the-surface advances in the way I want to do, repelled most of the people I ought to have addressed.

You have such a large philosophical background, and such a range of present philosophical audiences, that you take innumerable possible interpretations of your views into account. This has at times the effect to me that you pull your punches, where I should like to see the blow strike harder.

Now: there is not a one of the above attitudes that is "wrong." I am not even sure that any one is "unfortunate." In the long development of many men approaching as many ways, there is need for all. Especially in your case, you have got all the materials that are needed, and all the varied phases of the discussion, spread out before people so that they are all ready to be used, where a different manner of attack would have shut such people off from any grasp of the business.

Nevertheless, as I wrote before, I find it damned unfortunate that so many people go calmly ahead in discussing your work—either pro or con—and at the show-down are ignorant of what it is that makes it go.

Such being the case, I have a question. It is a genuine question for a purpose. I am not trying to "tell" you, but to find out whether my guess at what the next step in presentation should be is anywhere near your opinion on that matter.

My impression is that whenever a reference to the actively producing *Subject* comes up, you indicate that you have no need for and no use for it (I think I noted ten or twelve such passages in the *Logic*).

However, when reference to the *Object* is necessary, you indicate that the object is needed, and you are not trying to get away from it.

With an eye on the philosophizers, the practical need of these two affirmations is evident. You must not let the subject appear too individual; you cannot permit the object to disappear altogether even in fancy.

Your "psychological" is and has always been on the adaptational, biological side, as opposed to the in-growing cortex location side. More than that, it has been increasingly "situational" (on the basis of positions you took as far back as "Reflex Arc") with respect both to "other people" and to "outer things."

Your "person" becomes—and you so state it—a "region" in organic-environmental-social living. Your "object" remains, however (and here I am not so certain as above), a pre-organism object.

Now when you develop a logic or discuss other related topics, you assert the full situational background; you declare all valuations are to be held within it; but you proceed to discuss in a terminology referable to a "person" (to be valued as you have valued him) in his dealing with an object (to be valued as you have valued it).

You therefore employ a full cosmic-biological background, treating the organism in its cosmic situation; but nobody ever quite believes you when you say you are not needing the subject and are using the object as fully as it ought to be used—any more than Mead believed himself, or James developed himself, or than anybody retains a belief in my

92

possible sanity, once he has got it into his head that I "really mean" what I say.

I now suggest splitting the subject-region and the object-region formally into two specimens for each.

When you say you do not need the subject, say also that you do not need the kind of an object that goes with the kind of a subject you do not need.

When you say that you need the object, say also that you do need the kind of a subject that goes with that kind of an object.

(I do *not* want to stress the words "philosophy" and "science," but generally speaking, the two rejected specimens are the philosophers' specimens, and the two accepted specimens are the scientists' specimens.)

You then have this situation that both the scientific subject-phenomena and the scientific object-phenomena are descriptions in the sense that both are *regions* in space and time, and neither can have substituted for it in technical work a timeless-spaceless naming as dependable agent in *interpretation* (more adequate descriptions) that . . . [is] to be developed out of, and around, and beyond it.

I read (or rather peered at) your paper "Context and Thought," in [*University of*] *California Publications* [*in Philosophy*] about 15 years ago, while at Columbia. And I think this rather set me off on this line. I may be wrong, but I think "context" was sometimes linguistic, and sometimes experiential or objective, and this particular fused use of "context" was the difficulty I had in getting in touch with Randall's views at the seminar. I think this is a good point to stop. . . .

Best regards, *Bentley*

Key West, Florida, March 9, 1942

Dear Bentley:

. . . The funny thing is that many years ago, long before I was as far along as I am now towards behaviorism, I wrote on the utter futility of the epistemological problem—given their own [theo]rems, any "solution" is impossible. . . . But I agree with you that I haven't been direct and flat enough. One reason is that I've had to feel my own way along gradually—so gradually that it was a long time before I knew where I had got to. And, of course, it is true that to a large extent I felt my way along through the medium of other men's systems and ideas.

I am especially indebted to you for your remarks about "object." I guess you are probably right in thinking I should say something about "object" as explicit as what I've said about "subject" in later days. Since "object" is in ordinary use with no epistemological associations, it hadn't occurred to me [that] its use needed special explanation—that "object over there," etc. Its popular use is, I think, synonymous with "thing,"

93

save "thing" has a much broader use—no-thing, anything; "object" seems to be an equivalent of a "thing" with a definitely limited spatial location—such as is designated by a "concrete" common noun. And there are difficulties even in using the word "thing."

Russell [cf. his "Philosophy of Logical Atomism to July, 1919," at p. 51] criticized something I wrote by assuming in something he quoted from me that its use meant belief in old-fashioned "substance." I ought to have said "event," according to him—at the same time he used in the same article the word "thing" several times in its loose popular sense.

Now it is also possible that in my desire to avoid the "subjective," I have used the word "object" in a pre-organism sense. I am sure the word is unobjectionable in its idiomatic, popular usage, but it is also highly probable that the epistemological use is so ingrained that in any case its use should be accompanied by an explicit statement of the sense in which it *isn't* used. I was after the underlying problem in the *Journal* [*of Philosophy*] article on "Subjectivism-Objectivism in Modern Philosophy" [*sic*]. In its technical sense, objects as objectivism are *environmental conditions* "in general," i.e., detached from any *particular* organism-interaction, so as to get a general point for control of these particular ones, i.e., *looked at* in detachment from *special* reactions—general and especially abstract nouns. And I think the word "subject" can be given a legitimate behavioral sense along the same lines—a study of organism-responses temporarily detached from interactions with any specific environmental condition.

Undoubtedly one thing which influences [me] is that I believe that most philosophers have been getting at something genuine—that there is a germ of fact in their performances—and I've spent a good deal of time trying to dig it out. Probably too much, since quite likely I've been affected by the fact [that] I've earned my living teaching professional philosophy. But take the words "self" and "person." Philosophers may have (actually have) made more or less of a mess in what they have said about them. But they didn't invent [the words:] he, she, you, they, I, myself, yourself, himself. Nor did they invent the fact that the "modern" period is marked by a greatly increased emphasis upon whatever these words stand for—Newton's law, Edison's light and [Albert] Einstein's relativity. The thing I wrote about James started out as part of a preliminary study for an article on the self—with a social interpretation, and I have some notes entitled "Persons and Things" [to the effect that] normal human beings have certain distinctive properties, and the distinction between person and thing is a highly important social-behavioral distinction.

Well, this isn't by way of rejection of your suggestion, for (1) I doubtless have used the word "object" in a pre-organism sense, and (2) even when I don't, there are a lot of persons who probably assume I'm using it in that sense. [Basil L.] Gildersleeve once wrote that "objects" is something which "objects"—what it objects to, being the execution of some plan or aim or desire of ours. "Object" is also what is aimed *at*. I think these two meanings cover the ground pretty well. Anyway, many thanks.

. . . One of the difficulties readers have with your writings is, I think, that they are lost unless they can classify a writer, and they can't place you—it is a matter of secondary importance that an article of the kind you mention would assist, but it's of some importance. *The* important thing is a paper from you covering the points of language about the perceptive and sub-perceptive activities in the way you outlined in your letter. That would be something genuinely new and a challenge that couldn't misfire. I think your Columbia experiences would help you in driving it home where it is needed.

Yours, *John Dewey*

Paoli, Indiana, March 13, 1942

Dear Dewey:

. . . Your "person" and "thing" are what I had in mind as "subject" and "object." I might substitute "assertion" and "fact," or "mind" and "matter," or "organism" and "environment." I used "subject" and "object" because my recollection is that "object" is a word I had noticed you using in certain passages in which, in order to protect yourself from the cry "idealist," you emphasized the actuality of the outer world around the organism. This emphasis being not in the slightest a break with your position, but being of such a phrasing that the other fellow could pick it up.

I did not know I would do it when I wrote you, but since then I have drafted a paper called "Subjects and Objects" [unpublished], in which I have set down the characteristic blind spots the academic philosopher's eye has toward you, and toward a similar region in James. Then I have said [that] an independent or severed Subject set over against an independent Object yields an epistemological chasm. Next, that a subject no longer independent should have an object or an environment, etc., similarly no longer independent, both being carved out of one block. Third, that dropping the independent subject but not being equally sharp about dropping the independent object leads to confusion and misunderstanding. To this I have added two developments, one on the perception-languaging-sign business you mentioned, the other on the way [that] James's "pure" experience, if not read "mentally," and with language substituted for cognition, would yield a formulation fitting in its way with your "knowledge out of activity" development. Did you hear [Edwin Bissell] Holt the day you spoke about James [Dewey,

95

"William James as Empiricist"] at the New School in November? He said James's outcome was inevitable materialism [published in his essay, "William James as Psychologist"]. I should have denied this on the spot, but did not. My point is that James's outcome here is the very biological naturalism that you have developed logically. It is significant to me that on the first appearance of your early logical essays James shouted ["The Chicago School"]: This is my kind of meat. . . .

Sincerely yours, *Bentley*

Paoli, Indiana, March 16, 1942

Dear Dewey:

Regardless of whether it is necessary or not, I want to withdraw all I have written in recent letters, and apologize for them.

I shall go ahead sketching and throwing sketches away, until, to paraphrase Peirce, my conception of the performance is equal to my conception of the effects that might conceivably have practical bearings that I conceive the performance to have.

Of course, if you do anything more along the line of the "persons and things" or comparable lines, I should be glad to know about it. A horror to avoid is the appearance of conflict where there is no substantial conflict, though I find it almost as bad to have an appearance of similarity where there is actual sharp separation of paths.

Sincerely, *Bentley*

Key West, Florida, March 19, 1942

Dear Bentley:

. . . Language habits stick by, and while I can point out in history at large the way old words have distorted newly discovered facts, it's hard to escape their influence in my own case. I don't doubt that the pronouns, he, me, etc., are a mixture, but I think there is a strong social-behavioral content—probably overdone in legalistic deposits, but punishing and rewarding agents . . . [have] always been one of the chief human jobs.

No, the point about the sub-perceptive, perceptive, etc., series wasn't a development by me of something you said. It was taken quite literally from what you wrote. I was so much struck that I repeated it, for my own sake. I can't think of any one job as well worth doing at the present time. I have been trying to write for some two years now on "interpretation" of modern philosophy as a cultural phenomenon. [This manuscript was lost and never found.] I've written a lot about the epistemological problem as a product of the "subject-object" assumption, but I'm also trying to find some moderately reasonable explanation of why on

96

human grounds this situation developed. There was something in historic conditions that led to a rather sudden as well as rather extreme awareness of human nature as amounting to something on its own account and not just on account of the cosmos (Greek) or on account of God and his plan of salvation (medieval). When old institutional habits are felt to be cramping, there is an exaggerated sense of "individual" qualities—of being different. I have written chapters on "Persons and Things" and on "mind and matter," but [I] started all over again last fall, and haven't got back to those topics yet. What you write—and will write—is a great help in keeping me from falling back.

There is a lot in what you say about [my] use of "object." I had noticed before you brought up the topic a rather marked tendency on my own part to use the word "subjectmatter." "Assertion" and "fact" is a very helpful suggestion.

Yours as ever, *J. Dewey*

Key West, Florida, March 19, 1942

Dear Bentley:

. . . I hope I haven't said or implied anything to indicate either conflict or a feeling that what you wrote was anything but welcome to me. I'm immensely indebted to you, and in nothing more than the last two letters from you. I think your scheme of the sub-perceptive, etc., series the most helpful thing I've seen in a long time.

Sincerely yours, *Dewey*

Key West, Florida, March 28, 1942

Dear Bentley:

. . . I was at a loss to surmise why you felt you had to take back what you had said in your previous letters. It has since occurred to me it might be what I said about "subject-object" in my Whitehead article ["The Philosophy of Whitehead"], written, by the way, somewhat over a year ago. I have no copy here of that book and don't recall just what I said, but there was a discussion of "subject-object" that might strike you as indicating a difference between us, and possibly even that I was so confused that I hadn't known what I was saying in writing you. However, my treatment there was enough of a deliberately attempted stunt so that in fact it doesn't indicate (even at the time when written) the kind of unawareness of what I was saying [that] it may seem to—nor yet a deliberate suppression in writing you—though that wouldn't be as bad as not knowing what I was saying.

Aside from my genuine admiration for Whitehead—he is so much "thicker" in James's sense than all the other systematic philosophers—I

97

was in hopes that the fact [that] he took the subject-object relation entirely . . . out of the epistemological context and made it an aspect of every interaction of energies, so that either one of the elements might be called equally subject or object, might be used to boost things along somewhat. Of course, my hope may have been wrong, and I only made things worse. But I had a feeling that Whitehead would see the point of my final *criticism* even if others didn't. Anyway, whether this had anything to do with your last letter or not, I thought I [would] write it to you.

In any case the connection of your point with James and myself is not important in the sense that a statement of the positive serial development from the sub-perceptional activities up through language [is]. Believe me, I was more than sincere in everything I said about the importance of that.

Sincerely yours, *Dewey*

Key West, Florida, April 1, 1942

Dear Bentley:

. . . I've just looked at, but not read with any care Weiss's article ["Logic of Semantics"] in the current *Journal* [*of Philosophy*]. A beautiful inversion. Where signs are, there mind is also. Apart from mind, clouds are not a sign of rain. Apart from mind, *words* (yes, mind you, *words!*) are not a sign of *thoughts.* . . .

I was pretty damn discouraged after reading [D. S.] Mackay's article ["What Does Mr. Dewey Mean by an 'Indeterminate Situation'?"]. . . . I wrote and sent in a reply ["Inquiry and Indeterminateness of Situations"] to the *Journal* [*of Philosophy*]. I'll have to cultivate your technique of holding a writer to a responsible use of words. Instead, I asked for some evidence that I hold the views which at crucial points he attributes to me and [upon which he] bases his criticisms, and pointed out that they made nonsense of my whole book on inquiry. . . .

Yours, *Dewey*

New York, April 4, 1942

Dear Bentley:

. . . I have never regarded your suggestions as in the least officious. Not only do I owe too much to them both in general and in particular in helping me avoid and correct some "besetting sins," but my preservative "instinct" intellectually has usually made me interested in learning from criticisms even of an adverse character (I've sometimes been inclined to believe that has been the chief factor in my professional career as compared with that [in the careers] of my colleagues).

As to your comments, I agree with all except the first—that there is no "inconsistency"—for there is inconsistency. I think I've been headed in the right direction, but I've tripped on the way.

Certain differences between us are expressions of different problem-interests. Your different problem and approach . . . [have] been one thing that has made your writings, letters included, so useful to me—stereoscopic effect. Whether there is actually an underlying difference as to "cosmic object," I'll have to find out. Meanwhile I agree with you as to the need of explicit qualification when I use "object" for the reference of a common noun and also that I have failed on the language-cognitive side. Your problem has been closer to facts than my problem in that matter. . . .

Yours, John Dewey

Paoli, Indiana, April 24, 1942

Dear Dewey:

. . . Under two conditions only would I want to publish it ["As Through a Glass Darkly"].

(1) If you find nothing whatever off-color in my rendering of your position. (I do not want any reader to have a chance of raising or even imagining an issue between you and me.)

(2) If you think it has any value of "timeliness," so that there is a chance of a fly or two getting stuck on its flypaper.

The manner of presentation of analyses like this is something I must examine with a view to getting a method of writing that is less "personal." You spoke of my method of holding writers to account for their words. Some of my friends who like what I am doing always see it as a sharpened method of criticism. I do not see it that way at all. I see these writings lying spread out before me like natural phenomena—like bugs to a "bugologist." My attitude is that it is just as important to see how the sentences hang together (apart from the writer) as it is for an ento-mologist to see how a bug's tissues are organized, apart from considera-tion of any other nature. However, in writing, whenever I attempt a de-personalized statement, the sentences lose definiteness—they open possi-bilities of vague reference. For instance, I did some of this in terms of "theorist" and "critic," but every now and then a phrasing arose in which "critic" might mean me instead of Mackay. I have to pick out "lines" or "leads" to write about. This also weakens the analysis. If I should lay down the text, report my analysis the way I make it myself, and use no other aids to reading, I am quite sure I would have no reader at all. I am setting this problem of description down for later study some time.

About "inconsistency," I express my view in this paper. It is simply that when you select a certain phrase and discuss it from a particular point of view for a particular group of philosophers, the issue as thus formulated is often partial, and the phrasings used, while impressionistically good in the given instance, will not stand generalization. Then someone gets a chance to object. . . .

I am planning to complete three unfinished papers: one on Subjects and Objects (with an eye to such an audience as *Philosophical Review*); one on the difficulties of a theory of language (with a *Scientific Monthly* audience in mind); and one on the main propositions of a general theory of language (with an eye to *Language* magazine). [These were not completed or published.] Then I shall probably throw aside all the "unity" analyses, and postpone the book on the basic Peirce [never developed or completed] till I get the language theory constructed; that is, the rendering of language representation within a general system including sub-perceptive and perceptive signs "below" and perhaps the free-functioning "symbols" "above." . . .

Sincerely, *Bentley*

New York, April 28, 1942

Dear Bentley:

. . . Your paper ["As Through a Glass Darkly"] is a gem. I wrote a longer paper ["Inquiry and Indeterminateness of Situations"] which the *Journal* [*of Philosophy*] will publish, but I didn't take up the central issue, and you raise it fair and square, a between-the-eyes blow.

What you say about your method of procedure develops what I mean by your "technique" in a way that makes my own meaning much clearer to me. It is the technique of a naturalist. You illustrate your own theory about language in your method of criticism. You treat a man's language in a natural world.

I agree in substance with what you say about my "consistency" in your last [letter]. But I do make actual slips occasionally—it's hard to get away from early attitudes—and I do have the habit of coming as near as I can to the other man's views, which has both advantages and disadvantages.

Yours, *John Dewey*

Paoli, Indiana, May 1, 1942

Dear Dewey:

I have just had your ["The Philosophy of Whitehead"] . . . read to me. You referred to it a while back. It confirms all that I have felt about Whitehead. If you would have somebody sit down and list your praises and criticisms of Whitehead, I suspect you would find one general atmospheric endorsement, and about fifteen express disagreements. About half way through . . . I made the following memo to see whether the paper would come out with me or against me: The core of Dewey's position is to get the subject interpreted in "nature" in the sense of a "system," let it come out as it may. The core of Whitehead is a sort of opposite. [He] is always trying to read the universe in modified mentalistic terminology.

I have tried to read him repeatedly and never could find consistency or any other meat in any dozen pages. I have meant to ask you whether I ought not to persevere till I found it. My irreverent feeling is that he empties a pillow case full of feathers, and you waste a lot more time than is necessary in huffing and puffing them away. He worries me. When I read your remarks on his prehension, it reminded me—as I am often reminded—that it was oversight or ignorance on my part not to have stressed him in my recent "Factual Space-Time" paper, but when I shake the stuff around and inspect it, I am sure his treatment is exactly what I do not aim at.

I think I can illustrate to you from your text here the type of phrasing which leads people like Mackay and others in recent papers to falsely interpret you. On p. 645 your phrasing runs: ". . . that experience is a manifestation of the energies of the organism; that these energies are in continuity . . . " etc. There is no possible excuse for mis-reading, but when a man who says and reads only in one form, the mentalist, reads that "experience is a manifestation of the energies of the organism," he strips off all the rest of your construction, takes this one localization, modifies it to his liking, and proceeds at once to say that you, like himself, see all things mentally. This is my guess at it. . . .

Sincerely, *Bentley*

Paoli, Indiana, May 3, 1942

Dear Dewey:

I have been sampling a few more phrases in the [*The Philosophy of Alfred North*] *Whitehead* volume [P. A. Schilpp, ed.], and I cannot resist the following comment.

If I am off the track as always, I should be glad to be shown:

Our language is full of mentalist terminology (psychic, etc.). Both Whitehead and I take this language as indicative of fact. Whitehead takes it as presenting Gosh-awful reality, so that if you can just fiddle around with it enough, you do your job. In other words, he takes its main *nouns* as truth-reporters (that is true-fact reporters, or fact-reporters). The philosopher operates around the edges of these words.

I take this mentalist terminology culturally and historically as a first rough, imperfect stab at facts. The basic *nouns* are the items in it I regard as most unreliable. (In a sort of way, freedom to change the nouns is scientific; adherence to them is philosophy.)

You give me the strongest support I have in this line by your whittling the nouns down in all sorts of cultural ways (this being the lesser phase of support) and by your actually developing (this being the greater phase) a logic and other theories in which you proceed *Technically* without this apparatus. (This isn't any sort of flattery or wiggle-wording —so far as I can now see, it is straight fact.)

I now note that the uneasiness I feel with some of your discussions is that in your desire to be fair to an opponent in recognizing as fully as possible that he "means something," he is too often left in the belief that his "noun" meanings are that "something."

He then goes away and reports your reasoning to be specious, because he fails to get the point that actual technical procedure is more important than traditional belief. So long as he still thinks that *his* reference for *his* nouns is accepted by you, he will continue to think he is right in regarding your reasoning as fallacious. . . .

Sincerely, *Bentley*

[P.S.] If there is *One* sure statement that can be made about that which we call "science," as we have it today (and that is all I am talking about—taking it as good sound knowledge), it is that attribution to *actors* is the one technique science is surmounting ceaselessly, without deviation. Newton's second law meant this, and the passage into energy and out meant this. And infinities in mathematics mean this, and the "light" spectrum in wave terms means this. Of course, one can read a soul into a quantum if he wishes. But I am for Leibnitz. He told what a monad could be, and he did it for all time (all *My* time, I mean). . . .

New York, May 4, 1942

Dear Bentley:

. . . Fundamentally you are right, of course, about Whitehead. But when I neglect entirely his own panpsychic interpretation (and his ultra-mathematical organizations), and stick to his sense of temporal inter-activities, I get a boost from him. Also he is suggestive on a lot of things incidentally. See what he says for example about "scholarship" in *Adventures of Ideas* (Index and pp. 150–51). He is a scholar himself, and I don't know any other scholar who has such a sense of the dangers of scholarship.

When I was in Key West, I had a long letter, rather missionary in tone, from [Charles] Hartshorne, pointing out to me what an improvement it would be if I only went the whole panpsychic (mentalistic) road with Whitehead. (When and if I see him, I'll tell him Whitehead and I are both too old to change, but otherwise Whitehead has more to learn from me.) I got one thing from his letter which has left me with the feeling [that] I've got now the root of Whitehead's trouble (aside from mathematics).

It's the same as Bergson's starting from Newtonian physics; there *had* to be (as you've pointed out) another "world"—the mentalistic. Both Bergson and Whitehead were struck with the importance of time-qualities (*durée*, prehension, etc.). Then relativity and space-time came along, and Whitehead (but not Bergson) applied his temporal constructions to physics. But instead of seeing that, in doing this, he cut the ground from under his "mental-world," he used his old contra-Newton doctrine to mentalize his "Reality."

I'm pretty sure this is the explanation, and I think I'll write it out sometime.

Yours, *John Dewey*

New York, May 7, 1942

Dear Bentley:

. . . I hadn't read [Percy] Hughes' article ["Is Whitehead's Psychology Adequate?"]—and [I] had some difficulty reading it after you spoke of it. However, as an element in starting myself on a reform career, I wrote him a letter . . . since in the context he refers [p. 279] to my use of "transaction," and asked him if he hadn't made it clear that in my view the "transaction" was primary, and what he called "acts" were at best abstractions in it or from it.

Yours, *Dewey*

New York, May 9, 1942

Dear Bentley:

He [Herbert Schneider] felt (as I do) that it [Bentley, "As Through a Glass Darkly"] disclosed the source of the difficulty between Mackay and me, as my reply doesn't.

He also remarked (with no effort at extraction from me) that you made quite a dent in the Columbia seminar on the students.

I think I wrote you that it [has] often happened that ideas strongly objected to when first presented take root and modify later views.

Yours, *Dewey*

Paoli, Indiana, May 15, 1942

Dear Dewey:

In drafting the paper on "difficulties" in language theory [unpublished] I find myself talking about the "guaranteed perceivings" of an actor-perceiver. As I go along, I notice that this balances against "warranted assertibility." The material of consideration is common enough—but I wonder whether you ever balanced the perceivings against the assertings with something like a comparable "warrantability" discussed for each in its own class? . . .

I think the "difficulties" all work up in very good shape for the kind of a book Schneider has in mind—surrogate for the public lectures [on language] that never were delivered. But I have suggested to him that if, after each man has made his own straight development, he will make an equally straight criticism of each of the others as a separate section of the book, it might have real value. These mixed "what I think" and "what you oughtn't to think" are the bane of my life. It is almost impossible ever to tell where "I" leaves off and "you" begins, even in the texts of the strongest mental isolationists. . . .

Sincerely yours, Bentley

New York, May 16, 1942

Dear Bentley:

. . . I got an answer from Hughes saying that my questions regarding separate acts and transactions were "fundamental," but his letter gave no additional light. On the whole, he rather dodges by saying that what is primary for one type of inquiry is not for another, and "no type of inquiry can itself be designated as primary." And he says: "The explanatory efficacy of any scientific account depends upon its assumption of some special force or forces, e.g., momentum, genes." At the same time he seems to admit that courses of action or natural histories belong to another type of inquiry in which the "tendency expressed" is called a "force." I couldn't follow him. . . .

They told me a story about G. E. Moore, who is here this half[-year]. He said [that] the mind was different from the body and the self, or me, different from both of them, and that when he said, "the wall is further away from me than this book," it didn't mean it was further away from his body or mind. Someone asked which was further away from him, his nose or his foot, and he said, "Oh, everybody knows the foot is further away. . . ."

Sincerely yours, Dewey

New York, May 27, 1942

Dear Bentley:

Maybe I can save you time by making a statement of the gist of my position about proposition and judgment, free from collateral issues discussed in the Logic.

104

I take a proposition as something pro-posed—put before some group or public for consideration. Any proposition occurs, accordingly, in a network or complex of propositions—its force and bearing . . . [are] determined by the set of connected considerations that are or may be brought forward (including counter-proposals or negative propositions).

Judgment is the actual or overt acting upon a proposal, or proposition—which is the only meaning I can find for its "acceptance" or "assertion." It carries out or executes the *reference* aspect of a proposition; it is an accomplished interaction in which the prior environing conditions are modified in accord with the terms of the proposal as a plan. It thereby tests the proposition.

One rather important collateral consideration is that the judging process is more or less continuous and gradual. That is, the above statement refers especially to the final and most decisive phase. It doesn't preclude a fairly steady stream of intervening acts of application or execution which serve to build up and out the judgment to its decisive stage.

The account is based ultimately upon the view of experimentation involved in my *Logic*. Roughly speaking, a proposition is a plan for an experiment; judgment is the interactivity in which the plan is tried out in actual operation. . . .

Sincerely yours, Dewey

Paoli, Indiana, May 30, 1942

Dear Dewey:

Have you ever read a paper called "Does Reality Possess Practical Character?" in the James volume [*Essays, Philosophical and Psychological*]—I mean since you wrote it? It has everything. . . .

I do not think I ever saw this paper before, and I read it with too much immediate appreciation to watch it closely, but I noted that at the opening your rejection of mental states was limited to those "precedent" to objective recognition and requiring "transcendental" function to operate; and at the end, when you discuss "awareness" directly, you accept it as a differentiated fact, and make your report show that this fact is one that appears in certain transitions. . . .

My panacea, of course, if it works out as I hope it will, is to drop all "feeling" items to physiology; formulate all "cognition" in linguistic embodiments; under a widened "sign" scheme, organize the perceptional and cognitional behaviors in one development; and finally exterminate from my own expression all words indicating "awareness" except so far as the reader will understand the object-participation in the awareness to be as active as the subject-participation. In other words, as in the case of Nagel ["Operational Analysis as an Instrument for the Critique of Linguistic Signs"], the "event-sign-user" is the situation, it is the fact of meaningful-event itself, and it is not the logician's revival of an ancient fairy tale.

It is the arrival of your letter orienting proposition and judgment to each other that sets me off on this consideration. Fully as I can accept what you say, you do not quite reach to what I want said. You do not orient proposition-and-judgment to other subject-matters of research in the way I want. You do not give me a statement that I can lay across a construction in terms of "connection," "reference," "relation," and say: "just here" and "just there." . . . You do not state the materials—the kind of meat—which are proposition and judgment. They are human living, human behavior. They are to be taken situationally, interactionally, rather than personally and actionally. . . .

Sincerely, *Bentley*

New York, June 1, 1942

Dear Bentley:

I don't believe I answered a specific question you asked me about two weeks ago, namely whether I had ever balanced guaranteed perceivings against or with "warranted assertibility" in the case of perceivings. The answer, unfortunately for me, is No. You have struck a new lead in bringing the perceivings and subconscious responses into the same sequence with explicit discourse.

It is not a matter directly connected, but I raised in the *Logic* a question I didn't think it was necessary to answer in that book (pp. 55–56). My own belief is that the sentence on p. 56 beginning "Upon the whole" could read "exclusively"; as far as [the] explicit signifying or evidential capacity of things is concerned, I think it is, so to speak, an after effect of language. But there are stimuli and leads and consequences on the sublinguistic plane that are in sequential line. I don't doubt you can work out successfully a statement of warranted perceivings of a sublanguage type.

Yours, *Dewey*

New York, June 12, 1942

Dear Bentley:

I remember your saying once how you disliked to go back and read what you had written. I have the same experience. I haven't read that essay ["Does Reality Possess Practical Character?"] for years and years, and I am mightily pleased that you found it, after all these years, worth reading—that there are things in it that shouldn't be there I can well believe; I am surprised they aren't more numerous than you seem to have found, since I must have been more under the influence of my early habits then, which I've been trying to outgrow.

If I knew in more detail what question you specially have in mind with regard to proposition and judgment, I might be able to do better. Proposals are certainly dependent upon the existence of language for their material as well as being themselves forms of linguistic behavior. "Ideation" is, in my usage, the turning over of proposals to reach a decision—talking to one's self, if I may use the word "self" to distinguish a *particular* social communicator from other communicators. Anything becomes an "idea" or suggestion, a proposal of a possibility, when not taken to be a *fact* in the space-time order to which it *has* been referred, or when it is taken as means of better future reference.

I suppose I took my clue as to "judgment" from the "sentence" or "judgment" of a court, in settling or deciding a matter previously in controversy.

It is certainly identifiable as a way of behaving. If "ideating," "deliberating" (certainly a linguistic phenomenon) is implicit, inchoate (that is, pro-jected) behavior, judgment is transition to overt behavior. The former is interactive with environment in origin and reference; but is temporarily, for an interval, loaded on the intra-organic side. Judgment is recovery of *actual* interaction.

I don't suppose, however, that it is likely the above bears upon the particular question you have in mind. But the great advantage, it seems to me, language has over other forms of behavior is that the vocal organs, in connection with auditory activity, lend themselves in their physiological capacity to exactly the sort of thing that I called "implicit," "inchoate," "nascent," as distinct from "overt" behavior.

I don't know whether there is a difference between us, save that you are more scrupulous in use of words than I am—to my own loss. If there is, it may be connected with what you say about "feeling" being relegated to the physiological, and all cognition referred to as linguistic. I certainly agree with the latter, even if [I] fall down sometimes in my own language. I agree with the former up to a certain point; if there is a difference, it has to do with the location of that point. That anger and fear and love (sexual and parental) are primary biological behaviors, and that pain (as you once wrote me had been shown to be the fact) is physiological seem to be certain. But, as far as I can observe, they become affected, to the point of transformation, *by* interaction [with] language and what language as communication does; so that anger, fear, love, pleasure, and displeasure are then *psychological* modes of behavior; so that the facts make it necessary to distinguish "emotions" and "desires" from "feeling."

107

I don't know how to express in words the fusion that takes place when feeling as physiological and language (meanings) interact in a blend. I suppose we shall have to wait till we know a lot that we don't know now before we can tell how it happens. But that in the social medium of communication that is constituted by language, raw philosophical anger, fear, love, etc., undergo great transformation, seems to me undeniable. I don't mean that you do deny it; in dealing with cognition and its various connections you certainly are entitled to neglect it even if it exists, as I believe it does. But in all probability a good deal of what I've written has been in the context of problems which concern the attitudes produced by what I've called fusion or blend. This is certainly true of what I call philosophy, values, etc. . . .

Yours, *John Dewey*

[P.S.] . . . One reason that I have a soft spot about Nagel (as you have too, for what he might do, but doesn't) is that he directed my attention specifically to your book on mathematical language [*Linguistic Analysis of Mathematics*] after I had had it without reading it for some time. . . .

New York, June 13, 1942

Dear Bentley:

. . . It is a moderate statement to say that it ["As Through a Glass Darkly"] gave [me] a heartening that more than wiped out any discouragements I've experienced. You are too generous in what you say, but I realize that it is the larger issue you have in mind and at heart, and if anything could clarify that issue to those who are so much in the dark about it, it is your article. My reply ["Inquiry and Indeterminateness of Situations"] is a popgun in comparison; I had Mackay too much in mind. You have gone to the deeper issue and stuck to it.

After reading the article, I felt sort of ashamed that I had even suggested the possibility of a difference between us in any important matter. Should there be one, reconsideration of my own position is indicated.

But I've often thought that the fact that our backgrounds and our immediate problems were so unlike made your work helpful to me in a way that agreement from one with the same general background and set of problems could not possibly effect. . . .

Yours—more than ever, *Dewey*

Paoli, Indiana, June 22, 1942

Dear Dewey:

. . . If you have never read [Ernst] Cassirer's paper ["Le langage et la construction du monde des objets"] in *Journal de psychologie* . . . ,

108

1933, in the two or three hundred page issue devoted to language, you may find one part of it worth while. He argues strongly just what you referred to the other day from your p. 56 of the *Logic* about objects requiring language to establish them as objects. . . . He goes as far as either you or I could wish in the factual recognition; except that just when he arrives, he pulls his punch. In other words, instead of a naturalistic conclusion, it is reason in the guise of language which makes object *object*. (Accent the last "object" on the first syllable for Cassirer, and on the last for us.)

Sincerely, *Bentley*

Paoli, Indiana, June 22, 1942

Dear Dewey:

1. In your reply ["Propositions, Warranted Assertibility, and Truth"] to Russell you adopt [an] operational correspondence between "subject" and "object" with both partners open and above board. . . .

2. In the case of "objects" (physical and physiological), our "knowledge" no longer reports an object (say, fire) as doing something (say, burn), but instead it traces the processes (no longer mechanistically, but in full description), and has a goal of leaving none untraced.

3. In the case of "subjects" (as behavioral "objects"), we have a very considerable apparatus of *tracing* in fields of sensation and perception, but no reliable form of statement. I seem to regard Pavlov's *own* approach here as about the soundest I know.

4. In behavioral fields of meaning, reasoning, speech and technical "object-determination," we are almost wholly lacking in either apparatus or dependable formulation.

5. In these last mentioned fields (#4) you have a general background of organization (and so have I—about the same); but in your *Logic*, while you over and over indicate your background, you still make most of your development (perforce) in the terminology of the "actor" that "acts"—of the "thing" that "does something" (as in #2).

6. My proposition is that this whole field can be dealt with as "languaging," once we get the facts out in such form that people no longer *see* in language a "word-body" distinct from a "meaning-soul," but can accept languaging behaviors in complete body-soul-fusion. . . .

7. To do this, the "sign" generalization must be worked back into sub-perceptive and perceptive, and on through naming, and judging, to full symbolic coherence. The job—something mountainous—for which I am now exploring the foothills.

8. The problem I have been mulling over for months is how the blind . . . can be shocked into recognizing what one is trying to say to them.

9. I think your "connection," "reference," "relation" terminology will fit in fine. My job will not be done till I can provide a "verbal operator" to transpose your terminology in the *Logic* (including my old bug, "concept") into one steady form.

10. If there is a difference between us, it is probably in my search for a *direct* basic statement somewhat of the type of James's "neutral" which *may* perhaps develop differences in technique from your "biological"—but I wouldn't even want to guess about that yet.

Regards, Bentley

Paoli, Indiana, June 22, 1942

Dear Dewey:

With regard to what bothers me—or rather to what I want to get stated in better form—take your last letter about it.

You say "propositions" are dependent upon the existence of language for their material as well as being themselves forms of linguistical behavior.

I would say "propositions" *are* language in action, and nothing else. There is no difference between us as we stand, but there is a difference in developing a language theory. "Dependent upon" implies a difference in the nature of two different kinds of facts. You see a propositional language and, in addition, something that is language but not propositional. Certainly at a stage at which propositions are studied with respect to material, the proposition and, let us say, the non-propositional naming want to be held apart. But I want the main theoretical statement to cover both. Your theory *does* cover both. But your expression does *not* lead us astray, but I suspect it does lead others astray, when they are closed to your view.

Next you speak of "ideation" as the turning over of proposals. The idea is thus a proposal when not "taken" as fact, or when taken as a means. The "turning over" and the "taken" are specifications of actor, without other localization. Your hearer reads this as what a "person" "does."

To illustrate: Suppose someone says a tree's life is its growing in the world. This is unexceptional. But it does not specify anything about cells, or saps, or leaf-absorption of air, or radiation effects. It is this latter "what" [that] I want specified for "idea."

You *do* say, and have often said, that ideation is a "talking to one's self." . . . But I see two types of reference for the "turning over" and the "taking"—the first to a "person," and the second to the on-flowing streams of languaging (with reason and meaning involved or comprised). Your understanding is the latter way; your reader mostly reads the former way. . . .

Now as to *overt* behavior, reported in the form of an organism's action—I find a similar difficulty of expression. But I cannot state it even as well as the above. "Judgment" is advance in the linguistic-propositional train at a stage at which perceivings and object-identifyings are further reorganized than [they were] when the start of the special section under examination was marked down.

Some way or other, the perceiving, the judging, the languaging, the acting, the specialized propositioning, require for me what . . . I am calling "Best Common Denominator," a formulation which will not permit the reader to contrast one stage with another as if [it were] of a different "realm," "faculty" or "universe of discourse."

As to "feeling," I would fully agree as to the cultural presentation of emotions, desires, etc., or linguistic modification, as you put it. The only point I have intended to make about the "pain" business was that *if,* once that can be assigned to physiology, *then* a core of individuality is removed from the descriptive-social-person, and the contrast of person with social is further pushed toward elimination.

I am working fully in your line, and in what I select from Peirce and James as central factually in their work.

My points are limited to two:

1. Can I develop the language-reason-meaning process in a unified form?

2. Should not continual advance be made in eliminating "actor-type" phrasings from all reports? And is not the survival of much of this phrasing in your *Logic* one great cause why people who themselves work in "actor" terms fail to observe at all the more general theoretical formulation within which you establish your own use of terms derivative from the actor-type?

Of course, I have no objection to the actor-type phrasing where it is not misunderstood. And of course, it is impossible for any of us today to eliminate it entirely. And, finally, once the theoretical "interactional" formulation is secured, there will be an immense amount of work to be done in the "personal" form where "person" itself is just a description of one region of interactions. . . .

Sincerely, *Bentley*

New York, June 24, 1942

Dear Bentley:

. . . 1. I agree that "propositions" are language in action, and "dependent" was one of my loose uses of language. I know that what I *meant* was that a "proposition" is not formally and "outwardly" linguistic, but that it is so in content, subjectmatter, meanings or whatever. In-

111

tending to make an emphatic statement, I made in fact a greatly weakened one.

2. There is a difficulty I feel . . . [in] what you have written about the words "act" and "action." I recall that somewhere you mention explicitly the sense in which you are using and are *not* using the words. I agree in fact about the danger of reference by the reader to "person" or "self," in the isolated sense of the latter word, whether or not I always live up to [it] in language. But there is a sense in which events have a reference to a centre, although that centre is in a whole extensive network of events, and it is *they* which centre in a relational, spatial-temporal sense. I'm not mentioning [this] as against what you say, but as [an] indication of a problem that has occupied me, and which I have [not] got the ability as yet to state properly.

3. I still have to get systematically the matter of "persons" *as a social* term instead of [their being] set over against "social." As I've suggested before, if I knew more law, I could do a better job. You wouldn't object, I take [it], to the fact that certain business-men are insurance *agents* and others are *agents* with respect to other humans who are "principals." Of course, the word "agents" and action in connection with them is subject to misuse and, even if rightly used, to misunderstanding by readers. What I want to do is in effect to interpret the words "self," "person," etc., in terms analogous to the social-behavioral use of "agent" in such cases as I've mentioned.

I don't believe [that] the words are going to be abandoned in a practical, common sense, idiomatic usage. Therefore I think it is very important that their social-behavioral sense be firmly and intelligibly affixed to them. There is nothing far-fetched in what I'm trying to do, even though I don't make headway in execution. In certain respects Arthur F. Bentley is a name for something that says of itself "I" and that others say of it, "you," or "he," and the same of John Dewey and some hundred of other social components. Or more generally, [this is] an interpretation of John Doe and Susan Roe in social-behavior terms. Until this is done, the mentalists are going to have an edge, in claiming *they* are the only ones who can give an intelligible meaning to such words as the "personal" pronouns. There are certain ways of behavior characteristic differentially of human beings as against non-human things, just as there are of cats versus dogs and both of them versus ("versus" includes "in connection with") stones. This again is just to indicate something I've been working at (the James "self" article ["The Vanishing Subject in the Psychology of James"] was introductory), but haven't got ready.

What you said in comparison of my statements with the statement, "A tree's life is its growing in the wood" gives me just the specification (your meaning) I was in search of. I shall certainly bear [it] in mind.

112

I think it is true that I tend to take for granted without detailed analysis the type of subjectmatter you are especially engaged upon. Having another problem uppermost, I tend to fob it off under a blanket term, "social environment," alluding occasionally to the fact of its indefinite temporal-spatial extent, and also, since you called my attention to it, [to] the tautological character of the phrase "social environment."

Yours, *Dewey*

[P.S.] Your way is the key to it all.

Paoli, Indiana, June 30, 1942

Dear Dewey:

I have a pretty good draft of the paper "The Jamesian Datum." . . . Disregarding all philosophical appraisals or applications, and all direct psychological uses, I am trying to show that his "neutral" or "pure" phenomenon (omit the word "experience") is datum, fact, primary observation for anybody and everybody any time. Correction. I am not "trying to show." I am taking his statement to this effect, and stressing it apart from all other considerations factually. Then I am trying to show that it is small-scale datum, correlated fully with your large-scale "organism and environment in nature" datum; that the two hold together, along with Peirce's durational and functional efforts in the Darwinian background, bringing the three grades of knowing in the James scheme, "acquaintance," "about," and "inference," the last apparently added after your early logic essays, in one frame. Again correction. "Bringing" is not the word, since they are there already—"permitting further terminological ordering" is probably what it will come to. *Question* I. Do you recall any treatment of this type in which solely the issue as to factuality of this "neutral" is raised, with everything else thrown aside? *Question* II. I am not making any mistake, am I, about the three levels—as in [*Essays in*] *Radical Empiricism*, p. 53?

In your letter [of June] 24th you say of a proposition that—it is not formally and outwardly linguistic, it is so in subject-matter, content, meanings. If "formally and outwardly" means something to the effect that "when we specialize on grammar, we are not exhausting the full scope of propositional process," then I understand. But if the distinction is one of our "manner of examination," I do not see how it justifies an "is" or "is not" with respect to "linguistic." The statement "is not formally" but "is in content" is just one of the forms of statement that seem to me to permit misinterpretation.

I think a similar reaction on my part comes to your comment #2 on "person." So far as the statement is made in terms of "point of approach to study," o.k. So far as it is made in terms of "is," *Trouble*. Immense study has to be made, in the future, of person-centering phenomena, under full interactional formulation. . . . Privately, however, I am in-

113

clined to think "person" is "wider process" and "less centered" than "cell" or "bullet." The biologist is always centering on "nucleus" or on "gene," and finding out he is wrong, and needs to broaden out interactionally. In my view the "person" is much less "centered" than the "bullet," not much "more" so; I characterize "person" therefore at the far extreme from the current sociologist's characterization. But I am not pretending to develop in such terms as yet. . . .

But as to "self," I have felt that Mead completely destroyed "self" in all standard uses. If he had said so outright, changed his terminology, and given direct description of what he found, all o.k. As it is, he is always doubling back and stressing that he is explaining that which he has explained. . . . I agree, of course, that such words as "person" won't disappear. "Particle," however, needs "wave" to help explain it. *Et tu, persona,* says I.

Sincerely, *Bentley*

New York, July 2, 1942

Dear Bentley:

1. I guess I still made a mess of what I said about [the] formal and content linguistic character of propositions. I meant to repudiate the distinction, and simply say they are language-events, *any way* you look at them. My first statement was intended like this: Anybody will admit that a propos[ition] is made of words and is in so far linguistic. Well, one has to go further than that and admit [that] their meanings (content) are also language-affairs, determined in and through communication. It was an example of my tendency to try and start from some common ground with the other person, and of the danger of getting involved in his position by so doing.

2. There is obviously a difficulty in the word "center"—I wasn't thinking of it in anything like a mathematical sense, but in a sense which allows for interactional field and process as wide as observation may find it to be in any given case. An agent of New York Life Insurance Company presents *a* (not *the*) centering of the full scope of its undertakings, obligations, etc., however extensive they may be in space-time. Maybe a better word can be found—center*ing* may be better.

3. "Aware of itself as a social subject and agent"—"subject" is ambiguous and shouldn't have been used there. But a government official has to be "aware of" what he does in his capacity *as* an official, or government agent, and what he does in his other capacities—"aware of" equals "discriminate."

All this is consistent with your belief that I *do* tend to "ease off my statements into old forms" and thereby give ground for misrepresentation—and I'm trying to be more careful.

114

It had occurred to me that some of the difficulties about "action" adhere also to "Behavior." But then I thought at least there is no *noun* "behaveror," like "actor"; at least there is that advantage.

On the whole I don't believe there are any *words* which will *completely* avert misrepresentations—though there are degrees. I think the main problem is to work out a statement of the words on the basis of observationally verifiable data, consistent with a thorough naturalistic interaction[al] position. (But, of course, the word "interaction" is dangerous, as it is easily taken to imply *two* or more *prior* existences. Like "stimulus-response," the words "organism" and "environment" have to have a functional interpretation within events which are integral. I tried to guard against misrepresentation of "interaction" in a paragraph at bottom of p. 33 and top of p. 34 of the *Logic*, stating that "interaction of organism and environment" expresses a condition of partial disintegration of a prior integral event, rather than something primary.)

I was interested some years ago to note, from the dictionary, that "private" originally had the force of *deprived*—"public" being primary.

Your "Jamesian Datum" paper will help; Russell tried once [in *The Analysis of Mind*] to do something with James's "neutral," but he just made, or tended to make, another peculiar order of existence out of it, instead of the datum-interpretation you give it. Of course James himself wasn't wholly clear—at times he seems to mix his neutrals with a kind of jelly-like cosmic world-stuff of pure experience; which Peirce did at times too, in language, at least.

And now to answer your questions. I don't know any treatment of the type you indicate; Russell's use is rather at the opposite pole. No, I don't think there is any doubt of the three levels in James—though in some places he uses "acquaintance" too loosely, I think—as if, that is, *familiarity* could come first.

Yours, Dewey

Paoli, Indiana, July 3, 1942

Dear Dewey:

Listing (experimentally) various possible placings of a James "datum," I set down (experimentally) alongside various possible placings of your biological subject and object. I note the following (*Journal of Philosophy*, 1941, p. 541) ["The Objectivism-Subjectivism of Modern Philosophy"]. . . . (a) The "subjective" equals the operations of an accultured organism; (b) is like "objective" equals physical subject-matter; a *condition* of experience; (c) Every actual or direct experience is of some *this*, here and now. In (a) where I wrote "equals," your phrase is "using the word to designate." It is a "naming," a "convention." . . . I accept this 100%. In (b) you definitely make experience (that is, *an* experience) something different from this "subjective." The "subjective" apparently "exists as a condition," and precedes (temporally?, logico-causally?, probably both?) "an" experience. I am unable to make any such separation. I do not think you do either. In (c) your use of "is of" seems to make "an experience" have a locus "in" an organism of the type that could be established by surveying (trigonometry). The "is of" is not here explained, but I read it as the "operational correspondence" of your reply to Russell in *Journal of Philosophy* last year ["Propositions, Warranted Assertability, and Truth"]. . . .

The only general way of statement that satisfies me is that I put everything of research within knowledge, and you carry on a good deal of exposition as if based on items underlying, prior to, or conditioning, knowledge. For example:

You put the organism and object in nature, and rest there. You then proceed [as if] "knowings" could be stated in terms of organism and object in nature,

After a while you use phrasings that seem to imply that "knowings" are processes of the organism as opposed to the objects in nature. Whereupon:

(a) I automatically connect your phrasings and go ahead in terms of your basic system of organism-in-nature. (b) Technically, when I inspect your phrasings in terms of organism, they imply an item of existence which is just as unfindable by me empirically as if you made the statement in psychical or mental terms. (c) I then note the old-timers (Hughes, Mackay) contentedly taking your phrasings to imply all the old evils that you have thrown out. (d) I then (1) write you about the phrasings, and (2) wonder whether the Jamesian datum, or fact, in the small cannot be correlated with your biological natural "system" in the large. . . .

Sincerely, *Bentley*

[P.S.] The kind of thing I like is a remark of yours that our sense-reports have apparently changed very slightly if at all in a *homo sapiens* range, historic and prehistoric. And, if so, how come that people try to explain cultural build-up in terms of objective impact? Apparently a very trifling delivery from the "objects" is used to interpret an enormous transformation of the "objects."

How will this compare? My typewriter has just written down that in the case of animal-and-tree or man-and-book, we actually *see* perception. We see all there is to it—providing we permit extension of seeing for this case such as we permit for the physicist with his instruments. We see confrontation, and muscular tension and directed gaze, and pointed tail or eye-muscle motion, etc. *Yet* . . . [we so] . . . habitually use such a fictional verbal set up about our own private perceivings

116

—the intervening third item, or percept—or conscious state—that we apply it to the other cases (friends, animals), and when we can't *see* it there, we say we can't see anything of the "real" event at all. . . . It is, of course, by way of gloss on your "How Is Mind to Be Known?" (and that, by the way, is a paper which almost everyone asks me if I have read— and which must have dented a good many heads) . . . *If* the pain (and all simplest "feeling" reference) could be handed over to the physiologist as physiology proper—as subject-matter proper of physiological research —*Then* the guts would be torn out of *Psyche*, and that kind of confusion you were talking about in the case of toothache—between having and knowing—would be on the road out—maybe.

This "How [Is Mind to Be] . . . Known?" paper, by the way, is a damn fine paper. . . . But even though at the end you say you are not taking up conclusions about nature of mind, etc., I am just wondering whether I do not go a little further in this matter than you do—whether to "fare worse" or not, I would not say. While you still use the word "mind" as if something could be said about "it," I regard it as just a bad form of naming and talking; so that while the behavioral as distinct from the physiological and physical is our subject-matter, the noun "mind," or any substantive to go with the adjective "mental," is just as much surplusage as phlogiston or a substance "heat." . . .

Paoli, Indiana, July 4, 1942

Dear Dewey:

. . . Immediacy, Factual Immediacy, is a naming . . . but [I] can't state [it] well enough to be able to get anybody to admit he is looking at it the way I want it. . . .

It is factual, cultural behavior prior to a discrimination of social and individual. It is perceptional behavior prior to hypostatizations (and hence my present fussing about James). It is naturalism, not biologically affirmed, but developing the biological-environmental contrast within it, and yet working factually, not mystically. In the language case I can get this immediacy in the "word-meaning" and in the "spoken-heard" and in the full word-meaning-spoken-heard. And I can see the language-thought immediacy in a setting of subsign-subthought immediacy. And I formulate generally that the further the cultural-behavioral advance, the clearer the immediacy, not the greater the particularity (individual-ity)—leaving intense individuality to bullets.

But how the hell [to] formulate a dog-tree-perceptional-situation in a way that will never imply that "George the dog" is "doing" it? Probably the answer is in the full sign construction, as you have several times indicated. . . .

Bentley

117

Dear Bentley:

. . . I think you are getting ahead in expressing the immediate here and now situation more than you appreciate. Your *"seeing* perception" in the sheet you send, the whole *illustration* is effective. Re-education of a lot of people is required, *and it's a slow* process—but it will spread.

. . . I suppose we would agree:

1. The possibility of control depends upon knowing the conditions of the occurrence of an event. (I mean this is a necessary condition—not that it is *sufficient*.)

2. Taking the case of a disease whose occurrence we wish to "control." It is legitimate, in fact necessary, it seems to me, [(a)] that there be investigated environmental conditions, say mosquitoes, swamps, etc., and also intra-organic conditions, conditions of blood, temperature of body, etc. *Not* (b) that the latter exist prior to the disease, chronologically or logico-causally, as an interaction, nor (c) that the disease has its locus *in* the organism apart from the whole spatial-temporal stretch of events which *are* the malaria, but that the distinction is a part of the procedures of investigation (what at times you call "carving out," unless I get you wrong) prerequisite to the operation of procuring effective control. I don't mean separation, any more than a physician who gives quinine by that act denies the mosquito-part and the necessity of draining and oiling breeding places, etc.

There is no difference between us as to the total situation. I don't think that the modern historical emphasis upon the "subjective" is *merely* a holdover from old ideas of soul, spirit, etc., though philosophic statements were tremendously influenced by this holdover—through religious Christian sources mainly—think of the hold of the Catholic church for centuries. There was also an interest in control that was totally foreign to Greek and medieval periods and a discovery of *human* nature. Then the philosophical statements that ensued (they aren't just in what is conventionally labelled philosophy, but in political theory, economics, linguistic and philological theory, etc.) were a bad mixture of the interest in finding out about human nature, as an *interacting* set of conditions in behalf of control of what happens *and* separation of inner and outer, psychical and physical, etc.

Because, I suppose, of all my early training, and also likely by temperament, the problems of historical culture-movements, how people get that way in beliefs, are problems I can't get away from. Your comments come in pat; next time I tackle the subjectivism-objectivism history, I shall at least know more of the dangers in statement [that] I'll run into. . . .

Yours, *Dewey*

Dear Dewey:

. . . I do not sense the slightest difference between our backgrounds and objectives. The questions that rise are all about phrasings, and about these only as directed to special audiences. In James's case, I took a quick glance at the Gifford Lectures [*The Varieties of Religious Experience*] and noted the startling difference between the phrasing of the contents, and that of the text for the ears of the worthies who attended the lectures.

Do you know what made James come so suddenly out into so large [an] amount of construction in 1904? Was it by any chance the impact of your first lot of logical studies [*Studies in Logical Theory*]? I find between 1895 and 1905 a lot of experimentation and general orientation, but no construction (except the California pragmatism announcement ["Philosophical Conceptions and Practical Results"]). Then, suddenly, everything. The perceptional immediacy becomes sharp and firm. The relational immediacy is added. The "radical" takes new meaning. He goes on to a "perceptional view" of causation in the posthumous *Some Problems of Philosophy*.

I mentioned Cassirer's account ["*Le langage et la construction du monde des objets*,"] of [H. von] Kleist's "*Uber die allmähliche Verfertigung der Gedanken beim Reden*," * and said I think it was a bug of mine. I find James in the *Problems* saying he was often "surprised" by his "scriptorial causality." I have the loveliest case I ever saw in the *Mind* paper of 1884 ["On Some Omissions of Introspective Psychology"] where "stream" was not [used] as construction, but as figure of speech. In the cognition paper of 1885 ["The Function of Cognition"], I am pretty sure he did not *use* the stream procedure (though I have not verified it). This last paper was the most "atomistic" thing I know of his having done. Then in 1890 [*The Principles of Psychology*] the "stream" blossoms out in full objectification as activity. *And Further*, as you pointed out, it already contains "course of experience" without his having observed it. It is the prettiest case of my general construction of languaging as event taking place in people [that] I have ever noted.

[*Bentley*]

Dear Bentley:

That's a very interesting question you raise about the rather sudden turn in James. I think the Chicago *Studies* [*in Logical Theory*] may have had something to do with [it], and I'm quite sure Bergson had a good

* *H. v. Kleists Werke*, Erich Schmidt, ed. IV, 74–82.

deal to do [with it], probably more in some ways. I think the change was largely by [their] giving him courage or confidence to express views he held in a way when writing his *Psychology*, but wasn't sure enough of them to express [them] positively. I do not believe that the double strain of things out there, and states of consciousness "knowing" them, which he said was necessary for *psychology* at any rate, ever satisfied him. The assertion of direct immediacy of relations, *Principles of Psychology*, Vol. I, p. 245, is accompanied with "*so surely . . . do feelings exist to which these relations are known*"—he felt bound to double up everything. But a few lines afterwards he says, "If we speak objectively, it is the real relations that appear revealed; if we speak subjectively, it is the stream of consciousness that matches each of them," etc. I think even then he would have preferred to do what he called "speaking objectively," but was held back by the doubling theory.

I think James got something out of Bergson [that] the latter didn't know was there in the line of perceptional immediacy, and then what he had said in his *Psychology* about "feelings of relation" would come into play as relational immediacy. "Feeling," as distinct from "thought" or "association," is on the verge of immediacy, anyway.

When I said my background was different, I meant the many years spent in teaching philosophy courses and analyzing the history of philosophy to try and find out what it was all about. . . .

Yours, *Dewey*

New York, August 3, 1942

Dear Bentley:

I missed out on the 1895 passage [". . . the paper seen and the seeing of it are only two names for one invisible fact which, properly named, is *the datum, the phenomenon,* or *the experience.*" "The Knowing of Things Together," p. 110]. I think that passage represents what James wanted to believe all the time, but he yielded to the doubling up notion in psychology. There is a passage . . . where James says that Bergson gave him *courage* to come out with what he had always wanted to believe, but had abstained from expressing because of a certain logical difficulty [*A Pluralistic Universe*, p. 214]. Unfortunately, it was apparently because of Bergson's view of "intellect" that James was inclined to say to hell with logical difficulties. And in his *Principles [of] Psychology*, Vol. I, Ch. VI, James expresses a predilection for [the] Mind-Stuff theory, a kind of panpsychism, and says the doctrine of evolution seems to demand it—p. 149. But, p. 158, it is "logically unintelligible," also p. 161. Then, p. 182, "empirical parallelism" [is] the safe course for psychology—that is, the doubling theory.

120

I said "unfortunately"—from the standpoint of his whole system. But actually I think Bergson's panpsychical evolution enabled him to get rid of this knower-known dualism, and in that way gave him confidence to state his own *empirical* position without reserve. This seems a roundabout process, but the Lord moves in mysterious ways his wonders to perform, especially in philosophy.

After all, Peirce inclined to panpsychic cosmology, and in his case, too, it served to get [him] away from the standardised subject-object view. Given the state of knowledge at this time, including the newness of evolution, I don't know that his roundabout metaphysical way to get support for what is in fact an original, genuine, empirical insight is surprising.

The crucial thing in my interpretation, however, is the James passage about Bergson giving him courage or confidence. . . . "Unfortunately," his theory of pure experience got mixed up with a kind of panpsychism.

Yours, *Dewey*

New York, August 8, 1942

Dear Bentley:

. . . You don't claim that James developed consistently the point of view in question or even always appreciated how fundamental it is, but [asserted] that it is actually *there* and [that] it is both the phase of James which has received least attention and [the one] which most deserves and rewards attention at the present time. . . . A process of education does go on slowly. I realize more and more what we are up against in the way of the charge words carry. After all, the western world was brought up under the influence of the Christian and Jewish religions, and the significations words have in the whole range of psychological and societal discussion are affected by that fact—people have got their "philosophies" in the nursery, and from that point on . . . to give the words a meaning from inside instead of from outside nature is a long, slow job—especially, as a lot of persons who deny quite honestly that they are supernaturalists perpetuate the tradition in one way or another. Look at B. Russell's insistence [that] there is no science possible without *a priori* premises [*The Analysis of Matter*]. . . .

Personally, what you have sent has helped me a lot on one point. I find it hard in the present state of discussion to get along with no reference to "experience." But your account of the Jamesian datum has made me realize that it is a mistake to refer to *it* as experience; that calling it experience is a matter of ex post facto *interpretation* directly connected with analysis of it into an interactivity of organic and environmental energies—an analysis legitimate and necessary for certain purposes and

121

problems, but *not* given as part of the datum itself. This clears up a lot of things for me, and I hope will show in my further writings. . . .

What you say about the tendency of James to adapt himself to the audience he was addressing is sound and shrewd. Of course, we all do it to some extent, but James to an unusual degree. I think there were two causes. James had a democratic respect for the beliefs of others if they were sincere (he was inclined probably to be a little overgenerous in assuming sincerity), and he was an artist with the artist's desire to communicate.

Yours, *Dewey*

New York, August 19, 1942

Dear Bentley:

. . . My Spencer is in my office at the University—his [Herbert Spencer, *Principles of*] *Psychology* is typical for "inner" and "outer" in the good old material and mental sense. But "adjustment" is there and influenced James without doubt—p. 6 of Vol. I of [James's] *Principles* [*of Psychology*] says Spencer's phrase is very vague, but the idea is sound [and] then speaks of "mind" inhabiting the environment. [Karl] Mannheim's later book is *Man and Society in an Age of Reconstruction*. But what I got out of it was not general theory, but some insight into Germany through what he calls "mass democratization." I think he had something there. His general position is still confused and diffused—but the influence of English life upon him after he left Germany is humanly interesting. . . .

Yours, *Dewey*

Paoli, Indiana, August 20, 1942

Dear Dewey:

As I clean up all the outlying memos and notes for the James paper, I run across one or two that seem to specify a difference between your approach and mine—not any basic difference, just a provisional working difference. I put them down without re-"thinking" them—just as I find them.

I

You are inclined to take organism and environment "as you find them," using them in their system and in their distinction, as sufficient bases of reference for the inquiry you have in hand.

I am inclined to regard them as specifications of linguistic knowledge, *such that* our language-construction must provide for their production, and not be based upon them.

122

II

Would it be practicable to establish the following term-uses:

"Knowledge": to cover all linguistically operated object-discriminations,

"Experience": to cover all sub-verbally operated sign-behaviors? To note is:

    a) that the sign-process holds both levels in one system,

    b) that the border regions between the two would have vagueness subject to gradual clarification in research, just like other scientific border-regions.

For the knowledge regions we might say "symbol" process. For the experience regions we might say "sign" process. Underlying them would be physiological and physical process in "continuity."

[H. S.] Jennings has already run socializations through chemical into sign processes in above sense. (Two papers in *Science* ["The Transition from the Individual to the Social Level," "The Beginnings of Social Behavior in Unicellular Organisms"] [in the] last year or two.)

III

Referring back to "I" above, you retain a good deal of terminology that is organically biological, rather than situationally biological. Or in other words, you carry on a good deal of exposition in "action" terms, assuming that the other fellow will remember your pronouncements to the effect that "transaction" underlies "action." I am hoping to reach a "transactional" terminology as the standard, with the "actional" limited to closely held specialized cases. . . .

Sincerely, Bentley

Paoli, Indiana, August 21, 1942

Dear Dewey:

    . . . Did you ever note a similarity (if there is one) between your "generic" and "universal" [*Logic*, pp. 255 ff.], and Romanes' "recepts" and "concepts" [*Mental Evolution in Man*]? I pick it up from some of my old notes on James's *Principles* [*of Psychology*], II, p. 327. . . . I am not stopping to check myself. But I have a lot of material on Romanes, and very high respect. Cut out his "self-consciousness" as a manner of protecting himself from mob violence. Then he becomes patron saint of the adaptational, as opposed to Lloyd Morgan as the patron saint of the physiologists. I mean sometime to do a lot with Romanes, just as I mean to do it with Peirce; but I can never get to either.

Sincerely, Bentley

New York, August 29, 1942

Dear Bentley:

. . . I shall have to do considerable reflecting before I comment on your remarks about "experience" and "action," but I'll make an introductory stab. There are certain words that are, it seems to me, of direct common sense observational nature, but which have been given a peculiar quirk by a philosophical tradition which is in turn a manifestation of religious-animistic beliefs. I think the words "person," "thing," "you," "me," "they," "action," and "activity" belong here. I can't see that there is any necessary connection of action, activity, with the postulate of a separate actor, though I recognize that philosophy has tended to vitiate the words by introducing such a reference as if it were intrinsic. (And I don't doubt that in my writings I have at times been led astray by that infection, and I'm grateful to you for making me conscious of the danger.) But I don't think it is inherently involved. I think "activity" and "energy" are closely allied, and any position that throws out the former would have to throw out the latter. Activity being, so to say, a neutral datum, it becomes highly important to substitute *interpretation* of it in terms of transactive and interactive events for the one which refers it to an isolated doer or actor. But I don't believe it is necessary or desirable to throw the baby out with the bath.

"Experience" stands on a different footing. *It* is a term of philosophic interpretation. Upon the whole, it has served the purpose of a term of protest and attack upon supernaturalistic and transcendental, super-empirical theories. *Historically* it has been of great service in this respect. If, and when, all traces of this attitude have been eliminated, I think "experience" can and should drop out of use. Meantime, I think it is probably important to make it clear, when the word is used, that its significance is methodological rather than directly descriptive of subject-matter—and I haven't always lived up to this mark. As a lawyer might say, it belongs to the procedural rather than the substantive aspect. As a term of critical methodology, I am inclined to believe we aren't as yet far enough along so that the signification of the word has been absorbed into methods in actual use so that it can be fully dispensed with. There is, for example, a highly somnambulistic article on culture [David Bidney, "On the Philosophy of Culture in the Social Sciences"] in a recent *Journal of Philosophy*. To identify it as a mode of intellectual somnambulism as distinct from experiencing by way of observation seems to me the most effective way of criticizing it. . . .

Also I should add that I agree that "actional" terms should in many, perhaps most, cases be held down to specifically discriminated cases—carved out for a specified purpose in connection with special problems. But I think the first definition of "action" in *The Oxford Dictionary*, "exertion of energy," "working," "operation," is after all primary. The next two definitions are (a) Of persons, (b) Of things.

Yours, as ever, Dewey

Paoli, Indiana, September 6, 1942

Dear Dewey:

When it comes to the matter of terminology, I am attracted to your word "transaction." I found a sentence I had written referring to your "interaction (transaction)." I also found myself in revision crossing out the "interaction" and the parentheses and leaving "transaction" stand. "Interaction" implies two actors and an "inter," and Kantor so uses it, and has been using it heavily. "Situation," which I have used somewhat and you have used in the *Logic*, has the same defect. "Naturalism" or "biological naturalism" is a generality, good when talking atmospheres, but not [when] making specifications. "Transaction" is free from this, and even vulgarly detaches the transaction fairly well in naming, from the transactors.

So far as I know, the only differences between your *approach* and mine (there is an enormous difference between your wide range and my narrow one—but I am only talking about manner of looking) is that I have been striving for a *direct* naming of the "transaction," while you have been specifying that you deal with "transaction," but carrying on discussion in terms of coalescing participants. I want to specify the coalescence first and then get back to the participants. As "method," there can not *possibly* be conflict here, since the two methods are complementary, and bound to have swings forward and backward. One can postulate either way for a particular purpose. It is only when the feller makes dogmatic assertion one way or the other that the trouble comes. Neither you nor I do that. I doubt if you have done it since the nineties; and I think the last traces of it were in my publication of 1924 [*Relativity in Man and Society*, 1926]—or rather I think [that] that publication of 1924 was couched in an "it is so" form, and that steadily since then I have passed to the linguistic stress, in other words, to the postulatory. . . .

All right. I have got to have a word for the primary presentation. I might almost say "we" should have a definitely specified word. At the moment I vote for *transaction*.

Next. I shall before long be compelled to have two words—one for the sign-processes from name to symbol—the other for the sign-processes from below perception through perception up to the borders of naming. Perception and cognition are definitely *out*—the next "n" generations will understand them in facultative view.

. . . James was enormously right in spreading the word "knowledge"

125

from 1884 on across all the "consciousness," and using "feeling" alongside. His job was to bring behaviors together as process. But I feel pretty sure that for future work "knowledge" or rather "knowings" should be equated with the higher sign-levels (wordings and *up*). . . . If this were done, the form would have to be:

Knowledge (broader sense): lower limit somewhere between toad and dog (or down to paramecium, if one will).

Knowledge (technical sense): word-sign-processes.

The trouble with the broader sense is that it fused into, and possibly covers, the whole range of "behavioral" activity.

What, then, would be a comparable naming for the sign-process behaviors ranging below the name-sign-processes? It was only in this sense that I [considered] . . . the possible use of *"experience"* at this lower stage. There seems something for it and much against it. I am very glad indeed to have your account of the word "experience" in its philosophical use, and compared with words like "activity." From what you say, and from what happened to James, it looks as though when "experience" has served its time as a word, it ought to be thrown out altogether. On the other hand, we *Must* have some kind of positive name for the sublinguistic selective behaviors, when specified from the point of view of a separation between the organism and environment (1) *not* physiologically, (2) *not* ecologically, (3) but interactionally in a way that is as yet (4) *not* linguistic-symbolically operated.

One part of your discussion I can't follow—that is, so far as the word "energy" comes in. So far as I am concerned, "energy" is out. I want *description;* transaction, interaction, action, activity, will all translate themselves into it. "Energy" is resistant for all uses outside of physics— as much resistant as soul. Unless I have a totally false understanding of the trend of physics, energy in physics is far along the descriptive route already. . . .

Sincerely, Bentley

New York, October 6, 1942

Dear Bentley:

. . . I agree with what you say about "transaction" and shall use the word in further writing whenever it is a question of first-hand matters or primary presentation, and will reserve "interactivity" for cases in which it has been made clear that, for a special purpose and problem, one of the partakers in a transaction has been analyzed out. The *methodological* formulation of the "neutral" is, of course, just what is needed to clear up James—he himself was never quite free from a tendency to make a stuff out of it. In this connection something you've written about naturalism reminds me that [Joseph] Ratner told me that in something

126

he is writing he is using the phrase "methodological naturalism" exclusively. And while I think "experience" has served its purpose, I still find myself with a kind of hankering for using "experienc*ing*" as a *methodological* term. The fact I've written so much about education is one reason [why], I'm sure now, I clung so long to the word "experience." In view of what goes on in the schools, first-hand, vital participation needed emphasis in contrast with verbal symbolizations taught with no grounding and no application.

Now this *may* be in line with your suggestion about experience as a word for sign-process behaviors below word-sign-processes affairs.

I can see the need of a word to designate the sublinguistic, and maybe "experiencing" would do it. But then it occurs to me that the symbolically operated behaviors are also a kind of participating, though of a more indirect kind, and that tends to throw me back on "experiencing" as a generic term, since it is capable of being distinguished into a number of different modes, manners, ways, from the most primary to the derived, and from the sound and fruitful ones to the mistaken and misleading ones—as far as these are capable of generalized formulation *as ways*.

I won't defend my use of "energy," as its use has dangers, but I'm not sure that with adequate specification, it has to be thrown out; "powers" is another dangerous word in the present state of things, and yet the man in the street talks about power-houses, etc., the powers of a policeman, judge, etc. And a power in operation seems to be what is idiomatically meant by an energy. Maybe if we could speak of *an* energy and energ*ies*, as we speak of a power and power*s*, instead of power at large, it would help. However, all this is rather aside from any matter that is pressing—more like talking out loud.

There is one point in your letter I am not sure I get the meaning of. That is the use of "knowledge" as an *inclusive* term; its use on the upper —symbolic—level, I understand and agree with. As to its wider use, I'm inclined to feel pretty strongly what you say, that the trouble is it then covers the whole range of behavioral activities. I think that when I've used "experience" (as experienc*ing*) intelligently, I've used it as a word to name this range. But I also recognize [that] the word is mixed up with a lot of historical complications we have to shed.

In some writings I've been at work on, I've been struck [by] how often the words "formulation" and "formulae" enabled me to steer clear of "science." What you have written about knowledge and language has steered me to use the other words, I'm sure—and whenever I go back to your chapters on knowledge and language [*Behavior, Knowledge, Fact*], I see how damn correct they are, as I didn't see on first reading—that's the line to follow up.

Yours, *Dewey*

127

New York, October 6, 1942

Dear Bentley:

Just one further word to say that I am inclined to believe, I'm not very sure as yet, that in my emphasis upon "experienc*ing*" and upon *different* modes, ways, manners, of experiencing, in connection with the standing to be given various matters, I was engaged basically on the same problem that you deal with in your "forms of construction." Your expression undoubtedly is better in getting rid of certain hampering historical associations. In dealing rather directly *with* the history *as* something to be got rid of—which fills a lot of pages in what I've written—it was easy, and perhaps appropriate for the particular problems I was at work on, to use the phrase I did. . . . For putting knowledge in its place along with fact and language in the subjects of sociology, yours is much better.

Yours, *J. Dewey*

Paoli, Indiana, October 10, 1942

Dear Dewey:

. . . I remember, after I had written you a while ago how I would use "knowledge," I thought at intervals for days about all the standardized uses that would not fit. I would join you for "experience" covering "behavioring" if it were not for what has happened to you and James in using it. Probably I should anyway. How would you feel about issuing a proclamation about it? Do it strictly on your own. Make it unqualified and powerful. Cite some of the distortions. If you have not enough, I will send you my list. Bring in a minor "James too" as reinforcement. You have the standing and the power. No one else has. . . . I thoroughly agree with you about the symbolic behaviors being experience too. . . . If we could use "experience" in that way, it would be very simple to run a spectrum from the immediate through many grades of the mediated, and name them. . . .

I am reading one of the finest books—*Vision*, by S. H. Bartley. He is definitely trying, not to explain sensation, but to find out what it is phenomenally—how to talk about it. Of course he does not get through to sustained statement—thank God for that—since going that far would certainly today be confusion afresh—but he makes the start. As physiological experimenter, he begins: You folks talk about objects; not I, not your way. It's all right about the cow out there; but here we are in a dark room. Through a little round hole comes light; you see a disc; that's your object. Now watch me. I make the source more intense; I make it less intense; I narrow the hole; I widen the hole. Every time a "new" object. Sit tight, brother, sit tight.

Two young psychological about-to-be-doctors spent a good part of a day here a little while back. I tried to find out from them what an image on the retina "is," phenomenally. (Bartley's phrasing wanders—I don't think he has got to asking this yet.) I made no progress in getting the question before them, since manifestly images on retinas are of the general type to them of pictures in frames, only not so permanent. I switched to the lamp I saw in the mirror. They definitely started out with three "things." 1. The lamp on the table; 2. the lamp in the mirror; 3. the lamp behind the mirror, which apparently is both there and not there. I asserted that given "a lamp" on the table, the "straight" rays from the lamp and the "bent" rays *via* the mirror were "all the same" to primary statement, and did not multiply "objects." I got over with great difficulty a glimmer of a possible approach, but not enough so that I could proceed to "lamp-seen" as basic. . . .

Sincerely, Bentley

New York, November 3, 1942

Dear Bentley:

. . . Years ago I mentioned in an article . . . that in the 17th and 18th centuries the epistemological philosophers wished off a lot of their views on the psychologists, and now the epistemologists took it back with the "sanction" of a "science." . . . I realized in later years that in many places my terminology was still too much of the old type, "sensations," etc., though the main point was sound. I've been trying to write something fairly extensive to clear up some points and be sufficiently definite so that I wouldn't be badly misunderstood. It's been a hard job, and I'm not through yet—I have had to keep starting over again. . . .

In my *Logic* I took up briefly a matter akin, I think, to the three lamps (pp. 465–66)—the seen light in the heavens and the distant "scientific" sun, and tried to show that all that was necessary is a single inclusive space-time continuum—but nobody paid any attention. The point has to be worked out in detail and hammered in repeatedly, to all appearances. Anyway, the context in which I used this particular example wasn't the right one for the audience, though it happened to be right for my own purpose at the time. . . .

Yours, Dewey

New York, January 16, 1943

[Note to Bentley]

With some bearings on what you say . . . ["The Jamesian Datum"] about psychologists. I think it would help if there were an explicit statement that *if* the psychologists accepted James's primary fact at its face value, the nature of the "mental" eye, etc., would be something to be determined by a careful observational analysis of the history or course of happenings in *re* this primary fact—just as philosophers would have to try to understand "reality" and "truth"—in case they were interested— on the same basis. This is badly phrased, but the point is that you indicate what the psychologists would positively gain by starting with the primary datum that James pointed to and at. Otherwise some of them—that is, unless you indicate the positive alternative—may charge you with captious faultfinding.

New York, January 16, 1943

Dear Bentley:

The above represents all I can find to make even remote objection to in your paper after two pretty careful readings. The paper is as smooth in continuity of expression as it is weighty in substance. It's a gem. I think your treatment of [Ralph Barton] Perry is beyond adverse criticism; you make full allowance for verbal justifications of what Perry says and bring out clearly the profound basic difference. . . .

Yours, *Dewey*

New York, March 30, 1943

Dear Bentley:

I began my attempt to turn over a new leaf by reading some of the back numbers of the *Journal of Philosophy*. The enclosed ["Valuation Judgments and Immediate Quality"] is the first product. I shall rewrite the whole thing before sending anything in. . . . In rewriting I shall emphasize . . . my denial of the "subjectivity" of qualities and the fact that failure to take that denial into account is the commonest cause of misrepresentation of my view on a number of subjects. And I'll rewrite the closing paragraphs to come back to the point. In fact, that point is really all there is to the technical part of the paper—the latter is just an attempt to emphasize this point.

The first two numbers of the *Journal* for this year contain articles that are much worse than [Philip Blair] Rice's ["'Objectivity' in Value Judgments"], being, among other things, too confused in statement to be discussed. The extent of his [Bruce W. Brotherston's] own confusion is his acceptance of "pragmatic empiricism" as *he interprets it* ["The Genius of Pragmatic Empiricism"]: "The central disclosure of immediate empiricism is that the subject-object relation operated, prior to its rise to self-awareness, in the original unity of life-urgency." That is, according to him, it is there in "emerged" or latent state, and the "subject" aspect is really controlling; the mistake of all previous statements of pragmatic empiricism being that it took the original experience to be neutral to the distinction instead simply of being prior to explicit awareness of the distinction. And he expressly says that James was wrong in making the primary situation neutral to the existence of subjective and objective distinctions. His capstone is the declaration that what misled James was the dominance of the "realistic intuition" in occidental philosophy— as if James hadn't come to his position after years of accepting the other position as necessary. . . . From one point of view, it might be regarded, like Rice's article, as a step in the right direction—but it is so confused that it is a step backward, while Rice's article is at least clear in verbal statement. . . .

Yours, Dewey

Paoli, Indiana, April 2, 1943

Dear Dewey:

 . . . The main thing we need . . . I think, [is] the beginnings of a firm terminology—some verbal point, somewhere, that one can hold to. Take the word "knowledge"; if we could have agreed among a group— you and I, and any dozen others you could find—[on] three or four variant uses of the word; then label them K sub-1, K sub-2, etc.; and then make a disputant stay with one use or another, it would help. At present there is chaos. In your present paper you use "situation" a good deal, in the sense [used] in the *Logic;* but it suffers the same difficulty. Most people will read it as the environment of the organism; get some to include the organism "in the situation," and behind it they will have "a mental" outside the situation, though attached "at" the organism. "Experience" goes completely wrong. "Interaction" calls up two actors posited prior to the action. "Situation" requires re-forging the hearer before he accepts its presentation, as by you or me. "Transaction" seemed to me for a while the best term to work on—you are the only one who has positively employed [it]. . . .

As I see it, Peirce definitely put cognition into a naturalistic universe, and he saw that his phenomena were all durational, but he could not do a thing with the words of his day. James got [a] hard grasp on a central core of fact, but did not get to use it, or make anyone see he meant *fact.* You have covered the entire field (there is nothing I ever said or can say, I suspect, that I can't run across in your pages), but you have done it atmospherically so far as language goes—that is; I can not find a hard, fixed word-fact to build on. I think I can say I have added a direct social immediacy (primary description of event seen across people, instead of emanating bit by bit from individual specimens), but I have not even attempted to use a hard, firm word. If this line of procedure is going to make progress, it has got to be linguistically fixated somewhere, or rather some little bit of it must be fixated. . . .

Regards, Bentley

131

New York, April 9, 1943

Dear Bentley:

. . . Yes, the "Reflex Arc" piece has been republished. . . . It is in the volume *Philosophy and Civilization,* with the caption "The Unit of Behavior." I think I made a few verbal changes, but probably not enough to straighten out the vocabulary about "sensations." Some of the English [philosophers] have substituted the neutral words "sense-data" and "sensa," and deny they are mental. But they have carried over all the other mistakes about "sensations" in isolation from behavior that have accumulated. . . .

Yours, *Dewey*

Seattle, Washington, June 25, 1943

Dear Dewey:

Here is a detail about your work and James's about which you might have some comment. If not, forget it, and don't bother. It concerns the James's immediate datum, and its possible orientation to your "Reflex Arc Concept" paper.

In developing my "image" work (which now requires differentiation into four papers), I get:

1. direct statement of seeing-thing-seen (taken over from other work).

2. detailed destruction of a string of image-things intervening between presumed "mind" and presumed "thing-out-there."

Now unless I am very much mistaken, you have in the "Reflex Arc" paper a biting comment on the half-way-item that sits on the skin between the two "termini." . . . In other words, my present development points with equal strength to you and to James in sub-surface influencings and growths; your position entered in James's position of, say, 1904—eight years later.

The way this viewpoint came out was as follows: In the drafts, I came more and more to stress the "image" as used in optics as a representative of ancient psychological sense-items surviving in another field. I then introduced illustration from Descartes' amusing statement in the first five chapters of his *Dioptrics* [*La Dioptrique*]. I then definitely made optical-image an antique (outside of the mathematics) by getting intimations of constructive formulations physiologically and optically. With the development once pretty firm in that form, I noticed the connection, as above suggested.

I have a tabulation of some twenty *types* of image-word-use in optics. "Retinal" image is not a member of any one of these types. It is definitely out, and has status of superstition (this does not, of course, affect focussings and retina-cortical localization, but only the "picture" view of retinal image). However, it is this "picture" view which is the substratum of mental image, either present (percept) or delayed (as memorial).

What we have left is three varieties of geometrical or physical images (really symbols under your "relation" rubric); "floats," which are energy transmissions as phases capable of being picked up and used in optical systems for physiological systems; "enscreenments" (as in camera-ground glass, or on the degenerate retina at back of excised eyeball); and "embodiments," as in optical effects from statues, paintings, photographs, etc. A "retinal image" should be an enscreenment. I have a dozen varieties (perhaps) of enscreenments, and the retinal image cannot be any of them. . . .

Best regards, Bentley

Part II

Letters: June 25, 1943–December 29, 1943

Dear Bentley:

I've just been re-reading a letter of yours dated in April [2] of this year. You never said a truer word than that I write atmospherically, with absence of hard-and-fast words. Looking back, I don't see how I could have done otherwise at the time, and some people—a few—got something by breathing the atmosphere. But that can't profitably go on forever, and perhaps the time has come to do something in trying to fix a set of leading words. I don't seem to be able to write continuously, but maybe I could collaborate on words if you gave a start. You spoke especially of "knowledge." I suppose the thing, perhaps, to do first would be to list the different significations that can be found in contemporary writings, and then sort them out somehow. . . .

One thing would be to make out two lists, one of idiomatic uses, and another of epistemological-metaphysical meanings, usually presented as psychology.

In the first list I would put: (1) knowledge as what has been found out or learned. (The pseudo-significations would add on some reference to a mental organ or process by which something is found out.) (2) Then there is knowledge as something told or communicated—socially current information. News passing as report of actual events. Tidings, intelligence, in one of its senses.

Then there is knowledge in the sense of laying hold of, grasping, the meaning of a word or significance of an event—a kind of practical ability. (This runs easily into a pseudo-signification.) When one says he knows or doesn't know French or algebra, I think the meaning is that he can [or cannot] handle it—same, in the case of events, is "knowing beans"— can "tell" one thing from another.

I don't need to say that all of these three involve communication. There is one point about "fact" and "knowledge" that would have to be dealt with. I agree with what you say in your book about Fact, Knowledge and Language [*Behavior, Knowledge, Fact*]. But raw or brute fact, the Jamesian datum mayhap, seems to be material *for* knowledge, rather than *of* knowledge. There is a good deal of formal difficulty in making a statement of this point; we have to "know" what we are talking about, but we can communicate by *pointing* to something as that about which we might learn or be told. "What is *that?*" seems to involve knowing as far as pointing to one thing rather than another, but not as grasping signification (in the case of a word), or significance in the case of an event.

To distinguish, identify (recognize), is ability to "tell" one thing from another. Recount, count, and account are the early senses of "tell," according to *Oxford Dictionary*. . . .

I think a word like "situation" may be safely used, provided its use is accompanied by statement that it does *not* mean environment in the sense of "surroundings" of an organism. Same with "interaction," if it is made clear that it is a secondary meaning, analytic of durational-spatial events or transactions—*not* of or by an agent, but as a carrying on (going on) or over.

Perhaps one way of getting ahead with the word "designation" . . . would be to distinguish between primary names of events, and results of analysis made for the sake of some ability to handle or treat [them] more effectively.

Well, . . . all this is to get something from you that will help condense my atmospheric efforts into settled forms.

Yours, *Dewey*

[P.S.] I still think that certain words like "agent" are legitimate if it is made evident (told) in what context they are, and are not, applicable.

The *difficulty* of expression I mentioned is that there must be something to talk about and communicate. When actually communicated, it is *fact* of knowledge—before that, it is raw or brute fact, and yet it has to be somehow present.

Seattle, Washington, June 30, 1943

Dear Dewey:

Nothing would suit me better than a hunt for two or three stable words covering "knowings," and most particularly with your concurrent control over errant starts. In fact, I can never get a general theory of language out without a few such words dependably used. Beyond that I cannot hope direct conveyance of the procedure unless there exists an audience of a few people who will consent to use those words in those ways during the course of the inquiry. . . .

Just in reminiscence, it seems to me I was wondering [about May, 1942] whether we could fixate "experience" for the raw materials before communication, and "knowledge" for the communicable formulation via language. I do not believe this could be done by series ordering—so far [as] experience is concerned, and beyond that knowledge. I believe it would have to be done by phases, or rather something like an electro-magnetic spectrum—in which length gets stress at one end, and duration at the other—wave lengths *vs.* frequencies, each involving the other. For instance, in my present small scale work I have images at one end

138

that are embodiments (statues, paintings, photographs), but they are behavioral-cultural, and optical—as well as bodies; while transitions run right through the geometrical images at the other end that are verbal, symbolic, factual, in system, but not in "reference" to out-of-system facts —that kind of a spectrum—one end the extrapolation from individual organism-actor is symbolic, the other end it is bodily. What I am not at all sure of is whether those are the right words—the words that will fit most people most nearly.

I agree with your rendering of "situation"—understood as *event*. "Event" is a word that might have to underlie others, indicating that all matters considered were *temporally*-durationally considered. Personally, I tend toward your *"transaction,"* and have even had *"trans*fact" in my text, though I am cutting it out, as too hard for the addressees. I allege two types of transfact I am showing; one the "float" or light-image, as identified before it hits retina or screen, the other the after image seen as neither psychological or physiological, and thus a better central-fact than image. . . . I do not like "interaction," because it so definitely opposes the two "ends" as separate, and also because Kantor has firmly taken it over for a system primarily in a mechanistic background. . . .

The terms James took from [John] Grote, "acquaintance" and "knowledge about," always recur. You have a phrasing much akin to this, which I often see quoted. Can you recall the one I mean? . . .

Why could not "acquaintance" and "knowledge" be taken for a trial instead of "experience" and "knowledge"? Then adjust your old phrasing with it.

You remark on "communication" involvement everywhere. Can we perhaps separate "indirect communicative build-up" from "formal communicative status"? Suppose we describe this latter as "verbal embodiment," experimentally. We might then inspect a general communicative-social setting, within which we might differentiate:

a. Acquaintance (in a perceptionally developed form—and here the Cassirer argument cited in one of my James papers ["The Jamesian Datum"] goes a long way in aid as to perception requiring communication), and

b. Knowledge, using the term only for what is linguistically embodied or *fixated* with a permanence. Tradition then would be an early knowledge-form. (For me, I positively insist that each "item" must be capable of specification as "somewhere," as "present" or "existing" in a position.)

(Comment on this: Your term "agent" is necessary; we could not work along without doing a lot of the work in terms of "actor" or "agent" in that sense. *But:* I cannot look upon it as a proper term with respect to which our basic [i.e., underlying; broadest conveniences] terms can be discriminated.)

139

Your distinction of "raw" or brute fact from knowledge, the former as material for the latter, points at an important distinction, but I do not think it characterizes or names the distinction. Suppose you stress this "raw" as "material *for*," and then contrast it sharply with knowledge-material itself (material *of*); and suppose you use the word "agent" a little loosely; what do you have as the result of your communication-to-others? My guess at what you "have," in the sense of what other people hear-you-tell, is the old rejected psychology in which the ancient "mind" (diluted further, but still present) *makes* the knowledge out of world materials. This is exactly what you do not want.

You suggest Jamesian datum as perhaps on the raw-material side. I see it as set up there in a fumbling way as a starter. But I see it capable of generalization over all knowledge—a sort of holding-together background of presentation.

Your term "subject-matters" grows on me. That is, occasionally I glimpse it as wide-spreading—further than I have ever used it.

Would "subject-matter" and "situation" coalesce in discussion?

When you list (1) knowledge as what has been found out, and (2) knowledge as something told, and add (3) knowledge as practical ability in statement, I would be inclined to take (1) and (2) as different stresses in the statement of the "same thing," and (3) as an indication of the individual man's "local" position in the process. We might perhaps say: Knowledge is the linguistically embodied (your #2) working content (your #1) of human behaviors (transactional) up to date, which as "linguistically embodied" is behaviorally distinguished from operationally behavioral (manipulative) behaviors. It survives, exists, in rhythm, resonance, repetitive goings-on. We say it "is," and if the older space and time forms are not adaptable to it, we say, then, we postulate enough space and time modification to "carry" it. Your item #3 then becomes the limited individual organism throbbing transactionally in his limited setting. We start knowing we have knowledge; instead of spreading it to fit "old" space forms, we revise space and time forms to [fit] it. All by way of tryout.

But I would like to know what successful phrasing you used to use.

Regards, *Bentley*

Montville, New Jersey, July 15, 1943

Dear Bentley:

. . . Historically, it would be interesting to know when the mentalistic use of the word "image" came in. I think later than the Cartesian, *et al.*, *pictura*, which was probably meant literally. Descartes and Locke undoubtedly helped on a transition to "subjectivism," but aren't as openly such as they are now represented to be. Well, what I started out to say is that in Greek writings, images are treated as pictures (paintings, photos—if they knew about them), as reflections in water, but also as copies and imitations, and therefore as deceptive unless one is possessed of knowledge of the "real article." The nearest counterpart I can think of is counterfeit money, which is perfectly "real" as [a] piece of paper, but spurious and false as [a] medium of exchange. All this isn't important *re* image, but has importance in connection with ancient philosophy in its difference from modern, and also [as] background of latter.

. . . The reason I came to use it ["event"] less is instructive on the point that no word by itself is foolproof. Russell uses the word constantly as if "event" had a knife-edge thinness. He and others use it as if saying, "every existence is an event," were a definition or had an *exclusive application* the way a definition has. But I take it that [it] is equally true that every existence is an area or field. I fancy one reason for . . . [using] more and more of "situation" is that it does have the almost empty thinness that some contemporary writers assign to "events" in the contexts they give them. The writers who have criticized substitution of "event" for "substance" have something to say for themselves in view of the lack of thickness and extent (substantiality) in Russell's events— and he isn't the only one. Well, the point I am making here is that in every case some fairly extensive description with illustration has to be given in any terminological adventure. I have often noticed (without making any very systematic use of the observation) that adjectives are safer than nouns and adverbs than adjectives. "Situational" is probably better than "situation"—though, even then, it might be needful to say it isn't identical with "environmental" in an exclusive sense.

Of course, I agree with you about "agent." I imagine one of the first things to do is to make separate lists of words of first and second intentions or applications. A good deal of what I have done is in fact to show that words to which many philosophers have given a primary (or directly "existential") meaning really designate a function served by some primary "affair" (under conditions that have to be specified). [George] Santayana criticized my use of "affairs" in *Experience and Nature* in a review he wrote ["Dewey's Naturalistic Metaphysics"] as showing my preoccupation with American business! The Latin *res*, usually translated *thing*, is definitely *affair*. *Res publica*, etc. . . .

Yours, *Dewey*

[P.S.] Agent is like re-agent in chemistry—nothing is a re-agent *per se*, agent either. Same with such words, even, as "person."

The Greek used "subject" where modern philosophers have said "object." I think perhaps that influenced my use of "subjectmatter"—a subject in that sense is what you talk or write about—running off on the symbolic side into topic, theme. I am taken with your suggestion about a kind of spectrum spread from the bodily end to the symbolic. It's a darned good lead, I fancy.

Montville, New Jersey, July 19, 1943
Dear Bentley:

. . . Your . . . remark about "fact" as the best organization yet attained of meaning-behaviors with operating-behaviors is a conclusive contribution to the vocabulary business. I enclose some notes intended to be a response to your suggestion that I send something about my prevailing words—usages in the past. I haven't any of my writings here, but I think what I have said is reasonably faithful to my intentions, if not to my executions. . . .

Sincerely yours, *Dewey*

Comments on Words:

. . . "Experience." I doubt if it is necessary to use the word. But it has served a very useful purpose in the past in holding things down to what is observed and observable.

Regarding such use, it is, as James said, a double-barreled word, standing for experienc*ing* and for what is experienc*ed*. It is possible that it may prove useful to retain it in the first sense as a "secondary" or derived term, to designate any and every way in which organism participates or is engaged in an interaction. As such, experiencing is still double-barreled. It is agent and patient. As patient, it *undergoes* something in an interaction and suffers (undergoes) some modification; at the same time or in the same interaction, it is modifying that with which it interacts, and in that capacity is agent. The illustration I have used in the past is drawn from the standardized putting the finger in the flame illustration. Getting burned is the undergoing aspect. But just getting burned isn't an experiencing. There has to be the active aspect—the withdrawing—and, what is more, in order [for an experience] to be an experiencing, there must be *observation of the connection* of the undergoing and the *doing* phases of the interaction. The mere jerking back, as pure reflex, wouldn't be an experiencing any more than the mere getting burned would be. The child who sees the connection between putting out his finger (a doing phase), getting burned (undergoing phase), and withdrawing (doing) has an experience (experiencing)—and the last-named doing has its own counterpart, undergoing—and so on in continuity.

I think you will see the proportionality of this account with the "Reflex Arc" paper. Upon the whole, in my past writings I have used the term "experience" as a name for the whole "circuit," which I tried to substitute for the disjointed reflex arc business.

Habitual use of the word to apply to *every* kind of observed engagement or taking-part of an organism is probably the reason why I don't take to limiting the word to pre-observed, purely physiological, participations.

I don't think it is necessary to use the word "experiencing," more than perhaps to say that *if* [it is] used, it designates the foregoing sort of event. But the underlying analysis serves, I think, to clear up the words "excitation-reaction," "stimulus-response," "habit," and also helps in discriminating various modes or manners of being engaged, occupied, concerned, taking part, interacting—whether observing, liking, hating, trying, or whatever. In short, I think it gives the groundwork for a descriptive analysis of behaviors. (I think you would agree it is as possible, unfortunately, to use "behavior" in a loose, blanket way as it is to use "experience" in like fashion.)

Perhaps something can be done by developing a number of words that apply to different aspects of the same primary subjectmatter, e.g., "event," "eventuation," "eventful"; coming-out-of and passing-into; past and future dimensions. (I still think every event as an existence is a *history*, but I don't think it is necessary to insist upon that at the outset; it is more of an interpretation.

"Field," "area"???? Symbolically, a domain.

"Affair," "concern" (not as anxiety, but in [the] sense in which we speak of business as a concern, and in general of "going concerns"; business); "thing" in its idiomatic, non-metaphysical sense.

"Situation," as a name for the field-event in its own diversified-unity of qualities, qualifications. (*Not* limited to apply only to organism-environment interaction, though providing groundwork for it.) Following up what I wrote before about current use of "event," Russell, *et al.*, have used the word to designate a thoroughly artificial *simple*.

What has influenced my use of "situation" is the necessity for definite acknowledgment of the intrinsic variety of qualities in every event as a durational-extensional affair. I probably haven't been explicit enough about the durational spread, but I have always taken for granted, in my own mind, an indefinite shading off, both temporally and spatially. Spatially, for example, this room is in this house, this house in this region, this region in this world, etc.—and in such a way that house, region, world, etc., all directly qualify "this room." The situational aspect is that [which] makes possible and which invites or demands the analysis in consequence of which an *event* is capable of treatment as *complex*. Simples and elements as simple, homogeneous throughout, etc., are always products of some analysis of an affair or event which, though not "complex" per se, is such in contrast with the "simples" that are products of analysis.

Possibly some such description as event, field, affair, situation, in connection with your spectrum-spread idea would help clear up the terminology problem. That and the distinction between "primary" and "secondary" words.

I think we exchanged some remarks once about what is designated by such words as "centered," "focused." I am not able to describe what I observe (or think I observe) without some such words. It seems to me they are involved, along with the quality of indefinite spreading out and shading off, in any statement of field-events in their situational aspect. Limits, centres, seem to me to be two indivisible aspects of the same description or report.

"Contexts," "contextualist," "contextualism," seem to be (I haven't given enough thought to the matter) names referring to one aspect of the situational aspect of field-events. That is a reminder that the product of analysis is still connected with other aspects, phases, portions, of an original "situation" and can be understood (protected from being arbitrary) only in such connections. "Context" is a warning against the fallacy of simple elements, simple locations (points), simple durations (moments), etc.

More generally or *philosophically*, it serves as protection against the view that there is a *reality* behind what is immediately present in perception, the empirical fact being contextual connections that have to be search[ed] for and which when found constitute *understanding* that which is immediately perceived. (The "sense" and "reason" business.) When modifications become familiar, as in the case of familiarity, acquaintance, the results of excursion into context become consolidated into what is directly *present,* and we have *sense* as in the phrases "getting the sense of a thing," "it doesn't or does make sense," etc. . . . The term "sense-perception" doesn't describe anything that happens save as a way of referring to the physiological conditions under which something is perceived; in its common usage it is as if we had got in the habit of talking about "cerebral-perceptions" as if the words named something per se.

In the past, I have at times made a good deal of the distinction between "raw" and "refined" subjectmatter—scientific subjectmatter as such being a refined product. [Clarence E.] Ayres of Texas is doing something that may well be of importance in treating science as a technology. There are some difficulties in connection with raw or crude materials save as a term of contrast, but I think it can be developed so as to be free from the dangerous confusion you speak of. . . . That the "physical world" is a term of discourse (symbolic) standing for the subjectmatter of physics, not for direct, raw fact, isn't easy to say without getting into difficulties, but something of the kind has to be said—of course there is no "fact" *so* raw as not to involve connection with language. Your comments on my comments about knowledge are very helpful.

[Dewey]

Montville, New Jersey, July 21, 1943

Dear Bentley:

Re vocabulary. It occurs to me to say that perhaps my *intention* in my use of "experience" was to get a *generalized* expression for sights-seen, sounds-heard, pains-felt, textures-touched, hatefuls-hated, beloveds-loved, meanings-meant (intended), etc.

Yours, Dewey

Paoli, Indiana, July 29, 1943

Dear Dewey:

. . . Would it be possible to set up "Experience," not in terms of organism and environment, but in terms of "Duration" strictly and exclusively? Assume that we have a field of inquiry in a layout involving organism and environment; and limited to sign-procedure, indirection, whole-organism-action, and called "behavior," or whatever name fits. Then could we say: "Experience" is the passing segment, long enough to have hitch-up (a matter of seconds perhaps), and not so long as to have drained away—time organized in terms of night and day, blood pulse, the holding of attention, etc.—I mean "organized" in the sense of clues to the spans we assign to "experience" as a specific name. That is, not to be answered yes or no: but "is it worth trying out to see how it holds together?" . . .

"Having" *vs.* "knowing" (?) was your old phrasing that I sought, I think, [that] was so much cited. What would you say about the "having" now?

I am not just sure how you would set up "primary" and "secondary" words. Will you enlarge?

If we can hold "an organism" or "an individual" to its *local* point of view, then "experience" is world-locally-at-work, spatially as well as temporally. Various people have set this up in various phrasings, of which some may be good. . . .

Admitting that the adjectives and adverbs are safer than the nouns, we are at the point where we must have nouns or bust.

Your "focusing" or "centering." How will this do to characterize "reference," your *Logic*, p. 55, where definition lies within relation; and process, or function, or some such name, applies within connection? . . .

When all is said and done, we *must* have at the heart of a terminology replacements for the old "sense" and "reason"—to me, now, roughly, acquaintance, or having, or experiencing, on one side, and formulation, sign-substitution, languaging on the other.

Do you think "behavior" can be built up into a basic word, with respect to which "experiencing" can be the short-term representative? What possible alternatives have we? . . .

Regards, *Bentley*

Paoli, Indiana, July 31, 1943

Dear Dewey:

After I sent you some sketches on terms a day or two ago, it occurred to me I had omitted a remark on "we," as I have used the word. I never write without having a special point of view and an audience in mind. I can't get anywhere without writing and rewriting. In this case I cannot write as if from your point of view. I am not ready yet to place my own point of view; or rather, if I try, it will be too closely modeled to my pending work. So I took a view, *as if* from a position we could *both* occupy, thus enabling either party to bring out into the clear, and lop off, what in the other did not jibe with him. The finished form, if any, is not involved in this provisional procedure.

A successful—that is, effective—presentation will probably depend on what is presented as background or hypothesis, and what is set up as "thing named." This again will have to be decided with an eye on the particular type of reader addressed. It may be that it will be a good thing to write it in four or more ways; one addressed to philosophers, one to psychologists, one to scientists in general (as if for *Philosophy of Science*), and one popular. On this basis, however, there should be differentiated presentations for at least three types of psychologists.

Regards, *Bentley*

Montville, New Jersey, August 1, 1943

Dear Bentley:

. . . I think—anyway hope—I am beginning to clear up on the time-dimension property—an affair on which I've been rather hazy, as you have suggested sometimes. What you say about "experience" in your last letter helped. *Re* secondary terms as distinct from primary: "Transaction" would be a primary; "secondary" applies to what you have sometimes called "cut-out" matters; they are words that apply to transactions when the latter are viewed analytically, from an angle or in a perspective due to a special problem—e.g., "agent," "subject," not in its usual usage, but as "agent" looking at from even a more special view. I didn't mean to suggest the primary and secondary use of these

146

words; they are too loose; just used them as shorthand. There are, I think, a good many philosophical words which leave a wrong result or point in the wrong direction as they actually figure in philosophical writing, that have a sound meaning when they [are] described in the actual transactional situation with respect to their *functioning* in that situation. They are results of cutting out which are not recognized as such products.

Now, the connection of this with the matter of length of the time-dimension is that I begin to see that the cutting-out in question is a matter of reducing the time-segment, making it shorter and shorter. (The same thing happens on the *field* aspect of the transactional event.) I am only just beginning to get the full force of the point, but I am pretty confident I'll be helped.

I have a hunch that the distinction and connection of the *extensive-intensive* comes in here in an instructive way. Reducing the area of vision may intensify what is seen; extending it too far approaches a blank as a limit, as too much reduction has a bare point for its limit. What I have called getting hold of something in the function it exercises is a restoration of the *intense* phase into a field that is extensive. There is a rhythm of intense and extense. A "scientific" generalization as such is the legitimate limit on the extensive side—see mathematics, that applies to anything you please because it doesn't apply to anything "in particular."

I haven't got all this worked out—I'm writing it for my own benefit mostly. But I have a hunch it will help me on the vocabulary side as and if it ferments. "Experiencing" on this line applies to events in their peculiarly intense aspect. I heard a man say the other day: "That certainly was an experience"—and he wasn't talking philosophy. I imagine this line will help out on the "having" and "knowing" distinction. "Having" is the Jamesian datum as you interpret it, but viewed, I now see, from a certain angle for the sake of intensification; "knowing" is placing what is had in a wider and longer contextual event.

1. A man may be mad without knowing it; certain qualities then present themselves directly as intensely obnoxious—they are immediate qualities of the transactional situation.

2. He becomes aware that he is (or was) angry—a cutting-out within the total event.

3. He studies, investigates, to find out *what* "anger" is—involves among other things [Walter Bradford] Cannon's physiological researches, etc. "Scientific" knowledge—emphasis on extensive—gets away with symbolic relations from the qualities of [the] immediate, intense—from "experiencing." "Relations" take the place occupied by "qualities."

4. This scientific knowledge [is] used in a directly intense case to construct a new situational event.

147

The reason I stuck so long and rather obstinately to the broad meaning of experience was, I now see, because there is an immediate, intensive phase in the case of 3 above; when it is analyzed, it presents itself as something immediately had—it has an "experiencing" aspect.

The cause for my insisting on that is because so many epistemological philosophers have introduced the idea of "reality" and held that the subjectmatter of scientific knowledge represents the *real* world in a way which things in their immediate qualities do not. . . .

I have some notes on the topic of a self as knower, taking the position that the idea is one that arises when a belief or piece of knowledge is viewed in the context of social responsibility-freedom. I think this is what Mead was driving at in his talk about "subject." I don't think it was merely a historic holdover in his case, though he didn't get entirely free. Greek-medieval thought took "knowledge" as something entirely social in the *collective* sense of social. There was no provision made for discoveries that disturb the existing body of knowledge. The introduction of new points, of new and newly observed materials, thus came from sources that were *private* in contrast with the received body of knowledge—*socially private*, that is. In other words, the "individualistic" movement actually brought in something socially valuable, though "individuals," etc., were interpreted as if they were inherent instead of socially functional.

Yours, *Dewey*

Paoli, Indiana, August 3, 1943

Dear Dewey:

Where the devil did you get the oppositions, "excitation-reaction" and "stimulus-response"? I am sure I did not mention it in my last note, but it keeps bobbing up. No recent psychology I know has used this form of statement. The "distal" *vs.* "proximal" in [Egon] Brunswik is an effort to maintain the old confusion. . . .

If you reflect some other use in this matter, I would like to know where and what. If not, then "excitation-reaction" can be laid down in physiological terms, and "stimulus-response" in behavioral terms, and the two can be correlated as they develop, and not by wobble-words.

In the work I am doing on vision, e.g., the treatment from point-light-source (not object) through retina (without sense-image) into reaction can be in your first terminology, and the treatment in terms of object-seen can be in stimulus-response. *But,* the object in stimulus-response here enters as *Behavior-Object* [which is] built up by a lot of excitation-reaction processes and not as *real* or *external* basis for all inquiry.

Regards, *Bentley*

Paoli, Indiana, August 5, 1943

Dear Dewey:

I am beginning to see what must be done. This beginning of seeing is that we must:

1. Get our spatial-temporal-factual-verbal layout expressed well enough for our own uses.

2. Establish certain tentative specifications for "what ought to be named" to aid inquiry-behavior-types, knowledge-types, etc.

3. Choose the best-looking names for the specifications.

4. If possible, get some good eggs like Nagel to examine the names we set up, and suggest others as substitutes which will best reach the logical (or alternatively physiological or psychological) audiences we want.

5. Refine the specifications for the chosen names.

6. Probably then try to decide, each for his own work, how far he can use such names.

If we can get this done, I will be about ready to produce the "language-theory." Since I want this work to fit alongside your *Logic*, no better approach could be made. . . .

Spectrum-scheme:

Can't have a fact without a naming—despite the as-yet-unlearned.

Can't have a name without facts—despite Gods, centaurs, etc. (Something is being named-at.)

As limits (technically limits—approached, but not reached)—at one end: pure factuality (reals); at other end: pure namings (knowledge). . . .

Regards, *Bentley*

Montville, New Jersey, August 6, 1943

Dear Bentley:

I haven't anything here to go by, but I imagine the "excitation-reaction," "stimulus-response" is somewhere in my *Logic* [p. 29]. I used it in teaching for quite a while, but don't know about first publication. I'm sure I didn't take it as a settled distinction from anyone else. Glad you can use 'em in your vision paper.

Yours, *Dewey*

Paoli, Indiana, August 11, 1943

Dear Dewey:

. . . Anything behavioral (i.e., not technically, physical-chemical-electrical process), as, for example, a protozoan evading what-casts-shadow, has knowledge-quality. Assign knowledge in this sense to the organism,

149

watch it develop in evolution, and it does not stay in organism, but appears cultural-racial. Analyze that, and it is incoherent except as organic-environmental-situational-transactional.

If, then, we match knowledge with organism, we have it first organic, then social, then transactional, and finally we have the "transactional" spreading down over the earlier levels. Then we have to mark out what we mean by "knowing" as distinct from "behaving."

The other alternative is to have some word other than "knowing" for behavings up to a certain point, and after that speak of knowing-behaviors. This would be at the point of linguistic-entry probably; and equivalently in [the] older phrase of specialized consciousness under some kind of definition. Then knowing-behaviors, substantized as knowledge, would have to be set up only in comparison with language-behaviors.

Again so far as the word "knowing" is concerned, we can hold it all through to the organism (not as transactional, but as specialized "agent"). This seems to be the primary pragmatic approach. But then the word "knowledge" won't match with "knowing."

All of which raises a question put to me by someone: Have we *fact* enough to justify making a terminology?

However, in our field:

1. Language-manipulation alone (philosophy) gets nowhere.

2. Hard-fact set-up has yielded "minds" (also nowhere).

3. I am unhesitating in believing that we are on the right track—fussing with all the words and all the facts we can get at in order to bring them into some kind of system.

"Atom" is a physical word that ought to help patterning behavioral cut-outs. One had pebbles; one reduced them to smallest possibles; one got mathematical-verbal "particles"; then came chemical atoms, now as hypotheses, now as facts, finally as superficial descriptions of complex processes. And these complex processes in radiation today are no longer intra-atomic, but trans-universe, since they are in wave-form with infinity components. . . .

Sincerely, *Bentley*

Montville, New Jersey, August 13, 1943

[To Bentley:]

. . . As far as not having enough facts is concerned, we haven't got enough to settle everything, but I don't suppose that is the ambition of either of us. If we have enough facts so that we can use them to get certain inquiries and discussions on a better track than they run on, a track where there is some likelihood of their getting to *some* destination, I'd be happy.

150

In the protozoa-man spread, "signal" seems to be a good verbal pro-sign bet. Of course even lower animals have something more than excitation-reaction events; they are too short-spanned to keep any animal alive. "Stimulus," "signal," "sign," "symbol."

Yours, *Dewey*

Montville, New Jersey, August 13, 1943

Dear Bentley:

. . . "Physical," "physiological," "behavioral," are all terms of highly systematized research-forms. That is, I take it, "physical," as in the words "the physical world," stands for the subject-matter of a certain type of inquiry-research. "Behavioral" would stand for another, and it can be pointed out how its material of search is more inclusive—makes less cuttings-out—than the other two system-forms while making use of their findings—depending, in fact, upon such use. That is, with respect to *all forms of system-research*, it *is* a primary term, but not with reference to system as coherence in *manipulation*, with respect to which it postulates organism-environment distinction-connection. This, perhaps, or something like it, is what you have involved in mentioning "manipulative and expressive in *full* descriptional presentation."

You raised a question I never answered about "knowing and having." "Having" is undoubtedly a secondary word. It is tied up with the matter of the "raw" material I said once I hadn't got clear. I mean, I think, the word "raw" stands for something with reference to which knowledge—at least in "science"—is manufactured, refined goods. But I haven't been clear as to just its reference, which, of course, has to be carefully speci-fied. . . .

I never said anything, I believe, about the various senses of "knowl-edge" in yours of the 29th ult. (By the way, I've run into the "prag-matics, semantics, syntactics" business several times lately. . . . I fear the damn thing is getting standardized.)

The extrapolation idea is good phraseology, I think; new in this con-nection, but familiar in others. Fits fine into the spectrum handling. (And I imagine some of the popular astronomical speculations give good illustrations of extrapolation carried beyond the limits within which it is legitimate and necessary—for specified results.) The extrapolation formulation covers a lot of the ground I had in the back of my head in the "having-knowing" distinction.

I have been wondering a little about the word "operations." "Manipu-lation" is fine for one kind. It might be helpful if there was another as distinctive word for operations performed with symbols. Perhaps "opera-tions" should be limited to manipulative style, but it might be well to extend it to both forms of behavior if we got a good word for the expression end.

I never said anything either *re* your inquiry as to "acquaintance." I don't think I'm quite ready yet. But I can tell you where my own difficulty with the word came from. It was seized upon to designate a supposed kind of "immediate" knowledge, immediate in the sense of not only excluding (being independent of) mediation by inference, but any kind of mediation whatever—to endow "mind" with a special faculty; though they didn't say so in so many words, they *knew* things just by beholding them. Now, "acquaintance," it seems to me, is a product of a lot of manipulative operations, and in that sense is thoroughly mediated. (James himself once in a while fell into the snare of concluding that because definite systematized, symbolized knowledge didn't intervene; therefore, there was a kind of direct "intuition.") There is, as I see it, always an element of funding of prior operations in acquaintance. The distinction between knowledge *that* and knowledge *about* is sound, but not the interpretations, psychological-philosophical, that have been put on it. The category of manipulative behavior gets around the objections I've felt to a generalized use of "acquaintance" such as you suggested. (One trouble with me is that I am rather too familiar with a lot of abused uses [that] different philosophers have made of good words—B. Russell, as usual, is one of the worst offenders *re* "acquaintance.")

Sincerely, regards, *J. Dewey*

Paoli, Indiana, August 18, 1943

Dear Dewey:

. . . I suspect "meaning" is one word to which we must give definite behavioral setting, if the rest is to hold up. . . .

I do not think I got over . . . just what I meant about the two phrasings "excitation-reaction" and "stimulus-response." What I want is both sets of terms discriminated, the first for physiological statement, the second for object-subject statement, psychologically, not philosophically, and strictly adhered to. There is legitimate ground for using both. There is every reason in the world for not mixing them into a fruit-salad.

Your scheme stimulus-signal-sign-symbol covers the range factually as we need it. "Signal" has a bit too strong the feel of deliberately signaling. "Sign" is so ranged along with "word" that it may have to stay there. *But* . . . I would be inclined at this moment to make the order: stimulus (or excitation), sign (or cue)—sign is better—signal (or some modification) for word-range, symbol for the top relation-language range. . . .

I noted a neat analysis of Ogden-[I. A.] Richards [*The Meaning of Meaning*] by a man named [George] Gentry in *Journal of Philosophy*

["Reference and Relation"] . . . and dropped him a brief note saying I would just love a little of the same about Morris and his layout.

Regards, *Bentley*

Montville, New Jersey, August 18, 1943

Dear Bentley:

Just a word—not to interrupt the image business—to say that if I hadn't been so damn dumb, I could have brought the second section of my Rice reply ["Further as to Valuation as Judgment"] up to the key in which the first was pitched. The point is that you have finally got through my skull the necessity of sufficiently extensive durational-spatial events to describe anything scientifically. What I was objecting to in intent was Rice's chopping it off and whittling it down into a brief segment, if I had only known it at the time.

It's too late to remedy in this article, but I'll tackle the topic again sometime, independently of Rice, and make the point. . . .

Yours with regards, *Dewey*

Montville, New Jersey, August 22, 1943

Dear Bentley:

I got the "signal" word from [Max] Meyer, a behaviorist-psychologist at University of Missouri years ago—much better informed than Watson ever was—how far he reduced "behavior" to physiological phenomena I don't recall [Cf. Dewey, *Experience and Nature*, p. 176]. But I think he must have introduced the social. The illustration of "signal" [that] he gave, which . . . [as] I recall, is the clucking of a hen to its chicks— a specialized kind or preparatory kind of stimulus—the phenomenon to which he gave the name "signal" seemed to me intermediate between excitation-reactions and words.

Regarding the stimulus-response business, it's true I didn't wholly get your point of limiting it to the "object-subject" statement. I think when I made the distinction, I had in mind the difference between the short-span momentary event and the serial event within which the former falls. I was criticizing the doctrine that isolated the former and developed its theory on that basis—the "Reflex Arc" business over again. I recall the illustration of the sequential event of an animal hunting its prey and the *reactions* it would make, say, to rocks, etc., in the course of its pursuit. There is a real difference, but I can see the advantage of limiting "stimulus-response" the way you suggest. As far as "excitation" is concerned, it can be used with an accompanying statement of the distinction between a short-time excitation and an enduring one. I'm not so sure about the "reaction" word; it has got pretty well tied

153

up with the short, cut-off aspect of total event. Incidentally, the word "behavior" has got into general use—has been for a long time—in connection with descriptions of animals—"biological" seems to be a much wider word than "physiological," an analytic word within [the] biological (?).

The "meaning" question has, of course, to be tackled, and it isn't an easy matter for me. I think the key is proper attention to the *consequential* phase of a behavior—event in connection with its initial stage. "Meaning" will take on the peculiar *meaning* it now generally carries when the two end [phases] of an event are so separated as to be treated as separate events—then the earlier end [phase] is taken to have something called meaning on its own account. And as far as direct perception is concerned, we become acquainted with an event in a piecemeal way—we get the first end [phase] first and wonder what *it means,* points to, indicates, as its terminal end. This doesn't profess to be a straightforward and thorough behavioral statement (too atmospheric), but I put it down for what it may suggest, if anything. I think the distinction between an event of short span and [one] of enduring temporal and extensive spatial area is in the right direction. . . .

Yours, Dewey

[P.S.] The consequence statement applies both to such cases as "the clouds mean rain," "fall in the barometer stands for increased atmospheric pressure from moisture," and "the meaning of a word is thus and so." The word as an event has consequences directly as in the case of a command, and as a symbol in a statement, [it] has consequences in the form of other symbols. The statement about meaning would, of course, have to be so worded as to avoid any intimation of an intervening "agent." I think the consequence statement has been put forward, but with the idea that a mind produces the consequence and thereby gives an event or "object" meaning.

Montville, New Jersey, August 24, 1943

Dear Bentley:

I was writing a letter the other day in which, without thinking of any philosophy matter, I wrote the words "involved in." It then occurred to me that it would have made no difference in the sense of that sentence if I had written "meaning." Not that they are identical, but "meaning" might be the symbolic expression for factual "involved in." This is somewhat in line with what I wrote before about earlier and later phases of an event. . . .

Regards, Sincerely yours, John Dewey

Paoli, Indiana, August 28, 1943

Dear Dewey:

. . . "Event" and "Fact." The way we are handling them, are not "event" and "fact" the same? If so, we can drop the dubious "event," and use "fact." . . .

"Involved in." This, I think, gives the clue we want. In time I would have got around to the suggestion that "meaning," as seen from the point of view of the on-going organism (pragmatic), is all very well—and historically basic—but too narrow for general use.

[*Bentley*]

Paoli, Indiana, August 30–31, 1943

Dear Dewey:

. . . I am reading yours 7-19-43. . . .

Re experienc*ing* [as] both active and passive at once. Taking the finger and flame illustration. You say "getting burned is the undergoing aspect." But "just getting burned" is not experienc*ing*: the active aspect must come in too, the withdrawing. Also the observation of connection.

Memo. I seem to "focus" four or more descriptions here;

1. "burning" in physical statement.

2. "getting burned" in physiological-sensational statement—sense awareness.

3. reflex-withdrawing physiologically stated.

4. "observation of connection."

For your purposes and mine (2) and (3) are not separates, but one event or fact. I suspect it is they that are the active and passive "aspects." Your account seems to yield one passive (2) and two levels of active aspects (3) and (4). A catalyptic or hypnotic subject might have (1) without the others—we would not call it "behavior" at all.

But if (2) and (3) are the passive and primary-active (as patient and agent), are not both in terms of the organism? You would then have both experienc*ing* and experienc*ed* in terms of the organism. This would not be just what I called (rightly or wrongly) the Jamesian Datum—for this latter would have to be in terms of organism *and* environment.

We have in the above four fact-reports and three types of technical treatment (physical, physiological and behavioral).

You proceed to require for *experience* (4) above as well as (2) and (3).

I suspect if "experience" is used at all, it should be definitely used as organism-description; that is, as an enrich*ed* statement on the side of the organism, or from the point of view of the organism.

I think this clears the matter up for this word pretty well. I mean

155

the first stage of application of the word is clarified. It is not "neutral" in the sense in which I read "neutral" in James. It is built, however, in the same background. It covers the behaviorally-participant organism's participation in the full organism-environment setting.

You also proceed to show that the word "experiencing" will cover a large number of varieties of behavioral processes, and [that it] helps to clear them up. And you repeat that probably it need not be used at all.

This, also, I can clearly interpret (or think I do).

Experience or experiencing is not the old narrowly personal. It is the organism-behavior stressed as in environmental process. But it is too comprehensive in its coverage to be used safely at present.

Now, however, in my character of finger-pointer-at, I want to know factually what this phase (4) of "observation of the undergoing and the doing phases of the interaction" consists of. How [to] specify it?

Or: if one is to expand and account [for] from the organism's point of view of the (4) stage (the organism being both patient and agent), in what words, or on what basis, or by application of what detail names, are we to describe it? It is not up in the sign stage. It seems to be in the upper parts of the signal range—in the more complex perceptions—(broader-ranging perceptions). . . . Having gone over your page again, I note three things:

1. You say the above yourself (if I read it straight): You say you have used the word "experience" as "a name for the whole 'circuit' which I tried to substitute for the disjointed arc business."

2. I seem to recall [that] I have suggested in the past the possibility of using "experience" for the perception ranges, and "language" for the old rational ranges. (It makes me a little suspicious of my analysis here to note that I came out again where I have come out before.)

3. We have one possible form of "makings" for a distinction between "Behavior" (transactional) and "Experience" (interactional, from the organism's end of the "inter").

Further (4) in differentiation: you write that experiencing in this way is basic for clearing up behaviors. I change [this] to making it clear up the organic end of behaviors. . . .

Here is the hot baby in the above:

Given the organism as agent; consider him further as patient; can this patient characteristic be held to expression in terms of organism, or must it be expressed in terms of environmental-organic process?

Could it be that

Excitation-reaction	is the physical-physiological report?
Stimulus-Response	is the behavioral report?
Response	is Experiencing?

Stimulus   is Behavioral Object (i.e.,
object in transactional be-
havior, and not either pre-
behavioral nor post-behav-
ioral)?

Now. Interaction and Transaction are no longer opposing claimants, but organized and on their way. . . .

Your card 8-13 suggesting stimulus-signal-sign-symbol. Whether it agrees with the way I wrote before or not, I would make this

         excitation   (physiological)
         signal   (behavioral)
         sign   (behavioral)
         symbol   (behavioral)

Then I would equate stimulus with behavior-object and set it over against behavior-experience.

I am not concerned about the names at present, but the stuff to be named.

In short, signal, sign, and symbol would be specification of stimulus-object, and response would be experimental in the experienc*ing* sense.

I must confess a desire to [use] sign for the lower stage and signal for the verbal stage. But that is going to be a question of wisest communicative course, and needs study, with outcome as may be.

Your suggestions as to the general approach in which behavioral is primary, and the technical one in which it is secondary: It is clear that here we have got to advance to a pretty sharp statement. . . .

We postulate the organism in *inter*action; next, *trans*actional fact as richer fact-form; then, this transactional fact as stage of knowledge; finally (temporarily finally) and back of all: knowledge as *what?*

We can state knowledge as linguistically embodied and the linguistic as organism-in-action with organism-in-action as transactional.

What this comes to is that the cosmos (as thing) is a reification of language process in above sense, but also, language process is *a* phase or aspect of the cosmos (unreified? or reified?). . . .

The problem for us, however, is to make matter of fact statement about it, enough to carry our point and no more. It is (1) just the admission we are not God-omniscients and (2) that we abandon metaphysical "reals." Or: it is an ignorabimus without sentimentality, an unknowable with [un-] Spencerian solemnity. But how speak it out as plain common sense? . . .

You suggest "raw" for "science." Might not your occasional query about "raw" or "brute" materials be a surviving trace of reification? Does it not get representation in your *Logic* in the form of the indeterminate situation? Or, let us say, as a focused (temporarily), or reified or thingified, tentative kernel of the indeterminate situation? . . .

157

"Biological" *vs.* "Physiological." You do not directly say it, but you seem to suggest the possible substituting of "biological" for "physiological" in the classification of knowledge-fields I have been setting up. If so, we can hold it open till the last minute. I will try to dig into my own attitude towards it. . . .

Approaching "life" studies, zoology is the museum contrast to "physiology," the technique; and "biology" is certainly a wider word. The common use makes "physiology" a narrow, specialized term as you say. . . . ["Biology,"] I do not sense as technique [in the] way [that physiology is]. . . . I am wholly ready to substitute "biological," and it should be kept open, especially in view of the term "biological naturalism," which is excellent.

Which raises the question, *en passant:* Are we not approximating a *behavioral* naturalism? . . .

Regards, *Bentley*

Montville, New Jersey, August 30, 1943

Dear Bentley:

. . . I think the distinction between "name" and "term" (as a specified kind of name) is likely to be distinctly useful. (I don't know whether "sentence" and "proposition" might be used in a corresponding way.) I think it will hold out, though there may be border line cases—in a new topic, maybe, when terms are still undergoing development.

Some . . . [one], I can't remember who it was, but [I] ran into it when I was doing my *Logic,* said only nouns were names—verbs and adjectives don't name anything. Maybe it was Russell [cf. *The Principles of Mathematics,* pp. 42–52]—I'm not sure. . . .

Yours, regards, *Dewey*

Montville, New Jersey, August 31, 1943

Dear Bentley:

My life-habits as to writing are too atmospheric to be very serviceable in the present juncture. The sheets I enclose are more as "evidence of good faith than for publication"; faith in the importance of the undertaking. . . .

In my *Logic* [p. 55], I use "significance" and "sign" as names referring to "connection"—the indicative or pointing to, predictive function of an event; as in "signboards"—"symbol" as name for referring to "relation." There are, of course, symbols on a signboard pointing the hand at cross-roads and the "5 miles to Yonkers." But they function as an event to point the way to other events.

Sincerely yours, *Dewey*

[P.S.] My chief difficulty is telling how far to go in detail, the Scylla of cumbrous overloading and the Charybdis of leaving some words in the air. Not legislating as to [the] way words should be used, but telling the way in which we are using them.

Use of word "name," not limited to proper names, nor yet to "things." . . . Verbs, adverbs, adjectives, are names as well as nouns.

(This matter illustrates my difficulty as stated above; if we try to eliminate every possible miss [misunderstanding], the thing will get strung out.) . . .

"Field." It might be convenient to have a word for something corresponding as a matter of "relation"—that is comparable to "name" and "term."

Say "field" and "domain." . . .

Under "Behavioral Thing and Process," there might be mention of "situation" [as] a *convenient* word to guard against splitting up and isolation—as a reminder of the extent of an event and the sub-heterogeneities which are compatible with being *an* event: *specifications within* as capable of being made when an inquiry is served by making them. (If I recall, you used the words "situation and situational" for a while. Of course, there would have to be negative statement—that it doesn't name something *outside* or surrounding.)

Going back to another matter—"involved" is a name as to "connection"; "implied" as to "relation." "Meaning" to "reference"???

We (citizens of . . . [the] United States) are *involved* in the war-event. Possibly "situation" suggests something too static, though I haven't intended to use it that way. In that case it might be linked up possibly with "thing" as "an event looked upon statically for purposes of consideration" in cases when it is desirable to indicate range and complexity. (There are plenty of objections to technical use of "complexity" for "specifications within." But there is a plenitude of distinctions, refinements potentially in the event-knowing-known at the course end of the spectrum.)

In events as going concerns, e.g., the war-event, *what* is involved is not discovered short of an issue—and there is no finally complete issue. What does the war indicate, point to, for the future of . . . [the] United States, China, etc.?

Montville, New Jersey, September 1, 1943

Dear Bentley:
. . . One view that has a good deal to say for itself is that "fact" is a *term*, "event" a *name*. That is, "fact" may be taken to stand for an event when the latter is brought into definitive ascertainment and formulation: the "facts" *about* electrical events are thus and so. On this view, "fact"

159

as term is of the same order as "truth," though of a much more concrete sort, and without the emotional and moral glamor of "truth." "It is a fact *that*." In other words, this usage of fact has good idiomatic support; it isn't a holdover from philosophy. It has been formulated by someone as follows (I think C. I. Lewis) . . . : "Fact is the subject-matter of a verified proposition"—that is a more technical way of saying "it is a fact that."

"Phenomenon" has the disadvantage of a bad parentage. It has the advantage of popular usage, and can be used with considerable hope of being taken in a neutral sense.

In an earlier letter . . . you made more or less incidentally a remark about knowledge that was open to misunderstanding. Some would take it to be a denial of the occurrence of events before man arrived on the globe, though of course that wasn't the intent; and it seemed to extend the scope of knowledge so far as not to leave room for the unknowns still to be discovered. I mention this matter, not otherwise important, because it may have a bearing on the event-fact affair. There are some difficulties in referring to events still under inquiry as "facts;" "potential facts" isn't a happy term.

I have been speculating some about "data." As far as I have got, it seems to be a name for facts placed toward the lower end of a spectrum—if "fact" can be said to have a spread?

Sincerely yours, and with regards, *Dewey*

Paoli, Indiana, September 2, 1943

Dear Dewey:

. . . I badly need right soon a word to use for *applying a name* in steady contrast with *defining a term*. I am apt to write "specifying" or "specification." *Re* your "reference," it might be "referring," but that is too loose. Could [one] "focus" or "center" a name or reference? Maybe "term" is too loose for "defining," and you would suggest some alternative. Could we *define a "symbol,"* and divide "symbols" into "symbol-terms" and "symbol-emblems" (or "index," "cipher," "token," "mark")?

Here is another half-stab at a scheme for the word "knowledge":

I. Knowledge-behavior: full-functional; would require us to characterize what aspect of behavior it is; would be the primary form.

II. Secondaries: a. intra-integumental—1. know-how, 2. experiential, (aa) as of the moment, (bb) as in possibility of range. b. extra-integumental—the things-known as a "cosmos" or "universe discoursed about." c. super-integumental (Ha!)—the full lot of warranted assertions of time and place—in language—in libraries for embodiment and localization.

(Would II-b here rate description as "guaranteed perceivings," extrap-

160

olated as "things" just as II-c is extrapolated in libraries? And what kind of word could we use for "extrapolated" which did not imply an "extrapolator" behind the "extrapolating"?)

Regards, Bentley

Paoli, Indiana, September 3, 1943

Dear Dewey:

More memo as I go along and, My God, what a long road to travel and how many twistings. *Re* your suggestion: name-sentence, term-proposition, I am inclined to think the scheme should be: "word-sentence," "name-assertion," "term-proposition."

In other words, I must set up "word-sentence" as the most general characterization (naming) of linguistic behaviors. Then, out of these, I need names to use in your field of reference: where name is good, and where, I think, your assertion, based on warranted assertibility, should be used. "Term-proposition" seems assuredly indicated for the field of relation.

Looking at it either from my point of view or yours, I think as many of the critical words in your *Logic* should be employed for what-we-hope-to-be-soon-future-terminology as possible. Where you have alternative phrasings, we should stick to one. If we find a better word now and then, we should substitute it. For example, I think "subject-matters" should be introduced and made firm. I think it will work out as one specification of the process agent-objects, which itself is a specification of organism-environment in a particular range of activity; with organism-environment again as subject-matter of research.

"Subject-matters" is strikingly "behavioral" in transactional presentation. Requires subjects in both senses (organism and environment), both being "matters."

As for "assertion," it might be you prefer some alternative. I have not yet checked my notes on your *Logic* terminology. . . .

Every *fact-named* must have localization. It must "be somewhere" and it must "be somehow." In this it differs from a term which is relational-technique-in-language. No term may be used as a name under its own power.

This brings out a difference in treatment of "knowledge" by you in the *Logic,* and by me in the present enterprise. This difference *might* extend to a gap between us, but I think not; I think all that I am attempting is implicit in your *Logic,* though not yet (so far as I have yet noted) explicitly set down. In general, in the *Logic,* "knowledge" is the outcome or product of inquiry. This leaves its location in the universe unspecified, except as read back into a "head" or a "culture." P. 8, you say "the conception of knowledge as such can only be a generalization." This,

161

as I read it, has the effect of knocking out the "reading back" into "heads," etc.—but does not extend to a positive *placing* of knowledge. This matter of *placing* is vital to me—no place, no fact. "Placing" is possible (as I see it) in "behavior as organism-environment transaction." . . . "Continuity," "naturalism," "biological naturalism," "cultural naturalism," "continuum of inquiry," "naturalistic logic," "behavioral naturalism" (your *Logic,* Ch. III). . . . The first five you either use or specify closely. Is "continuity" any different in feel from "biological naturalism"? "Continuity" has too many current uses. "Biological naturalism" is frequently mentioned in current papers. Is it the best thing to stick to? It certainly draws attention most closely to the right spot in the present decade. . . .

Regards, *Bentley*

[P.S.] I am getting an idea that if you could develop your *Logic* in a very short form with a hard-boiled terminology, each name specified, and no alternative phrasings used—[a] straight-out presentation, and no attention to philosophizings—it would be a knock-out. . . .

Montville, New Jersey, September 3, 1943

Dear Bentley:

Re yours August 30–31. . . . I didn't mean to present the receptive (environmental) aspect and the reactive (organic) aspects, the under-going-doing, as at all significant in our present search. The statement was, rather, *reminiscent,* telling how I *did* use the word ["experience"] for Environmental-Organism interaction, and with emphasis upon unity constituted by *connection* of doing-undergoing, neither having any priority absolutely, and either being capable of [being] taken as first in given cases of analyses. My reference was intended to be retrospective to a development out of the "Reflex Arc" article—that I think can be left behind, unless it should come in handy in reference to some quite specialized matter—so specialized as not to belong in a general terminological survey.

My present preference would be to avoid the word ["experience"] entirely in such a survey, unless, in connection with some other point, it be stated parenthetically that if the word is used, it *is to be used* to designate that particular matter.

Otherwise I would drop my earlier undergoing-doing aspects of the Environmental-Organism interaction in favor of "experiencing" as the short-span, here-now segment of an extensive field-event. And I doubt if, in a preliminary formulation, even that is necessary. (In a more extensive, less terminological discussion I probably would make that point, and would also want to say that every knowledge statement at the other end of the spectrum has this aspect, or, in other words, there is no "sight"

162

so extensive that it doesn't have its aspect of here-now seeing. In short, I agree with you . . . , it is wiser to steer clear of too elaborate developments.)

. . . You are right about clearing up the organic-end of behaviors rather than behavior as such. Returning to the reminiscent stage, "patient" in "agent-patient" is on the same level as "agent"—the Organism-Environment *inter*-action viewed from the Organism end—important distinction to make from the standpoint of some special analyses, but not now relevant.

. . . I am not in the least insistent on any particular placing of "signal" —undoubtedly its usual usage refers to some kind of agreed-upon code— definitely the upper or verbal stage. The type of intercommunication that goes on between animals, sexual and parental, seems to be intermediate in development of language as an important kind of gesture, and to need notice in *that* connection—à la work of Meyer I mentioned [*The Psychology of the Other One*], but it doesn't need to come in here, nor to be called "signaling" when it is noticed anywhere.

(Incidentally, the language aspect of knowledge is interestingly indicated in such words as "noting," "noticing," "remarking," "telling apart," as synonyms for "observing.")

. . . My reference to "raw" was reminiscent also. I now think what I had in mind works out at the lower end of the spectrum—where naming applies to short-span aspects of events—"sense" perception.

. . . My feeling about "biological" is mostly a hunch. "Physiological" is often used in contrast with anatomical techniques. But it is true that those words carry a sense of operational techniques of inquiry not conspicuous in "biological." The latter seems to be an *aspect* of behavior— physiological technique—reference within it. It may be that there is a trace of reification in my feeling about "biological." Anyway, I am not ready to try to pin it down out of the atmosphere.

. . . My remark about animal behavior was simply in line with [the] difficulty of finding any words that are foolproof by themselves—also possibly associated in feeling with biological; plant and animal behavior, and man's behavior *qua* animal. The fact that a lot of people take "behavior" to stand for something formal and external just can't be helped. Some of *them* may be helped, and some can't.

Yours, Dewey

[P.S.] Your comments about cosmos and language are in line, I think, with my remarks about knowledge and world. But in any terminological survey we can be as agnostical as we want to be. Personally I enjoy speculating, but it's a luxury.

Dear Dewey:

. . . You suggest "event" as a *name*, "facts" as a *term* somewhat akin to truth, in the sense of "it is a fact that." I think I am pretty close to you here except in calling "fact" a "term" (until we have specified "term" more closely). ("Phenomenon" should be out entirely, I think—it has some *hope* of proper use, but not much.)

I much prefer "event" as the name, the reference of which will be characterized by "it is a fact that." I have only been building in terms of "fact" because you had had trouble with "event," and said you had almost dropped it in use. I am glad to try out any word. My alternative writings are "interior conversations" helpful to me. Now, with an additional close "conversation" with you, much more help comes.

"Event" (the reference) for me has the great advantages that: 1. it is primarily used in the specific case for *An* event; 2. it carries with it *duration*, a time-span covered, a description in time, to almost every hearer's ear.

I suggest that we formally specify, and unvaryingly employ, the word "event" as a name for anything and everything that is *connection* (as distinct from relation and reference, which are linguistic behaviors), on the understanding that connections must be *factual* in the sense that they are established somewhere in the spectrum-like range:

    Assured Perceptions,   (These three not "compartments,"
    Workable Namings,   but transitions, with focused
    Warranted Assertions.   namings for stages or levels.)

And, further, that they are to be characterized always in terms of durational description (extension implied) and as specific instances with any desired temporal length. (Your *Logic* does not index "event," but I recall your saying it is something "judged" as to beginnings and terminations [*Logic*, p. 223].)

Use it on the further understanding that the events of connection cover *all* events, including knowings and the whole psychological tribe, either in primary full-functional namings, or in secondary namings with respect to organism and environment.

Now as to "fact." Lewis [e.g.] may be all right (and I am keen to assemble cites from anybody or anything helpful), but as long as we have "warranted assertibility," I am not interested in the "subject-matter of a verified proposition." . . .

If we are going to use "terms" for words set up in "relation" where "relation" is the "symbolic" process of language, "fact" cannot be a "term." "Fact" cannot even be a "term" (I suspect) while it still remains "in" a proposition as the outcome-in-language. Or rather the word "fact" is not germane to the technical outcome. Also it covers named and perceived situations.

I think we can set up "fact" all right as a type of naming with specified characteristics. Is not this what you have done for "truth" in the *Logic*? Have you not eliminated "truth" in the ordinary views and substituted something better? Cannot same happen for "fact"? Indeed have you not produced it already?

One thing very important to watch for is phrasings of the kind you mention in some letter of mine which either (a) imply no events before man, or (b) seem to shut off future discoveries. My position gets misread this way, or used to, and I have had some vehement arguments thereabout. On the other hand, when I read your texts, and find references to "raw" or "brute" materials or facts, I find a corresponding misreading indicated.

The antipodes are: If everything is *in* knowledge or involved in knowledge, what the hell has become of the factual world? If there is some raw material outside of knowledge, how the hell does it get in?

My solution is, like yours, "transactional."

You work with the higher-up "logical," starting with "materials," . . . I work from the neutral datum (not originally the Jamesian, but my own "social") and sometimes seem to leave "everything" out—to have no basic point-of-support. I think my "feel" in this was expressed at the end of Part II, *Behavior, Knowledge, Fact*. . . . My position is, I think: that our sciences are developed namings; that our earlier namings are primitive efforts; that our sciences as techniques have everything open before them and are not limited to interpreting things already known (and merely adding new things to the number)—and can organize and reorganize everything.

If, now, (1) we get the full business transactional, and (2) we get a transactional technique of signal-sign-symbol, and (3) we get a definite way to talk about it, we should get somewhere.

From the high level of "logic" you have "materials." From the full behavioral viewpoint, you see those materials as "subject-matters." If they are subject-matters, they are no longer "raw." Or: if they are "raw," what assurance have we that they are "there" at all?

We jointly oppose the view that sensation "gives" what "mind" "handles." . . .

Regards, *Bentley*

Paoli, Indiana, September 6, 1943

Dear Dewey:

. . . It is clear that I have used "reference" in a more limited way than you use it. (*Logic*, p. 55.) I have reduced it to the maximum-available definiteness of "naming fact." . . .

What would you say as to the three words, "involvement," "connection," "inference"? How separated, or how overlapping?

Is not "connection" without use of "involvement" an adequate word for "that . . . sustained by things to one another"? (your p. 55).

Is not "inference" an adequate word for the determination of namings that work (or "involvement," or any other word you prefer—but one word only, not two)? Should not "involvement" be assigned to "reference"?

Is not Aristotelian logic a process of name-determinations-that-work-in-practice? That is, "inference" or "involvement" in this sense?

Is not the doubling up of the names "connection" and "involvement" a method of slurring over the "raw material" or "behavioral material" issue? . . .

I suspect my own (undeveloped) procedure would be to say that the whole perception-action-behavior (our tentative "signaling"—also the guts of Bridgman's "operations") manipulated by words as names (our tentative "signing") yields "named-things," of which the good firm ones (did I say yesterday "workable namings"?) are "facts." The high-powered relation-process, of course, assumed as a symbol-stage. From the dates, I would assume Aristotle would not have known of Euclid, and there would not have been enough of the "hypothetical procedure" in the geometry of Aristotle's day to stand out prominently; or was there?

"Facts" would be the layout of the age, as developed in warranted assertion. . . .

For our purposes, the named-things attaining warranted, factual status would be not static things, but *Events*, specific as things, but fully durational in form; with "knowings" and "knowns" equally "events." As static things, the "knowings" and "knowns" could not assimilate; as "events," they can (we hope). . . .

Regards, Bentley

[P.S.] Perhaps I can put my difficulty in another way.

On your p. 55, *Logic*, you let "symbol" run over the full language range which we are now proposing to differentiate into "sign" and "symbol." Does the following state our present differentiation as you see it:

"Sign" (for language), the use of word (or words) to "stand for" or, in effect, "name" events.

"Symbol" (in language only), the term-definition-implication system?

On p. 55, "symbol-meanings" represents both of the above.

As for "relation," the "assertion" on p. 55 is equivalent to our present "assertion."

As for "reference," you set up symbol-meanings in process with (relation to) existence.

As for "connection," you set up [as designating] "things to one another"; which, I take it, is equivalent to an "assertion" we would now make.

But for "connection" (and "involvement") you also say "in virtue of which *inference* is possible."

Question: Should not the "involvement" and the "inference" be transferred from "connection" to "reference"? Or: is not just this the "reference" process?

Can our set-up be (not in formulation), but as cues for use between ourselves:

"Connection": the cosmos extrapolated as the "known" within the ongrowing knowing-knowns, including all that we don't yet know, and covering connections of "knowing" and of "knowing-knowns" as well as other extrapolated "knowns."

"Reference": the knowing process, viz. sign-using (i.e., language in the sign-stage), thus concentrating into namings, these namings being, however, namings of *events*, i.e., of descriptions, rather than of extra-descriptional "existences." (My own position would always place action-verb-language primary to thing-language. But the known get action on the known-side in the form of event, and on the knowing-side in the form of behaving; and may have no conflict.)

"Relation"; as we take it, mathematics, implications. . . .

[*Bentley*]

Montville, New Jersey, September 6, 1943

Dear Bentley:

. . . The decided advance you have made over previous statements is in introducing "provisional reifications" for "cosmos" in connection with physical research, for life, and for behavioral facts. That disposes, both for ourselves and for others, with a number of matters we might otherwise get mixed up in. I believe it will continue to hold water; we need words to designate matters *still under* inquiry, actual or potential, and at the same time [to] make it clear that they have reference to inquiry, and inquiry to them. And I think your formula does both of these things. . . .

I'm not clear yet either about a name for applying a name. As I said . . . , I've used "specifying" or, more formally, "identifying-demarcating": it somehow picks out and frames what is taken for fact in inquiry. But that is no nomenclature. In another connection, I've fooled around with "de-signation," but that is more of a synonym for a sign name. It does carry the idea of definitive selection—or election; denomination is more of a nomination than an election. But this is a kind of playing to see what would happen.

I have wondered about "field"—whether the usage of the psychologist, who has made a mess of it, . . . is sufficiently in general use so it has to be ruled out. There are field equations in physics, aren't there? I was rather stuck . . . [for] some word for the space end of time-space that will do what "event" does for the time-aspect. . . .

Long ago you asked me a question about "judgment," and I didn't get the point of your question when I tried to answer. I think I can come nearer now. "Judgments" (primary) are events that occur in transactions between parties in a law court or an arbitration tribunal and [are] recorded in law books as far as they furnish rules (precedents) regulating further legal behavior. In a transferred sense, they are anything of the nature of advice or instruction that has the effect of settling some matter previously in dispute, or, more generally, that is undergoing inquiry in such cases as present alternatives . . . to fact[s] still open. I think along this line it is possible to give [to] "judgments" [a] spatial-durational description as events.

. . . I think, as the discussion proceeds, it will be necessary to have names for "fact" as *outcome* for inquiry, as "provisional reification" subjectmatter, as per your [suggestions] of 8-31-43, and also for "fact" indicated as possible, worth exploring, by "facts" in the first or decisive sense—also to indicate that they—the latter—are not themselves facts, in the sense of being out of bounds for further inquiry, when, as, and if, indicated to be needed.

There is a kind of spectrum spread in "fact," all shades being, of course, in reference to inquiry.

Judgments are measurements, in process or completed, [from] loose to more accurate. They refer to something undergoing construction or formation at a given time and place, *or* to its result as far as that constitutes a cue, or, more strictly, a rule in future transactions of that kind.

As to "signal," I don't see how we can do better than stay by Pavlov, since he is the one who has done actual work. The cue-force, or value, or function, of words can be treated, I think, as a specialized case of signaling (development). Quite likely Meyer's use was a loose derivation from Pavlov's stricter use.

Sincerely yours, With best regards, *Dewey*

Paoli, Indiana, September 7, 1943

Dear Dewey:

Could it be the case that "fact," in everyday use, is directly double-barreled as "firmly-named-thing"; whereas "speech" and "thing" (although we construct them as double-barreled) are not at all so recognized by the user, but used *as if* literally and assuredly far apart in different realms?

We might have then: Transactional Pole—our approach; intermediate usage—"fact"—semi-transactional; "thing" (and "agent") interactional. Interactional Pole—the usual approach (conventional and philosophical), separating the two ends, and requiring fiat (epistemological or other) to bridge between them.

It strikes me the main thing for us to do with the word "fact" at this stage is for *you* to envisage material-proposition-activity as man-in-action (behavior) on the sign-name levels; next push the organism end away from the environment end for immediate purposes of analysis; then decide what phases of what part of what process the word "fact" names. As I write this, I identify "fact," "the fact" with your "determinate situation" as outcome. But this is not enough.

In a completed propositional form (material), is "fact" the verbal outcome in the form of a "firm name"? Or is it the reference of that name? If for such a reference we choose the name "event," then we have both names again and the previous difficulties.

Is there such a process as fusing the *word* event with the *fact* event in a "justified scientific reification"—and then letting the word "fact" be the *name* for such a reification or fusion? This yields two kinds of "naming," one fused, one at arm's length. Does ordinary logical development exhibit two kinds of namings of such kinds? . . .

Regards, *Bentley*

Montville, New Jersey, September 8, 1943

Dear Bentley:

. . . I am beginning to believe that I have done most of my work that amounts to anything in an intermediate field and that I am chiefly sensitive to names in that field. It has to do with names of things (subjects and subjectmatters) taken not directly, but . . . functionally, or [with] reference to their uses. Take, for example, the word "evidence" (better word for most uses than "sign," which I've probably used too much). Every case of evidence must, of course, be one of fact. But not every case of fact need be one of evidence. (I imagine, though I wouldn't bet on it yet, that this is at the root of my old emphasis upon having-knowing, as I have pretty habitually confined the word "knowledge" to cases where use or functioning as evidence comes in.) A large part of my criticisms . . . [has] consisted in giving a "functional" interpretation to words to which a reified or "inherent" signification is habitually assigned by philosophers. Now, just where do we place a word like "evidence"? It's a name, isn't it, not a term? But it's a *reference* name, not a name like cat or Silurian period. Should we have *three* sorts of words? "Connection names," "reference names," "relation terms"?

The grammatical connectives "which" and "that" *are* connectives, I suppose; "if" is a relation word; *therefore,* "so" is sometimes a relation word—in "logical" use—but it sometimes stands for fact insofar as that fact is reached by evidence. The color of that flame *indicates* (in some cases, [one] could say *proves*) the presence (factual) of sodium. The word "suggests" stands for a fact, I think, but a fact of *reference,* [a] weakened case of *indicates* as that is a weakened case of *proof* (I'm using "proof" here, not in the Euclidean sense, but in that of adequately made out and tested—adequately under given conditions).

Having got thus far, I am beginning to wonder whether the whole class of words to which mentalistic import has been given are not *reference* words.

The above may be out-of-place-and-time. If so, let it go for the present. But I got to thinking about . . . [reference], the kind of work I had done, and it struck me I had never cared much about the field of symbols, nor yet the field of facts in their direct (or non-functional) occurrence, but about that of uses to which events are put—which are facts, of course, but a fact of the order of a tool, instrument, etc. (I shouldn't wonder if that is my "pragmatism"—I certainly never could go [for] all the statements James made under that heading.) It probably accounts also for my affinity for the organism-environment approach.

All this may be of some value as giving you my general slant on things, my bias, and direction of emphasis. Otherwise, let it slide, though there may be something in viewing *behavior* names on their organism-end as reference words.

What you say about my mixing up terms, meanings, etc., in *Logic* is correct—the most that could be said is that when a name had a formal feel to me, I probably was more likely to call it a "term."

As for *quality,* I certainly don't believe in it apart from behavior—all qualities are qualities of behavior, and I didn't intend to give any other impression. (As a matter of cosmic speculation, there is probably something in the *immediate* occurrence of pre-human events which from an evolutionary point of view prefigures qualities of human behavior.) As far as I now recall, my concern in the *Logic* was to distinguish between "quality" and "trait" ("characteristic," "feature"), which are function or reference words. ("Character," as I used it, is a *relation* word—not important at this time.) I agree "quality" [is a] strictly neutral behavior word—probably doesn't need specification in a present statement.

With regards, Yours, *John Dewey*

[P.S.] My talking about "meanings of terms" is an inexcusable case of the sort of thing that happens when *sounds* and *words* are confused.

Dear Bentley:

Re yours of 9-5-43. Am glad you are back with "event" and are so independently of the issue *re* "fact." I'll have to be more careful about my casual remarks. I didn't mean by what I said to object to the word "event." It's a swell word and does something no other word does. I was sort of apologizing for not using it as much as I had formerly—but it is paying too much respect to Russell, *et al.*, to permit them to monopolize it in a wrong use.

If we settle on "event," precisely as you state it, I think something will stay settled for quite a while. As for the space aspect of event, as temporal-spatial, maybe we can begin with a circumlocution if we can limit it enough. I've always liked the philosophy contained in the idiomatic expression "takes *place*" [as] applied to any event—it recognizes localization as part of an event. But it won't do for terminology as we need the latter.

And I think we can manage "fact" without bothering about "propositions," or "judgments," or any such word. They are events specified with respect to the characteristic of being *known*—in an emphatic sense of known-as-certained as such-and-such. I'm not offering this for acceptance—it's still atmospheric—but as in line with your setting up "fact" as a naming with specified characteristics.

I can't give a satisfactory answer to your question about "raw"—which is a good reason for leaving it out. What I was feeling for in distinction between "raw" and "refined" was, I think, in the direction of a knowledge-spectrum. I certainly intended both words to be taken comparatively, not absolutely. It had nothing to do with the "senses" as so-called sources of knowledge; it had more to do with such cases as "That is wood," when I don't give a damn about wood save as something to burn at the time and place when fire is needed in a short-temporal span, short and locally narrow transaction. But the word "raw" isn't needed. I don't believe, though, that in eliminating the "raw" or "crude," there is commitment to the conclusion that what is "out of knowledge" can't get in. . . . I don't see why the event called knowledge shouldn't occur as something new, just as extending the range of interacting events produces in the case of other events in other matters a rearrangement having a new pattern of organization—as sodium, rather dangerous by itself, and chlorine gas, a poison, constitute salt when they come together under certain conditions, with the result that a set of very different consequences takes place when salt enters into interaction with still other things. . . .

My habit of using "term" loosely is likely going to take some time to break; I'll try though. . . .

I wanted to say that I "guess" I was off the rails in calling the facts

I was trying to talk about "reference" words. They couldn't exist without words, as far as I can see; they are a kind of fact of which the existence of words is a causal condition—but it isn't words which are named, but events being evidence, subjectmatter, suggestion, indication. And, as I said, . . . my habit of locating "knowledge" in this range is probably why I had a need for "having" and for the "raw." . . . You are much better at firm naming than I am, and so far I've seen nothing I don't agree with, even if it takes me a little time to get into full practice. . . .

Yours, *Dewey*

[Montville, New Jersey,] September 11, 1943

[To Bentley:]

Haven't got far with [a] word to take [the] place of "specify," "identify"; "particularize" occurred to me as usable sometimes, but [I] don't think it is firm enough for a terminological system.

It's a nuisance [that] there are not words to distinguish between *dictionary* definitions (of usages) and *logical* definitions—that set standards *for* usage in certain instances; that of "symbols" and "relations." Thus, in [the] Aristotelian system, "terms" were taken to be names of limits, boundaries set in and by "nature" (between fixed species, for example), and definition had to do with them. It was "real and true" knowledge.

. . . I share your doubts about "non-existential" in *Logic*—[I] wasn't well satisfied in writing—[its use was] more or less a concession to "mathematical logicians"; otherwise I think [it] a protection or protest against a kind of reification (the "realism" of your *Linguistic Analysis* [*of Mathematics*]), firmly established in cosmology up to the time of at least Locke and Hume—and basic in Kant and his followers. . . .

[*Dewey*]

Paoli, Indiana, September 11, 1943

Dear Dewey:

This matter of confused uses of words—you know what I am after. If there ever was a man who had "everything" and had it organized coherently, it is you. You attained it by free handling of words. But now and then a time comes to hammer down a few words, as we are trying it now.

Visitor here has been showing me your *Experience and Nature*, p. 176, reference to Max Meyer and "signals." Here "signal" in your text is used for communication [by] sub-vocal forms. This is a bit different from what we are now trying to do with "signal" as any perceptive cue. I have no choice (at any rate, as yet) about any of these names.

172

You have the transactional statement, p. 179: "Meaning is primarily a property of behavior and secondarily a property of objects." * Unmistakable to your audience at the time (though, of course, unrecognized). Would it be correct to say of our present terminology:

We drop "primarily" and "secondarily,"
We would hardly use the word "property,"
We transfer "behavior" from organic-end to full situation, and dig up another term for the organic end? . . .

Best regards, *Bentley*

[New York,] September 13-14-15, 1943

[To Bentley:]
Terminological:

1. "Thing" (original usage). Name of a *public* assembly: court of conference. 2. Then a matter, cause, suit, pleaded before such an assembly, passing into 3. "That with which one is concerned (in action, speech or thought); an affair, business, concern, matter."

I think there is plenty of good cause to ignore "entity" and "substance" significations. In contrast-comparison with "Fact" (see next), I think a fair paraphrase would be "layout of the age" as exhibited in discussion, dispute, argument, inquiry, as distinct from your

"Fact." "Layout of the age as developed in warranted assertion." Note: It now seems to me that the firm opposite of "Fact" is "Fiction." "Fact," something made *out*; "fiction," something made *up*. Yes. Firmly named-events are "Facts." *With respect* to "knowledge," every event is a fact(?). This is the best I can do with using the word "potential."

"Evidence," "Inference." (What follows is descriptive of the way I have used the words, rather than my opinion as to how they should be used. I think I've used them with more than usual firmness, for me.)

Only an event can provide (be) evidence. I have limited "inference" to cases of drawing conclusions from "evidence." The ordinary usages, even in supposedly formal treatises, strike me as inexcusably loose. [They] . . . cover drawing conclusions from observed events (facts) and from symbols related by implication, ratiocination, reasoning. I don't say that "inference" should be used as I have used it, but that reaching conclusions from events as evidence and from relations of related symbols—propositions—need differential names.

"Connection," "Involvement." I have used these words, "connection," as least, loosely, and as if they were synonyms; if they are, of course one of them is plenty. But there seem to be three main kinds of bonds, ties;

* The exact quotation is: "Meaning is not indeed a psychic existence; it is primarily a property of behavior, and secondarily a property of objects."

173

lack of a generic word is the reason for my double use of "relation," perhaps; that and the fact that I started with pointing out it was used ambiguously. All events are bound together somehow; space-time(?). As near as I got to a steady use, this is what "connection" stood for. Then there is the way symbols are bound together: "Relation," constituting reasoning: Ideal type, "mathematics."

Whether correctly or not, I used (or would have, if I had been steady about it) "Involvement" as that species or sub-kind of "Connection," that ground use of events as "Evidence." To be *an* event is to be "in connection with" other events; otherwise, no duration, nor extension (I, telling my *feel* about it in use of words). But in a given case, where "a" or "an" be employed, there has to be a special kind of connection between specified events if one of them is evidence for another one, or grounds *an* inference. (In usages recorded in [the] dictionary, "imply" and "involve" are often synonyms; this seems to me another case of confusion of the two different kinds of "drawing a conclusion." Historically, the confusion comes, I think, from the fact that the Aristotelian logic identified them by making "necessary connection" in "Reason"—there was no other kind of *necessary* connection—metaphysical—the basis of "inference," in my use of that word.) The "mathematical logicians" do the same thing . . . holding that inference from events as evidence (their "induction") can't give "science," since only deduction, "demonstrative and necessary reasoning," can do that. "Implicated," but not "implied," is a synonym for "Involvement" as I used the word.

All this leads up to "Reference." I can best elucidate my use of the word, when I used it with an approach to technical firmness, by starting with [the] historical point just noted. I wanted a word to stand for the fact that it requires a special *event* (operational) to *apply*, and more generally [to] decide the *applicability* of, conclusions reached in discourse or from *terms* to events—in other words, inference from evidence [is] more fundamental than conclusions from reasoning, the latter becoming a part of knowledge of events only through the *Application*, itself an *Event*, namely, that of *an* Experimental *Operation*.

(Unfortunately I used "existence." No "events" in [my *Logic*] text. This motivation is expressed on p. 75 in the sentence: "Finally, the *test of the validity* . . . ," * in contrast with the next sentence: "They were no longer taken to be 'true' as constituents of *rational discourse in isolation*.") [Emphasis not in the original text.]

Now, I am in a state of doubt. Maybe I was so overinfluenced by opposition to a very influential historic doctrine (still influential) that I got away from a more fundamental matter, namely, the connection of

---

* The entire sentence reads: "Finally, the test of the validity of conceptions formulated and developed in rational discourse was found to reside in their applicability to existential qualitative material." (Eds.)

knowledge (upper end) with *language*. But it accounts (p. 55, middle) for linking "reference" to "symbols."

The *word* "reference" ranges, I think, from a loose use, e.g., "alluding to," "mentioning," "speaking of," to an "overt" event of *Application* (as overt as applying a plaster to the back, or mucilage to stick pieces of paper together), i.e., bringing events in *direct* "connection" that were previously only connected by intermediates. This *bringing* into direct connection is what I take to be *experiment* as *test*. Mathematical conclusions, e.g., are applied in "inference" (my usage) when they indicate *an* operation to be performed which tests their capacity to bring events into *such* connection as produces an *observed event* agreeing with *calculated* conclusions. The test of a *direct* event of observation is the criterion underlying the whole thing, independently of *reference*. Or a *name* can be *firm* only when *confirmed*, tested, in this fashion. "Light," a name; "light" as electric-magnetic hypothesis, arrived at by mathematical reasoning, a symbol-term; "light" *is* electric-magnetic; a *name* arrived at by an operational event of direct application of events to one another as directed or dictated by hypothesis, and testing the validity of [the] latter.

Now, I am going into this length because I am much more convinced of the general scheme than I am of the word "Reference," which I know I used loosely. (One dictionary definition of "Application" is: "To put a thing into practical contact with another"; "practical," I take it, is "direct.") Another one is: "To bring a law, rule, test (principle), into contact with facts," to put it into practical operation. Now, what I didn't make clear enough, I think, is that there is no such thing as a direct application of a law or rule. It occurs by employing the law or rule for what it is, theory, hypothesis; namely, a formula for performing an operational event to bring *events* into "practical contact with one another." . . .

There is *a* connection between "reference" as an event and "inference" as an event. But, as I used them, they are not identical. "Reference" is a *test* of the validity of an inference when the latter is still in the intermediate condition of an hypothesis; making a sign a firm *name*. (In so far I was one-sided, for the historical reason mentioned above, in linking "reference" to "symbols." . . . When I used the word ["reference"] carefully, it wasn't just "sign using," but includes *testing* of use of word as *name* for a given event (guaranteed name).

"Knowledge." I am not going into this generally here, but just to reply to your suggestion of a possibility we are *apart* [with respect to "knowledge"], ("gap," yours of September 3, bottom of page 1). I don't think there is a difference *in fact;* there is [a difference] in that in my *Logic*, because of its subject-matter *as* Logic, I gave the word a narrowed use. I used it for *warranted* or tested results. But I don't think there is anything in that fact which stands in the way of a wider (psychological) use.

My problem took me into the field limited by that strict sense of the word. You are right in calling attention to the weak sense of "referring," "mentioning." P. 8 [of my *Logic*], I say "Knowledge as an abstract term" . . . —and that is what I was limiting discussion to—though, doubtless, at times I had to make forays into more "concrete" affairs. If there is anything in it, [my] *Logic*, that prevents or militates against the treatment of it as a kind of event in connection with other events, I hereby take it back. I don't doubt rephrasing is needed, but I don't believe there is a serious gap, aside from that set as mode [of] approach by the problem in view. . . .

(I've intended several times to mention that Greeks [and] (scholastics) used [the] word "subject," where moderns say "object," and [use] "object" very explicitly to name a subject as before the mind in process of knowledge. We could almost go back to "subject," only they used [it] as [a] name for *substance* in [the] logical context of substance.)

"Means-Consequence." What I am going to say now has no direct bearing upon terminological discussion, but is intended to indicate my background. Since starting our terminological discussion, I've been led to go back over my philosophical writing in a general way to see if I could tell what it was I was up to; I never pretended to myself to know at the time beyond this and that problem. What I see now is that if there is any general survey, it amounts to this:

I have taken words to which most philosophic writings give an "inherent" nature and treated them as words that stand for an office, use, or application; i.e., as means to consequences that can be specified. For instance, I have, of recent years at least, pretty systematically treated words given an inherently mental signification as names for "biological" events, used, under observable social conditions, as means to certain observable consequences. I have usually spoken of this as describing events with respect to their *function*, but now think perhaps that word is too physiological. Should perhaps use "application." I got started in my classes this way years ago by distinguishing: (1) "Events" connected in cause-effect, action-reaction, type of interaction: *Physical;* (2) "Events" connected in stimulus-response (I called it then) type of interaction: *Biological;* (3) "Events" connected in means-consequence type of interaction: *Psychological: Proper* use of "mental."

I am inclined to believe that everything I've done in philosophy that amounted to anything has consisted in restating affairs usually reified in terms of (3).

Under (1), I came to the same conclusion you mention . . . as to setting up the motion of each billiard ball separately. That's what I intended by "action-reaction" formula—probably also [my] reminiscence of Newton. What I did with it specifically was to treat it as the basis of

176

function (use, application) of *substitution,* making possible equations and other mathematical operations.

In general, I put this down as knowledge of background [that] may be of use. Particularly, it is the ground for a question: How far *down* and how far *up* do you carry "knowing how"? Downwards, everything physiological above tropism? [And] does it extend far enough *up* to include what I've called "use" and "application"? In that case, "reference," when I have used it in the right way, not as synonym for "mentioning," is a case of "knowing how" at the upper end of *that* spectrum—if there is one. This would enable me, if [it is] practicable, to make a cleaner, straighter statement about "knowledge" than I've ever done before. Walking, dancing, running an automatic machine, mowing grass, are cases of knowing how? Then, so is talking and naming? *Knowing how to name* so that names would "function," operate, as means to knowledge *as* warranted assertion, would, I think, take me out of the slough I got into.

Otherwise, the only things at all firm here are opening paragraphs about "Fact" and "Thing." I think we are in agreement now about them. And something is said under "evidence"—which is, again, [a] case of knowing how to use named events as means to consequence of more (tested) knowledge.

1. Color red, say. Name for a seen event; 2. Theory of vibrations, term, symbol; 3. Red color, as so many vibrations per unit of time-space. *Name* for passage from 1 to 2, 2 to 3, a case [of] knowing *how?*

"Knowledging" is case of technology, running the gamut, like smelting crude ores, and other technologies, from relatively primitive, undeveloped technologies to relatively highly developed ones—latter are "sciences." This is the point I got from Ayres. But I wouldn't have thought of the "knowing how" aspect, if you hadn't asked me those questions about "reference." . . .

"Response." Obviously a transactional word—*Answering.*

"Tell." A "know how" operational word when equivalent to counting for something. Telling blow; the attack told on enemy. As distinct from Irishman's "How do you do, Mrs. McCarthy? Not that I give a dom, but to keep up the conversation." So, it did "tell" a little after all. Account *of*—so as to account *for.*

[Dewey]

[New York,] September 20, 1943

Dear Bentley:

. . . As far as I am concerned, I'm willing to settle on "Fact" as "something established," not absolutely, but enough to go on, "something which is actually the case," i.e., accepted as basis upon which to go. In law, for example, it is a fact that a person not heard from for so many years is (legally) dead. There has to be something upon which to go. I'd line it up with truth, only with event located and dated *specifically* or singly. *On* which "to go" in *any* kind of operation.

I am not sure . . . just how you use "isolate"; probably, because I've tended it to use it as synonymous with "vicious abstraction," *illegitimate* cutting off; by assigning characteristics due to context to an event absolutely. Chemists, however, "isolate" "reactions" and "substances." Is that your sense? And quarantined persons are "isolated." Etymologically, an *island,* also. I think, probably, [an] analogy with chemical use is the most usable; but has to be described carefully, or we shall have an "individual" of the kind we don't want on our hands. Or do you use "an isolate" for that to which "an" can legitimately be prefixed, as in "an event"?

Somewhere or other I imagine we'll have to face the single (*an*) connection issue; single, one, an, separate—joined, linked, together with. *Any* event is connected with other events. *Every* event contains (consists of?, is made up of?) [other] events.

"Name" stands for "an." "Assertion" stands for *an* in-connection?

"Knowledge." As far as Anglo-Saxon origin of word is concerned, *Can* is skill, ability—still found in "canny"—cunning—know *how,* and "Con," learn to. ("Can" in sense of "able" is derived from more special sense of ability as skill.)

It seems to have been a name for acquired, or *learned,* skill-like, have learned to talk, learned a trade. Con—"Get to know"—this seems to be the original sense of acquainted with—*become;* to "acquaint" was "to *make* known"; *come* to knowledge of. "Introduce" one's self or somebody else. . . . Know, note, recognize in the sense of admitting, confessing, claims of, acknowledging. *Note* is the primary root. This doesn't amount to anything—just fussing around, trying to get hold of hues in the spectrum.

Dewey

Paoli, Indiana, September 29, 1943

Dear Dewey:

Maybe, what we mostly need is the right verb, and then a verb-form with gerund-gerundive values. I noted "Fact," "Event," and "Knowing" in terms of "determine." All such verbs are double-barreled. (*All?*)

Here a knowing is determinating; a fact is an event in determination; and an event is a determinate fact. (Only none of these ways of putting it are usable.) How's to catch a good verb and modulate him to fit?

A. F. B.

New York, October 1, 1943

Dear Bentley:

. . . I think probably "knowing how" should be the alpha—connects more directly with physiological, and leads up to scientific inquiry as a highly developed case of knowing, how to know.

It struck me, in reading, that "behavioral event" gets rid of some of the difficulties that might arise in the case of "behavior"; it's hard to get wholly away from an overload on the organic side with "behavior"; "behavioral event" seems to bring out *transaction* better.

As I look back, I think I used "experience" as a double-barreled word, about as you use "behavior"; calling it experien*cing*, when the emphasis was on organic selection; experien*ced*, when on environmental side.

. . . Do we say anything about behavioral events not of any of the knowledge types? Being mad, afraid, etc. Do we differentiate different types of behavioral events? not separate, but as names for different emphases.

Regards, yours, *John Dewey*

Paoli, Indiana, October 5, 1943

Dear Dewey:

You certainly ask a pointed question in regard to namings, whether "being mad," "angry," etc., gets attention. The answer is: "Not by me." And, then: "It ought to."

I salve myself by (1) assigning feeling (in the sense of "pain," etc.) to the organism physiologically; (2) regarding the rest of the content as "situational," "transactional"; (3) letting it thus have cultural, descriptional status. After this much, I don't do anything. Maybe I should. I seem to be a sort of social-fatalist with respect to human passions and . . . [acts]. The passions and fates are there, but what of it?—I seem to think. Once in a while, it occurs to me that maybe, in this respect, I have an awful lot to learn and, maybe, I will learn it some time "the hard way," by being bowled over on account of it.

I think you are right . . . to make "knowing how" the alpha; and certainly "knowing how to know" is corking. I think my problem has got too far out on the "language" end, and should be hauled back into a know-how base. . . .

Best regards, *Bentley*

New York, October 8, 1943

Dear Bentley:

. . . The enclosed . . . probably is of more use if I ever revise my *Logic* than in the "Terminological" affair. But "determinant" or an equivalent term may be useful in "Knowing How to Know." . . .

Regards, *Dewey*

179

Notes.

"Events": Determined and undetermined, but determin*able, un-,* not *in*determinate.

"Knowing": operation of determining: (1) An event in *process*—indeterminate, *as far as*—in process (not otherwise) of determination; (2) in outcome, product—determined; equals Fact. "Fact" is Determinate Event; (3) In further use or producing: Determin*ants.* "Facts" as means of Knowing. Since Knowing is an Event (spatial-temporal), determining, determination, determinates (facts), and determinants are always as of, say, October 8, 1943, in a given region of . . . [the United States] or the globe, i.e., not *absolute,* or final, or exempt from later determining events.

Determination has aspects: with respect to an event as determinate or "Fact," it is *description.* Determination of traits (characteristics, features) by which an event is recognized (ac-knowledged). Equals determination of the regular, uniform (standardized) connections (spatial-temporal) of an event. Equals the *kind* of event a given event is determined as. The product is a *name.*

With reference to an event as a Determin*ant,* it is "Definition." Determination of the *grounds* ("reasons") upon which an event is determined to be of a certain kind. (In loose language, a statement of the "nature" of an event.) The product is a "Term." (In loose language, an "abstract" noun.) The bearing of this on distinction between "name" and "term" as already made ("connection" and "relation") has to be worked out; I think it can be. Description enables an event to be identified, demarcated: *Specified.* It does not, thereby, of itself determine the "power" of the Fact thus named in further (transactional) events of determining [the] undetermined events.

Description as coefficient; definition as exponential? A Name and Term in operation is "Reference." This indicates that it is necessary to qualify somewhat what was said . . . about determining—determin*ants.* A description or name is determin*ant* with *reference* to specification. A definition is determin*ant* with *reference* to use of the terms (in the sense of conditions) of a specification of a *system* of knowings. Equals an hypothesis or theory.

(This has to be worked out more carefully. If it is any good, it should help tell why, and how, there are symbols in relation, as well as names in connection.)

[*Dewey*]

Paoli, Indiana, October 16, 1943

Dear Dewey:

Even if you do not feel like considering details of our project, I should certainly have from you, in case of unfortunate need, your attitude

180

toward what we have done thus far. How firm an outlook we have? How definite a statement we can make? What probably is the best opening-up? What type of workers we can perhaps find most receptive? Whether such a "naming" as was suggested by alpha's and phi's in the last draft, looks hopeful? Whether the evolutionary- and functional-height classification (as represented by the alpha's), set over against the one-short-organism scale toward the many-long-social-living (as represented by the phi's), is promising? or needed?

The alpha's would represent, perhaps, levels of transactional process. The phi's, in contrast, would present, rather, product accumulation and storage. (I have no idea how the phrasing would come out to best advantage.)

I believe I could go ahead and make a development representing *you* distinctively, rather than me. In other words, after setting down as surely as possible the large background common to both, I could then specialize: (1) from the position of the organism acting, and (2) in terms of his evidencing and judging activities. Without surveying our material, and using just impressions as we have gone along, I set the above down as the stresses you introduce as distinctive from the stresses I am apt to use.

I ought to be able to hold the development in such a form. If I wished, I could then supplement [it] with a somewhat different point of view—developing under my own stresses, which are usually in terms of what we at times call . . . [cross-section of activity] across the masses of individuals.

One might, in this way, get two formulations, corresponding to "particle" and "wave" presentations, lifted into the behavioral field. The variation between us is certainly that of stress in work, not of knife-slicing down the middle.

One thing I should certainly have in case of need. The names of two or three men whom you would pick to appraise what I did as with your eyes.

I do not mean that I *want* to separate the developments—only that it *might* be safest.

I have found, however, that on practically every suggestion you have made toward (1) above (organism's standpoint), I have recognized it as desirable for me to adopt (certainly at this stage of work, and without prejudice to any possible outcome). On the (2) point (the evidencing), I have noted it as something for which the layout must be kept open, and for you to decide upon.

Sincerely, *Bentley*

181

Paoli, Indiana, October 17, 1943

Dear Dewey:

. . . Following yours of [October] 8th, we get:

"Events" classified into determined and undetermined, and, in another way, into knowing events, non-knowing events. "Knowings"—Determining events. "Facts"—Determinate events; i.e., Events Known. We establish this in an on-going system, centered in organic-environmental situations, as the heavy factual stress of our era. (This you have developed *far* beyond anyone else.) "Fact" is central as transactional. "Events" and "Knowings," stated otherwise than in the factual cores, may drift out endlessly in language, the way she is used, but they don't bother us.

You now distinguished "events" as determinate and as determinant. Distinction recognized by me O.K. (Perhaps "determinant" is too positive, and a near-synonym "determinative" might answer—this just as the use of the word—for "determin*ant*" has a rigorous effect, probably from its mathematical use—too deterministic—where "determinative" is freer.)

As to "description," "fact," "name," "specification," "characterization," I follow you to the last detail. You introduce this "with respect to an event as determinate or fact."

Your next paragraph you introduce: "With reference to an event as a determinant." I cannot follow you. A line of distinction is sharper here than usual (though it has been up before). In the first place it is not "event" simply, but "fact-event" that is a determinant. In the second place this fact-event *as* determinative procedure is heavily on the "knowing side" rather than on the "event" side (that is, in stress, phase, "emphasis," as you wrote it once).

You proceed as follows: (1) You (at least seem to) produce "definition" and "term" in parallel with "specification" and "name." (2) You certainly allot "term" and "definition" a "power" effect in the determinant process which you do not allot "name" and "description." (3) This leads you to combine both processes with respect to "reference." You write, "A Name and Term in operation (as event) is Reference."

Here I have one positive distinction, and a minor question or two. My scheme, as I have been writing it, confines "Reference" to cases of "Name-to-Fact" (or "Event," if we prefer)—i.e., either, optionally we name a fact, or fact itself is event-naming. It does not permit "Reference" to apply to "relation of terms"; or if the word "reference" is used here, it will be the reference of one term to other terms, or, in other words, it will *be* relation, and so should not be used *both* for "name-reference" and for "term-relation." Of course, I don't care about the words we use. The point is the events. I see such a radical difference between the application of "name to fact," and the application of "term to what?" that I must separate them. In the naming case, I make "name" refer to fact. In the "relations-term" case, I make the whole set-up (the system of

182

"terms," the "theory," the "postulation"—any one of these phrasings will apply, as one wishes) to event.

I have a brilliant illustration in geometrical image. The geometer *postulates* ray—nobody anywhere any longer calls *ray* a fact. He then proceeds to *focus*, usually calling it a fact, but I have found two cases which treat focus as *symbol*. All, however, proceed to treat *image* as fact. And Hell pops incoherently. Geometrical image is a collineal projective (geometrical) construction from postulated ray and focus. Make it a name of a fact, and it is chaos. Keep the whole postulatory system, ray-focus-image, all at once symbolic, and apply to research as a whole; then all clears up. Now, on this basis, I want to keep distinctive namings. As I see it, we advance linguistically into namings. We then advance linguistically still into symbolizations. It is higher-power stuff, but not more precise naming. Or rather, it is more precise, and *If* you still call it naming, then it must be made clear that the word "naming" covers two kinds of events (a) application to things, and (b) application to not-things.

I can go all the way with you on your general assertion that every word is a "name." "Inside" and "since" look like namings to me when used in naming schemes. But not when used in relational—let us say, mathematical equational procedure. "One" can be a name. But "one," in one plus one equals two? Is it a name in any such sense? The "infinitesimal" was a desperate effort to establish a "name" in operations of the calculus. It had to be abandoned. A "name" technically, with "technical" reference to a determinate-fact—an infinitesimal, did not work. . . .

If we use the build-up: "sign," "name," "symbol," *then* the differentiation between name and symbol is one of the most important items we have. If so, *Why* use *"reference"* for both cases. . . . I am not saying my procedure here is right—I am only saying, if so, terminology should be sharp.

My guess at your position is that, having developed on the logical side, and having separated the existential and procedural propositions, you hold them together in a sense that the procedural feed directly into the existential. As over against Carnap's irrational severance of syntactics from semantics, you are far superior, of course. As for the present use of "reference" in two fields, and probably as for holding "procedural" subordinate (if I am correct in the "feel" of this), it seems to me your statement is not quite fully developed.

You in the *Logic* use both "judgment" and "language," making your development in terms of "judgment," and indicating its basis in "language." I think I have the advantage of you terminologically here, in consolidating the meanings and sounds in *one* language-logic presentation. (You went as far as anybody could go in your California address

["Context and Thought"] in stressing "word" and "meaning" as one. I have noticed a good many people picking this up—picking up . . . cues of it—but no development. It does develop here—if the procedural-relational becomes an advanced stage of languaging-behavior, splitting itself off from specific reference.)

There, in the last phrase, is one form of solution. One could distinguish "Specific Reference" (Naming Reference) from "Relational Reference." Suits me. But I think, nevertheless, the processes of name and symbol will turn out in the end to have such widely different ranges that no one word should be allowed to bind them too tight. . . .

Best wishes for progress, *Bentley*

Paoli, Indiana, October 18, 1943

Memo to Dewey:

The distinction we are making between "sign" and "symbol" ("name" and "term") is a long further step (possibly a circle-rounding constructive step) in eliminating the control of the putative existential.

The pragmatism of Peirce, James, and you (not [F. C. S.] Schiller) put the business practically in the stream of time. Your *Logic* completed the development, so far as appraisal of all materials and aspects is concerned. It did not sharpen the names. This firming-up of names is what we are now after.

I used "precision" earlier (I think) on the symbol side. "Precision" ought to be retained on the "fact" side—in the precise sense of "precision tools"—far ahead of ordinary procedure, and the very best attainable at a given time.

Concerning the extrapolated "existential reality," which is always a bother—for it puts us in the wrong if we appear to "deny" it, and yet it is incoherent to admit such an "unknown" in control of the "known": My phrasing now says this assertion of the extrapolated existence as a typical linguistic procedure; it is, however, a low-grade linguistic procedure; it is not scientific-linguistic procedure. This latter reaches out a little way, and appraises very carefully what it pulls in, without "big talk." . . .

The threefold arrangement: "Event," "Fact," "Knowing." I see now why I made naming-knowledge, alpha-knowledge, and sign-knowledge beta-knowledge. A threefold arrangement is sound description on the naming level. It is not sound on the sign level, where basically we have not three, but two—organism and environment; and the very value of signing-process is that it handles it thus.

(The old mentalism ran "threes" in everywhere, and Peirce busts on that flaw.) . . .

I suspect that "pattern" laid direct against "event" (twofold, not three)

184

is what we get in "Symbol," after we knock out reference-naming, from the symbolic set-up proper.

We may then—*just possibly*—have an exhibition [of] a broad theoretical scale in which the "trinity" business is limited to the *naming* level (where, notoriously, it both does its good work, and falls into its characteristic errors). Above and below we work organism against environment direct. Neat little shebang if it works. . . .

[*Bentley*]

Paoli, Indiana, October 22, 1943

Memo to Dewey:

Application of our distinction of "name" and "symbol" to my work with "image." My classifications have been set up with a special group for the "symbol" at one end, and with an extension of the word to items more object-like than image-like at the other end, and a large group of confused uses of the word in an intermediate group. I have treated the last two groups as "namings," and I have been doing this all the way along after the earlier sketches. But I have not anywhere near exhausted the analysis. Hardly a week goes by without some fresh stage of analysis. I have just been observing very sharply how the "term" processes over-ride the "name" processes, first building them up, then corrupting them. I shall have to develop a set of factual namings for the various focuses and physical image-processes. At the present time the symbolic, the physical, the physiological (on several levels), and the pictorial-behavioral are all still in tangles. This is merely a note to the effect that the distinction "works," and takes "work" to put through.

[*Bentley*]

New York, November 8, 1943

Dear Bentley:

. . . The enclosed isn't intended as a contribution to terminological statement, save as it may suggest something indirectly. It's a kind of revised development of my *Logic* book in the light of what I've got out of your correspondence and your other writings. A sort of attempt to bring myself more nearly up to date.

Yours, *Dewey*

Jottings—hardly memoranda:

"Knowing"—finding-out, learning, searching.

(A) As interaction of organism-environment, prelinguistic communication, equals learning-*how;* from side of organic factor equals habit as skill, technique; from side of environmental factor, transformation of an

185

excitation into stimulus(?), a "stimulus" being an environmental-organic-interaction in a serially or sequentially ordered interaction-continuum. (What is "habit" as referred to organic factor, is "stimulus" as referred to environmental?)

(B) As behavioral transaction, knowing or learning, finding-out, is inquiry, investigation, re-searching. (Connected with linguistic communication?)

From side of organism, result of finding-out, learning, is wariness, taking account of environmental conditions, giving heed to. From side of agent in transaction, it is a-wareness, perception, apprehension, in its broadest possible sense; sense-perception being an artificially—or analytically—constructed distinction within portion as knowing-knowledge (knowledge-knowing). So-called "rational" perception is also [a] polar distinction in the single transaction of perception, aware—taking notice of, instituted for a purpose. (Linguistic communication required in any transaction involving an end-*in-view,* or "purpose.") Without linguistic communication, "ends" are events as results, outcomes, so-called effects. A possible result when *fore*seen or linguistically present is an end-in-view. What is skill in terms of interaction becomes *method* in transaction . . . finding-out; knowing-how to know.

(C) Admitting, acknowledging, recognizing, is a primary phase of learning both interactional and transactional events. "Taking into account," reckoning, is passive-active; subject-agent; submissive-responding so as to utilize; result phi-knowledge(?). Meaning of "social," cultural???

(D) Communication as transmission?

New York, November 9, 1943

[To Bentley:]

Further about your comments in letter of 10-17.

1. Don't know whether my point in distinguishing "events" as undetermined and determined facts was clear. It was a way of avoiding the objection that everything in our statement is already *within* the scope of knowledge, while, at same time, maintaining that it is potentially, though not in actualization, within its scope or range. In other words, leaving room for knowing as learning, finding out what *was* unknown for inquiry and knowledge as *its* issue. Whether "determine" is the best word, I don't know; unfortunately, it seems to link up with "term" at the expense of "name." A *going* concern (intrinsically going, not accidentally or from some outside cause) is, I think, the basic fact.

2. It was careless on my part to mention "event" as determinative (I abandon "determinant" for reason previously stated); you are, of course, right. Only a determinate event, or fact, can be determinative; I tend to be elliptical often when I should state the transactional fact.

3. In connection with "name" and "term" and "reference," I've already said I got mixed up. What (I fancy) was in the back of my head is that application in reference and relation have both to be seen as themselves *events*, that knowing (research, inquiry, examination, and whatever) are events (capable of and *requiring* specification? determination? as facts) having to do with, concerned with, other events. Likely, this sounds confused. But to get a smooth-running, going-affair, it seems to me, there must be specific recognition of knowing as an *event* in connection with other events. My confusion in making relation a case of reference was due, I think, to transferring what holds of *connection of events* over to events as known or fact. In consequence, the only genuine point was badly mangled, namely, that knowing is itself an event in specifiable, describable connection with other events. Incidentally, this point may help in getting away from a prior *existential* "mental" and "mind," and in describing, as far as statement is needed, the latter in terms of search—research-events. Anyway, I agree fully with your comments in criticism of what I said in my earlier letter.

4. Perhaps, the significant point in treating both the naming and symbolizing phases of knowing as events is that it links up with the distinction and connection of "sense" perception and "rational" perception, and enables symbolization to be located as a definite kind of event, one in which a connection is treated as a possibility, serving thereby as a hypothesis or theory in direction of further inquiry. *Some* unnamed connections are indicated and postulated in the short period, narrow extent of "sense" perception; as an objective of *inquiry*, a symbol functions in the search for some thing involved in, but not named in, the immediate subjectmatter of sense. "Language" as symbol stands for a *possible* connection in a way capable of specification, and that directs search for a connection as fact. (This "4" is just part of my effort to bring statements in my *Logic* into line.)

5. I have been speculating (somewhat idly) on "telling" and "saying" as forms of linguistic communication. In the terminology of my *Logic* (see p. 120) "telling" links up with assertion; "saying" with affirmation. Language as "saying" is a kind of tentative doing-behavior that enables knowing-behavior to get outside of what we already have effected in knowing, and this is a condition of directed inquiry or research. It seems to point out one important connection of language and knowing.

Where I say (p. 120) "direct existential," translate to "direct reference."

I agree that "existential" is a dangerous word to use; too suggestive of prior independent "reality." But literally "ex-istence" is allied to "e-vent," the latter word stresses "coming out of" . . . an "event"—"ex-istence" emphasizes *standing-out*, so as to be distinguishable.

This is not an argument for using the word. The "philosophical"

187

usage has got too far away from the idiomatic. In the latter, "exist" is usually synonymous with "occur," as accessible to perception—"extant."

[*Dewey*]

Paoli, Indiana, November 11, 1943

Dear Dewey:

. . . About the only thing I don't like in your professional career is the number of re-publications of essays, *undated*, in your volumes. I always want to know when anything was published *so* I can reconstruct the audience better. Your "Naturalistic Theory of [Sense] Perception" [Originally "The Naturalistic Theory of Perception by the Senses"] in *Philosophy and Civilization* is something, so far as I know, I never saw before. I should suspect it as about 1910–1912,* or at any rate a footnote would indicate that. Where you use illustrations from vision, your attitude is very close to what I demonstrate in detail in the "image" papers—especially as regards the "where," the *situs*. I have included reference to [the] "Reflex Arc" paper in the image development, and now add this. If there is any technical understanding of "where," in this sense, in any psychological work, I have never observed it. I wonder if you would restate to me in a couple [of] sentences the introductory oppositions—and in a paragraph, the positive affirmation as to sense-object-existence.

Here is a better form of request. How would you feel about taking the two old papers, "Reflex Arc" [and] "Naturalistic Theory of Sense Perception" (and possibly the [Carl A. Murchison, ed.,] *Psychologies of 1930* ["Conduct and Experience"], which I have not checked yet), disregarding the philosopher problems, and writing a straight factual statement, up to date, including the factual base of our terminology? Address it straight to me, and as compact as you think I can stand? I would like to see it. I can supply a developmental hint as background (not for use in such a paper). You reduced the creaks in the mechanism in 1896. You had "*inter*action" and "field" and "interactor" in 1910(?) [1925] perception paper. You stated "transaction" in the 1930 paper. You had a full system statement, as I recall, in the opening pages of the [*Essays in*] *Experimental Logic* [1916]. You have the investigation of all the logical labyrinth in the *Logic*. And you have a pretty good demonstration of distortion in such items as [essays by] Mackay, Rice, Sisson, and Brotherston. You also have all along the way snapshots at *word-meaning* as one behavior, not [as] separate branches of research. But you have not utilized this last systematically. If you care to write such a paper (as I said, not for philosophers) in straight naturalistic organism-

* The actual date is 1925. (Eds.)

environment-evolvement formulation, I think it would carry us a long way forward. . . .

You have a better statement of "sign" [in] *Philosophy and Civilization,* p. 197, than [I] ever can hope to get. . . .

I want to get a matching and organization of your "experience" (older use) and "experiencing" (1930 use) of the act of experiencing at the organism-end, and the content at the outside-end; your custom, that is— over against my tendency to seek a cross-[sectional] statement for the organism-environment situation. My business makes sense to me from some approaches, and not from others. It seems to me we ought to be able to spread out an organism and environment, and carve it up. We both of us, in agreement with James, leave out the "intervening" item. We both have a biological view (your word "biological," I come to find better than the "physiological" I have been using). There ought to be a chance for definitely corresponding observation and naming.

The essay "Conduct and Experience" as you have it in *Philosophy and Civilization* does not seem to me to have all the stuff I recall in the way it appeared in *Psychologies of 1930.* In other words, there was some personal psychology development in the first form that seemed to me divergent from the main thesis, and that I do not note as I go over it now, although you endorse it in the form of "life-career or individualized activities" (p. 257). Note here, however, that you wind up [p. 270] with an endorsement of C. I. Lewis on conscious*ness;* something you have been arguing against. The passage you quote seems to me to destroy "system," tolerates the thing-kind of "emergence," and while denying substance, substitutes something else like it (all except in name) to take its place. . . .

As this paper ["Conduct and Experience in Psychology"] stands—and I skip through it again—I cannot tell how far you would maintain—just taking this paper by itself—a distinction between "conduct" and "experience," the latter in the sense of "experienc*ing.*" P. 269: "Some modes of behavior have distinctive qualities, which have consequences with distinctive properties, and, in virtue of the distinctive properties of the consequences, are to be termed mental and conscious." * That is a little tough (as I have paraphrased it) on the innocent bystander. I don't believe, however, there is anything in this to cause difficulty, since both forms of expression are biological activities. And in what sense the experience differs from the conduct-*ing* at this stage is not important to us.

That development of the "where" in the "Sense Perception" [essay] is a corker. Does not the whole paper come awfully close to a literal

* The exact quotation is: ". . . some modes of behavior have distinctive qualities which, in virtue of the distinctive properties of the consequences of these acts, are to be termed mental and conscious." (Eds.)

factual development of what James made a terrific jump at in the form of "neutral" datum? Do you not lo*cate* the facts neutrally? . . .

Regards, Bentley

Indianapolis, Indiana, November 18, 1943

Dear Dewey:

   . . . I noticed [in the *Logic*] also your use of "integration," around pp. 33–34, as a stronger form of "interaction"; and it struck me that, in a way, my tendency is to start with the stressed "integration" in the *neutral* sense, and that this sort of start is about what my continual insistence on direct observation of the situation amounts to. You have quite a number of stages between independent items through necessary interaction, with the stress on the "inter" up to integration and transaction. I do not mean here to confuse my use of "situation" with yours of "integration." I only note that when your statement attains to integration, that distinction of ways of approach is less marked. . . .

Regards, Bentley

New York, December 16, 1943

Dear Bentley:

   . . . The thing I was laboring about in our conversation is linked up, I see now, with "signal," and I think when I am a little more myself, I can state it. Then there is a question about "sign." Does it stand
$$\begin{cases} \text{signal} \\ \text{symbol} \end{cases} ?$$
It has occurred to me that "de-signation" may be a handy word somewhere. . . .

Yours, Dewey

New York, December 17, 1943

[To Bentley:]

   . . . The point I wanted a little help of expansion on is "a changing of the use of the names": sign and symbol. I take it the change is to signal-symbol, with sign as wider, but want to be sure.

Yours, Dewey

Indianapolis, Indiana, December 21, 1943

Dear Dewey:

   . . . One thing I want to put up to you strong for your decision. This is the word:

190

"Fact." Look over your *Logic*, consider the use of the word "fact" there and elsewhere in your texts. Ask whether the word "fact" cannot cover the entire range from indeterminate situation to warranted assertion —in other words, the entire range of *inquiry*—which is probably about the same range as that of *naming-speech*.

In this way "Fact" would be something-known-as-known, in such a way (1) that it was not an interaction of a knowing and a known, but a transaction, and (2) did not imply anything "real," either in the subject or object direction; the "reals" being eliminated altogether.

To use it thus, I would hold "fact" primarily to this region of naming-knowing, and would not let it run either to the perception or the mathematical-symbol level. In other words, I would not (to start with) say that earth was *fact* to an earthworm, or that infinite-dimensioned space was fact to Einstein; but that dogs were facts to men, etc.

Now suppose I use "exist" in the sense of your recent note as "identifiable occurrence" in place of "event" for a particular case of "exist." I would then have "exist" (in fact) and "name" (in fact) as equivalents of "the known" and "the knowing."

This procedure requires a full durational inspection as on-going activity, so that fact is not merely "named by me now," but the durational growth and forecast, and the spatial extension across cosmos, all held together linguistically, where language is full durational behavior itself.

We would then have: "Exist": in various concentrations of inspection (your word is "focusing," and it goes fine here), such as "situation," "event," "object."

"Naming": as a central evolutionary stage in "Sign" (if this proves the best word to use), with the earlier stage of "Signal" (covering perception or Pavlov's conditioned response) and a more subtle stage in "Symbol" (mathematical, etc.). (I mean to make "Sign" the widest term here, and "Signal," "Name," and "Symbol" the three stages of increasing subtlety.)

"Reality": totally, completely, and forever eliminated as child's play with words.

The big preliminary question here is: Will This Use of the Word "Fact" Square with Your *Logic?*

With regard to the words "Signal," "Name," and "Symbol," we have had a few tentative agreements, such as: that naming is good, sound process, and there is no sense in refusing to call it by its own name, and pretending to improve its status by subsuming it under "sign"; and to say that naming *is* itself knowing, right on the spot, and not as incidental tool of some mysterious upstage "knower," is an improvement.

If we take this position, then we recognize that, as an earlier stage, both historically in animal life, and as "simpler" or "more direct" in our own everyday affairs, we have perception which is a "cue" process, with stages

191

of gesture, say, between seeing and naming. Also, as a more subtle use of language where the direct name-work of the word is stripped off and a symbolic system established, we have mathematical process, etc. Call the two stages "Signal," and "Symbol," with "Name" in between; and we have the word "Sign" (if we wish) for the whole cue-business all the way up.

Another thing this requires is elimination of the artificial, conventional distinction between perceiving (as sense or mind) and action as bodily. Seeing is as much action as running. Running involves a perceiving just as seeing involves an acting.

Also, your suggestion of the organism's straining—striving-trying-manipulating (you thought I had a word for it, and I think you have the word somewhere) probably matches the "signal" range. At any rate, one form of development that comes naturally (and I suspect the name-behaviors is [sic] bound to dominate in a behavioral theory of language) will place the name-behaviors over against the manipulating-behaviors, as representing them. Which is to say: *If* I make behavior [a] transactional inclusion of environment and organism; *If* I make both the striving-producing behaviors and the naming-representing behaviors forms of such transactional behavior; *Then* the namings fit onto the strivings, all in one sweet system.

Just how "symbol" develops best, I don't know, but it seems to me the *fact* is overwhelmingly present that, when you develop number-theory as in mathematical induction, "one" and "two" are not names of some special existing "oneness" and "twoness" in the manipulating region, but they are components of a system which, when applied as a whole (i.e., two and two make four, and to hell with anything else), works wonderfully. . . .

"De-sign-ation" is a damn good word, with "sign" in the middle of it. But here "sign" seems equivalent to "name." At least, I do not envisage "designation" except in the range of namings. I have used in my texts "specification" for a name as collateral to "definition" for a "term." Then I have used "reference" of the name to the existence (that is, of the name-in-fact to the existence-in-fact . . . taking "reference" from your *Logic* scheme, p. 55). "Designation" would not do for the general layout: "signal—sign—symbol"; and it is a little too much like the act of the designator; I seem to prefer "specification" as more "transactional." Goody; there is not a bad hint; if we can pick all our main terms for their "transactional" feel, and build up a transactionality to replace the old (external) objectivity, it will be interesting. . . .

"Connection" would hold as within "existence-in-fact"; "reference" from "naming-in-fact" to "existing-in-fact"; and "relation" would be within language with "reference" cut off (but there is a lot to develop here for firm statement). As for the "sign-symbol" scheme as compared

192

with that of your *Logic,* you do not keep a steady differentiation between "sign" and "symbol," or between the referring and relating processes of language. In other words, the *Logic* covering a long period, and involving progress all through, has not yet got the "sign-symbol-signal" terminology in a (consistently) maintained form. I am *not* saying that the layout I have made is right, nor the naming, but this is a region in which some change in the terminology of the central chapters of your *Logic* will be necessary, because we have got to get the thing *sharp* one way or the other. This, incidentally, so far as I know, is the only place in the *Logic* that an express alteration of terminology will be required. . . .

Suppose we should say that you and I undertake to secure for our personal use a set of names to which we can supply accurate specifications, and which, if we are satisfied, we will undertake to try out. One trouble is that one would have to provide a set of postulates within which to proceed. Or, could one introduce all this material also in "names"(?). Another trouble is that almost every word used in the specifications would itself require specification within the framework. I have been writing as if to an audience, and have repeatedly changed my type of audience and type of address. It gets more muddled all the time.

I believe I will try this. Set down some names; give them specifications; get a lot of them; let it appear in time whether they can get organized; find out in the end what dicta have to be introduced, what goats set apart from what sheep. Maybe, you will feel like picking up some central names this way before long; and certainly, when we get far enough along to include the logical names, it will all be up to you.

Regards, *Bentley*

Indianapolis, Indiana, December 24, 1943

Dear Dewey:

. . . I happened to note *re* "excitation," "stimulus," "reaction," "response," that as *inter*action, "excitation" (or stimulus) and "reaction" go well together. But as *trans*action, it makes no sense to set up "stimulus-object" and "organism-response" over against each other prior to giving them secondary status. . . .

Regards, *Bentley*

New York, December 27, 1943

Dear Bentley:

. . . I want to say this as strong as I can make it. I am not stuck on anything in the *Logic*—certainly [not] on its vocabulary. My own development was slow and tentative. I can claim only that I never permitted pride in what I had written in the past to slow it up. In fact, I rarely look at what I've written in the past. When I do, it's for some special reason, and when I find something that I still like and hold to, I'm tickled stiff. And I worked my way along largely by means of habits formed in lecturing to a class—trying different modes of statement, if, by the grace of God, I might hit some, and save 'em from philosophical perdition. So this correspondence with you has been the first conscious, serious effort I *ever* made to get a firm terminology. So, there is really no big question as to whether what you say (as in yours of [December] 21st) squares with my *Logic*, or not. I'll be glad to make a fresh start whenever it helps. . . .

Yours, Dewey

New York, December 29, 1943

Dear Bentley:

I have no confidence in my ability *re* terminology. If I can do anything much, it will be in the line of mentioning some background considerations that may have a bearing on the matter of terminology.

I. "Perceptive-manipulative," "naming," "symbolizing" (mathematizing), with recognition (1) that seeing, hearing, etc., are just as much bodily acts (which are always inter-actions with some environmental conditions) as are so-called reactions to them, and (2) recognition of the *spatial-temporal continuum*, in which bodily environmental conditions *directly* involved in (or constituting?) here-and-now interactions, is, I think, the sound and firm point of departure. (It gets wholly rid of the disjointed "sensori-motor" business.)

In this connection, either "perceptual-manipulative" should always be used as a single expression, or some other device should be found to avoid ambiguity and make clear the difference between it and the perceiving that involves naming, and which (for the purpose of present identification, but *not* for the terminology) I'll call "reflective." Perhaps, calling the latter "observation" and maintaining a sharp distinction between "perception" and "observation" will do the trick. (According to Murray [*Oxford English Dictionary*] observation is noting, remarking—both imply language—and, scientifically, is "carefully watching and noting"—the watching being comprised, of course, in the perceptive-manipulative—*in respect to the connections* of what is observed. The dictionary wording is "noting a phenomenon *in regard to* its cause or effect or of phenomena *in regard to* their mutual relations"—and adds the silly statement, "these being observed as they occur in nature, and so opposed to experiment" as if experimentally observed events don't "occur in nature.") In short, the difference between the "perceptive-manipulative"

194

and "perceiving-with-naming" lies in their different behavioral setting and consequences. . . .

II. Yours of 12-21-43 *re fact*. I think "Fact" as covering the entire inquiry-range is 100% right—whether I live up to it in my *Logic* or not— for indeterminateness is *determinately* a *fact* in respect to inquiry-operations. The distinction to be made is *not* between the determinate as fact and the indeterminate as something else. When we *name* signaling, the perceptive-manipulative, they, of course, are facts. And this is as an aspect of the circular-continuum which eliminates completely the "reality-mind" business. (Only as themselves named are the perceptive-manipulative "facts," but *as named,* they are facts.) This, I take it, is the holding-off, in and for examination, inquiry, that goes by the name "objectification"—which, probably, we don't need to use unless to explain that it is holding at arm's length for purposes of observation. (I forgot to mention *re* "observation" that the earlier usage is "observance," the action or practice of *keeping,* or paying attention to, a command, law, ceremony, set time, etc., giving heed to—certainly a behavioral transaction.) [Fact is] comprised in the ongoing "circular" temporal-spatial situation, with its elimination of mind-reality, . . . [the] moment, what is not *directly* in the subjectmatter of inquiry is *named* in that particular capacity or respect, [or] regard, it is [a] fact that (1) there is such subjectmatter, and (2) that it is connected, linked up [with] what focally and directly is the subject ("object") of inquiry. The postulate is that what is observed, is linked with what is not observed, or even observable at the time—or that there is nothing inherently non-observable. . . .

III. This links up with the short-span, here-now phase of knowing (naming) in its distinction from the longer and wider space-time continuum. In all naming whatever (as distinct, say, from symbolizing behavior), there is a *this* (proper-noun linguistically) phase: (1) "Specification" or "particularization" in the old logical terminology aspect, and (2) an aspect of indefinite spatial-temporal extension. And, "and" here doesn't mean "added on," but something that must be expressed hyphenatedly, although one or other aspect of the indivisible subjectmatter may be emphatically uppermost. In the old logical vocabulary, there is "particular-general," not particular *and* general. The twofold import of "and" is mentioned in a technical way on p. 338 of my *Logic.*

Naming specifies—generalizes—proper-common names—at every stroke, where, of course, "proper" includes *this, that, here-now,* and not merely Bill Smith and New York City. There are two "that's," very different in import. According to Murray [*Oxford English Dictionary*], the original "that" was the one which introduces a relative clause, and was akin to "the"; its use as a demonstrative was later. What is more interesting is that "this-these" was etymologically formed by adding a particle signifying "lo, behold." The perceptive-manipulative must deal with what

195

is here-now; it carries over into observational naming, while its significance in the latter is transformed by intrinsic reference, regard, respect, to connections in the durational-extensive ongoing continuum without which demonstratives and proper nouns are nonsense. In so far I was right in my treatment in the *Logic* (for example, pp. 125–26, 437–38 and under "this" in Index), though if I [were] writing now, the mode of statement would be simpler. At least, for our purpose no reference to "judgment," "subject-predicate," is needed.

I think there is an important point in what is said in the previous paragraph about the necessity of hyphenating "specification" with a correlative word indicating the intrinsic connection of what is specified, though the wording isn't the best possible. . . .

Yours, Dewey

Part III

Letters: January 5, 1944–December 27, 1944

Paoli, Indiana, January 5, 1944

Dear Dewey:

. . . You tend to set up terms interactionally on the organic end. I tend to set up transactionally. Both are needed. We match then:

My	Your
Signal	Perceptive Manipulative Action
Name	Observation
Symbol	Symbolization

Your two points, perception is action, and all is in spatial-temporal frame of observability—I fully accept. The matching of observation with naming seems to me like an extra fine point to use. Also, I can see we need a different name for Perception, with the full activity included in the name.

Of course, below "signal," I have the whole physiological process—tropistic—using your word "excitation." . . .

I am only using "specification" for the verbal account of the application of a name. On the "existence" side, I am shortly introducing "situation," "event," and "object" as a first stab at the "what is specified" organization.

Regards, *Bentley*

Paoli, Indiana, January 10, 1944

Dear Dewey:

. . . "Designation." Your recent suggestion. It suddenly struck me today that the word might fill the place in which I have used "naming" opposite existence within fact. It took time to soak through. Maybe, it will. It prevents an awkward multiple introduction of "name." It does not seem to me today to be over-organism in its stress, as I first felt it.

"Accuracy." "Precision." Probably, go pretty well to correspond with name and term.

"Factually behavior does not so exist" is a sentence I wrote, where "so" meant as "intra-organism" fact. It then struck me the sentence held closely to the terminology proposed as to "fact," "exist," etc. And, interestingly, it makes the *adverb* the strongest word, as you have several times said it should be. . . .

About the aspectual . . . (after the old style of particular-general) from "specification into cosmic connection," I do not quite see the point as to "correlative word" at the moment. I do see very strongly . . . that it must be clearly shown where "specifying," "naming," or it might be "designing," is introduced, that this is a stressed *inter*-act within a *trans*-act. My text may have failed to stress this—that naming is a limitation. But, by doggie, we have "naming" and "existence" balanced, so that limiting "naming" limits "existence" just where we want it limited. The procedure [does] at times—or is beginning to be able to—"make hay." This is when it looks good to me. When I reflect on how thorough it ought to be and how complete before it hatches, and how much it must cover, then is when I get scared, and write letters. . . .

Regards, *Bentley*

Paoli, Indiana, January 15, 1944

Dear Dewey:

. . . It may be that "Event" can be put back into the terminology in place of "Existence," making the basic scheme: "Fact," "Event," "Designation." . . .

We then have: "Fact" falling as actually into event and designation; "Event" spreading spectrum-like from "Situation" to "Object"; "Designation" represented by "Naming" as a central stage in the levels Signal, Name, Symbol (central both as stage of evolution, and as type of process), where "signal" is in general perceptual and "symbol" in general mathematical. . . .

The above suggestion has the peculiar effect of making the "fact-existence" couple do over again in a different way what the "name-event" couple does. But, maybe, this is not so bad. Thus:

Fact

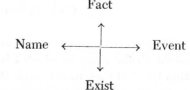

Exist

Yet, how describe what you are doing after you have done it? Does one name an event? And assert factually its existence?

Regards, *Bentley*

Paoli, Indiana, January 19, 1944

Dear Dewey:

"Hard fact." I take it this is sufficiently allowed for both in your *Logic*'s development, and in our scheme. If "hard fact" is not absolute monarch over all other approximations, then the business is "factual" under present approach, all the way from any indeterminate to any determinate. But it may be desirable to have a "name" in "fact" form, in addition to one in assertibility.

"Raw" or "brute fact." I take it this gets covered by bringing the "signaling" into system with the "naming"-perception as earlier sign, followed by "naming" as later sign, with "symbol" still later as higher-powered function. However, as concerns "Hard Fact," we can exhibit your *Logic*; we cannot help out "Raw Fact" in this way, as my construction holding the stages together has not yet been published (and will not be for a couple [of] years at best). This will probably need more characterization.

"Symbol." I have frequently said that the "sign-symbol" arrangement was the one important change of terminology from the *Logic*. Maybe, this is not necessary. I have been using "symbol" for the term-relation procedure as opposed to the naming procedure with "reference." But, as I write along, I seem to have no need for "symbol" when I have once set up "term" and "name" in contrast. Further, "symbol" is one of the [most] mixed-up words we have around, and by that test should perhaps be tossed overboard like "experience" and "epistemology."

Later. I am not so sure. As I go on writing, I find places where I just got to (at present) say "symbol." One possibility would be to adopt "symbol," force it in here, and assign "term" to a specialized linguistic-logical use, coupled with "proposition," etc.

Bentley

Miami Beach, Florida, January 20, 1944

Dear Bentley:

. . . A rewritten *Logic* isn't a bad idea; I could certainly do a much better job now, and cut out a lot beside—or as part of doing a better job.

Here is one general idea before I get down in a few days to any specific contribution. It ought to be possible to get a statement after, and upon, which as background we could speak, when needful, of *a* knower and *a* knowing without danger of being [mis]understood. The background is the distinction and connection of the here-now and the connective aspects of *every* event. The events named as sunset fact are indefinitely long temporarily and broad and deep spatially. But the entire complex focuses or centers particularly [on], and in, an unbroken succession of heres-nows. Same with any, and every, other event. If we can get a clear statement of this point, much clearer than what I just set down, there would be no embarrassment or danger of misunderstanding, barring [those] . . . who will misunderstand anything, in speaking of John Smith as knower in a specified knowing-event, that is, there is nothing peculiar or unique. It is a specific case of the universal fact that every event can be named only as an indefinite spectrum, spatially-temporally, with a locus, or focus, or centering, of its own. There is nothing more peculiar in the existing of John Smith as a knower than of electricity as a flash, and of John's knowing a particular dog than of the flash in question being one that strikes a particular tree. I think if we can get this point stated properly, it will do as much to get rid of the mind-reality "Concept" as anything. It will help remove the apparent need for it, if we can show that what goes by that name is just a special case of a universal fact. It will line up with the description of the sense-perception-rational distinction-connection; placing the first as the here-now focusing and the indefinitely extending aspects of the same fact. I think the world [of scholars] can be safely defied to name a case of naming "this" [that] doesn't have "this" and a range of connected events as its own indivisible aspects. While the aspects are indivisible, they are distinguishable. So-called scientific naming selects and emphasizes the connectives, so that in the case of water as H_2O, [and] as what we drink and bathe in, it takes a special training (learning another language) to know they name the same fact. But the first names *this* water, leaving the wateriness as such in abeyance, and [the second] . . . leaves the "this" in [this-water in] abeyance. Maybe, I overview the importance of this affair because it has been such a fundamental problem of the whole modern *philosophy* of knowledge.

Yours, *Dewey*

Miami Beach, Florida, January 20, 1944

Dear Bentley:

. . . I think "event" is a better basic word than "existence"; "e-vent" [is derived from, and conveys the sense of, its Latin root]: comes out of and goes into; "ex-istence": sticks out, stands out—like that part of an iceberg above water; it's, so to speak, a more static word and seems (though this is just my feeling) to emphasize especially the directly perceptible aspect of an event. . . .

Yours, *Dewey*

Seattle, Washington, January 27, 1944

Dear Dewey:

I got a chance . . . to go over part of your letters. . . . Your interaction-continuum builds up transaction, for example. Your full discussion of the uses of "reference" may result in considerable rearrangement of terms later on. . . .

Also, I think, I see better what has bothered me, and caused me to write fearfully at times. I have been sharper than you in asserting

202

transaction to be "a" thing. It queers other people with my work. If I have gone too far, I am washed up. And I have not wanted to involve you, just by the flowing of the stream, so to speak, in the portions in which I may be out too far on the limb. But you have been just as far out on the limb, and indeed much more broadly, except in specific naming; so, I am going to stop bothering.

The "Fact" terminology helps greatly. If "Fact" is transactionally stated, if we can present "Event" and "Designation" as differentiations that can be viewed as in interaction, the first as environmental and the latter as organic—if we can then justify this differentiation as "aspectual," rather than as "thing-emergence"—we have a good, clear presentation. . . .

Regards, Bentley

Seattle, Washington, January 27, 1944

Dear Dewey:

. . . The point between the long-time and the here-now, I simply don't get. . . . You have had it up before, and I have it noted to examine later. Possibly the reason is you are facing it (according to our cooperatively established way) on the organism side, and I on the full factual-transactional-so-designated.

As I am building [it] . . . the naming *is* the knowing—that is, it is *the* knowing we are working on. (Your old proposition about it isn't a word unless it has a meaning—word and meaning are one—is what this comes to.) Now [the] word "water" vibrates through me a million [other uses], no two fully alike. Word "H_2O," direct or implicit substitute for word "water," vibrates through [a] limited number with slight overflow at high-school levels. It is all one doing, one knowing, so far as I am concerned. And this, because I do not have *your audience* to adapt myself to. Frankly, I do not see why the *connectives* are more connectivious in one case than in another. . . . We are agreed that perceiving takes build-up and naming, and simple-water-naming has less build-up than H_2O naming. In other words, conversion of knowing into naming and conversion of naming into upper-signing (i.e., signing above signaling, but below symboling) wipes out the issue for me, if I get the issue properly. (Of course, all knowing is not converted into naming, but that does not affect the kind we are studying under such conversion.) . . .

If you [are] building object out of situation logically (and, of course, set in a sub-cellar of similar building), then the here-now and the connectives are not different. If I proceed by saying that I *never* see an object, but *always* work through clues or cues (and this is commonest common sense, since no one ever saw all-an-apple at once, but only

203

hints), then what is the distinction as to connectives? . . . Why maintain the separation of connectives? . . . [when] the full layout handles it. . . .

To your express question as to how to speak of *a* knower and *a* knowing without being misunderstood, I would answer: speak of them as *an* organism and *a* naming in the present set-up—*Subject* to your telling me whether I am getting the point.

Regards, *Bentley*

Seattle, Washington, January 28, 1944

Dear Dewey:

You are in favor of grouping sciences as "Physical," "Biological," and "Behavioral." I sometimes start to do this, but always find myself working as "Physical," "Physiological," "Behavioral."

It strikes me the reason is that physiological and behavioral are *both* biological, and that when technical methods of inquiry are at issue, the technique is physiological, and the word "biological" is too broad and covers too many kinds of treatment. How about it?

Regards, *Bentley*

Seattle, Washington, January 29, 1944

[To Dewey:]

. . . This issue of "Fact" and "Event" is, of course, not one of true or false, but, in this particular case, of the way the terminology is set up.

(a) I suggest "Fact" as "event-designated." You, on the contrary, in this particular inspection make "Fact" as "event *definitely* designated," and "Event" as "fact taken in *process* of determination."

(b) You incline heavily to "fact" as "hard" for your basic use. I incline to "factuality" as expressive of name-knowing-procedure, however feebly begun, and all the way up.

(c) If you can reach hard fact (warranted assertion) that will *stay* hard (warranted) forever (or for a good, long time), then your use of "fact" is probably the most significant use. I, however, assert that, in an age when the Newtonian space, time, and particle have proved inadequately factual, your stress on the "hard" is not dependable. This is an age of "close approximations to" and not "certainty of." . . .

I cannot recognize "transition from interactional to transactional."

To me it is the other way around. Being given the transactional (i.e., this being our richest statement), we secure the interactional as an ancillary procedure of less richness.

Use the interactional technique to the limit, but always interpret results (or reinterpret) transactionally. . . .

Regards, *Bentley*

204

Dear Dewey:

"Real." You have had radical trouble with statement here for thirty years or more—I recall passages, I think, in [the] James Memorial volume ["Does Reality Possess Practical Character?"]. In the good sense you stress reality, actuality, as heavily as anyone. Rejecting it in the bad sense, you at once fear . . . that you will be subject to attack as idealistic. You, therefore, hedge. Hedging has brought no fruit. I am against any more of it.

The procedure here, I think, is to separate the duplex uses of the word so thoroughly (and largely by enumeration) that "word-flicker" on the reader's part will be reduced to a minimum.

"Real" [in] *Bad Sense.* Reject substance, substrate, absolute, and every use of "existence" which supplies a presence asserted as ultra-spatially-real, or ultra-temporally-real; in short all hypostatizations. . . .

"Real" [in] *Good Sense.* Retain all the actuality there is in descriptions in space and time for what they are worth. Make them take the place of the "real" (bad sense). . . .

"Exist" and "Event." While "existence" can be retained for "real" in the good sense, we both are agreed that "event" is better. "Existence" can then be made applicable to event, or otherwise modified as desired.

"Fact" and "Event." We may postulate either:

(a) a flow of events (nature), (existent), with respect to which certain included events (organic-biological) and the use of language in inquiry, establish Factuality (Warranted Assertion) as to certain candidates for existential-event-status. (This is in effect the way you work it out.) . . .

Or (b) a range of existential-assertion (factuality) (named-events), with respect to which the "range of events" (a preceding) is aspectual, and, likewise, the naming-behaviors (organic), and so that (aa) while the range of events is subordinate aspectually to factual assertion, nevertheless, (bb) this very factual assertion (naming) has status only as one stage in the "range of events"—the earlier (lower) being perception-actional-responding (signal), and the later (higher) being symbol-relation-mathematicising; leaving Designating (existential—factual) as the mould, and (c) this situation being the characteristic form that Circularity takes in our type of construction.

Now, for our *most general* purposes, I hold that *my* postulation (if I am right about its form) is superior to yours, because it (as it seems to me) is *trans*actional whereas yours becomes *inter*actional, and we want the interactional secondary to the transactional.

I could go so far as to say that your procedure . . . that "Fact" is the firm outcome from Event retains something of the extra-knowledge, old-time "real." . . .

None of the above argument is primarily concerned with the assignments given the words "Fact," "Event," and "Existence," in our present project. It has to do with the materials to be named. I think in the choice of names I am entirely controlled by your own comments and approvals.

If "Fact" is to be the outcome of inquiry by the organism upon the Events (cosmos), then it is the organism's report, and a product of interaction, and Events "exist" in some sense behind "fact."

If "Event" (cosmos-as-we-know-it) is to be the outcome of factual research, it . . . retains a certain flavor (I would think) of the older "real."

It is to be understood, Of Course, that making Fact top-postulate, instead of Event, is not to make "everything" take the form of name-using-existential-assertion. You have frequently pointed it out. The toad hops into a tree or eats a bug, without saying "Lo, a bug"—in older phrase, without being "conscious" as a matter-of-fact about entomology. Mathematics does not have to assert existence, but it "gets there just the same"—more entomological reminiscence.

In Event "namings" and existence-assertions are placed (dated).

But Event *in toto* is linguistic-factual set-up, and so *in toto* to be appraised.

Regards, Bentley

Miami Beach, Florida, January 30, 1944

Dear Bentley:

. . . I am not sure I know what you mean by "Transaction" as "*a* thing." Apparently, you mean more than that *a* thing and thing*s* are transactional. I get it from that end, and probably would get it from the way you say it, if I knew just what is meant.

I think the difference in our approach, the one which has made me select and overemphasize the organic-environment aspect, is that I have been interested in the method of inquiry as the means of attaining knowledge in its "eulogistic" sense—that is, assertible—the sense in which I have used the word "logical." You have taken up the whole background, getting "knowledge" in all its senses as event-facts (errors, false beliefs, mere opinions, etc.) back into their common and inclusive setting. This is the way it should be, for the differentiation I have been interested in making falls within this total context. But, aside from being interested in this particular question, I have never known enough scientific subject-matter to tackle the question from this wider and deeper approach.

Making the distinction between "reference" and "connection" names is just one of my wobbles and is properly disregarded. All words, including propositions, are namings, and the difference in the latter that

can properly be made, is not in them as namings, but in *what* they name—
as much so as in the case of the names "cat" and "dog." . . .

Yours, with regards, *Dewey*

Miami Beach, Florida, February 1, 1944

Dear Bentley:
 . . . The trouble with my contribution to this terminological-nomen-
clature business is that what you write stimulates me to go over my previous position and try to bring it up nearer to date, so that much of what
I write is more pertinent to revision of my own previous views than it is
to the work in hand. I only hope some of it will be useful as background
—but, for heaven's sake, don't pay attention to it when it doesn't fit in
fairly directly. . . .

Yours, with best regards, *J. Dewey*

Miami Beach, Florida, February 1, 1944

[To Bentley:]
Comments—mostly by way of getting my own background cleared up:
 . . . Of organism-environment, in connection with knowing.
 1. Organism-Environment "Interaction" is a distinction-connection *in*
knowledge. That is, the facts to which the names Environment, Organism, and Interaction apply are facts in and of knowledge. There is no
knowledge of organism and environment [as first] separate from each
other, and *then* interacting; they are known *as* interacting.
 2. Organism, Environment, and Interaction can each be inquired into
in specified, here-and-now cases in temporary detachment. The common
mistake of regarding Organism and Environment as separate things,
sometimes happening to interact with each other, is due to supposing
that, because the processes of the organism can be studied *in special
cases*, such as blood circulation, muscular contractions, etc., food digestion, by themselves; therefore, what holds in special instances can be
carried over to Organism in general, or as such. Actually, even in special
cases, interaction with Environment conditions is involved, very directly,
in breathing, walking, taking food (birds flying, fish in water), and the
same holds of cases cited above, save slightly less directly.
 3. Moreover, only by temporary detachment for purpose of inquiry-
knowing *in process*, can ability to regulate, direct, [and] utilize interactions be achieved. That is, there are the cases in which modifications
taking place in time in Organism and Environment constitute simply
the next Interaction in time. Then, there are the cases in which modifications of some processes in Organism are produced for the sake of producing some modifications in Environment-conditions, with a view to

207

the modification of subsequent Interactions thus effected. (Example, any use of tools.) I am afraid this isn't stated clearly enough to be clear in meaning. But it's a generalized statement . . . about my tendency to start with Organism-Environment interaction, because I was interested in problems centering in regulation of processes going on. . . .

Idealistic philosophical systems . . . express a revolt against the separation of knower and known and a feeling they should be in the same universe or cosmos. But they contradict their own aim by retaining the mental and then swallowing everything else up in it—hence the quarrel between "idealist" and "realist" goes on and has to go on forever —until they give up their common premise. But, as far as it goes, it rests upon a sort of recognition, neither of them can help, of the "circularity between knowings and known." . . .

Most of what I've been saying is to the effect that the distinction between "fact as *we see* it" and "fact as it is" is bound to occur when knowing takes the form of a deliberately executed art requiring specialized equipment or apparatus (partly "physical," but also mathematical). The false philosophy comes from making a complete and unlimited generalization out of a practical operation which can be specified. . . .

I think some of the writers on sociology of knowledge have begun to get hold of something—knowledge as social event-fact, socially-conditioned and socially-contributive. They seem to have some sense of the context in which the theory of knowledge is to be placed, which is an advance upon the epistemological context, though their particular treatment is often muddled enough.

Dewey

Miami Beach, Florida, February 1, 1944
[To Bentley:]
Incidental Notes:

Brute fact, raw fact, seem to me closer together in quality than either of them is to "hard" fact. Brute fact, something you've run up against; raw fact, a little less opaque, candidate for connections that will give it place and setting, but *only* a candidate. Hard fact seems to suggest something made out, that can be stood by; decisive under the conditions.

The factual ground back of "real" lying outside of knowledge is the fact that [in] any given time and place, there is much not-known, to-be-known. This remainder, present in every knowing, gets lumped together and [sets] off [by itself], and is called "reality." Moreover, it is so connected with what is knowing and known that it exercises a compulsory influence upon it. In knowing as a going concern (inquiry, investigation, reaching conclusions, decisions), what is then and there known is subordinate to what then and there is not-known. This functional superi-

208

ority of the latter was, I believe, a factor in suggesting it be called "the real."

I am of the impression that something called "reality" was not thus set over against knowing and the known until knowing became an art, industry, carried on like other arts, deliberate as a special technology. In Greek philosophical theory of knowledge, there are different degrees of Being, from perfect Being down to non-Being, Emptiness, the Void. And each one of these grades of Being has its own proper grade of knowing, from rational intuition and demonstration, down through opinion, sensation, to the non-being of ignorance—which is "really" correlative on this scheme to "ontological" non-being. I do not think there was any separation of subject-object, reality-knowing mind, in Greek philosophy. Knowing was something [that] nature—the cosmos—*does*. "Mind, reason" was not an agent, but the highest order of Being itself. It operated *through* certain organisms, parts of the cosmos, by strictly natural means, to reproduce itself; the reproduction being according to the grade of the organism—some being capable of taking on demonstrative science; others, opinion; the lowest social class hardly capable of rising above perceptions that had to do with appetite and its satisfaction. . . .

When knowing became an art, it became an occupation carried on by man, not something done by nature through man. And it was a struggle with and against that which resisted the art. (Old Professor Gildersleeve once said in an article that an "object" is that which objects.) "Subject" used to stand for subjectmatter—what modern philosophy has called objects—and "object," then, was a name for *it*—the cosmic subjectmatter —when attention is directed to it. The only difference between subject (matter) and object was that the former slipped, so to speak, in and out of vision. If one stops to note how accidentally, in the sense of lack of deliberate purpose and control, most of our "knowing" goes on, and that the Greeks did not have our experimental techniques, it will be seen that they kept pretty close to their facts, while the modern subject-object business is a mis-reading of facts attending deliberate search—knowing as a specialized art. The specialized art of knowing with the Greeks was carried on *in the head*, without having to *do* anything with or to environing conditions.

[*Dewey*]

[Miami Beach, Florida,] February 2, 1944

Dear Bentley:

. . . 1. It is true I have preferred "biological" where you have said "physiological." It is also true that I hadn't thought of the point you justly make—the behavioral is also biological. What had influenced me, I suspect, is that, in its usual usage, unless I am mistaken, "physiological" is distinguished from "anatomical" rather than from "behavioral" and is referred to processes as they are specifically referred to an organism, while "biological" involves the interacting environment. Hughes (who influenced me too much at one time, producing one of the aberrations—my doing, not his—[which] you have called attention to) used the word "biotic" to name, as I remember it, the wider sense of "biological." Probably, the best way is to use "physiological," but make it plain that the word is not used in its narrower sense, either as respects distinction from "anatomical," nor as including "physiological," in narrower sense, *and* anatomical, but taking environmental interaction for granted, without specification.

2. Incidentally, I have had some bother, which I haven't mentioned, with the *word* "behavior"—not with what you use it for, but the word. I have been accustomed to speak of the behavior of the solar system, a molecule, etc., and I think that accords with common usage. I can see why you would hesitate to use the word "psychological"; it certainly lends itself, enthusiastically at that, to misapprehension. But I have wondered whether "behavioral" could be kept as the inclusive designation, when a generalized name is wanted, and adjectives be prefixed, [e.g.] physical behavior, physiological, etc. Probably, however, the best way out of the verbal difficulties is to introduce the names, transaction, interaction, action-reaction; first explain them, and *then* identify whatever names are further used, like physical, physiological, behavioral, on the basis of these three names. (By the way, it just occurs to me that probably the original meaning of "categories" in Aristotle was types or kinds of *namings*.)

3. More important point, of course, is the event and fact business. I have wobbled about. In one communication, as I recall, I agreed fully with what you say, saying something like this: "It is [a] fact that a given (specified) fact is indeterminate." You are doubtless correct in thinking that my tendency to use "fact" as event definitely designated, or as (at a given time) warrantably asserted or named, is a holdover from the logical approach. I've used the event-fact a number of times to cover what is properly just Fact. It just came to mean something I needed. . . .

4. Of course you are right in saying that in full factual statement . . . the interactional is within the transactional. But in *knowing* what the transactional is, we are guided by taking a genetic or developmental view—perhaps, a rough analogy is the fact that an (some) adult comes before an infant. But we know the adult that this developing infant moves toward better by tracing in detail the "transition"—the developmental process—from infancy—first *its* infancy and then placing it in a still longer temporal genetic process. [It] seems to me that [this] is the essential Darwinian contribution to understanding knowledge. Let me

210

know if there is anything basically wrong with this. If it is wrong, I'm off on a wrong slant.

In any case, what got me off, in my own history, on this slant, is the fact that a lot of things that gave me difficulty in historic and current theories of knowing seemed to get cleared up when, taking inquiry as search, I genetically affiliated it with simpler physiological processes— search for food to keep living going; the stimulus, in general, being a state of tension, identifying the fact of *need* also—such processes as escape from an enemy—harm, pain generally, etc. That was my route out of separate mentalism into what struck me as naturalistic description. And doubtless, it affects and largely determines my point of view and, emphasis. I believe that it can be so stated as to complement your approach, but, doubtless, it has to be safeguarded from selective overweighting. What I wrote yesterday about knowing-inquiry as a technological art may help explain the *practical* sense in which an Inquirer is *outside*.

5. Probably, the most significant issue you bring up is that about my "here-now" and "connections." If I seemed to *separate* them, I wrote very carelessly. What I intended to do was to introduce a distinction of two connected phases, neither of which occurs without the other. I might start over this way. Words are of two kinds, and each kind of word must be used to describe [or] narrate any fact. They are Demonstratives and Designations. Examples of demonstratives are this, that; they point and locate. They are so far from being separate that a demonstrative does not and cannot point to the here-and-now phase of the total solid (spatially-temporally coextensively continuous) fact; contextual connections are understood. (In my *Logic* I have definitely criticized the theory of the separation of demonstratives from meaning.) [L. Susan] Stebbing (following Russell, if I recall) said a "this" came first, naked-pure so to speak, and that it was then characterized as such and such. I pointed out that without a minimum of characterization as a ground, there is no way of telling whether later occurring characterizations are about "this" at all. (I think "This" in the Index will show the passages—an Index being, by the way, itself an illustration of a Demonstrative.) Now, on the other hand, unless, when something is said purporting to be a description or extended naming, it is nailed down by an attendant demonstrative (usually not expressly stated, but always "understood"); it is completely in the blue—mere speculation, and floating at that. No matter how extensive and solid what is known—or what is *to be* known—it remains in the domain of relations expressed by symbols, unless it has some here-now focus—some *demonstrable* place and time. Otherwise, it is neither an ex-istence, nor an e-vent. Inquiry is an invitation: Come out of the dark and *show* yourself.

In your statement about never *seeing* an object, but only hints (I emphasize the seeing as against your emphasis of "never" and "object"), the hints, cues, clues, constitute or *possess* the demonstrative aspect, that which you [work] through and toward, [and which,] in their distinction (but not separation) from the hints, signs, data [used] *as evidential*, constitute the connections. In fact, you make here just the distinction-connection I was trying to describe.

Using the words "see" or "perceive" in a rather strict, or at least limited, sense, it might be said that an *object* is all you ever do *perceive*. H_2O is not *seen*. However, this is aside from the present point, and it might well be unnecessarily confusing to go into it. The positive fact at which it points is that all knowing involves what, when they are distinguished (and in traditional theories are separated), are sensory apparatus (peripheral) and cerebral (central) in cooperation, or "sense-perception" and "intellect," "reason," "understanding"; and either phase is subject to selective *emphasis* (giving occasion to a *phase*)—as when we engage in inquiry to make out clews, and when we theorize and mathematize to make out the connections that give the raw fact its import. I don't think you intend to make out that the water we see, drink, wash in, etc., is in any way illusory as compared with H_2O, or that, when known in those connections, the result is less knowledge than when known in the connection H_2O. Though the connections are much less extensive in space-time, they are *the* connections which answer the needs of the situations while the chemical formula answers another. The first is practical; the second is cognitive. But I don't think you intend to perpetuate the classic theory that makes the latter intrinsically of a different and higher order.

Quite likely, I have over-elaborated here beyond any call for it. But, like some of what I wrote yesterday, it is to make my own angle and line of possible contribution clearer, not for direct application. . . .

Your question about how far back goes the admission that "subject-object" involve each other, I can't answer—don't know that I could find the answer, even if I had the books handy. I spoke of the reversal of the use of the two words. Descartes still used the words in the classic sense. "Objectiver" meant viewed in relation to knowing mind; "subjectiver," as it is in itself. I'm reasonably sure the English writers from Locke on introduced the reverse use without knowing it; so it probably goes back to some scholastic school—likely [the] "nominalists." I do not believe that anyone has undertaken this particular job before. Probably the scholastics were more careful about terminology than anyone has been before or since. Peirce had great respect for them in that particular. . . .

Best regards, *Dewey*

Seattle, Washington, February 2, 1944

Dear Dewey:

About "transaction as a thing," what I must have had in mind was that I have steadily stressed observation "across skins" dating back to my cross-sectional in 1908 [*The Process of Government*]. You have not only developed [transaction] in terms of logical inquiry, but you have centered this in formulation as "of and by" the organism. You have limited and obligated the organism to the full extent to belong in a natural world, but (for your audiences) you have continued to try to "educate" them by using personalized words they can understand. The interesting thing (the thing that makes this present enterprise possible) is that no matter how I develop from my manner of approach, I *always* find you have fully anticipated any statement I can make—though setting it up as conditioning of what you say about the organism, rather than as direct formulation.

In other words, as to the above phrase "transaction as a thing," we both require all our data to have spatial and temporal characteristics. Your "indeterminate situation" is as much naturally factual as your "warranted assertion" in outcome so far as general background is concerned, although, for the immediate purpose of an account of inquiry, you stress a firmness of fact in the outcome that was lacking in the indeterminate situation as subject-matter. I then go on to argue that *If* interaction is as between two objects (for the moment styled "things"), *Then* a transaction fusing the interacting objects is a "thing" in that sense—a transactional thing. *Also* a transactional (confused) start, not yet differentiated into interaction things, is itself hazily "a thing." And so on, and so on. When you . . . stressed "an affair" (to Santayana's . . . disapproval ["Dewey's Naturalistic Metaphysics"]), you did about all I probably had in mind.

I am more and more inclined to think we can get a double speech-form for behaviors, one on [the] side of agency, the other on the side of cosmic transaction—and it will certainly be an improvement in talking which . . . [will have an] influence in the future. . . .

Sincerely, *Bentley*

[P.S.] Here is an illustration of your remark that all words are names— the great question being *what* they name. I wrote "factuality" a little while ago, and at once observed that "factuality" does not name a characteristic of fact in its aspect as "events," but in its aspect as "being named." In other words, the word "factuality" names, not outer cosmos, but linguistic process. So, also, I have long said of "concept," and now can say of "percept."

[Miami Beach, Florida,] February 3, 1944

Dear Bentley:

. . . I must have expressed myself badly *re* "the real." The only question I intended to raise was about the *order* of statement. I agree com-

213

pletely with your position; we wouldn't have anything to say worth saying without it. But I thought if the positive position were developed first, there would be more likelihood of proper understanding [and] if the negative statement about the "real" . . . came later. In fact, after a strong statement of the positive position, I can see how dyed-in-the-wool bourbons can—and will—disagree, but I don't see how the most wilful can misunderstand. I can see also how my seeming to give "event" a prior status to fact would fall back to the wrong view of the real. What I was after, though my expression was poor, was to make it clear to the reader that there is nothing in the position that every possible statement falls within knowledge, that is at all incompatible with the statement that one of the things known is that, in any given case of knowing, there is a lot which is unknown. I agree with you that *event* is not prior to fact, and when it is explicitly distinguished, it is that *kind* of fact that eventuates when fact is held off for examination. (Your mode of statement is better—I'm awkward about it, but I have no wish to differ.) One sort of fact exists before another sort of fact, but the idea that event as such exists before fact (the materials so named) knocks spots out of what we are trying to do. It's quite true that my problems have centered about an *intermediate situation,* and probably I tend from habit to make that phase too conspicuous, but I accept the position that it falls within the transaction. I've long noted that, what a person most fully takes for granted as the background of the problem he is concerned with, he doesn't mention. In fact, most advance arises from digging back into what one has taken for granted and seeing it in a problematic connection.

As to "materials to be named," . . . I accept what you say as basic to our whole attempt, even if I wobble sometimes in the naming when I shouldn't. . . . When I have used the expression "event-fact," it was to designate the "relatively" *hard* fact that emerges or eventuates from a given inquiry—which is serial and ongoing, its terminus being just a period. . . .

Yours, with regards, *John Dewey*

Miami Beach, Florida, February 8, 1944

Dear Bentley:

. . . 1. As to material about "experience" . . . as far as the word is concerned, this is water over the dam. I think the word can be cut out entirely. I wrote once [in *Essays in Experimental Logic*] many years ago that since it was an "infinity" word, standing for everything, it has no differential signification. But, as to the points you raise, "burning," in the sense it bears in physical research, was not intended to be something separate and prior in the illustration I gave; it was postulated as a physical name when taken with fuller scope (wider and longer), when, by

214

means of biological intermediaries (interactive), it becomes (in present terminology) transactional. And the "reflex-withdrawing" is not intended to come *before* perception of connection; for the introduction of perception of connection indicates that the *organic* phase of the total is on a plane of behavior experience excluding anything reflex. In other words, it is meant to describe an experience in terms of an "organic circuit," to the exclusion of any reflex arc. The "experienc*ing*" and "experienc*ed*" of those earlier writings were intended to express two *aspects*, disclosed by *analysis*, not two prior "facts," though quite likely the analysis, since it tried to link what I was talking about in "genetic continuum" with the physical (a case of combustion), and with the physiological or biological organism-environment interaction, gave a wrong impression. . . .

Well, the only point of all this . . . is that perhaps mention of the intimate linkage of the genetic and the analytic in scientific research would serve to convey to readers how it is that transactional behavior is both primary and final, and yet requires for its scientific naming an account of conclusions of physical and physiological research.

About the words "physiological" and "biological" once more: I had taken it for granted that the "ology" part of two words stood on the same level, designating or referring to inquiry-techniques, while the "bios" part indicated that all which lives in its capacity as living is the subject-matter; "biology" thus serving the same purpose here that, you point out, is served now by "physical," in bringing into connection subject-matters once split up among a number of subjects. Identity of "subject" in this sense (astronomy, botany) with specified "subject-matter" would seem to illustrate the knowing-known unity. It abolishes any basic division between, say, botany and zoology, between vegetable physiology (emphasis upon organic aspect) and ecology, with emphasis on environing aspect. This is not a plea for use of [the] word "biological"—but to indicate that, whatever word is used, there will have to be some cautionary measures to point out to what materials it applies.

"Having-knowing." I don't know whether the importance I have ascribed to the business of distinguishing-connecting "having" and "knowing" is a relic of some kind of unjustifiable dualism or not. It perhaps overemphasizes the organic aspect. There certainly can be no reference to "having" outside of knowing, and if the distinction-connection in question suggests there is such a reference, it is viciously bad. The *intention*, I think, is quite in line with our present effort. There is something which just *is* at the beginning and at the close of any given knowing (inquiry, search, research). The *kind* of factivity marking the particular warranted assertion of a specified inquiry does not have to be named as a case of *knowledge*—it is a case of *what* is *there*, that *which* is *done, made,* till there is occasion for further inquiry. "Having," as I have said, bears down too heavily on [the] organism side. But, in the analysis

215

of a whole, it points, I think, to [the] verifiable or assertible fact that a given knowing or piece of research has resulted in something to be taken and used.

Cosmos = World (?)—not world as this globe. But, as name for all that is, or can be inquired into—what "can be," being of the space-time *continuum* as that which is known, and, hence, is in space-time connection with it. Knowledge of it when reached is not knowledge of something else, but is increased knowledge, and improved or extended of what is known at any previous date and place. . . .

After you called my attention to it, I saw the objection to the words "social environment," though I had been in the habit of using them. But there seems to be a need for some distinctive word to name the environment of human beings *as far as* it is determined *by communication*. A sucking human infant seems to be an organism interacting with environing conditions in the way that is subject to techniques of physical-physiological inquiry. A human being who marries or votes or who calls in a physician, etc., . . . is engaged in transactional affairs with environing conditions. Unless I am mistaken, the words "social environment" came into use with the intention of distinguishing facts of this kind from facts of physiological interactivity. This undoubtedly is from the side of an organism aspect, but it is legitimate to describe inquiries analytically as transactions that involve organisms having certain specified properties and environing conditions of a certain specified kind —just as a loan involves one identified or specified borrower and another identified as lender—in an extensive environment of the kind usually called "economic" or "commercial." Now, the question and issue I have in mind are directly up the alley you have been working in for years. Is it possible to use "sociological research" to specify a certain technique, that of research into transactions, as "physical" and "physiological" are used to specify areas of the techniques of other knowings? The "ology" differentiating it from the much too wide word "social." Now, I am not attaching any particular importance to this particular name. But symmetry of distinction-connection seems to indicate the need of some word when naming of intercommunications, mutual participations, *explicitly* determines the special properties of the materials under *direct* investigation.

Or am I going wild?

Yours, *John Dewey*

Key West, Florida, February 14, 1944

[To Bentley:]

. . . There might . . . be a note to the effect that the original meaning of "conception" was not mentalistic, but was that of a rational prin-

216

ciple or ground sufficiently basic and wide in application to have a determining or regulative effect on other narrower and, relatively speaking, derived ideas—in their earlier nonmentalistic sense—ways of looking at and interpreting; "cosmic" rather than mental.

Yours, *J. Dewey*

Lincoln, Nebraska, February 16, 1944

Dear Dewey:

. . . I am noting your phrasing [2-8-44] that "transactional behavior is both primary and final, and yet requires" the scientific work in between. But I hope you will not let the accompanying argument on genetic and analytic disappear. Here, incidentally, is one of the overhead-planning issues—how far we run toward professional philosophical or professional psychological appeal, or how far a statement on what assumes itself to be a common-sense, observational, or empirical basis can be made? by main force, or any way whatsoever?

"Distinguishing-connecting." I see you have used this phrase (word) several times lately. Could we maintain it officially? I have written of aspectual differentiation, or specification. A standard name of striking efficiency would be great business. It strikes me: The "ing" form is more on the agency side. The "tion" form (often objectionable) may have some transactional value.

The having-knowing issue ought to be solvable by a better organized terminology for knowing such that:

1. there was a covering word for all sign—all behavior—so far as cognitive, in the understanding that without some sign, some cognitive, we did not have behavior at all, 2. a word for signal-knowing was adopted, 3. a word for existence-name-knowing was used, 4. a word for symbol-knowing-about entered, and 5. (perhaps) a name for sunk-down-in "having," of the kind that followed 2 and 3, would also be required.

This was what the alpha-knowledge-phi scheme was verbally ready to apply to, if ever the facts were ready to be named.

. . . I have set up "transaction" as the most general account, and "interaction" as a more limited account, with the remark that you can get along pretty well in old physics without knowing about transaction, that Newton went part way with action-reaction, and that later physics has gone transactional with Faraday, Clerk Maxwell, and wave in general.

You seem to suggest: "action-reaction" for the physical, "interaction" for the physiological, "transaction" for the behavioral.

I (now) do not think that will work. I would modify to gradations of technique. The transaction is essential base *before* we get an empirical behavioral inquiry, although we can do some interaction subordinate work in behaviors. Physics, however, went through the whole development of mechanics, and Newton's universe, without ever thinking of transaction until recently. . . .

Regards, *Bentley*

Lincoln, Nebraska, February 17, 1944

Dear Dewey:

. . . It has occurred to me that since "Experience" is the Devil, and you have wide acquaintance with him, and, further, since your reports have suffered so many aberrations through the academic spectacles of your critics, it might be a good thing if you wrote a preliminary paper on "Experience," or "The Word 'Experience.'" I would envisage a short paper, with a minimum attention to philosophizing arguments, and a maximum to variation with respect to organism and environment, transaction and interaction; with the very best analysis of the possibilities we can make, and with whatever conclusion we can come to. Such a conclusion might be (though I have no idea whether it will be, the case being one of *solvitur scribendo*—if such words exist) that:

Whereas the word was introduced to hold Subject and Object together;

Whereas, nevertheless, everyone reduces it to the subjective side by overstressing it thus; as witness (a) The "neutral" being dropped from James's neutral experience, and the experience retained as subjective; and (b) the frequent recent distortions of your own work, in which you have steadily given it a transactional setting, which is steadily ignored;

Now, therefore: 1. you will degrade it from [a] leading position; 2. establish a full transactional presentation in some other words; 3. use "experience" subordinate to this other word, as at the organic end; 4. hold "experience" to the signal-range, and not make it cover naming or symbol-using (except in a still more limited sense).

(As for the full-transaction naming, you may, or may not, be able to stomach "behavior" in the end—and that does not matter—but I am setting up the words, "sign," "signal," "name," and "symbol" in *full* transactional use, and not as organic specializations.) . . .

Regards, *Bentley*

Lincoln, Nebraska, February 18, 1944

Dear Dewey:

. . . Could "know*ing*" be used for the agency phase? (Incidentally, if "phase" is a good word for this position, it should be standardized for it, and have no near synonyms in our use—so that it would *always* present aspectual or connection-difference.)

"Meaning" has very little of the "ing" effect left. Is there any chance it could be raised to a transactional level like "sign," etc., and held there? (Incidentally, I do not believe I have made it clear how *fully* transactional I want "sign," "signal," "naming," and "symbol" to be. Not that I want these words in particular—but some words—and these seem best fitted. [I want them fully transactional.] So that "sign" would *never* mean either the "thing" used for sign, nor the . . . mental sign-using process, but always sign-in-being as transactional "function" with no reduction, except as secondary process, to organic agency and environmental thing.)

As to "social environment." If you divide the world into (a) one organism and (b) all the rest of the world, and call the rest "environment," then you can lump off the other men of [the] same race and time as a social environment. It is crudely interactional. It is a perfectly good step in an early stage of inquiry, but objectionable when mouthed over by sociologists as a substitute for inquiry. I don't think I ever object to the casual use of such phrases.

If you make "communications" a special field of research to be styled sociological, what will you do with psychological? You mention . . . this sociological and put it alongside physical and physiological, but you do not mention psychological. If you do this, and spread communications over the region of "namings" . . . plus some signalings of the gesture and shriek type, and call these transactional, and make them sociological, I *suspect* that the region of perception-manipulation (styled "Signal" . . .) will have to enter as psychological under more or less of the view that they are *not* transactional. This would eject the Jamesian "neutral," which is not important, if true. But it would also interfere with a unified treatment of signal and name (and how about symbol?) as behavioral. And this is what I work toward. . . . I consistently treat what is called psychological and sociological as one field.

This is half a question of choice of names, and the other half an attempt to use facts which we are just beginning to learn, as a base of distinction. I am open to any scheme, I hope, but I don't seem to flow in this direction. . . .

Regards, Bentley

Lincoln, Nebraska, February 19, 1944

Dear Dewey:

. . . You once asked whether words for "feeling," "emotion," etc., were needed. Would you think so now? We are specializing on the knowing-aspect. A completer study would need them. Our study would probably suffer by attempts to force them in.

Your remarks on "context" in a letter of July 19, [1943] contain a char-

219

acterization of "understanding" which exactly meets the needs of a man who recently wrote me about the word; but, in general, you treat the use of "context" as a warning and a protection. I have objected to "context" in current uses because I could not tell how far the "context" intended was verbal and how far perceptive-manipulative. In your discussion you consider the whole business in the form of "products of analysis," which again fuses both the naming and the having in a joint process. . . .

Regards, *Bentley*

Lincoln, Nebraska, February 20, 1944

Dear Dewey:

I am back at my "image" work, the first time in almost four months, and I should begin to get some tips "from the soil."

I have an idea that in our terminology work it is now essential before further development to settle on the word to use where I have been using "behavior."

You object to "behavior" properly because:

1. It can be used for "chemical" behaviors, and similars.

2. It has been specialized (after Watson) for overt behaviors, with "mind" left out.

3. It has currency in the form "animal behavior" as something inferior to human conduct.

4. Perhaps, other reasons I do not recall.

I approve the word because:

1. (and mainly) I know no better word, and none nearly so good.

2. Your 1. is generality of usage with which all scientific words (except new coinages) are affected; as fish with respect to whale.

3. Watson's "behavior" is fictitious, not factual, and is not on the rise, but on the decline.

4. Animal behavior seems to me a good precedent rather than objection.

5. We stress all the time purposiveness ("sign" in our materials) to such extent that none . . . can list us as Watsonian. . . .

6. I think in time we can establish *our* usage.

Physics as inquiry has had for subject-matter, materials named as matter, electricity, electromagnetic wave, etc.

Physiology as inquiry has living tissue, secretion, nerve-conduction, etc.

Psychology has psyche, mind, sensings, reasonings, purposings, etc.; and all, as things and as actings.

You can't get a close name for either materials of physics or physiology, nor can we expect it for our field.

Roughly, physics has before it the [inanimate?] material (inclusive of the undulating). Physiology has living matter. We have *behaving matter*. We now name ours: Behavioral Event. . . .

Regards, Bentley

Key West, Florida, February 22, 1944

Dear Bentley:

. . . The enclosed comments are just by way of emphasis, by way of amplification of your points as I get them. . . . If the knower had not been isolated as an immaterial soul, I doubt if the "known" would have become so seemingly self-evidently isolated as it has been taken to be. . . .

I think we can leave "experience" out, save, perhaps, for a footnote saying that while some philosophers had worked definitely toward a transactional view—as in James's insistence on its double-barreled nature—it has become so identified with the subjectivistic, mentalistic view, especially in psychology, that we judge it better to exclude mention of it. . . .

Yours with regards, Dewey

[P.S.] I am inclined to think philosophers have not, upon the whole, gone as far as psychologists. Ofttimes my own statements have been more "inter" than "trans."

Lincoln, Nebraska, February 22, 1944

Dear Dewey:

I note that one time you remarked that "Term (limit) and de-fining go together." Definitely. Yet my arrangement . . . does not provide for this. I have "definition" with "symbol" and (I think) no provision whatever for "term." That is, common words are characterized, names are specified, symbols are defined, but when I disassociated "term" and set it up as special range with "proposition," etc., I did not introduce a name for the process of hardening it.

I have "convention," "accuracy," and "precision," for "word," "name" and "symbol," again leaving "term" uncared for in this respect.

This is apparently due to the wavering development as for the use of "term" and "symbol."

It has occurred to me (once or twice, and then been neglected) that the proposition business (Aristotelian) *is* the naming business.

I seem to have:

Word	characterizes	conventionally	connections
Name	specifies	accurately	with reference
Term			
Symbol	defines	precisely	in relation

These distinctions are of course behaviorally actional and functional, and never compartmental. "Term" runs across both its neighbors. It is the best operation of "naming," and yet in the region of symbol it still carries the odors of mortality. Here is a case where my preference for bludgeons over rapiers is not doing so well. . . .

Regards, *Bentley*

[Key West, Florida] February 23, 1944

[To Bentley:]

What influences me is, I suppose, a strong prejudice against every theory of science that holds, explicitly or by implication, that science is *the* superior mode of knowledge, save for a specifiable class of problems and uses. . . .

If I recall the dictionary aright, "perception" was once a broad name, about synonymous with noting, noticing, laying hold of sign-values, twigging, grasping significance. Limitation to "sense"-perception, later development: largely, I think, in effect, a protest against the verbal manipulations of later scholasticism—and a means of calling attention to the necessity of observation for scientific results. The fact that observings have sensory-behavings as one of their *conditions* then was treated as an *inherent* part of a perceiving. It is possible that *a* perceiving can best be treated as the narrow, temporally immediate or here-now, aspectual phase of an observation, which has been cut off from its proper connections because [it is] regarded as the activity of a special organ or faculty of a "mind." (I think it is often helpful to indicate how a wrong steer came about—though it can be carried too far, especially with respect to the extent of a given document.)

Re "experience," once more. . . . I sort of hesitate at saying anything that indicates that what is named, and even relational formulations, are not experienced. With reference to the functions the word has served historically, the implication would be taken to be that there is something "rational" about them—which, of course, there is, but not in the sense in which rational means an organ or faculty that is super-observational and *a priori*. . . . "Distinction-connection," by the way, is better than my "ing" form—the latter is useful when it is desired to bring forward the behavioral aspect, but not otherwise.

About "physical"—My trouble is due to the fact that I haven't got habituated to thinking in present terms; what I said was, probably, from [the] standpoint of Newtonianism: forget it, and I'll try to. I agree with you my "action-reaction" won't work—reason just given.

I didn't mean to set up a special environment as social—you pointed out that error to me some time ago.

The question about "sociological-psychological" *is* a question ma-

222

terially and not just formally, I think. The anthropological use of "culture" seems to me to be in effect a device to effect a union—though, doubtless, most anthropologists are not aware of that fact. What I had in mind was not setting up "sociological" as a separate, but just what you say—"sociological and psychological" as *one* field. Roughly speaking, I would say that the "psychological" is the "biological" (narrower sense) [as it is] transformed through "social" factors centering in and radiating from language as communication. The "ological" in "sociological" brings in the factor of a technique of inquiry. My use of the word was as one way of taking the word "psychological" definitely out of the mentalistic, on one side, and cortical behaviorism, on the other. I meant to indicate that I thought some special statements were needed on this point—not to object to use of "psychological" to apply to the transactional as distinct from [the] interactional. The topic I had in mind is not the *names* themselves, but what is said in connection with them to clarify terminological usage in the apprehension of the reader. . . .

Yours, Dewey

Lincoln, Nebraska, February 26, 1944

Dear Dewey:

. . . "Affirmation" and "Assertion," "Description" and "Narration."

Here are a couple of specializations from your *Logic* that may need to be fitted in.

"Assertion" cleaves to *name* and the existential implication for event-named. Do we need something comparable for "word," "term," and "symbol"? . . .

. . . "Event and Fact." . . . I am interested in one sentence especially. You write "Event is Fact as definitively designated." This is O.K. Yet I have been writing "Fact is event named." Yours sounds better to me than mine; . . . providing we can say what "Fact" *is*. But to say what "Fact" *is*, we have to include the naming-knowing, which I do. Your expression (upon analysis, or what seems for the moment to be analysis) would assume "Fact," and then specify that, under a certain condition, namely, its "definite naming," it becomes "Event." So inspected, your phrase sounds worse than mine.

The only issue I know is: which way can we talk and stick to it most easily? I suspect in your phrasing the word "existence," where used, would equate with "Fact," whereas in my use (as above) the word "existence," if used, equates with "Event." . . .

Regards, Bentley

Dear Bentley:

. . . "Reference": I think your general use for this term is the best. But, for my purpose in the *Logic,* there was need for a word that expressed the *indirect* bearing or application of symbols, as contrasted with the direct connection of "things" with one another, and direct relation of symbols with one another. To "refer" etymologically is to carry or bear *back;* that, probably, influenced my choice of that word. Symbols are human products. Transactionally, the application of symbols to "things" is cashing promissory notes, in contrast with (a) cash transactions (connections) and (b) foreign and domestic *exchange*—transactions of debits and credits (relations). I think some distinctive word is needed to name the fact that a special *intervening* operation is required to effect its reference—in the broad sense. I fooled with "Application," but that, like "reference," is so broad as to *apply* all the way through. Maybe, for present purposes, no special designation is called for.

"Phase" and "Aspect": In ordinary use, these words aren't synonyms. "Phase" refers to (names) aspects that are temporally *successive*—as phases of the moon. "Aspect" refers to (names) distinctions that are contemporaneous; various *em*-phases or *views,* facets. I think (at the present moment) that the distinction-connection of "aspect-phase" could be standardized for know*ing* as agency, as you suggest. . . .

"Hunting," "Striving," etc. One phase of Living; but *living* also has the phase of finding; "consummatory," I've called it. I'm inclined to believe that the rhythm of (relative) disintegration-redintegration needs attention in transactional as well as in the interactional mode that I emphasized in [*Logic*] Ch. II, pp. 27 ff., p. 221, paragraph near bottom of page. . . .

But I think something of the nature of tension-resolution marks the physical, physiological, and behavioral, and, while especially marked in perceptive-manipulative transactions, also characterizes symbolic relationships. . . .

"Behavioral Event" and "Behavioral Agency." What you say under head of "Integrate-Interaction" about my approach and the difference between us is undoubtedly correct. As far as I am concerned, my approach is conditioned by the fact (aside from infantile ignorance of physics) that what I know best is the history of beliefs, philosophical and (up to the time of the ultra-specialization of psychology) psychological. I have worked out my position largely against this historical material. My view of the main course of philosophy as exemplified in the larger names is perhaps different in color from yours. I was educated in that field and taught philosophy professionally for years, and I believe that, upon the whole, the men classed as philosophers were superior, not inferior, to their contemporaries—provided they are interpreted . . . [in] socio-cultural terms, not in terms of what they themselves supposed they were doing.

Chapters II and III of my *Logic* thus give in substance the background or prepossessions with which I approach the subject. As the net outcome, I undoubtedly express myself more easily in interactional than in fully transactional terms, even when I recognize that the interactional belongs in the transactional and can't be understood or properly stated except as placed [there]. As for sectional papers, I feel I may need to work out one on genetic-functional, or temporal-continuum, method (what I have called "historical-geographical") and one to try to account in cultural terms for the conspicuous role of the self, subject, etc., in the philosophy of the last three centuries—the latter to help purge myself, in part. . . .

If you would expand somewhat on what you call your vagueness "as between transaction crossing name-event and transaction crossing connected events," I think I might get a better grip on the matter of "behavioral event versus behavioral agency." (In fact, if I had a firm grip on the way you use "crossing" and "across," I think I could adjust my statement better.)

"Behavior." I didn't intend to object to the term; I think it is highly necessary, especially in adjectival form. I only mean to suggest the need of some careful qualifications to guard against misunderstanding—as if we were denying or excluding something we don't at all do. I wouldn't change the word.

"Term" and "Symbol." I think I was probably too literally etymological in what I said about "term" as limit set in defining. Aristotle's theory of knowledge took definition as the highest kind of existential knowledge— and fixed limits as cosmic determinations, e.g., the fixity of species, of substances and essences. Probably a footnote would take care of "term" to the effect [that] words, names, and symbols, all of them, tend to select some aspect-phase and hold it up to view or for consideration with a kind of fence around it. In other words, it is a rather loose word, once the Aristotelian point of view is out.

I think a short paper might be written on such words as "Telling," "Calling," "Saying," "Noting," "Remarking," "Marking," etc., in connection with "Naming," as illustrating the determining influence of language, communication, upon the basic and primary attitude *naturally* or naïvely taken toward knowledge. Even "proposition" as proposing, as placing *before*, submitting, for discussion. Not for the terminological paper, but as a side-issue support.

"Sociological–Psychological." I should have said more or much less. I shot blindly in the air at nothing in particular in what I wrote. . . . What I had in mind was that the physical-physiological is (becomes?)

the psychological when, as, and if determined by *communication,* language, as the sociological distinction-connection characteristic. At the same time, the physical-physiological can be named, identified, specified, only in terms of (conditions set by) the sociological-psychological. The negative part of what I was after was to get rid of the psychical-mentalistic, separate domain, notion of "psychological." (I guess that was the positive intent, not just the negative.)

"Term." The use of "term" in previous paragraph may possibly suggest the standardizable usage of that word, e.g., "the terms of a contract." Instead of hitching it up with "symbols" and "definition," as I have done at times, perhaps it should stand for the precision-limit of a name. But I am rather in the dark about this matter.

"Word." I have used this word very loosely, to save trouble (I imagine) in getting the precision needed. We might possibly have a kind of spectrum (spectrum because of intermediate shade zones): "Word-Name-Symbol," a progression from communication, as talking, conversation, exchange of information, advice, etc. "Word," never by itself, since the meaning of any single word depends upon topic, theme, subject of conversation (the boy who cried "Wolf"), [relevance] to knowledge.

Technique of Inquiry and/or "Event-Fact" side. . . . The "ological" part of terms we have used suggests that, in a certain sense, the underlying techniques or methods determining knowledge are what we are primarily concerned with—*not* in the agency or interactional sense, but as?? A good formulation eludes me, but, among other things, as elimination of the prior "reality" business, and the distinction-connection of state of knowledge with Fact-Event. I haven't been able to think of a form of statement that doesn't seem to be weighted on the agency side, but I think it is possible to find one that would indicate the centre (and circularity) of the document. . . .

. . . The "stimulus-response" formula may link up with ongoing continuum (question-answer series), where each "answer" serves to make more precise the underlying subject that binds or holds [them] together, while "excitation-reaction" is short-span and immediate—because not taken up into "discourse." . . .

With best regards, Yours, *Dewey*

Key West, Florida, March 10, 1944

Dear Bentley:

Personally, I am in favor of publication; on the whole I think the Columbia *Journal of Philosophy* offers the most promising outlet, but, if you have any other suggestion, [I] am not set on it—the fact [that] it comes out fortnightly is an advantage, other things [being] equal. I see no reason for holding it after its shape satisfies us. I think your last suggestion, confining the first paper to main issues, with [the] following one for secondary points, is well worth considering. As far as my name is concerned, for many reasons I should be glad to have it associated with yours—the only out is that you have done so much more of the work.

. . . It has occurred to me, maybe I'm off, that "transaction" and "interaction" haven't, after all, been sufficiently linguistically identified; doubtless, the reason is in me and my habits. But, if I get shaky, other readers are likely to be even more so—I think we can't take too much care on that matter. Another suggestion has occurred to me about publication: a statement toward the close that our paper is a program to be worked upon and out, and inviting all interested in the general line and accepting it "in principle," [to] join in its development.

As to "sociology of knowledge"—I think I know why you damn them—they are badly confused. But I have a feeling that they are working away from a mentalistic statement toward one in social-cultural terms and therefore don't need complete damning—some of their followers *might* be allies of ours. . . .

Yours as ever, Dewey

Paoli, Indiana, March 13, 1944

Dear Dewey:

. . . Kaufmann sent me a copy of *Philosophy and Phenomenological Research* with three papers on "meaning," by Lewis ["The Modes of Meaning"], [G. W.] Cunningham ["On the Linguistic Meaning-Situation"], and himself ["Verification, Meaning and Truth"]. I had heard about the Lewis paper and looked these over at a library. I am sending the magazine to you, just for tips and hints on the present status of terms for our terminology. (Your remark that "term" has dropped from Aristotelian strength to current looseness, I will incorporate heavily.) . . .

Lewis steps on his own feet "mentalistically." It seems to me to be terrible writing and thinking. . . . Kaufmann just becomes more plainly "un-natural" at every "advance" he makes. Cunningham amused me. I read his summary first. I never would have dreamed he thought he was working along your lines. Then I turned to the opening paragraph, and found that was what he said he was doing. This simply emphasized the importance of care in our publication.

Cunningham and Lewis both seem to accept *meaning* as an existent (an event in our terminology) answering to the word "meaning." Then they start to organize what they can say to such an existent.

You and I, in contrast, continually drop the word "meaning" out of use, saying that the word is a vague approximation—it is on the subject-matter end, not the object-end of inquiry. In our present paper all we do is to *point toward* meaning. Or, more broadly, we equate meaning-fulness with behavior—the full range from infusoria to Einstein (or should I say [Alfred] Korzybski?). We thus are free, they are in chains to a word. (We are not really free—but we are straining toward freedom) . . .

Regards, *Bentley*

Dear Dewey: Paoli, Indiana, March 17, 1944

I am delighted with the "By Nature and by Art" [paper]. First part went fine, and last part grandly. There was a little part in the middle that I stumbled over. . . .

The difficulty I have is with the opening paragraphs of [Section] III. . . . Assuming art as of nature, and the separation a practical convenience, you first, as I read it: (a) make common-sense knowledge direct (nature); (b) qualify this by proviso that historical background enters into immediate knowings on both sides, organism and environment; (c) make all things-seen, etc., "by art."

Here seems to be a difficulty of terminology about range of knowings. You have [elsewhere in our correspondence] stressed "observation" as requiring "naming," which is "art," in a way, on its low level. Possibly, common-sense knowledge as a product today seems "direct," compared with knowledge that is being worked for today, which has art-process. But if we went back into early acquisitions, this common sense involved its art-process, too. I think a slight rephrasing as to "common sense" will remove the uncertainty I seem to feel.

Regards, *Bentley*

[P.S. With respect to "By Nature and by Art"] It is obscure to me what this "larger part" consists of, that is, "by nature." I think of the whole perceptive-manipulative range, of the old sensation, of our signal.

But all of the above is to me "by art," in the wide sense, running back to earliest protoplasmic behavior. You view this also so. Your distinction is specifically special here as to nature and art. Nevertheless, that does not sharpen the reference. . . .

I personally cannot accept (or interpret) the phrase "without intervention of artificial means." I am not correct in this; I *can,* I think, *interpret* it. You are considering heavily the contrast of science and other knowings on lines you have mentioned in recent letters. For that specific purpose, your distinction is doubtless O.K., if sharpened a bit in phrasing. But the general scheme you have set up is (to me, as I read it, anyway) much broader than your specially focused problem. Hence, I feel a clash.

. . . The phrase "product of transactions." This clashes with me (as I sense it at the moment), for I think I would say here that "transaction" cannot *have* a product, but rather *is* the fact seen as product, when and as, technically convenient. . . .

Your phrasing "search" and "research" might possibly be useful. You could take a physiological level of search "by nature," supplemented by a scientific level of research "by art." . . .

Coral Gables, Florida, March 21, 1944

[To Bentley:]

I couldn't make out the topic or subject of Lewis's paper ["The Modes of Meaning"], and [it] didn't seem worth the energy that it would take to try to find out. So, I'll have to confine myself to some incidental comments.

1. He seems to be extraordinarily loose about what he calls "words," "expressions," "terms." In his first sentence he identifies "words" with ink-marks and sounds which *"convey* meanings." Then . . . there is a ready-made "verbal symbol," which must be prior to meaning since it is *associated* with the latter. And what a *fixed* meaning is, he nowhere tries to say. If he said that an arrangement of ink-spots or sounds can be used to fixate a meaning otherwise loose and floating, I would, at least, have had some idea of what he was driving at. Then he contradicts himself by saying that a symbol is an "abstract entity." Then a "linguistic expression" *may* be a term, but no attempt to define "expression," beyond the aforesaid association of a verbal symbol *with* a meaning. Then a "term" is an "expression" capable of naming, applying to a thing of some kind—then (top of p. 238) the "denotation" becomes the class of all things to which that term "correctly" applies! Here we have "things," "existents," and, where has meaning gone to? Then p. 239, *"abstract* terms are those which name what they signify"—on page 237, every symbol *is* an "abstract entity." Further down on the page, to name is identified with "speaking of" something. Page 241, near bottom, meaning drops out again. "A proposition is a term capable of signifying a state of affairs"—or "signifying," if it is a synonym for meaning, is the function of indicating, pointing to, standing for. Then, p. 242, "the state of affairs is the *signification* of the proposition"—according to which a proposition as term *doesn't* signify, but merely "names" (speaks of) a signification already there. Then application to existents, or to a state of affairs, seems to turn up as a *special* kind of meaning, called "sense meaning," "able to apply an expression in the case of *presented things or situations.*" * I say *seems* because it's all so vague as to be "seemingless."

* The exact quotation (p. 247) is: "*Sense meaning* is intension in the mode of a criterion in mind by which one is able to apply or refuse to apply the expression in question in the case of presented things or situations." (Eds.)

About all I get out of the article is confirmation of your thesis about the inseparability of names and facts, by demonstration of how, on any other ground, discussion has no guiding principle whatever, and one is bound to all sorts of incoherences.

I thought Cunningham's article ["On the Linguistic Meaning-Situation"] was at least of higher order, though he, too, gets mixed up in talking as if "words" had a kind of existence of their own.

Certainly, both articles show forcibly and clearly the necessity of distinctions to be drawn between words, names, and terms in order to get anywhere. . . .

J. D.

Coral Gables, Florida, March 22, 1944

To Bentley:

Re Kaufmann's article ["Verification, Meaning and Truth"]. . . .

Not a very profound study, leaves me with the impression that he is about half over [to our position].

His base proposition seems to be the necessity of two distinct order[s] of approach, or criteria, in science, one "factual," the other "logical." P. 267, line 5, or, as [he] states it later, matters of observation, "*empirical* rules of procedure," and of "internal relation between propositions." The matter of grounded incorporability of a proposition in the body of science is, however, set up as the supreme test, which is divisible into these two subordinate ones.

On page 272 he admits that rules and methods of procedure may be, and are changed, in the course of scientific procedure. This would seem "logically" to admit that what he has called "logical," is itself the result of analytic observation of facts concerning the factual procedures by which scientific bodies are "in fact" built up, and that the distinction between "factual" and "logical" is at best a distinction within procedure, which it may be helpful at times to . . . [employ]. But, on the same page, he says that is an affair of lower and higher orders of rules, the first being scientific decisions, and the second, methodological decisions. He seems thus to restate his original dualism, in other words. At all events he doesn't anywhere, as far as I can see, subject the distinction to any critical analysis.

I do not think that "logical" incompatibility of observed facts is, in scientific procedure, equivalent to "falsification." I guess that in most cases it is taken as an indication of a problem for further factual investigation. And, without adequate knowledge of historical facts, I should suppose that in mathematics, which seems to exemplify what he calls the "internal relations of propositions," change of procedural rules has been the chief source of scientific development.

It looks on the surface as if his "preference rules" and "basic rules" were again the same thing; in other words, the former being "subject to modifications as inquiry proceeds" and the latter (strangely enough, in view of his earlier remarks) being those "which are not intrinsically related to scientific goals" (p. 274). What in hell they are "related to," he doesn't say—a game some persons like to play, maybe. Or, his statements about logical grounds, methodological rules . . . as not intrinsically related to scientific goals, are simply survivals of Kant's *a priori* (that is, supplied by the mind) conditions of knowledge, lugged in because of inability to forget.

His wobbling is well illustrated on p. 276. A theoretical law cannot be falsified in its strict sense—but can cease to be regarded (used) as a working rule of scientific procedure—in other words, it is falsified *only* in a scientific, but not a strict sense!

[*Dewey*]

Paoli, Indiana, March 23, 1944

Dear Dewey:

. . . I am in trouble again about "Event." If only "Existence" could be read back to *sisto* [cf. L. *existere, exsistere,* fr. *ex,* out + *sistere,* to cause to stand] and stand forth in durational-transaction, instead of being dead, static, it would be the better word. Maybe, one can keep "Event" as is, and then put in a heavy black-face line to say "if ever anybody will give 'existence' a chance, a bit of life, we can run it back in."

You ask about the vagueness I felt as between name-event-transaction, and event-event-transaction. I think that is straightening out. At least I have not run into more hesitancy. It is the business of our taking a technical process (transaction) and identifying new objectifications by its aid and in its terms. (I suppose this is the age-old business of taking a predicate and making a subject out of it, and swearing by all that's holy that the transposed predicate is basic reality.) For instance, consider a *law* in a nation. Take a farmer, two hens, two dozen eggs, a thief, a sheriff, a judge, and a book of statutes. Try to apply them mechanistically. No one ever yet was able to say *what* a law was. Now I come along. I say, let's take the whole business transactionally instead of interactionally. I notice that piecemeal everybody does that every day—one does it when he uses the word "culture," for instance. But when one tries to go whole-hog with it (as I do, when I deny that one should say social environment, since, without the environed man, the environment would not be there environing—in the generalized case), then there is hell to pay. Still I have faith that some day some one will give specification to the name "a law" in transactional form. (The

231

electromagnetic wave contrasted with the corpuscle in physics is, I think, a similar case.) When in your *Logic* you advance from indeterminate situation to object, you establish object as a transaction, but then put that object over against other objects as in interaction. This is all O.K.—in pieces, with more trouble as a general construction (*Teste* Mackay).

Now we are going on and repeating the transactional advance for the big case of all knowledge. We take mind and real thing and fuse them into *Fact*, then we re-establish them as agency and event, as interactions within transaction, legitimately (and not frozen). But in this case we split naming (or, later on, mathematical symbolizing) off from the event-named and event-symbolized. (Maybe, this should read: object-named and event-symbolized—in my layout, one does not symbolize a "thing" or "hard object" by applying a single symbol to it, but applies a large . . . symbol-scheme to a wide event-situation.)

At any rate, where we had been viewing transaction as an improved connection in the range of event, now we are running transaction across event and designation. I just got to slipping around a bit. . . .

A suggestion . . . that, maybe, we have not yet developed transaction and interaction sufficiently, is entirely in line with my view. I think it is coming. I think it is going to be safe—in fact, both of us have been working toward it for so long that it is going to be just too bad if it isn't. But caution is the word now.

Your development began in interactional terms (as you have remarked several times), and you have introduced "transaction" (am I right about this?) as a more emphatic word, intending thereby much the same thing as interaction. (Suppose you answer this specifically—namely, prior to this present project, what distinction would you have put between the two?)

My development began with a heavy transactional statement in a limited field—that specialized as man-to-man (in other words, the cross-sectional of *The Process of Government*). It was not till 7 [or] 8 years ago that I extended it for man-to-thing. I only did this because *all* the psychologies, among which I expected to find a usable one, broke down in application. (Had I known of your "Perception" essay earlier, I would have made earlier progress, for you have there a "localization" assertion that it took me a lot of work later on to develop, in ignorance of your paper "Naturalistic Theory of Sense-Perception.")

Now we have two techniques, which tend to assert themselves conflictingly as to "things" (as in first part of this letter).

As a methodological development (if we were making one), I would, with a reminiscent reference to Comte, say that they were two differentiations of positivistic approach, arising in a historical setting of (a) person-magic (soul) in place of Comte's theological and (b) substance-magic (verbal reifications) in place of his metaphysical.

For the full scheme, we would have to add your "relational," my "symbolic," in the higher mathematical areas.

This makes the "transaction[al]-interactional" a differentiation within the procedure of designation—one more nice bit of circularity. . . .

Regards, Bentley

Paoli, Indiana, March 24, 1944

Dear Dewey:

There is one feature that I did not properly introduce in the letter of the 23rd. . . . This is degeneration-deterioration. We are considering interaction. You are treating it largely in its *good* form, pepped up as transaction. I am considering the name as covering many degenerate forms.

I assume that all the old magics were good in their day, but now degenerate, no matter how dominant still in the psychologies and sociologies (this time, I will leave out the philosophies). Same with everything else; and at this moment with interaction.

Roughly I would say: Newtonian mechanics: *inter*action at its best. Modern physics, nevertheless, today requiring certain *trans*actional presentations in addition.

"Subject-object": an aping in the behavioral field of the *inter*actions of physics. This now appearing as rotten; and knowledge as *the* field in which it most certainly is no good.

"Transaction," as we set it up: a stab at getting a better statement. We thus set up transactional "Fact," with respect to which "Designation" and "Event" are taken as in a subordinated phasal interaction, but *only* when held aspectual[ly].

This leads to the establishment of "Cosmos" in terms of "Fact" instead of in terms of "Event" (existence).

Our own transactional presentation of "Fact" will degenerate, first chance it gets. Indeed, if we are not deadly careful, to most readers it will have a life span (like some transmuting atoms) of half a millionth of a second.

All your life you have been against the subject-object and mind-body types of problem-posing; and getting stronger all the time.

Can we not fix it so [that] in this interactional-transactional connection-differentiation, we generalize the procedure of subject-object analysis, no longer facing the problem (say of mind-body) on its home ground, but subordinating it to a general technical "grow-and-then-decline" procedure in knowings? . . .

Regards, Bentley

Key West, Florida, March 25, 1944

Dear Bentley:

. . . I'll change the wording [in "By Nature and by Art"] to make it clear that, when I distinguish "knowledge" that is an art, from what I call . . . "by nature," I am using "art" as equivalent for a technology, not as a synonym for "skill"; and that the characteristics which, as I use the word, demarcate it from the perceptual-manipulative skills of amoebae and the animals, including man—as far as his perceptual-manipulative skills [are concerned]—do not involve extra-organic, "artificial" implements, apparatus, instruments, devised so as to obtain a certain specified kind of facts as the consequence.

Thanks for calling my attention to these points. Also I'll change the "common-sense knowledge" passage, as it is so vague as to be open to misapprehension—I was using it in the sense in which it is marked off from science in my *Logic*, virtually equivalent, I think, to perceptual-manipulative operations using only bodily organs. . . .

Yours, *Dewey*

[Key West, Florida,] March 26, 1944

[To Bentley:]

. . . Our inquiry to attain knowledge of knowledge is thus radically marked off from the start from epistemological inquiries purporting to attain the same conclusion, meaning by "epistemological" inquiries those which proceed by postulating subject-object, or mind-world (or consciousness) as basic pre-conditions, in terms of which, or in reference to which, the account of knowledge must be given. . . . To some, including ourselves, it seems a strange procedure, if not absurd in the sense of self-contradictory, to assume knowledge of what is designated subject-object, etc., prior to and conditioning any knowledge of knowledge. But, at this point, this fact is not mentioned as an objection to the epistemological procedure, but as a way of indicating, by means of a sharp discrimination, the nature of the procedure in arriving at knowledge of knowledge, which will be here adopted and described. We begin with what is accepted as knowledge, at the given space-time period, on the ground of the best existing authorized (that is, tested) methods of inquiry, and undertake to observe and report them as facts by further use of the methods by which the knowledge under study or inquiry was itself arrived at. In short, what is already known is the data for knowledge of knowledge. The subject-matter of recognized sciences constitutes the subject-matter data arrived at by the most thoroughly tested and competent methods, and in consequence, that which has been most carefully and systematically named. Employing such knowledge as subject-matter of investigation does not (as already indicated), in any way, purport to say or imply that other modes of knowledge are of slight or no account. It points to the fact that when they are named and reported, they come, in virtue of that very fact, within the scope or "domain" of knowledge that is named and known.

Dear Bentley:

This [above] . . . is evoked by your [comments]. . . . Of course, the wording is not meant to be adopted as is. It sets forth "in principle" what was suggested as to order of statement by your pages. I think this mode of approach, in improved verbal form, would lead up to (1) perceptive-manipulative knowledge, and (2) to agency, organism-environment reports as strictly within the transactional, [held] out and held off, temporarily for inspection.

I think your suggestion about "search—re-search" can be adopted generally.

With best regards, *Dewey*

Key West, Florida, March 28, 1944

Dear Bentley:

. . . I want to say a few words *re* "interaction." It has occurred to me that part of the difficulty is that I have been used to using that word with a broader and deeper naming-potentiality than you are used to giving it—due, in case such a difference exists, to emphasis upon the *inter*. For example, Lewis' "association of marks and sounds with a fixed meaning" strikes me as a denial of interaction, not as a case of it. And I had been accustomed to treating Newton's "action and reaction are equal and in opposite directions," * in connection with his theory of independent corpuscles, as at least *pre-interactional*, not a virtual denial of it. If he had placed his action-reaction within an interactional situation, [it] seems to me his framework would have been quite different. Perhaps, the point I have in mind is covered by what you write about proper and illegitimate uses of "interaction"—which is a good thing to insert, in any case. But I have a feeling that explicit emphasis upon "inter" brings it closer to "trans," and explains some of the difficulty I have had in the case, for example, of *organic* conditions and *environing* conditions. (I believe, or at least hope, that it has been a long time since I've used the wholesale noun words, interaction of organism and environment, instead of protecting the statement by using adjectives and the words "conditions" or "processes.")

* The exact words of Newton's Third Law of Motion are: "To every action there is always opposed an equal reaction: or, the mutual actions of two bodies upon each other are always equal, and directed to contrary parts." *Mathematical Principles of Natural Philosophy,* p. 13. (Eds.)

The above is not intended to apply in our formulated document. It is said by way of helping clarify my past usage and my tendency to use the word "inter" where "trans" would be to the point.

Re your statement about transactions not having consequences—or products (I forget the word used)—I agree in a certain sense of that word, as indicated by your statement, that "transact" is the thing itself. But I think it also has to be made clear that *a* transaction is a member of a system of transactions (as, for example, in the case of borrow-loan, credit-debit), and that other specifiable transactions (plural A's or An's) are *its* consequences in constitution of the system. But, of course, it must be made clear that they—the consequences—are transactions themselves.

Anyway, I am leaving out that part of my article ["By Nature and by Art"], including the discussion of perceptual knowledge and knowing how as "by nature," to which you properly objected. . . .

Yours with regards, *Dewey*

Key West, Florida, April 8, 1944

[To Bentley:]

. . . In my revised "Nature-Art" piece I said the traditional rational-sensible knowledge problem was to be resolved by identifying the "rational" with the developed system of knowledge as that functions, and the "sensible" with here-now subjectmatter which, when fused with the other, has scientific properties, while it also anchored it and kept it from being hypothetical. I think this is right as far as the distinction-connection links up with it as *going* concern.

[*Dewey*]

[Key West, Florida,] April 8, 1944

Dear Bentley:

. . . It is interesting and encouraging to note how often we tend mutually to anticipate each other—as in the case of "trans—inter." What I wrote wasn't for the sake of changing the terminology in the document, but to explain my past usage. When you definitely raised the question on the former point, after thinking it over, I came to the following conclusion: "Trans" is proper word for the actual fact-event as primary and total—that is, in its own occurrence, without respect to analysis. "Inter" is, in comparison, a name for a secondary fact-event—analysis of *a* trans-fact into constituent conditions, e.g., any case of human behavior is a transaction, which, however, in respect to some particular problem may be resolved into interaction of specified organic-environing conditions, neither of which has any factual-event status, save with respect to trans-actional behavior.

236

There is . . . [your] point . . . [that] has to do with "judgment-proposition," and my seeming lapse from a completely fused "meaning-name" account. I did not intend by any means to desert the integration by starting with Judgment as independent of language and make language a more or less incidental aid, though my wording may be so awkward as to give that impression. The subjectmatter I had in mind is that pointed to by evidence and pleadings in a court trial (called propositional in the sense of proposal-subjectmatters), and the decision or determination of controverted problematic material under inquiry. This, of course, is itself linguistically stated, and that fact should have been made clear. But while the language-formulations during the trial take effect in further prosecution of the trial itself, the decision of the case (through jury-judge) takes effect in fine, damages paid, or prison term, or payment of costs, or established and final exemption from such events.

In short, I used "judgment," not to stand for a mental event, but for a factual end or termination definitely reached, and "proposition" for a process as still in process, and, hence, still tentative and relatively indeterminate. I think the distinction-connection has to be made as a specified case of the means-end distinction-connection. If the distinction is rendered more prominent or emphatic than the intrinsic connection, it goes contrary to my definite treatment of end-means. As respects terminology, I should probably have referred to two phases of the status of propositions, one relatively tentative, a determinate and decisive proposition in process, and a determinate proposition as the relatively finished or accomplished proposition: relatively since subject to further inquiry-processes and to revision later. With respect to subject-matter, a definitive proposition (what I called "judgment") while in process is like a house in process of erection; each proposal or means arrived at is *used* (functions, operates) in further building; the house when built is *used* for the operations of carrying on domestic life, use as factory-store, in which language is fused with very different system of meanings. I don't mean to say that I made these matters plain in my *Logic,* but that this is the factual subjectmatter that warrants a distinction-connection of the kind I was somewhat blindly driving at. . . .

Dewey

[Key West, Florida,] April 10, 1944

[To Bentley:]

I think I can make a clearer statement of what I tried to say the other day about "propositions." I did not intend to use the word "proposition" to cover every kind of verbal linguistic form. On the contrary, I was engaged, as far as subjectmatter is concerned, in pointing out two subjects so different that they need explicit recognition by different words.

One of them consists of relatively tentative statements put forth as *proposals*—of material to employ and the course to follow in reaching the kind of statement that is determinate or decisive at that time and place. I proposed to call the former "propositions"—and since the things called "propositions" by contemporary writers are, as matter of fact, of this kind, the name wasn't wholly arbitrary. *Their* "propositions," in other words, make sense only when understood in this fashion. Linguistic statements of the concluding and relatively conclusive kind, to which I gave the name "judgment," are of a more direct sort. Their office is not to promote obtaining of warranted statements. They are the kind of statement that accompany transactions undertaken on their own account—not deciding whether there is debt, for instance, but the deed of having to pay or the state of being legally absolved. The language that is appropriate has a different kind of subjectmatter. I don't mean I made this clear, but this is the way what I said lines up, when translated into the terminology we are trying to fix. My earlier treatment was misleading as far as it gave the impression that judgment was independent of any linguistic statement, instead of being language having a very different subject-matter than that of what I called "propositions."

[*Dewey*]

Key West, Florida, April 20, 1944

Dear Bentley:

. . . I have got so used to writing in analytic terms, in the hope that I can get some other philosophers to see the error of *their* analyses, that I slip away from the primary transactional fact into the "how come" form of statement. I have written to and for other philosophers so long that I don't [easily] break myself [of this habit]; for teaching and for writing to philosophers—also teaching—the "how come" mode of statement is the most effective. Your habit is that of scientists—putting the "as is" first. . . .

Yours, *Dewey*

[Key West, Florida,] April 21, 1944

[To Bentley:]

I was struck in reading the quotations on "Fact" [in "On a Certain Vagueness in Logic"] by the fact that the incoherence in all of them has a common source. It arises from starting unconsciously or deliberately with the subject-object, mind-world, self-external relation as primary—what I have called the "epistemological" approach. In consequence, "fact" is bound to turn up in two guises fundamentally incompatible with one another, once as "reality in its own right," independent of cognition, and then as the "veridical" element in knowledge as over against the fictional; then follows the attempt to get over the contradiction by making the latter a correct or true grasp, apprehension, cognition, etc., of the (previously) independent "reality."

What I had in mind, in opposing what I called the "logical" to the epistemological, was that the factual, as distinct from the fictional, in the knowledge field is an affair of connections between items already in the field—in short, a question of specific *evidence*. The writings of the type you quote don't directly tackle the so-called "transcendence" of [the] knowledge problem—how mind, consciousness, self, subject, etc., can get outside itself and lay hold [of]—apprehend—what by nature is "external" to it. They merely are so habituated to *it* they take it for granted, and then are totally unaware of the resulting incoherence in their treatment of factual.

I don't mean all this should be gone into in the document; it is too definitely on the side of "inquiry" and away from the primary transactional fact. But I think it would help the reader if in a few sentences it is pointed out that the incoherence isn't arbitrary and personal, but the inevitable result of an original separation that goes contrary to the fact of knowledge as a fact-event; since the only way of avoiding the incoherence is to start with transactions of knowings-known and work from them, there is a definite confirmation of our position. . . .

[Dewey]

Paoli, Indiana, April 21, 1944

Dear Dewey:

Here is something which we may never have taken up explicitly, although it has been around incidentally.

I am inclined to equate "knowing" in the broad sense—in any and every *broad* sense—with "behavior" so that they can be used interchangeably. The narrow sense, or set of senses, may then be determined within the behavioral frame.

James in [the] 1884 papers ["On . . . introspective psychology," "Absolutism and Empiricism"] consolidated cognition and feeling. It has been basic to me since I first went into action in the nineties. The new "sign" set-up, which officially makes all behavior to be sign-process transactionally viewed and organizes sign in the stages signal-name-symbol, implies this.

I do not call to mind anything express in your position as to this, as I do about most issues. I would suspect: 1. that, structurally, since [the] "Reflex Arc" paper, you operate this way; 2. that habits of talking to teachers and general public pull your expression away from it and over to the "personal" side.

239

The question seems to me [to be]:

If, and when, we use the word "know," do we make prominent a characteristic that enters into all animal behaviors from protozoan to tensor analyst? Or: do we make prominent a characteristic that distinguishes certain types of behaviors from other types?

Of course, in our paper we have done the latter for temporary purposes in using namings as knowings, but at the same time we have implied the former in saying namings were only one level of knowings. But neither of these steps tells us whether we are going to decide that knowings range from protozoa to tensors or not.

Regards, *Bentley*

Paoli, Indiana, April 23, 1944

Dear Dewey:

The difficulty I have been having is probably due to my being technically "stale." I am going to do other work till I freshen up. But if I get a half-thought anywhere along the line, there is no reason why I should not slide it in.

You have not said anything to this effect, but I suspect as between us, the following gives you some pause: You use a biological naturalism. I use a linguistic behavioralism. I place my behavioralism as a phase of your naturalism. You rate your naturalism *qua* knowledge as a linguistically engineered behavior. In your free expression you frequently use expressions that I do not like as they stand, and that I want expanded. Similarly, my expression affects you frequently. The same kind of reaction runs as to patterns of presentation. I have been doing the writing. I get all my side of it in first. I suspect—indeed I feel quite sure—the effect to you is that we are too far out toward the end of the limb. I am equally sure that if you had been doing the writing, I would feel you had been building too emphatically in terms of historical organisms, making them as "existing facts" rather than as "the way nature is now formulated" in the general scientific status of the day.

I wonder if we can beat the game as follows (and I am talking strictly of organization of presentation):

Take out of the introductory matter the assertions that we are dealing with the organism in nature as evolved. Make this into a preliminary exposition. It might be short. Maybe, a page would do it. But make it strong. Put it at the front. . . .

Then say: This naturalism is used by us, not as "real" or "forever so," but as cultural knowledge of today.

Then proceed with most of the development. . . .

Then follow this with the next-to-be-written paper based on evolutionary-contemporary signal-name-symbol behaviorial stuff—that is, with the development suggested biologically in the short introductory passage. . . .

Regards, *Bentley*

[Key West, Florida,] April 24, 1944

[To Bentley:]

Answering your specific question of the 21st, there is no doubt I am not habituated to using "knowledge" as broadly as you do—as equated with "behavior." My habit is to use it as characteristic of [a] distinctive *aspect*—not kind—of behavior, not as inclusive of feeling aspect. I am talking here about my habit, not about what is proper. I'll have to think the thing out in its implications. . . .

J. D.

[Key West, Florida,] April 25, 1944

[To Bentley:]

. . . I don't think the card I sent was at all clear. So here goes.

I think you are right in saying that the signal-sign-symbol position is a commitment to recognition of a knowing-known aspect or phase in all behavior from protozoa all the way through, with further discriminations made within this broad use. I don't believe I have ever expressly taken this position in the past, but I am glad to take it now explicitly.

What I am not so sure about, as yet, is that this recognition is identical with *equating* knowing with behavior. I'll have to look up the papers, 1884, of James when I get back; I can't recall them now. Offhand, consolidation of knowledge and feeling, *save* as connected-distinguished aspects or phases of behavior, tends to give me the shivers. But I am open to persuasion if the papers give adequate reasons for a literal equating. Behavior as transactional is bound, it seems to me, to present distinct-connected aspects. (1) In its continuity, it is life as conserving process, having impetus or momentum (I don't use these words technically, only as hints of an aspect for which I can't supply proper name). (2) It is marked by hesitations, need of re-adaptations, change of immediate line of direction; the feeling or emotional aspect is rooted here from protozoa through to human interest or concern, as, for example, to find out about tensors, etc. (3) In the transactions that are behavior, certain elements are constituted in these hesitation-re-adaptation phases of behavior to be signals-signs-symbols.

It is obvious, I think, that this account is definitely from [the] biological standpoint—which, so far, I don't . . . [think] can be avoided if the protozoa-man sequence is brought in at all. What I have labeled (2)

241

above is the ground of the "problematic," on the directed inquiry level, dealt with in my *Logic*. In calling them "aspects" or "phases," I intend, of course, to affirm [that] they are distinction-connections brought out in analysis, not separate factual items. Now, so far, I don't see how the statement we are trying to make in terms of behavioral transactions can avoid falling *within* the inclusive fact of knowing, signal stage included, as connected with an operation of re-adaptation in a continuing transactional process. As such, if the general account is correct, *it* involves selection ("analysis") and rearrangement ("synthesis").

The above is for the sake of making clear the ground upon which I have been proceeding, so if there is any difference between us, it can be located—and any needed "re-adjustment" be made. It isn't put down as a finality, by any means. But, so far, I haven't been able to escape from interest, concern, as giving direction to knowledge—I mean I haven't been able to go [to] a literalistic view of knowing. (The *words* "interest," "concern," are of course dangerous to use at present—they are too loaded with "subjectivistic mentalism." But, as I recall, in your *Process of Government*, you have shown that "interests" must be used in another way to make sense; one compatible with the transactional standpoint as basic.) . . .

[*Dewey*]

[Key West, Florida,] April 26, 1944

[To Bentley:]

The following is not even preliminary, save as being preliminary to an attempt to clear myself up. I seem to think better with pen or typewriter in hand, so this is written for myself rather than for bearing on the document.

I think you are right in saying that the original objective has somehow vanished. I am wondering if the trouble did not begin when the shift was made from the original simple "Terminological" title to "Naturalistic Specifications, etc.," with the result, as you say, of giving the impression we are telling the world something new about knowing. I believe the fault for the shift lies at my door, with you as accessory, because you were too willing to adapt your treatment to my previous terminological excursions. Now, as I think I've said before, I have used language *ad hoc* to try to get over a particular point to a given class of readers, without much respect for coherence in system. (There are probably, I hope, some exceptions of a fairly basic quality.) In addition, I have worked hard in the past to get philosophy over to a more naturalistic base and function, and that has kept creeping in too much when I have written you. So I think the article should (1) definitely return to the original

242

objective, (2) with its emphasis upon finding a set of usable names, (3) as free as is humanly possible from misleading associated significations due to extraneous sources; (4) to secure this emancipation, we have, probably, to illustrate what is meant by extraneous by some pointed and reasonably brief references to epistemological assumptions as conditioning the signification of names used, and what is intrinsic (non-extraneous) by some reference to—illustration [of]—scientific naming—these things not as a question of correct and incorrect, but as a matter of what we are doing—trying to do—the medium in which we are operating. (By the way, I have sometimes tried to use the word "medium" to escape the externality of "Environment"—this has nothing to do with present topic, but using the word made me think of it.) I think, imagine, that towards the end some reference to the naturalistic approach will be pertinent, as a sort of signboard-hand putting the reader wise to the general context or medium. . . .

I see clearly now that treatment of "Transaction" should come before reference to "Fact," etc. More illustrative indications are needed of "Transaction"—loan, etc., good—but you need also something of the kind you have written (in a letter, maybe) about such words as "Culture," and emphasizing the meaning of "across." In one of my earlier writings I made a point about what I called "gross" and "refined," and the necessity of carrying the latter back to the former. What I said in a letter about primary and secondary names was likely a reminiscence. If I had associated earlier in the game what you name "transactions" with what I was trying to get at with my "gross," I guess I wouldn't have got off the track so easily. (I wouldn't have tended to substitute the adjective "transaction*al*" so frequently for the noun.) I hate to admit I was so stupid, but I am afraid I'm only just now getting the "whole hog" fact in its wholeness and hogginess. . . .

You are about 100% right, I think, as to our different approaches. The linguistic behaviorism is your baby, and things *have* to be stated that way before a "linguistically engineered behaviorism" in terms of accultured historic organisms will get a show of being understood. And, besides, I have had, and may continue to have, plenty of chance to state things from my own angle of approach. So your letter only confirms my idea that the foregoing is at least headed in [the] right direction. . . .

Now I've finally come within sight of the objective, I'm all for holding down the paper as far as may be to what you call "the way nature is formulated today in the general scientific status of the day"—in the culture in its scientific aspect of 1920? 19??

I don't think the two modes of approach and statement conflict; on the contrary. But we have allowed them to be mixed, me as principal, and you as accessory, in hopes. I'm sure you are right in saying that my approach will continue to be distorted and taken for what it isn't meant to be till something definitive along your line is available.

[*Dewey*]

[New York,] May 10, 1944

[To Bentley:]

. . . I imagine my sticking point has been something like the following. Interaction depends, as you point out, upon prior knowledge of the engaged factors taken *apart* from transaction, while in every transaction such separation is impossible. But when we wish to know a transaction *with respect to a certain type of problem,* we proceed by analysis into an interaction of distinguished factors. For example, take the transaction borrowing-loaning. *Re* "transaction." It is absurd to treat it as inter-action of distinct factors. But there may (and does) arise a type of problem in which it is needful to inquire into the causes which led A to borrow and B to loan, and also into the respective consequences of the transaction upon the subsequent careers of A and B respectively. In other words, in *further* knowings a transaction is placed in a new and inclusive time-space setting in which, ex post facto, it is viewed (treated) as an interaction. In other words, in dealing with the subjectmatter of knowings, attention may have to be given to particular dates-locations of the extensive space-time cosmos-knowledge.

The passage you mention from my *Logic* [pp. 33–34] in which I treat of "Nature" becoming "Environment" is more than a hedge in accommodation to possible readers. It was a definite slip. But there was something factual behind it, I think. What was behind it, but not brought out, is a distinction between what is actually in knowledge at a particular or given place-time and what is there "potentially"—that is, with respect to knowing-knowns as a continuous, extensive transaction; a distinction-connection I probably have at times called by the words "explicit-implicit," "direct-indirect." But which in terms of our present attempt may perhaps be specified as that of the *named-unnamed* at a given place-date. I think I spoke once of the fact that some readers were likely to give an "idealistic" twist to some statements in our document, and the consequent need of distinguishing between "Nature or Cosmos" as known at a given time-date and as subjectmatter of continuous extensive knowing.

The above is, of course, more or less an afterthought rather than a statement of what was definitely in my thought when I made that distinction between "Nature" and "Environment." It isn't, however, an attempt to explain my slip away, but is intended to suggest the need for a specified distinction-connection of the general character (it now seems to me) of the named-unnamed as found at every stage and phase of the knowing-known transaction.

244

Knowings-knowns as a progressive transaction is a continuous naming of what was previously unnamed, and such naming involves more or less *re*-naming of what was previously named.

While I can't locate any express passage, I believe that I have at times said that nature or cosmos in its totality is present, through its consequences upon qualities, properties and connection, directly or explicitly noted, in every case of inquiry-subjectmatter. If I had been sufficiently aware of what I was about, I would have made this clear in the nature-environment passage.

(Incidentally, though not for our document, I think there is somewhere in the foregoing a key to the consciousness-unconsciousness business, when the nouns are reduced to adverbs.)

[*Dewey*]

[New York,] May 10, 1944

[To Bentley:]

Undoubtedly, "fact" doesn't "take place." It is that which has taken place, does take place, and will take place, not just as event, but *as event designated* in full transactional statement.

[*Dewey*]

[New York,] May 12, 1944

[To Bentley:]

. . . Introduce "reporting" along with the words in parenthesis; "naming, establishing," etc.? Question mark is because "reporting" might seem to introduce a split between naming and what is reported. But there are many uses of "report" in which events are not complete until they are reported. In court proceedings as well as in scientific investigations the report—account—is an integral and terminal, but not finally terminated, completing, part of the event. The only thing that raises this point above verbal triviality is that it may serve to emphasize the continuing durational property of knowings-knowns. To *expound* is to *expose* or lay open to observation, and no line can be drawn between observing and describing.

. . . I haven't a good phrasing for it, but the distinction here drawn between knowledge "at" a time and place, and knowledges as themselves extended and enduring, is so important that it might well be amplified—maybe the reader could be invited to consider the difference between knowledge as a fact that is cumulatively growing over long periods and found in books, articles, libraries, with the common treatment of it as something done at a particular time-place by a particular Agent—whether a bodily organism or a mind—and to consider how the latter mode of treatment has resulted in complete departure of the prevalent theories of knowledge from knowledge as a fact that can be observed and described. Some emphasis here upon the difference would, I think, help readers see what our standpoint is and what we are trying to do. Probably, at bottom, the tendency to deal with knowings and knowledge as something confined to specified locations and dates is one case of the "epistemological" approach, but I believe it should receive separate—distinct—recognition.

. . . I agree with what you say about dropping "experience," as not needed. I should like the mode of treatment a little more sympathetic —probably because of my own past struggles. I think it might be said that the word once served a useful purpose as a protest against introduction, under the name usually of "reason," of unobservable entities, and might be even viewed as an approach to the fusion of knowings-knowns —a tendency that became explicit with James's insistence upon the "double-barreled" nature of experience and upon "neutral experience." But when that fact is established, the word "experience" is no longer needed, and we can get rid of the subjectivistic or mentalistic colorings so often attached to it, especially in writings purporting to be psychological. I put in that last clause because I can find a good many specimens in philosophical writings, even those of different schools, in which the word is used as always "*of* objects," not as mental. I don't mean they got over to the knowing-known identification, but they have certainly used the word as a halting approach to it. But when we get that identification, "experience" can be abandoned in the interest of clarity and definiteness.

I agree as to the possibilities and desirability of avoiding the mass of (mainly) emotional aspects that now saturate the world. . . . When, and if, truth is used in [a] theoretical statement, it should be in connection with the extensive and continuing operations of *test* (repetition of experiments with changed conditions, etc.) under which events acquire the status of fact or knowns. I think it is wholly legitimate to use the moral connotation of truth in connection with communication as cultural (so-called "social") behavior to illustrate the cooperatively extensive and ongoing character of everything entitled to the name of *knowledge*. I'll write something about "meaning" when I get my wits together after further reflection. . . .

[*Dewey*]

[Indianapolis, Indiana,] May 13, 1944

Dear Dewey:

. . . I had lost sight of the closeness of our procedure to the kinetic and potential energy of physics. Physics does not care about those words

246

—it is not harmed by them—it knows that potential energy is not mystically potential, but actually "present," even though quiescent.

We must get our *naming* as actually present, even though quiescent. But potential is not the word—since it gets off to the unconscious *vs.* conscious. Against a conscious as real, and [an] unconscious as something else—all foolishness. But making the conscious the passing poke-up, providing we can name the cosmos that contains it properly, will work. It is damn luck we are dealing with specific namings as knowing-exhibits instead of with knowing-generalities. Now, if you can go a step further and get that more solidly phrased than we have yet, it will be fine.

"Known at a given time" *vs.* "continuous extensive knowing": I would not want to say . . . "knowing-knowns as a progressive transaction is a continuous naming . . . etc.," because we must steadily allow in phrasings for other knowings than naming-knowings. But we might say . . . : Naming-named is a continuous transaction, progressive from barely hinted namings, involving re-namings of what was previously named, and open to better naming of the best present named.

I see still another question enters as to your phrasing (for I have just remodeled yours more than I had expected). You write "a continuous naming of what was previously *un*named." There is a sense in which a good naming exhibits what was previously unnamed in the *poor* naming. Here "naming" enters in the here-and-now form. But if we should carry that so far as to imply a *complete* "*un-named*" in the broadest general sense, I suspect we would fracture our construction. We would have something "outside" or "beyond." This, however, does not hold when we have built namings into the long evolutionary series signals-names-symbols. In that sense we have a legitimate "beyond"—that is, it is "beyond specialized namings," but not beyond the general sign-behavior procedure within which existial [existential]-naming is the great exhibit; or, more specifically, the percept-knowing is not yet name-knowing, while, nevertheless, in the broad scheme both are sign-knowings in a construction in which all knowing is sign-knowing (and no other kind of knowing).

I always get back to that phrase of Peirce in his youth: "All knowing is in signs and requires a time." [*Collected Papers*, V, 151.] * (I am not sure his word was "knowing.") I always have felt that this short sentence was the most pregnant I have ever seen. . . .

I found this from [Georg] Simmel: "Truth is not selected because it is true [(to reality)]; it is true because it has been selected." [James Mark] Baldwin [*Dictionary of Philosophy and Psychology*, II, 720] cited it and paraphrased: "Reality is not that to which truth must correspond;

---

* The exact quotation is: "To say, therefore, that thought cannot happen in an instant, but requires a time, is but another way of saying that every thought must be interpreted in another, or that all thought is in signs." (Eds.)

truth, on the contrary, is that to which reality must correspond" (thus . . . weakening Simmel down to about a quarter of what he intended). . . .

Regards, *Bentley*

New York, May 21, 1944

Dear Bentley:

   . . . It's rather late in the day, but I am beginning to wonder whether some of the statements about knowledge aren't more sweeping than the present job calls for—as if, to use what you wrote not long ago, we were telling something new. . . . But instead of saying or implying (1) that knowledge goes back to the unicellular organism, and (2) that it is all inclusive, it would be more consistent with our main purpose to (1) say just what phase, aspect, or stage of knowledge we are dealing with; and (2) that while it is taken for granted that there is genetic and functional continuity with earlier pre-linguistic events, and that there is an important, indispensable field for inquiry here, we are not now concerned with its particular nature beyond the basic naturalistic fact of continuity with no introduction of conditions or factors from without; and the fact (3) that nothing can be said about the prelinguistic events, save in terms of that knowledge with which we are here concerned, which, accordingly, as far as an account of knowings-knowns is concerned, is all inclusive.

   I suppose what is back of my bringing up this matter now is that in my earlier writings I've made a distinction between what I called "being and having" and "knowing"—between, e.g., being angry and knowing what anger is, and having blue before our eyes and knowing what blue is. I was enough of a naturalist to hold to continuity of development, but I also identified "knowledge" with "statements." Now I am quite willing to modify my terminology, and I wouldn't want to have anything put in our document that in any way suggested the exclusion of use of knowledge to cover prelinguistic transactions and, especially, nothing that would militate against treating knowing through designations as the all-inclusive knowledge, in terms of which all the events I called being and having are themselves observed, described, etc. In fact, it was this latter point that had [led] me to make a distinction. (Incidentally, I used the word "experience" as a name for that of which knowledge, as I treated it, was one distinguished-connected aspect. I don't mention this as relevant to the present document, for "experience" has convinced me that we can get on more intelligibly without the word.)

   The relevancy of the above, if any, to the present discussion is to the *unnamed-named* point. Your comments upon my way of putting the matter are sound, but I think the unnamed-named distinction-connection has to be stated somehow to avoid some pretty fundamental misapprehensions. . . .

I think the division of papers a good one. I don't know about there being any need for the fourth—the orientation with my *Logic*. Maybe, later I could write something as to certain modifications, at least of em-phasis, I would make if writing now. . . .

Sincerely yours, *Dewey*

[P.S.] I've been re-reading your *Behavior, Knowledge, Fact*. What you say about "local" times expresses better than I have done one of the points I've been working at and on. I wonder if the substance of your discussion shouldn't come in somewhere.

[New York,] May 22, 1944

[To Bentley:]

. . . 1. I think "designate" O.K. We needn't be thrown off because others use it in a different way. By the *Oxford* [*English*] *Dictionary* I find that "design" in its first use (now obsolete) was synonymous with "designate"; "design" as plan, purpose, is derived usage (and we have plans of buildings, etc.). A definition of "designate" is to point out, indicate, particularize, specify; another one is "to point out by a name or distinctive appellation, to name, denominate, entitle, style"; still another, "to stand for, be descriptive of." The "sign" part of the word is certainly all to the good. . . .

In my *Experience and Nature* (1926) [actually, 1925] I used the words "denote" and "denotative method." After saying "experience" does not stand for subjectmatter, but for a method, I said it stands for "denotative method." The *Oxford* [*English*] *Dictionary* under "denote" says "to mark; to mark out; to distinguish by a mark or sign" and "to indicate, to give to understand, to *make known*." And under "denotative"—"having the quality of designating." I think "designate" is better than "denote"; less technical.

2. I agree with you about "cause" and "causation." In my *Logic* I say in effect, but not so bluntly, that it is used in reference to a connection between broken events (incidents) that are arbitrarily isolated from the extensive event to which they belong, an isolation justifiable only as it serves to indicate the nature of that event and, when the latter is made out, has to be dropped, having served its purpose. (We don't need to go into that; just don't use the word; causational *interpretation* is O.K.) . . .

I am wondering whether there shouldn't be later a special paper on language. You should write it, as you have all the materials in your *Behavior, Knowledge, Fact*. You only have to generalize in the instances where you may have seemed to limit your remarks to sociological inquiry.

I thought of this in connection with the list of words "tell," "note," "call," "report," "mark," "remark," "pro-positing," etc., "de-scribing" (writing down). "Tell" is a very significant word. It *counts,* has weight, etc., and makes public, communicates. Then there is synonymous use of "tell" and "relate" (a story, event); account-recount. Then there is "denote," as to *make known.* And to *inform* is to *make known,* publish. I don't believe development of this point belongs in the present set of papers. It brings out the connection—fusion—of known with communication—its sociocultural, non-private mentalistic nature. And this is more a matter of telling facts than about use of names.

Something might be done (by way of later illustration of *trans-act*) with a list of double-barreled words, "consideration," "interest," "affair," "concern." No, I guess this is too thin.

"Named-unnamed." Of course, we have to avoid any suggestion of anything *completely* unnamed. And "potential" is, without doubt, a dangerous word. But naming certainly brings out into the open, makes public, *makes* known, overt, ex-plicit, something previously im-plicit, in-volved, im-plied. It focalizes and centres what was loose and scattered. . . .

I am confident we have to take care of the "legitimate beyond," though I don't see very well how to do it, *unless* it is by the signal-name-symbol matter. There is, it seems to me, a marked distinction between even radical re-naming (say in the case of "atom") and naming that which was previously indicated, pointed to, signaled (and, hence, involved) but *not* noted-known, or *re*-marked. Something of this kind was back of what I was used to saying about the difference between "being-having" and "knowing," and about the latter as but one aspectual phase of "experience." If it can be worked out, I should still prefer such a phrase as "sign-*event* of or sign-function" to "sign-knowing," not to preclude their identification, but to leave it open as not essential to the special job in hand. "De-signing" would then come in handy.

You have something about the variety of uses of the *word* "knowledge." "Knowing" as *cunning,* which is *canning,* or ability to do, involving a quality of indirection, justifies the sign-knowing phrase. But unless we should go expressly into the different senses . . . in order to justify the extensive use of "knowing" wherever the sign-function takes place, a wider word—such as "sign-event" or "function"—strikes me as better.

I have just looked up again the *Oxford Dictionary* on "know." It admits that the word now stands for things that earlier were designated by a number of words. It tends to reduce the latter to *two* [three], "can," [or] "ken," and "wit" (German *wissen*), and then it tends to identify (in the explanatory introduction) the former [can, ken] with "knowledge by the senses," (but it also says that it is held by some that knowing always has to do with fact—and that to *know* a person or thing is to know some fact about it; what particular fact being shown by context), and the latter [wit] with "knowledge by the mind"; to ap-prehend and to comprehend or understand; which is just the result of recent epistemological psychology, in my opinion. . . .

[Dewey]

Paoli, Indiana, May 23, 1944

Dear Dewey:

. . . [Alfred] Tarski in current *Philosophy and Phenomenological Research* ["The Semantic Conception of Truth"] . . . is more sarcastic about other people's "semantics" than I ever was. He does a beautiful job on the word "truth." It is a pleasure to read it. But he arrives, by using a meta-language on an object-language, at a practicable, blank statement about "truth"; "a sentence is true if it is satisfied by all objects, and false otherwise." But he nowhere states the conditions that there be objects, nor the fact that these objects are developed by sentences. I want to use him. . . .

I suspect the great difficulty in preparing these papers (since we once got the fact-event-designation scheme clarified) is that we are crowding too much into too short a form. It is too late to change. But I have wondered once or twice whether something else was not practicable. (This being a mere suggestion now, and not capable of determination till after the papers are published, and we see how we like them.) It is: Make a book by taking the four (probable) present papers—precede with your essay on "How [Is] Mind [to Be] Known," follow with extracts from your three main psychological papers ("Reflex Arc," "Naturalistic Theory of [Sense] Perception," and the one in *Psychologies of 1930* ["Conduct and Experience"]) and with the historical point from "By Nature and by Art" as to how knower got grafted on souls; and with some of my papers, a dash of "The Human Skin," etc. A title might be *Knowings and the Known*. My paper "Factual Space and Time of Behavior" should go in, probably. . . .

Books and traditional skills, libraries and technological institutions are knowledges, not as particle-acts of isolated men—but as broad cultural behaviors out of which the particle-acts differentiate and into which they feed back. The broad form is as "human" as the narrow. The broad form states what the narrow form neglects. Here, in actuality, is wide dimension and wide duration of human knowledge. . . .

Regards, Bentley

Paoli, Indiana, May 25, 1944

Dear Dewey:

. . . You suggest "perhaps, symbol may be transaction in the abstract." Why not other way around? When we get "symbol" worked out ob-

251

servably, it should give some sort of meaning to "in the abstract." If "abstract" gives meaning about anything to anybody, it fails to do it to me.

Regards, *Bentley*

New York, May 26, 1944

Dear Bentley:

I've been confining myself lately to comments on special points. I am going to engage now in a general survey.

In writing I've often had the experience, when I get toward the close, of finding that what I said there involves considerable change in what I said in the early part of my discussion; probably, many persons have the same experience. So I find that your second paper ["Interaction and Transaction"] gives me some suggestions, not only about it, but about the first paper ["A Terminology for Knowings and Knowns"].

1. One of them, which I am not at all certain about, is whether the substance of the second paper should not, or could not, profitably form the first paper—after the Introductory section I. It seems to be less formal and to get down more directly to bedrock. However, I know you had your reasons for holding [that] specification of fact, event, naming, should come first. It seems to me that possibly what has to be said about them would come better after the trans-, interact material. This is suggestion only, and I'm open to reason about it.

2. I feel reasonably sure that, if the present order is kept, anything said about "reality," "experience," etc., would be more in place and more intelligible (and with less repetition) in the second main paper.

3. I want to add something to what I said in [an] earlier letter about "experience." I don't believe that "experience" was in its origin a "philosopher's device." . . . The original signification of the word was "to put to test or trial"; then it passed over insensibly to "put to trial by means of observation as the dependable source of knowledge"; the last clause, "as a source of knowledge," is more or less a philosopher's formulation—Bacon's and Locke's, especially—but it was only a formulation of a usage of the word that was already fairly idiomatic. I quote from Peirce [*Collected Papers*, V, 428], when he quotes from Locke's saying that all the "materials of reason and knowledge come from experience," * namely, "Our observation employed either about external sensible objects, or about the internal operations of our minds." The external and internal distinction is, of course, traditional and has to go out—but in its origin, even it was popular. But the *observation* is fundamental. Peirce

* The exact quotation is: "Whence has [the mind] all the materials of reason and knowledge? To this I answer, in one word, from *experience*. . . ." (Brackets supplied by Peirce's editors.) (Eds.)

then says this definition should be "accepted as definite and as a land-mark that it would be a crime to displace." And what he means by this comes out a little later when he says [V, 429], "The idea of the word 'experience' was to refer to that which is forced upon a man's recognition, willy nilly, shaping his thoughts to something different from what they would be." * Then he virtually cancels the "internal-external" affair by saying, "Philosophers of experience, as of other schools, forget to how great a degree it is true that the universe is all of a piece, and that we are all of us natural products, naturally partaking of the characteristics that are found everywhere throughout nature"—so that [it] is "in some measure nonsensical to talk of a man's *nature* as opposed to what his perceptions force him to think." Vol. V, pp. 428–29.†

In another place, after talking about man's "internal world" of fancy, reverie, etc., and the "external world of fact," he says man "defends himself from the angles of hard fact by clothing himself with a garment of contentment and of habituation. . . . I call forcible modification of our ways of thinking the influence of the world of fact or *experience*" (italics in the original text). Vol. I, p. 160 (1903).‡ P. 169 of same: "I think it is probably true that every element of experience is in the first instance applied to an external object. . . . It is [the] special field of experience to acquaint us with events, with changes of perception." [Brackets of Peirce's editors were omitted by Dewey.] P. 37 of . . . [Vol. V], "Experience is our only teacher. . . . But how does this action of experience take place? It takes place by a series of surprises. . . . It is by surprises that experience teaches all she deigns to teach us. . . . Experience says, Open your mouth and shut your eyes/And I'll give you something to make you wise." § (1902, I think.)

In connection with both the last two passages there is [a] very definite statement of "double-barreledness" though it is stated in terms of "Inter-action," not of "Transaction." "In perception two objects really do so

---

* The exact quotation is: "The idea of the word 'experience' was to refer to that which is forced upon a man's recognition, will-he nill-he, and shapes his thoughts to something quite different from what they naturally would have been." (Eds.)

† The exact quotation is: "But the philosophers of experience, like many of other schools, forget to how great a degree it is true that the universe is all of a piece, and that we are all of us natural products, naturally partaking of the characteristics that are found everywhere throughout nature. It is in some measure nonsensical to talk of a man's nature as opposed to what perceptions force him to think." (Eds.)

‡ The exact quotation is: "For this reason we call the world of fancy the internal world, the world of fact the external world . . . [man]. . . . defends himself from the angles of hard fact by clothing himself with a garment of contentment and of habituation. . . . I call such forcible modification of our ways of thinking the in-fluence of the world of fact or *experience*." (Eds.)

§ The exact quotation ends: "But precisely how does this action of experience take place? It takes place by a series of surprises. . . . She says, Open your mouth and shut your eyes/And I'll give you something to make you wise." (Eds.)

react upon each other." A double consciousness—the expected idea suddenly broken off on one hand; on the other hand, the strange intruder in his abrupt entrance. . . . "The old expectation, which is what he was familiar with, is his inner world, his ego. . . . The new phenomenon, the stranger, is from the exterior world or *Non-Ego*." * The double "consciousness" (i.e., perception) is that they are two ends of the same event. (Vol. V, [pp. 39–40].) "It is the compulsion, the absolute constraint upon us to think otherwise than we have been thinking that constitutes experience." (Vol. I, p. 170.) The "doubleness" is that constraint and *resistance* are two aspects of [the] same fact.

I have combined two things here—one is the fact that Peirce is formulating what may be called the classic British notion of "experience," and that is exactly the opposite of the idea of it as "subjective" or [as] a state of consciousness. This latter view is historically late—I should say not before the first half of the 19th century—and came from the "psychologists," not from philosophy. The other point is Peirce's anticipation of the singleness of knowing-known, though he states it in rather physical terms and not as trans-action, and not so much of knowing-known as of know*er*-known—ego-non-ego. However, the *behavioral* attitude is at least implicit in what he says.

I don't go into this detail for the sake of anything to put into the papers, but to clear up background stuff in some detail. In [the] Greek treatment, the "empirical" was the routine, practical, matter of course, order of nature. "Reason" was the intelligible, rational order of nature; beginning with Francis Bacon, the positions were reversed. "Reason" stood in their [early British empirical] criticisms for a kind of combination of personal preferences or "fancy" and a crust of habit. "Experience" was a name for what broke through, and was instructive—standing then for the new and growing. . . .

On the whole, since we can't avoid misunderstanding by those who don't want to understand, I think we'll get better understanding from those who can, by sticking closely to our own knitting in these papers. And, heaven knows, I've pursued the opposite course in my past writings, as a whole.

Coming now back to the papers. You speak of a tendency to scatter. I think it exists, naturally enough, in putting down material at the outset. I am inclined to think that our purpose and position would be clearer if in this set of papers we confined ourselves to a positive statement of that intention and position, cutting out practically *all* reference to the position of others. This wouldn't be because I object to what is said about [C. J.] Ducasse, Lewis *et al.*, but because I have come to think

* The exact quotations are: ". . . in perception two objects really do so react upon one another, . . ." "The old expectation, which is what he was familiar with, is his inner world, or *Ego*." (Eds.)

that some of what we have, tends to get the reader to think in terms of [the] *others'* position, and distracts from a clear-cut statement of our own, and understanding of it. I think you should follow up later with a separate paper on current confusions as to *fact*. (I think, likely, I could give you some more instances.) Some reference to "real" and to "experience" would, as already indicated, be relevant in the second paper to transaction-interaction, as illustrative. In short, make all our own statements positive and clear-cut. . . .

We use the word "fact" to present the direct and forthright, competently reported cosmos, etc., cutting out the negative reference, save perhaps for a *footnote* saying: "It will be noted by the informed reader that this usage contrasts sharply with those interpretations which place 'fact' in a limbo intermediate between indubitable 'reality' and indubitable 'mind' or 'consciousness.'" I think in a footnote it will not interrupt the positive flow, and the phrasing [is] too good to lose. . . .

May 27, 1944

. . . Knowledges are taken as themselves enduring and extensive—with illustrations you have in your letter of 5-23-44, for instance, including "Books and traditional skills." . . . Such knowledges . . . [have] to be placed and understood as they occur in the extensive context. . . . There would be an analogy suggested with the particle-acts of physics; that would carry back to what you say about encouragement from change in physics. . . .

The impression I get from reading present text is that it is rather slow . . . [in] getting down to brass tacks. Fact, event, designation, should be somehow moved up and *out,* more of a "bang," and qualifications come later and more condensed.

(The apparent necessity of introducing reference now and again to transaction-interaction . . . is what suggested to me, whether after the introductory material, trans-, inter paper could come first—that is, fact-cosmos treated first, names as events, facts, in it next. Of course, the trans-, inter gets at once into the knowing-naming procedures, but [we] can't help this circularity anyway.) . . .

About *potential.* I recognize dangerous associations with [the] word. But there has to be some recognition of a distinction between the field, domain, scope, or whatever, of knowledge and what has entered knowledge-naming at a given time and place, and this even with the widest possible extensions of times and places. Taken literally, it isn't true that "What takes place enters knowledge," not in the way that sentence will be understood. The fact that there was such a thing as Mycenaean civilization (and pre-Mycenaean) and that there are lost dramas of say, Aeschylus, has, tautologically, entered knowledge and naming. But lots of things that took place in those civilizations—and in the dramas—haven't

255

entered knowledge, and there is no ground for holding they ever will. Capacity for, availability for, are safe terms. Positively speaking, we have the facts that (a) what is known-named at a given date-place stands in continuity with what has been known and what will be known in an extensive continuum, and (b) that this very continuity involves things *still to be* discovered; the latter may have entered knowledge in some sense, but, certainly, not knowledge as naming. I don't see how both (a) and (b) can be recognized without use of some equivalent of potential. Growth, development, change-in-continuity, in fact, any statement that what takes place is *ongoing in itself* and, not just in [a] time-space [that is] supposed to be an external vessel in which it takes place, seems to involve it. I am not pleading for express use of "potential." But I don't believe the facts of the position we take can be made clear beyond misunderstanding, without words ending in "able." After all, coal, oil, wood *are* inflamm*able*, even if specimens never burst into open flame, and while chemically they are engaged in combustion at *any* time, what is going on as to combustion at a given time and place is subject to a course of events still to occur. Some wood just rots, some is burnt in a stove, some turns to fossilization, according to the subsequent course into which *it* enters.

I know these are commonplaces, and it is silly to write them down. But we don't want any mode of statement that some readers will take to involve their denial. Without some substantial naming-recognition, I'll bet dollars to doughnuts some of the statements about knowing-knowns will be hailed as "idealisms." There is the cosmos *open* to inquiry, to knowing-naming, to "noting," but I don't think it is as wide as the cosmos that enters indirectly into our manipulative behaviors, which as takings-place are continuous with what has previously taken place. All I want is a mode of statement that doesn't *seem* to shut that out. I think it can be stated without getting into the conscious-unconscious foolishness; something in the nature of "named-unnamed." . . .

Yours, Dewey

Paoli, Indiana, May 29, 1944

Dear Dewey:

. . . My position is (personally, but not, at the moment, for insertion into the paper):

1. At the line at which the psychological or behavioral differentiates from the physiological, we begin to find distinctive markings. There are choices, indirections, "lines" of conduct. Men speak of them as "conscious" sometimes.

2. From here on up there is something of the "cognitive." (In this connection I mention James's union of cognition and feeling aspectually.)

3. The word "knowledge" runs hither and yon from belly-learning to "knowledge of God."

4. It is one of the words we would like to "specify."

5. It is a word, however, that we are hardly yet in a position to specify for general uses by everybody.

6. I have never expressed an opinion, no matter what sketches I have made, in earlier stages of our inquiry.

7. I have asked you whether *you* wanted to run it all the way down. You do not. Neither do I.

8. I would accept any dividing line on the way up from perceptions and small habits.

9. The only place I know where I could differ from you would be that if knowledge was said to begin with naming-existence (probably, an excellent place—or possibly—even though we had to say, maybe, that a dog did not "know" the rabbit it ate), *then* I would have reasons for excluding symbolic mathematics from a "knowing" category.

10. I would not want to take this last step now—don't have it fully enough worked out.

11. This knowledge business seems to be two-dimensional—one, expressive; and two, habit-established. Almost everybody gets excited about "dimensions," at some time. I wonder if they have been applied this way to knowings. Not that I want to do it. . . .

Regards, *Bentley*

Paoli, Indiana, May 31, 1944

Dear Dewey:

Here is a letter that is apt to be long. . . .

Your eight pages of May 26 and 27 offer a pretty complex problem. Certain large structural suggestions I can readily adapt myself to, whether they are, or are not, what I might primarily suggest. Certain of the minor suggestions I might debate, though most are improvements, but there is one which, if of more than local significance, might blow the procedure sky-high. I don't expect that, but I am well enough used to such results in my own work—if things work, they work; and if they don't work, they don't, and no harm done.

Structural

1. I have no objection to tossing Nagel, Ducasse, and Lewis. Adding Tarski and Carnap, and maybe Morris, I would enjoy making a separate paper, with you joining or not, as you wish, when the job is finished. A title might be, reminiscently, "On a Certain Vagueness in Logic." I do not regard these, however, as illustrations, but as critical demonstra-

tions that something is wrong in the old background. I would therefore like to see the paper go in advance of the others.

2. As to putting the "Transaction" paper ahead of the others, it may well be done. The *argument* belongs in the introductory matter preceding the introduction of "Fact" in our manner. It was there originally, but it took too much space. . . . If the "Transaction" paper goes ahead of the "Fact" paper, I would want it very clear that it is merely there as a technical device, not claiming glory of its own.

3. As for the general revision . . . I doubt if it can be done by minor repair jobs such as you suggest. I think worse of it than you do. The trouble goes deep. It involves objectives and organization. When we straighten this out, the paper will quickly clear up, just as the "Transaction" paper did when given a chance to itself.

Historical

We started at your suggestion to find a few "leading words" for "knowledge." After a while we settled on Fact-Event-Designation as our first line of namings. Set over against these, we adopted Signal, Name, and Symbol, the first for the perceptive-manipulative, the second for designatory-existential, the third for mathematical-symbolic. This means two complementary papers.

We have had an understanding that these two papers would be developed alongside, each freely in its own terms, but neither to be regarded as acceptable till the other was finished also.

In developing the first side I found myself pushed back and forth between a desire for a sharp, short dictionary-like assemblage of names, and the need for protecting the names against misunderstanding as we brought them in. Swinging back and forth between large and short forms of presentation, I find myself convinced that three protection measures *must* be taken before our uses of "Fact," and "Name," and "Event," can be clearly presented in distinction from the current uses that differ from us. These are:

1. That we have no intentions [interest] in or designs toward *reals* beyond knowledge.

2. That we use scientific specification, and not symbolic definition.

3. That we are not compelled to accept "things" as naïvely observed by us and treat them causationally, but that instead, we have the right to build up transaction as well as to break down interactionally.

"Postulations"—Sec. IV

The above "conditions" are Postulates #2, #3, and #4. . . . To them I have prefixed the general durational postulate #1, and have appended (as I wrote you, or asked you) a #5 on basis of a suggestion of phrasing

258

from you: "nothing inherently unobservable." This new postulate, in rough first phrasing, . . . is:

5. Nothing "inherently non-observable" is presumed; the very words "inherently non-observable" are absurd in growing research. Observation and description go together, hand in hand. What is here and now observed links both in event and in observation with what is here and now not observed; and what is here and now being described links in the same way with what is here and now not being described. The reports of the moment must be read into the wider reports, rather than being treated for the most general purposes of construction as the isolated building blocks from which the wider reports are made.

Query: If we are going to shorten the preliminaries of the paper, can we possibly get along with less position-taking than in these five points?

Query: Remembering that this is all provisional phrasing, with no attempt as yet to tighten it up, what shadow of difference is there between what I am setting forth, and your view . . . 5-27? . . .

Certain Details

The issue you raise about . . . "know" is in error, and due to my condensation of phrase. . . . When I first noted that we could select a region of knowings and treat it as namings, I felt it was one of the guiding schemes, as it freed us from the usual vagueness of such discussions and gave us something observable to talk about. . . . Touched up, . . . it now reads: . . . "The range of the events to which the word 'knowing' is at times applied by current writers is very wide. Types of application run all the way from the amoeba's simple engulfing of food to the lore of the dog in the forest, the dealings of a worker with his tools, of a scientist with his specialized observations, or of a teacher with his texts, and from these on to symbolic knowledge through mathematics' powerful aid." I might have added here "to the mystic's communion with God" to balance the amoeba. If the amoeba bothers, we can readily begin with a toad's knowing a fly—indeed, I think that would be better—but it makes no difference in what is being said. Note the amoeba cannot engulf food without discriminating it.

I note another phrase that was careless on my part which seems to lead to misinterpretation. . . . "What takes place enters knowledge." It should not be read as "All that takes place," but as: "Only what takes place can enter knowledge and be available to science." Even then, it is poor phrasing. But it certainly does not indicate divergence of views. The worst thing about it is [that] the use of "knowledge" [is] wholly vague and undefined. If that word was out, there might be no trouble. . . .

As for the words "take place," they are your suggestion, though I have over-done their use. They come in excellently in a loose passage, but should not be used as I have. . . .

The One Serious Peril

You propose to strike out a . . . passage [that] states that naming is a form of knowing. It is the very heart of our project. It is the most radical thing we have. . . .

Take this out, and we have nothing left. This position is primarily your own—you have taken it atmospherically for years. Here we have it developed and made the core of a report on knowing. It makes things definite. . . .

What Worries Me

Not any of the detail that can be remedied. . . . It is the fact that naming-knowing is not strongly enough brought out.

The situation is this: I developed the Transactional differentiation on the needs of the naming-knowing. In earlier drafts . . . these held together. But they grew far too long. Then, when the "Transactional" became a separate paper, the naming-knowing was left in the air. . . . I have done something to correct this. If we definitely move the "Transaction" paper ahead of the "Fact" paper, the thing will probably solve itself.

A Challenge

Your treatment implies that we can get in the "Fact" paper to a statement of Fact in three or four pages without all the preliminaries. In fact you say that. Take the specification for "Fact," "Event," and "Designation." Set them down. Forget all my work. Toss it away. Proceed to write an introduction and a set of leading-up passages such that you are confident the reader will get your meaning without distortion. . . .

A Request

You evidently feel that a lot of my positions are divergent from yours. Instead of implying it, and discussing my text, why not set down in a row the positions in which you think I diverge? Then show development lines or passages or arguments that diverge. (Chance words have no importance at this stage at all; for I have made no attempt to refine phrasing in incidental passages. There must be no chance words in the end, but if you expect me to refine details before I can see the larger plan, you are going to be disappointed. I will fail.)

Personal

You have covered an enormous ground, and have a great number of followings, to whom you have talked in a variety of forms of expression, as you have often said.

I hold that central to your work is a sound observation, an empirical control, and a steady development not consistent in the logical sense, thank God, but thoroughly coherent in the scientific sense. I believe your *Logic* exemplifies this, and is a couple of generations ahead of anything we now have.

So far as I know, I am the only person who looks upon your *Logic* in this way. Plenty of men use bits, and plenty express admiration. Your logical readers, like your other readers, split off when the test comes. They take a few colors or shadings and flee the rest.

I am no good at personal or biographical appraisal. I don't pretend I am right in above remarks—it is only the way it looks to me.

Consistently throughout our work till the last few letters, you have participated in development along this line. These latest letters read as though what I was doing had been getting away from your approved central line of development.

The one thing I do not want is through mere contact or joint interest to get you involved in something that you will not look back on favorably. I might easily do it, through moving sideways myself somewhere instead of forwards. I have repeatedly suggested caution, and it was for this reason . . . I wished you would get some friend, seeing things from a different angle, to check up.

The only point about all this is that if the work seems to continue to go wrong, and if it does not straighten out, I want you to feel perfectly free—indeed I would urge you—to postpone it or toss it aside altogether. It won't make the slightest difference to me. I am used to it. . . .

Regards, *Bentley*

[P.S.] After Sleeping on It (6-1-44): *One possibility.* I may be thinking too highly of, and putting too much stress upon, our central Fact-Event-Designation conclusions. But I think not. I have examined some of your writing and some writing about you. Generalities are everywhere and insignificant. *Your* development has centered both in observation and in expression-forms on the agent—on results for (to benefit) the agent. (It is this which has permitted Mackays, e.g., to subjectivize everything you do.) I think we have gone definitely beyond this, and if so, we *should* center on it. We have equated "Fact" with "Cosmos" (not with outcome, as measured to agent); and we have positively put "Agent" in "Cosmos" in this particular respect. This is much more than proclaiming organic knowledge organized to organic centers with a cultural binder.

Another possibility. You have for several months included discussions of the here-now *vs.* long-time type, of which I take your remarks on potential . . . to be specimens. I have not worked them into the text, probably because I felt the text covered them already, and did not "get" the issue as a differential to examine. Perhaps, this is what I was feeling for in "A Request." . . . To be frank, I feel that I have gone further along this line than you have—not to go further back, take the paper "Factual Space and Time of Behavior" . . . regarded not as renewal of generalities but as a technical program for inquiry. If you feel a defect in my approach in this (or any other respect), it would help immensely if you took it up direct, instead of via inferences from the wordings of tentative place-holding passages. . . .

So far as I know, however, there is no essential difference at any point between your view and mine. Differences of stress at stages or report, come of course; also differences of manner of opening up new observations and organizing them. If I thought there was an essential difference, I would quit; and if you think there is one, you should quit (as I see it). It does not matter whether we work this job out. It does matter whether we work straight, or not.

If there is any deeper split that I have not got hold of, the main thing is to bring it in[to] the open. . . .

We take a cosmos. In it we take "naming-knowings" as *a stage*. (This for the next paper.) Yet this whole cosmos we agree upon as a name-known cosmos. . . . We have no "is" about either—only the circularity of technical inquiry into knowledge, always present, which we now bring into [the] open.

We have been in agreement on these points from the very start. Our very subordination of Designation to Fact (though without letting Fact run either idealistically or mechanistically wild) handles the main issue of your [remark], I am inclined to think. Possibly, if I had developed the "Agency" paper without waiting to straighten out the "Fact" paper so far, it would have gone better.

[New York,] June 2, 1944

Dear Bentley:

I hasten to answer one point in yours of 5-29-44 . . . I *don't* want to limit "knowing" and "knowledge" to naming instances. On the contrary. I think not only that knowing-*how* precedes it, and that naming-knowing grows under specifiable conditions out of how-knowing, but that naming-knowing tends, when conditions are ripe, to pass into knowledge in which naming is merged—practically submerged. The face-to-face presence of something in a physicist's laboratory is the ulterior end of namings, as well as of mathematical manipulations of symbols—face-to-face presence is a poor metaphor, but there is just something-observed-there. If there is any difference between us, which I don't think there is, it is more likely to be at this *post*-naming end.

I brought up too many matters; all I had in mind was to make it clear that in these papers we are discussing the naming segment or aspectual phase of knowledge.

The post-naming terminus is what I had in mind when I wrote once that knowledge in its most vital sense can't be conveyed or communicated from one to another. What can be communicated, on the experimental basis, are directions [on] how to obtain an observed subject-matter with an indication of what will be observed if the proper conditions are set up.

Yours, *Dewey*

Paoli, Indiana, June 5, 1944

Dear Dewey:

Yours of June 2 makes clear a definite *split* between us. However—it is not a split of construction, but one of *personal interest* at a certain point. We trot along together until we get *Naming* established as well as it can be. Then we say: Oh, what a nice little fellow. After that your interest runs to enriched living. I wonder if the "having" of your old contrasts fits in—or "feels in"—here.

My interest, however, stays on, on the research side. It runs not aesthetically, but mathematically. I inquire how mathematical stuff (which is definitely *not* naming—*teste* infinitesimals, roots of −1, etc.) aids knowings, by destroying old namings, rebuilding new ones, making them aspectual, and destroying them again, in turn—and always helping out the "doing" (hence, also, I would say—though it is none of my business—the living and having). Perhaps, my main theoretical contribution (if I ever get it stated) will be here: How no mathematical symbol (symbol replacing name or term) is a name; how mathematical systems (layouts, together-hangs) can be taken complete (must be so taken), instead of as built up out of existential namings; how the whole hang-together (but not parts apart) operates like a naming, i.e., how one in research *applies* not a component-term (symbol), but the whole consistent-scheme, and—bang—gets a radio (worse luck).

Regards, *Bentley*

New York, June 6, 1944

Dear Bentley:

. . . After going over recent exchanges, I'll see what I can do in putting things *together*, instead of making comments here and there, which I recognize have often tended to get off center.

No, I haven't held out on you as to differences; if I had any of importance, I'd put them down in black and white. There is an undoubted difference of background and approach, due, I think, to our having been interested in different main problems. But that should be all to the good. I know that trying to see things from your angle has given me a sense of my own position becoming more three-dimensional. The difference of problems strikes me about as follows: You are concerned with knowledge as a solid, extensive, sociological fact, whose nature has to be made out with some definiteness if there is to be a solid basis for sociological theory in directed inquiry. I have approximated your conclusions in many respects because of what I have called the *cultural* transformation of biological (physiological) transactions. But my main interest hasn't been in the body of knowledge as a single extensive fact, as determined by "culture," but in its *further* extension, through *use* of the existing body (taken for granted), by means of *inquiry*. Probably, as a statement of different standpoints of approach, the above isn't very satisfactory. But, maybe, it will suggest how and why they should be complementary. . . .

I repeat, I *don't* feel a lot of your positions are divergent from mine. I think our different modes of approach complement each other. I hadn't expected at my age (I'm 85 in October) to get a "refresher course" that really refreshed. I feel I've got it through this contact with you, and that I can restate my own mode of approach and its results with my feet more on the ground than in the past. . . .

Yours, pending, I hope, something a little
more unified on my part, [*Dewey*]

New York, June 7, 1944 B

Dear Bentley:

Of course, there is a divergence in *interest*—not, however, a split, I believe. People are not interested, as a rule, in what they are not good at, and I am better at least in matters of function than of structure, where I am next to no good and have to take for granted; while functions are, without doubt, matters of "enriched—or impoverished—living."

But I must have expressed myself badly in mine of the 2nd. Just because mathematical symbols are *not* names, and the proposed documents are confined to that naming section of the whole field, I intended no more than the innocent remark that we have no further concern with symbols in these particular papers than their physical, physiological, psychological application extends. . . .

I find your statement of your own interest and contribution, which I don't doubt you will make, clear to the point of being fascinating and exciting. I'm too incompetent to grasp the forms of the hang-together, but I think I get the idea—and the ultimate bang is certainly a case of what I called above, "function."

Yours, *Dewey*

[P.S.] Clarence [E.] Ayres has sent me a copy of his new book, *The Theory of Economic Progress*. In one place, p. 159n, he makes the same remark about "technological and instrumental" that I made in a footnote of my article—only in reverse direction—he thinks "instrumental" less open to misapprehension! . . .

[New York,] June 7, 1944

[To Bentley:]
First Paper. Introductory statement of aim and desire; of standpoint; of connection of work with that of others; those included, those left out; included those who accept the conclusions and methods of science as providing the data for forming a theory of knowledge—that is, of reporting and describing knowings-knowns—on the ground of what is known and how it is known, as of the present age; revisable, developing, just as the findings of science and improvements in its procedures. Those who are left out—those who set up criteria, "norms," etc., for knowledge outside of and prior to the body of knowings-knowns.

(I don't know whether it is proper to introduce the phrase "knowings-knowns" at this point. It may seem as if something had to be brought out first about "transaction" to justify the hyphenated word. On the other hand, it may be possible to use the phrase as a shorthand designation for an attitude or standpoint which systematically considers facts known and methods of knowing in steady, firm connection with one another, without going into the transaction matter; it is possible that such an introductory approach might, temporarily at least, avert the tendency to interpret "Knowings" in the usual "psychological," individual-mental sense, by fixing attention in connection with knowings upon methods as actually used in advance of scientific knowledge.) I hope foregoing is in line, as to knowings-known, with your standpoint, because if I'm off here, I'm sure to be off in what follows. I believe the chief obstacle we have to contend with is that the moment we say "knowings," readers will think of mind and the whole outfit of sensations, perceptions, conceptions, reason, etc. . . .

Yours, *J. D.*

[New York,] June 7, 1944

[To Bentley:]
Here are some notes I made to help clear myself up. Maybe they will have some suggestive value.

To name is to specify; to specify is to note or mark or ob-serve, remark —[notice] the double-barreled, transactional quality of these words. *A* note and *a* mark, and *to* note and *to* mark. He remarked: "He made an

265

observation." Did he *say* something, or did he use a telescope? To specify, name, note, is to identify-by-distinguishing; to elect or select; that is, to pick *out* something from other things and identify it by its difference from them. Observ*ance* in the sense of *keeping* or obeying is a much older English usage than observation in the sense of standing off and looking at something. *Paying heed to,* attending, observing, is first a definitely overt ("practical") behavioral act and then gets thinned down into a cognitive, "intellectual" act. But the latter is still behavioral, though it takes effect in or upon a body of knowledge instead of in or upon some special case of overt conduct. The purely "psychological"—mental—interpretation of observation is wholly, I think, a matter of a particular academic theory; I doubt if it can be matched in a single idiomatic case. Why don't you look out, pay heed, mind what you are about, pay attention, observe, notice, note? And then perform these acts for the sake of what you will find out and add to the knowledge system.

Names—from *proper* names, picking out this, to *scientific* names, which state tested *methods* of picking out "thises" through an indefinitely wide range. Intermediate are pseudo-names; e.g., "general" often means being so vague that its application is left in the dark. Or, perhaps, in this case they are half or quarter names as against such pseudo-names as may excite an emotional reaction, but which designate nothing that can be *observed.* Like the preacher who could make his audience weep by the way he said "Mesopotamia." Value words have to be distinguished from penumbral words where there is deliberate provision for more to be found out. A proper name is at first highly selective, but it leaves specifying characterizations open for indefinite further acquaintance.

[*Dewey*]

Paoli, Indiana, June 10, 1944

Dear Dewey:

Your comment (6-6-44) on the difference of our trends contrasting "body" with "means" of inquiry is better than my recent one so far as our immediate problem is concerned. I think I stressed your goal in "having." But the two fit together, for the "inquiring" and the "having" both develop on the "agency" side. I hope it will not take so very long now before I can sketch the "agency" aspect for the later paper.

I am slower with the "Vagueness" paper than I expected because I have had to go much deeper into Carnap. For the first time in my life I have sympathy for him. He has got far enough along to note repeatedly the type of problem we are working on, and say it is [an] open question, and that he is puzzled. I can put him in with better tone now. . . . Incidentally, he spreads "designation" out to cover "sentence" in line with what we do. Of course, for him the designation of a sentence is its

266

"meaning," i.e., the correlated "proposition," which is just duplicity. It tickles me to find Nagel's review of the Carnap [*Introduction to*] *Semantics* regarding Carnap's "propositions" as "hypostatic Platonic entities," although there is hardly a shadow of difference between Carnap's and his own in [the] Cohen-Nagel book [*An Introduction to Logic and Scientific Method*]. I find Cohen-Nagel quoting Peirce (i.e., *our* side of Peirce) on symbol and language emphatically, and then calmly proceeding as if Peirce had meant *their* side, splitting the meaning from the words-proper. . . .

Incidentally, I am building the "Vagueness" paper as to "propositions" strictly in the comment that to make the man's talk one thing, and his behavior or "self" another, is apparently the source of the trouble, and that we will try a consolidation just for the sake of appraisal. This gets along without using [the] Transaction theses at all. Then, at the end I can broaden the man-doing thesis into a man-thing-doing thesis, and suggest we will see whether we cannot construct that way.

You speak of explicit identification of our job with "science." That is what that . . . tentative introduction was to accomplish, except that I used your "naturalism" positively and let "science" sneak in only as an adjective. Every damn fool calls himself "scientific," and whenever I write the word I aim to eliminate it. When we get cleared up on organization, I think we can get those points down in pretty sharp shape.

As for the third paper . . . we started out for "Terminology." . . . We have got nothing but "Fact," "Event," "Designation," and comments on a few connected terms such as "real" and "exist." The plan then was to . . . take [the] following steps:

(a) briefly organize under "Event," and as event: "Object" on the relatively fixed side, and "situation" on the relatively fluid (or not yet developed side). This is strictly on the lines of your *Logic*, except for using the main name "Event."

(b) Next take "Designation" and set it up within a scheme:

Sign equated with behaving. Signing, or sign-behaving *trans*actionally viewed, so that no such behaving enters except out of both organism and environment viewed in one process.

Subdivisions of Sign process (i.e., the layout for orientation) both in evolutionary stages and in levels in daily behaviors would be:

(1) Signaling: perceptive-manipulative range, the Pavlov conditioned reflex.

(2) Differentiated Naming: carrying up from the (Designations) primitive namings to the most adequate scientific namings.

(3) Symbolizings. (Here the difference between Designations and Symbolizing is functional. New linguistic function. Designation alleges existence. Symbolizing does not.)

Sharp illustration. An infinitesimal and a differentiation. As a name, infinitesimal did harm. Thrown away as a name, it no longer did harm—the process went on.

Again: The naming pinches down. Say electron as a named thing. By and by, it is pinched *Out*, regardless whether such a "thing" as "one" electron can be isolated; [then] comes to rule the world, subject to the still more elusive electromagnetic wave specializations.

(c) *After* this set-up is made, we proceed to differentiate "Behavioral Object" and "Behavioral Agent."

(d) Differentiate *functionally* the Physical, Biological, and Behavioral. Just how to introduce this—whether earlier than (b) or here later as (d) is a question of *expression*. I have tried it over and over each way, and (just like "Transaction," with reference to "Fact") I have not found the best way. Whichever way I have tried, you have suggested the other—which is a sound representation of the status quo. But this will take care of itself.

(e) Introduce "Connection," "Reference," and "Relation" from your *Logic* as is, to represent "Event"-layouts (physical). Designations (name to event) and Intra-linguistic organizations. Some variations possible, but not serious.

(f) Proceed to the *Inquiry* stage in terms of Subject-matter, Content, and Warranted Assertion, from *Logic*.

(g) Whatever else seems firm, and nothing but what seems firm.

Regards, *Bentley*

Paoli, Indiana, June 11, 1944

Dear Dewey:

You frequently say, inspecting some reaction I make to some remark of yours, that your expression must have been inept. And I as frequently note (though without saying it) that it is my reception and expression in response, and the stresses in both, that . . . [have] actually been inept. As you know, I think that the right kind of critical stuff on the work of men like Carnap and Nagel produces the strongest argument for . . . *our* point of view. . . . The work should, however, be done, not in terms of the big, shiny lumps of coal that come out of the mine (as biographical, personal), but in terms of the run of the mine; or, as I think I remarked the other day, somewhat entomologically, the word-hills should be studied like ant-hills.

Somewhat the same way, I am immensely interested in both the parallelings and interlacings of our operations, and the divergences. If we can get them clear, we have a big constructive aid. For instance . . . you said that your view was the "inquiry" as over against my search for "body," whereas I saw your stress on the inquirer's "having" as over against my interest in the functional use of language[, which] in a non-naming way I call "symbolic." Yours is the better statement, but the two are essentially alike. More generally, you stress behavioral agency as transactional, whereas I stress the inspection of transactions as that of which behavioral agency and behavioral object are "aspects" in first statement, and "phases," perhaps, on closer study. But every wriggle we make in getting these characteristics in the clear is going to help out that "Agency" paper. . . .

Regards, Bentley

[New York,] June 12, 1944

Memo to Bentley:

I. We desire to secure usable specifications for knowings and knowns as aids to naturalistic knowledge about or of knowledge. By "specification" is here understood determination of *names* for what is subject to *observation, description,* and *report.* By "naturalistic" is here understood that approach in inquiry which regards knowings as events that are similar with respect to their being known and knowable to such other events as eclipses, fossils, earthquakes, galaxies, etc. "Nature" is employed, in conformity with the practice of knowing, as a name for the domain of whatever inquiry is concerned with, to the exclusion of concern with Nature as an entity independent of research.

This[, of] course, . . . because it conforms strictly to the standpoint and the procedures by which the "sciences of nature" have achieved their success, since in them "nature" stands only for what is known by them and what they strive to know.

II. The above equating of usable specifications with names as names [that] are factually used in knowledge, is based upon the fact that in any and all knowledge satisfying the criteria that mark knowledge off from casual and unverified opinion, *observation, description,* and *report* are inseparable; any one of the words taken by itself stands for an aspectual property of one integral or undivided knowledge-system or body. We do not make this statement on the ground of any logical, psychological, or epistemological theory that such *must* be the case, but on the ground that observation, description, and report of the actual structure of what is known shows that such *is* the case.

III. The base of departure and procedure in what follows is, then, the fact that there exists in fact a body of knowledge [and] that this *outstanding corpus* can be inquired into for what it is in its own factual state, the same as any other set or system of factual events. It not only may be studied (observed and reported) for what it is, apart from reference to conditions supposed to be imposed by some agency (whether soul, mind, consciousness, self, individual, organism, nervous system), but *must* be so studied from the standpoint and procedure here adopted, since anything *known* about such alleged agencies falls *within* the body of knowledge of known things, and only *after* being so placed and viewed can it possibly have anything to contribute to knowledge of knowledge. There is here expressed no denial, nor desire to deny, that *as* constituent parts of [the] body of knowledge, an account of knowing agencies may have something to contribute to knowledge of knowledge. What is here emphasized is that *only* under the limiting condition just stated can such an account have anything relevant to say.

IV. The words "knowledge" and "body of knowledge" here used freely and loosely to stand for something which just is. A botanist might say his inquiry is concerned with "plants" without assuming prior "definition" of plants; or, stated positively, without any other postulate than that "plants" for the purpose of inquiry stands for the facts which are established in the process of inquiry.

Footnote: It may demand something of [a] wrench on the part of many readers to treat knowledge as something existing "out there" (so to say), because of engrained habits or viewing it only in connection with an agency or "knower" whose existence is postulated as an outside condition. But, unless one is willing to make an effort to take this standpoint, what is said here is sure to be radically misunderstood. It should not be too difficult for those who are not over-sophisticated to think of the known facts of physics, chemistry, astronomy, botany, zoology, physiology, history, anthropology, etc., in their capacity and status as a body of facts. A moderate degree of practice in taking this standpoint should make it possible to see that a self, ego, mind, organism, cannot possibly be introduced, once the attitude is firmly held, as if it were a condition of what is known, since what is said about the agencies in question and their operation has cognitive standing only *within* the body of known facts. . . .

Libraries may be said to contain or represent knowledge, and so may finger-musculature in connection with tools. The one condition that is of importance is that the inquiry which is undertaken in order to yield knowledge of knowledge be not checked or distorted by assuming in advance a "definition" that dictates what knowledge must be. Meantime, we have what is known by, say, mechanics at work in shops, and by men at work in astronomical . . . [observatories], [by] farmers in the field, [and by men] in all sorts of laboratories, in field-exploration by land and sea, and in libraries, as indications of the kind of material to be used in arriving at knowledge of knowledge. It is [as] absurd to suppose that we have no preliminary indication of the *material* for inquiry in the case of knowledge of knowledge as it would be to suppose, in the case of the botanist, that because he is engaged in finding out what plants are, therefore he has no data upon which to base and by which to direct his inquiries. What is here insisted upon is the same right to keep inquiry into knowledge open and growing that is assumed as a matter of course in the case of every "special" science, i.e., in every portion of the knowledge-corpus.

In any case, what is said at the outset of this paper limits the present study to one specified region of the wide range covered by the word "knowledge"; namely, the region of knowing by, through, under, or in *naming* operations. We adopt this course because it is [the] region most directly open to observation and report, not with the implication that this mode of knowing represents the supreme and final form of knowledge. On the contrary, it is selected with express recognition that the connection of this region of knowledge with other regions is an important subject for continued investigation. For the present, it suffices that wherever and whenever anything is said about any form of knowledge, it is said through or in the medium of naming, so that, *in this respect,* naming-knowing is inclusive.

. . . Stated in the form of postulates, the postulates of this inquiry are, then, the following:

(1) Naturalistically we face a single system or body of knowledge—a single cosmos of fact in which animal life appears and evolves into language-using human forms, and in which language-using itself develops into *namings* that specify and report (know) the very cosmos in which language-using behaviors in general and knowing by naming in particular occur. (Something here about *circularity* of procedure [should be said].)

(2) Knowledges and namings are themselves fact-events in the cosmos and are to be studied in that connection and *only* in that connection. Hence, they possess *durational-extensional* characteristics (?) exactly as do the fact-events they specify and describe. They are to be studied, not as appearing "at" a date as measured by a clock, nor "in" a place as determined by a yardstick, but as themselves enduring across an indefinite period of time and over an indefinite territory in space(?). . . . (Insert "across the skin," etc.) The mode or manner in which durations and extensions enter is itself something to be determined in inquiry; it cannot, e.g., be assumed in advance that they enter as matters of mechanistic assumption or in a way that limits knowledge to what is "physical."

(3) Nothing inherently non-observable is presumed; the very phrase "inherently non-observable" being absurd in the growing research that constitutes knowledge. Since specifically the observed and the described . . . [go] together, and cannot be separated from each other, it is absurd (see III above) to limit the range of application of "observation" and the "observable" by reference to some presumptive or alleged agency as a condition. What is observed links, both in event and in observation, with what is not then and there (or here and now) observed, and what is here and now under description links similarly with what is not here

271

and now under description. The reports of the moment (to which "definition" of observing-observed in terms of an external agency would limit the events) are read in knowing as a going concern of indefinite duration and extension [and] must be read into the wider reports constituting the knowledge-corpus, not treated as isolated building blocks out of which the wider reports are built up.

(4) Naming is used as an intrinsic constituent of observing-describing-reporting. . . . (The word "accuracy" seems to me to need some amplification—[its] contrast with "consistency" in definition is, of course, O.K. and goes in; "accuracy" is self-explanatory, if taken in its etymological signification, careful, caring-for; but it is likely, I fear, without some further qualification to be given by many readers a narrow quantitative interpretation.) Something further about "specification" through use or *application,* as controlled by reference to the whole knowledge system, might help.

(5) A bringing together of . . . "Fact" in contrast with "Reality," and with "the real," but also, perhaps, with brief notice that "real" as an adjective is etymologically synonymous with "factual"—*Res,* a thing—hence [the] dictionary usage (*Oxford*), having "foundation in fact; actually happening or occurring," and again, "actually existing as a thing"—"thing" is, probably, idiomatically the widest term of all for anything in any way under consideration or discussion or mention. I think it might be good tactics to take advantage of the idiomatic use of "real" versus the philosophical use of "reality" and "*the* real." I have been contemplating the possibility of a statement in which it would be brought out that when *spatial-durational contexts* are systematically taken into account, as they are in all factual inquiries; illusions, dreams, etc., are facts (or are "real"), i.e., are events actually occurring, being subjects of investigation—e.g., the problem of insanity as medical and as "social" and legal —criminology. Only when taken out of their proper durational-extensional setting are they non-factual or *un*-real.

If it is decided to put [the] transaction-interaction paper first; it would come naturally at this point, the foregoing material being introductory. And, I think, something to the effect of not engaging in propaganda, welcoming cooperation, etc., as per your earlier statement, would come in properly as transition. . . .

[*Dewey*]

New York, June 13, 1944

Dear Bentley:

The enclosed [the immediately preceding Memo to Bentley] represents an attempt primarily to clear up *myself,* especially with a view to getting your report on the degree of convergence I have reached. It is without doubt put in my mode of language, but that isn't very important, provided there is no serious divergence from your approach. If such is the case, the difficulty I have had in my own case is probably symptomatic of the difficulties others will have, since I certainly was more sympathetic with your position at the outset than most other readers are going to be. What I have said about taking knowledge as an extant body or corpus and the wrench that has to be undergone to take it that way, grows then out of my own experience. It is quite likely that even if what I have written is in the right direction, the wording of "knowledge body or corpus" isn't especially right. But, first, is it convergent; if not, where does the divergence come in?

Yours, Dewey

[P.S.] The right word would help. "Knowledge System" is O.K.; only it implies more coherent unity in organization than actually obtains. . . .

Paoli, Indiana, June 17, 1944

Dear Dewey:

Re your p. 287 ["By Nature and by Art"] and your question about short-term and long-term. (I am writing this before studying your long set-up —my first reaction to it being that I would be willing to join in as it stands—as far as the development has gone.)

I do not see how I could dissent at any point. On the other hand, when it comes to picking out a "body of knowledge," I have not been developing on that line. We started with your suggestion of the variety of ways knowledge was applied (i.e., knowledge, the "word"), and then we considered two or three sets of namings to cover the points of view we used. All the time, however, "knowledge" was before us as a word applying to a general region of discussion. It was the name of a preliminary "situation."

Now I do not know whether the following is correct or not. I will try it out and see. As I went along, I got further and further away from any attempt to specify the word "knowledge" for determinable "objects." I threw it more and more back among the vague, impressionistic namings. So also did you. I would say that in terminological layout the word "fact" replaces the word "knowledge." "Fact" in our presentation is the fused thing-known, but regarded as transactionally prior to the differentiation of the knowing and the known aspects, these latter entering as "Naming" and "Event."

Now, when we come to a final layout, you, with a long background of attacks on knowledge-problem, want to establish what we are doing in terms of "knowledge" to your satisfaction. I have not been working that way. I have not anywhere in the later drafts used "knowledge" as . . . an adequate name for any "phenomena," or as if I was trying to establish adequately *what* the phenomena accurately were which the word "knowledge" (as a necessary word) should be required to name. (If I have used it that way, I would be glad to appraise the passages, for stage of development, etc. Perhaps, here is why you were disturbed by my abbreviated phrase as to what knowings covered, while I could see no reason for bothering any more than slightly to adjust the phrasing.)

You say in footnote to yours 6-13-44: "The right word would help" and suggest "knowledge system."

Suppose I ask specifically: Is not "Fact" as set up in the paper, "Fact, Event, Designation," an attempt at such a name, doing justice both to organism and environing nature? . . .

Regards, *Bentley*

Paoli, Indiana, June 17, 1944

Dear Dewey:

Re "Body of Knowledge" or "Corpus." . . .

Here I start, "We have used the word freely and loosely" . . . and say, We had better let it go at that. I also say there is a bare trace of the makings of what we mean by knowing in all sign-process . . . all the way up from where "behavior" begins.

In other words, I, so far as I go, have postponed the "knowledge" characterization—the application of the word—till we get further along.

You in yours, 6-12-44, with entire correctness of judgment, bring our introductory statement back to terms of the Knowledge-problem. In a bully way you set up the makings of the issue between body of knowledge and knowing-behaviors.

However, so far as I can see, you (we, I,) do *Not* have the makings of a firm terminology useful to our fellow-citizens as and of *Knowledge* at this moment. So your presentation (in my opinion) should be kept just where you have it in general terms. And "Corpus" is as good a word as any for the purpose.

Next step will be our "Fact" used in substitution for "Knowledge" in intermediate ranges. Once get that out, and we can return to knowledge. If we can in the end make a hard and firm statement that primarily the word should apply to *Naming* procedures, it will suit me fine. . . .

Regards, *Bentley*

Paoli, Indiana, June 20, 1944

Dear Dewey:

. . . Showing a visitor your view of language and logic, I turned to p. iv of the *Logic*, where you say no general theory of language exists . . .

274

"in which form and matter are not separated." This is equivalent to your old "word and meaning" are one. It is the guts of my theory of language. It is the guts of our present development of "Event-Designation." It is omitted from your presentation of what we are about in your present sketch. . . . It is the point I wrote back to you was critical for me.

Now I do not want it put in with your set of points. "Often, often, but not too much at once," said Old Papa Swann in [Proust's] *"Du Côté de chez [Swann]."* And I am all for that. It does not need to come in at the start. But we want to be clear at the start that we haven't yet begun there.

In yesterday's letter I spoke of your "Knowledge-Corpus" as the equivalent of "Fact" in later development. I do not think I mentioned it as the equivalent of "Cosmos," not only in our development, but in general usage. . . .

About that matter of your possible use of your letters that I mentioned yesterday, you know from experience that I am apt to mention anything that occurs, long prior to reflection, and just as material for it. But it does strike me that if you took the transcript, eliminated from it *all* reference to me so that merely a shadow addressee remained, and eliminated a good many of your casual references to yourself, retaining, however, those of biographical build-up, and touched up phrasings a little, but left the free and easy form of "work-in-progress," you might have something you could set aside for future use, or leave for literary editors to use at some future date, which (the way you are going) I would estimate at well over 15 years from now. (And let Leonardo hang his modest youthful head in shame.) . . .

Regards, Bentley

New York, June 21, 1944

Dear Bentley:
    . . . Let me say first that I didn't write what I sent you as a substitute, but, as I said, first to help clear up my own mind, and at the same time get your reaction as to how the substance of it, rather than the form, was in line, and how far it was off. I realize that my background and prevailing interest tend toward getting off on another track where there are switches at junction points, and I have learned so much in the attempt to get my train running along your lines, I wanted to find out how I was getting on. The same way about my question as to passage on p. 287 ["By Nature and by Art"]. I have spent an awful lot of time in the past on the sense-rational, perception-conception problem, and from a different point of view—from that of the whole historical British empirical-continental rationalistic controversy, and Kant's attempt to get them to-

275

gether. The paragraph in question marks an attempt to get the gist of the matter out of this historical context into one where it would stand up on its own account. My query wasn't from fear of lack of sympathy, but for my own encouragement if you thought it was O.K. It isn't easy with my old habits to shift a standpoint and see things in and from a different perspective, not even when I am confident there is no fundamental disagreement between the two standpoints and perspectives.

This in general. More particularly, I didn't intend to tie down any interpretation of "Knowledge," or get away from the open, impressionistic reference of "knowledge" by what I said. I was simply trying to get a pointing or denotative word, leaving the "meaning" open; as far as "meaning" is concerned, I intended to adopt completely your "freely and loosely." I suppose what I said that points to a somewhat definite kind or range of objects was due to the desire to get over to the reader what we *weren't* doing by limiting discussion in advance [and] by holding the meaning down to some agency-conditioned form. My attitude is something like this: Men set out to study cancer; they don't know *what* cancer is—that is for their inquiries to find out. But there are certain events capable of being pointed out and at, to which their inquiries are directed—if anyone asked them what they were studying, they could point to this and that clinical case, and say, Here are our data. By study of them and similar cases—both broader and narrower as inquiry proceeds— we want to know, and find out, what cancer is or signifies. Meantime, here is a rough denotative indication of what we are about.

More specifically, my material was not intended to be a substitute for discussion of "Specification" and "Fact." . . .

I took it for granted in what I sent on that there was to be a definite, extended discussion on "Fact," and of "Specification." "Naming"—"Designation" later on. From the standpoint of substitution, my piece had reference only to an introductory statement of what we were at or about, as a directive or steer to the reader. . . .

Yours, *Dewey*

Paoli, Indiana, June 22, 1944
Dear Dewey:
. . . I do not think you ever told me what you thought of the "Transaction and Interaction" paper as a whole, apart from details of development. During the early sketches you seemed to think this line was of greatest value; then we had times when we both felt it defective. It is the final form I want to know about: Are the defects overcome? I thought it was a good job. There is one way a change could be made. Namely: "Interaction" covers three things, which, from a different point

of view, might be more sharply separated. I felt and still feel that using the same word for 1. Primary standard physical causation, 2. Legitimate aspectual, 3. Illicit hypostatizings, is the best scheme. I may want to fit the paper in, and would be glad of your more general view. . . .

Regards, *Bentley*

New York, June 22, 1944

Dear Bentley:

I appreciate your suggestion about correspondence. I remember that once you said something about [how] difficult it was for you (this is the way I recall it) to go back to what you had previously written. It awoke an answering echo in me. What lies ahead seems so much [more] interesting—it's the other side of a field for the berrypicker. Going back seems back, not going. And as long as I can go through the motions of going ahead, putting time in on old letters is an annoying idea. The things that beckon are somewhere else.

I think "connection" for facts-events and "relation" for symbols much better than my earlier treatment. I was mixed about "reference," as you once pointed out. I should now be inclined to say that *signs* refer—I just looked up p. 246 of the *Experimental Logic* essay ["The Control of Ideas by Facts"]—and it wouldn't be so bad if "sign-reference" were used instead of "signification-relation." I wonder how it would be if we specified an equivalence of "naming" not with a "sign" but with "sign-reference." Without having gone over the old paper, I'm inclined to think "meaning" is used much too loosely, though with some anticipation of the sign-reference specification. I have an idea that in that paper "fact" is equated too narrowly with "datum," but, maybe, it's used so as to suggest covering the whole range from the fact as datum for further inquiry to fact as made out by means of inquiry. Anyway, the whole range is within knowing. In any case, my previous work is not involved in the present job in any way that should affect the latter—it may do so at times, but that is one of those accidents that at times are unavoidable.

I think we should stick to the "signal," "sign," "symbol" business strictly. There are "sign-connections" of things; "sign-references" of names; "system-relations" of symbols. ("System" isn't the right word, nor is "postulated"; maybe "defined" relations, or "definition-relationships"—I'm not trying to suggest words for final use, but just to say how I see the layout now, no matter what I have written in the past.)

I'll have, if I live, which I expect to do for a while, time to do some pieces from the standpoint of [my] own idiosyncratic interest. I want to get squared up with yours for the present papers—and that is a matter of interest to me—of self-interest for my own later operations. These remarks are in connection with what you said about breakage on my part. Thank heaven, I've always been breaking with my past more or less, that's my strongest point. . . .

Yours, *Dewey*

Paoli, Indiana, June 23, 1944

Dear Dewey:

. . . Looking over the "Transaction-Interaction" paper, I see about half of the contents is your own suggested phrasing or developed in correspondence and approved by you. I could not use it as my own under any circumstances.

The point is—I have said it so often, yet it always bothers me—you have a definite position and a steady, clean, central advance. I am professionally erratic all over the map. The stress is not on whether *I* could influence *you,* but on the fact that in any such contact any participant is apt to move erratically—temporary perturbations of orbit, we might say —due to propinquity of another celestial body. I am off the track most of the time, but that does not matter.

Of course, in this paper the construction (the end) was mine, but only as worked out in steady pressure of correspondence. . . .

I note one difference between the tone of your draft . . . and our previous drafts. You attack the problem of knowledge direct much more heavily than the problem of *technical* approach to dealing with knowledge. I have carried the technique (i.e., postulations as tentative) more heavily in mind than the problem of knowledge itself. Often my expressions have slipped into the other form (especially, in the many efforts to find the shortest possible way to get rid of epistemological duplicity), but always I have had in view eliminating those stresses, and getting back to "what are the best tools to work with?" . . .

Notice that the stress on "observables" is your contribution (I mean, by never letting me neglect it). And the general remark that word and meaning are one is yours from away back. The immediate identification of Naming as itself a form of Knowing, and as such an observable and transactional and factual form, the consistent hammering on it, seems to be my contribution to this work. Also twice, without meaning to do it, you have passed up this naming-as-knowing stress, while you develop from the viewpoint of "Knowing" along your older established terminological lines. . . .

My argument is that *Naming-as-Itself-Knowing,* as observable knowing itself—with no non-observable knowing (subjective, mystic, or other back of it; this being your own view)—should somewhere in your papers come out hard and strong. It is, perhaps, really a question whether we are going to speak that way at times, but develop some other way, or whether we will develop that way. The first way is soft, the second is hard. You yourself have frequently told me how . . . with not a great deal of success at the main point. . . .

In other words, when the right time comes—namely in the "Fact" paper—I want to develop this *Naming-as-Itself-Knowing* (not all knowing, but a region of it) good and hard.

Regards, *Bentley*

Paoli, Indiana, June 26, 1944

Dear Dewey:

. . . Your suggestion of an equivalence of "naming" with "sign-reference" (not with a sign). This is absolute[ly] O.K. in principle. But, with one *Exception* in detail:

Namely: Signal, Name, Symbol are human behavioral levels, well known to all. We want a word to *hold them all together* in system and permit growth of observation-description report *within* the system. We gotta have a working word. For that word I want "Sign" (and not for naming specifically). . . . Then under "Sign," we have the three stages above.

The equivalence of naming would then be not with sign-reference *in toto*, but with that range of sign-reference which is worded and enters evolutional development *after* perception, and earlier than complicated mathematics (otherwise to be called "Symbol"). . . .

Regards, *Bentley*

New York, June 27, 1944

Dear Bentley:

I've already mentioned, I think, that the earlier papers were labeled "Terminological." I am reminded of that fact by running across (in looking over old correspondence) your mimeographed sheets on language at the Columbia [University] seminar. I have a feeling that what I've written has had a tendency to steer discussion too much away from the original subject, and that while you agree with the sheets I sent . . . for what they are, you feel that what they are is more on the topic of knowledge than on that of language-naming.

. . . Idiomatically the word ["real"] is used as practically synonymous with our "fact." (This is a sample of what often happens—often the idiomatic usage is O.K., but then a sense grows up that is influenced by some special "philosophical" theory, and the best tactic is to get back to the idiomatic usage, rescuing the word from a distortion due to a particular doctrine.)

. . . The three "interactions" of your letter [of] June 22 [are] specifically O.K. I think it might also be mentioned that in some cases "inter" has the sense of "trans."

I am inclined to think that "account" is a better word than "report," when we get around to the observation-description-account affair.

Yours, with regards, *Dewey*

[P.S.] About "inter" as "trans"—sometimes (*Oxford Dictionary*) "inter" has the force of "between" in a spatial-temporal sense (interpose, interject—different from our "trans"); sometimes it means "with," reciprocally (or mutually)—close to transact. I think Peirce generally used it in that way.

New York, June 29, 1944

Dear Bentley:

I think your friend has put his finger on the difficulty under which we labor generally. If we compress, we don't get it over, and if we expand, especially with needed illustrations, the papers run to great length. . . .

I forgot, for the time being, the need of a word like "sign" to cover the three cases. If I could suggest some other word to serve that purpose, I see some advantages in using "sign" for the naming function, such as connection with de-signation; sign-language; signboards. I have been to my standby the *Oxford* [*Dictionary*]. I didn't get special aid as to another word for "sign" in its inclusive sense, but I did get a lot of incidental confirmation of our general standpoint and procedure. "Mark" —it is first a boundary (like "Term" in original use); then marking a boundary, *de*marcating; then a sign, token, indication, symptom; a distinctive feature by which a thing is identified. To *Mark* is to notice, watch, observe, attend to, give heed to. . . .

The net result is that there are three functions or services which run into one another and blend. Marking out and off, hence identifying-distinguishing, paying heed to, observing; hence, making known, declaring. I don't know that we can do anything with this, but as I said it all indicates, points to, is evidence of, the fact that we have a sound, idiomatic, common-sense base.

"Signal"—double sense of sign, token, indication and conspicuous, outstanding, remarkable.

In several places in the dictionary, in connection with Signal, Indication, Mark, and Sign, the word "communicate" is used in connection with "making known." Maybe, at some place we can do something with "making known"; public.

My wife's grandfather was a man with practically no school education, but wise. I recall once in speaking of something, he said, "Sometimes it

will be found out and not only found out, but *known.*" Knowledge and
ac-knowledge were once often used interchangeably. . . .

Yours, Dewey

Paoli, Indiana, July 3, 1944

Dear Dewey:
   If you have Morris' [*Foundations of the*] *Theory of Signs* by you, I
would be glad to have comment on his use of "names," middle p. 7, both
for his own development, and with reference to our proposed uses.
   Morris sets up: "implicate" in the field to which we assign "definition"
—(your "relation" in the *Logic*); "designate" for the *Kind* of object (p. 5)
. . . "denotes" for [each actual existent object]; "expresses" for what the
mind [of the interpreter] does. . . .
   (Incidentally, Lewis [*Philosophy and*] *Phenomenological Research*
paper ["The Modes of Meaning"]. . . . makes denotation of the *class,*
and suggests that some say "designate" as to "the *thing* that it names"—
here, if he refers to Morris, he says opposite use from Morris'—Carnap,
also, is mixed. Lewis prefers to retain "denote" for things, and "denotation" for class-business, admitting the muddle, but liking it (probably,
because of his material implication—if he has the name correct).
   I think my question is: Should we introduce stuff on "designation" and
"denotation" differences—"thing and class"—in above sense—or can we
let it slide, as we have done thus far?
   My tendency, of course, is to regard relation-logic as a technical device,
but not as setting up a new *Kind* of nature.
   Whatever I have written down by use of "designation" covers both
naming and classing. . . .

Regards, Bentley

[New York,] July 5, 1944

[To Bentley:]
   The "Logic Vagueness" paper, it seems to me, will help put back the
succeeding papers on the rails [that] we started off on and that comments
of mine tended to get away from, viz., specifications through language.
Morris *says* [*Foundations of the Theory of Signs*]: "It is possible to include without remainder the study of knowledge [science]"—our knowledge of knowledge—"under the study of the language of science" (p. 2).
And that group starts, as we do, with signs as the determinant of anything
called knowledge. So Morris *says*, "To supply a language in which to talk
about, and in so doing to improve, the language of science" (p. 3). I
wouldn't set out myself on the job of improving the language of science.
But the more modest job of improving the language in which science *as*

language is talked about (taken account of, reported, observed, and described) is worth undertaking.

I think one basic ambiguity in this group is wavering between [science] *as* language and "language *of* science" [Dewey's italics]—which latter expression carries with it an indication that science has an existence outside of language and then uses language in some distinctive and important way. (1) If science and language are *first* separated and then afterward brought together, it would seem to follow that reference or application of linguistic signs to something else (designata and denotata) is different from or in addition to being a *sign*. But if science (knowledge) *is* a sign-system, that idea is nonsensical. And (2) *if* language (namings) is a behavioral development of which scientific naming is one special (cultural) development, then it is nonsensical to treat "its relation to persons who use it" [p. 29] as a special subject of study [pragmatics]. Signs are isolated (by Morris) (1) from what they designate. And then (2) from the behavioral events in which alone they *are* signs. Language is one thing; "using" it is another! There is, it seems to me, a continual giving with one hand and taking back with the other hand.

Then on p. 4, he *says*, " 'sign,' 'designatum,' 'interpretant,' and 'interpreter' all involve one another," * being *aspects* of the same process. Here verbally he tends to get back to knowledge *as* a sign-system. On p. 5 he says "the general theory of signs doesn't need to commit itself to any specific theory of what is involved in taking account of something through the use of a sign." † In other words, [he] dodges the fundamental point—for, without a statement on that point, it is very easy to split things up three (or four . . .) ways. Then on p. 6, after expressing a preference for a behavioristic theory on the point regarding which no theory is necessarily involved, he says, "To take account of D by the presence of S involves responding to D in *virtue of a response to S.*" [Italicized words are Dewey's.] Here response to S becomes a *separate* thing, instead of S, *as* taking account of, *being itself* the behavioral response under investigation and report.

Signs, a language system, is treated as being there on its own account. Then we respond to it, and by some miracle in so doing, we also respond to objects, which are also out there on their own account, and respond to them in such a way as to take account of them—an *account* being presumably the signs which we started out responding to!! Can you beat it?

---

* The exact quotation is: " 'sign,' 'designatum,' 'interpretant,' and 'interpreter' involve one another, since they are simply ways of referring to aspects of the process of semiosis." (Eds.)

† The exact quotation is: "the general theory of signs need not commit itself to any specific theory of what is involved in taking account of something through the use of a sign." (Eds.)

The foregoing was suggested to me by your pages *re* Morris. I put it down because I have a feeling that there is something here which may be usable in a paper, emphasizing at the start, the matter of names as signs, or as specifying, in the attempt to get names in knowledge of knowledge—and, I think, without breaking the "flow," if we start from knowledge as a sign-system.

Would it be possible to take as our first postulate that knowledge and a sign-system are identical—quoting Peirce, maybe? Then the second postulate: names as one kind of naturalistically developed signs—limiting the scope of present discussion to a specified subjectmatter. . . .

[Dewey]

New York, July 10, 1944

Dear Bentley:

. . . I have a quarterfledged idea: Is it possible that "syntactics" is a case of failure to see that symbols are *not* matters of relations of "things"? I can't see that the analogy of grammar (syntax) and mathematics holds. Do Morris and Carnap . . . *et al.* make the same failure to distinguish between "symbol" and "existence" that you speak of, only concealing it by making "mathematics" (syntactics) formal relations—of what?

What is the meaning, anyway, of making "syntactics" *coordinate* with "semantics" and "pragmatics"? And calling "syntactics" "investigation of the structure of scientific language"? I haven't found in Morris any definite statement about mathematics. Either he is very cagey, or [he is] very loose.

Yours, Dewey

New York, July 12, 1944

Dear Bentley:

I'm sorry to be of so little use on the Logic paper ["On a Certain Vagueness in Logic"]. I had never taken Morris' paper [*Foundations of the Theory of Signs*] seriously enough; it seemed to me so obvious that he was splitting things up in order to evade the real problems. I am rather shocked now that I have read him with care. Certain fundamental considerations are left totally in the dark. For example, what does "interpretation" name? In ordinary usage, to interpret a sign would be to restate or translate it into other better known signs—to "elucidate." But that isn't the meaning in Morris, and there is no statement as to what is meant by it; the vagueness makes it possible to cover up and beg a lot of other questions. His "interpretant"—separated from "interpreter" is even worse; he made up the word, and doesn't tell what . . . [he] intends by it, though he makes it the basis of his "pragmatics." His nominal statement is "that *effect* on some interpreter *in virtue of* which the thing in question *is a sign* to that interpreter" [Dewey's italics], p. 3. I can't see how anybody can make head or tail of this. Taking something as a sign has an *effect* on the one so taking it; in virtue of this effect (which comes *after* taking it as a sign), the thing in question *is* a sign. I think the reason others have taken up Morris' statement as much as they have . . . is that [it] encourages them in a kind of looseness so that they don't have to face the issues.

On page 4, there is the express statement "The takings-account-of are *interpretants*." This is not only a radically different statement from that of the "effect" made on the interpreter *by* taking account of, but verbally, at least, it identifies "interpretant" with the entire "semiosis" process, which in the very sentence previous to the clause just cited says, "Semiosis is accordingly a mediated-taking-account-of," which, verbally, expressly identifies it with what is said about the "interpretant" in the next clause. Then, in the next paragraph we have still another account: "a taking-account-of-something is an interpretant only insofar as it is *evoked* by something functioning as a sign" [Dewey's italics]—this in connection with the statement that his three-four terms "involve" one another, and are ways of referring to aspects of semiosis, or "are relational properties which things take on by participating in the functional process of semiosis." Whether "aspects" and "relational properties" are identical, and *how* they are, isn't stated.

On page 6, "pragmatics" is introduced as the study of the "relation of signs to interpreters"—the word "interpretant" having dropped by the wayside. On page 7, it is said that the "relation of signs . . . to interpreters" is that of "expression." "The word 'table' . . . expresses its interpreter." Here we seem to have the reverse of *"effect* on some interpreter" [Dewey's italics]. On page 10, the word "pragmatics" as a name for the "relation of sign to an interpreter" is tentatively illustrated. "The pragmatist is inclined to regard a language as a type of communicative activity, social in origin and nature." Of course, this is thrown in incidentally. But *the* or *an* interpreter, who is alone and separate as far as formal definition is concerned, has now got multiplied—the "effect" or the "expression" (whichever it is) is now *across* human beings and not just from one "thing" to another. But there is nowhere any discussion of the fundamental issue: the connection, if any, of the two kinds of transaction with each other. (I don't know whether it is significant, but on page 12, "Writing, painting, etc.," are spoken of as products of behavior, while oral speech is a *part* of behavior.)

On page 30, there is for the first time an illustration of what is designated in the concrete by "interpretant" as the "effect" relation on the interpreter. After saying that the traditional view is that the effect in question or the "interpretant" is a "thought," he goes on to say that under the influence of *Peirce* "the interpretant is the habit of the organism to respond, because of the sign vehicle, to absent objects which are relevant to a present problematic situation as if they were present" (p. 31). [On] page 33, it said that "to discuss adequately the relation of signs to their interpreters requires knowledge of the relation of signs to one another" (syntactics), and incidentally, the same thing is said of the relation of signs to things—that is, semantics presupposes syntactics. No proof, and no discussion. Earlier, p. 29, we have the following: "Syntactical and semantical rules are only the verbal formulations within semiotic of what in any concrete case of semiosis are habits of sign usage by actual users of signs. 'Rules of sign usage,' like 'sign' itself, is a semiotical term and cannot be stated syntactically or semantically." Take your choice.

One more thing. On pp. 12–13, he discusses sign systems or the interconnectedness of signs. The issue as to the relationship of linguistic signs to "natural signs," he disposes of as follows: "That the syntactical structure of language is, in general, a function both of objective events and of behavior, and not of either alone, is a thesis which may be called *the dual control of linguistic structure.*" And in this connection he expressly says that "the sign factors *in perception*" [Dewey's italics] (as thunder is a sign of lightning) are a "case of signs drawn from materials *other than behavior* or the products of behavior" [Dewey's italics]. The "*dual control*" is from the "interconnectedness of events on the one hand, and the interconnectedness of actions on the other."

I don't think the foregoing is of any use, save as an indication of how extremely difficult it is for me to do anything with Morris. He can't be held down to anything.

I have been looking over some back numbers of *The Journal of Philosophy.* One thing that strikes me is the influence of Richards. The formula that "names *stand for* their reference" is probably only a formulation of an old traditional doctrine—but it is almost incredible that it should be taken as the starting point of some new and important insight. "Words standing for"!!—and nothing about words pointing to, directing to, and thereby making known. I think the origin of it was probably that "ideas" stand for things, and then words "express" ideas, and so indirectly stand for things. . . .

Yours, *Dewey*

[P.S.] Further reading makes it certain that Carnap-Morris take mathematics as a special case of "syntactics," not as special language, but as growing out of the relations signs bear to one another in ordinary language. This may account for the fact that they have done so little with mathematics—and spent themselves upon comparatively trivial "formal," so-called, logical relations—à la attempt of Russell to get logic back of mathematics.

285

New York, July 14, 1944

Dear Bentley:

I have read Nagel's article on signs ["Operational Analysis as an Instrument for the Critique of Linguistic Signs"] in *Journal of Philosophy* . . . and a longer one in the volume of essays [Krikorian, ed.] on *Naturalism [and the Human Spirit]*, just published . . . the latter entitled "Logic without Ontology"—not bad at all, I judge from a hasty reading. [The] general idea is that certain logical distinctions that have been supposed since Aristotle to have "ontological" counterparts can be better treated as having a regulative, operational, function in direction of inquiry. . . . It occurred to me that there might be a footnote to the effect that later writings by Nagel seem to involve departure from positions quoted from the Cohen and Nagel *Logic [An Introduction to Logic and Scientific Method]*. As a matter of fact, Nagel wrote that under the influence of Cohen, and at that time held that fundamental logical invariants were counterparts of "ontological" invariants. In an article ["Can Logic Be Divorced from Ontology?"] in *Journal of Philosophy*, XXVI 1929, he criticized an article by me ["The Sphere of Application of the Excluded Middle"] which takes the view he takes now, that the laws of identity, excluded middle, etc., state criteria to be observed in obtaining consistency. He then held that Logic couldn't be divorced from ontology. . . .

Yours as ever, *Dewey*

[P.S.] Looking up Peirce, I find, what I had forgotten, that Morris gets his word "interpretant" from Peirce, as well as his triadic relation. [On] p. 51 of Vol. II [*Collected Papers*], Peirce says: "A *Sign* is anything which is related to a Second thing, its *Object*, in such a way as to bring a Third thing, its *Interpretant*, into relation to the same Object." * On p. 52, an Interpretant is spoken of as that which signs "aim to determine." Then he goes on to say that terms and propositions leave their interpretant to be what they may, while "an *argument* is a sign which distinctly represents the Interpretant, called its *Conclusion*, which it is intended to determine." By "argument" he means a relation of propositions of the nature of inference—or reasoning; so, of course, a conclusion is what it aims to determine. Morris completely shifts the meaning of "interpretant," mixing it up (as far as I can make out) with an interpreter, so that he sometimes has three and sometimes four members, and, aside from this, ignores the fact that, according to Peirce, it is only a set of signs ordered in a certain way that determines an "interpretant." In a footnote (of Peirce's) on p. 391, "limitless intermediation" is said to be the business of reasoning.

* The exact quotation is: "A *Sign* is anything which is related to a second thing, its *Object*, in respect to a Quality, in such a way as to bring a Third thing, its *Interpretant*, into relation to the same Object. . . ." (Eds.)

New York, July 18, 1944

Dear Bentley:

  . . . I'm trying to do something new with "Signs," "standing for," "objects." Following Peirce, I think the only meaning to be given "objects" is "conclusions." I think this lines up with "facts," and also applicable in case of "symbols," "standing for," "representing," is the set of (behavioral) operations that terminate in the *conclusion*. [I have] . . . good statements in Peirce of the operational nature of signs, e.g., vol. II, p. 189 [*Collected Papers*]. . . . "The peculiarity of this definition—or rather this *precept* that is more serviceable than a definition—is that it tells you what the word lithium denotes by prescribing what you are to *do*." * What *you* are to do equals *what is to be done*.

Yours, Dewey

Indianapolis, Indiana, July 19, 1944

Dear Dewey:

  . . . I will be glad to put in [a] footnote about Nagel. He deserves it. . . .

About six years ago I spent several months on the Logical Positivists and their "Unification of Science." I ran across several papers recently on such subjects as "What Price Unity?" and "What Is Interpretation?" I never did find out what "Interpretation" is. . . . Carnap does not know. No wonder you had difficulty. I have a memo . . . that sometimes Carnap says a semantic system *is* the interpretation of a calculus; and sometimes he says an Interpretation is a third thing in addition to Semantics and Calculus. . . . You have taken this confusion up in several ways. I don't believe it can be worked into our present paper. It runs aside from our close-held *terminological* job. Takes too much space. If you see any specific point that can be injected in the present paper, please shoot it in. . . .

Most of the basic discussion I do not undertake with Carnap. I throw it out. On the same ground, I do not see how we can get your particular present analyses in. "Designation," I should say, is the most confused spot in Carnap. I have just touched on it directly, though I have skimmed it all through. "Designation" is meaning—except when they want to use meaning differently. It is naming, with the named object nearly always omitted, and with a half dozen sliding stages from syntax, Interpretation, Rules, semantics-L, semantics-F, absolute concepts, absolute terms. . . .

Regards, Bentley

* The quotation ends: ". . . by prescribing what you are to *do* in order to gain a perceptual acquaintance with the object of the word." [Dewey italicized the word "precept."] (Eds.)

Dear Dewey:

Re "Objects" as conclusions. . . . I wonder if we cannot apply our terminology (such as we have it) so as to differentiate different *ways* of handling such a problem—complements, not opponents.

Taking an object and an organism in rough first report, we may block out:

I. Pre-pragmatic (epistemologic)—Object known *by* organism (as mind).

II. Pragmatic—Object known *to* (or probably better *through*) organism-activity. We have this developed in two stages. First, ideas as consequences under test; second, objects as consequences under test. Cancelling "ideas" and substituting "language," we get both words and objects in pragmatic values.

III. Transactional—we develop the pragmatic further by considering every entry as transactional. Thus: on the perceptive-manipulative level we postulate organic-objective activity as a richer, deeper statement than object *plus* organism. On the existence-object level we identify the *range* of existence as the *range* of namings, and such that we use "Fact" for the transactional statement. (The symbolic level, if properly so separated, does not need to be introduced at this moment.)

We have thus [a] natural-transactional-perceptive-manipulational account to give. Also, we have a named-existence account to give. And the two to build up into a joint report. . . .

As to "Object" as "conclusion," it comes to this. In the sense of "he concluded that," it might sound pre-pragmatic. In comparable uses, but qualified, it might be said pragmatically, but still with a slant of presentation as in terms of the organism. In the sense of "the session concluded," it would run transactionally.

Regards, *Bentley*

Dear Dewey:

The ["On a Certain Vagueness in] Logic" paper is now in such shape that, if I were doing it privately, I would now proceed to finish it up for use. . . .

There may be some minor slip. There probably are two or three points subject to mis-reading or to challenge on other grounds. However, many such points have either established themselves already, or already been eliminated. The only one that comes to mind for the moment is what I say . . . about "proposition" in the meta-language and "proposition" in the object-language. I don't see how I can help being right, but I want to reserve [it] for more thought. He [Carnap] is setting up a word in a meta-language, and doing all his talking in muddled words of an object-language; and I do not see how he *can* be talking about the meta-language word, although he makes it look like it. If the point is good, it ought to stay. . . .

Regards, Bentley

[New York,] July 26, 1944

Dear Bentley:

. . . I am writing out some stuff on "standing for," "representing"; continuing (i) a brief behavioral-operational, (ii) some selections from Peirce, (iii) some things from Morris to show what a mess he made of Peirce, and then (iv) a brief conclusion restating the behavioral "pre-scription" views.

I have no present intention of doing anything with it when I finish.

Yours, Dewey

Chatham, Massachusetts, August 9, 1944

Dear Bentley:

. . . In connection with the reference to Peirce . . . you say truly enough that while the cosmic pattern is taken from Peirce, it doesn't represent his fundamental attitude. I think it might help if his own "basic envisionment" were stated, as it will serve to indicate why the criticisms made on the writers discussed are a good deal more than more or less verbal matters of casual inconsistence. I . . . [could] supply some brief statements of his that would serve this end, if I had my Peirce with me. I have one notation, and perhaps it is sufficiently typical to bring out the main point. After having given a certain illus-tration of the scientific use of "lithium" as a sign, he goes on to say: "The peculiarity of this definition—or rather of this precept that is more serviceable than a definition—is that it tells you what the word lithium denotes by prescribing what you are to do in order to get a perceptual acquaintance with the object of that word," * *Works*, Vol. II, p. 189. What is "denoted" and "object" in passage cited are obviously the referent and designatum of these other writers, but taken along with the passage you quote [and] which Cohen and Nagel quote from Peirce, it shows that his "cosmic pattern" is *not* of two orders brought into connection by a third intervening thing as sign, but that the so-called intervener is the *man* behaving, or the sign prescribes what he is *to do*. I think the passage suggests, if not more than merely suggests, what he means by

---

* The exact quotation is: "The peculiarity of this definition . . . is that it tells you what the word lithium denotes by prescribing what you are to *do*. . . ." (Eds.)

"thought" and why language is the essence of good thought. It certainly explains the basic ground of difference between his "cosmic pattern" and that of the men dealt with.

I go into this [at] the foregoing length because, I believe, the only lack in your paper as it stands is that it needs, from the standpoint of most readers, a pretty continuous indication of why the "tour" of inspection is necessary and what it is getting on. If that can be brought home to the reader, I think your paper is as revolutionary an introduction to those which follow as it is unanswerable.

. . . Some of these writers (and some of your readers) will say, "But we aren't trying to deal with Fact any more than with Reality; we are dealing with formal relations as far as *logic* is concerned." (And, as distinct, à la Morris-Carnap, from "semantics and pragmatics.") Thus Cohen's and Nagel's book is called [*An Introduction to*] *Logic* and *Scientific Method,* not . . . *Logic of Scientific Method.* I don't mean I think you have . . . to emphasize the division between logic and scientific method. But I think you can avoid the objection that may be raised if you *begin* your discussion with the material about scientific propositions, not saying anything at first about *fact,* and then deal with the entanglement of facts with propositions. This would involve omission of middle paragraph on p. 3, save, as you said, that you begin with propositions and their connection—or lack of connection—with facts, and mention of the fact that the first case you examine tries to begin with a purely formal treatment of propositions as "logical" and then goes over to their relation to facts as nonformal in the section on scientific method—and the difficulties they get into on the whole subject—and wind up again with emphasis on the reason—the threefold name, thought (sign, reference), object-things, pattern. Then, when you come next to Carnap, it will take only slight verbal change to indicate that he tries to get to greater unity between the purely formal and the scientific or factual by the device of giving propositions "two different concepts." . . . I may be wrong, but I think this mode of exposition (of introducing it) emphasizes the point of the impossibility of any coherent statement that sets out with the threefold cosmic scheme, but then has to cancel [it] by bringing 1 and 3 into union (called "reference," "designation," or "proposition" as distinct from "sentence").

It is possible that I am in error by tending to introduce material (or rather a *standpoint and approach*) that properly belongs in the following papers. But, on the other hand, it may be that some hammering on the threefold scheme affords the best introduction . . . [as against] one which begins openly with names or designatings as a total and inclusive operation.

Maybe, I'll be able to send something later. But, on the whole, my firsthand knowledge of the material dealt with is too slight for me to be of much use.

I think you have a powerful document. . . .

Yours, Dewey

Seattle, Washington, August 9, 1944

Dear Dewey:

. . . The large-scale open question as to whether injustice is done [to] Carnap might arise if anyone could aver that there was actually something definite and sharp about Carnap's "designatum." I had intended to go through technically all of his formulations (definitions and theses) from this point of view. But his shiftiness with respect to the underlying entities . . . designata, objects, facts, absolute concepts—none of which, so far as I know, can be firmly distinguished from the others—would seem to make this unnecessary.

Regards, Bentley

Seattle, Washington, August 13, 1944

Dear Dewey:

. . . In the *Naturalism [and the Human Spirit]* book I find two papers (and two only) to use. A reference to the vaguely atmospheric character of these discussions at start of the postulational paper should serve admirably as background to focusing on our direct biological-evolutionary-naturalistic localization of knowledge process. Then, as to the special papers:

(a) [Eliseo] Vivas ["A Natural History of the Aesthetic Transaction"] uses the word "transaction" and almost approximates our transactional view, though his most specific formulation (top, p. 106) falls away. Anyway, this is good stuff as showing problem.

(b) [William R.] Dennes' discussion of "event" ["The Categories of Naturalism"], and his connection of it with "attribute" and "relation" will be good foil for our development in the "Fact-Event-Name" paper. He has not a trace of the "human behavior" in his treatment. A "sign" is a "thing" used by an "agent" to mark another "thing." On the showdown he falls back to a Carnap-Morris type of a world of dice-like things cast helter-skelter, while "men" scurry around with definitions trying to make them hop, skip, and jump like the dice (designating, denoting, etc. —a magic process very different from our behavioral-naming of behavioral-objects). . . .

Regards, Bentley

Seattle, Washington, August 15, 1944

Dear Dewey:

. . . There are reasons both for and against [rewriting the section on "fact" in "On a Certain Vagueness in Logic"]. You see it in terms of how formal logicians will react. I see it in terms of our main objective.

We are not criticizing formal logic but only its realistic embodiment—this is [the] factual setting. Here is a reason for keeping "fact" to the front.

Also I think it will be startling to all but some dozen or two constructing logicians to see what bad shape "fact" is in in their work—that is, to have this emphasized.

Finally, we may have our heavy *Fact* specification in the next paper to follow (that is, if your scheme of a start gains way over mine—mine being still to use your naturalistic postulates early), which is another reason for having the "Fact" gun fired hard. . . .

Regards, *Bentley*

Chatham, Massachusetts, August 15, 1944

Dear Bentley:

. . . The material you quote from Cohen and Nagel contains the material that enables you . . . to make the definite reference to "Fact" and the ambiguous position in which it is left, as outside of propositions, and that by which their "truth" is determined, if ever, or . . . possibly as the "object" of propositions, and as themselves propositions. I believe that keeping, as far as possible, discussion of "fact" till [or] towards the end, and as led up to through discussing their own statements about propositions, brings out the point clearly—and, as I've said, makes it unnecessary to make any allusion to the difference between "logical" and "scientific" method.

. . . Your treatment of Carnap is a gem of the first water and deserves to become classical. I'm sending this on without waiting to go over the rest. . . .

As far as my signature is concerned, I would be proud to sign it just as it stands. But I should be suable for false representation; I have contributed zero to it. I'm not sufficiently familiar with the subjectmatter to have done anything, and for these last weeks I've been out of touch with the books—I could have done a better job, I think, in what I wrote before about Cohen and Nagel if I had had a copy of the book . . . here. I think the fairest thing all around would be a statement from you, perhaps in connection with the reference to further papers, that while I . . . [will] join in the later articles and while I have read the present article and fully agree with it, the immediate responsibility for it is yours. You understand that this isn't because of objection on my

292

part to either the substance or form of the article, but from a sense of common decency.

I think a better way is for you to have a footnote on the first page that this article is preparatory to a series of later articles written by the two of us in conjunction. That would be the fact and would serve the purpose, I think. . . .

Yours as ever, Dewey

Chatham, Massachusetts, August 16, 1944

Dear Bentley:

. . . My complimentary reference to Nagel's paper ["Logic without Ontology"] was largely based . . . upon his backing down on the earlier Cohen ontological base, and some sentences in which he said expressly [p. 240] that some logical propositions which have been given "onto-logical" status "serve rather as indices of modes of conducting inquiry *into* that subject matter." He doesn't seem to get the full generalized import or consequences of that statement, but, at least, it seems to put him ahead of a lot of the others. And so with another statement: [signs in the natural sciences] "function as means for integrating inquiry by indicating how different experimental data may be brought into mutual relation." Not very clear-cut, but at least starting on a right road. His negative statement [p. 240] that "signs employed (in the theoretical sciences of nature) do not, *in general,* serve as mere labels for the experienced qualities of their ostensible subject matter" * is a good example of what I mean by his not getting the full force of his statement—he seems to assume that there are some "signs" or combinations of signs which are "mere labels," whatever "mere" means. In fact, the "merer" a label (like that on drugs or chemicals), the more obviously it is [a] direction as to what to do. I can't recall now that he anywhere gives any indication that there are no signs outside of sign-system or organization. . . .

Yours, Dewey

Seattle, Washington, August 19, 1944

Dear Dewey:

I could list half a dozen reasons why you should sign this first paper, and several why you might not want to. Your argument that you have done little specifically is no good at all. Neither is any argument based on personal liking. I can boil everything important down to one statement on each side:

* The exact quotation is: ". . . signs they employ do not, in general, serve as mere labels for the experienced properties of their ostensible subject matter. . . ." (Eds.)

For Signing. We need big artillery. You're it.

Against Signing. The stuff is tricky. There may be somewhere some specific merit in the developments of Carnap or Tarski which I overlook. Small flaws are almost certain. You ought not to be involved. It is not good strategy to have you involved.

The possibilities as of yesterday were: your suggestion that I put in a footnote at the start saying you approved. Suggestion rejected by me. My suggestion that you put in a footnote over your name (such things usually in brackets). . . . If we can hold the introductory matter over joint signature strictly to the *main issues* (and I believe I have done this), and if you can get it phrased to suit you throughout, I believe it ought to be O.K. to you as well as to me.

Anyway, you are up to the neck in this business—as deep as I am— historically, in fact, much deeper. I am not at all inclined to fire off a boom-boom opening gun at random. I want you tied in. . . .

Regards, *Bentley*

Seattle, Washington, August 19, 1944

Dear Dewey:

. . . You speak of "common decency," which might be all right if the conditions required it and the particular contributions per each per page were the test.

In the first place, this is a part of a big job, which is built in your background, and with the aid of some hundred letters covering maybe 75,000 words in the last year.

In the second place, you have contributed more than you probably realize even to this special paper.

In the third place, and this is the *Important* thing, what we want is action. We want to get this lousy mess out of the way. It is important to us personally. It is important to the thing we are interested in. And to get action, your name on it is worth fifty times what mine is. Of course we do not want to distort anything, or ghost-write, but suppose we estimate you at only ten per cent in this paper of actual energy output, certainly in those postulates for naturalistic dealings with knowings you will come out 90 per cent to make up for it. Anyway, what the hell, what counts is not typewriter-hours, but goal-reaching.

Would you consider using both names, and then your putting in a footnote to the title, signing, say, with your initials, saying that the whole project has been a joint one under way, though in this particular paper, while you are in agreement, I have done most of the work.

What impresses me mostly as against . . . using your name is that the hammer and tongs procedure is not one you have been employing— the attitude is raw, instead of polite. On the other hand, you have said sharper things to some of these epistemologists than I ever said—I recall especially some of the cracks in the paper in the William James memorial volume ["Does Reality Possess Practical Character?"].

It is perfectly satisfactory to me to do it either way. As you know, I always want to be careful not to let some of my cave-man procedures overflow into your range, or to get anything twisted from the past. There is more of the stamp of my way of performing than of yours on this paper. That is why I suggested you rephrase here and there on lines that would be recognizable as yours.

But if we don't use your name for the paper, we should at least have an attached footnote with your name signed to it, as endorsing it for use in carrying on.

Regards, *Bentley*

Seattle, Washington, August 24, 1944

Dear Dewey:

. . . As for the publishing, it will simplify the matter to have both names, and such a footnote as you suggest will be desirable from several points of view. It is true I have done most of the work, and that it is a specialization of my type of procedure, and also that the technical responsibility should be mine. It is also true that without your co-operation I would not have done it—for instance, you sent me a long time ago the Carnap prospectus, noting the absurd claims; it is not that I had to be shown about that, so much as that I was fortified by your independent observation. Much the same as to Morris. . . .

Bentley

Chatham, Massachusetts, August 23, 1944

Dear Bentley:

I don't think much of the reasons you give in yours of the 19th either as to why I should sign or [as to] why I shouldn't want to. The reason for my signing is [a] desire to be associated all the way through; the reason for my not signing is that it assumes work on my part I haven't done. I like the idea of a preface to the whole series. . . . All work of this kind, any sort of critical analysis or construction, is more or less a gamble in the present state of the subject, and if there are flaws, and I don't believe there are serious ones in fact, they would be just as likely to be there if I had had a more active part.

It's true [that] my manner of approach in writing is likely to be different from yours. Partly temperamental quite likely, but largely due to the fact of many years of . . . teaching class, with an audience directly in front of me, which cultivated the habit [on my part] of trying to find some common ground, or trying a flank movement that would get around or under their prepossessions, instead of making a frontal attack. But I certainly have no unwillingness to sign the present [paper] because of your approach, either in substance or [in] form. . . .

Yours, *Dewey*

Chatham, Massachusetts, August 29, 1944

Dear Bentley:

. . . Our letters have crossed, and so I'll say that I think your later idea of a prefatory note to the whole set, with statement that the series as a whole is joint, while the responsibility in some is primarily that of one of us, that of the present paper being yours, [is best]. Then, when it comes to [a question] of the vocabulary of my *Logic*, back reference can be made, with note [that] the primary responsibility in its case is mine, etc. . . .

Yours, *Dewey*

August 29, 1944

[P.S.] . . . Comments *re* "Fact." Whatever the proper use of "object," "objects," it is not in connection with the theory of knowledge. We may speak of the "objective" of the latter as that which inquiry, or know*ing*, is concerned with in particular cases. But it is not engaged in collecting "objects" as a child collects pretty pebbles, or a connoisseur pictures, or a buyer samples of wares. (These cases are intended to suggest the context in which the word "objects" has pertinence.)

There are "subjects" of inquiry—topics, themes—and some aspects of these subjects of study may be properly called "objectives" or ends-held-in-view, as directives of behavior. But the substitution of the word "objects" for the word "subject," which latter word was alone in use in connection with the theory of knowledge until the seventeenth century, is wholly a product of the epistemological, mentalistic, mind-world metaphysical dualism in which mind as knower retained the *super*-natural attributes of soul or spirit while being set over against the *natural* world of science—which [natural world] was then exclusively *physical*, and "material" in its traditional disparaging metaphysical sense. ("Physical" is a word applicable only in connection with the subject-matter of certain aspects of knowledge which have to be specifically identified.)

We can speak intelligibly of "subjectmatter" of knowledge, the word naming the *range* of what is known and to-be-known in specified *subjects* of examination.

296

The one word which is exclusively and inclusively distinctive or characteristic with reference to the field and scope of the subjectmatter of knowledge is "fact," "facts."

Seattle, Washington, September 2, 1944

Dear Dewey:

. . . With regard to "objects," we differentiate "Fact" with respect to the aspects "knowing-naming" and "event-under-naming." Then we must differentiate "event" with respect to (1) "situation" (broadly set off), and (2) (?) (sharply set off), and (3) the intermediate thing-in-process (this latter commonly being called "event." For 2 (where I put the ?) I am using "object." Here "thing" is common naming; "isolate" would be O.K., if selection were understood. The distinction of 1, 2, and 3 is one of sharp margins. "Situation" is a cell with nucleus specified so that nucleus and rest of cell are studied together; "Event-intermediate" is an account of a minute or second of cell-change; "Thing" (object) is cell setting up on its own as small *deus* for a generation or two.

Now I am 100% for your discussion, and stress, on subject-matter on both sides (Fact). (And where I do not get this stress in—at the right place—I hope you will remember to write it in.) "Subject-matter" [is] better than "object" and in wide range of discussion should be used. But these seem to be cases of "object" as *of* knowledge, or of being known. On the other hand, "object as *in* knowledge" (or as *in* Fact) has to have names for its gradations of sharpness in selection, isolation, holding-for-a-while. What is the name I should stick in there?

Thus far I make "Event" the "named-phase" of "Fact" (as opposite to the naming-phase). And also I keep "Event" for the intermediate transition-phase, thus having "Event" differentiate in spectrum-style with the phases "Situation," "Event," and "Object." (For "Sign," we do better by having "Signal," "Name," and "Symbol" as its stages.) If you can solve this problem, for "Event" and "Object," it will be [a] good thing.

Regards, *Bentley*

[P.S.] What I am trying to say here is that your elaboration for subject-matter *vs.* object seems to me to run against the cases where "object" is set over against "knowledge." Also, in general discussion of the methodology, it is immensely preferable to use "subject-matter" instead of "object" (you have been increasing stress on this phrasing right along). On the other hand, we need a name (and it is at this moment my concern) for the sharper identifications *within knowledge*, i.e., for *this dog Fido now* seen not as subject-matter, or situation-in-environment, or process-going-on, but as identifiable thing-of-the-moment. And what should it be?

[To Bentley:]

Slight Additional Comment *Re* "Fact," etc. When "objective" is used for "object" of knowledge, it is obvious that it does not name that with which knowledge is concerned on its own account, but only in the special status the latter occupies under certain special (and specified) conditions.

"Thing"—this word is the vaguest, most neutral, and noncommittal of all words. Its sense is best gathered from the everyday usage of "something," "anything," "nothing," which refer to "anything" whatever; affairs, topics, actual and possible, ghosts, illusions, and [which] do not in any way stand for or indicate an "object" in its epistemological sense, much less one that is "substantial" in a metaphysical sense.

(This comment on "Thing" may seem quite unnecessary and can certainly be improved in wording, but two or three lines in glossary form might be useful.)

Dewey

New York, September 6, 1944

Dear Bentley:

. . . I don't believe "Things" and "Object" can be said to be synonymous, save as "Object" is given a much wider and vaguer use than is customary either in technical or [in] ordinary discourse. An *object,* I think, is *thing* much circumscribed.

"Thing" was originally an "assembly," especially of a judicial nature; then, any cause or matter that came before it. Then (and this, I think, is now the primary idiomatic usage) "that with which one is concerned (in action, speech, or thought); affair, business, concern, matter, subject." (Murray's *Oxford [English] Dictionary.* . . .)

Yours, *Dewey*

[New York,] September 8, 1944

[To Bentley:]

"Transactions"

I. If there are cases in which existences which are independent and separate (in the sense of not belonging to or inhering in a system) act upon or with each other, the changes which occur are said to be Actions-Reactions. The development of physics since the time of Newton has significantly reduced the number and scope of cases of this kind, of which the impact of two billiard balls, isolated from everything else, is a standard illustration.

II. Cases in which such action and reaction effect, or tend to bring

298

into existence, a system in place of previous separation are said to be cases of Interaction. Thus certain materials, say grasses, when acted upon by certain tissues of animals [and] while acting upon the latter, become *food,* and the tissues at the same time become organs (in this case of assimilation or digestion). There is *Interaction,* not just action-and-reaction. Because of, and by means of, reciprocal activity, components are *now* in system.

III. Cases in which the components of a total event are in system throughout are said to be cases of Transaction. The changes which take place are then said to be *Developments.* Thus, the phrase "development of physics" (as employed under I) postulates that physics as science consists of transactional material. The same principle holds for cases of Growth: Life, that is, and . . . [for] all material to which *Historical Status* is assigned.

Thus, while grass and tissues may be assigned independent status in the illustration given in II, the same is *not* true of, say, *Environment* and *Organism.* As a man is, say, husband, father, buyer, seller, tenant, lessor, only *in* transactions of marriage, commerce, leasing, so surroundings are environments, and structured tissues are organisms *only* in the trans-actions which constitute life. Some form of living-events is possible without the *particular* thing, grass; and without the particular tissues constituting the digestive organs of, say, [a] cow. But living events are not possible without inclusion of environment, nor without inclusion of organism.

All events to which life (that is, living or being alive) is attributed are transactional. So are all events which are the subjects of sociological inquiry; such names as heirs, creditors, consumers, officials, agents, crim-inals, prisoners, student, teacher, tools, assets, capital, labor, utensils, implements, articles of furniture, have no standing save transactionally.

Just what respective subjectmatters are to be treated from the stand-point of action-reaction, interaction, and transaction is a matter to be decided in, and by, the actual progress of knowledge. But it should be clear that knowings-knowns fall wholly within the scope of transactions, and that failures to treat them in that context can only result in confusion. If, for example, such words as "subject," "mind," etc., as *knower* have validity and intelligible coherent standing, it is only as involved in trans-actions in which *knowns* are also involved—and the same for objects, thing, etc., as names for that with which knowledge is concerned.

Without attempting to pass here upon the question of the factual scope of, or range of, application of action-reaction and interaction methods of statement, it should be noted that when the case of the two billiard balls is taken as one event in a system of events, prolonged in time and extended in space, as in the case of a game, and then in the case of the game as a component of life-histories of players, the transactional treatment is required. . . .

There is need then of *names* which firmly and without ambiguity present the transactional property of all words employed in inquiry into the theory of knowledge—e.g., "Fact," etc.

[*Dewey*]

New York, September 11, 1944

Dear Bentley:

[In *re* a draft of Bentley's essay "On a Certain Vagueness in Logic"] . . . As to the two "sides," "sentence under designation," "the same sentence as an active assertion." Does this mean simply that sentence is active assertion and as such is to be distinguished from the (meta?) logical? sentences which deal with sentences *as* assertions—or does it mean that the sentence itself has these two "sides"? In the former case, it seems innocent and proper. In the latter, it would seem worth notice, in an amplified statement, as falling back into the separation of sentence as language and sentence as knowledge (assertion?) I'm too ignorant to know whether there is any point or not to this suggestion. . . .

Yours, *Dewey*

[P.S.] Might have something early in the next paper to the effect that the statements criticized in the "Vagueness" paper show one property in common which can be taken as an advance—recognition of the importance of language in knowledge—while their incoherence reveals that confusion necessarily results when the place given to language is merely tacked on to older doctrines with slight modifications of their tenor. . . .

[Paoli, Indiana,] September 11, 1944

[To Dewey:]

"Transaction," etc. Dewey's treatment (. . . dated 9-8-44) covers the ground in a way that varies at some points from mine. I would not say which is best, until further study.

I have been distinguishing:

A. Self-Action: When one feels that if you describe *the actor*, you have done the job. Here the ancient magics, modern "faculties," and pre-Galilean physics (probably) would illustrate.

B. Inter-action: When one has materials which one feels one can describe as apart from any joint-operation; but which when in joint operation affect each other, and in critical treatment "affect equally." Here I would use Newton's second [third] law of motion as illustration; likewise all provisional studies or part-studies of transaction.

C. Trans-action: In the same sense as Dewey; when you just can't tell the story or adequately describe either component without implying the other.

Dewey now does two things in a different way than I have been doing them: (a) he applies the terminology "action-reaction" under A; (b) he uses Newton's second [third] law to illustrate A instead of B.

As to the first of these, I am inclined to think the terminology of "stimulus-reaction" or "stimulus-response" in psychology really belongs under A, and under A on the organism side. (The very term "stimulus" is established from the *organism's* point of view, not from the environment's, and that is not fair play.) But "action-reaction" I do not feel clear about: I do not know in just what sense John Dewey is using it here. I do not picture any physical situation in which the "action" element is distinct and separate from the "reaction" element. It might have very well been *before Newton*. But Newton's law said that action and reaction were equal and gave a technical expression in "force" for each component [and] brought them into *system*. But to be in "system," according to John Dewey, would be interaction. The system is mechanical in this case. [Henri] Poincaré *demonstrated* that if one mechanical interpretation [is] possible, an infinite number are possible (Preface to his . . . [*Les Méthodes nouvelles de la mécanique celeste*] for his statement). That *Is* system—hit it from any corner, and you come out O.K. This takes my "b" difference as well as "a."

In John Dewey's "II" I do not understand the "effect, or tend to bring into existence a system." If we look at all materials as subject-matters, I would phrase it rather that the "interaction" was in the subject-matter. Our technique of inquiry brings it out, of course; and from that point of view "tends to bring into. . . . " But what it "brings into" is not "existence," but rather "conclusion of research." (Not that I am violating our first principles here by going too far in separating "event" and "naming"— but, still, what is under stress is the system which *was* event and *is* event, [and] is now getting *named* (known as) event.

My questions are:

In what sense are action and reaction used in John Dewey's "I"?

What (apart from magic, faculty, etc., or pre-Galilean physics) illustrates "I" as different from "II"?

The digestion illustration is bully for "interaction." But what it shows is that, within the wider subject-matter, there is a differentiated region (or rather sets of regions) in which a technique different from the physical must be applied. It does not show that in developed knowledge we can rate the physical as "action-reaction" and the physiological as "interaction."

What we have here, I would say, is one type of interaction that we handle physically, and another type of interaction we handle physiologically, and a third type behaviorally. All of them will tolerate trans-

301

actional envisionment, and all will tolerate interactional breaking up for examination. And that our present stage of knowledge is too far advanced to justify "self-action" discussions (which latter survive in philosophy, logic, psychology, and sociology).

It is plain that the most successful "interactional" report was physics in the Newtonian era. It is also plain to *us* (and that is the bottom of our present job) (i.e., "bottom" equals "heart") that for the knowledge problem a vigorous transactional envisionment must precede solution.

But I am not clear on the distinctions of "I" and "II" as John Dewey uses them. And I may miss the point altogether. . . .

A. F. B.

New York, September 13, 1944

Dear Bentley:

I was sort of carried away by your first terminological paper and hastily jotted down in writing the things I sent you. I should have considered them longer and sent them in a legible form. I enclose some further comments which at least should be more legible. . . .

I have been thinking some about the suggested paper at the end. I think I probably shall be glad to write something on knowledge and language, not *primarily* on the terminology of the *Logic*, which in some matters I should alter as the result of our correspondence, but in a way which might supplement yours by approaching it from a different angle, with incidental references to my *Logic* when they come in naturally. (By the way, did Kaufmann send you a copy of his new book [*Methodology of the Social Sciences*]? He sent me one with a complimentary reference to my *Logic* in the Preface—I haven't got at reading it yet. He makes a sharp distinction between Logic proper—formal deduction, Syntactics? (though he doesn't use the word)—and scientific methodology. I'm most O.K. on latter, but wrong [according to Kaufmann,] in not making the separation.)

I should begin with language as *communication* maintaining group organization, and then go on to language as not having *directly* any such reference—my old hobby horse about the intermediate function of "science." And I also have quite a lot of notes bearing on identification of naming and knowing, Noting, saying, telling, etc., that I should work in. I don't think a paper dealing *mainly* with my logical terminology is worth while. This other one might sort of supplement, stereoptically, yours.

[*Dewey*]

September 13, 1944

[Notes to Bentley:]

The scheme of the paper just received ("Terminology for Knowing," etc.) is fine. The idea of beginning with what is *needed* and why (how) it is, is a stroke that simplifies the whole business of effective statement. There are, perhaps, a few cases in the paper where externally or apparently the process is reversed—where you begin with the name itself and not with the distinction it is needful to make and observe. You will undoubtedly detect any such cases yourself when you go over the paper with this in mind. The instance that strikes me particularly is in connection with consideration of "sign." . . .

The paper, as it reads now, seems to take too much for granted, instead of telling first just what the great *need* is. I can see the difficulty here in getting over too much into the material that belongs to the later discussion. Perhaps here, the reference to the previous paper as [a] sign of the growing general acknowledgment of the need for considering *language* in connection with, or as a significant part of, the theory of knowledge would suffice. [I think] that the previous paper gives sufficient evidence of the need of deciding upon the word "sign" in the present state of discussion.

The other possible case is in connection with Physical-Behavioral. If any introductory material is needed, a brief statement to the fact [effect] that traditional discussion of the subjectmatter involved has been mostly in epistemological-ontological terms instead of in terms of the state and process-progress of knowledge would suffice—then point out [that] the treatment proposed answers the urgent need for the latter mode of treatment.

That is, point out that the theme is in no way a new one, but, on the contrary, has long been a stock subject of "philosophical" discussion. . . .

. . . "Names." Some words probably needing specific if brief glossary attention: "System." You use the phrase "in system," and I have picked it up from you as useful—and necessary. But as it is not self-explanatory, perhaps a brief exposition should be given. Also "Organization"?

"Action," "Activity." Probably in connection with "Interaction," "Transaction," simply a notation to the fact that they stand, when used alone, for either of the above words in cases where further specification does not need to be made in that particular context. "Process"? "Operation"?

(About "Action-Reaction," I think, perhaps, what I wrote about that the other day (9-8) represents unnecessary caution on my part. It may be there are *No* such cases, in which case the reference would be only to an earlier phase now untenable. But I was anxious to avoid "telling," and so I put it in as a factual matter to be determined in the process of knowing. Maybe the change in physics has already settled the matter. You can judge much better than I can.)

It seems to me, perhaps, that just as "Process" emphasizes the dura-tional continuity of the factual event, so "Operation" emphasizes what is usually called its causal aspect—doing something, or the "activity or action," as conducting to a specifiable outcome, a further state or aspect of the ongoing activity-process.

It also calls attention to "organism" participation in a transaction, possibly too much so to be a safe word at present—but that holds of "ac-tivity" also, save as guarded, as we are doing, by reference to "inter" and "trans."

"Term." You have properly called attention to the loose and confused use of this word. But I think in the proper place, the positive force of the word should be brought out: The cases in which a name specifies *conditions to be observed*—or, in short, when it is accomplishing the *function of specification*, while that fact is given attention as the needed, explicit noting of the fact that names do specify and *how* they *do* it—setting up limits, boundaries, conditions—connection with "de-term-ining," "term-inations."

"Proposition." The confusion [and] vagueness in *Logic*, simply treats "term" as a casual constituent of any proposition, with no coherent view of what a proposition is or what it is to have terms for its components. A sentence as a linguistic expression is a proposition (or may be "termed" that) when concerned in the knowledge operation of de-termining—making specific, definite, precise, some factual subjectmatter. "Terms" are the instrumentalities of effecting (reaching, securing the existence of) this determination. Hence, every *proposition* is in serial system with other propositions—in that continuing process of determination, specifica-tion, which is knowledge. (It may be that this matter belongs in [the] article on language. But, maybe, it and "Term" should be subheads under "Specification.")

Re your remarks about "meaning." I've been interested to see how easy it is to substitute "is" for "means" and how much gain there is in definiteness when this is done.

"Definition," "Description." . . . I agree that "Definition" in strict sense should be limited to relations of *symbols*, mathematical statements. But I think the connection of the word with definiteness, or with the most firm and precise determinateness, specification, attainable at a given time should receive notice. Hence, what I said about "De-scription"—which has the advantage of being, literally, a language-name—[being] writing, noting *down*, marking *off*.

Dewey

Dear Bentley:

Re "action," "inter," "trans."

Doubtless I was, and probably still am, overinfluenced by my long use of "inter" in connection with the physiological. I don't think highly of my inter-action formulation. I was hinting at its difference from full trans-actional. I am, doubtless, also influenced by the literal sense of "inter" as conveying betweenness—a sort of reciprocity or mutuality. And my knowledge of physics is slight in comparison with yours. But I venture to set down my understanding of Newton.

1. His minute particles are structurally unchangeable. They change direction and velocity rate when they act *upon* one another, but not their primary properties, which are immutable.

2. After an action-reaction, or acting upon, everything is just as it was before save changed direction of motion in space, and rate of motion. (This is "1" over again.) System, order—as, for example, the solar system—is in consequence the product of divine design in creation—and occasional intervention when *system* shows signs of running down. It belongs, I should say, to his theological science rather than to his physics. In fact, he uses the *logical* outcome of his physical system as ground for inferring the *necessity* of activity of a Divine Being, the contrast between these consequences and the actual state of things being so great as to need special explanation. Whether, and in what way, Einstein on relativity marks change over into *inter*, I am not competent to say, but should imagine it does, and then [may] the post-Einsteinian physics [mark the change] into *Trans?*

3. "Self-action" is associated in my mind with pre-Galilean physics or cosmology. According to Aristotelian physics, "matter" was purely passive; couldn't even *re*-act. There was an ultimate pure self-mover, which he identified with *Be*-ing in the full sense—i.e., God; the stars of the heavenly firmament that move the same forever were then next in order —rank—of Being. As we come down to earth, "matter," or sheer passivity, became more and more a leading property of events. The same thing held of his "elements"—fire was most self-active; air next, then water; lowest was earth.

The relevancy of the above to Newton's physics is that he revolutionized the scene by attributing self-activity, in the way of motion in space to *all* ultimate physical beings—namely, minute particles or atoms, giving them the same eternal fixity of Being and inherent structure that had belonged in the classic cosmology to God and the "heavenly" bodies or "fixed stars." Self-action thus lost its old meta-physical character and was taken to be scientifically physical.

Your criticism of my "Tend to bring into existence" is thoroughly justified; it is terrible. It illustrates by contrast the immense value of "Fact"

305

as name, since the latter brings the matter definitely into research and knowledge.

My only answer to your inquiry about the sense in which I use "action-reaction" is Newton's own use—"equal and in opposite directions." That they occur simultaneously, with simply a change in direction—and in more compound cases of acceleration—doesn't seem to me to involve system. If "mechanical" is taken strictly, *does*, or doesn't *it*, and "system" destroy each other?

To go back to pre-Galilean cosmology—it held that, except in the case of perfect Being and the fixed firmament, all bodies in motion tended to come to rest—in various qualitative degrees according to the graded amounts of Being they contain. The revolution began with Galileo's assertion that, on the contrary, moving things, *of themselves*, continue forever in motion. The transfer in the *locus* of "self-action" made an immense difference. But it left over "self-action"—at least, that it is the way I read Newton; maybe I'm wrong. But, logically, I don't think his excursion into theology was an excrescence. And the same holds for the whole deistic "design" argument that eased over the old supernatural theology into what took itself to be "rationalistic" [theology]—and was so taken by representatives of the old theology.

From my point of view, your "self-action" has a decided advantage over my formula as the *primary* one. What difference there is between us is that I think the old self-action carried over into pre-Einsteinian physics, although without *at the time* seriously interfering with the needed kind of actual research. From a certain point of view, I may seem to be exaggerating the importance of historical considerations—even if I should be right in [the] report upon Newtonian premises. On the other hand, it illustrates the mixture, and the failure to work free in the earlier stages of the continuous known-knowing process, from old naming which is everywhere characteristic—and which is seen in the present holdover of the old subject-object formula, which also once served a positive end, at a particular historic juncture.

I add I don't see how Newtonian *absolute* space, time, and motion works out on an interaction-interpretation of his second [third] law; correcting my bad statement of bringing system into *existence*, instead of into ascertained fact.

What you say about what my digestion illustration "really" illustrates is, of course, sound. My statement was elliptical. It assumed, instead of intending to deny, that the difference was that between a shorter-span, narrower extended piece of knowing and that within which, temporally-spatially, it takes place! A matter of the special problem at the time.

That in historic effect Newton's self-action theoretical formulation worked in actual (practical) knowings in the interactional direction, as you state it, I don't doubt. But was this fact theoretically observed or

306

named at the time? Was the Einstein "revolution," in fact, not so much of a revolution as it was an explicit naming of what *had been going on,* which corrected incoherence in the previous namings? . . .

Yours, Dewey

[P.S.] It occurs to me to add that the chief source of the differences that turn up between us is due to the fact of my interest in specifying historical settings or contexts; while instead of historical interest *in that sense,* your interest lies in the whole panoramic sweep. The two interests ought to be capable of working out together in a coherent picture.

[New York,] September 15, 1944

Dear Bentley:
     . . . As far as I assumed, or seemed to do so, that physical, physiological, and behavior corresponded to action, interaction, and transactional, it was sheer carelessness.

Of course, your statement [that] . . . the type of methodical approach . . . [depends] upon subjectmatter (the main point) and that only the transactional is competent in dealing with knowledge, is the only correct one. And I don't disagree as to the statement that in *effect,* or in actual *outcome,* physics has been the successful example of [the] "interactional." But I don't think that the postulates of the theory were stated interactionally, or were so regarded, as far as naming, in distinction from doing, was concerned. Hence certain incoherences in theory-naming. And, as I suggested, maybe the separation of chemistry from physics was one of them. In chemistry the obvious occurrence of transformations in the case of combinations was, I think, the source of the separation—incidentally, maintaining a certain continuity with al-chemy as concerned with certain attempted transformations. Chemistry as strictly physical is a fairly modern accomplishment. . . .

Yours, Dewey

[New York,] September 15, 1944

[Notes to Bentley:]

Actional

I haven't a copy of the *Principia* at hand. But I have some quotations. When Newton is arguing about the fixity of the ultimate minute particles, he says in behalf of their inherent immutability that if *all* particles [in] all bodies could be broken, they would wear away; in that case, the "nature of things depending on them would be changed," and "therefore, *that nature may be lasting* [my italics], the changes of corporeal things are to be placed only in the various separations and new associations and motions of these permanent particles." One other passage: "God in the beginning formed matter in solid, massy, hard, impenetrable particles."

I don't believe that the fact that he [Newton] gave self-action to his ultimate components of nature alters in any way the bottom or "heart," of your statement. (1) It indicates that *self-action* is primary and my "action-and-reaction" is derived. (2) It gives a good illustration of the fact that a theory of knowledge must be based on what takes place, what is transactionally done, not upon what is said, and (3) that in important matters, there is a very considerable lag in the latter as compared with the former. . . . (4) [The lag is] very marked in the theory of knowledge, so that we are simply reporting in language that describes what has observably taken place in knowledge—when it is observed on its own account, free from the influence of namings which are [the] product of earlier and now outgrown states. . . .

In other words, what was *done,* what took place, in physics was interactional, but the generalized naming or theory about it was self-actional. When we get on to express consideration of "inter-trans"—I think you can effectively correlate significant advances in science with specific shifts over to explicit interactional [uses] that have already occurred. In your letter of July 4, 1944, you suggested [that] I offer some instance of gradation from "inter" to "transactional." My scientific knowledge is not much of a resource. But instances all the way from "self" through "inter" over to "transactional," taken from the developing process in knowledge (knowledge as process or continuing durational events), would be effective. What you said about genes suggests the old worship of cells as kind of Newtonian atoms, with external combinations in physiology and its enforced abandonment, [and] the vogue of [August] Weismann's "biophors" in his theory of heredity. On the other hand, I take it the rise of the ecological in botany is "inter" and, probably, fairly well on into "trans." Psychology, of course, is full of cases, while the fact that transition has not yet been effected, accounts for its confused state. The scandal of "individual" in social theories (economics, politics, ethics) introduces deeply controversial material, but it should be O.K. to point out that the controversies turn on self-actional versus trans-actional [uses], leaving [it to] the reader to draw the moral. . . .

In connection with this matter, it occurs to me that, in dealing with special items in the terminological list, it will give unity and body, and at the same facilitate brevity, to state their actional status, e.g., stimulus. . . .

. . . Names to receive attention:

"Connection," as distinct from "relation" of symbols. (I find it extremely hard in consecutive writing not to use "relation" at times as a synonym of "connection." I don't suppose it does any particular harm if

308

the context makes clear its proper use.) Obviously the discussion of inter- and transactional is about *Connections*. It would be a good thing, I believe, if we could get a word that corresponds in this matter to "Self-action" in the other range, to name what is taken to be out-of-connection. "Self-actual" is awkward, but has a certain kinship to "self-action."

"Isolation." Note ambiguity in its use. Sometimes to name that which is taken to *be* out of connection; sometimes, as in the case of isolates in chemistry, as a name for something derived—product, extracted out of something more compound. I don't know whether there would be any advantage in employing "extract."

"Reify," "Hypostatize." Words that name *vicious* isolations, resulting in giving Self-actuality and Self-action to matters . . . [that] can be observed and described only in connectivities. Some examples: "Thing" and "Entity," "Object," in certain prevalent uses in the theory of knowledge.

"System": (1) Number, variety of things (i.e., affairs, concerns) and/or events in connectivity. Solar, planetary, digestive. . . . (2) Also used in case of matters in *relation*, that is, according to some method manifesting the know*ing* aspect of the knowledge transaction: Copernican system, Linnaean system, natural system of classification, Platonic, Newtonian, etc. Distinction between (1) and (2) is only one of phase or emphasis, and provides marked illustration of the known-knowing character of Knowledge and Fact. . . .

Dewey

Indianapolis, Indiana, September 17, 1944

Dear Dewey:

Re "Transaction." I don't think there is any doubt at all about your being right about the Newtonian position—that is, about the way Newton interpreted and viewed his work and its cosmic outcome. You make a heavy case, resting in Aristotle and connecting the theology. This is something we must get *into* the paper when it comes. I can add something. . . . "Force" was looked upon as an *actor* even down to 50–75 years ago. Today "energy" is treated by all the old-timers and many of the solemn younger ones as a *performer;* they speak of it as though you catch and cage a quantity of it all by and for itself.

What I was really doing (or trying to do) was to contrast "system" as built up under the Newtonian mechanics—i.e., *mechanical* systems—with "system" as it has developed under wave theory of light, the electromagnetic scheme, and the Einsteinian layout in which, for example, gravitation is not treated in the old way, but rather as a characteristic of the universe (space-curvature, etc.). . . . I add my own bug. "Infinity" treated as place or thing makes no sense. "Infinity" as a linguistic characteristic of a symbolic scheme as a whole does the job without friction.

I would therefore remodel as follows:

Self-Action: magic, souls, and faculties, pre-Galilean physics, Newtonian basis as Newton saw it.

Interaction: Newtonian mechanistic system as it slowly purified itself, so that the second [third] law of motion was not just an account of the action of immutable particles—but all-the-way-round statement (Poincaré). (Notice that by a particle today, the mathematical physicist means simply *any* unit you select, from a theoretical electron to a theoretical sun, providing you work it in mechanical system—technical mathematical mechanics. . . .)

Transaction: Where physics generalizes; what psychology needs to get a good start; what is basic for a theory of knowledge.

You remark that the absolute space-time-motion of Newton does not work out interactional[ly] in second [third] law. I agree. They do not. What worked out was the historical development yielding a full interactional mechanics. The difference between us thus again is merely that I had my eye on the matured Newtonian scheme; you had yours on Newton's place (and attitude) historically. . . .

Regards, *Bentley*

Indianapolis, Indiana, September 18, 1944

Dear Dewey:

. . . Your *Logic, to me,* has thorough central consistency—the empirical kind—it takes a problem and keeps straight toward its goal. As we agree, you have used almost every possible form of phrasing you could to get your point over. This leaves the little minor precisionists a chance to act like smarties. On the other hand, *to me,* the ordinary logics have a great pretense to braininess, but with rotting guts. Now in our papers we are shifting one of the partitions used in the signal-sign-symbol terminology; we may have some slight change of naming in other respects; there is a good deal of your more technically logical terminology we will not get to; and while I have a page, you may recall, in an earlier draft showing how our Fact Scheme is explicitly the Fact Scheme that was used through the early chapters of the *Logic* (and of course the rest but less explicitly), that probably will not be all that is necessary. Also the scheme Connection-Reference-Relation in the *Logic* wants to be stressed as structural in what we are doing. All of which together makes me think a special paper by you designed to clarify the presentations for new readers would be very helpful to all concerned.

I have checked all your suggestions. . . . The only one I want to discuss is "Definition and Description."

I would say, subject to further examination and possible error, that by "Specification" I intend precisely what you intend by "Delimitation," or by "Definition" in the sense of "delimitation." I suspect that by "Characterization" I intended very close to what you would by "Descriptive Definition." The problem is strictly one of what names we are going to use. The first name to decide on is "Definition." Here I am provisionally committed to throwing it on the symbolic side. As to the other names, as to whether "Specification" and "Characterization" are best, I am open. (So far as dictionary definition is concerned, we can pass it over—it is a collection of usages—vulgar speech.) But in technical use I have a very emphatic *First Principle:* if we are ever going to get anywhere, we must establish and maintain throughout the discussion a clean distinction between a name for name-application and a name for mathematical- symbol-development. Everywhere I turn, people believe that when they have perfected symbolization, they will have perfected naming. This I regard as superstition, ignorance, magic. The great test case is the infinitesimal. The mathematicians were unhappy and hampered until they finally got it into their heads that they could use the infinitesimal process without catching a little infinitesimal bug and keeping him in a cage while they did it. Now they are free from it. But to my mind everything in the whole sphere of existential naming from "Cat" to "Beersheba" has got to be freed from it. The existential names (say genera and species) will hold good while they work. They can be applied so far as they work in the form of name applied to a thing. The symbols hold good while together. They cannot be applied, any of them, single symbol to single thing, but only in the full *system.* And in full application they work wonders. I push this distinction of "name" and "symbol" clear through. Of course, it is not compartmental but aspectual. Historically the symbol-using expands out of name-using, just as name-using had earlier done out of prelinguistic sign-using. But as distinction within the factual transaction, it is necessary at this stage. . . .

I accept "definition" for the symbolic range because the tendency is that way in Carnap and Tarski, and many others. (Of course, I would be willing, if you showed something better, to use "definition" in place of "Specification," and get a different word for what I have called "definition.") Assuming we place "definition" in the symbolic range, then I would fight against anything like "descriptive definition"—that is, not against your "process" to be named, but against . . . [this] use of definition. Manifestly, to put the adjective "descriptive" onto the word "definition" after having denied "definition" all descriptive value is not so hot. It is *Namings* that we are after here primarily, and at the moment almost exclusively. If we want name for the kind of namings that begin with *dog* in current use, develop as *canis* in taxonomy, and widen out into a huge chemical terminology with *accuracy,* I do not think "description" is good. It is a little too free and easy. That is why I have "Specification" and "Characterization" alongside of "Definition." Is not "Specify" almost as sharply delimiting as "Define"? Mind you, I don't care about these words—which are chosen—at all. I think "definition" should be held to its widest, or rather, most centralized application, *provided* that that is in the line of probable development. Otherwise free. You yourself widen "descriptive definition" out as a "summary statement of the conclusions of knowledge (of existence)—say of a given date." A name is just that. . . .

And here is another thing. Suppose we use "Situation," "Event," "Object" ("Event" here narrowly, not broadly). If I say that we *name,* or specify in all three cases, I make "name" stretch pretty far. But it is one of the essentials of whole treatment to keep "name" (designation) properly elastic. Suppose I should *specify* an object or an event, but *characterize* a situation. That again would be to transfer technical procedure to object-side as existential. This is just one of the minor involvements.

Regards, *Bentley*

[New York,] September 20, 1944

To Bentley:

. . . I did not intend any change whatever in the fundamental point or principle. But merely a little amplification to avoid readers' misapprehension. The utmost precision of terminology on our part won't insure of itself against interpretation in terms of currently fixed associations in the minds of readers. (I probably tend to exaggerate the latter factor because of experiences as teacher.) Just to make sure: I never thought for a minute of substituting "Definition" for "Specification"—nor "description" either. The former is fatal; the latter confusing since "specify" is the primary name and "description" is a further characterization of "specify": at best and most, it is that *only.*

(I might say in behalf of myself in *Logic* that I made a distinction between "characteristics" as descriptive (specifications) and "characters" as defining in our present sense "relations," symbolic developments. Not, of course, that the words must mean that, but that there are differences that should have some name. That is also the way I used "Universal" and "General." This point doesn't need mention in the article, but might come in in my language article.)

I don't recall whether I mentioned in connection with Morris (and presumably [this] applies to Carnap) that his attempt to make syntactics simply a matter of formal relations, and his identification of mathematics (and logic) with syntactics, fail completely to note or take any account of your basic point about mathematics. He may escape from using

312

mathematical symbols as names of things (as *entities*), but he certainly makes them names of relations—of some strange sort—*between entities*.

I suppose my two forms, as against your three, is my present tendency to slur "objects"—curiously enough, that fact is due mainly to your own influence on me. But I looked up my *Logic* [p. 119] and find "The name *objects* will be reserved for subject-matter . . . [so] far as it has been produced and ordered in settled form by means of inquiry. . . . For things exist *as* objects for us only as they have been previously determined as outcomes of inquiry."

I think with you "name" should be kept elastic, and be used of the entire range of the non-mathematical.

Incidentally, I think I have run down the source of my earlier wobbling about "Fact." Because of connection with what is done or made, I tended to feel it should be reserved for "eulogistic" naming—well-established cases—and this in spite of my other emphasis upon inquiry as a continuing process. It shows how hard it is to root [out] all traces of earlier misconceptions. In spite of my own position, I was tending to cling to something finished (absolute) as the *proper* use of Fact. . . .

[*Dewey*]

[New York,] September 21, 1944

[To Bentley:]

In a letter of 7-5-44 you said, "Name is a grand old name," which it certainly is, and [you] went on to make some remarks, about "sign," directed especially against trying to derive "name" from "sign," instead of vice-versa. Starting with [the] fact that "name" is primary and "sign" derived, should anything be said specifically on this point, or [should we] confine discussion of "sign" to section on "signal-sign-symbol"? I take it "name" is treated first, has priority over "signal-sign," etc., discussion. Perhaps, something could or should be said there about sign as a further name for a name on a special use or application of the latter, referring to later heading for more detailed statement.

I am not sure whether I wrote . . . that you might introduce . . . a brief reference to the previous paper, ["On a Certain] Vagueness [in Logic"], to the effect that the authors there discussed, or most of them (and the entire modern interest in "semantics"), had indicated a promising movement forward inasfar as they were sensitive to the intimate connection of language with knowledge, but had definitely increased rather than reduced confusion by inserting it as [a] third thing between the old mind [and] thing. . . . It is proposed to see how things stand when the connection is taken seriously, i.e., with elimination of the carry-over and treatment on the Knowing-Known basis. . . .

About all that is needed is that knowers are in the cosmos along with

313

what is known and to-be-known, that knowings are there too, and are to be studied (observed) in exactly the same way (that of observation-report-specification) as other matters. Then, that can be used to specify naturalism-naturalistic, instead of using the latter to characterize our procedure. (This would eliminate, I think, the danger of reading our article in the sense of naturalism as another and rival metaphysical scheme.) . . .

"Object." I think you have it already well in hand. The statements I made a few letters ago reacted backward altogether too far—what I had in mind was that facts as objects are those not undergoing specific investigation but, rather [are] being taken and used ready-made, as finished goods, so to speak. And it should be pointed out that, neverthe-less, the *outcome* of a knowing in which they are so treated may modify them as "objects" for further knowing-process, and that in the course of time minor shifts of this kind may cumulatively determine a different "object," decidedly or notably different, that is. (I hope the quotation on "Object" I sent from my *Logic*, p. 119, is not out of line with your use. The modification of "objects" is dealt with rather clumsily on p. 29 —the illustrations are better than the statement. I think it is equivalent to the fact that an object is a short expression for something of a certain kind which is still undergoing determination.)

"Entity." Scholastic word, originally abstract (*ity* termination), then concrete. . . . I think . . . it safe, however, to say something to the effect that the word, as currently used (without the technical precision it had in medieval scholasticism), is a word conveniently used whenever writers (writers on logic?) who hold to the doctrine of [abstract classes of] things, objects, existences, wholly apart from specification, wish to refer to them in the vaguest possible fashion. . . .

Hence, ["entity" is] a word to be definitively eschewed in a scheme having the postulates upon which we are proceeding. . . . In substance, all the objections [that] there are to "Existence," are multiplied to infinity, because "Entity" does not have the saving grace of *ex*-isting, standing out, in a process (like e-vent, coming out).

"Phenomenon." I haven't the *Baldwin Dictionary* [*of Philosophy and Psychology*] at hand. But I wrote what it says there, and it was to the effect that it should be given a purely neutral signification (as against the distinction between "phenomenal" and "real"), making it in effect a synonym of "event," "occurrence," if the word is used at all. I think that covers its proper use, together (with warning against its epistemo-logical use), perhaps, with remark that in its scientific use, it often names the kind of event which for reasons in the existing system of science stands out conspicuously as having critical importance for inquiry. . . . If it weren't for the damned metaphysical-epistemological associations, the word could be used to illustrate knowing-known, . . . an *event-as-*

observed. This, I think, is the way it is used in scientific writing when they stick to science; with, as per [Baldwin] *Dictionary* quotation, an intimation that observation is not as yet complete specification. Whether it would be worth saying that while we do not use the word, it could be used, consistently with the approach we adopt, in *that* sense, I don't know—probably hardly worth it.

"Datum-Data." My earlier use here, as you have doubtless noticed, was decidedly narrower than one you often use. I reserved it for those *particular* facts which serve to set a problem to test proffered hypotheses and solutions in *specified* cases of inquiry. Your usage has often been more extensive—to cover the whole damn business—James's neutral, etc. I do not think there is a conflict here; the latter usage may be a generalization of that I adopted, thereby taking the word out of the temporal loci, to which I confined it. Etymologically, the "given" [is] what's there, so [to] speak, but not just *out* there in the sense of away. I think we need further discussion on this word—unless there is no conflict and it would suffice to point out the wider and narrower application[s]. (I imagine that, maybe, "experience," as I used it in my later writings, had about the same application as your "datum.")

"Thing." Idiomatic usage seen most clearly in *something, anything, nothing.* Philosophical usage often distorts this by using "thing" technically as equivalent to "entity." I wrote before about "thing" as equivalent for "concern," "affair," "matter," "subjectmatter." Desirability of some noncommittal word for *what* or *that which* is under specification, leaving both its range (spatial-temporal extent) and properties open in inquiry. Often a virtual synonym for "what" (what's the matter? What are you talking about?).

[Dewey]

Paoli, Indiana, October 5, 1944

Dear Dewey:

I have spent quite a bit of time on Kaufmann's book [*Methodology of the Social Sciences*]. Probably it was worth it. How so keen a *Kopf* can do such a bad job, I do not know. He can't accept your theory of meaning, does not state what it is he cannot accept, and definitely has no theory of his own. He just assumes concepts-propositions-meanings behind the scenes. A lot of evasive or false statements. How he can think that by announcing a Principle of Permanent Control (i.e., control by a mind), he can improve your *Logic;* or [do so] by abandoning your wide cosmic "situation" and [by] examining what he calls [a] "scientific situation," meaning thereby a mess of propositions, I do not know. . . .

Regards, *Bentley*

315

[New York,] October 12, 1944

[To Bentley:]

Got a carbon . . . on Nagel's letter to you. Have written him that the reason for my not commenting is the same as reason for my signature not appearing [on the essay "On a Certain Vagueness in Logic"]— my lack of acquaintance with Carnap's text—but that I knew from prolonged correspondence how hard you had worked to get Carnap straight. I also said he was mistaken in taking your "bouquets" satirically and as slurs, and that if there were brickbats, personal epithets, they should [be struck] . . . out.

J. D.

Paoli, Indiana, October 12, 1944

Dear Dewey:

. . . I have a scheme for high-lighting our proposals—from keeping readers away from easy slipping into reading the opposite of what we say. It is to use certain carefully selected books for a background—*not* by muddying the text, but by footnote references to the *opposite* of what we are doing—and this not haphazardly, but systematically, although in merely curt indicative sentences. . . .

There is a fine contrast to our "Fact" in the Einstein [Herbert] Spencer lecture [*On the Method of Theoretical Physics*]. (Papers by [Niels] Bohr and Einstein: *Physical Review* . . . [1935–36] valuable alongside.) Einstein says the "basics" are fictitious. All he means is that they prove not to be "real." But his supposititious "real" is to us "fictitious." This sets free the "basic" as merely stage in Fact where Fact is Knowledge-fact. A thing like this ought to turn the spot-light on. . . .

The main work, however, [that] I have in mind is Coleman R. Griffith, *Principles of Systematic Psychology*. . . . Griffith writes that there are two great ways of getting down to business. One in the form of "I see an object" and the other in the form of "There are objects." But in this he is totally blind to your "experience." He quotes you from *Logic*, p. 521, on his p. 37 on behalf of independently existing objects (where you were just denying the idealistic, and making the common-sense assertion that things can be handled apart from handler-men). But no quote at all on your over-and-over asserted view. He quotes James on irrelevant items. He refers to my "Situational" ["Situational vs. Psychological Theories of Behavior"] paper in two places, but not the point of it. In short, he does not go beyond his two schemata to introduce a third in the form of "neutral experience" or "sight-seen." . . .

Also he is hell-bent on being "functional" up to the neck, but he is really strong for "gnomic mind," which is the old mind-hunks in a new hitch-up. Thus he has "individual items of information in the gnomic mind of man." . . .

The man, nevertheless, is good. He comes *almost* up to our technique-distinction of physical, physiological, and behavioral, and then lapses back as he does with "gnomic" mind. Similarly with "behavior," the word; he almost gets a statement, then slips back. . . .

Regards, *Bentley*

New York, October 17, 1944

Dear Bentley:

. . . I tried also to set him [Nagel] straight about supposed "slurs," but you made the more important point. . . . Considering the readiness of readers to misunderstand, I think I was rather dumb not to have suggested sharpening your point by having the reference [in "A Search for Firm Names"] read something like "in view of the competence of the writers who are discussed, the confusions and inconsistencies which are found can be attributed only to something defective in the underlying assumptions which influence their approach." But it is impossible to foresee and guard against all lines of misunderstanding, especially when the text seems to oneself to be clear beyond their possibility. . . .

It has occurred to me that the words "function-functional" in their non-mathematical sense don't appear in the list of names dealt with, as far as I remember. Maybe there is no call for it, but in looking over my *Logic* for something the other day, I noted the frequent appearance of these words. I don't mean that is a reason for including them, but I concluded, in the light of what I've got since from you, that what I was getting at is closely connected with the "transactional" in its space-time extension; that is, I was using the words to indicate the need of taking events (facts) in connection with context of antecedents and consequences, or in a space-time continuum, and as protest against short-span, narrow-spread treatments. Perhaps, under "transaction" a reference could be made to it, including what is meant by a "functional treatment" (sample of my use, pp. 268–70). If I ever rewrite a short version of my *Logic*, "functional" will largely disappear by replacement . . . with "transactional," as more basic; the same thing is true of such words as "operational," "instrumental," "purpose," and even "inference." I think it is sheer misunderstanding to give the latter words a "mentalistic" interpretation, but I would or will restate the status of inference so as to leave a minimum of room for misconception, making it clear that inference is simply the completion of an observation which has been narrowed in its space-time scope. Maybe I can best bring in some of these points in the article you suggested to come from me in the present series. . . .

Yours, regards, *Dewey*

New York, October 20, 1944

Dear Bentley:

. . . I don't see why it is necessary to call attention in print to the fact you may have made an error. And I think it would be a good thing to insert in the manuscript ["On a Certain Vagueness in Logic"] what you suggest so definitely in your comments on Nagel—that if some of your points seem finical, it is because the text is so slippery that it is extremely difficult after prolonged, careful study to make sure of what is said, so that things which might not be important in casual writings become important when the writings in question purport to [analyse them]. . . .

You can emphasize in [the] text that it is not error, but vagueness with which you are concerned, . . . the wrong method of approach is bound to produce vagueness, no matter how ingenious the writer who employs it. . . .

Yours, *Dewey*

Paoli, Indiana, October 27, 1944

Dear Dewey:

I have just read your recent paper on "[Some] Questions About Value." That is the kind of a thing, of course, which gives me a lot of pleasure— linguistic dissection of importance. But there is one sentence in it which holds me up—an incidental sentence . . . the third sentence in Sec. III . . . "communications are, *ipso facto*, not *propositions*." [*] I think I could add a word or two to any communication that would make a proposition of it, and maybe I would argue (at some time or place) that, life being a going process, these added words were always implied. But I am not interested in that. What I would like to know—just as a guide as we go on—[is] what particular discriminant you had in mind in writing the sentence—what the correctly accepted distinction would be in the background you were working in at the moment you wrote the sentence—just what, in other words, you take for granted in that particular sentence. . . .

Here is one phase of my procedure in knowledge which may need watching by you, as we proceed. It is a matter of stage-development on the agency or personality side. The thing I "abstract from."

By hypothesis for me: No behaviors, no matter how far down the scale, [are] without cognitive aspect. No cognitive behavior, no matter how far up the scale, escapes from behavior.

___

[*] The quotation is: "Is there anything unique or distinctive about valuation-propositions *as propositions*? (If they merely enunciate to others facts already in existence, this question does not arise, since such communications are, *ipso facto*, not propositions.)" (Eds.)

318

Hence: No cognitive presentation by me, no matter what expression I temporarily give it, pretends to escape behavior. It is always aspectual. O.K. so far.

A different question is whether there may not be, perhaps, very important cognitive aspects, which I do *not* allow for in my layout, and which should be provided for.

Most of these I reduce (correctly or incorrectly) as they appear. The latest one I may mention, as a region in which I perhaps need the watchful eye upon me. It is Heck [Hector] Chevigny's dog from the Seeing Eye.

Chevigny is the man who went blind while I was in New York last winter. "My Eyes Have a Cold Nose" in *Reader's Digest,* October, [1944] tells about his dog. Such details as the dog's tendency to lead him into barrooms are easy. But the transition point in training, when the dog's routine performance for a more or less casual master suddenly transforms into active responsibility and partition of labor by the dog, is another matter. Without this transformation clear and plain, he says, dog and man may not go forth.

I am not bothering about dog-and-man as one organic system. There is no more reason why they should not be such a system than why heart and hand in one organism should not be one. The point is strictly the transition from routine to comprehension, whether in dog, or in man, or in dog-and-man. Possibly I have already answered myself. This is just an instance of widened awareness, akin to all awarenesses despite its spectacular appearance. . . .

Bentley

Paoli, Indiana, October 30, 1944

Dear Dewey:

. . . You have a tendency to get your statement in the form of a classification of "fact," or "given materials." I have a tendency to get the statement entirely in form of technology, organization as of a given date in our history, or in the pending inquiry of our times. Here, I think this is the *safer,* and probably broader, manner of statement. No clash at all. . . .

"Interaction-Transaction": One fine way of opening this up will be through the word "field." We have hedged around on this word, but the double use of "field" (as in the conflicting cites [that] the Griffith book puts side by side without recognition of the split) is exactly what *we,* by further analysis than anyone else appears to have made, are destroying. . . .

"System": You suggest, 9-13-44 memo, "Names," . . . that we should explain use of this word, also [of] "Organization."

319

How would it do to use "System" most generally, in the way you have suggested "Thing" should be used most generally? We need verbal oars to row the boat before we get the engine and propeller hitched in. Maybe an early introductory statement on several help-words, including "Thing" and "System," would be in order.

"Term": Yours, 9-13-44. You discuss it as specifying conditions (like Peirce's definition that is prescription), as accomplishing the function of specification, as explicit noting that names do specify.

Can we, perhaps, say that any *name* (where one *names* not merely the dog and dogs, but the color, bark, or kind) is a *term* when in formal propositional (or assertive-statement) use? How on your own phrasing . . . are we to distinguish between "name" and "term"?

"Proposition": Yours, 9-13-44. You make it [a] sentence in knowledge-specialized action, with "term" its instrumentality. You do thus in the broader case [of] "proposition" what I was led to suggest for "term." But I think we can omit words like "instrumentality" and get [a] whole statement for "name," "term," "sentence," "proposition," direct. . . .

"Interaction," etc., again: Yours, 9-14-44. I can see [a] very sound reason for expanding from my old scheme by splitting "action-reaction" apart from "interaction," getting at least a four-stage scheme instead of three. Thus, maybe, the self-action is [for] little gods, while Newton cleared all the little gods out and concentrated them up above. Would his theology [be where] he drained off the putrid stuff formerly in the physics? . . . In fact, you go on to develop [the idea] that the self-action was converted into mechanical action for each particle, which is equivalent to saying the free magic was drained off of the particles. . . .

"Relation": A minor point of disagreement, but only practical. You speak of [the] difficulty of avoiding the word, and hope it does no harm. I think it does harm always and everywhere, because of meaning too many things to too many men.

"Object": Your 9-20-44 cites your definition from *Logic*, . . . [p. 119], and yours [of] 9-21-44 refers to illustrations, . . . [p. 119], and says you hope the definition is not out of line with my use. I laughed when I read [the] preceding, because I will take oath [that] my position follows your total position in the chapters on situation growing into judgment, culminating in this definition. . . .

"Datum": 9-20-44 you mention your particular use, and think mine [is] broader. I cannot recall ever using the word on my own account in a significant way, though probably [I] have. However, I think you take my probable attitude from [the] title "Jamesian Datum." What I had steadily in mind there (of course the word "datum" was just one of the Jamesian wordings) was the specific case—that the raw fact—each raw fact, . . . was neutral. I thus probably implied a usage corresponding not to your "Experience" broadly used, but to *an* experience. I

320

am free for any application of the word that recommends itself as we go along. I have no involvement of any kind in the general philosophy of science search for things like that.

"Context": should go on list of official trouble-makers like "Phenomenon." The boys use it so [that] they do not have to distinguish with grief and care between verbal and manipulative environments. . . .

Regards, Bentley

New York, October 30, 1944

Dear Bentley:

Re my value sketch ["Some Questions About Value"], I think my sentence is so elliptical as to be blind—this is my impression on re-reading. But I didn't say that "communications are, *ipso facto*, not propositions," but . . . "Such propositions [communications] . . ."—the sense of "such" being fixed by the preceding hypothetical clause. On p. 452 the question is asked "Does a valuation-proposition merely communicate the fact that a thing or person has in fact been held dear. . . . If so, what is the function of deliberation?" * Now the sentence on p. 453 [see Bentley letter of 10-27-44] refers to *that* alternative, and was meant to indicate that mere transmission of information does not *of itself* constitute a proposition in its logical sense. However, (i) on the preceding page, I had used the expression "valuation-proposition," so there seems to be a verbal contradiction, but there isn't one in fact, since in the first case "valuation-proposition" has the force of valuation-*proposition*, or that valuation is, in fact, a proposition. However, it was careless writing. The word "proposition" should have been omitted. Also (ii) . . . the passage reads, "Such communications are, *ipso facto*, not propositions." That was very careless writing, for it seems to deny that they are propositions. What I should have written [was] "are not, *ipso facto*, propositions," i.e., are not propositions in virtue of the mere fact of passing on information. They may be propositions, but, if so, it is in virtue of "the word or two added or implied." Thanks for calling my attention to the matter; I hope sometime I'll get to the point where I'll check my expressions more carefully before publishing. I can't recall just what was my intention when I wrote. But I think the background was the same as that which led me to distinguish in the *Logic* between "proposition" and "judgment." A sentence (a "communication" message) is a proposition in virtue of what I called a "judgment" ("deliberation" on previous

---

* The exact quotation is: "Does *valuation* affect or modify things previously valued in the sense of being held dear (desired, liked, enjoyed), or does a valuation-proposition merely communicate the fact that a thing or person has in fact been held dear (liked, enjoyed, esteemed)? If the latter, what is the function of deliberation?" (Eds.)

page)—that is, an inquiry terminating in statement of *connections*. Some *reason* for engaging in message-behavior is, without doubt, implicated in all sane communications and, insofar [as this is the case], a communication *is* a proposition.

Saying this reminds me of a paper I wrote (or spoke) on "Context [and Thought]" several years ago. Not that I wouldn't state it differently now, but I think there are signs I was trying to move in the direction of our present position, though still hampered by a heavy load of tradition. The word "thought" can be read [as] "inquiry," I think, without particular violence. And on re-reading now, I think the paper shows I was struggling to get a unified transactional view without explicitly making it and also [that I] was after, under the name of "context," . . . a wide space-time context, called "background" in the paper. The word "transactions" on p. 211 is, unfortunately, merely casual. "Interception" and "concurrence" are, I think, useful words. The second paragraph on p. 209 is the nearest to [my] present position. . . .

I'll write later about the cognitive behavior business. I certainly agree with [the statement] "no cognitive behavior escapes from behavior." And I think I agree with the other: "no behavior without cognitive aspect." I have written a good deal in the past about behavior "experience" as non-cognitional and cognitional as special development. But then I had knowledge of the scientific kind—at the upper end of the scale in mind—and was ignoring the aspectual business. But I'll think things over before I write.

Yours, *Dewey*

Paoli, Indiana, October 31, 1944

Dear Dewey:

. . . . Your suggestion from Peirce about the set of behavioral operations . . . etc. You introduce this (yours, 7-18-44) in connection with "symbol." It never got through my noodle till this moment that this is almost precisely (probably) what I am after in trying to get in developing use of "symbolic system as a whole" when applied to existential-phase of Fact. In other words . . . I make "reference" (as I have been doing since "image" studies developed) run, not from a symbol to a fix-fact-Object, but from full symbol system to full subject-matter-in-inquiry. . . .

Regards, *Bentley*

Paoli, Indiana, November 3, 1944

Dear Dewey:

. . . Why have we not noted in our text in connection with the word "Experience" how positively "Fact" in our use replaces it? This protects the substance formally, while justifying the terminological change, and cautioning against misuse on the "Fact" side. May need stress. My statement is partially wrong. You use "Experience" much more broadly (down to sub-namings) than we used "Fact," held to the naming-named region. . . .

"Term-define." In one of your early letters you couple these two. This tendency always arises, yet lately we are throwing "Define" to the symbol-relation side, and "Term" to the firm name side. The arguments balance so closely on both sides. We may not be done with this yet. I probably go further than you in insisting that there be no miscegenation or inter-marriage between the functionally designational and the functionally symbolic; and that the basic evil of logics is struggling to force a fusion, and make symbols scheme deliver ultimate or proximo-ultimate namings. Hence, where "Term"? and where "Define"? is deep trouble to me.

"Existent." It struck me we might use "Existent" in place of either "Existence" or "Event" in proper place in our scheme. Some way "Existent" seemed to *flow* gently out. And I wondered whether modifications of common names might not be the solution, instead of either taking common names over, or making new ones. But the *Century Dictionary*, my heaviest arsenal—if I began life over, I would do so after your style with Murray [*Oxford English Dictionary*]—seems to present the "Existent" as that part of the Absolute which sticks through into the phenomenal, "but is wholly removed from them and not cognizable by us." * This was [G. H.] Lewes' description of the "Unknowable" philosophizers. . . .

[Bentley]

New York, November 4, 1944

Dear Bentley:

I am again impressed with your thorough, careful way of working when I get your sheets with references to my letters to you. I also need to say once more, don't take them too seriously. I often write things on the spur of the moment, trusting to you to make what you can or wish to out of them. Here, however, is one more.

"Expression." This, I believe, is the most inclusive, and hence the vaguest, of all language words. I'd almost written "expressions." I use the awkward "expression" language-forms because I think it is more inclusive than words or speech—including sometimes, coughs, winks, gestures, etc. It covers equally, I think, exclamations of assent, dissent, admiration, disgust, whether smiles, frowns, poutings, etc. (Darwin's

---

* The exact quotation is: "but is something wholly removed from them, and in no way cognizable by us." (Eds.)

Expression of [the] Emotions [in Man and Animals]), . . . serious treatises and "mathematical expressions." In other words, it needs firm specifications of qualifying traits and connections to be used intelligibly. "Names," "Terms," "Symbols," "Sentences," "Propositions" and the "expressions" dear to the Semanticist come within its range. I consulted the *Oxford Dictionary*. I wasn't surprised to find, under the word "Express," that the latter's earliest English use was in connection with statues and paintings, to portray, depict; then to be an *image*, likeness of; then to *represent* "in Mathematics to represent by a figure, symbol, or formula"; also chemical formulae. (I think this use of image and representation in nonmentalistic sense is suggestive.) Also "to token, chiefly in connection with feelings and personal qualities," * then "to represent in words, to put into language, set forth a meaning; give utterance to an intention." † And the first definition of the noun "Expression," after the literal "squeezing out," is Representation, Manifestation. (I wrote something on another sheet about the inclusive and indeterminate use of "Expression" when unqualified before I looked at the dictionary—and the above covers works of art, emotional manifestations and explicit statements.) From this point "Expression" seems to be a word worthy of attention from which to go [on] to specify "words," "names," "terms," "sentences," "propositions," etc. Also, in effect, ["Expression"] links up with "Signal-Sign-Symbol" series. . . .

"System," "Organization." What you say [is] O.K., I believe. "Terms." I've said something before about use of [the] word in "terms of a contract bargain, treaty," setting conditions. I think this can be generalized. Terms are those of a *transaction* as transaction. When a transaction is "expressed," stated, when its conditions are named, we get *terms, not* otherwise.

I fancy that possibly the broad use of "expression" links up with what you wrote about the extent of the cognitive. Animal behavior is "representative" (i.e., cognitive) to other animals when it evokes responsive behavior. It then "says something" *de facto*. And in some rough way this seems to link up with the traits that differentiate physiological (biological) from physical. Says something also about "social."

I left Richards-Ogden, as well as Signs and Peirce, hung up in the air. I got switched off to some extent by a lot of articles about the impossibility of a "natural science" of social subjectmatter because values and valuations are so bound up with the latter. Some of these articles would justify an article on "A Certain (or Highly Uncertain) Vagueness in

* The exact quotation begins: "To token, now almost exclusively with reference to feelings or personal qualities . . ." (Eds.)

† The exact quotation is: "To represent in language; to put into words, set forth (a meaning, thought, state of things); to give utterance to (an intention, a feeling)." (Eds.)

Writers on Social Science." Some articles by [Frank H.] Knight ["The Rights of Man and Natural Law"] and [Hans J.] Morgenthau ["The Limitations of Science and the Problem of Social Planning"] (both of the University of Chicago) in *Ethics* beat for contradictions and confusions what you found in Carnap, *et al.* And as to "*Fact*," [add] [Wolfgang] Köhler's outgivings on the Relation of Value to fact—and the assumption that "natural" and "physical" are synonyms. . . . [Cf. his book, *The Place of Value in a World of Facts.*]

Yours, *Dewey*

[New York,] November 4, 1944

[To Bentley:]

In my zeal about "representation" as expression, I narrowed the cognitive animal in a way I wouldn't stand by. Of course, the ability in selecting food materials is cognitive, though this behavior isn't (I think) as much in the line of cognitive evolution as is behavior toward other animals.

J. D.

Paoli, Indiana, November 4, 1944

Dear Dewey:

. . . This is not the issue to me, i.e., the way you make it [cf. Dewey's letter, 10-30-44]. I don't care whether the *ipso facto* comes before or after the "not." I want to know for our purposes [how] the communications and propositions are to differentiate. I know a lot [now] of namings, *Ausdruck, Aussage*—I forget the main ones—none definite to me.

What we are getting to is proposition not as a different *thing* from a sentence, not as a positive entity opposed to a naming convention (Carnap), but as a behaviorally differentiated function. Or rather, that is what *you* have got to in the *Logic*, and what I am trying to fixate terminologically. What I have got is a differentiation of symbol function from name function in a sharper way than others have it, probably. But I do not have the differentiation of communication from propounding in any good form. When boss Deer goes on the alert with tail, nose, ears, and eyes, the other deer in the herd being trained to continuing receptivity, he not only communicates (in deer-sign), but he also makes the proposition "danger there." I would be inclined to think that the differentiation of communicating from propounding was a highly stilted device of inquiry at a highly aloof stage of technical naming and observation.

You assimilate this problem with the "Judgment-Proposition" development, but at this glimpse it does not seem to me to work out as you say. Not communication-judgment-proposition; but pre-proposition, stir-up, post-proposition; like the pre-fact (raw) and the post-fact (settled, firm).

If we could get something like "Factant" for the entering stage and "Factate" for the provisionally settled outcome-stage, it would help. We would have "Observant" and "Observation," and "Proponent" and "Propounded" (I don't mean these words, but such stages) to correspond. The dictionary shows a great variety of words beginning with *fac-* or *fact-*, and then organized to "hard fact"—many quite the reverse—so, "factitious," "factional." Maybe, there is something in this.

If your "Context [and Thought]" paper is the University of California address . . . I will welcome it greatly. It contains the strongest statement you ever made that word and meaning are one linguistically—I made it key-slogan the moment I found it.

Regards, *Bentley*

[P.S.] "Function" here means organic transaction first (instead of snipped-off item) and so leads to Organism-Environment transactional construction.

Paoli, Indiana, November 5, 1944

Dear Dewey:

Here is something good. It pays for boiling slow and waiting. What we are doing is to pick names out of current vocabulary, and try to firm them in their best applications. (If we used non-coinage, it would carry just such specifications as we gave it and would be creaky and useless.) It occurred to me that the way to handle this might be to take a word (say "Fact"), indicate its range of applications, divide the range, and set up "Fact" for a part and other words for other parts. We are indeed doing just this—but I mean we can go beyond it and describe it formally as guide to procedure. But that ain't nothing yet.

What we can do, formally and descriptively, is to take a *group* of words, any "Real," "Exist," "Fact"; point out that these overlap in a range—that the range is not well organized by the very fact that the distinctions wobble—say that we will reorganize this whole range at once—and then assign the old words to sharpened functions in the range. Thus "Fact" to knowings-knowns durationally-extensionally in back and forward sweeps; "Exist" ("Event") to the sound determinations of our age within fact, as *seen* apart from Name-Knowing; "Designation" to the name-knowing as aspect apart from Event, or as a special event over against the others; and "Real" (or maybe "Pseudo-Real," or "Extra-isolate") to the out-of-bounds on both sides, real thing and real mind. This is, of course, what we have been doing in detail. Point now is we can escape confusions by setting up badly organized field of several word-applications and reorganizing it.

We have not bothered with "Substance," I suppose, because it is tossed out anyway. We want to throw "Real" after it. Have we a good way of indicating under a single word both the Real Mind and the Real Object?

I think we had better organize "Terminology" to (or away from) "Term," if we use the former in the heading. Also perhaps set up as a word group: "Term," "Terminology," "Name," and "Concept" (with the latter [a] hermaphrodite between "entity" and "language"). (I recall I developed [this] in terms of "Word-Clusters" somewhere [*Linguistic Analysis of Mathematics*], but I forget how; this may be reminiscent or justification, or altogether different—I don't know). . . .

Our sustained analysis that the word "Fact" implies both ends (being and naming) holds; it yields the top transactional status to the jointly-named. But it does not prove that "Fact" is the best word for it. You yourself persistently want "Fact" for the warranted. Probably it ought to stand, therefore, for the warranted under the recognition that warranting is involved. At the moment this seems overwhelming to me.

But what have we left for the main-guy word? "Cosmos" . . . is all I can think of. "Reality" is what we don't want. "Nature" might do, despite all the emotionalizings and distortions. "Existence" might serve. And here "Existence" could not escape beyond bounds, because in direct inspection it would be held to the "Factual," and would itself branch into both "Fact" and "Naming," or rather into "named fact" and "fact-naming." Maybe, even "The Existent."

If this were done, we could start with heavily stressed existence as always known-existence, and not the beyond-knowledge-real . . .

"Phenomenon": Could that good old horse go back to work under heavy specification that it applied to durational-extensionals *only?* It seems to have three type uses: mere appearance, apparent fact, striking fact. We might hold it the middle way, i.e., the ordinary, scientific use. I mean [to] put it in and hold it there without increasing confusion (I have evaded it for many years).

Regards, Bentley

New York, November 5, 1944

Dear Bentley:

One more word. I was slow in getting at the full import of your name-functional (proposition) and symbol function, and I'll probably slip, but I know you are right. And [you are] right about carrying communication clear down, and differentiating "statement" expounding [?], propounding, from it—as communication; there is no difference between

Eskimos rubbing noses (if they do), shaking hands, a kiss, and the performance of animals in respect to one another clear down the line. (You have something in your "Factant," "Factate.") *Oxford Dictionary* —suffix ("fic"—e.g., pacific–*ficus*), making, doing, forming adjectives from substantives, with sense of making, causing, producing (weakened root of *facere* to make, do); and suffix "fy" pacify, specify, liquefy, beautify—same original source. "Fying," "fic," seem to line up with "factant"; . . . "facient," however, seems to be good English. . . . See factor. Factitious is one kind of "fact." Fiction comes from *fingere* to fashion, form. . . .

[Dewey]

New York, November 6, 1944

Dear Bentley:

Some of your questions I'll have to think over. But as my recent letter shows, I am now wholly for "term" as a firm-sign name. I don't know what I had in mind earlier. "Symbol" covers the ground for symbols. . . . I don't see how you can "define" point, 1, 2, etc., in the traditional sense of "definition." However, I haven't tried this out, and anyway it doesn't affect "term." When we say "terms of discourse," I think we mean limiting conditions of discourse as transactions.

Yours, *John Dewey*

[P.S.] . . . I thought [Morton G.] White [*The Origin of Dewey's Instrumentalism*] was good, but not tackling the "fundament."

Paoli, Indiana, November 6, 1944

Dear Dewey:

. . . "Meaning"—"Sign"—"Behavior." In our set-up these three words cover practically the same range; here "practically" is a wobble-word. Either they do, or they don't. "Knowledge" goes with them, but we have (if I recall) pretty good agreement to hold "Knowings" to the *naming* ranges of sign—the great middle human specifi*cation* stages.

The three words are, of course, not the same. They are different "technologies," "instrumentalities" (*see* [comments on these words by] you and Ayres.) "Techniques" is what I have been saying for quite a while. "Aspects" of behavioral transaction is not the right word. "Phases" is much worse. "Characterizations" might do along my scheme (if we hold to the naming) of Characterization, Specification, Symbolization. "Behavior" is specifying the type of transaction and can be done either as "Trans" or as the organic end of "Inter." "Sign" is the discrimination from physiological inquiry. "Meaning" is (or should be) a transactional specification of what old terminologies called "relation." Your older

328

construction certainly made "meaning" transaction[al], but your phrasings never became sharp enough to hold your audience to that stress, and they treat it (like Kaufmann) as a psychic variation.

Queries: 1. Would you want to limit active use of word "meaning" to an interior range, as we probably will "Knowing"? Or would you speak of "meaning" wherever there is "sign"? 2. Does some technical word suggest itself to name the *kind of discriminating* we do when we let "meaning," "Sign," "behaving," and, broadly, even "knowing," be coincident in range (i.e., all behavioral as contrasted with physiological, and not . . . [as] a compartment of behavior, but each a specialized stress in knowledge about it)?

"Operational," as a broad term to cover both perceptive-manipulative and linguistic operations. You have had that up. We may need decision and use. Can we say: "Operational" shall *always* cover organic-environmental doings? That would make "operational" another word in addition to the four above that had the full behavioral range. It would make it a pretty legitimate name for the organism end of each transaction (or, at a glance, it looks for a minute as though it would) when interactionally studied, and here would fall into the two types: namely, the signaling (perceptive-manipulative) and the linguistical (which latter again subdivides into naming and symboling, as progress goes on). . . .

"Term." (*re* my 9-2-43) Here is the $64 question. Are we going to use "term" for symbol-consistency; or for the sharpest and best specification of "name" at a given time? You know *My* clamor is going to be steadily that the two *must* be held apart by distinctive namings, and that the slipping back and forth from one to the other (or rather the continued effort to consolidate the two, and the belief that such consolidation is the goal of logic) is the great *Evil* of *Logic* today. Without checking up, is not your generic and universal a form of this point? Do you go through to a finish with it? Would it furnish us any terminological suggestions? I believe this is the most discussed feature of your *Logic*. . . .

"Term"–"Proposition." . . . I see (in) 9-3-43 I suggest "Word-Sentence" (which is O.K.), then "Name-Assertion," and "Term-Proposition." But the way it looks now, almost certainly, "Name"-"Proposition" belong together, and since "Term"-"Proposition" belong together, we would get "Term" as the sharpened propositional use of "Name." Also "Assertion" would probably be the looser use of "Name" prior to sharp propositional form.

Now move to "Relation"-"Symbol"-"System" consistency. Here "Symbol" enters, following "Signal" and "Name" as the higher functioning form of "Sign," the most general descriptive term. We do not really need "Term" here if we have "Symbol" in this sense, since the two would be alike, as "Symbol" is not something to sharpen, but the sharpening itself. What then would correspond here to "Proposition"? In the Syntactic development [of the logical positivists] they use "formula," and "formal," or perhaps "theorems"—in Carnap, his Calculus (syntactic) presents definitions and theorems, as compared with the semantic which has definitions and propositions. (I note, for the first time, that here he uses "definitions" officially in both fields, but "propositions" in semantic and "theorems" in calculus.) But *we* are dealing with living behavior. We do not want "formula" or "theorem." I vote at the moment for "Relation," the word on your p. 55 [*Logic*] I shouted for. We might then have [for] Technical Knowledge: "Word-Sentence"; "Assertion" at the characterization level; "Term-Proposition" at the specification level; "Symbol-Relation" [on the "pure" mathematical level]. There are other words to bring into line. I recall experimenting with "Accuracy" for propositional-assertive naming and "Precision" for the symbol level. "Consistency" belongs in Symbol. . . .

I am not strong for the above naming. "Word," "Sentence," "Proposition" and "Symbol" seem soundly placed—the rest questionable, but, nevertheless, tentative offerings we *must* have in a very few months.

"Domain and Field." Do you feel the need, at this stage, of a Domain for relations as against a field for Connections *or* for Reference? We left that in some confusion. My impression is that *re* the presentation of a Logic, you needed some such namings, both, however, lying in a "universe of discourse." I, however, have not that immediate urge. So far as Field is concerned, it enters for me as a current name in the general region of Inter-action–Transaction, to be further examined.

Regards, *Bentley*

[New York,] November 7, 1944

[To Bentley:]

Organization: Is it worth while to deal with (i) brute (literally) Knowledge; (ii) ordinary (common-sense) Knowledge; and (iii) scientific [Knowledge] on the basis of differential modes of organization? I don't see anything the matter with the position taken in my *Logic*, that scientific knowledge is organized on the basis of the knowledge continuum, that is, direction given to extending what is already known by means of incorporating further knowledge. I am now inclined to think that the point can be formulated on the basis of space-time connections. An intermediate knowledge in my *Logic* was said to be organized with reference to use-enjoyment. I think that can also be covered in terms of less extensive, more direct or immediate, space-time connections—I use "space-time" as a short name for the whole set of connections with which

330

science deals. That would leave us to find some formula to cover brute knowledge.

It may be that I am falling into my old mistake of trying to tell things instead of sticking to the name business, but we have to give some indication of what it is the names name. Anyway, the above paragraph is in response to your point (11-3-44 letter) about distinction of "raw or brute" and "developed knowledge." What I have called the "intermediate" is largely an affair of knowing how to do or make in reference to what I summed up under "use-enjoyment"; the space-time connections bound up with transactions in living at a *given* period in *given* surroundings. Scientific knowledge is knowledge organized as an affair of how-to-do-and-make-knowledge. (The traditional notion that if it is science (True), then it is eternal, is, I believe, a sort of confused product of the distinction of scientific knowledge from that knowledge which is rather definitely [in] connection with local areas and durations.) . . .

Incidentally, I believe that my use of "Experience" was to attempt [to set up] a name that covers the whole range of transactions within which the needed distinctions have to be made, from the brute through the scientific. And I am inclined to believe that in mentioning how "Fact," as now used, replaced "Experience," the word "Experience," when freed from mentalistic and states of consciousness standpoint, has just this force. It carries back, when so used, to the original sense of "Experience" and "empirical" which limited the word to recurring space-time connections, so narrow in scope that they were not "understood." . . .

"Existent": definitely an improvement on "Existence." Suggests connections, and the "ence" ending [in "Existence"] is isolative in effect. What was said in the earlier portion is meant to apply to the more general point you raise about my stuff in your . . . [letter of 11-3-44]. My general tendency was to call material *for* worked-up knowledge "*non*-cognitive"—"experience," materials in processes and operations of Living (transactions), in which knowledge was not itself the primary aim, but was incidental to other transactions (eating, fighting, making houses, etc.) and, on the other side, scientific knowledge tending to terminate in *Post-fact. This* intermediate position of scientific knowledge was what I tried to indicate by the name "instrumental"—*out* of something and into something else.

But the broad use of "Fact" is better, if for no other reason than it drops out a lot of traditional confusing issues.

Not but what some persons will be confused by this broad usage.

J. D.

Dear Dewey:

"Term": I said yesterday that your comment (11-4-44 . . .) was "too general to help." "Term" bothers me each morning when I try to go to work. . . . I should have said your comment was not "too general," but "condensed-elliptic." I believe, however, you have settled the matter for me. But if you have, if I am right as to how to read your comments, then it is up to you to tell me specifically whether I am right or not, and second, by Doggy, to stick firm in future phrasing. To work thus (if correct):

Terms are of a transaction. The transaction is one in which the differentiation is one between "linguistic sign" and "event," i.e., this particular transaction is across knowing-known. (Incidentally, why is not "word," simply as it comes, better than "expression" as substitute?) If you say "terms are of a transaction," and the transaction under consideration was one of Connection (your *Logic*)—i.e., event regarded as detached from naming—then the "terms" would be "events." But here there would be no reason to speak of them as "terms."

The terms that we are seeking are:

1. on the expression side,

2. (in your phrase) "of" a transaction where,

3. the transaction in question must be an expression-event-transaction, and,

4. under our procedure this particular expression *must* be "Designation" or "Naming"; therefore,

5. "Term" stands as a variety of "Name."

6. It may never by us (in this build-up) be applied to Symbol-procedure.

7. It will be the "accuratest-available" form of Naming (Name).

8. "Term" . . . will name a kind of "Name," and not "name" an "event," leaving the word "Name" to designate the event-naming (this is not coherently said as yet).

9. "Term" will remain hitched up with "Proposition," and, beginning to extend the problem further:

10. If we distinguish between "Proposition" and "Judgment" (both expressive—and no difference of "kind," but only one of stage or "phase," as in your recent interpretation to me by letter), then,

11. (I was going to ask) Will we use the common word "Term" both in "Proposition" and in "Judgment"? But,

12. The answer seems clearly to be: We will.

This layout would seem to settle my bother the last day or two over stages of propositions. Question: Do you want to make good, strong, heavy statement that "Proposition" and "Judgment" must not be contrasted in type? But rather as phase? (Here "phase" becomes a sound word, because settled judgment is settled only in *phase*, not in independence, and is ready to start in on the wheel of knowledge as "indeterminate situation" all over again.)

Considering that temporarily O.K., we now must determine the terminology in the region of symbol (mathematical, primary, and future approximations thereto).

Let us take "Symbol" as a sign-behavior that has differentiated itself as richly from "Name," . . . [as] "Name" [has] differentiated itself from "Signal." "Symbol" is, not symbolically, but genetically, *not* "Name" (i.e., by naming, it is not itself a Name). "Proposition" ceases to apply in this region, if we are to be accurate in our namings. I should be a little inclined for a try-out to set up Carnap's word "Theorem" as replacement here of "Proposition" (I do not know whether this use is explicit with Carnap, or whether it is only happen-so).

Question to you: Out of your logical range can you suggest some two names better than "Symbol" and "Theorem"? If there were a better than "Symbol," we should have stubbed our toes on it before this. But how about "Theorem"? "Equation" is too limited. "Equivalence" is used. . . .

We are torn between [a] desire to use "Fact" for the settled knowledge of event, as you frequently do, and note that you do, and want to do; and to make it the leading guide to the whole scheme. Put up into position with "Event" and "Naming" subsidiary, it has served us well as a guiding light for six or eight months. But that is no reason why we should not change if we [can] get a better showing. I suspect most people, regardless of the issues of knowing and known, simply think of "Fact" as "what is so." Then, if we can hold "Fact" to "what is *so* in knowledge" and get a proper naming and description of naming in the top place, perhaps a change is indicated. . . .

Regards, Bentley

Paoli, Indiana, November 13, 1944

Dear Dewey:

In your letter (12-29-43) you discuss terminology for "Perceptual–Manipulation." To offset this, you set up "Reflective" tentatively, and "Observation" or "perceiving-with-naming." You stress need of namings here. Since standard methods separate perception and manipulation, and we combine them (you have stressed this for decades), we should evidently hold to the joint naming: say, "Perceptive-Manipulative." This is definitely the region of Signal when transactionally seen. The next region is that of Naming when transactionally seen. It might not be at all bad to call this "Perceptive-Reflective," and equate this name with "Observational." Studying this to see what distinction I would make between these two expressions on one side, and "Signal" and "Name" on the other,

I do not know that I would make any. I certainly do not want "Signal" and "Name" (as phases of "Sign") to be treated as organism-activity. "Sign," I take [it], must be set up transactionally as key to whole development. It is the best place to pass from isolates and *inter*-actions to *trans*-actions. We can make a strong statement that in any meanings we give either to "Perception" or to "Manipulation," there is no perception without manipulation (or, except as manipulation) and no manipulation except as perceptional.

"Here-Now": . . . Suppose we take our series "Situation," "Event," "Object" (as also in your *Logic*, transition from indeterminate to determinate). In the perceptive-linguistic procedure you (and we) get out "object." Could it be that your background here-now in a continuity would be the similar process on that level? Anyway, I hope you will have an eye on this, and see it gets in right. . . .

The grand difficulty is that in our field everyone reads *into* what is offered him to read, just that which he is prepared to read—reading his own reflection, not what is offered. Discussing Morris at Columbia three years ago, Nagel argued for two days that that was the only way one should read—try, namely, to find out what the guy was trying to say—and don't be critical about what he actually did say. . . .

I had a striking case recently from one of the young men who likes my method, and who knows that you and I both work on the factual side *always*. He more or less complained of my applying "consistency of expression" tests in recent papers, especially the logic one. Yet I have never done that on any point. My present argument is (1) that none of these logicians talk a common language or use negotiable terms; (2) that we find inconsistencies in their habitual uses of terms; (3) that in logic, at least, there should be steady effort and some progress in getting rid of such inconsistencies; (4) that we see no progress, and that when we find masses of inconsistencies, much alike in every member of a group of logicians, we have [a] fair right to infer (and this empirically) something [is] wrong in their terminological set-up. . . .

Best regards, *Bentley*

[New York,] November 18, 1944

[To Bentley:]

"Entity," "Thing": What follows is wholly exploratory on my part. Propositions as "Entities" (Carnap). What is an "Entity"? Is there any place, any need for the word? What, if anything, does it *name*? Apparently (I'm following remarks in your "Vagueness" paper), Carnap's own account consists only in distinguishing it from a "sentence" as the designatum of the latter. If, as may be the case, a "sentence" is identified with *mere* "words" and/or *mere* "language" (supposing there are or can be any such things), it is, then, that which words, or *some* arrangements of words, "stand for." Apparently, in other words, language as a sign-organization is first split into two different things (entities?): one, sounds or marks, which, as such, are certainly not words nor language, and the other, what the marks stand for; and, then, the latter are regarded as capable of independent treatment on their own account. They are no longer just what is named or designated by sounds or marks in their language capacity, but have a kind of existence or being on their own account. If we use the words "stand for" as necessarily involved in any account of words [or] language, then "stoods-for" are capable of being viewed and treated on their own account; or, if we use the word "represent" in connection with anything which is language, then there are certain "representata" which are such inherently, independently, or on their own account, and it is by the miracle of reference to them that certain sounds or marks become words or language.

So far, I don't think I have said anything you haven't already covered. But [now], as to "Entity." Does the word, as here used, stand for, designate, represent, anything that is now covered by the expression, "Language says something or other"? "Thing" in this connection is equivalent to "What"? It is Fact with a minimum of commitment or assertion; as in the expressions, "The thing we were just talking about," "There are quite a number of things to be taken into account," "There is something the matter," "Is there anything new?" that is, "Entity," if it says or names anything, is a synonym for "subject," "topic," "theme," when it [has] undergone reification, just as "thing" is sometimes reified in metaphysics into "substance" as [an] independent entity.

[*Dewey*]

[New York,] November 19, 1944

[To Bentley:]

"Propositions": "Communication," *says* something. "You said something, brother." "Communication," all down the line—e.g., your deer illustration. Noises, movements, Strictly Behavioral. All communication is *trans*.

Something of the above sort is, I am reasonably sure, our starting point and ending point—the check for reference.

Now just what does *speech*-communication *do*? What is it as differential communication behavior? (If we can answer this, we can say all [that] has to be said about propositions.) I am more and more inclined to think we can forget about "sentences" save as authoritative decisions—as by a court in delivering sentence (which influenced what I said in *Logic* about "Judgment" as distinct from "Proposition." A "sentence," as far as I can now see, is what grammarians call [and] what logicians [call] a "proposition." According to *Oxford Dictionary,* etymologically and in early usage, a "sentence" was an uttered or expressed opinion. And grammatically, as far as I can see, a "sentence" is whatever comes in print between two periods, and orally, to whatever corresponds in the way of inflection to periods in print. I don't think a "sentence" can be defined (described for purposes of identification) without including the *periods.* A period is (1) primarily a cycle—the period of the earth's, sun's revolution. Then (2) the completion or end of the course or cycle. (3) A pause. If we wanted to go into subtleties, we could say that a "proposition" is a treatise or dissertation, while a "sentence" is one of its distinctive periods, or relatively complete constituents —like the year period of the earth's revolution in its connection with the earth's ongoing movement. After all, the earth doesn't stop to celebrate, and time didn't stop the other day when I "celebrated" my 85th birthday. I think this distinction is legitimate, but I don't see that it is needed or important for our purpose. Though I do think that writers like Carnap— and quite likely the whole traditional theory of Propositions—have been affected by giving finality and independence to sentences, which after all are purely periodic or cyclic differentiations.

But, for our purpose, it suffices, I think, to point out that "Propositions" are constructions, structures of varying extents of space-time complexity. From, say, calling Fire or pressing a fire-alarm to a treatise on the physics of combustion.

To get back to the main question: What does "saying" or "stating" do in a differentiated and differential sense with respect to "communication"? Well, the answer to that in a detailed way is a treatise on logic, and we aren't writing that. In contrast with the deer case, it holds onto the communication in a way which makes it indefinitely available for future use, and this far beyond the group originally influenced behaviorally. [Comparable to] capital funds and new machinery for new technological developments. It also gets it into the open for examination, development, and test. Still strictly behaviorial, but with indefinite spatial-temporal extension. Relation of a code of law to prevailing, but unstated customary practices; [of a] statute to common laws—from compiled court records to legislative action; [of] systematic book-keeping, including planned budget, to ordinary expending and receiving money, etc.

This is about the best I can do in reply to your remarks of 11-4-44 about communication as propounding. My treatment of "Proposition" in my *Logic* was influenced by [the] idiomatic habit of calling, say, a ball pitched to a batter in a ballgame, a "Proposition"—anything submitted or placed before [someone] for responsive behavior. So you proposition "danger there" in [the] case of boss deer behavior. But it doesn't remain put before us in the latter case—and that makes an immense behavioral differentiation. After all, the ball in the ballgame, as

336

an integral (periodic) phase of [the] latter, is part of an elaborate construction of art, and in so far differs from [the] noise made by an animal
as [a] danger-signal.

In short, I agree with everything you say, save the stilted nature of
the device—I think the stilting is something done by the Carnaps, while
the evolutionary development is from grunts, etc., through words, oral
sentences, written languages to treatises.

[*Dewey*]

Paoli, Indiana, November 19, 1944

Dear Dewey:

. . . You are speaking of "knowings" as *equated* with "behavior," and
contrasting that view with the view of "knowings" as *aspectual* in "behavior." Then you speak of certain elements of behavings which in
adaptation phases are constituted as signals, names, symbols—signs.

Now I could never have intended (no matter how I phrased it) to
"equate 'knowings'" with "behavings." My point would be that here
we have two words, both of which, when fully expanded, cover the be-
havioral-adaptation range. On the other hand, with the word "behavior"
widely employed and the word "knowledge" narrowly employed, they
do *not* cover the same range. Again, I would not want to literally equate
"knowledge" and "feeling." I would only leave it open to say that no
life detaches its feeling-living from its knowing-living, nor vice versa, so
that we cannot count on finding detachable feeling-lumps or detachable
knowledge-lumps. Here I am sure our positions would not differ, especially as I am putting no stress on this at all, and have no need of
mentioning it. . . .

Now as to "feeling." The test with me would be solely one of technique of research. I think pain can be handled by physiologists in their
own technical language, and shows, by its variations and ranges, normal
physiological characteristics—this as a suspicion, not an essential or
stressed point.

As to the "behaving-knowing." So far as your phrasing makes an element of behavior (physiological or psychological) any kind of a sign,
I am opposed. Vital to my position is that if one wants to set up any
kind of a sign (signal, name, or symbol) and do it successfully, one must
do it, *not* on the designation . . . [side], and *not* on the event side, but
primarily and emphatically as transactional-fact. So that there is no
kind of *sign* before us at all, without both organism and environing [con-
ditions] entering transactionally (and not merely inter-actionally). This
as technique of inquiry.

It is in this way that I make the *range* covered by everything that is
behavior (as distinguished from physiological) the same as the *range*

337

covered by the word "signing." Which, again, is very far from saying that when one has investigated sign-process, one has investigated all of behavioral subject-matter. All one has thus far is a systematized set-up of one line of inquiry as far "up" as we know anything about from a "start" where physiological techniques default—say, anywhere beyond the tropistic-chemical, etc. . . .

Another point: "interest"-"striving." I think we have that O.K. I work on a basis of living interest and going-concerns. Need special attention from other points of view. But never reification in the way older physicists still reify "energy." . . .

Regards, *Bentley*

[New York,] November 20, 1944

[To Bentley:]

"Fact"

I judge [Otto] Neurath [in *Foundations of the Social Sciences*] uses "statement" about the way we plan to use "Fact." I have been wondering whether we might not run a list like Unknown, undiscovered (as of a given place and date) facts; dubious, questionable facts; vague-distinct facts; facts-under-inquiry; unstable-wavering . . . facts; or in-process-of-knowing; hypothetical, tentative facts; ascertained facts (as of a given date and place); indeterminate-determinate; particular, generalized, facts; fictional, fictitious facts (fictions as actual fact-events); hallucinations, delusions, paranoias, as facts; etc. Theories as facts.

This might be put in direct connection with the fact that we recognize a departure from ordinary usage which identifies "Fact" with what is *warranted* in knowledge; and our reasons for departing from that usage. (Some of Neurath's remarks are quite applicable.) Such as, what is warranted fact is always of a given date, place, under specificable conditions, and any other view runs into just the ontologizing of "fact"—putting it outside and beyond knowledge—we are getting away from. If the reification of this latter position, and the confusions which result (*Vide* your paper . . . "[On a Certain] Vagueness in Logic"), is so recognized, such an extension of "Fact" as suggested above is both legitimate and necessary. Or, if any better word can be found having similar scope and flexibility, not limiting knowledge of knowledge by setting up in advance conditions to which it must conform, O.K. with us. Meanwhile, the apparent objections—those which occur offhand—to the use of the word as we are using it, are really arguments in favor, since these objections all depend upon a metaphysical ontologizing or reifying, which is the chief obstruction to development of a theory of knowledge which treats "knowledge" as something to be known progressively (i.e., in space-time) as other things are studied and known. . . .

I haven't said anything, I believe, about the sharp differentiation of "name-symbol," to which you have referred a number of times lately. I can only say I think it is indispensable—you can handle the details better than I can. I should judge "theorem" is the proper counterpart in this layout to proposition in the other. Also "Organization" for Name-Knowledge and "System" for Symbol-Knowledge.

I've used "Meaning" so much and so loosely that I am now uncertain about it. I find in looking at my *Logic* [that] it is used, generically, for "representative capacity"—standing for, p. 46. But on p. 52, I propose to connect "sign" and "significance" with each other and "meaning" with "symbol." But here "symbol" is used much more widely than in mathematical reference—namely for such things as the word "smoke" when released for development in discourse, while "sign," "significance," are used for the evidential function of observed events. Pointing to, indicating, leading to other events as distinct from words leading to other words in development of "meanings" in discourse. I am not citing this as a model; on the contrary, it fluctuates between and mixes words and (mathematical) symbol. But a word isn't always a *"sign"* in the sense in which a signboard with a pointing hand is, or in the sense in which expansion of a metal under certain conditions is a sign—evidence of increased heat. At times I have used "denotation" for words that look to —refer to—other events, which words as *events* often do, e.g., *here, now, proper names.* Is mathematics *pure* discourse, i.e., free from any denotating reference or naming? Now I am getting into another matter I am far from clear about. Nouns, adjectives, verbs, and adverbs are names. Are prepositions, connectives, names in the same sense, or rather are they such *always*? "The house of my neighbor." Here "of" names fact of possession. So, "His house is a long way *from* here." But how about, "Propositional form B is derived (logically) *from* form A"? The double use of "if" is perhaps more obvious. I seem to be raising a useless puzzle, but there seem to be connectives that name connections of events, and other connectives that serve discourse about events. Well, I guess it is simpler than I'm making it out to be. They are all names, but some are names of *connections,* and some of *relations.* The distinction isn't in names, but in *what* is named.

From a hasty reading of Neurath, I think his exciting vitality is derived from the fact he has a strong sense, which underlies what he says, though he doesn't put it in words, that knowledge and knowing are natural, sociocultural events and have to be treated that way.

[*Dewey*]

Bloomington, Indiana, November 21, 1944

Dear Dewey:

I have read the Whitehead short lectures [*Nature and Life*] (1934).
I made a memo, as I see a good way to mention him in the "context." . . .
If my attitude veers from yours, please tell me. Of course, this comment
is not for use. It just locates the tone.

I have partially glanced over Cassirer's new *An Essay on Man*. He
uses signal along with sign for animal stuff, and symbol for namings. This
compares for our sign for the full organized process, with signal where
he has it, name present in its own right, and symbol for the post-naming,
mathematical-systematic-consistency process.

Cassirer's main stress thus far seems to be that

Man Is Higher Than the Animals.

There is a paper by a dead Russian, [L. S.] Vigotsky, in *Psychiatry*,
vol. 2, about 1938 [1939], on Thought and Language ["Thought and
Speech"] which repelled me at the start. But I made out that "thought"
for him was on-going activity other than verbal. That is hunky-dory,
and I shall examine [it] more carefully.

The phase you want developed terminologically—that of agency on the
organism-person side—and which I have not picked you up on as yet—
may get help here. (Whether the [Clark L.] Hull striving does any
good or not—Hull probably will show up mentalist in the end.)

About all Whitehead and Cassirer do is to put new clothes on the old
spooks. That is why the spook-addicts like them. . . .

Regards, *Bentley*

[P.S.] What I started this note for—and, of course, did not get in at all
—was to say your stuff about sentence and proposition and essay is full
of development.

New York, November 22, 1944

Dear Bentley:

I am certainly impressed with the thoroughness [with] which you
work. It should be a warning to my hit or miss, impressionistic methods
—save, perhaps, my more studied writings. . . . As to yours of 11-19-44,
I don't think [that] with your further statement there is any difference
between [us]. I think you used the phrase "equating knowledge and
behavior" in a letter to me, and it seemed to me to need qualification.
It was more the word "equating," though, that I objected to, than your
intention as now stated. But, when I wrote, I was more inclined to limit
"knowledge" to the middle region than I should be at the present time.
It was a holdover from the problems I was occupied with in my *Logic*,
the need imposed by those problems of pretty definitely specified limita-

tion of the word. I now realize the corresponding need of placing this special meaning in the larger total range, including the whole behavioral range. I treated the latter as [a] necessary matrix, and verbally insisted upon continuity of development; but I didn't have as worked-out a survey as I have now attained—though I fall back at times. As far as I used "signing" as an "element," instead of [as] the whole transactional event, that was all wrong, of course. The "feeling" matter I don't find it easy to lay hold of firmly—"*pain*" doesn't seem to me a feeling, any more than red, or hard. Pleasurable and emotional qualities seem to be on a different level. But, fortunately, we don't have to go into this matter in detail in the articles, and I certainly stand by your statement that feeling-living is not detachable from knowing-living. . . .

"Expression." I didn't mean, of course, to use or suggest it as equivalent to "name"; rather the opposite—to cover all kinds of behavior that are adaptively responded to—behaved to—like the attitude of our boss deer. I don't think Darwin's "Expression of Emotion" a happy phrase as far as it suggests that emotion is one thing and behavior another. His own treatment negates that idea; "emotional expressions" *in man* being shown to be reductions to partial and somewhat inchoate form of what in animals below men were complete behavioral operations. The animal isn't "expressing"; he is behaving, transactionally. The responsive behavior of other animals is what institutes the "expression" trait. In other words, it doesn't communicate because it is expression, but [it] is expressive insofar as it communicates. This, I think, is in line with what you write about "expression" as stretching into signals and symbols—perhaps I would prefer to carry the stretching somewhat further, and then make discriminations within the total stretch.

"Organization." The word perhaps suggests something too formal, and qualifications might be added to cover, in the region of namings, [from] Neurath's "clumps" ["clots"] and "*Grégats*"—[to] clusters, and loose constellations. Beyond that, in my *Logic* I make the difference between common-sense knowledge and scientific knowing a difference in the purpose (consequences) of their respective modes of organization. I don't think this is relevant now—as to the principle involved in the two cases—but it may be relevant to point out that there is no single ground of "organization" and that indefiniteness of space-time—*scope* and range—characterize non-mathematical scientific knowing.

Yours, *Dewey*

New York, November 24, 1944

Dear Bentley:

. . . I know his [Whitehead's] *Adventures of Ideas* pretty well, and in my opinion, it is far ahead of the writings of anyone of the group of contemporary philosophers to which he belongs. There is a certain amount of putting new clothes on old spooks, but also a lot more. E.g., "The brain is continuous with the body, and the body is continuous with the rest of the natural world." This [is] in connection with the statement that "experience" is a natural activity "involved in the functioning of such a high grade organism" (as the human), and the further statement: "The actualities of nature must be explanatory of this fact." And, "It is a false dichotomy to think of Nature and Man. Man is that factor in Nature which, etc." [And], "The world within experience is identical with the world beyond experience." . . . [He] attack[s] . . . the "bifur-cation of nature." He expressly denies that the "subject-object" can be identical with the "knower-known." Now I don't doubt that he leans over definitely on the side of interpreting "nature" in terms of "man," but this involves placing the *physical* aspect of nature in a more extensive be-havioristic organization. Not that he works it out consistently or without falling back on mentalistic language. But his sentence you quote, about the "energetic activity of physics," and the "emotional intensity enter-tained in life," can be understood from a unified (technically, not meta-physically unified) behavioristic organization. (I criticized Whitehead once for converting continuity of functioning into identity of *contents—* and think he is very guilty.) But in his line of movement he seems to me in a class by himself compared with Russell, Moore, Santayana, [Bene-detto] Croce, and (probably) Cassirer.

Yours, *Dewey*

New York, November 26, 1944

Dear Bentley:

. . . Neurath is in a way the father of the whole "unified science" movement. I met him some years ago, and he gave me a fairly full story. He and some other intellectual workers in Vienna used to meet informally, calling themselves the Vienna *Kreis*. They were anti-clerical and also anti-Kantian, the latter throwing them out of step with most of the philosophical anti-clericals. They were more "positivist" than anything else, though I've forgotten whether they used the name "logical posi-tivists." They were influenced chiefly by [Ernst] Mach and [Franz] Brentano, they were Austrians, i.e., not under "German" influence. Then, in Neurath's own words, "Carnap came down and Prussianized us." But this attitude was purely for informal, conversational purposes; officially, he stood up for Carnap as if, while he himself didn't care about that sort of thing, it represented an important phase of the whole movement. His new paper [*Foundations of the Social Sciences*] reads as if he thought the time were approaching for a break. He certainly is much nearer us than to the Carnap-Morris bunch.

I wrote a piece ["Unity of Science as a Social Problem"], rather slight, for the first number of the [*International*] *Encyclopedia of Unified Science*. The article isn't important, but the fact that I did it at the express wish of Neurath, and also followed rather closely suggestions which he made, may be of some importance in the light of present developments. It was definitely at his suggestion that I put in a sentence saying a unification of science movement "need not and should not lay down in advance a platform to be accepted." I think now he wanted something as an offset to the Carnap influence. "Building bridges" is also, I am pretty sure, his phrase. Something corresponding to the French *Encyclopédie* of the 18th century was definitely his model.

I'm rather sorry he uses the word "physicalist." But it is clear enough that he uses it as identical with "space-time" formulations, and not in the sense of the special techniques of "physics." In original Greek, "physics" was synonymous with "nature," and I am not sure he wouldn't consent to the "naturalistic" if it were put up to him.

I've read Neurath again more carefully. I think the strong points of his piece are (1) his insistence on taking knowledge where it is at a given time with all its inconsistencies and gaps, whatever they may be in fact (which, I think, is in line with our position both about fact and knowledge), and (2) the one transaction including speaker, speech, and what is spoken of. On the whole, I think it is rather poorly organized otherwise. But as far as it goes, it is all to the good—save its wandering features make it easy for a good many to discount what is sound in it. . . .

Yours, *Dewey*

Paoli, Indiana, December 1, 1944

Dear Dewey:

. . . Your 11-20-44 . . . as to all words being "names." "Of" in "the house of my neighbor" is a name. But, you question, how about "from" in "this proposition is derived from that proposition." Is not the answer that the name in question is "derives from." Transferring to active from passive phrasing, we get "A originates B" instead of "B is derived from A." Transfers into either active or passive forms should be made for all items compared, before comparison is made, and words (verbal components) should be determined regardless of printer's set-up or grammarians' dicta.

As to names of connections *vs.* names of relations, there is still a little slippage here. I never can get a clear inspection. I think perhaps we ought to apply interaction-transaction to it. Take an interaction between two "things." Talk about the "things" as if not in interaction at the moment, but as sitting on the side-lines capable of it. Such talk speaks of their "relation." Name the relation. *But* transposes from *a*-and-*b*-in-interaction to the *trans*action *ab*, or better to the transaction *c*, which

343

can be aspectually observed with respect to namings *a* and namings *b;* then one does not have a relation on the spot to name. And relation tends as in your *Logic* to transpose into symbol-system. I will have to wait on this, as on other matters.

Feeling: Your 11-22-44. I have same attitude to pain as you mention. A question? My provisional way is to say pain is physiological in the sense [that] it can be dealt with by physiological techniques—those New York experiments of range [Schumacher, *et al.,* "Uniformity of the Pain Threshold in Man"] I once was excited about. Neurath's "objectless-feeling," I regard merely as a hangover from his old psychism—much as I regard his "statement-base" (p. 2 of this letter) as a logico-positivist's hangover. When we get further along and get statement of agency, I think we will "get" this where we want it.

Regards, Bentley

Paoli, Indiana, December 2, 1944

Dear Dewey:

. . . Speaking of the way Carnap sets a proposition over against a sentence as its *repraesentatum* or something such, you speak of "concept" [11-20-44] in similar status with respect to "term."

Would it develop that we could show that in long, implicit, historical usage, "concept" got set over against "word" or "term," as either [the] meaning or thing which word referred to? Then, that Carnap, steeped in this usage, . . . proceeded to transfer the steepishness to "sentence-proposition"; producing therefore a wonderful reductio ad absurdum for the future to use with awe?

As you know, I have claimed for years either that "there ain't no concept" or that "concept" is the same thing as word. I have always qualified the latter as a crude statement, and [held] that the linguistic status of "concept" had to be painstakingly investigated. . . .

Regards, Bentley

[New York,] December 3, 1944

Dear Bentley:

I ran across the following from Morris—which explains a lot about him, I fancy—not otherwise important. "Since social groups are composed of individuals, the pattern of a society can only be the pattern of the types of personality of its members"—good old John Stuart Mill stuff watered down by the quasi-mystical introduction of "personality."

I didn't mean to indulge in anything like a wholehearted defense of Whitehead. In fact, I think his thought is slippery—but the slipperiness is of a kind in which I think the alternatives are either to leave him alone or engage in a highly technical discussion—in our case I favor the first alternative. . . .

I think philosophy has had another aspect [than that of a forerunner of science]—namely, that of suggesting programs for social action—either by way of defense of existing institutions or by criticism of them and proposals for change. I've stood for this position so consistently I don't want to seem to go back on it—since I still hold it. The change I suggest doesn't commit you, however. . . .

[*Dewey*]

Indianapolis, Indiana, December 7, 1944

Dear Dewey:

I found the Einstein-[Leopold] Infeld book [*The Evolution of Physics*] on my shelves—apparently never read. Examining it for field. P. 152, *re* Newton: "The earth and the sun, though so far apart, are both actors in the play of forces." "In [James Clerk] Maxwell's theory there are no material actors—they do not connect widely separated events—the field *here* and *now* depends on the field in the *immediate neighborhood* at a time *just past*." *

Also, pp. 216–17, they contrast motion as a sequence of events with motion as "something which *is*"—just what we do in "Transaction-Interaction." . . .

Regards, *Bentley*

Key West, Florida, December 11, 1944

Dear Bentley:

. . . This is just to say that I think your paper on "Names" for *Knowings and Knowns* one of the best things you've done—it sticks to the *naming,* and I think might well be the first paper of the constructive act— with some development, but no great change . . . maybe we don't have to go into the naturalistic postulates *by themselves.* We state them indirectly—that is, in the paper on names, we say in so many words that the naming is done from the standpoint of man-in-nature and nature-in-man—giving whatever synonyms for nature seem advisable—language (naming) itself a natural event—explaining "natural event" by other examples—rain, lightning, digestion, etc.

If necessary, it could be clinched by pointing out what it is *different from;* e.g., man over against the world, subject-object, mind-things, etc.

---

* The exact quotation is: "In Maxwell's theory there are no material actors. . . . They do not, as in Newton's laws, connect two widely separated events. . . . The field *here* and *now* depends on the field in the *immediate neighborhood* at a time *just past*." (Eds.)

345

—raising the question (as a question) whether historically these are not heirs or ghosts of the *super*-natural soul.

I think I was originally responsible for the telling (as distinct from the naming) on Naturalism.

Yours, *Dewey*

Paoli, Indiana, December 13, 1944

[Draft of an essay by A. F. Bentley for the *Journal of Philosophy* with suggestions from Dewey, September 4, 1944]

A TERMINOLOGY FOR KNOWINGS AND KNOWNS

Science uses names efficiently. Such names serve to mark off certain portions of the scientific subjectmatter as tentatively acceptable, thereby freeing the worker's attention for the close consideration of other portions that remain problematic. For efficient work the user must be able to hold such names steady, not only at different stages of his own procedure, but also in converse with his associates.

Theories of knowledge provide their workers with no such firm names. They may find themselves using impressionistic words, words of pre-scientific and indeed often of primitive cultural origin and implication, or else using collections of words they call "terms" with little more than occasional insecure pretense to do service as names. Agreement upon word-employment as between various workers in this field is, notoriously, the exception to the rule. Until reasonably firm names are gained, research here can hope for little progress.

We believe the time has come to undertake the establishment of a few firm leading words *of this type* in this field. We believe further that only upon a naturalistic basis, where "naturalistic" primarily means "factually organized," with the knowing man a factual component of the known system of nature, can names be secured such that a worker can depend upon them in his own study, and in discussion and report. Our expectations, to start with, are none too high. If a few names are obtained which are as dependable for us as are, say, words such as "quadruped" and "camel" for the zoologist, it will be a great help. Can such definite status be established for words indicating fact, object, event, field, interaction, and situation? By their aid, and by the aid of various correlated words, can sharpened names for knowings and existings be dependably developed? Here is our problem.

The difficulties of such a task need no stress here. Names of the type we seek must (1) be based on observation; (2) the observation must be attainable by every ordinarily competent person; (3) the use of the observation must be postulational, hypothetical, tentative, its aim being to improve further observation, rather than to give a purportedly "finished" report on "reality"; and we may add (4) inquirers must become acclimated to procedure under hypothesis instead of in the bonds of express dogma or tacit convention. Given this much, then (1) established creed, habit, or belief, is no bar to alternative forms of study; (2) the fact that a form of observation is adopted which is commonly disregarded or rejected as trivial or unusable is no bar, since the purpose now is to test it; (3) the fact that from a kernel of observation a wide construction grows is no bar, since again the aim is operational test in work, and the project makes good or defaults, not by assertion, but through such [an] operational test. We face a need; we work toward satisfying it; to avoid wasteful confusions of discussion, we propose maximum explicitness under hypothesis as to our form of approach.

In a preceding paper [A. F. Bentley, "On a Certain Vagueness in Logic: I, II"] we displayed the astonishing linguistic chaos that has developed in the [modern] logics [of Russell, Carnap, et al.] from the use of primitive observation and naming relied upon, despite, and to the neglect of, the keener and fuller observation, which perhaps every specialist makes at one time or another, but which, so far as we have noticed, no one proceeds to use. Primarily for the logics, we found necessary the abandonment of their inherited custom of detaching *words* from their users as if the words were a new realm of fact; secondarily, we indicated how the detachment of the *things* a man deals with, from his dealings with them, and [from] his wordings about them, as if they were independently present, results in similar confusion. Without developing it (the point was plain enough as it was) we proceeded on the understanding that the three-realm procedure of the [modern] logics is basically the primitive subject-object procedure of the [modern] epistemologies, plus the addition of a third realm, that of language, recognition of which had forced itself upon [philosophic] students. Any recognition of the indissoluble connection of language with the distinctively human forms of knowing contains the promise of positive and progressive advance in the theory of knowledge. But the insertion of language as a third "thing" * between knower and known, as our earlier paper has shown, greatly increases the difficulties of the epistemological subject-object approach, and in the end yields an emphatic disclosure of the incoherences it involves. Recognition of the need for experiment and construction of a new type, we believe, is everywhere growing.

The observation we shall employ is of a type that brings together in combination, in one sweep of the eye, details which previously had

* "Thing" is another of our vague words, and very useful as such. It is everywhere in good standing. Where no stress of the types involved in such words as object, entity, phenomenon, enters, we shall freely employ it.

347

been treated as basically separate, and assumed to require organization and interpretation to be supplied to them from without. Later in our observation we shall name this changed form of observation "transactional." The inspection of speakings and writings, with all their contained meanings and constructions, as man-himself-directly-in-action requires observation of this type. We make speaking-as-event to be as readily observable as is a bird-in-flight, and [consider books] in print to be observably man-in-action in no different sense, so far as observational requirements go, from observable nest-building, egg-laying, or hatching. To observe man-in-action, not as radically set over against the environing world, but as component of . . . and in a world-situation is observation of this type. To inspect any event occupying a duration of time as descriptively one, rather than as made up of the addition or other combination of separate instantaneous existences is an exhibit of such observation. . . . Procedure of this type was continuously used by Peirce (though he had no favorable opportunities for developing it *) and was basic to him from the time when in one of his earliest papers he stressed that "all thought is in signs and requires a time." [Peirce, *Collected Papers*, V, 151] The "immediate" or "neutral" experience of William James was definitely an effort at such a form of direct observation in the field of knowings. Dewey's development in the use of interaction and transaction, and in the presentation of "experience" as neither subjective nor objective, but as system and organization (no matter how persistently his commentators have falsified him in this respect) is strongly of this form. And in his *Logic* of 1938 and the preceding Logical Studies of 1903 and 1916, he has developed the forms of inquiry in a situational setting. Bentley's *Process of Government* sought treatment of this kind, and his later analysis of mathematics in language, his situational presentation of psychology, and his factual treatment of behavioral space and time, all fall within this line. [A. F. Bentley, *Linguistic Analysis of Mathematics; Behavior, Knowledge, Fact; Inquiry into Inquiries*]

The first step we propose to take in developing a terminology for knowings and knowns is to note that something called "fact" is of outstanding importance in this era of science. If we want to attack the knowledge problem directly, "fact" ought to furnish first-class subject-matter for examination. But what *is* "fact"? What cosmically, in terms of the organisms-in-environments [that] the cosmos presents, *is* the factual situation, or status, or condition itself which is indicated or intended by the word "fact"? To *what*, in short, practically and with common sense, does the word "fact" *apply*? Recall the dubious status of fact in the logics we have examined and in the confused dictionary and magazine phrasings which we have cited. (Sections II, III, IX)

* See [Bentley, "On a Certain Vagueness in . . ."] Logic paper, Sec. I.

[Bentley's "On a Certain Vagueness in Logic."] We shall hold that if there *are* facts, and if they *have* enormous importance, and *are* vital in the issues of knowledge, then it is of importance for us to be able to characterize "fact" as such—to be able to say . . . that we know what we are talking *about*, when we use the word "fact," and that what we are talking about is itself something in the range of fair observation and linguistic identification. In short, our terminology is involved in fact, and fact in our terminology.

To establish anything definite as to "fact," *qua* fact, it is required that *both* an identifying activity, and a *what* of identification be taken into account, *and* that they be taken into account each as participant in the other, and never either as isolated from the other. This is equivalent to saying that knowledge includes . . . (and requires) both knowings and knowns. (We shall postulate, both in respect to fact and in respect to knowledge, that we find no "thing known" and no "fact identified" wholly apart from the knowing or identifying of it; and, conversely, that we find no knowing or identifying activity wholly apart from the *whats* that are being known or being identified. "System" in knowledge is taken by us in this sense.)

The above we regard as a simple, clean-cut report on the status of the words in question, i.e., knowledge of fact, and on the manner of their application. The report is one of simple *observation* of taking men in action in the world. If it is not, we do not know where to look for any simple observation and report. The usual custom in our field of inquiry is to admit more or less vaguely what we have just set forth, and then to forget all about it. Here, in contrast, we propose to use this observation and to construct by its aid. . . .

In proceeding, however, we shall face the need of a great amount of elaboration and discussion to give [us] protection against probable misunderstandings and misinterpretations, most of which arise from the defects of our conventional vocabulary, and especially from its lack of adequate propositions. Our language is not grammatically organized for the statements we have to make. It is impracticable to take up thoroughly and at length each such issue as it shows itself. Should we try it, it would lead us so far afield that again and again our objectives would be lost from view. In the present paper we shall limit ourselves to assembling the main names that we believe should be established, indicating, to start with, rather what is *needed* than what precisely we have to offer. We shall leave elaboration of discussion for the papers that follow. We may even, for provisional practical reasons, employ namings in the present paper which we shall drop later in favor of others that we believe more desirable, but which are not safe to employ until discussion is further advanced. (This should be a separate section.)

Another practical point of the greatest importance in our procedure

349

is this: While we intend to examine knowledge, we do not intend to let ourselves be deluded into thinking that it is necessary to mix in one single stew everything on heaven or earth to which the word "knowledge" is applied. Such everythings run all the way from an amoeba's contacts with food to divine omniscience, with plenty of room in between for intuitions and magics, as well as for perceivings, manipulatings, and set habits. Too many cooks spoil the broth, but also too many broths spoil the cook. We shall limit ourselves at the outset for our present inquiry to the sharper knowings, the communicable ones, in short to the knowings and knowns that lead up through search into research, and establish themselves thus. This region of our inquiry we shall call the region of naming-knowing. . . . It is in general the region of warranted assertion and of asserted existence. Just how far the word "knowledge" or the more definite words "knowings" and "knowns" should [and may] be applied beyond the margins of naming-knowings, will be an issue of high import, no doubt, at some future time, but it is not profitable today, and we refuse to let it hamper us. For our present campaign, in short, we divide to conquer, and make no bones about it.

Let this be clear [re] "cosmos," "term," and "fact": For the purposes of further research, we are *not* going to proceed as if we had to do with "things existent" entirely apart from men, and with "men existent" entirely apart from things, the problem being to force them into some sort of organization. Instead, we shall proceed under acceptance of organisms—including men—developed in and living in a cosmos such that all their procedures including their knowings and knowns can be viewed directly and together as *one* system. Knowings and knowns thus enter as differentiations *within* a factual cosmos, not as elements of prior validity that have to be combined to produce a "cosmos-knowledge-fact." Language here enters as [an] intra-cosmos process, and no longer as [a] blundering intruder upon the ground of rival camps. It enters aspectually in spectrum-like behavioral spread of meaningful application. The terminology for inquiry into knowings and knowns must develop with the elasticity that the terminology of genera and species presents within a biology-in-growth, and free from the taxonomic rigidities that tend to appear in biologies-quiescent and that characterize epistemological endeavorings wheresoever. Such oppositions as the antique body-soul, mind-matter, sheep-goat types have no place.

We do not assert our position to be "true" nor our presentations to be "real" in any of the radical applications of such words. We simply say: thus runs our observation; and further: given general bankruptcy in epistemology, let observation grow.

With regard to the word "observation," we are connecting it with the range of name-usings, with notings, namings, and tellings. We stress as observation, available to each and all, that when a knowing-known is before attention, it may be observed (inclusively of the knowing and the known), and that this be so capable of inquiry. Will anyone venture to assert today that he can properly "observe" a mind beyond all action—in our case, beyond all knowing—or a real beyond all that is known, as that upon which the fact is based? Current construction goes thus, but observation not. To the contrary, we assert [plain] observation in any reasonable sense reports that that upon which the fact-character is based in any given case consists of what are also (or are taken to be) facts.

Our suggested terminology, as we have already said, is designed to bring to view the regions most in need of firm naming, to set up names for them, to use in this first paper, not so much the names we may ultimately prefer, but rather names which we feel will be less open to misinterpretation, and to do this on a basis of sufficiently frank hypothesis so that resulting discussion itself may be frank.

We shall begin with the cosmos as within knowledge, [and shall be] doing justice to the knowing- and the known-aspects in one presentation. We shall call this presentation "fact." By fact we shall not intend what any one man knows, nor what is known in any one geographical region or human grouping, nor (comparably) what is known in any short, limited time such as our day and age. Nowhere in all this range is the Fact of Knowledge [taken to be] rigid or stable. It is all in change; it is all in the manner of change [that] we commonly call development or growth. We take it not as rigid, but as growing, as spread over durations of time. These durations, as we know them, are not merely decades, but centuries. For all we know, they may stretch out indefinitely; to decide about that is not our province here. Knowings and knowns, we take as they come. The distinctions are not those of fact and not-fact (nor in the analogous form of true and false), but they are those of poorer-named fact and better-named fact. This will remain for development in later papers.

Within this factual cosmos—this range of Fact—we recognize everywhere the distinctions of naming and named, of identifying and identified, of knowing and known. We make this differentiation the basic differentiation within the factual cosmos for the purposes of our inquiry into Knowledge. We expect to maintain the name "fact" throughout, and we will build up the case for this decision in a separate paper later on. For present naming of the differentiated aspects we expect later change. For the present we shall call the named, known, [and] identified, "event," and the knowing, naming, identifying, "designation."

We secure therefore these names:

Fact;
Event;
Designation.

351

We prefer to say in place of "Designation" simply "Naming" or "Name," but this "name" itself is full of such varieties of implications that, as a starter, we consider it unsafe. We shall justify it later. The name "Event" has the value that it preserves the durational aspect throughout, and this is of the highest importance. It has the defect that it also is used in many ways, and particularly in more recent mathematics [physics] for a time-space instant. But if we should say "Existence" in place of "Event," the word would carry much implication of instantaneous status and much of a reality beyond knowledge, with both of which we have no affair in an inquiry into Knowledge.

Whatever words we establish, we must maintain in progressive development. But other words we use casually; we caution against hearing [them] as fixities. The word "knowledge" in particular we are using in these papers as rough impressionistic rendering of the subjectmatter of inquiry. Most positively no reader is justified in understanding ["knowledge"] in some way peculiar to himself and trying to force our text to fit it.

Let us consider now what differentiation we need on the side of Event. Event most broadly comes under attention in preliminarily characterized situations, in processes, and in sharply determined objects. In all of these, we have subjectmatters of inquiry—of human search and research. (Note that subjectmatter, as commonly used, places "subject" on the "object" side of the distinction, which is one most excellent reason for eliminating [the] basic use of the subject-object differentiation altogether.) Our suggestion for terminology here is that Event ([in the] broader sense) be differentiated thus: *Event; Situation; Event* (narrowly) [in] process [of] Transition; *Object.*

Observe that just as "event" and "designation" differentiate within "fact," and are not at all [to be] taken as separate, preliminary materials by way of which fact appears, so here "Situation," "Event-in-Process," and "Object" are differentiations within "Event" more broadly stated. Object is durationally in process . . . [in fact just] as much as is situation or event, and correspondingly situation and process are naming-knowing-identifications as much as objects are; so that "object" participates in the free "situation," while the freest "situation" in knowledge has some of the identifiability of the firmest "object."

Turn next to the side of "Designation." We shall again differentiate, but this time we shall inspect "Designation" not as separating into three types, but as itself one of the three types in which human cognitive-behavioral process (most broadly viewed) can be dissected. It happens that knowings, knowledges, are most closely organized in namings. It is the naming-knowings we are centering on [in] them. Therefore, under "Designation" we orient naming-knowings to perceptional-manipulative behaviors, preceding them in the historical-evolutionary scale on one side,

352

and to symbolic behaviors arising out of them, and in that sense following them in the evolutionary scale. It is common today to talk about a name as a sign, without trying to find out what "sign" is supposed to be, and to then talk of words as signs, as if it [that] helped matters. When later we substitute "Name" for "Designation," we shall endeavor to give naming such full behavioral value that it can stand in its own right. "Sign" we shall choose as a broad word, not "the same as," but with variation of stress rather than scope, covering the same regions of cosmic process as the word behavior, knowledge (most broadly used). We shall then differentiate

Sign
Signaling
Naming
Symboling

(The following perhaps should have been in introductory matter. I write here as if it were not there. There is a hint of this two or three pages above.)

"Signaling" (the word is taken from Pavlov's use for adoption here) will cover the range of perceptional-manipulative behaviors (not, remember, as commonly understood, but under the procedure hereinafter described). "Name" will cover the general range of event-known-named-identified, i.e., "existence." "Symbol" will be specialized to sharpen precision procedures for which mathematical equation gives the model. It is to be *kept in mind throughout* that our present inquiry into knowledge does not pretend to be universal, but it takes up *knowings in that central range of namings* to which we can give intelligent attention without too much divagation.

We may take the following general statement on our procedure at this stage. So far as existence in the sense of what is under knowing or identifying is concerned, we take it up as involving namings. This is not to deny any other process. It is to assert that here is a great central region which can be made subjectmatter. We then find that such knowing-namings cover not only the region of knowing-naming, but regions of signal-knowing, and regions of symbol-knowing; in both cases, however, with the word "knowing" having very different applications from what it has in the "naming" regions—and indeed with absence of the "existence-affirmation" characteristics, the "event-specification" values which naming gives. We have here *circularity* about which we are explicit, not casually implicit. The naming is set in wider behavioral ranges; but those wider behavioral ranges are present as event under designation (naming) and not with full rights existentially apart from their designational determination.

We stress again, but in changed phrasing. . . . [that] Fact, so far as it is specified, is specified by naming. Naming, nevertheless, is a fact-process. If we distinguish event and designation within Fact, then we find situation, transition, and object characteristically differentiated forms of event, but we find naming itself one form of a wider behavioral range covering signal-name-symbol, all parts of which are themselves existentially differentiated through naming. There they are—reports in observation of the way men work and talk. We adapt ourselves to them.

However, if the words we have used, such as "sign" [and] "name," or "event" [and] "object" are read in the older forms of elemental isolations, rather than in the form we use of differentiations within a cosmos that is factually set forth, all will be falsely read. We shall now set three [new] types of distinctions, all belonging within the framework above and all necessary to properly present it linguistically. The first of these is distinctions of: *Characterization; Specification; Definition.*

The word "definition" we shall hold to the range of symbolic procedure. This is for our purposes, and as a necessary distinction. This limitation is in line with the more common recent usages, although *sharply* holding to it is not common. Dictionaries offer definitions, which are more or less accurate characterizations of current usage, very interesting, but not usable with dependency on inquiries into knowledge. To say that an animal [that] has four legs and barks, is a definition of a dog is possible, but not useful. We hold "definition" to regions in which mathematical consistency serves as best illustration.

The typical scientific statement, as different[iated] from symbolic statement, seeks accuracy rather than precision. We shall not speak of "definition" here at all, but instead of "Specification." What is wisely scientific in our generation, observing the succession of Einstein to Newton, is satisfied with doing the best it can, not claiming to be at the limit of precision, but leaving the way open to renewed improvement.

Everything done in our set of papers is by specification, nothing is by definition. In our subjectmatter the symbolic procedures involving definition are a long way as yet from being developed to apply, or from having materials to which to apply.

Another distinction of the greatest importance is one involving *Self-action; Inter-action; Trans-action.*

Our procedure here we shall show later, as of our particular subjectmatter, and particular stage of inquiry, to be transactional. By this is to be understood the approach to inquiry not by setting up two separates and organizing them but by getting a fresh view of the full subjectmatter, seeing it in system, and reporting observation [on it] in such terms. The epistemological procedure we have mentioned before, which opposes real-existence on its own account to mind on its own account, is, in its more developed form, interactional, and crudely so. Its less

354

developed forms—more primitive forms—run to self-actional report and may be self-actional in terms of mind alone or of matter alone (in the extreme cases) where "mind" and "matter" are words, it is true, but both of them words with very primitively useless naming values. The one thing one cannot ever find out is the *what* that either of them names. All superstition. To place knowing and the known in a single factual system is manifestly transactional compared with contrasting procedures which bring separates, isolates as separate, together in organization. We shall develop this at length in a separate paper later on.

Associated with the above sets of distinctions is one that includes *Physical; Biological—Physiological; Biological—Behavioral.*

Having set up for consideration a general cosmic fact-system, it is evident that we should not be expected to regard the physical, vital, and psychological as three different kinds or classes of things in a world; but instead [as] the three great scientific divisions, recognized and accepted almost everywhere in inquiry, as different manners of approach to a common subjectmatter of inquiry—the cosmic world of fact. It is really more the other way around. Because we have come to accept the sciences as inquiry-forms rather than as compartments of things, we are able to proceed to the wider envisioning of the full knowledge process that we here adopt. Everyone knows that if a man shoots a rabbit, the full transaction can be studied physically, physiologically, and psychologically; that some transactions occur in which we find physical but not physiological or psychological directly applicable, and some that we study [as] physiological without needing the psychological directly; but that in the final analysis the study itself involves the psychological and that this shows itself in the very characterization of subjectmatter as in wave-particle alternations and in the [Heisenberg] principle of uncertainty as to momentum and position.

Hardly a word is available to use in a specification which is not apt to be read by various readers in various ways. Nevertheless, we shall offer preliminary characterizations of the words we have marked for attention above. We hope [that] in no case is a loose word used in such manner that its defects corrupt our statement.

Fact The cosmos of advancing knowledge, with knowings and knowns
involved
Event Differentiation of Fact in existential stress
Designation Differentiation of Fact as in identification
Situation Event entering broadly as subjectmatter
Transition Event-in-process under specification
Object Event in its more permanent fixations
Sign Characteristic of all behaviors transactionally
Signal Sign in the perceptive-manipulative ranges

Name Sign in object-identification ranges

Symbol Sign in symbolic precisions, under the discard of name-identi-
fications

Characterization Best applications we can give words prior to scientific
determinations

Specification Scientific applications, always in progress toward better,
or open to it

Definition Symbolic precision of statement

Self-Action The antique attribution of initiative to objects, mainly surviving today in the psychologies and logics

Interaction Where participants to inquiry enter as distincts for which
organization must be sought

Transaction Where broad observation sees system, within which the
analysis of components follows

The Sciences Main types to be differentiated by techniques used in
investigation

Physical By the techniques of the physical laboratory

Physiological Biological of the physiological laboratory

Behavioral Biological adaptations and adjustments, not statable in terms
of extra-dermal energy interchanges, but requiring direct trans-dermal
observation.

Inspecting the above, one can identify the region of naming which is
the special subjectmatter we take, and see that fact with its differentiation of Event and Designation is establishing this region, while, nevertheless, proper naming in this region limits it to something far short of
ultimate determiner of all knowledge, it itself being bounded within
the very factual procedure it sets up to be regions of signal and symbol
which are not existential-producers.

It will also be apparent that [this] procedure rejects definition and
proposes cautious advance from characterization to specification, appraising this as scientific, and locating the establishing [of] the right of
transactional inspection as need arises under the guidance of a differentiation of the sciences via technique. . . .

[Alternate arrangement by A. F. B.]

Fact The cosmos in its knowings and its knowns as known in its knowings

Event Fact known as taking place

Designation Fact in the taking place of its knowing. The taking place
of knowings in Fact

Fact The cosmos as known in—[or]—to its knowings

Event Fact known as taking place

Designation The taking place of knowings in Fact

Without using knowledge words, we are in trouble. Knowing and known are so incurably our way that they flutter down. Here all we have to do is to make them inclusive each of the other, and to secure consideration of the special region of knowings we examine: viz., namings and the named.

(Alternative)

In compact form we now have the main landmarks of the needed terminology. . . . We propose specification, not definition; we proceed transactionally, and neither magically nor mechanistically.

Fact Cosmos as before us progressively in knowing through naming
Event Fact named as taking place
Designation Namings as taking place in Fact

Specification Accuracy of designation in the lines through which modern science has thrived
Characterization Processes preliminary to developed designation—including such items as "dictionary-definitions"
Definition An evolved symbolic procedure—not subject to designatory tests. . . .

Behavioral, Physiological, Physical Differentiations in modern science, of techniques in modern science, which mark off subjectmatters under their own advance. . . .

Transaction Observation of [things in] system where before organization of [individual, separated] components had been tried
Interaction Organization of components seen at its best in Newtonian mechanics; in biological regions, found in many recent endeavors to get a full play of organisms upon environmental objects, and vice versa
Self-Action Primitive views of independent "actors" at work, still dominant in most psychology, and (we believe) in all the logics and epistemologies we have noted
Situation Event more broadly seen; usually less definite as subjectmatter. To be taken *always* transactionally under given spatial-durational attribution
Event (Transition) Event observed as in process, and so specified
Object Event in its more stabilized fixations. Always, nevertheless, subjectmatter for further inquiry as the time arises

Sign Characteristic of adaptational behavior, transactionally viewed. Used for the aspect of behavior with which knowledge-inquiry is concerned
Signal Sign in the perceptive-manipulative ranges

357

Name The specialized linguistic control developed among *hominidae* though heralded far earlier, but specialized in the characteristics our study examines only among *homo sapiens*

Symbol A linguistic development of recent [vogue?] gaining certain great powers at the expense of others.

Key West, Florida, December 15, 1944

Dear Bentley:

The enclosed is something I did with your paper of 9-8-44 . . . [probably, "Transaction and Interaction"]. I did the job partly to get a feeling that I was earning my keep as partner, but more to see if I was getting things straight myself. If I am making headway in that direction, there may be some advantage in my re-editing [it]. Having had to work myself to get it, and yet being much nearer you at the start than the average reader, I may be able to judge where the sticking points in understanding are likely to be. On the whole I have tried only to expand what is in your paper, having in view the difficulties readers will have, who are, even in spite of themselves, more or less saturated with the epistemological point of view. [N.B. Enclosure is not printed.]

The . . . sheet that is enclosed [on "Fact"] represents a kind of pilgrim's progress on my part. You may recall that at first I rather wanted to use "fact" only for that which was "warranted," without recognizing that thereby I was abandoning my own position about the inquiry-continuum. Maybe I've carried the making-doing business too far, but it seems to me it holds in line with the man-acting-in-the-world business.

As you will see, I didn't use the word "naturalism" at all—on the whole, I think at the outset "cosmos" and "world" are safer than "nature." I've introduced the word "transactions" two or three times without explanation. I thought it might be a good idea to get the reader sort of used to it before any explicit description is given.

Yours as ever, *Dewey*

Key West, Florida, December 19, 1944

Dear Bentley:

. . . The chief trouble with [my paper "Concerning Signs"] was that it was not placed within knowing in its full sense. The enclosed is an attempt to remedy that defect. . . .

"Things" in their occurrence are not "signs"; they are "signs" only when taken or used as evidence, as indications, directions, pointers; things functioning in a specified way. That is to say, "things" are "signs" only in connection with a knowing-in-process at a particularized date-place. When the process is completed, when the fact is done or taken (that

358

is, *used*) as done or made, the name "sign" has no further application. Clouds under certain conditions are an indication of coming rain—but only when so used. And in the event (eventuation) of rain or non-rain, the clouds-in-question are simply parts, constituents, of a single fact more extensive spatially and more prolonged temporally than the clouds (of limited observational scope) previously used as evidence of a possible or probable future rain event.

The intrinsic reference of things-as-signs to a particular knowing-in-process is exhibited in the fact that when there is nothing questionable or problematic in the thing, it is reacted to or used *directly*. Is that thing salt? Tasting or trying some mode of tasting to find the answer: the indirect *or knowing*-doing. Using the shaker to season food, the direct doing or making. A knowing is an indirect, mediated, postponed, way of making-doing. (Links up with pause, hesitation, in acting.) Knowing through naming is, *as such*, an *incomplete* making, doing. (This seems to follow if the foregoing account is correct.) . . .

Behaviorally speaking, things-as-signs are connected with habit in respect to both conditions and mode of further operation.

As to conditions of origin, they are a matter of learned, acquired, behavior; expertness of sailors, trackers, of skilled artisans. A particular behavioral action, doing-making, through habit, is loaded with selected consequences of previous doing-makings. In itself [it is] a physiological matter; acquired skill of animals through training. [It] becomes a different kind of *knowing-how* when *naming* enters. Memory (organic) becomes re-membering, re-collecting; preparation, readiness, skill, becomes fore-sight. Alternatives are always involved in observation.*
As to modes of further operation, that is to say, what is skill, efficiency, in direct doing becomes [so] when affected by naming [and] observation of alternative consequences through tendential stimulation of differing (more or less conflicting) modes or ways of doing; which effect (is) the behavioral pause or hesitation.

Yours, *Dewey*

Key West, Florida, December 20, 1944

[To Bentley:]

I don't think I ever answered your query about "proposition-judgment." I agree with your comment about the difference as one of degree. Perhaps, "judgment" doesn't need to be brought in, [in] spite of the amount of attention it received in my *Logic*. But it could be said that *if* "judgment" is introduced as a name, then . . . etc.

* If developed, this has something to do with reflection, inference, as an intrinsic constituent of observation.

359

I would now state the difference on the ground of what I've written about a knowing in process, making-doing ("proposition") and that which is done or made ("judgment"). But, of course, the distinction is relative because of the continuum of knowing-known. Just as a tentative proposition may become settled or "judgment," so the judgment may in the course of knowing become problematic and tentative, a "proposition."

But, in any case, I think this way of stating is secondary to the fact-observation variant of it for the sake of covering the ground.

[*Dewey*]

Key West, Florida, December 21, 1944

[To Bentley:]

It has occurred to me that organization of names might be aided by employing a few central lines of distinguishing, such as:

1. Names—symbols—connections, relations—not that there is anything new here. I remember getting into trouble about "reference." It seems to have dropped out in later sketches. I think I was wrong in speaking of "names" as referring. "Names" *apply* rather than refer. Reference to, respect to, regard to, concerning, seem to me now to be linked up with specifying, particularizing, when in process—*a* specifying. In my *Logic* I used "reference" to designate the operation (and . . . [its] consequences) by which symbols are applied to or brought to bear upon "existential subjectmatter," mathematical formulae employed in physics, or legal definitions applied by court to specific issues.

I think this matter should be covered somewhere, but I think "Reference" isn't the word to do it by. It's more like "touching upon," "bearing upon," "about"; in any case, not confined to "symbols."

My present feeling is that it drops out as coordinate with "connection-relation," and comes in as secondary along with "specifying." . . .

2. Transaction in entirety—taken in part, or a-part. For example of latter, "event"; nothing new here either; just [a] matter of applying it throughout as far as it will go.

3. In the case of *a* knowing—*a* known, the distinction of doing-making and done-made. I've given some examples of this. I would add another. "Affirmation" as doing, establish*ing* as firm, i.e., trustworthy, steadfast in use, constant, firm, opposed to "fast and loose," deuces wild, wobbly. "Assertion" as done: maintaining in use as established, settled—until, of course, observation gives ground for changing, in which it becomes in-firm and needing *af*-firming. Maybe I'm hipped on this distinction, but it strikes me now as one of general line-up.

There is one other possible line of distinction, which, if it exists, is basic: Pre-naming knowing; naming-knowing; post-naming . . . -knowing intermediate-transitional. This may be only a survival of some of my *Logic* framework which should be dropped. But there is a kind of absorbed enjoyment and of confident, wordless going ahead, which seems [not] to depend upon prior knowing-naming, but to be its fruitage or consummation; also aesthetic. It doesn't fall within our scheme to deal with or discuss this, but whether it, like pre-naming knowing, should be noted down [is a question].

When I refer to possible assistance in organization, I'm raising the question whether it is desirable to make express statement of these lines of distinguishing in one place as running through the entire scheme. . . .

[*Dewey*]

Seattle, Washington, December 21, 1944

Dear Dewey:

Concerning your notes [of the] 19th on "signs." I don't find a thing to take exception to, but I do think there is a way of broadening the procedure, and this I feel necessary for more general purposes of statement.

Agreed that a sign is a sign only in use, and that we can talk of it as being present as an object apart from its occasions in service as sign. But where are we when we get back to the stage in which "object" is being built up out of "sign-process"? This may happen to mud-turtles, or to physicists in laboratories (assuming that mud-turtles get to objects, and that what physicists get at these days, such as waves, quanta, etc., are properly to be called "objects").

It is back here that we have to make the whole statement *trans*actional. In other words, a developing cosmos develops its organisms which, as they go along, fold back on the cosmos and develop it as a known cosmos (which it certainly was not before) with all the deficiencies of a being-known. And that neither can be properly stated except as of the transaction (of course, with whatever limited, minor, interactional statements one wishes as one goes along).

Which yields an interesting comment. It is universal to say that valuable as language is, language always distorts more or less. Here language is looked at as distorting with reference to, or by the test of, some sort of perceptual actuality. My position certainly is that the perceptual is a distortion to start with, a lower-grade distortion than the linguistic-super-percept (language upon perception) successor and representative. Nothing to this: it is just another way of throwing a rock at the "real entity"; the phrasing interested me as a change.

In your development in this letter, you seem to be inclined to use the word "sign" as a special procedure in which an object is involved; and I inclined to use it as the general procedure under which objects

361

become identified, or arise, or enter as objects. You would use it as one among many behavioral procedures; and I as an aspectual name for the behavioral range in general. There is no conflict here—it is a question of form of statement—unless, possibly, there might be a question whether a sign-evolved object always remained a sign-event (my view) or whether it, so to speak, graduated and got promoted to a higher class with the degree "object." I do not object to giving it the academic degree "object," providing it remains mortal, and subject to all the ills mortals etc., are heir to. Here we are at one. The cosmos is certainly mortal. And this mortality is transactional-behavioral.

On a knowing, as an indirect, incomplete making-doing, I note only a slight difference of phrasing. In the papers I am now working [on] I write a "naming-knowing" where you write a "knowing through naming." My phrase (so far as I succeed in maintaining it) indicates that a naming (in its habit-set, of course) *is* a knowing. Yours carries the implication that a knowing may be identified in one locus, and treated as applying a naming as its implement in some other locus. Phrasing only.

Regards, Bentley

Key West, Florida, December [?] 1944

[*Draft by John Dewey that became, with revisions, parts of I and II of the essay in* The Journal of Philosophy]

A TERMINOLOGY FOR KNOWINGS AND KNOWNS

I

We wish to have and use names for knowings and knowns which satisfy, positively and negatively, certain conditions. (1) The names are to be based upon observations such as are accessible [to] and attainable by everybody. Negatively, this condition excludes, by its statement, any observation whose nature or conditions confine it to a single observer, as is the case with so-called introspection. (2) The status and use of what is observed is to be tentative, postulational, hypothetical. This condition excludes all material, however derived or arrived at, which is asserted to provide "foundations" for that which is accepted as knowing or known. It excludes all fixed principles asserted and to be used as original and necessary premises for anything entitled to the name of knowledge. (3) The condition just stated leads into the condition that names be such as to promote and improve further observations, which in turn have a similar aim and use. This condition excludes all names and namings which are asserted or assumed to give or be of the nature of finished reports of "reality."

The above conditions amount to saying that the names wanted have to do with knowings and knowns in continued operational use and test in and by work, in which any knowing or known establishes itself or fails to do so, not on the ground of any outside alleged foundation, premise, axiom, or *ipse dixit* assertion, but through continued operational test.

It is not asserted, for example, that the conditions stated above are "true," nor are we arguing in behalf of them. We are stating them as conditions to be satisfied by the kind or type of names for knowings and knowns for which we are in search. The procedure indicated does not then bar study of knowledge by others on the ground of established creeds or prior tenets, since it but states the ground upon which we ourselves wish to operate with the belief that there are others who may be glad to cooperate in its development. It is an attempt then to apply to the study of knowledge the same postulates and methods which have advanced knowledge of other facts. For science has learned to use names efficiently. Names having scientific [standing] mark off portions of subjectmatter as tentatively acceptable, thereby leaving the attention of the inquirer free for considerations of other portions that remain problematic. For efficient work, the user must be able to hold such names steady not only throughout the successive stages of his own work but also in that communication with other workers which is an integral factor in the operations of inquiry.

Inquiry into knowledge of the kind that would result in knowledge of knowings-knowns (or knowledge) does not have at present possession of such firm names. We believe the time is ripe to undertake the establishment of a number of leading names of this type. The difficulties in the way are serious; but we believe the difficulties have their chief source in the injection of traditional notions formed when, on [the] one hand, an observation was in such relatively primitive state as to its controlling methods as not to provide subjectmatter which is now abundantly available, while, on the other hand, cultural conditions (such as are made familiar by anthropological students) then favored the introduction of factors which have now been shown to be so irrelevant to the operations of inquiry as to stand in the way of formulation of a straightforward theory of knowledge—straightforward because setting forth conclusions reached through inquiry into knowledge as fact.

The basic postulate of this procedure is that knowledge exists as an observable fact, exactly as do the subjects which knowledge is about. A glance at any collection of books and periodicals discloses the immense number of subjectmatters which have been studied so that knowledge of various degrees of establishment is the result. It does not require argument to warrant the statement that this wide field of knowledge (possessed of varying depths in its different portions) exists exactly as do the things it is concerned with. We believe that with respect

363

to both its main procedures and some of its main results, the chief obstacle to forming a theory of knowledge by the same general operations which have advanced knowledge of other facts is dependent upon standpoints and views framed in a period of relatively primitive observation—that is, prior to development of present methods of knowing and the institution of what is now known.

In a previous paper instances were pointed out, in contemporary writings by competent students, of the extraordinary confusion that exists, we hold, because of uncritical transfer into logic, as theory of knowledge, of forms of primitive observation, if not to the utter neglect of the fuller and keener observations now available, at least to such a mixture of two incompatible types of observations as inevitably produces confusion. It was affirmed in that article that advance required complete abandonment of the customary isolation of words from both man speaking and from things spoken of or named. In effect, and often overtly, words were spoken of as if they were a new and third kind of fact lying between man as speaker and things spoken of. The net result is to effect a separation of the things which are involved in man's transactions from the man dealing with them. While the logical writers in question have professedly departed from the earlier epistemological theories framed on the basis of mind as subject and an external world as object, we believe that competent analysis will show that the separation which is the source of the confusions in their writings is the ghost of the seventeenth-century epistemological separation of knowing subject and object known—as that in turn was the ghost of the medieval separation of a "spiritual" soul from a "material" nature. The importance (in what precedes) to the establishment of firm names is the direct result of employment of observation of knowledge as a going factual concern. For observation brings together in combination in a single sweep matters which have been treated as isolated and hence as requiring to be brought together ("synthesized" is the traditional word) by some outside agency. The seeing of language, with all its speakings, writings, together with the theoretical constructions and organizations which the speakings and writings contain, as man-himself-in-action-dealing-with-things, is observation of the type which sees matters as they exist in connections with one another, not as isolates. Here primary speaking is as observable as is a bird in flight. The inclusion of books and periodicals as a case of observable man-in-action is no different from the kind of observation of the steel girders of a bridge that connects them with mining and smelting of ores, the operations of a mill and of bridge-building. For . . . [that] matter . . . it is no different from observation extended enough to take in, not just a bird while in flight, but the bird nest-building, egg-laying and hatching. Observation of this general type sees man-in-action, not as something radically set over against an en-

364

vironing world, nor yet as merely acting "in" a world, but as action *of* and *by* the world to which he belongs as an integral constituent.

To see an event filling a certain duration of time as a description across a full duration, rather than as composed of an addition or other kind of combination of separate instantaneous or short-span events, is another aspect of such observation.* If there should be difficulty in understanding this use of the name "observation," the difficulty illustrates the point previously made about the introduction of material from an extraneous source. The current philosophical notion of observation is derived from a psychology of consciousness (or some version of the "mental" as an isolate). The current conclusion reduces what is observed either to some single sensory quality or to some other "content" of such short time span as to . . . have no connections, save as they are provided by "inference" as an operation outside of observation. As against such a procedure in obtaining a description of observation, the procedure we adopt reports and describes observation on the basis of what the worker in knowledge (astronomer, physicist, physiologist, etc.) employs as test observation in arriving at the conclusions accepted as known. We proceed upon the postulate that *knowing* is always and everywhere the inseparable correlate of the *known*.

II

"Fact" is a name of such a central position in what we propose to do in forming a terminology that we begin with it. For if there are such things as "facts," and if they have such importance that they have a vital status in the matter of knowledge, then we should be able to characterize fact; to be able to say, that is, that we know what we are talking about when we use the word as something which is definitely identifiable in the range of fair observation and firm naming.† The primary consideration in fulfilling the desired condition with respect to Fact is that the activity by which it is identified, and the "what" that is identified, are both required and are required in such a way that each is taken along with the other, and in no sense as separable. This repeats in effect the statement that knowledge includes and requires knowings and knowns together. Anything named "fact" is such both with respect to the knowing operation and with respect to that which is known.‡ We establish for our own use, in terms both of fact and of

---

* Your reference in your [Bentley's draft] p. 3 to Peirce, James, Dewey, and Bentley was accidentally omitted. It should go in—perhaps as a footnote.

† The prior paper, ["On a] Certain Vagueness in Logic" indicates how far present discussion comes short of possession of this ability.

‡ It may be well to repeat here what has already been said. In making the above statement, we are not attempting to legislate meaning . . . but are stating the procedure we are accepting.

knowledge, that we have no "something known" and no "something identified" apart [from] its know*ing* and identify*ing*, and no know*ing* and identify*ing* apart from the somewhats or somethings that are being known and identified. Again, we do not put forth this statement as truth about "reality" but as the only position which it is possible to take on the ground of that reference to [the] observed which we take as basic. The statement is one about ourselves as observed in action in the world. From the standpoint of what is observable it is of the same straightforward kind as is the statement that when chopping occurs, something is chopped, and that when seeing takes place, something is seen. We select the name "fact" because we believe that it carries and suggests this "double-barreled" sense (to borrow a word from William James), while such words as "object" [and] "entity" have acquired from traditional philosophical use the signification of something set over against doing [and] acting. That "fact" is literally or etymologically *something done or made* has also the advantage of suggesting that knowing and identifying, as ways of acting, are as much ways of doing or making (are as much behavioral?) as are chopping wood, singing songs, seeing sights or making hay.

In view of the state of the language currently employed in discussion of knowledge, a great deal of protective elaboration is needed to avoid probable misunderstandings. For the purpose of facilitating further inquiry, what has been said will be restated in negative terms. We shall *not* proceed as if we were concerned with "existent things" or "objects" entirely apart from men, nor with men entirely apart from things. Accordingly, we do not have on our hands the problem of forcing them into some kind of connection or organization. We shall proceed by taking for granted human organisms developed, living, carrying on, of and in the cosmos. They are there in such system that their operations and transactions can be viewed directly—including those which constitute knowings. When they are so viewed, knowings and knowns come before us as differentiated within the factual cosmos, not as if they were there provided in advance so that out of them cosmos-system-fact-knowledge have to be produced. Fact, language, knowledge, have, on this procedure, cosmic status; they are not taken as if they existed originally in two irreconcilably hostile camps. This again is but to say that we have to do with knowings both as to material and workmanship, in the sense of ordinary science.*

* It is practically impossible to guard against every form of misapprehension arising from prevalent currency of language-attitudes holding over from a relatively pre-scientific period. There are probably readers who will translate what is said about knowings-knowns into the terms of epistemological idealism. Such a translation misses the main point: Man and his doings and transactions have to be viewed as facts within the natural cosmos.

366

The reader will note (that is, observe or give heed to) the great superiority of our position with respect to observation over that of the older epistemological constructions. Who would assert that he *observes* a "mind" in addition to the organism which is engaged in carrying on the transactions proper to it in an observable world? The fact that . . . [this] position can be held only by construing observation as private introspection is sufficient evidence of complete departure from any procedure having scientific standing. And the assertion or belief that things or "objects" outside of and apart from human operations are observed or are observable is an obvious flat contradiction.

Observation and name-using are directly connected in our procedure. We would not say that a lion observes as he springs at the throat of his victim. For observation involves a phase, however slight, of pausing; some, but not too much, of hesitant action. For a considerable portion of actual observation lies in border regions between direct action of and through the senses and explicit names. Nor would we say that a mathematician observes as he calculates or as he constructs with tensors—save as a phase of uncertainty enters in, which is identical, in so far, with his not operating *as* a mathematician, since he pauses to find out what is mathematically required.

If we have succeeded in making our position clear with respect to the type of names for which we are in search, it will also be clear that the types of names come in clusters. *Observation* and *fact* are central names, and around them cluster other names shading off as we move toward the periphery into names that are still vague and which can be firmed only after much serious cooperative work that lies ahead. But in any case we cannot hope to succeed by first setting up separate names and then putting them in pigeon holes or bundling them together with wire provided from without—à la Kantian "synthesis." Names are indeed to be differentiated from one another. But the differentiation takes place with respect to one another in cluster, and the same thing holds for clusters that are differentiated with respect to one another. This procedure has its well-grounded precedents in scientific procedure. The genera and species of botany and zoology are excellent examples—provided they are taken as determinations in process and not as taxonomic rigidities.

(How about the determination of chemical elements and compounds as another illustration?)

Because *fact* is a name for doing-done—a making-made, an operation carried-*out*, the word is not to be confined to the extreme of eulogistic or honorific use to which fact is sometimes reserved—in which case it becomes not only a synonym for *"truth"* and "reality," but being true, is taken as a finality and hence outside of process and operation. Things are wrongly and defectively constructed; as history shows, every utensil and every product exhibit a succession of improved forms. The first automobile was an automobile in spite of its clumsy form and inefficient performance as compared with later forms—and the "perfection" of the present form is not inherent but relative to the past. It *invites* further change instead of setting up a claim to finality. Whether fortunately or unfortunately, there is nothing done in this world that is not capable of some degree of later re-doing and un-doing.

As things done or made by human beings operating-in-and-with-things-in-single-system, facts are also of all sorts. Fictions are facts, although not the *kind* of fact that will win acceptance when observation is more extended and refined in respect to space-time conditions. Upon the ground of pre-scientific practices, it may seem absurd to speak of doubtful, problematic, vague, indistinct, and mis-taken facts—to say nothing of *fabulous* or *false* facts. When, however, it is said that what is fact at one time and place is not fact at another time and place, we are not stating a doctrine but making a straightforward report *of* facts. Again we are not attempting to legislate for those who identify fact with "truth" and "reality." We are, however, decidedly pointing out that such an identification is based upon considerations that are foreign to observation as that is determined in and by scientific procedure . . . and that the latter course is the only one open to those who would frame a theory of knowledge on the ground either of known subjectmatter or approved scientific methods of knowing. We are not, then, propounding a "Truth." But we are saying, in effect, that the present state of affairs imperatively imposes the need of making a choice.

Key West, Florida, December 27, 1944

Dear Bentley:

. . . I have read over my sheets of 12-19-44 and can't comment very well on your comment of 12-21-44 because I don't get the reference to "Object." I don't think the word (nor the idea) occurs in my comments. Evidence is not a matter of pointing to an object, but to a conclusion factual in nature. That a "good" sign (not necessarily a *right* one) points by means of indicating operation is *a* knowing-in-process—not directly— I didn't say; but I took it for granted as not needful to say. Instead of referring to, or bringing on, "objects," I said [that] when the operations are carried out, what had been used as a sign becomes taken into the factual outcome. Status as object has nothing to do, that I can see, with making and using signs, but with the matter of later direct response. E.g., when I am carrying an umbrella and it begins to rain, I raise my umbrella. As far as that behavior approaches a reflex, and I don't investigate the thing nor the desirability of opening it, I react to it as an *object*. At least I thought we had settled on *"object"* as name for the sort of thing that was so well determined by previous behavioral operations as to be used directly "as is."

Quite likely, I missed the point of your comments. But you say that I "seem to be inclined to use the word 'sign' as a special procedure in which an object is involved," and in any case, I shall be glad to learn what gave you that impression since it is the opposite of my intention. . . . But concern with evidence does seem to me to be a distinctive procedure, connected with the pause or hesitation which you noted in behavior.

Yours, *Dewey*

[P.S.] . . . If your point is that *a* (particular) knowing-in-process is but an aspect of inclusive knowing-known; of course, I agree. I think I said in an accompanying note that the main trouble with my previous sketch was that it didn't place the sign-business within [knowing]. But I should suppose [that] the aspect distinction needed recognition in connection with a satisfactory name-systemization.

[Seattle, Washington,] December 27, 1944

Dear Dewey:

. . . You suggest illustration for . . . contrast between scientific and other naming. If I started development here, it would take a whole paper. I doubt if the ordinary working scientist would ever get the point. . . . This "Terminology" paper cannot possibly do anything but *state* positions in advance. It worries me more because it has too much detail rather than too little. Suppose you keep a running list of your own of points that particularly need specialized development as we get to them. Then you can check where I miss giving it later. . . .

In your *Logic* you have done this job of transition from "situation" to "Warranted Assertion" and "Assured Fact" to the Queen's taste. I proceed on that basis, and consequently may overlook the importance of bringing it in explicitly in our present procedure.

Where the trouble comes in for your *Logic* is in the beginnings and surroundings and endings—here Mackay cannot "get" your starting "situation," and Kaufmann likes your open finish, but wants to peg it onto a "thought." Here also we have decided to use "Fact" for the full open situation, and not for the "hard," "finished," or "done" situation. This is because it is vital to the whole scheme that the "done" be not done forever—that the finish can always be re-finished. (Where I said about "the trouble comes in," I mean only in the acceptance by readers—not in the development itself.)

What we are after is a terminology which will exhibit the open situation within which the finish and the done (temporarily) are secured. Therefore, when you raise this point, I am inclined to postpone it. I do think, however, now, that we ought to have a strong protective assurance that we (you) can get as much hard-fact as anybody, and just as good a quality, out of a procedure from situation and to situation as anyone can from creation to eternal bliss.

Maybe this should be in the first "Search" paper. But just at this moment I am inclined to think that it is [the] very kind of thing that should be in what I call "postulates" or [of?] "technique" or "natural" inquiry" and wait for the second paper. . . .

Regards, Bentley

Part IV

Letters: January 5, 1945–December 28, 1945

Seattle, Washington, January 5[?], 1945

Dear Dewey:

. . . In your *Logic* you used terminologically a general way of talking about "sign" and "symbol" as though—at the given stage of action—"sign" was used to name what already was a "thing" to the organism; while the "symbol" named what was still fluid in his end of the total performance. Now, as you and I go along, and expand "transactionally," we bring the "thing" up into the behavior as well as the "symbol-thing." In other words, the particular line of division between "sign" and "symbol" which you used in *Logic*—while valid for the situations for which you used it—is not valid for our most general attacks. Therefore we faced the issue: either to keep "sign" and "symbol" as you used them, and find new namings for our more general situations; or to widen the characterization of the words "sign" and "symbol," retain them thus widened, and go ahead, thus marking a slight break with [the] terminology of *Logic*. The latter was the decision. . . .

Regards, *Bentley*

Seattle, Washington, January 8, 1945

Dear Dewey:

As far as I can see on going over it, and without having as yet gone into details in full, I would be willing to substitute your . . . "Terminology for Knowings and Knowns" as it stands for the first nine pages of my enclosed draft. . . . It looks as though the rest of my [draft] could follow right along as "III" of your paper. . . .

You will notice how heavily I have used *Subject-Matter*, which has steadily taken a stronger place in your terminology since the *Logic*, where you had it strong already. You have several times mentioned your liking for it, and here I find it holding subject and object together very competently. . . .

[*Bentley*]

Seattle, Washington, January 13, 1945

Dear Dewey:

I have got back to work today. I have not gone very far, but I am practically certain your introductory draft of 12-15-44 is much superior to mine. At any rate, it has recognizably fresh material and fresh points of view, and good organization. This last holds even to the introductory paragraph—in all probability.

I have found several words used that I will want to make remarks about and one form of phrasing that I suggest modifying. . . .

You speak of "knowledge" in a way that sets "it" over against the "subjects it is about." Similarly . . . "knowledge" is contrasted with the "things" it is concerned with. In my draft, right at the start, I have set the word "knowledge" down as a vague word, which cannot as yet be used by us specifically, but only as a general reference. Take your instances of use just cited. I ask: "If the 'knowledge' is separated from the 'thing' it is about, then what kind of thing is the knowledge?" The only answer would seem to be: "It is the subjective end; it is the naming (if we can later stick it) or it is mind-locus." This is far from your intention. It is purely [a] matter of phrasing—to be fixed.

I note the following words also. . . . "Operational" . . . I have avoided, largely because it implies Bridgman and other point-mentalists like S. S. Stevens. "Introspection" . . . [I] think will stimulate the wrong things. . . .

Incidentally, I think we are right in making "Fact" the leading word at this stage. I have suspected that, at [the] end, in place of Fact-Event-Designation, we can use Fact-Existence-Naming. But I would not be surprised if in the end we came out in the form: Existence-Fact-Name. In other words, I am optimistic enough to think that before we get done, we can purify "existence" (the word) so that it is usable.

Sincerely, *Bentley*

[P.S.] Where . . . you write that "knowing is . . . the inseparable correlate of the known," I do not find such an objection, though tentatively I have inserted after "known" the words "twin aspects of one fact." It is the damn word "knowledge" as a contrasted "thing" that miscarries in implication.

Seattle, Washington, January 14, 1945

Dear Dewey:

These are just remarks—as if I could look up across a desk and comment—made as I proceed. . . .

"Exist": this word is used somewhat freely by you. I have no objection to any case I find as casual. But since "exist" is a word to straighten out (dry-clean), it ought not to appear in a running text unless we drop a footnote that it is a "vague sister"—probably not even then since we have heavy duty (perhaps) for it later.

"Senses": used by you occasionally. I doubt whether this should appear. I omit it always. You have not meant the common meaning of the word since 1896 or thereabouts. Every time you use it, your reader reads you as common meaning. Hence, much misunderstanding. (The relation of your "Reflex Arc" paper to James's neutral experience ought to be investigated by somebody—I can't remember that I took it up in the ["The Jamesian] Datum" paper.) Actually we are reconstructing the *whole Sense Business.*

I am knocking out the word "naturalistic" wherever I find it in . . . [our present paper]. Thus, page 1, "scientific" can replace it. I'll knock it out in your text similarly—if present.

Feeling our way, instead of making determinations of names. When you read . . . [the present draft] you were quite enthusiastic (September) because of this change of attitude. I also thought it was a great advance. Sharp expression of it has vanished from both our present drafts; yours and mine.

What is lacking from your paper is a sharp statement that this paper is an introductory memorandum on what is to come. (I also have got away from the point.) What I dislike in my draft . . . is that it is not staccato enough. Your draft is less staccato and more ruminative on almost all matters than is mine. Now I would not be surprised if your introductory treatment was *Better Than Mine* so far as discussion orientation is concerned. But I think both drafts want to be pepped up as layouts—programs—of our project. . . .

Observation: Your further development on "observation" in your draft is very important. I have felt the lack of it, or rather the inadequacy of presentation in my draft. . . .

Regards, *Bentley*

Seattle, Washington, January 15, 1945

Dear Dewey:
. . . Yours 12-21-44 concerning "organization"—with reference to preliminary advance statement in present paper. What is to [be] included? You refer to (numbering is yours on page 1 of the letter):

1. Name-Symbol-Connection-Relation. I think name-symbol [is] now in sufficiently. Connection-relation can follow in special treatment. O.K.? (I know some of this was written by you before you had [a] full draft. This is just my check-up to get further comments, if any.)

2. Transaction. Same as preceding.

3. Affirmation-Assertion. You are far from "hipped" on this. It has top rank. But it [is] a thing we are out after, not setting out in advance. In other words, you have developed it in your *Logic*—we are now firming up organization names—I take it that the field *Specification* . . . covers the working of proposition-judgment—affirmation-assertion, and is set up to hold those processes distinct from careless language (characterizing) and symbolic specialization (definition). . . .

As I see it now, after the pending paper, I want to write three or four pages (as a try-out) on "postulation." Then this would be followed by the paper . . . where I am more and more certain that "Specification" must be the preliminary part . . . and here the development would come. Tell me if I have not yet seen all there is in this to use.

4. The suggestion of a post-naming wordless enjoyment which needs orientation to naming, just as the pre-naming knowing gets it. You are here, it seems to me, specializing the "know*ing*" as "agency": that is, legitimately under our scheme, you are specializing the organism for descriptive attention by itself. Here (legitimately) you inspect the "know*ing*" as organic, rather than (at the time) as in full transactional presentation.

On the other hand, my series takes a pre-naming sign-transaction, continues to a naming-sign transaction, and from that to mathematically-symbolic-sign transaction.

Both are legitimate. In a general way we have agreed that our transactional treatment should *precede* our agency treatment.

But it does not follow that your "agency-series" is properly omitted from our main naming list. Indeed, while I have not taken account of the stages you suggest, I have thought that "Agency" should be in our list. Probably it is not there because I did not get a good balance . . . to set down. Perhaps I can put "Agency" and "Environment" in the table, and a bit of comment in the text to carry it. Let me try it (the phrasings are not good yet):

. . . Where the organism is given specialized attention within a transactional setting—and this is always legitimate in all forms of inquiry (?) so long as it is deliberately and not confusedly undertaken —we may speak of *Behavioral Agency* with respect to *Behavioral Environment*.

. . . Behavioral Agency: To use for organic behavioral activity, somewhat in the sense of Reagent rather than of Initiator.

Behavioral Environment: The environment under interactional inquiry with respect to agency.

The above will *not* introduce your series in the treatment of the first paper, but it *will* indicate the place where it is to appear.

Let me have your impression.

. . . On "Refer," "Apply," "Name."

This also should be dealt with under Specification. . . .

Similarly, the words "Accuracy" and "Precision" can be differentiated there with respect to "Specification" and "Definition." I suspect you are right in distinguishing "reference," as perhaps applicable for "characterization" or "loose talking," from "apply" for "Specific Naming" (and whether or not "Apply" also holds for a mathematical formula put to

376

work in physics). ("Apply" seems good in both places and in a unifying way.)

I have not faced this, largely because I work under a general slogan frequently set forth by you that *all words have naming* service to perform. Thus the preposition "of" performs indicatively along its special lines as much as does "hair" or "dog" in "hair of the dog." Consequently I have postponed the naming. I doubt whether we need it in [the] opening paper. Indeed it is risky to go too far till other things work out better.

Side Remark. That *very* short paper on "Postulation" I want to draft . . . ought to be styled "Postulation For Behavioral Inquiry." It is not specially for knowing, and it certainly is not "naturalistic" in any of the popular senses (I think I told you how I wanted [at] one time to drop the word). It should contain the up-to-date essentials of your "Reflex Arc" and "Sense-Perception" papers—of the Peirce continuity and "pre-script" and time-form, and of transactional freedom, provided free durational-extensions are *required*. . . .

Yours, 12-27-44, concerning my comments, 12-21-44, on your sheets, 12-19-44, on "sign." I am like you—I cannot just see where I brought an argument or comment in. Probably, your remark that I may have been stressing the "special" procedure is correct. I use "sign" in the most general way to cover all cases that are cognitive or even have a cognitive smell. Then I use it with transactional stress throughout. This is not because I like it particularly, but in default of better wording. Then I let "sign" differentiate into "signal," "name," and "symbol." I think all I had in mind was phrasing. We both of us certainly (a) see object in use as sign, and (b) see object-identifications as themselves sign-doings. The only difference seems to be that you are a little more inclined to call the object the sign and supply for it the full transactional business as background; while I am more inclined to use "sign" as a background statement itself, so to speak.

This again is very apt to be the difference between an agency treatment and a preliminary transactional treatment. And it is not a sign of conflict, but a case of God-be-praised that we can get both points of view together, without conflict, and only with the qualification that talk-forms must be watched all the time. . . .

Regards, *Bentley*

Key West, Florida, January 15, 1945

Dear Bentley:

. . . There is only one general point I would raise: The advisability of saying a little more about the word "behavioral." Good working scientists speak of astronomical facts in terms of behavior, and it is used equally widely by physiologists, and without, as far as I can see, any objectionable implications. The point of this remark is not to object to the usage. . . . Cn the contrary, the point is to raise the question as to whether it is desirable to note its technically limited use *here*—not as a matter of principle as over against the kind of [use by] astronomers and physiologists spoken of, but as a matter of technical convenience with respect to the need for some distinctive term not injured by prior associations—as in the case, for example, as to "psychological." Of course, in another sense in full transactional consideration, physical and physiological *are* behavioral—or I have missed a point here. Not that this latter point, even if correct, needs treatment here.

Before I had read the latter portion carefully, I had thought of suggesting the desirability of saying something more along the line of my remarks on the portion previously sent you about the difference between names that are mainly indicative pointings to a range of subjectmatters under inquiry and those which mainly summarize and convey attained results. It was to some such effect as the following: Scientific knowers, when *at work*, use names in terms of (as conditioned by) the work they are doing and read the statements of work done by others in the same terms—on the same basis. This understanding demands attention to the work as a whole. The theorist, not engaged in the work, attempts to give names used meanings as if [they were] inherent in them—that is, without attention to the work that is . . . [being done]. Since this is literally impossible, it amounts practically to their translation over into another and alien work-context—that provided, namely, by traditional ontological metaphysics and/or epistemology. What we are attempting is to understand (observe), report, in terms of work-done, doing, on the *extensive* scale of knowings-known, but subjecting the latter to the same kind of observation-report the working scientist employs in a limited factual range.

After reading your paper I saw [that] this development doesn't belong in it, would weaken it by divergence. But maybe, something of this sort would fit in somewhere else. Of course, it is contained in what you have written, but it might help the readers to *tell* them [so] in so many words. Especially, in connection with such cases as the physiologist's treatment of, say, digestive processes on the basis of intra-organic events. In his *work* he takes for granted the whole transaction or business. To the reader who is not habituated to observe in terms of work-doing, the standpoint taken and things said from it readily appear to be the whole affair. . . .

Yours, *Dewey*

Dear Dewey:

. . . "Object." I have a query as to whether it would be possible to establish "Subject-Matter" in place of "Object." But I think "Object" has so much (in all philosophical use) of what we want that we can well retain it.

Specification. Yours, 9-13-44 and 9-20-44, have some remarks on bringing the distinctions out very plain. I do not know whether my latest text handles this or not. But [I] am anxious to have it appear right, and if you find uncertainty as to either definition or description still, I will be glad of suggestion.

"Symbol" and "Definition" (incidentally, yours 9-20-44, page 1, speaks of my effective statement in my letter, 9-18-44, bottom p. 1 and top p. 2). In your "Context" paper ["Context and Thought"] p. 205, you put it thus (symbols of mathematics): ". . . where the system determines the meaning of any particular symbol." What I do, on your base, is to sharpen it thus: (a) We will use symbol for just this particular type of situation and never for existence-naming; (b) in this case the particular symbol—used in system—does *not ever* "name" anything direct. I should have put the (b) before the (a) and stated this not assertively, but hypothetically. (It's your line way back yonder.) . . .

"Characterization." I take it that there is no question, but what this word stands close enough to "Characteristics" in the *Logic*, and far enough from "Characters," to be the proper word for our employment (yours 9-20-44).

"Objects." I have been avoiding citations, for if once started, there is no end. But some day, somewhere, we will want to display our past records. However, just for one right now: What do you say to putting your reservation of the name "objects" for subject-matters ordered by inquiry (*Logic*, p. 119) as footnote? . . . Anyway I have marked my copy of . . . [the present draft] for such [an] insert. . . .

Regards, *Bentley*

Dear Dewey:

. . . 1. The word "Behavior." This definitely needs the attention you suggest. Would the following footnote answer what you have in mind:

Our use of the word "behavioral" has no "behavioristic" implications. We are no more behavioristic than mentalistic, disavowing (under our procedure by hypothesis) "istics" and "isms" of all types. The word "behavior" is in frequent use by astronomers, physicists, physiologists, and ecologists, as well as by psychologists and sociologists. Applied earlier to human conduct, it has drifted along to other uses, pausing for a time among animal students, and having had much hopeful attention from mechanistic enthusiasts. It belongs rightfully, we believe, where we are placing it. Such a word as "conduct" has many more specialized implications than has "behavior," and would not serve at all well to supply the name for a great division of research. We shall be open to any substitute as work proceeds, but thus far have failed to find a more efficient word to use. In such a matter as this, long-term considerations are much more important than the verbal fashions of the decade. . . .

5. Designation. Naming. Designational. Designations as names or as nam*ings*. Now we come to the tough nut; and I certainly am glad you caught the effect.

I think I agree with everything you say—and I will go over the items one by one. But I gave a phrase-effect that looked the opposite. And it is important to deal with. I wrote:

"Designations, therefore, *are* Events. Similarly Events *are* Designations."

Now in the first sentence I am clearly thinking of the active temporal process of designating, or designation. Only in that sense are designations events, and [only then] can we speak intelligibly of *a* designation or *an* event.

In the second sentence I *almost* reached the same effect, but not quite. It is this difficulty between the thing and the action that has blocked our advance in expression from the very start—made it so that I have never been satisfied with any phrasing on the cluster Fact-Event-Designation and shouted with joy over the phrasing just quoted as an approach.

The only reason I know (or recall at the moment) for substituting "Designation" for "Name" at the start is because designation is verbal-form and name is crystallized noun-form. Until I can get "name" understood always as "naming"—"behav*ing*"—I don't dare use it. But I still have the statement such that you can smell the Name-fixity behind it, and convert designation to fit. My phrase requires it of you. The only protection I gave was comment on two meanings of "are" in the two sentences, but that was not enough. It needs more.

Incidentally, the reason for staying with the particular word "designation" is (1) that we have found no better, and (2) that it is being quite commonly used by men like Carnap, Lewis, etc., and never with any great certainty as to what they intend—always as a way of escape from some implication they want to seem to avoid, or pretend to avoid, while still sticking to their old fly-trap arrangements.

Now as to your suggestions.

Designation is (to me, as to you) definitely wider than Specification. It covers also "indication" (I quote you and agree). That is its value. It fits for both Characterization and Specification (in our table); it

380

excludes (under our layout) symbol and definition; it leaves the place open (as we do and intend) for aesthetic, imperative, etc., language.

I would say, not that names designate, but that namings designate, characterize, specify, etc. (if we make further differentiations), and that naming-behaviors are therefore designatory, designational, behaviors— or in short (as behaviors) they are *Designations*. . . .

The word "Event" involves in any normal use the extensional and the durational. The word "Designation" for our purposes *must* likewise be taken so. The Designation we discuss is not a designation taken as *a* sound or *a* mark and applied *as* a name *to* an event. Instead of this, it is the action, the activity, the *behavioral* activity, of naming through which event enters as knowledge, or Fact; it is the identifying aspect that yields the identified aspect in the full process of identification-through-name-using. Wherever "designations" are directly spoken of . . . activities, not the dropping of activity, are indicated. . . .

Regards, *Bentley*

[Key West, Florida,] January 22, 1945

[To Bentley:]

. . . If I diverge from you on any fairly basic point, it is that you seem to me at times to make the cognitive swallow up everything. I just can't. I'm willing to admit a cognitive aspect to the amoeba's behavior in, say, deglutition, but I can't see swallowing, absorbing, and digestion as itself an instance of knowing. I don't think appreciative enjoyment of a poem or a painting is a case of knowings, though it can't exist without a cognitive aspect. But phasically (not aspectually) speaking, it is postcognitive—and so is the absorption of knowledge into functions of behavior that are habitual—till challenged. . . .

I think an effective treatment of "specification" will solve most of the "proposition-term" perplexities. I think it possible [that] only incidental attention may be needed. I personally should identify "terms" with names which have been scientifically determined—which are in an extensive system, and have their force, meaning, determined by that fact —like the terms of a contract or other legal transaction—conditions which are specified with technical accuracy; that, as far as possible, point and lead in one behavioral direction only. This may look again as if I were limiting statement to agency alone, but I doubt if it works out that way. . . .

I agree that "object" can be used safely, if carefully specified; "subject-matter" is an excellent noncommittal word and should, I think, be kept for use when detailed specification is not in place.

I don't seem to be altogether clear on the subject of behavioral-agency-object. If "Behavior" is our most extensive descriptive word, what other kind of agency or object is there? I have become aware of difficulties or dangers in [the] word "environment" as getting us away from trans-actional into interactional [phrasing], and perhaps behavioral objects is a protection. If I recall aright, French physiologists have used "medium" where English writers usually say "environment."

[*Dewey*]

Key West, Florida, January 22, 1945

[To Bentley:]

Referring to yours of 1-13-45. 1. As far as anything I have written indicates or even suggests that knowledge is set over against the "sub-jects it is about or is contrasted with the things it is concerned with," it is, of course, cockeyed—so cockeyed that I was surprised that even in my loosest writing I had fallen into it. So I looked up my passages and was relieved to find that, context taken into consideration, I hadn't been guilty. Doubtless, the wording can be improved so that a reader won't get that impression, but I think the meaning is fairly obvious—namely, that a *theory* about *knowledge* can be and should be framed by exactly the same kind of study of something there for observation as has ad-vanced special knowledges in chemistry, astronomy, physiology, etc. (I used the plural word, and, as far as I can see, the only contrast is between study of knowledge as itself a fact of an extensive or general kind, lead-ing to a theory about it based on observation, and study—knowledges of —the *special* facts known.) I think the point is so fundamental [that] it should be made—or else I have failed to see what it is we are trying to do. But, of course, the wording should be protected from any suggestion that in these latter cases there is any contrast of knowledge and what it is concerned with. I don't set "knowledge" over against what it is con-cerned with. (I don't find the word "subjects" in my text, but am point-ing out that while there is a difference between study of knowledge to frame a general theory and study of physical, astronomical, physiological fact to frame a theory about them, the method pursued must be the same in both instances.)

The objection to "introspection" and "operational," I don't get—"intro-spection" is definitely ruled out as tenably observational. Bridgman may have misused the word [operational], though to my mind he made an advance, but if we don't use any words that someone has misused, we won't have any words at all. . . .

Yours of 1-14-45. I had thought it possible to use "existences" loosely and vaguely till we got around to it, just as I would use "things"—but you [are] probably right, it may mislead. "Senses." I don't get the force of your objection, but I am not wedded to it. It seems to me a safer word on the whole than "meaning"—more idiomatic and less mentalistic, as

382

"There is sound sense in what has been said"; "It just doesn't make sense" —sense as sensations is a degenerate, non-idiomatic usage.

I agree with you—my paper isn't staccato enough. That is one reason I . . . prefer yours.

I, too, like an amplification, along the line of my remarks about "observation," but probably it should come in later—without some protection, it is much more subject to distortion, I think, than is "sense." Same for "fact"—better [for a] later paper.

Yours of 1-15-45. I am not at all sure that it is necessary to say anything at all about "affirmation-assertion"—unless in some place where it is advisable to distinguish between [what] is *deliberately* taken tentatively and what is taken as (at the time-place) relatively settled or determinate—enough so for use as dependable, though "tentative" in the *whole* knowns-knowings business. Because of the state of logical literature when I wrote the *Logic*, it seemed advisable then to make considerable of it. . . . But I'm like a snake in one thing—I rather enjoy shedding old skins.

[*Dewey*]

Seattle, Washington, January 26, 1945

Dear Dewey:
. . . I certainly tend to throw the phrasing into an all-cognitive form —upon which I should be stopped every time. But certainly I don't think of digestion as "cognitive." . . . (So far as one wants to apply "cognitive" to sign-process as distinct from physiological process, it is O.K. with me—or O.K. not to.) Now Sign-Process is a process of the going-living-breathing-feeling-stinking-and-whatsoever animal. I am inclined to hold that a lot of the "feel" can be physiologically studied, and that where you have it otherwise (say, in ordinary use of "emotion" as different from "feeling") the distinctive mark is sign-inclusion. . . . I specialize my work on this signing. You have equally much on the cuff for the "enjoyment-possession" end. You mention it. . . . And I am sure I will go as far as you want in expelling the "cognitive fallacy."

"Behavioral Agency" and "Behavioral Object." . . . Darn if I know whether "Agency" is best word. Also when you ask "What other kind of agency is there than 'behavioral,' " I can't answer. The history of the word is this: You suggested "agency" in the sense of "reagent" within a situation—quite early in our procedures. Now I cannot justify putting the "behavioral" before the "agent" and certainly not in putting it before the "object." "Behavioral object" was used, I think by Mead. . . . But that meant a tentative selection of behavioral quality in objects. We have generalized that. You are certainly right. "Behavioral object" says no more than "object." Probably "behavioral agency" says no more than "agency." I howl when people say "whole organism." I should howl here too. . . .

Passing far beyond the soul-mind-brain series, we have such words as "person," "individual"—*der Einzige* [*Einzelne*]. We want a phrasing that can be maintained in the clear. Of course, it may be possible to hold "Person" to this use. . . .

We have the following: To explain gravitation we have to have different objects (particles) in a system of organization.

To explain heredity, we have to put it in a setting of organism-and-environment-as-situation before we get results—even though the present stage of work is in terms of the organism-*qua*-separate.

To explain behaviors (1) the old scheme is to individualize them in a special companionate mind beside organism. (2) Our scheme is to pass over to transactional statement as primary in this region.

To explain knowledge behaviors (3) we are in effect saying that these are the extreme cases in which the fullest transactional (fused) view is essential (instead of being the case, as epistemologies and logics assume, where individuality is the sharpest, and the individual form of decision (thus, Kaufmann's rules, Lewis' meanings) is dominant.

Now, however, every transactional statement, after it has set the "key," so to speak, needs to be broken down in all sorts of ways for inquiry. This is legitimate and essential—to be taken for granted.

Here you and I have different trends of study (not differences in set-up, but in specialization):

(1) I tend to hold that, for very large numbers of "social" things, the "cross-sectional" statement runs so far through and so deep, no "personal" statement is necessary. Thus the word "cow" as applied to "with-cow-behaviors" seems to me to need no "agency" discussion. There are, of course, differences between boy-learnings, and man-intonations and man-applications, but "things" in general are "others" rather than "sames." Point is we do not "interpret" via such differences. (I am not trying to tell you anything—I am just laying out the case for decision on a word.) . . . I would go a very long way up the scale and say that when we get the right form of statement and the right gathering of well-stated facts, we can get 99.9% of the Einstein achievement stated as a continuing variation out of Newton, the name "Einstein" being a sort of caption or key-word for the social achievement, variation, or whatever you style it.

(2) While I "tend" to go that far, I am not shutting any door to different outcomes, as to "agency," etc.

(3) Apart from that difference (cross-sectional *vs.* organism-orientation) there is a wide field of inquiry in all sorts of "personal" forms—affectional, enjoymental, clinical, maladjustments, etc. I doubt whether "Agency" is the appropriate word here. . . .

(4) We must have this naming in our scheme. We ought to have it forecast in present paper. We might just set down a space for "name needed." . . .

Sincerely, *Bentley*

Key West, Florida, February 2, 1945

Dear Bentley:

. . . I was probably wrong in thinking there is a difference as to the scope of "cognitive," though as you say, thank God, there is a difference in interest. My interest has always been in what I would now call the growing points—but just calling them that, makes an approach to your position, as it is the whole corpus or body that is growing—the cross-section on the go—while before, I think, I tended to talk as if it was just the growths that were growing. I suppose the emphasis that comes from my interest is that unless and except for the growing-points, the whole . . . thing would be dead. But if and when I tend to write as if the only living part is on the "agency" side, that is a throwback I don't want to stand for. The "organism" aspect is no more active, nor more *an* agency, than is the environmental; and even in my earlier days I always, at least for many years, held that introduction of self was superadded—[a] political-legal matter, to use large words for the simple fact of the need for locating responsibility in certain circumstances, whether for credit or the reverse. Historically, the most interesting phases to me are those in which some events are treated, whether for praise or blame, reward or punishment, as dangerous revolts or as promising innovations —generally both at once. But, of course, in the entire account, these "individual" manifestations are just as "social" in conditions and consequences as are the conformed and conforming habituations. . . .

There is a terrible exaggeration of "individual" at present, demonstrably a case of *social* pathology. But the correction lies, as far as I can see, in getting it placed in its legitimate perspective, which again has something to do with actively growing points where and when the growth involves some aspect of opposition-struggle. After all, Galileo got into trouble, and the fact that (in the whole cross-sectional business) he was simply carrying on, and the fact of "trouble," are two aspects—*qualities,* I would say, but you don't like the word very well—of the same affair.

But, as to what I call or intend by "enjoyment," or used sometimes to call "being-having," I don't have in mind anything personal or of the "agency" phase—on the contrary, "post-agencial" of the resolved, cross-sectional, easy-functioning order. But I don't think there is anything here that needs particular attention. . . .

Yours, *John Dewey*

Seattle, Washington, February 3, 1945

Dear Dewey:

I have an awfully nice comment from Kaufmann on the papers—the first comment of any kind that has come. Although he knows that this stuff strikes at his own procedural heart, he writes: "My first impression is that it is a true masterpiece of criticism. . . . I hope that the philosophers who are its targets will take it as seriously as it ought to be taken. If they will, then I shall exclaim with [Ulrich von] Hutten: *Die Geister werden wach . . . is ist eine Lust zu leben*" [cf. *Opera*, I, 217].

It struck me that it would be a fine thing to have Kaufmann read the new manuscript. It is most important to get out all phrasings that elude [us] worse than [is] necessary. . . .

Regards, *Bentley*

Seattle, Washington, February 13, 1945

Dear Dewey:

. . . I appreciate fully, as I go over this matter, the sound basis for your attitude of caution toward all the postulate groups we have had up in the past. In the matter of our special namings, we got nowhere until (last September) we suddenly saw we could take up the namings and the named tentatively in joint system. Now in the matter of postulation, similarly, I can see that the postulates must be taken up tentatively and in their "settings" (your *Logic*—as out of the subject-matter). But I think (maybe) I can best you on a generalization of this (even though I have not been living up to it). I think I have a chapter in the *Behavior, Knowledge, Fact* (a short one toward the end) [Chapter XXX] which says that every sociological job will have to be taken up duplexly—studying the scientist-in-his-setting along with, and just as fully as, the work-he-is-examining, in-its-setting.

Regards, *Bentley*

Key West, Florida, February 14, 1945

Dear Bentley:

. . . I don't know whether I ever told you that twice I have started to write a "social" interpretation on the history of philosophers—if not of philosophy. I accumulated a lot of manuscript, but it never would jell. When we get this job done, maybe I'll go back to it. . . .

In spite of the emphasis in my *Logic* on the "Inquiry Continuum," I think you are probably right about my failure in making clear "direct durational presentation"—the temporal continuum emphasized was on the procedure side rather than on that of subjectmatter. Of course the latter was implied, or else the other was nonsense, but it wasn't made explicit. . . .

I think the hitch in your statement about Logicians trying to run science was its personal form; if it had been stated in terms of a supposed necessity for foundations outside of knowns-knowings which logic had to provide, [Julius] Altman—and maybe others—would have got the point quicker. One of the difficulties [that] people have with your writings—unless I'm mistaken—is that so often you put your criticisms in personal terms, while your positive statement gives that element only an incidental place, not to be grasped save in terms of the inclusive business. Maybe I've got something here.

Regards, Dewey

Key West, Florida, February 21, 1945

Dear Bentley:

. . . I don't share your aversion to "possibility," though it is more ideational [and] less behavioral than "potentiality." But in this case I think it could well be replaced by some expression that involves on-going movement—that would line up definitely with the durational and make it clear that duration involves the future as well as [the] past. . . . I want to say something about "Experience" especially—I've used it so much and often that I don't want to leave the impression that I have gone back on what I used the word to stand for, for as I used it, it came nearer to the unity of knowns-knowings and [the] transactional than anything [else] I've written, to my mind. It also has the advantage of being inclusive of non-cognitive behavior and giving the ground for linking up the cognitive with the non-cognitive. This doesn't mean that I want to go on using the word, but simply that I now think it is possible to cover the things I used the word to designate by expressions which aren't as open to misunderstanding as is the *word* "experience." But historically the word has never had the exclusive mentalist meaning it seems to have taken on with psychologists. Peirce, somewhere [*Collected Papers*, V, 428], mentions [that] Locke, I think it was, says it would [be] a "crime" to depart from the "objective" i.e., coercive, sense the word has [cf. Locke, *An Essay Concerning Human Understanding*, Book II, Ch. I]. I think "experience" adds some distinctive traits to "behavior," of which otherwise it is a synonym.

There is no doubt you are right in feeling that we are leaving out lots of good stuff, but it isn't as if we weren't going to have a chance to write more in the future.

Yours, Dewey

Dear Dewey:

. . . I am finding it takes quite a bit of time to sort and sift all these postulations. . . . We have gradually tossed out all my more extreme phrasings about the absurdity of saying one knows something more than (deeper than, foundation for) that which "is known." However, I am not so sure but what rash words are best.

The same thing applies to this matter of hard-words and sharp analysis of logics, etc. . . . The dilemma is that if we handle the specimens by name, we seem to be making personal attacks; if we don't use names, we slither off into the meaningless regions of our current philosophizers, slippery-mouthed and slippery-eared. I think we get nowhere faster this latter way than the former. *Teste:* the conversion of pragmatism into solipsistic opinions, and the steady distortion of your views in such cases as Mackay and others. . . . I hold you should take the text "as is" and go to it. You can't do this latter without naming the villain. . . . You soft-soap the understanding away; and I holler it away. At least those are two typical procedures. I bet on mine. Nobody loves me, but that does not seem to make me any the less happy—considering the kind of lovers in sight. A case like Kaufmann's is rare. I never hit anyone harder or more continuously than I have been hitting him. He knows why, and likes it. . . .

Regards, *Bentley*

Key West, Florida, February 25, 1945

Dear Bentley:

. . . I might find objections to your "soft-soap" characterization, but as I know what you mean and recognize its aspect of correctness, I won't. I do stick by the general proposition that controversial criticism, to be effective, must take account of the reasons why the man takes the position he does take. Of course, the exceptions are in the case where the man just isn't honest or says what he says because of jealousy—a not uncommon academic trait. . . .

Maybe we should have a postulate to cover . . . an aspect of proceeding according to self-corrective, self-testing, self-developing, scientific procedure. I didn't get things any too straight in the *Logic* by what I called the autonomy of logic, [but it] was certainly headed in "our" direction of movement.

To back a little. I think there is some medium between hard and soft words. If you hit a man hard enough with stones, you knock him down and out, in addition to making him sore. If you just throw hard words at him, you are likely to make him so sore that he has no interest in understanding—but only to hit back. This may seem like a plea for being mealy-mouthed. But I don't think it is. As I've said before, I learned by years of teaching how difficult and slow is the process of getting one to understand when understanding involves any change in a man's previous set of working beliefs or ideas. Forthright and direct statements by all means in setting forth your own position; the more so, the better. But criticisms of another man's views—save when he is dishonest—demand a certain amount of strategy of approach. Of course you have cases . . . on your side. . . . But there are other cases of men that began with a highly antagonistic attitude that were brought to understand, and so to accept. I have no objections to the way you handled Morris in the articles published; he was shilly-shallying about, playing both ends against the middle, and that sort of thing should be pointed out. But well established—I don't mean well-founded—historic positions need another kind of criticism, one that can point out why they came to be. After all, the case isn't one of being popular or unpopular, but of getting understood. I can say for myself that I was never really happy about my position until it was violently attacked by Catholic and some other reactionary philosophers.

Yours, Dewey

Key West, Florida, March 3, 1945

Dear Bentley:

. . . Should something more be said about what *we* understand by postulates? The phrase used a little later, "attitudes of workmanship," seems to give a good point of departure. (Also, directions of organization.) . . . The semanticists, even Kaufmann in his criticisms, seem to give the word a kind of extra-worldly sacredness. Brief reference to work already done—in science—and embodied in knowings-knowns, and something about their use, or function in further knowings-knowns could be put in a few sentences and not expand [your] article much.

And something of the following sort may be inserted somewhere: We believe that a sufficiently large number of workers are actually employing, without formal notification, such postulates as we list, so that explicit statement of them may procure cooperation in bettering the formulation we are attempting, [and] thereby [may] clarify an important subject now confused by introduction of material not derived from later work done or now in process. . . . I think a specific reference to one form of so-called "behaviorism" might help. Watson is now himself pretty well out of the picture, but many persons still identify . . . behavior with Watsonian treatment. . . . But Watson's isolation of language—naming as physiological processes of vocal organs—is a fine ex-

389

ample of the grossest kind of neglect of the transactional. He didn't even get as far as environmental *inter*-action. . . .

Regards, *Dewey*

Key West, Florida, March 7, 1945

Dear Bentley:

. . . There are three current meanings [of "Definition"], and confusion results from failure to mark them out and off.

1. There is the meaning appropriate to mathematical subjectmatter; and it is this meaning to which we shall strictly reserve the word. (Looking over my *Logic*, I was rather pleased to find the following— p. 47: "The elements [of mathematical subjectmatter] are what they are *defined* to be; constituted by definition and nothing but definition" [Dewey's brackets]—the entire passage shows I hadn't got the whole affair straight, but at least I was moving in the right direction.)

2. There are descriptions of ordinary sociocultural usage in a given language—of which dictionary "definitions" are representative. They set forth or give an account of common, customary modes of speech, but are not in any logical sense "definitions."

3. There are *delimitations* characteristic of scientific procedure; e.g., atom, electron, water, iron, combustion, have meanings delimited by their efficacy in respect to precision and breadth (scope, "comprehension") in conduct of systematic inquiry. They set forth or describe a certain kind of usage, but are marked off from the kind of description of "2" by the restriction just indicated. (Historically, traditionally, and etymologically, "definition" and "delimitation" are identical.) This identification was proper in Aristotelian cosmology of "forms, essences, genera, and species" in which geometrical (Euclidean) and arithmetical terms and propositions were regarded as directly descriptive of physical subjectmatter. The change in both physical and mathematical present-day science renders the identification not only inappropriate, but a constant source of confusion and incoherent treatment.

The first point—mathematical definition—needs development, and the other points are rough indications. . . .

Yours, with regards, *John Dewey*

Key West, Florida, March 9, 1945

Dear Bentley:

. . . As to "circularity," I think it is striking example of Kaufmann's inability to get the point—combined probably with a subconscious recognition that if he did, it would wreck his whole scheme. If anything, I would be in favor of expansion of the point. Kaufmann never says anything, as far as I know, about what I called in my *Logic* the "autonomy of logic," because of the autonomy of inquiry when it *is* "inquiry" and not an exposition of ready-made notions. This "autonomy" business— the fact, not the word—is where I came nearest to your position—at least I imagine so. . . .

Yours, Dewey

Key West, Florida, March 18, 1945

Dear Bentley:
   You will have got a copy of Kaufmann's reply to me. You were right in thinking that he was intending to amend my position by putting in something I had failed to note or gone wrong on. However, I'm far from sorry that I took the tack I did in my letter; at least he has committed himself definitely as to what he doesn't mean. As far as his statement of what he takes to be my position is concerned, I think his reference to my supposed theory of *justified* and *unjustified* doubt, and the consequent need of criteria and rules, gives the clue. In general, as I now see it, the difference between us springs from the fact that he thinks that there are *antecedent* conditions and rules, and his "methodology" takes account of them, while, of course, I hold that it is a matter of what takes place in ongoing, continued inquiry and its consequences. His body of "established knowledge" seems to be established beyond peradventure. . . .
   I'll have to postpone writing you about the "definition-delimitation" matter. I wasn't proposing a substitute of "specification," though probably I would have written more clearly if I had "specified" the connection of what I said with "specification," and, possibly, with "characterization." But I was thinking simply of the special paper on words and not of any more inclusive application. What I was trying to point out was simply that "scientific definitions" are descriptions of usage, but of a specialized technical usage by which they—the descriptions—are differentiated from descriptions of ordinary popular "common-sense" usage, while both are differentiated from the strict or mathematical definitions. . . .

Yours, as ever with regards, Dewey

Key West, Florida, March 22, 1945

Dear Bentley:
   No, I didn't intend to substitute "delimitation" for "specification." As I indicated the other day, the "context" in which I wrote wasn't . . . [that] in which we try to set forth our own position, but that in which we list various words in common use—common, that is, in philosophical discussions—and make some critical comment on them. Of course, this

involves reference to our own usage, but I failed to bring that out because I was thinking exclusively of ambiguities in usage, and I used "delimitation" as a word for one of the usages of "definition" that fostered confusion. It would be well, of course, to include in whatever is said, if it is judged well to say anything about that matter, that because of ambiguities, we avoid the word "definition" and use "specification"—and what you say in your letter about scientific specifications and "developed scientific naming procedures, elastic, flexible, powerful, with margins of Bridgman haze," might well be inserted.

As to dictionary "definitions," what I had in mind was that they are "descriptions" of usage, and that the sociocultural usages that are described are of all grades from primitive to those developed under sociocultural conditions which are themselves of advanced (or scientific) development. Thus a good dictionary might under "atom," say, have "jet," "mite," a small supposed elementary bit of anything, the Newtonian usage, i.e., *particle* as he "defines" it; and, if the dictionary is up to date, indications of present tendencies in scientific usage. It is quite likely that "characterization" is synonymous. But I had in mind also something looser and more primitive; Newton's "definition" is undoubtedly an attempt at characterization. The more primitive specimens are characterizations in *effect*, but it doesn't seem likely to me that they were such in *intent*. Which only means that my own feeling about "characterization" is of something more elaborated, more specifically "intellectual." There are some cases of what I called "dictionary definitions," meaning by that literally what one finds when one looks up a word in a dictionary. . . . However, this isn't what I was after in what I wrote; but simply to point out that while it is important to know about the usages of specified words, past and present, they *aren't* definitions. (Aristotle's definitions, to which I gave the name "delimitations," were in fact somewhat elaborated sophisticated characterizations.) My failure to employ "specification" more freely was not intentional; it was one of my oversights; I took for granted what you said [without] fully taking it *in*. I certainly didn't intend to substitute "delimitation" for it. I used that word simply to tell what I thought a lot of philosophers were actually at—the close resemblance of definition to making a "meaning" definite—and the *etymological* common reference of "finite" and "limited." I agree that it would be well, without making too much of a fuss about it, for us to use "precision" in connection with symbols and "accuracy" in the case of other names. (By not making a fuss about it, I mean not insisting that it, the words, have been used or must be used that way, but that there is a distinction that has to be observed, and we use these words so as to name that distinction.) . . . A scientific name (e.g., atom) is developed with respect to accuracy in specification

392

of both particularity and extent. (It is probable that in ordinary usage, specification is . . . loaded on the side of what in the above sentence is called "particularity." I think scope, range, extent, is also specified in a scientific name.) . . .

[Dewey]

Paoli, Indiana, March 22, 1945

Dear Dewey:

Kaufmann seeks Rules that Rule. You seek Rules that Belong. You politely identify Kaufmann as belonging in your general field, and push the issue on a technical matter. I hope this is the way to do it. . . . As I see it, Kaufmann gives lip-service to your naturalism. Deeply, how-ever—so deeply he does not know it himself, and cannot even recognize a question about it—he is made of *Geist-Seele-Vernunft-Verstand.* . . .

There is one word you use ("consistent") as applying in a physical region. Although I forget it often, I am sure, if we separate the existen-tial from the symbolic as we do, we must have two words. If we use "consistency" for the symbol region, we must have another for the existential—where I have occasionally inserted "coherence."

Regards, Bentley

Paoli, Indiana, March 24, 1945

Dear Dewey:

Here is a little memorandum making possibly more explicit some-thing we are always trying to get said in sharp form.

Three manners of Application of the Word "Exist."

1. Practical. In cases in which the act of knowing is closely de-limited, as to start and finish (as my own known-knowing), to the validly assumed presence of the object in substance, heart, or core, substantial, about-so, *prior* to the beginning of the now-knowing act.

2. For any Natural Theory of Knowledge. Allotting a longer dura-tional sweep-cultural, rather than "now": to whatever is known, or within knowledge, ranging from the firm factual cases to the crudely and vaguely named cases, through possibilities and probabilities, and allowing for dropping out of used-up namings, as centaur, to be replaced by horse-man. This being the region of our attempt at firm naming.

3. Ontological or Metaphysical. Superior to durational scope: so that [something is] said to be known to exist apart from its being known. . . .

Regards, Bentley

Dear Bentley:

. . . Your remark about the transaction[al] character of "shadow" as "signal" should go into the text. I think it could be shown that Designation-naming in idiomatic (practical) procedure is also transactional, but not having the benefit (as far as it is recognized as a stage) of the procedures marking off scientific naming designations. The out-of-line bulge (the total departure from developmental locus) is the product of sophisticated philosophical treatment that gave practical conversational (communicative) procedures an ontological meaning. I've tried to show this in the case of "substance" (nouns as substantives) in the *Logic*, pp. 127 [*et*] *seq.*, though the treatment there is more technically "logical" —in terms of subject-predicate—than anything we need. So the *gist* of the matter became an ontological *essence*.

I imagine the whole matter could be best covered by a short paragraph on *objects*, their practical communicative reference being to distinctions-identifications previously made out and later taken for granted as there in common to speaker and speakee, and then ontologized per Aristotle . . . [*et al.*], as is conveyed, perhaps by the statement on top of p. 128 [*Logic* which] may be simplified: An object "is a union of connected distinctions such that it may be acted with (*not* "upon" as in the text) a whole," * with the further qualification that it develops as further transactions produce more distinctions—which, of course, an ontological object can't do. I am not suggesting this as a model to follow, but as indication of what I mean concerning the side-tracking of the developmental procedure of transactions by irrelevant ontologizing. . . .

When Aristotle is placed in the historical context of [the] Sophists-Socrates-Plato, it is clear (to me, anyway) that "object" as substance was simply that which had to be the same for the different parties in a communication if the latter were to understand one another and "really" communicate instead of just appearing to do so. . . .

The "conventional" you mention is of two kinds—there is the conventionalized reference in the sense of what is in common use and hence is common to and understood by the members of a given intercommunicating group, and there is the further ontological standardization of this cultural convention in usage of words—which itself gets into common speech as a super-convention.

Yours, with best regards, *Dewey*

---

* The exact quotation is: "an object . . . is a union of connected distinctions so held together that it may be acted upon or with as a whole." (Eds.)

Paoli, Indiana, March 25, 1945

Dear Dewey:

[Kantor: *Psychology and Logic,* Vol. I] is difficult to pin down at any point, and does not anywhere develop positively. Nevertheless, I think it has a potentially fine core. I might put it this way. If your *Logic* stands as *trans*actionally cultural, the one Kantor advances would be *inter*actionally personal, such that, properly developed, it might fit in as a specialized treatment. However, the incoherences of *inter*action developed in the knowledge range are brought out by his doings more strikingly than ever. For example, he is greatly pained when he faces the possibility in *your* work that "objects are created in the act of knowing or as the result of inquiry"—but I can find a dozen passages when he has his own scheme to "create" them, and evade them, and fail[s] to develop them . . . [systematically]. The point of his construction is this:

He uses "system-building" all along as a general behavioral process of which logical work is an advanced type. In his main formulation (five types of logic) he introduces a section "Logic as the Science of Order," which apparently is system-building and means his own procedure, though he is not clear about it. He is strong, and his logic is a "specificity logic"—a long, dark way of saying he deals with logical events. In other words, he presents logical behavior as arising in a setting of sub-logical ordering and arranging behavior. That is, of course, all to the good, if properly developed and set. But he does not even clearly state what he is doing as a program. He certainly is confused as between actor and object. He is unclear about language, denying that it is essential to logic, demanding a sharp severance, yet stating that complex logical operations are impossible without it, and always more interested in keeping his skirts clear from other workers' work than in working out himself. . . .

Regards, *Bentley*

Paoli, Indiana, March 28, 1945

Dear Dewey:

. . . Take "definition." My feeling is about 90% that it ought to be used on the dictionary-fact-Aristotle-science side. At the start we couple it with "term." Under the influence of recent logical development we threw it out of that place and connected it with "symbol," and the whole mathematics-type procedure. We can cover all the in-between places with other names, but "dictionary-definition" is a sort of stumbling block, just because "definition" is used there for any kind of an account. These are what you described as "descriptions of usage."

Now, despite my feeling that "definition" most generally "ought" to

395

stay on the science-fact side, I am sure enough—satisfied—we are right in throwing it to the symbol end, for our purpose, in order to keep things clear in our work.

This leaves us to take care of (without using the word "definition") of the following: general descriptions of usage as in dictionary; main cases where the word is considered, not so much as a variety of words all with the same literal form, but rather as in each case separate, as word-hitched-to-event in a special way, and here the division between rough practical use and technical use must be set up. . . .

Regards, *Bentley*

Paoli, Indiana, March 29, 1945

Dear Dewey:

. . . I found a suggestion that the vague word "knowledge" would only get sense in a full activity-presentation. This we did not use in comment on the word in the "Terminology" paper. . . . As activity, the knowings-knowns get systematic status on both sides. Then the "inquiry" gets definite event-presentation as one phase of knowledge as knowing-known. Then also logic, if it is to be in any way naturalistic, or scientific, as specificalized inquiry into goings-on, has *got* to be a *theory of inquiry*—much as physiology is the goings-on of the living. I do not know that I have seen anybody object to your limitation of logic to inquiry—I mean, I just haven't noticed the point. However, this is precisely what Kaufmann does—wants to establish the realm of control that rules the petty waves of inquiry; while Kantor every now and then denounces the idea that logic is inquiry—this being partly to wash his hands of any idea that he might be following you. . . . If Kantor dropped his postulates of things-known existing before knowings, and product-things growing out of knowing processes (also existential)—and if he associated himself with your *Logic,* he might have something very neat to develop in his pre-logical, logical-prelinguistic, and linguistic-logical levels (that is, *if* he could demonstrate such differentiations). The point of this paragraph is not about Kantor, but that the knowledge-inquiry-logic terminology is worth development some time when it fits in.

Regards, *Bentley*

Paoli, Indiana, March 31, 1945

Dear Dewey:

What I cannot understand is why the impact of the single blunt statement about Cohen-Nagel in the "[On a Certain] Vagueness [in Logic]" paper does not blow up logic like an 11-ton town-buster. I don't mean affect the standardized academic men. . . . I do mean affect young, untutored minds. But I don't think I have a reaction of that type anywhere. It is true I held off in uncertainty for six months myself—but that was [my fear that] they might have qualifying phrases I did not observe. When satisfied they said what they said as they wanted it, then to me they were mush. (I mean that they made proposition to be something *sui generis,* and not a component of any recognized region of modern knowledge-statement, neither mental, physical, nor linguistic—*at the same time* that they said all Fact was proposition, i.e., that proposition was important.)

I am writing this because there may be some cue in such a situation as to how to proceed in further expression. . . .

Regards, *Bentley*

Key West, Florida, April 4, 1945

Dear Bentley:

. . . You hit the nail on the head. His [Kaufmann's] rules aren't regulations; if they functioned to regulate, they would be within inquiry, originating there and developing with its development.

One thing, I imagine, which confuses him is the "genetic" business. He can't understand it as a means of locating, specifying, as zoologists use biological development to distinguish and identify "species." And he keeps supposing that "validity" has to set completely apart. If he could once get the idea of a going concern, he would be able to see origin and validity as affairs of its two directions of movement—out of and into. After having being criticized for so many years for adopting James's formula about consequences as tests, [I can understand why] Kaufmann seems to ignore that old aspect. But what he doesn't get is inquiry as continually moving event, process, goings-on, or whatever. Your comparison to physiology as the goings-on of the living must be used somewhere. It's more direct into the eyes than any way I've put it.

After so many years of teaching and writing I can't share your surprise at the apparent lack of response to the "Vagueness" articles. It takes time for things to seep in, and when they have soaked in, there is usually more or less forgetfulness as to where the damn thing came from. And aside from silly pride, there is often more response than appears at first; there is a slow movement in a new direction. . . . I got one flat denial from a colleague, [William Pepperell] Montague, of logic as [the] theory of inquiry. He said it has always been regarded as the theory of proof, and I was taking liberties with the word "logic." He was too friendly to me personally to use that word, but that was his implication.*

* Montague's most extended printed critique of Dewey is in his *The Ways of Knowing,* pp. 133–72, but this 1925 analysis was not supplemented by any essay on Dewey's 1938 *Logic.* (Eds.)

397

I suppose separation of "proof" from "inquiry" is what ails Kaufmann at bottom. . . .

Yours, with regards, *Dewey*

Paoli, Indiana, April 5, 1945

Dear Dewey:

As to how we got "Specification" and "Term" connected . . . my recollection is somewhat as follows:

In earlier sketches we mostly set aside "Term" for mathematics and symbol systems. I recall your saying one time that the *only* place where "Term" has definite employment was in Aristotelian logic. (Its definite use in mathematics as component of an equation, while derived from Aristotle's use of a component of a proposition, is of a different type today—almost a settle-down resident.)

Gradually we came to feel that in this dilemma of mathematics, Aristotelian and other modern logics, and common colloquialisms, we could use "Symbol" with much greater accuracy (I mean with less chance of confusion) if we held it for mathematics. This set "Term" free. The next question was, probably: Should we keep it for the Aristotelian set-up which aimed at identification of "word" with "thing"? Or: Should we retain it for our purified (scientific) naming procedure? The answer to that (as nearly as I can reconstruct) would be that since it was so widely used, and had preferential implications and words, we had better retain it for our improved scheme.

Hence, if we accept "Specification" for the scientific process—or whatever other name we select for the process in place of "Specification"— "Term" should hold in this region. . . .

Regards, *Bentley*

Key West, Florida, April 9, 1945

Dear Bentley:

When names are listed in the paper for the sake of comment, including those we don't use, or don't use in the current fashionable way, "proposition" should be included, and the comment upon it should contain the substance of your remark in yours, 3-31-45 [cf. 11-8-44], to the effect (on the non-use side) that it is not something *sui-generis,* etc., but if used at all, must be used (just as you have it in your letter) as [a] component of a specified region of authorized knowledge statement, with a footnote reference to the "Logic Vagueness" ["On a Certain Vagueness in Logic"] papers. I don't recall any quite such neat summing up of what you were hitting at in the papers themselves—talk about neither flesh, fish, nor fowl. The younger men you speak of might have been challenged by such a statement to ask what proposition is anyway, when a whole gang are making it carry the whole load. As to finding it hard to detect, I have to admit that I didn't get the *whole* force of your criticism until I read the formulation in this letter of yours. *It* is a blockbuster, all right. It may even be well to say that at just the present juncture, the interpretation of "proposition" is so crucial a matter that readers may well be asked to stop [to] ask themselves what it is. . . .

With regards, Dewey

Paoli, Indiana, April 11, 1945

Dear Dewey:

Your mention of Montague's comment on proof and inquiry was illuminating—a real guide for direction of attention. . . .

I have suggested to Kaufmann that he make me a little set of postulatory hints, saying to him that if "apprehension of meaning" is so important, then he should at least be able to state definitely whether "apprehension of meaning" is one postulatory component; or whether "apprehension" is one, and "meaning" is another. . . .

What I stuck this sheet in the typewriter for was to ask you whether you could suggest a word that would name the *legitimate* use of de-spatialized and de-durationalized namings. For instance, I know that such words as "quality" and "abstract" have legitimate references. I know when you use them, you see them as squints at situations, but I know also your phrasing will easily slip into a form which leads many of your readers to think you are talking about what they think they are talking about, when they allot "existence" to, let us say, qualities conceived as extra-spatial and extra-temporal, alongside of the spatial and temporal "existences" they otherwise confront. My long uprising is, of course, against "concept," which I envisage clearly as linguistic behavior durational and extensional, but which most discussion assumes to "exist" somewhere on its own account, super-spatial and super-durational. . . .

This comes up in connection with the pending postulation thus: You keep calling my attention (and it is one damn good thing) to the need of holding open the scheme for full attention to behaving organisms in provisional specialized detachment from behavior-objects. All we want to do is to take the realistic edge off the person and off the environment. But we want to take this off for good, and good and plenty. Take it off, so that full statements will be in a "factual" frame (our specification of "fact"); then we want to provide for the maximum freedom of inquiry into the "person" and the "thing." This is an extreme case. Probably "space" and "time" set up as "things" is another. But the great ruck is of minor cases.

Now when I come to attempt to phrase the protective clauses or, better still, some positive assertion on the differentiating side to accompany the positive assertion on the connecting side, I find all sorts of ways to do it. There is hardly a place in the postulation where one could not plausibly stop and write in, "But, nevertheless, it is practicable, etc." This applies not only to person, but to "reals" outside of or beyond inquiry, to the use of namings in "specification," etc. These are the important stoppages, but others lie around. I have not yet found a way to work it in right.

O.K. You suggested (as to naming) primary and secondary namings, a long time back. I never get that in the text. Up to date it does not fit. The primitive naming is the very concretion or impaction we want to get rid of. Historically, our stress is secondary.

In a general way, with "specification" we control all names.

You have a developed differentiation between "that" demonstrative and another class. I can't stop to look it up now. Lies just beyond where I have worked. I see there is plenty [of] material when I get to it. But the query right now is how best to get indication in the postulation. Probably all this does is to "wise" you to a difficulty that will probably still remain when I send you [the] next manuscript. . . .

Regards, *Bentley*

Key West, Florida, April 15, 1945

Dear Bentley:

. . . There are obvious objections to our use of "common sense." But I tend to recur to the distinction between short-time span and narrow-space applications and long-time extensive ones to cover the same point— with the spectrum or haze shading from one to other, or the spectrum from immediate to highly mediated. Anyway, I think we need to protect ourselves from the charge that we say or imply that there is something inherently erroneous or false in naming used in ordinary spoken and written language. This may seem rather trivial, but the capacity for misunderstanding and distortion is almost unbounded. . . .

I wonder if it might help to indicate that reference by name to a writer is the same *sort* of thing as mentioning the date in connection with an event. Perhaps a better illustration would be the title and date of a scientific periodical along with the name of the author in the case of a scientific article. It's practically "important" for more reasons than one —including the repute or standing of the periodical and reporter and author of, say, an experiment, but the knowledge status of *subjectmatter* is something else again. Somewhere in my writings I indicated that "you" and "I," or Newton or Galileo, when used in connection with knowledge, are "moral," quasi-legal terms, having to do with such things as credit, blame, penalty, repute. I only had the point, however, on the side of the personal pronouns, not as you have it on the side of knowledge [cf. *Experience and Nature*, pp. 232 ff.]

Regards, *Dewey*

Key West, Florida, April 15, 1945

Dear Bentley:

. . . As to "quality," it's a new one on me. I had noted you didn't care for the word, but it never occurred to me that it was used as if applying to something de-spationalized [*sic*, de-extensionalized] and de-durationalized. . . . I'm sure you have reason for saying what you do, but I am not familiar with that context. "These goods have a fine quality," or "This cloth is poor quality," or "The red quality in that curtain jars with the other color-qualities of the furniture," etc., are, so to speak, spatial and durational plus—"I don't want that piece of goods"—"That color will fade too easily."

Well, after writing this, I recall that I've read, in, I think, some of the G. E. Moore–Russell crowd, a statement that "qualities" are pure "universals"—but I had always associated that with the sort of thing you attack in your ["On a Certain] Vagueness [in Logic"] papers and thought it was a kind of preciosity limited to a small group. You have in mind something more extensive, I'm sure. . . . If so, it's years since I've read any orthodox psychological literature.

I think I can say something about "abstract" as a legitimate word—in substance, something held in suspense with respect to past and habitual use in order to be applicable effectively in new factual conditions—as Newton "abstracted" the fall of an apple from apples, stones, etc. to apply it to the planets in their movements—or the economists' "fixed capital" is concrete and their other kind—financial—is abstract. In substance, concrete and abstract are paired, and if one goes, the other does too. But I don't know in what connection you feel something should be said about either quality or abstract. Abstract I can see goes with knowing in temporary disregard of the known—though actually dealing with one aspect of known fact as it operates in a specified knowledge-promotion undertaking. But hot and cold, soft and hard, don't seem to me to have that much suspension.

I am of the opinion that outside of technical psychology and philosophy, 90% of use of "concept" is legitimate, but I may be wrong. I should say it was used to designate any idea or point of view that exercises a regulative force—as a synonym, less technical and less dignified, for "category."

Yours, *Dewey*

401

Key West, Florida, April 16 (?), 1945

Dear Bentley:

You spoke . . . of my calling your attention to the need of holding the scheme open to take care of behaving in specialized detachment from behavior objects. Since I didn't do it "on purpose," it shows the more strongly where my interest has always been—at the other pole from yours, which isn't a bad thing, provided they are poles of the same globe. But what I want particularly to say is that given my angle, the way for me to avoid the kind of detachment which is fatal is to stick unwaveringly to the extensive range of "Fact." In a certain sense, there *is* provisional detachment from behavior "objects," in the proper naming of objects, but, of course, there isn't even provisional detachment from "fact." To some extent, though not explicitly enough, I saved the discussion in my *Logic* by use of the word "subjectmatter" in an inclusive way, "objects" being subjectmatter pre-determined (pre in the sense of temporarily prior) to be ready for use "as is" in further inquiry. Perhaps reference to the extensive naming effected by "fact" will serve to protect whatever is said about the legitimacy of specialized treatment of behavings. All this, of course, is covered . . . in what you say about "factual frame." But somehow it has just fully dawned on me that detachment from fact, given "fact" as the name it is, isn't even provisional in this specialized treatment.

Yours as ever, *Dewey*

Key West, Florida, April 20, 1945

Dear Bentley:

. . . My net impression [of "A Terminology for Knowings and Knowns"] is of an extraordinarily solid piece of work—the fact I've done so little of it ought to give me some right to say so. It is a substantial diet that is offered the reader and is in the main so revolutionary in the present state of the subject that even its clarity won't guarantee willingness and ability to masticate and digest it. But I'd predict that in time it will stand out as a classic; as marking a turning point, though there may be snipes and sniping like that of the one you wrote about in New York. . . .

Incidentally, your phrase "meaningful conveyance" on one of the galleys is what I intended by using the word "report" along with "description." It is, so to speak, the noise the description makes—the readings that the writings perform. . . .

Yours—with congratulations and regards, *John Dewey*

402

Dear Bentley:

. . . I looked up page 19 and page 23 in my *Logic*, and in the sense involved in those passages I certainly believed in emergings—not as a doctrine, but as a name for a fact. In the phrase, "Emergent evolution," "emergent" seems to be a doctrine and a rather absurd one. In other words, what I am trying to say is that to say that something emerges or is emergent, names a certain aspect of a certain phase of an event as durational. To speak of it as "the emergent," or probably even as "an emergent," conveys irrelevant doctrinal associations. But in any developmental event or, for that matter, in fact as durational, there must be, I should say, occurrences which would be described as emerging— whether as mutations or not being a matter of specific evidence. Or, taking a case from the account of knowings-known, doesn't it make sense to say that specifications have emerged from characterizations in the durational course? I'm not arguing here for use of the word anywhere; I don't see where it is needed, but coming-out-of, growing-out-of, arising-from, seem to me to be factual, and "emerge" a synonym. I think we share the same objection to "causation," but arising-from, coming-out-of, seem to me to be practically necessary descriptive words, at least at present. However, it is quite likely your footnote refers to some doctrinal usage of the word which (the objection) I would agree with. I think, though, that occasionally you tend to object to a word that has good idiomatic use and standing because it has been used in an objectionable doctrinal context. . . .

Yours, *Dewey*

Paoli, Indiana, April 24, 1945

Dear Dewey:

. . . "Inquiry": You know occasionally someone suggests you are not quite "sound" as to time [cf. Ernest Nagel, Review of *Time and Its Mysteries*]. I suggested caution in phrasing a while back. But think of this: Inquiry is process, process is across time. A logic of inquiry as opposed to one of proof is 100% on-going. It always comes out that way. I am reminded of your recent remark that you happened to hit on "subject-matter" and the phrasing saved your *Logic*. Quite the contrary; it takes steady pressure to get from "realms" to "subject-matters."

One thing we need is a word (probably not for official position—but just for use) such that when we use it, "duration" cannot mean just a span laid off by ticks, but certainly and always will indicate [that] the "thing" and all its "thinginess" is *a* growth—is *the* growth itself—so that no description of it as [something] apart from the extension across a bit of the ages is a description at all. In the course of time the old dead time sloughs off. I doubt whether physiologists go astray much now, no matter what term they use, or how they write—but our case is tougher. . . .

You put it that "experience adds some distinctive traits to behavior of which otherwise it is a synonym." I would put it that experience, as Event, *is* behavior of a specialized or distinctive type, and that as a "word," it names a specialized or distinctive region of behavior. That is merely a matter of phrasing, but it is a good deal like "emergence." . . .

Regards, *Bentley*

Key West, Florida, April 28, 1945

Dear Bentley:

. . . In looking up things in the *Logic*, I discovered that my treatment of *observation*, if not *all* wrong, is very defective. I limited it, under the influence of so-called psychology, to short-time span, immediate "sense" perception subjectmatter. In the "Vocabulary" ["A Terminology for Knowings and Knowns"] paper [and the "Postulations" paper] I'd like to put in a footnote with my initials calling attention to my error. . . . [See *Knowing and the Known,* pp. 96–97, n. 11.]

Yours, with best regards, *John Dewey*

Paoli, Indiana, May 1, 1945

Dear Dewey:

. . . Your 4-15 with remarks on "quality." Your illustrations are O.K. They all illustrate action of behavior. But you don't mean to say, I suspect, that when the rank-and-file philosopher discusses qualities in objects, he is talking our transactional language and never means anything but behavior. My guess would be that when "quality" . . . [is] mentioned in *Journal of Philosophy* articles, it always means some mysterious property of an object, requiring erudite philological vocabularies to manipulate. And, I note that in the passage, top p. 128, *Logic,* about "object" to which you referred a while back . . . you wrote: "capable of becoming a unity of interconnected distinctions, or 'properties.'" *
In other words *you* put "properties" in quotation marks in the text to indicate you did not hold to the common use of the word. This, as transferred to "quality," is all I mean. I don't think these words are safe to use. If we distinguish a legitimate ribbon-counter use of "quality"—and a weird B. Russell "pure universal" use—is not the ordinary philosophical use definitely on the bad side?

---

* The exact quotation is "capable of incorporating into itself other predicated qualifications until it becomes, as such, a unity of inter-connected distinctions, or 'properties.'" (Eds.)

"Concept." You say probably 90% of the general use of the word is legitimate. Maybe. I would say "indifferent." (1) I have never objected (in any careful statement) to the everyday dog-in-the-street uses. (2) I have never objected to anybody who will come out flat and say that a mental item exists to be called a "concept." That is his business. But (3) I have objected to all the heavy discussion using "concept" pontifically as if something were being said. And (4) my main howl has been to try to get people to tell me specifically *what* they are talking about—where and what is the referent—when they say "concept." It is this question that drives them wild. And *you* don't tell me a thing when you say it is "an idea or point of view that exercises a regulative force." "Idea" is merely a substitute term, and I don't think you would go far developing it on its own, instead of merely using it as casual phrasing. "Point of view" is fine, if developed, but I doubt [that] development would show it as a "thing called concept." The other words "exercise," "regulative," and "force," are just what need explaining—in the sense of more thorough description. This is just a little defense of my idiosyncrasy on the side. . . .

About the words "physical" and "psychological." In the paper now in type we have discarded "psychological" (for our specific uses) and substituted "behavioral" as much more readily transactional. In the same paper, "physical" is set up as differentiation of subject-matter. Both subject-matter differentiations. "Physical" assumed as possible viewpoint for "all" (as we can get at it now) cosmos. . . . But that leaves "behavioral" (1) as specialized physiological, and (2) as providing the naming-knowing system by which physical and behavioral themselves are differentiated in knowledge—i.e., in *all* we have got about Old Man Cosmos. You ask about further bring[ing] them in? Any time you see a place. Certainly in the "sign-behavior" paper. (And I feel a pang at having passed over [the] chance to cite "experience" in the paper now in press.) . . .

Regards, Bentley

Paoli, Indiana, May 3, 1945

Dear Dewey:
. . . Altman had a long discussion with Kaufmann a couple [of] weeks ago. He seems to have hopes that we will get somewhere. I don't see why. Here are a few points:

Kaufmann has a basic relation between autonomy of discourse and apprehension of meaning—here one should force the issue with him.

Kaufmann, when pressed, admits his assertions about "apprehension of meanings" are not "factual," but no urging would get him to say *what* they are if not factual. Except, perhaps, that: since description presupposes apprehension of meanings, no description of meanings themselves would be adequate.

Altman told Kaufmann that he confused two issues: (a) the need of meaning in a particular description; (b) the general locus of meanings. Said he must answer as to the latter.

Altman asked Kaufmann how the issue between your type of autonomy and Kaufmann's type would be settled, if factual determination would not do it. He got no answer.

Kaufmann said if discourse (logic and mathematics) was not analyzed in its own terms, such difficulties arose as were to be seen in your *Logic:* namely, nominalistic view of universals; failure to recognize "clarification" as mental function; insufficient attention to postulation and consistency. (Altman said to Kaufmann: are they not pressing the issue of postulation all the time and you avoiding it for your own case?) . . .

Regards, *Bentley*

New York, May 5, 1945

Dear Bentley:

. . . We have never, as far as I remember, said anything about "idea" as a name or a word. It may turn out difficult to say anything about "conception" without bringing in "idea." On the other hand, it may be that any reference to it actually gets us involved in the whole matter of a behavioral interpretation of "psychological" terminology—which is a good job to be done but not as part of present series. . . .

Yours, *John Dewey*

[P.S.] I have a long letter from Kaufmann. . . . For the first time I tried to indicate the difference between "doubt" as "pathological" and as "unjustified"—he makes me out as implying that I mean it proceeds from a person who is pathological—in general.

I ought to have asked him what in hell he means by "justified and unjustified" doubts, and will when I write him. It's not so important as yours about "apprehension of meaning," but it is psychologically important as an indication of his state of muddled opinion.

[New York,] May 6, 1945

[To Bentley:]

. . . I imagine Kaufmann may have some provocation, but I hope not justification, for his interpretation of my *Logic* in my treatment that suggests inquiry as consisting of a set or series of acts occurring at different times. It occurred to me that instead of seeing that what I called "resolution of an indeterminate situation" describes *inquiry*, he thought I meant that some independent act brings about that resolution; I think if I were writing the book now, I could protect it from that kind of interpretation.

. . . We certainly meant to say, firmly, that as far as Knowings-knowns are concerned, the transactional is primary and inclusive, and that any "interactional" treatments are developmental analyses of a transaction. But [how] to word it?

Your final "comment" *re* non-observable. Somehow the point could be made, I think, in connection with the durational—i.e., non-observ*ed* and possibly lacking proper techniques for observation at a certain specifiable ("highly localized") date—but never *intrinsically* non-observable.

Re yours of 5-1-45. . . . I don't know whether anything needs to be said about "quality." I suppose I have got so habituated to identifying it with hot, dry, soft, angry, etc., that except in extreme cases—like Russell and some of the English Moore group—it doesn't occur to me that even philosophers use it any other way.

"Concept." I think I wrote that if we deal with conception, we have to say something about "idea." In my casual description, of course, "force" has to be replaced. "Exercise" and "regulative" seem to me fairly everyday terms; the burden falls on "idea." Query: Do we have to say anything about "conceptions"? Perhaps, a note somewhere objecting to the mentaloid and mentalistic usage—which I still think is confined mostly to psychologists, even philosophers mostly use it in a logical sense—as a somewhat weakened expression for a principle. Of course you are entitled to ask what "principle" is. The whole business seems to me to find its best place in a special treatment, giving a behavioral account of a number of "psychological" terms. The need for a "more definite statement" is undoubted, but I should say it belongs in such a paper—and probably in your suggested paper, on the critical side of your proposed paper on other writers' postulates. . . .

There is no difference between us as to "emergence," I think. It's one thing to note it as factual, and another thing to make a "category" or a conception "exercising regulative determination" out of it. . . .

Yours, *Dewey*

[P.S.] I've read so little in the last few years that just now I can't add to the list of authors whose postulates should be discussed, unless it is B. Russell—though he has changed so many times [that] a book representative of one period would have to be selected and dated, probably. . . . The book to select is the one that is most completely "atomistic," old model, in which he says an ideal language would have a separate name for [every] single existence. I've forgotten the title; will try and look it up.* He might be combined—as far as [the] article is concerned—with G. E. Moore. The latter's basic postulate is naïvely stated in his autobiographical article ["An Autobiography"] in the book [Schilpp, ed., *The Philosophy of G. E. Moore*] on him. "I do not think that the world or the sciences would ever have suggested to me any philosophical problems. What has suggested philosophical problems to me is things which other philosophers have said about the world or about the sciences." † (p. 14)

I don't know how you plan to go about it, but in Russell's case, at least, it might be done by a set of numbered, quoted extracts—of course, that method might raise the question of the justness of the selections— but so would any other kind of statement.

[New York,] May 7, 1945

[To Bentley:]

. . . *Re* "Observation." I've done a little reading of my *Logic,* and am more convinced than before that I slipped up rather badly, e.g., pp. 108–110, though I still believe or hope that there was a genuine point behind. I use it as if the word applied exclusively to short-span, temporally and spatially narrow ranges of observation—through *immediate* involvement of eyes, ears, hands, etc., what is traditionally called "sense-perception"—though in one of my books [*Art as Experience*] I had objected definitely to similar limitation of "perception." But even in the passage mentioned, I say, p. 110, "To 'look at an idea' is not a mere literary figure of speech." On p. 231, in speaking about data of historical knowns, I guard the statement by the phrase "what can be *contemporaneously* observed [italics added here by Dewey]," and on p. 67, I speak of "focal" observation. The underlying point is that these direct seeings, hearings, touchings, are what serve to locate the problem of given inquiries and to test proposed or hypothetical solutions, and are accordingly distinguished as to their use or function from the observations that remark, note, take into account, heed, the system of fact with which the narrower observations are connected, and through which they derive their "significance" or importance. The same thing in general holds of what I called (doubtless, in a way that facilitated misunderstanding) "perceptual and conceptual objects," distinguished in the theory of "judgment," but also correlated or conjugally connected. All this, on my part, is a product of my long study of historic facts in the theory of knowing— especially, probably, the Kantian analysis. As far as I am concerned, it

* B. Russell: ["The Philosophy of Logical Atomism," in four parts]. [Part 1] reprinted in *Contemporary British Philosophy,* 1924.

† The exact quotation would be: ". . . philosophers have said about the world or the sciences." (Eds.)

was necessary as a bridge—thanks mainly to you, I've now walked across the bridge and wouldn't need it—save in footnote . . . reference to cultural history. But it still affects without doubt the feeling that in spite of the abuse of the word, there is [a] legitimate place for the word "conceptual," to describe one phase of observation—the kind of behavior with respect to long-run observation you and I are now engaged in, in distinction of "contemporaneous," "focal" observation of, say, my typewriter and the marks on this page. Not merely historically, but in view of the current state of beliefs, it seems still important to call attention to the functioning distinction and connection of the two sorts of observation—there is still too damn much "empiricism" on one side and "rationalism" on the other—not just in philosophy, which wouldn't be so important—but look at most any newspaper, with the split between the "news" columns and the editorial columns for illustration—the split between more or less isolated short-span and local items (which describe at their height what is "sensational") and the attempt at equally isolated contextual identifications. There isn't a schoolroom in the country that isn't marked by a similar split. Well, so much *apologia pro mea vita*. . . .

Yours, as ever, *Dewey*

Paoli, Indiana, May 8, 1945

Dear Dewey:

. . . Query. Will the following develop usably? Or, what does it need to make it usable?

We are used to sizing up a thing-across-space as "one thing." Thus a dog in a region a foot long and six inches wide, etc., is "a dog" or "one dog."

We are not so well used to holding one thing together as one thing in time—across time—its durance. Thus, puppy to dog. Thus an iron bar may be said to be the same thing a year from today as today. This says that what was one thing in space today, will be one thing (the same one in space) a year from today, but does not say that there is cross-time-change-one-ness in the sense we admit cross-space-one-ness.

When it comes to egg-into-hen or gene-into-egg-into-hen, we do not use a one-ness at all.

When it comes to cultural one-ness—as of a word across a century—we lack a constructional-naming for it. In other words, the ethnologies and sociologies present it, but their formulations about it are circuitously phrased, and direct statement about it lacks direct words to use.

This is getting our general time expressions down to the concrete. In such gettings-down one may easily go wrong—say things, not as he wants to say them or likes as he inspects later on.

In a general way, lack of getting-down is why "situation" and "inquiry" in your development get continually distorted and misunderstood by Mackay, Kaufmann, etc.

Which is why I put the Query: Just how can we make a usable comparison between thing-across-space and thing-across-time?

Regards, *Bentley*

Paoli, Indiana, May 9, 1945

Dear Dewey:

. . . My only question is as to the value of this word "conception." One fault is that it is mis-read everywhere in the same way Kaufmann mis-reads "justify" and "doubt" in your text. . . . I say (1) we have observation and language—in our range—knit together; (2) this particular "conceptual" we use is on the linguistic side; then (3) why not build it up as the linguistic function? (I always recall how Bridgman [in *The*] *Nature of Physical Theory*, who is vehemently "subjective," describes thought and language separately a few pages apart, but with almost identical phrasings. He makes them *do* the same things, but is appalled to think of them *being* the same.) However, this is on the side. This thing will work out as we proceed—to good expression, I am sure.

Regards, *Bentley*

[New York,] May 9, 1945

[To Bentley:]

. . . The kind of *behaviorism* we repudiate . . . is suggested by the footnote reference to Watson [in "Postulations"], but [it] might be explicitly said. A paper Clarence Ayres sent me ["The Ordeal of the Social Sciences"] quotes from . . . [F. A.] Hayek: "The whole question [that of the social sciences] is nothing else than whether the social sciences could possibly discuss the kind of problems with which they are concerned in purely behavioristic terms—or even whether consistent behaviorism is possible," adding in explanation that "while at the world of nature (!) we look from the outside, we look at the world of society from the inside." * (Quotation from *Ethics*, October 1943, p. 6, "The Facts of the Social Sciences.") Hence we judge the behavior of others solely on the basis of "knowledge of our own mind." (The "our" is wonderful in this connection.) Ayres adds the pertinent remark: "People do not resist inspection. They only resist having their cherished beliefs exposed to the cold scrutiny of science." . . .

John Dewey

* The quotation begins: "The question is nothing else than . . .". The brackets are Dewey's. (Eds.)

410

[To Bentley:]
Odd comments.

"Agency"—Looking over some back material of yours, . . . you speak of doubts as to whether "agency" is the right word for affectional, enjoymental, clinical, etc. I doubt it too. For a long time in discussion of "experiencing," I said it was conjoint doing (or making)—undergoing. The undergoing aspect is prominent in the materials you mention. I think the same thing applies when "behavior" is substituted for "experience." We behave receptively, "suffering," as well as "acting." The inclusive name would seem to be "agent-patient." (Incidentally, "passion" and "passive" were originally allied words.) Perhaps when we get in a later paper to "agency," the compound word will be useful. The "patient" part will at least indicate that there is a place in the scheme for a lot of things which we aren't concerned to discuss in this set of papers. . . . We shall, I believe, save a lot of misunderstanding, and obtain more cooperation if we indicate how and where within the cross-sectional there is a legitimate, and with reference to some issues, a required place for an agent-patient statement. The "continuing variation" mentioned in your letter probably covers the ground. For you have to treat Newton as a variation in a continuum as well as Einstein. And the whole durational, enduring (duresome) [dureful] aspect postulates variation. Staying still or frozen isn't en-during. I am inclined now to say that the known in your sense was taken for granted without needed explicit statement in my *Logic*, which is concerned with the procedures and techniques by which advances of favorable variations are secured, and with the characteristic forms which are involved in such variations. This has certainly been the focus of my interest. ("Focus" may serve at times when "nucleus" is doubtful.) I am inclined to think that your interest has been in the other phase and you have tended to take for granted the variational process. It's quite likely that my critical study of historical output in the theory of knowledge, from Aristotle down through Locke and Kant, etc., is based on the fact that they take knowing-known purely statically—even "empiricists" like Locke and Mill—and in a way which in effect took knowledge spatially out of earth and put [it] in the heavens and temporally out of time into eternity. Also, however, I criticized the modern movement, as in Locke [and] Mill, for making the variant (so-called "Individual") the whole damn business, instead of that *through* which the variation occurs. In fact, I guess all I want in the present papers is that *Through* gets placed in the *Across* scheme.

Obviously, what I am driving at here is something more basic than the name "Agency." . . . As durational affairs, knowings-knowns endure *through* and by continual variation—this word is better than growth, development, which named aspects of variation. Heres and theres are

411

cases of *throughs* spatially, and nows and thens the same temporally—the self, person, subject, organism, or whatever, ditto; it's a now and here knowledge variation. . . .

Continuing my intellectual confessions, I see now that I've always had an interest in erroneous variations—how and why they came about. I'm sure that the "great names" in philosophy are not names of fools, nor yet mainly of those engaged in fooling others—[in] spite of theological and anti-theological bias. A large percentage of my "diplomatic" or irenical way of writing springs from the fact that I think most of the great names had something, but got it twisted, mainly because of the sociocultural movements of their times; which [movements] also went *through* them for better or worse—same as [through] you and me. *Your* letter to *Fortune* [unpublished] was swell—all but the sentence about "down the sewer." If these men in the past had gone down the sewer, we'd be a hell of a lot worse off than we are. Amen and hallelujah.

Yours, *Dewey*

[New York,] May 10, 1945
[To Bentley:]

Glancing at a highly technical mathematical paper in *Transactions of National Academy of Sciences*, [I] find "concept" used seven times. Sometimes as, I should say, synonym of "topic," "subjectmatter under discussion," sometimes as synonym for "term," used to indicate a well-known, important principle.

J. D.

[New York,] May 11, 1945
[To Bentley:]

. . . Kaufmann's paper * on [genesis] and statements in his letter about [Genesis] (which are typical of a whole group at present) spring, at bottom, from just the failure to observe things in durance which you point out. And *undue* emphasis upon "genetic"—as upon "emergence"—has the same root. They are both cases of *transi*tions or bridges that, however, never get *across*. "Transitive," "transitional," are other examples of emphasis on the short-time span, *Through* aspect; more emphatic still is *"transitory."* The point in all cases, including the "transi*ent*," *"transitory,"* is a fact observed across a selected *section* of a *cross-section*, the section itself being cross-sectional. Query: Is it a fact that we can *name* anything save as cross-section of some more extensive duration—which, when named, is itself an observed cross-section of something more

---

* "Scientific Procedure and Probability."

412

extensive—and so on *ad infinitum?* But to your question about how to make a usable comparison between thing across time and space, I don't know save by some amplification such as contained in your letter. . . .

[*Dewey*]

[New York,] May 12, 1945

Dear Bentley:

. . . I looked over my old paper . . . "[Concerning] Signs" and started rewriting it. *After* I had done quite a job, I ran across your comment, 12-21-44, on the previous sketch. I italicized "after" because I was pleased to see that, independently, the chief change I was making was in strong emphasis of what you said then—that I seemed inclined to use word "sign" as a special procedure in which an object is involved, while you are inclined to use it as "the general procedure under which objects are identified, or arise, or enter as objects." You kindly said the difference probably was one of phrasing—of course, it was a lot more than that, and I mention this matter because my emphasis in the revision [is] upon the fact that a word as a sign or designatory name and its "referent," so-called, are determined conjointly by one and the same set of procedures—in other words, I've made some progress because of our correspondence. This "referent" business in "semantics" is something terrible—maybe what will finally emerge will be a paper on "Referents." I also intend to develop the previous sketch to include something about signs as "vehicles" of meanings.* . . .

Yours, *J. D.*

Paoli, Indiana, May 13, 1945

Dear Dewey:

. . . Note: In the current (May) *Scientific Monthly* there is a paper by [Carl B.] Boyer on "Quantitative Science without Measurement." [He] discusses Aristotle and Archimedes and how they got good work on the numerable without gauging the measurable. This should be highly usable to us sometime in defending our procedure as "scientific" against the mensurators. . . . Incidentally, the guy quotes Nicholas of Cusa (15th century) as guessing that Latin *mens* came from *mensurando.* . . .

Incidentally, *re* the range of "knowledge." *Scientific Monthly* for May has an almost startling article [William A. Albrecht, "Discriminations in Food Selection by Animals"] on fine discriminations by cattle, hogs, rabbits, etc., in food selection. E.g.—two stacks of hay; one grown on spe-

---

* For some elaboration of these points, see Dewey, "Peirce's Theory of Linguistic Signs, Thought, and Meaning." (Eds.)

cially fertilized soil, the other not; cows will clean up every spear of one before taking the other. This is then connected experimentally in significant cases with beneficial and undesirable nutrition characteristics. We know a lot of such stuff—suspect some—but here is experimental precision on a kind of "knowing" which is not any kind of "knowing" we "know." The homing pigeon is child's play, I should think, compared with this. We had a lot of layouts for various "types" of knowledges (applications of word "knowledge") early in this work. Fortunately, we abandoned all and centered on "namings" which we know something about. . . .

There is no doubt that your "Situation" in the *Logic* covers the "known" in present sense.

The whole thing illustrates my thesis: We never *know* what we are doing. It grows. Especially in theoretical (i.e., linguistic) build-up, it is slow, painful process. This is why I write these things over and over. Slowly and again more slowly, a little chicken peeps his head out. You can't do it all at a Minerva-brain-crack speed. For instance, I think the chance coupling the other day of consistency-existency (I remember writing "Wow" after it) is a great gain whether one ever uses the phrasing or not (and I think it is usable much later on and just illustratively). It brings the two divisions Name and Symbol into separation-combination—just the kind of thing [which] you are always after—and [which] we must develop sharply at some stage. Recall what James said in almost the last pages he wrote—something about looking at his printed page with astonishment at what his scriptorial activity was getting away with [*Some Problems of Philosophy*, p. 213]. . . .

Regards, *Bentley*

[New York,] May 14, 1945

[To Bentley:]

Vocabulary.

"Proposition," "judgment." Judgment is a proposition in as far as it marks (is taken, used, functions) as a *conclusion*. (I haven't found a case yet when "conclusion" can't be substituted for "judgment." This is a reason, in spite of my recurrent use of [the] word in previous writings, for dropping it out and [confining?] it to this vocabulary mention.) [This] illustrates the "cluster" business, which I think should be explicitly mentioned in prefatory remarks to [the "Concerning a] Vocabulary [for Inquiry into Knowledge"] paper [cf. the "Postulations" paper].

"Expression." In cluster: word, name, designation, term. The identity of naming with knowing (of a certain range of development) is illustrated by the common use of [the] words "calling," "appellations," etc.

"Term." Names are terms with respect to a certain emphasis or phase of knowing-known: Viz., a name is a term when it states, has the force of stating, conditions to be observed in further naming: E.g., terms of a contract. All legal names perform this function and hence are terms. Similarly, scientific names are terms.

Observation (very cursory). In a cluster containing noting, remarking (both words covering "taking notice of," and "saying," "uttering," "setting forth and/or down"); "keeping, following a rule, law, custom"; "practical adherence" (from *Oxford Dictionary*); "needing," "marking," "observant," "care" (*Oxford Dictionary*), "careful watching," "military and scientific," in reference to "cause and effect"—i.e., viewing an event or occurrence in its extensive durational context. An "utterance," "So and so made this observation." If I had consulted the *Dictionary* in writing the *Logic*, I would not have found a single case of restriction to "sense-perception," or short-span facts. (The "conforming to custom" aspect seems to illustrate the spatial range of observation. "Seeing," "viewing" used in wide sense. "Seeing," [in] the wide use [is] almost as early, according to *Oxford Dictionary*, as the narrow use with restriction to the eyes. To perceive in its wide sense; to take account of, as in an argument. "We have seen," "ascertain by inquiry, experiment," etc.; "ensure by supervision or vigilance," "see to it," not to seeing a bet in poker.

[Dewey]

New York, May 14–15, 1945

[To Bentley:]

Memoranda: Odd Topics.

Looking [at] some back stuff, I found the following phrase: "Scientific is not assumed in advance to signify reduction to physical or biological terms; but, as is the case with scientific investigation of concrete matters generally, leaves the scope of the subjectmatter to be determined in the course of inquiry." There is nothing new in the passage, but an equivalent of the last phrase might come in, in connection with physical, physiological, behavioral.

Perhaps, something to this effect is usable in connection with [the] prefatory statement regarding postulation—that instead of being "assumed" in advance to control further observation [or] discussion, they present summaries of the direction in which scientific knowings-knowns have steadily moved and are formulated as guides in further approach and observation.

Vocabulary.

Concept. In reference to expression, name, term cluster, economy and understanding would be served by dropping out "word" in behalf of name "Term" as defined—see my recent statement.

415

Definition. As used in [the] last sentence, it is evidently a synonym for discriminated, identified, delimited, marked off, and specified with the degree of firmness that is attainable. Probably, in this sense it doesn't differ from precision and firmness of specification—if so, all that would be needed would be to set it off from mathematical definition, on one side, and statements, à la dictionary of popular usage, on the other.

[*Dewey*]

Paoli, Indiana, May 14, 1945

Dear Dewey:

. . . Yours, 5-11-45, about naming cross-sections of endurances. We have quite a bit to work out in the next paper ("Specification," I agree, is best to take next). . . . We must make every name a naming; every naming a behavior; every behavior a transaction; the namings so heavily transactional for our purposes; they must be so kept in mind. Both the naming and the named enter as durational. *Through*-transit. We cut off the unknown beyond-knowledge, beginnings and ends of the trip. Specification becomes approximation in ever-increasing accuracy. I would say we give "dated" namings to "dated" events (referring to human-age-durations); that our sound namings are in the durance form; that our frozen namings purporting to cut off from the "transition" are secondary help-namings, and not master-namings. . . .

Regards, *Bentley*

[New York,] May 16, 1945

Dear Bentley:

Sorry I kept harping on "conception" business; it was defensive as far as my past use is concerned, but it wasn't meant to be a defense of further use. . . . I think "term," if carefully formulated, will serve all needed purposes. From logical point of view I have a need for a word that applies to such cases of observations as "I see what you mean," but in other communication I used "conceptual observation" only as a short means of identification, not to promote its further formal use.

Re your reference to Bridgman: Quite a long time [ago] I started a memo on obviously language words that are used for knowing, like "telling," for discrimination-distinguishing—telling apart; for taking account of, etc. Maybe, I'll get back to it sometime. I agree with you that "basic" is a dangerous word. One trouble with me is that in writing you, I often use words loosely because I trust you to see what I mean; that is, intended for you rather than for formal statement in paper. Primary and Secondary (or derived) are better, but I don't know [that] there is any call for them in these papers. . . .

Yours, *Dewey*

[To Bentley:]

. . . I don't know whether any postulate about "Logic" is needed. There could be a clause . . . to [the] effect that knowings-knowns had [been] continuously (in their whole history) and would continue [to be] in the future, if scientific procedure is adhered to, . . . self-testing and self-correcting. A formulation of this kind avoids useless controversies about "Logic."

There is a quite different matter—which strikes me every time I look up a "term" in the dictionary. We stress, properly, scientific usage as pattern [with] in which to operate. But as far as *idiomatic* usage is concerned, while it is greatly inferior in technique of procedure, it is always, as far as I've noted, behavioral or practical—much more definitely so than "scientific" vocabulary on its face. Take idiomatic usage of "Observation" as reported in *Oxford English Dictionary*, for example; also "heedful," "attentive," "watchful," "mindful," "minding" (as one's business or the baby). (The fact that "mind" and "remembering" were very close in original usage is, I think, pretty good evidence of temporal spread.) We see "motion" when we mind or observe in other than technical, "physical" sense. I don't mention this here as a matter for any immediate attention or "notice." . . .

[Dewey]

Paoli, Indiana, May 17, 1945

Dear Dewey:

. . . Now the radical difference between Kantor and what we are trying to do is that Kantor is committed to "things" *and* organisms prior to behavior or inquiry; and, further, this leads him to commit himself to *things* that are *products* of behavior as *existing* apart from the behavers; i.e., a book is a "product." . . .

Regards, *Bentley*

Paoli, Indiana, May 18, 1945

Dear Dewey:

. . . You do not expressly say, but imply, that it will be all right for us to set up either Statements, Scientific Definition, Mathematical Definition; Or Dictionary Definition, Scientific Definition, Mathematical Definition.

Now there are not very many things I will argue with you long and hard about. But this is one of them. The *only* question I have open here is what names to use for the three cases. I hold that the worst evil in all current logical discussion is the confounding of the two latter items both

417

called "Definition." I hold that the *only cure* for this malignant disease is to get two separate names for the two procedures (passing over the dictionaries for a while).

1. The procedure of seeking maximum scientific accuracy in naming and a manner of approach which commits us to assert that we shall reach no ultimate truth-reality ever, but shall continue the open line of inquiry *forever* (in our sense of words like "forever," which always [so far as we know, *ad infinitum*] includes the qualification *so far as we know*).

2. The procedure in which the words (symbols, terms) do not *name anything*. They hold together by fitting tight in system and have their full operational value in the fitting—and so that if they start work as names of something outside the system, their consistency (and consequent value) fails. (In a sense, a symbol can "name" an operation within the system—but that is different from the existential naming we have in mind.) . . .

I will accept any naming scheme you like, providing it does *not use the same word* for these radically opposed procedures. In general you assimilate "definition" to "delimitation." You are completely right.

In general, I note the heavy use of it on the syntactic-consistency side in recent works. I have been inclined to feel it could be strengthened here when divorced from the scientific application. My argument is that this ultimate-consistency application narrowly (and "feel" generally) will destroy any progress we make *if* we apply "definition" on the scientific side—and despite the fact you are teetotally right on the delimitation-status. . . .

Regards, *Bentley*

[New York,] May 18, 1945

[To Bentley:]

. . . *Re* animal discrimination. When I was interested in that subject [grandchildren], I heard the latest thing in feeding babies was to give up adult prescriptions based on "science" and give a variety [of choices] and let the babe select kind and quantity. When you first . . . [spoke] about the knowledge of the amoeba, I think I was momentarily shocked, but thinking it over, saw you had to be right. I think, too, it is a kind of knowing, *some* humans know—there is evidence in savages, if not in babes. You and I have a kind of smell on "intellectual" subjects which is of this general order—in reading an argument, I "feel" a contradiction before I spot it—a kind of physical jar. . . .

More *re* "*Observation*." Since I wrote the other day about my being misled by psychologists and philosophers in my limitation of word, I have realized that current use by scientists was also responsible—they pretty habitually use it for subjectmatters like the turning of color of litmus paper, transit of Venus, etc.—they want something, I suppose, to mark such cases off from "hypothetical" and "theoretical" considerations, and I wanted just that in writing *Logic;* so I adopted their use without due reflection.

I'm with you a hundred per cent that we don't "really" know what we are doing till *after* it is done. My conversion, my seeing the light, dates from when I first realized that particular [word] *Factum* [means]—thing done. That is where animal, cattle, knowing has it all over us—though maybe they get a stomachache sometimes. You have made me see, in addition, that it never *is done* in the sense of finished once for all, though I was smelling in that direction before. . . .

John Dewey

[New York,] May 22, 1945

[To Bentley:]
. . . While "physical" is what occurs most immediately as what is to be guarded against by reference to natural as subjectmatter, I got a new slant on approach to epistemological idealism, i.e. mentalism. A whole school of writers has held that "natural" subjectmatter is "psychological," (i.e., mental, consciousness, thoughts, sensations, etc.) and that "physical" is derived. I remarked in a paper a good while ago [that] this kind of theory had been wished on philosophy by the psychologists. G. H. Mead is far from being a clear writer, but I owe a lot to contact with him in getting me over to a biological-sociological approach. (If I ever write a paper closing my accounts with epistemology, I'll point out that if our transactional approach isn't used, there is [no] ground for choice between universal physicalism and universal psychicalism, and that the old historic round will be repeated—the only new thing being the insertion of language between—and in the long run, the problem will be raised whether these intruders are themselves mental or physical—or just plain . . . bastards.) . . .

J. D.

[New York,] May 25 (?), 1945

Dear Arthur:
. . . One of my girls said, when a student at Barnard, . . . that the more advanced the subject, the less certain in expression the teachers. Philosophers and psychologists were most sure; sociologists next, then biologists, then chemists, and, lastly, physics teachers. She had a good gift of discrimination even at an early age; at the age of two or three [she] remarked, to account for her unfriendliness to a visitor, "I don't like the smellings of him."

. . . I don't think it will work in anywhere, but it occurred to me offhand that History is the perfect example of the naming-named. It's what happened, and it's the story or account of what happened and you absolutely can't separate one from the other, and the account or naming is itself a part of what happens as a going event. It takes a place in that which it is about as well as taking place itself and then becomes something to give a further account of—*ad infinitum*. Or in terms of Knowings-knowns: History as Known is an integral subjectmatter of further knowing while, as knowing, it is a part of what is Known. As an event, it [is] a carrying on and variation in "the events it is" about. . . .

Some time ago you suggested an abbreviated version of my *Logic*. I wasn't far enough along then to get the point or a point of the suggestion. Now I do. The statement would be abbreviated, not only by leaving out some of the technical chapters (of "Scholarship"), but because I have now got hold or am getting hold of a simplified and much firmer hold of the subjectmatter—thanks to reading what you have written and are writing. . . .

Yours, John

[New York,] May 27, 1945

[To Bentley:]

. . . It always braces me up when I find out that while we [are] working on a new line in psychology-philosophy, we are getting them back on the good old line of speech as common, everyday human behavior.

It also rather pleases me when I can note that sometimes in the past I [had] hit on something by taking and sampling [it] without having the wit to develop it, by taking it in connection with other things [so as] to give it logical development—that is, development of *Logos*. So I just looked up pp. 166–7 of *Experience and Nature*, where the grasp and taking [of meaning] is expressed rhapsodically. P. 169, critical, is a more sober anticipation. But I never followed the "aperçu," as W. T. Harris used to say, up and out systematically.*

[Dewey]

Paoli, Indiana, May 31, 1945

Dear John:

. . . One of the things I like most about our present situation is that we do not have to "derive" any postulation from any other. (Of course,

---

* See, however, Dewey, "Meaning and Existence," a reply to a critique by Everett W. Hall, "Some Meanings of Meaning in Dewey's *Experience and Nature*." (Eds.)

we *could not* if we wanted—point is we do not feel [the] need of trying.) They all work into each other so that the point one begins at is directly selected with a view to entry into (burglar tools?) the needs of the audience, then let [the] rest flow along after. Maybe I have said this before, but I made the point to a young psychologist (major in army, personnel work) who was here the other day. He could never expand on our lines. His work will be in limited spots. He might not think much of our wide, sweeping formulations. But even if he uses "behavior" as of the organism, he will mean by it something that fits into the situation, and not something clashing with [it from] out[side].

Page 246 of "T" ["A Terminology for Knowings and Knowns"] in *Journal of Philosophy*. We have "behavioral" as subject-matter selection along with physical and physiological. We also have behavior-agency when the organism-participation is segregated to study.

I wonder what "a behavior" should be? "an instance"? We had "behavioral event" for the transactional thing. But certainly "a behavior" has got to be "a behavioral event." Same old puzzle. . . .

[*Re* postulation] Suspicion arises. My memo says "hard fact" must get a show in the postulation. What it actually gets is a casual reference in postulation draft. . . . Insert another entry: The hardest of "hard fact" is the strongest "warranted assertion," both to be understood within the frame of "fact" as nature, and in no case with fact-as-event getting out of hand into a region of its own beyond knowings-knowns, or facts. (This is just a stab at entry—not yet phrased.)

This also achieves something not yet (I think) in the postulations—a reference to warranted assertion, without having to make it stick its head out in the logical form.

I certainly like the remark you cite (5-25-45) about uncocksureness, as knowledge grows—made by one of your girls when at Barnard. I see I mis-read it. It was the content of assertions that were comparable. I, with mind set on revision, studied my own phrasing. Here is where her observation becomes the head of the corner. . . .

Regards, *Bentley*

[New York,] June 5, 1945

Dear Bentley:

. . . Sunday, an old doctor friend [Huston] from Austin, Texas, turned up, having come here mainly to see me. . . . He is one of the most intelligent men I have ever known, . . . has what seems to me an extensive and sound physiological-chemical knowledge. But the most interesting thing to me is the way he conducts his practice, with patients, in terms of behavior, without drawing any hard-and-fast lines anywhere. He was talking to me last evening and remarked [that] the Kidney is a most intelligent organ; it knows a great deal more chemistry than all the chemists in the world; and he doesn't draw any fixed lines between that knowing and . . . [knowing] in books. Not in virtue of any formulated philosophical position, but just by constitutional habit. . . . It has been a good bracer to find an intelligent and competent man who proceeds, as if by organic habit, in discussing things in his own field along our general line. What he is just now concerned with is the problem of learning, because (as far as I can see) he regards the problem of the medical practitioner as that of directing relearning along the physiological levels by starting from the behavioral level, and he is much intrigued with the question of the connection between them.

Yours, *Dewey*

[New York,] June 7, 1945

[To Bentley:]
Notes *Re* "Postulations."

. . . All of this talk about "knowledge" implying—or whatever word is used—"truth" is just too much for me, especially as it is usually offered in the name of "realism"—for they have to acknowledge circularity in every specific instance of a "truth." The fact that they don't attempt, in the case of the general noun "truth," to derive the general from analysis of specified instances is sufficient proof in itself of subordination of the whole inquiry to prior unexamined and unexaminable assumptions. (Don't want to go on expanding the text, but maybe there is . . . [some place] there for a single sentence about what our postulations *aren't:* [they are not] unexaminable, no matter what.) . . .

[*Dewey*]

[New York,] June 8, 1945

Dear Arthur,

. . . I often stick something in when writing you that is intended for inclusion in the paper which set me off. This is the case as to history as double-action.

Inquiry *vs.* proof belongs in later paper, without doubt. Perhaps, along with *un*-proved *re* postulates goes the same allusion as to their being beyond examination when laid down as fixed "foundations." Maybe, only.

Have already written about what I think of imperative need for space-time open to inquiry *versus* Newtonian space [and] time as fixed *pre*-conditions of physical inquiry. Of course, the charges of materialism (not important in themselves) and of complete inability of science to discuss certain important matters—to inquire or say anything about them

422

(which is important)—stem from just the use of "space-time" as [if] they were *pre*-determinations conditioning the scope of science. So I don't think you come down too markedly or firmly on this point—in a way, it is the meat of the approach side of the double front, as far as its range of application is concerned at the present juncture. So power to your elbow. . . .

Yours, [*Dewey*]

[P.S.] *Re* Kaufmann. I get more and more confused about what he is up to. My guesses so far have turned out wrong. I am being forced to the conclusion that he is just terribly confused and doesn't know himself. Take the analysis of "Scientific Procedure and Probability" paper you sent me. First he says "Knowledge implies truth"—and then he goes on, in practically so many words, to say [that] that statement contrasts with everything known about every case of actual knowledge.

I went back for light to an earlier paper of his "The Structure of Science," *Journal* [*of*] *Philosophy*, May 22, 1941. It opens sensibly enough—that any given science "should be defined in terms of rules of method rather than as a system of propositions"—the word "rules" is indicative of danger, but roughly one can agree with what he is driving at. But then he proceeds at once to say that there are two stages, the *first* being that in which "rules of method" are "*rules of the language of science*" and the second of which is "defined *rules of the procedure of science.*" The "defined *rules of the language of science*" are said to be "exclusively concerned with meanings as such." "We have to distinguish between [*sic*] three different points concerning a proposition in relation to the procedure of a given science S."

1. Its meaning. This is perfectly determined by the rules of the language of science. No reference to scientific procedure must be made in determining it. On the other hand, this meaning is presupposed in all rules of procedure when applied to it" (pp. 287–88). I imagine these passages contain the nub of his doctrines with respect to what he accepts and what he rejects in the *Logic*. But I don't know what he wants to say. My impression is that he belongs definitely in the group you criticized in your ["On a Certain] Vagueness [in Logic"] papers, inserting language, propositions identified with something called language, in between. . . .

Mention of "intuition" is additionally confusing; the only thing that is at all clear is the unique place of "meanings" which have top priority and can't be put off the plane for any mere "scientific procedure" passenger. But why and what of any importance happens in case such *is* the case, I just don't know.

[New York,] June 11, 1945

Dear Arthur:

. . . I am not aware that I have any special doctrinal position about "quality"; I was simply standing up for idiomatic use of [the] word to designate "red," "hard," "sweet," "troublesome," etc.—and as expressing something which must be *had*—as a blind man doesn't have "red," etc. Maybe the latter involves a doctrinal position—about "experience," perhaps. But I don't know just what you are getting at about either my view or [about] your own. If I were to go into the theory of the thing, perhaps I'd say that what the psychologists have called "sensations" can be better called "qualities," and that amoebae *have* food before they name-know it, and "qualities" represent or are the havings on the first and "lowest," least-developed stage of name-knowings. (This is perhaps something like what you would use the word "experience" for—while I want to use the latter word, if at all, for the whole range of behavioral transactions.) . . .

Sincerely yours, *John D.*

Paoli, Indiana, June 19, 1945

Dear John:

Specification in our *provisional* naming is the range of namings that arise out of the practical, become the scientific, strip off the ultra-human and pedantic-logical, and eternal-real pretenses, and hold to increasing accuracies but no God-given certainties. Represented by Peirce's fallibilism (I suppose—though I am judging by name); the pragmatism he forecast and you developed, the "open world," and the "biological naturalism" of your type. (Is not Peirce's "prescript" [precept] of the litmus-paper illustration the same thing as his conception-and-conceivable-effects of 1878?)

Our program shows under provisional namings: Characterization—your common-sense range; Specification—your scientific range; Definition—the mathematical symbol range. . . .

I think the main hesitation (maybe the only one) about your development is the old matter of the word "sign."

Facing all prelinguistic behaviors, in the signal range and clear back to protozoan, is not "sign" the best word for that which is characteristic of the behavioral as distinguished from the physiological? It covers also naming where namings are behavioral. I think I will know how to make it cover symbols when we get there (namely, it is not sign like "jump"; nor sign like "That thing is"; but it is slapping a whole scheme like radioactivity against a whole universe and getting more action like radar).

424

My point is: If we use "sign" so broadly, we should *never* in our development, after we once get going, give it lesser uses.

Here is another thing: You remarked the other day that "sign" tended to express the over-there phase—the outer. Now we know that "behavior" tends to express the in-here—the organism (with which we replace the mental of the older time).

If so; and if we make "sign" and "behavior" equivalent, in what I take to be the technical sense of that word so that (a) sign always implies behavior, and (b) behavior always implies sign, then we have the two tendencies (strainings-apart of the two words) overcome by binding them together forever and ever till God do us part (I mean "death do"). If I knew what Nagel's "entail" meant in the case of "knowledge entails truth," I would prefer "entail" to "imply" as more up-stage. . . .

Regards, *Bentley*

Paoli, Indiana, June 20, 1945

Dear John:

. . . Query: What is [the] difference between "quality" and "perceptional behavior"? Query: If a quality is such a signaling, then what is the "force" of the specialized word "quality"? What is it after? What is the distinctive stress? Is the distinctive stress one we wish to maintain? Query: Is there any purpose of discourse (our type) in which "quality" should be given a special compartment-classification in a different compartment from "object" or "event"? . . .

Strange Interlude. I made a speech to [a] visitor the other day. He wanted to know how our set-up, as between symbol and naming, would deal with a great number of standard logical problems. In effect, I said it left them aside. (If I had been remembering the *Logic*, I would have referred him to that.) Then I said what I proposed to do when I got to the point was not to fuss with those things; but to take a handful of working physics and another handful of mathematical symbolic construction, and put them together as working behaviors. (I haven't done it yet—I trust to the hunch—"Lead Kindly Light"—and may we come no croppers.)

Now see what a peek at "quality" throws me into. Your account of "characteristic" and "character," "generic" and "general," "reference" and "relation," pitches out the class-logic the way I (in far reflection, but applying our present organization) remarked would happen, in a letter a few days ago. You assimilate the character-relation-general-proposition procedure to the mathematical symbol form (I am not sure just how far or explicitly—I am not going into it now). You then assert [*Logic*] (p. 263) that this "propositional formulation is inherently necessary for controlled inquiry."

425

I have been aware that the issue was in here, and was due to come up, but I have been primarily interested in becoming sure "observationally," that the naming and the symboling procedures had a good basis of continued maintenance in division.

It is a pretty considerable question with me whether when you work out the relation-general-procedures, you get anything different from what syntactics will be if clearly worked out. Also whether when name-and-class logic is worked out, it is anything different from genera-and-species, liberally stated. So far as I know, the Aristotelian logic is not worth a damn in knowledge-advance, except to clear away kindergarten-bugs. I imagine the only use it has for Russell-type inquiries is to make people hope that maybe they can clear away sophisticated bugs. . . .

My idea as to what is needed is to take such a vivid illustration as the one about "square" in your footnote, p. 260, *Logic*, and say that for all technical purposes we need two types of namings. We are going to hold them apart vigorously. Here enters, of course, the use of the word "definition"—for one class only. . . .

Regards, *B.*

[New York,] June 20, 1945

Dear Arthur:

. . . I've just been reading [Arthur Koestler] *The Yogi and the Commissar.* In one essay he has a lot of remarks about [Joseph] Needham and a little about [J. H.] Woodger—in terms of "hierarchical levels of organization." [In] the last essay in the book, what Koestler misses, and I judge Needham does too, is that the levels are to be dealt with in connection with the "double front." By leaving out the front of approach, of method and techniques, the "levels" become inherent—the miracle of "emergence" is then called for. Here is a nice subjectmatter job for you to tackle later. What they don't see is that there is a subjectmatter, sociological, behavioral, or what have you, which overpasses, covers all the "levels," which are then differentiated with respect to [one's] way of approach—which in turn is, I take it, connected with the kind of problem under investigation.

This idea of levels of organization had quite a run once; . . . I came near falling for it, but somehow couldn't make it go and so left it alone. A prejudice I couldn't overcome, I guess, against any feudalism with its fixed hierarchy of lowers and highers.

Koestler in his essay diagrams it [levels of organization] as a staircase; a given science, physics, physiology, etc., works on the horizontal levels all right; but science is stumped by the verticals. At the same time, he doesn't call in any outsider to account for upward jumps. And in spite of the series of elevators, he sees that any account of one "level" has to employ the subjectmatters of lower levels. Reading him made me get more clearly the fundamental character of my objection to emergence as a doctrine. John and Susan rise from the ocean, but I doubt if Venus did.

They had to get into it, to submerge, before they could emerge.

Yours, *John D.*

[New York,] June 21, 1945

Dear Arthur:

. . . I've written him [Felix Kaufmann] . . . asking if the contrast between the insistence on the development of *situations*, put in contrast with his emphasis on decisions made or to be made by personal inquirers, A and B, did not perhaps locate the difference between us—adding that I could not see any logical issue when the inquirer and his "decisions" are dealt with as if occurring outside of the situation under determination.

If this isn't it, I'll have to give up in despair.

It looks as if Kaufmann were taking the predicament [that] a given inquirer may find himself in at a given time, as *the* logical problem. . . .

Yours, *John D.*

[P.S.] "Instance", "Case"—Your hunch about "Instance" is fine. Consulting my bible, the *Oxford* [*English Dictionary*], I find the original meaning is "presence," with sense of *urgency*, pressure. What could be better? On the instant, Latin, *instare, instante*, to be at hand, to be present, to urge, press upon; one might (but won't) say, to demand attention. It's just the word to denote the immediacy, short-span, narrow extent, aspect of the continuing extensive event.

A "Case" is (perhaps) an Instance in its "representative" or designation aspect. This (instant) occurrence is a case of malaria, etc.

"Occur," to run against or into; befall, present itself (Oxford), bears the same relation to an event as an instance does to an event, but with a somewhat different emphasis; an occurrence involves something of an interruption, a "happening"; an instance apart from its being a *determinate* sign, or *an* instance *of.* . . .

"Classes"—ticklish subject. But I am sure, on short consideration, that you are right in saying they fall by the wayside as between "specification" and "definition." I believe also that this conclusion was involved in what I say, repeatedly, about the logical ambiguity of certain verbal expressions. On p. 308 [*Logic*], towards [the] bottom, I say a "proposition" of relation of kinds as it stands "is not logically a complete proposition," being logically "preliminary to further inquiries." *

---

* These quotations are from this passage: "Propositions about a *relation of kinds* are also relational, having no logical subject-predicate form. When it is said that

427

[P.P.S.] It's true I didn't drive the matter home; but it is also true that it was because I didn't see its bearing on the current logics with any definiteness. So I thought it sufficed to point out the ambiguity and incompleteness [of the term]. Of course, it lines up with the whole taxonomic business. (The one bearing I did see clearly was the way it knocked out the Aristotelian logic; I was aware of *that*, but didn't have the knowledge of the newer formalisms to see its bearing on them; that is the reason I couldn't join actively in the ["On a Certain] Vagueness [in Logic"] paper. My education wasn't up-to-date—and I had a respect for Aristotle as standing for *something* which I didn't have for the new crowd.)

"Sign"—I am with you about its broad use; I haven't looked up, since getting your letter of 6-19-45, my "[Concerning] Sign[s]" paper, but there are probably traces, maybe more than a trace, of my former limitation of word to de-signatory signs or representatives. I intended to differentiate this last paper from the one I sent you earlier, which you properly criticized, by making it clear that I was confining myself to a specified sign-range. If anything in that paper is usable in the "Specification" paper, this point should of course be established—that is [the] place of specifying signs with reference to prelinguistic and post-naming signs. I haven't thought about it enough to be clear, but my present "instant" feeling is that something firm has to be said here about "signals." I rather assume that current psychologies avoid the issue by the way they use "stimulus." There's an animal sort of lying around in space at some time, and something happens to bump into him or he into it—and that's a "stimulus." Of course, we can't go into a full development, but perhaps enough can be said to make it evident why "sign" applies, and in full transactional sense.

Perhaps the time is more ripe for this physiological point than for most anything else we have to say. When we come to specifying "signs," we might say that the crowd that has stuck in words between the knower and the real have at least performed, though in a terribly confused way, a useful function: a fact that helps [to] explain their pretended reliance upon Peirce.

Incidentally, I should say that "entails" is an existency name—"implies" a logical symbol.

Yes, knowledge *"entails"* "truth"—also error and falsity. Fact "entails" knowing, and knowing entails facts—of different varieties, in short.

'Iron is a metal' the proposition does not appear to be relational because we cannot convert it simply into 'metal is iron.' But the proposition as it stands is not logically a complete proposition. It does not indicate or even suggest its own grounds. At most it is either a sentence communicating information or is a proposition preliminary to further inquiries." (Eds.)

Paoli, Indiana, June 22, 1945

Dear John:

It may be possible to work the Kaufmann positions . . . through the use of your word applied to him about "decision," to somewhat this form:

Logic is a study of decisions in scientific research in order to establish the rules under which they are made.

It is thus a modernized version of the older logic taken as concerned with "laws of thought" by the two main tests that (a) the decisions operate upon contents of a nature with respect to which (b) such decisions are *sui generis* and not "natural."

In the case both of "laws of thought" and rules of decision, the action may turn back upon itself yielding "logic," as well as turn out upon nature yielding "science," thus being *"sui-generis"* to the second power. . . .

Bentley

[New York,] June 22, 1945

Dear Arthur:

. . . I hope I am now ready to drop out the historical problems, which make a lot of what I said in the *Logic* irrelevant to present work.

The matter comes, I imagine, to about the following:

1. The "qualitative-qualifying" subjectmatter is covered by perceptual-behavior signalings. It differs pretty radically from traditional psychology of perception in that it is definitely transactional, organic-environmental, thus including the "motor" joined to "sensory" and (in) the guts, respiration, etc., as well as the "special" senses, and this includes *emotional* as well as indicative signaling . . . This can be stated, I think, with no reference at all to "quality" (unless in a footnote) when signaling, as distinct from designatory-behavior, is mentioned.

2. "Qualities" as designatory signs (traits, characteristics) are discussable, if at all, in connection with whatever is to be said, if anything, about traits and characteristics, and therefore again without emphasis upon quality.

And to answer your special question: "characters," as I used the word, are definitely *not* qualities, but are, when not mathematical (in its standardized sense), syntactical. [They] belong under symbols and definitions, not specifications.

I hope the foregoing clears up some of what seems to be a mess in the *Logic*. I believe and hope I've got by the need of dealing explicitly with the historic problems, save when advisable to dismiss them. But I had to go through with them, and wouldn't have come out where I hope I now am unless I had gone through them. And, as I've probably indicated before, my teaching experience has led me to realize that there

429

are a lot of other people, not confined to the professional philosophical class, who have also to be cleared up on these points. For the historic philosophers didn't create the problems; they only formulated them out of the state of "culture" [which was] prevailing when they wrote, and which is still widely current. And it was a service, not wholly a disservice, to formulate them; that was a necessary condition of cultural purge and ejection [of the unwarranted formulations].

Yours, *Pro Meo Domo, John D.*

[New York (?),] June 25, 1945

Dear Arthur:

I don't think there is any difference between us as to "conception," which linguistically I much prefer to "concept," as I prefer perception to percept; the concept and percept forms are reifications, the "tion" forms are at least compatible with action-behavioral interpretations. (i) We both are down on the mentalistic use common with writers of psychological texts. (ii) Being aware (perhaps another case of *Pro meo Domo*) that philosophers have not for the most part given it a mentalistic, but a logical interpretation, all I am after is that in the "Vocabulary" paper ["Concerning a Vocabulary for Inquiry into Knowledge"] this *logical* usage be recognized, but (iii) also with an express recognition of its *mistaken* logical interpretation—virtually, I think, Kaufmann's "rule of decision"—and a positive statement of its hypothetical character as a method of organizing otherwise isolated (unorganized) details or "particulars"—equivalent to short-span observations. Then (iv) say that because of this serious ambiguity, we do not use the word at all.

The rigid rule of decision, giving a "term" ability to de-termine beyond a "working hypothesis" in inquiry, and subject to test by results of inquiry, is, I take it, what you object to as "pontifical"—and *that* is certainly as obnoxious as any other form of dogmatic superiority.

In short, all I have been trying to say is that I think it is [advisable], in the interest of not being unnecessarily misunderstood, to point [out] that it is *possible* to give "conception" a legitimate logical interpretation, that is, in terms of inquiry-constitutions or operations, but that, owing to [the] abuse and consequent ambiguity of [the] word, we shall not use the word, but state what it legitimately stands for in a direct manner. I don't know whether, on the basis of the above, it is important or needful to say anything about "term" and "proposition"—my immediate reaction at present is *not* unless as a footnote pointing out an analogy when and if anything is said about "term" and "proposition." Maybe, the whole business is going too much into detail of logical theory, though I think that in any case we ought to be "firm" about conception. . . .

The application of the signaling-naming distinction is illuminating. It

430

suggests an issue that I have thought about some, casually—viz., the persistence of signalings after, in some other affairs, naming is achieved. They don't, probably, persist as undiluted signalings, even completely unmodified by namings, but they aren't in the naming range; maybe—this is thrown out offhand—they fall in the characterizing as distinct from the specifying range.

Another matter: "Range" is used here casually. We need *a* name to get away from the "level" notion; something that suggest[s] brackets and parentheses instead of a flight of steps. "Field" has [a] certain claim, but is also objectionable for reason[s] you've point[ed] out. "*Range*" has (*Oxford Dictionary*) the advantage, as far as it goes, of connection with "*rank*" and with "*arrange*," suggests the horizontal rather than the vertical—though "rank" has taken on a . . . [somewhat] feudal sense in ordinary use—literally it is to "draw up *in line*."

Yours, with regards, *John Dewey*

[P.S.] "Scope"—one meaning [is] the sphere or *area* over which an activity operates—*range* of application. *Ar-range*, arrangement, perhaps better than "organization" when the latter word is too tight.

Re-reading Cannon's [*The*] *Wisdom of the Body* with "transaction" in mind, I find that he specified [Claude] Bernard's "Internal Milieu" as a *matrix* . . . in a way that makes sense of what is meant, though nonsense of interpretation or usage of "milieu" as "environment" in the sense of surrounding conditions—though consistent with "milieu" in the literal sense of "medium" or what is between—in the middle of—provided, of course, "between" is not taken in a geometrical sense, but as a go-between or active intermediary in ways that can be, and more or less *are*, themselves specified.

The liquids are the matrix, i.e., blood, lymph, and plasma—and, of course, everything said about them as matrix is as to what they *do* as intermediaries of continuing transactions—receivers, excretors, transmitters, transformers, suppliers; go-betweens in transactions, not just in large, indefinite ways, but in carefully specified ways—where *what is done and how it is done* are inseparable.

I think it will make sense to hold that selves, persons, agencies, etc., are matrices in the sense in which blood is one, also that as *knowns*, they are the what and how of intermediaries in maintaining and carrying on certain specifiable operations—though as yet they are *unspecified* because they have not been observed as intermediaries of-and-in extensive transactions, which have themselves to be first specified! They can be studied apart as and only as blood is so studied. . . . As you pointed out a good while ago, "internal environment" when it is translated into factual events, is a complete destroyer of the usual sense of "environment"; when you get both an internal *and* an external environment, Which is Which? . . .

431

Paoli, Indiana, June 25, 1945

Dear John:

. . . In Clerk Maxwell's *Matter and Motion* I have looked up his use of "aspect." As he applies it to physics, it checks wonderfully for our uses. His use of "transaction" is ours, and he even suggests that buyer and seller are merely aspects of "trade." . . .

Your paper on [the] growth of pragmatism ["The Development of American Pragmatism"], reprinted in [Dagobert D.] Runes [*Twentieth Century Philosophy*], I read this morning. You mentioned James's specification of purpose and plan as discriminate for *mind*. This fits in beautifully with the sign-behavior layout (I never noticed it before). But "mind," in the purpose levels, is a level of sign-procedure—for specialized attention. If *one* wants to apply mind clear to protozoan behavior, it would run over it—I don't want to apply it. Perhaps, in this layout "mind" and "brain" are about on a level.

Regards, *Bentley*

Indianapolis, Indiana, June 29, 1945

Dear John:

. . . Yours, 6-25-45, on "conception." You add development to the treatment. It fits in fine despite my anarchistic bumptiousness on past comments. But—to my mind one thing is lacking to get proper positive statement. Where does conception take place? It is *not* in a mind. It is *not* in a physiologically investigated brain. It is in the organism-in-environment, of course—but that is generality of position-taking. Where? . . .

My way of doing it is now: (a) to specify language (languaging, language-behaving) so as to cover wording-meaning; (b) to isolate conception as a form of wording-meaning (and here I can doubtless follow you a full 100%); (c) to say that "a concept" is "a wording" in the sense that nouning or verbing is wording. (I might like to say "concepting" instead of either "conceiving" or "conception" or "concept.") . . .

A. F. B.

[New York,] June 29, 1945

Dear Arthur:

I am about ready to call it off with Kaufmann; I have a note from him in reply to the postulation from the paper I sent him (he mentions having a copy of entire paper), and he says he agrees with it 100%—that he didn't take the position taken by "sensationalists" and by Russell that there are "hard data exempt from testing and possible invalidation." Then he says that the issue isn't whether there [are] changes in the status of factual

432

assertions and of criteria of assertibility in the long-run course of inquiry—since he admits that—but whether, as in the case of the discussion of the two biologists about the transmissibility of acquired habits, that view is warranted by *now* accepted facts and by *now* adopted rules of procedure, i.e., what is taken for granted in a "particular context of inquiry," but need not be so taken "at other stages of inquiry."

In short, it seems as if what he is concerned with is the logic of argumentation—which fits in with his use of legal analogies, rules of decision, etc.

That takes me back to saying O.K. if anybody is specially interested in that sort of thing, but I can't see its importance for the general theory of logic. Only underneath I have a feeling that's an evasion on my part, just a verbal compromise, and that there is still an issue as to the position held . . . [whether of] "dialectic" as logic of argumentation or [of] "reasoning" in respect to the processes of inquiry. So I'll look up my *Logic*, for I'm reasonably certain [that] that is one of the "background problems" I have discussed—especially since that is essentially what the classic (Aristotelian) logic and the "canons of thought" logic [were].

I fully agree with you that if the word "operations" is used, it needs specification; I have felt the same, perhaps more so, about the words "activity" and "actions," since "operation" carries to my feeling more the sense of *specifiable work* (*opus*) done against the vague generality of the action words. . . .

I doubt if there is any difference between us as to "abstract," as to its legitimate and illegitimate usages, but, on the other hand, I don't know any reason for bringing a discussion of it in; it would be rather a "background" refinement, I fancy. Same about "quality," only I don't feel that I know what the point or issue is in connection with "quality," save with respect to transition from the perceptual-manipulative to the designatory of scientific type—qualities being as such "ineffable," literally, not mystically, yet behaving as signals.

The details of what I wrote about "sign" are of no importance; it is quite likely I was too much on the "ing" side. The matter that was back of what I wrote can be put as a question: Is it desirable to say anything about "Sign" in [a] general sense in which it covers all three: signal, designation, and symbol? If it isn't important, matters are somewhat simplified. But readers may raise the question. . . .

Yours, *J. D.*

[New York,] June 30, 1945

[To Bentley:]

In 1939 at a meeting of the American Philosophical Association, Cohen ["Some Difficulties in Dewey's Anthropocentric Naturalism"] and [Wil-

433

liam Ernest] Hocking ["Dewey's Concepts of Experience and Nature"] criticized my philosophical position and I replied ["Nature in Experience"]. I ran across a reprint of my speech the other day. Some of the things I would say differently now, but I was glad to find the following: "There is [a] circularity in the position taken (by me) [Dewey's insertion] regarding the connection of experience and nature. Upon one side, analysis and interpretation of experience [nature] is made dependent upon the conclusions of the natural sciences. . . ." (Then a passage saying that "dependent" does *not* mean reduction into terms of subject-matter of physical sciences.) "The other aspect of the circle is that it is held that what is experienced contains the materials and processes which, when they are laid hold of and used, lead to the methods and conclusions of the natural sciences: namely, to the very things that provide the means for forming a theory of experience. That this circle exists is not so much admitted as claimed." *

And speaking of the double-barreled status of experience, I harped so much on the inseparability of experienc*ing* and the experienc*ed* that back in the middle twenties some of the graduate students at an evening meeting put on a parody about "the Twins, Ing and Ed." . . .

[Dewey]

Indianapolis, Indiana, July 1, 1945

Dear John:

. . . If I prepare a little later a paper on language-theory based on Columbia seminar ["Memoranda on a Program of Research into Language"]—as you once suggested—that will settle the "concept" matter for me. But I shall have to keep hunting around. Of course, anything I say as to concept-procedure as linguistic is based on an immensely broader view as to what linguistic covers than the ordinary. On that basis I would like to ask:

Suppose (admitting that physiological formulations, though always possible, are *partial*) we look at generally differentiated brain-procedures (but never considering sharp separations)—

Suppose now we distinguish:

1. perceptional-transactional events—we can point at these in our movement among, and handling of, things. In other words, the name has a referent.

---

* The exact quotation is: "The other aspect of the circle is found in the fact that it is held that experience itself, even ordinary gross macroscopic experience, contains the materials and the processes and operations which, when they are rightly laid hold of and used, lead to the methods and conclusions of the natural sciences; namely, to the very conclusions that provide the means for forming a theory of experience. That this circle exists is not so much admitted as claimed." (Eds.)

434

2. conceiving activities other than linguistic.

3. linguistically meaningful activities of the more complex kinds; we can point at these in speakings, writings, and libraries and follow their organizations with the perceptional.

Having something named and observable for 1 and 3, what do we have comparable to observe as the referents of words like "concept" in 2?

Perceptional events build up and organize. Linguistic events build up and organize more explicitly (no sharp lines here between implied and explicit). But how about a region of conceivings as specialized, with no *central* prominence of either perceivings or linguistings [*sic*]?

You suggest an illustration. I suggest provisionally a prisoner alone, silently, never speaking, plotting his escape, and putting it over. Does he exhibit a strongly differentiated region of behavioral event, neither to be grouped as perceptional (signal) nor as linguistic (naming)?

If this is not a good illustration for your purpose, you proffer one.

I will say this: If there is an intervening region, then our tabulation wants to be revised by inserting another field between signaling and designating.

On my side, notice that the ancient faculties did not have a special one between sense and reason. Their third was emotions or will or something.

Romanes inserted recepts between percepts and concepts. He is about the only operator of that type. As I recall it, James did not speak very favorably of this scheme (in his [*The Principles of Psychology*], Vol. II). The recepts, as I recalled, were a sort of upper-percept, lower-verbal event and would not answer for the place that a concept as distinguished both from perceiving and designating would have to hold. . . .

Regards, *Bentley*

[P.S.] The words "explicitly" and "implicitly" . . . are not so good. What I meant was that perceptional organizations were perceptional (in a general naming all along). But linguistic organizations have a highly specialized, openly observable technique, which is responsible for our setting them over against the perceptional as a different range of behavioral event.

Now what we call "thinking" or "conceiving" is found . . . in perceptional ranges and also and much more prominently in language-ranges.

Has thinking or conceiving got any kind of a marked-out range intermediate between the two others? If so, what actional behavioral event shows up for it, such as things and words show up for the other two?

The word "thinking" thus would operate over both perceptional and linguistics (signaling and naming) ranges.

The word "concept" (unless a special locus shows up) would be manifestly linguistic behavior and not perceptional, primarily.

435

Dear Arthur:

I didn't attempt to suggest any answer to such questions as you raise in yours of 6-29-45, because I wasn't arguing for the use of "conception" —on the contrary. So it didn't occur to me that they were relevant.

Suppose we drop the word entirely and take the question of "subject-matter." 1. There are attitudes, dispositions, habits, which operate continuously and for the most part steadily or stably. ("Habits" is perhaps the best word because it is a transactional word, while the other words emphasize the transaction in its "organic" aspect; but only in that *aspect*. They are transactional names, *attitudes* being always *toward,* and *dispositions,* arrangements, *of* something.) . . . Just as the physiological transactions named are such as operate over a considerable spatial and temporal stretch of life-processes (being directive and regulative of local or particular actions, transactions), so with the name in respect to a set of other namings. This, it seems to me, is the factual event back of what "general" stands for.

As far as "conception" has been given a logical, as distinct from psychological, specification, it is what "conception" has indicated or pointed to. I repeat that I am *not* desirous of rehabilitating the word; it is enough to point out the ambiguity which is the ground for not using it, together with the subjectmatter for which it would stand if legitimately used. I don't take it that you deny there is a factual subjectmatter of the kind I have indicated—however poorly—above. If you did, I don't see how you could use "space," "time," as we have to use them—or indeed any distinctively scientific name. If there is a difference between us, it is that I believe it conduces to understanding to indicate the factual subjectmatter . . . [to] which words that have a long logical career behind them were blindly and confusedly employed to point . . . —otherwise, there will be a feeling on the part of many readers that in sheer rejection of the words, we are rejecting something that is factually significant.

As far as I can see, what I am trying to get at is in 100% agreement with what you say about wording and "concepting" (a good phrase) as a form of meaning-wording—"wording-meaning" and "meaning-wording" is exactly what I think "conception" should be. So if you ask *where* conception takes place, I would say in the Womb of language as specifying discriminated-identified events—it is just as transactional as mammalian conceivings. If I didn't *say* a conception was a linguistic-behaving, it was because I was taking it for granted that was where we had to locate any word or expression to which we assigned any possible kind of legitimacy. . . .

Yours, with regards, *J. D.*

[P.S.] Put in another way, my reason for feeling that in the "Vocabulary" paper something positive should be said about "conception" is to show that in the terms of our system something very direct and straight forward can be specified. Otherwise there will be readers who will say— Aha, see how they got stumped.

[To Dewey:]
Memo—"Concept"—"Habit"—"Language" . . . [*in re*] JD letter 7-2-45.
    JD. Habits of the organism as transactional. We name them. The organism-environmental transactional habits are "the factual event back of what the name 'general' stands for." I.e.: the word "general" names such habits. (I am transcribing and changing phrases. Tell me if I go wrong. AFB.)
    JD. We should keep in sight (or mention) what the words so long "were blindly and confusedly used to point for." (This is basic procedure to me. Work it out, identify it. Show what the words are used for—and how well. AFB.) If "concept" is the word in mind, I don't consider I want to reject it. I want to identify it more exactly. AFB.
    JD. Conception is a linguistic-behaving. Conception takes place "in the Womb of language." (On this basis, we have no argument, except a little further specification of detail for "womb" in this kind of conceiving. AFB.)
    However, I am not at all so sure of my own stressed assertions. And you stimulate me to a little further elaboration.
    Take "Habit," with reference to generals and concepts. You originally (I think) introduced this presentation to give a "where" to the process of conception in the organism without need of a companionate mental. It did its job fine.
    Now, however, once so given its "where," we have a number of varieties of "habit" to consider. For our immediate purposes and in our gross classification of "sign-meaning-behavior" we have the signaling side and the labeling side (designation) (labeling is bad—too narrow).
    A difference in the "events" we have in mind at once shows itself. You see the organism experiencing and interpreting the events that the words are used to name—i.e., the behavioral habits as events. I have been thinking largely in terms of the continual funny uses of the word "concept" that I run across in the current literatures. This leads us probably to different manners of expression.
    Consider:
    1. A rat is conditioned to a triangle (equilateral, point up) for food, and circle for "no food." The triangle is then used point-down, or a right angle triangle is substituted. If the rat "gets" it fairly well and fairly soon, he is said *by the psychologers to make a conceptual reaction.* (A

dozen big reports were made a few years ago all in terms of "concept" but never specifying for the word.)

2. A dog has a tremendously accurate reaction to separate men. Presumably, he has his habit of reaction to "all men" or "any and every man." He has a remarkably develop[ed] habit on the signaling side. Has he a "concept"? I don't know what we should say. It is undeveloped territory, and naming is crude analogy in this region at best.

3. Bridgman discusses the "concept of gold." He means merely the physicist's best reports on experimentation with gold.

4. If Bridgman discusses "the concept of light" instead of best description, he means some physicist's best guess-of-the-moment and has rival concepts interplaying.

5. We also have the "concept of virtue." Mostly specialized individual poop-poop. . . .

In the case of (3), as Bridgman found out by checking his own work, he could omit the word "concept" and merely say "gold" in matter of fact way and improve his delivery.

In the case of (4)—where an open problem was around—the need of some form of expression to indicate naming as imperfect is very great, but some such word as "guess" will do as well or better.

"Gold" in (3) is very general, even though it does not have its "individuals" stick out as sharply as individual "dogs" under the name "dog."

If you take the logical case of "general," the concept is, as you say, a name for a languaging-process. It runs thus along with term and proposition. If you take the specialized case where the *behavior of conceiving* is itself the event-that-is-being-named, then it is a habit that is being named; then also the naming-habit may be itself being named; or the organic-action-habit may be what is named where it lies in the signaling (as distinct from naming) behaviors. This, I suppose, is the Womb of language of the concept-type.

I don't pretend to any clarity here except in the upper-sharper language uses of the word "concept," and these are not only linguistic, but bad-linguistic.

I am very glad you have broadened the discussion to the underlying habit-base. And the main thing, I think, is not that we have any difference in this matter, but that our scheme of approach is leading us to widen the problem and attack it more thoroughly.

But here is one formally phrased, but not too serious, objection against the way you introduced the habit basis at the start of your letter.

Cases 4 and 5 above are definitely not cases in which the concept or the general are in the form of "habits." They are emphatically cases where *no habit* has appeared and the guy is wriggling around to find one to develop.

[*Bentley*]

Dear Arthur:

Your paper on Cohen * is a nice job. He sent me a copy of his book [*A Preface to Logic*]. . . . What impressed me was that in the early part (Foreword) he expressed his admiration for [George] Boole, Peirce, Schroeder, [Gottlob] Frege, Russell, Whitehead (not only a heterogeneous collection, but reciprocally opposed, many of them, to others in the collection), while his later chapters are a criticism of the formalism which is the characteristic thing about some of them. This confusion is rather typical of him, I think. He started with a wholesome reaction against pure formalism, but also with a great admiration for anyone like Russell who handled symbols. Q.E.D.—first the split, and then the artificial organization you fasten upon. His heart is in the right place, but his head is too choked with erudition.† Kantor, I haven't read, and unless I should, I'll take your word for it. White's essay [book] [*The Origin of Dewey's Instrumentalism*] came out when I was under hospitalization, and I never did get around to giving it more than a hasty glance through. His briefer articles and reviews [that] I've read are headed in the right direction. Probably I should cultivate acquaintance with him, intellectually speaking. He has more stuff to him—not stuffed in him—than most of the younger men who are writing. He at least has resisted going out into the wilderness after current false idols—not that there are any true ones.

I jumped through Hegel, I should say, not just out of him. I took some of the hoop (continuity, anti-hard-and-fast separations) with me, and also carried away considerable of the paper the hoop was filled with. He did me one service—he saved me from the Kantian bug, which was all the vogue—and, in fact, more than once. I doubt if I had "one general field" in our present sense, certainly not firmly, but I was probably looking for it, and as it headed *away* from subject-object, individual-social, mind-matter, etc., isolates. In that sense White is probably true to form in emphasis on what I was against. . . .

Yours, *John D.*

[P.S.] [Albert G. A.] Balz sent me . . . reprints of articles ["Matter and Scientific Efficiency I, II"] published late last year in the *Journal [of Philosophy]*. . . . But on the early pages I found the following . . . "The work of Thomas [Aquinas] may fairly be regarded as *preparatory for scientific inquiry*. . . . Thomas perceived this in his metaphysical efforts to determine "*what scientific inquiry must seek to know.*" (Italics naturally mine.)

---

* Ms. draft of "Logicians' Underlying Postulations." (Eds.)

† For a more rounded and favorable evaluation of M. R. Cohen's work, see Dewey, "A Philosophy of Scientific Method," and Salo W. Baron, *et al.*, eds., *Freedom and Reason: Studies . . . in Memory of Morris Raphael Cohen.* (Eds.)

After reading these pages I sent Balz a copy of our "Knowings-Known" paper, asked him how come [there were] knowings before there were Knowns, and called his attention to our circularity position and the necessity of starting with the Known *as* Known.

I doubt if he gets the point. But I never myself saw so clearly before the source of the "Realism" in modern epistemology and of the opposed "Idealism" that said we had to "know" the knowing powers before we could tell what "could and should be known." It's damn neat in a way. The particular point about "inner diversification of matter" is, of course, just one illustrative technical example; [it] could be replaced by a dozen or more other technical issues without affecting the underlying assumption —[one] can hardly call it a postulate. But it is glaringly illuminating of the whole course of the philosophy of knowledge to see that up to very recent times, there has been no choice, save the necessity of knowledge before knowledge, to tell what the knowing powers had to conform to, or else knowledge before knowledge of the cognitive powers in order to tell what ("things") could and should be known. Cheers.

Paoli, Indiana, July 10, 1945

Dear John:

. . . Kaufmann says "consistency" and "compatibility" are correlates. Here, concretely, is the kernel of the whole argument. If he can hypnotize me into believing him, well and good. If I do not hypnotize, and ask for explanation of the process, I hold that I am entitled to it. . . .

I am more than ever impressed with this point being identical (except for phrasing) with the *saltus* in Cohen, who requires an "hypothesis" to correlate "validity" and "science"—and who insists that this hypothesis is "necessary." . . . If an hypothesis is what one is not sure of, and necessary is what one cannot help admitting, and if logic is based on the declaration that it is necessary to admit what one is not sure of; and if that sort of stuff fills all the wave bands unchallenged, one might as well lie down and die in peace. . . .

Regards, *Bentley*

Paoli, Indiana, July 12, 1945

Dear John:

Examining your *Logic* for a different matter, I note, page 287, that you make propositions symbolizations, and neither [an] external garb, nor yet something complete and final in itself. (Preceding . . . [statements of Dewey's] reject propositions as linguistic expressions of logic, or as the logical result [actually, objects] of judgment.)

All of this rejects the divorcement, and is 100% with what I agree. How-

440

ever, I keep always wanting to say that the doings are linguistic, where I use linguistic as precisely what you call symbolization.

And the reason, of course, is that I can *observe* the language at work symboling; but never can I observe the symboling at work non-linquistically (or, rather, at work without observable sign performance, either of perceptive-signal, naming, or full mathematically-symboling). . . .

Here is a little sharper break in phrasing: *Logic* p. 117. Two kinds of operational: the ideational or conceptual, and the observational. P. 118, ideational and existential. "Symbols . . . are necessarily required in [. . . both]." The last sentence makes no trouble, because it uses symbols as linguistic, so that the intent is to say that language is involved in both the ideational and observational at the level of inquiry. I imagine the other two will adjust on the lines of proposition-into-judgment as all one process, of which there are plenty of expressions in the *Logic*, easy to find and clear, following your express affirmation. I, of course, would tend to render ideational as languaging. . . .

Regards, *Bentley*

Montauk, Long Island, New York, July 16, 1945

Dear Arthur:

. . . (1) You call attention (yours of 7-12-45) to my break on p. 117 of *Logic*. It's there all right, and that is the reason I wanted the footnote in the article taking it back in behalf of "observation" of two phases of subjectmatter. Perception-manipulation is an unambiguous name; perception by itself isn't—we say: I see or perceive what you *mean*—where laying hold is in the medium of language, not of direct manipulation. Possibly "perceptual observation" would cover the phrase [which] I wrongly limited "observation" to, in the cases in which it is relevant to make a distinction. (I don't think there are any cases in our articles in which the distinction is called for.) But in scientific inquiry there is a division of labor; astronomers turning the battery of their apparatus on an eclipse event to get new data, and the "interpretation" by which the data are organized into system in connection with subjectmatter previously formulated through designation and symbolization devices. However, the chief reason I put so much emphasis on this point in the *Logic* text was because of the historic strife of philosophical systems—"empiricism" for sensory perception and rationalism for organizing "principles." I was trying to point out that, from the standpoint of inquiry, at most there is a division of labor in carrying on the work of inquiry, and it was work *doing* rather than work *done* that I was interested in—and that, maybe, is also the special theme of *Logic*. Anyway, the system of knowings-known as extensive in space-time gives me now a much simpler and more direct way to state what I was struggling to get at. What I used "observation" to name in the *Logic* was the local, short-span phase of observation, and by sticking to that I can get away from and beyond the historical controversial system.

(2) "Womb of language" was just a metaphor that occurred to me while I was writing—a playful answer (i.e., not to be taken seriously) to your question about *where*. As I have said, I am perfectly satisfied with your formulation of "conception," and I needn't have made so much fuss about the word, only in some of your earlier writings you seemed to write as if there was nothing the word could stand for except a pseudo-mental something or other. What you say about "gold" goes. It was on this account that I once suggested (at least, I think I did) that "term" could be used as a substitute for conception—"term" as a specified kind of *name*. But I decided "term" probably raised as many questions and was as open to mis-taking as "conception." . . .

But as far as what Kaufmann is trying to do about rules for *acceptance of* propositions (as distinct from rules stating how they are reached in competent scientific practice at a given time), I think Kaufmann isn't trying to say there "might be" another job for methodology. I take Kaufmann to be saying there *must* be a job *outside* of "methodology." Of course, a trained person becomes very skilled in inspecting *"relation of meanings"* as that is distinct from connection of events, while in "relation of meanings" as, e.g., to contradiction and excluded middle, the "meanings" are not referred to any (then and there) specified events. But why Kaufmann fancies the *Logic* and we make no provision for "relations of meanings" and don't see [them] save as set[ting] up a "realm of meanings" independent of factual events [and] having pure logical "canons," instead of [as] just the working "rules" of methodology, [I do not know]. In short, [in] spite of what he *says*, it goes back to the old dualism of form and matter.

Yours, John D.

[P.S.] Expert skill in observing "relations of meanings" is, I guess, what Kaufmann calls "intuition." An expert *in a given field* gets similar skill in "intuiting connections of factual events."

Paoli, Indiana, July 27, 1945

Dear John:

. . . Incidentally, I am finding a lot of good in Moore—his start in common sense—his great care in statement at times about important issues. His interpretation of common sense as common talk. But he does not go out to hitch talk and action in a system; he seems to think analysis of language (concepts) alone will do. And (for his merit),

442

while totally shorn of his Knowing start, he is totally unassertive about the results of his analysis. I can boost him a bit. . . .

Regards, *Bentley*

Montauk, Long Island, New York, July 30, 1945

Dear Arthur,

Enclosed are some belated comments.* You haven't got anything I shouldn't be proud to put my name to, but I shouldn't want it except with a statement that the article is 99.44% pure Bentley, with a few slips and tucks by Dewey. . . .

Yours as ever, *John*

[Notes] . . . According to Cohen, as I understand him, *Universals* are a part of nature which are sufficiently akin to mind (reason) so that they are directly apprehended by the latter. How far Kaufmann's *meanings* are similar to universals, I don't know. . . .

In looking over Cohen's *Preface* [*A Preface to Logic*] hastily, I was struck by what seemed to me a sharp conflict in his statements. At the outset he gives his blessing to the formalists who hold that logic—or logisticism—deals with a separate realm, sphere, or what have you (including Peirce's name among them, if I recall aright!) and then later criticizes the notion that logical forms can be properly understood apart from the known subjectmatter. . . . Here he is nearer to Peirce than to the names he cites; also more in line with historic "rationalists." I don't know whether this point is relevant . . . [but] (I believe) what he here calls validity in relation to "existence" is the logical material of the formalists. This point, if correct, does not affect at all—save to emphasize it— your point about his *tour de force* in having to bring together what he has first split in two. But, at least, he stands apart from Russell in having a sense that there is some kind of intrinsic connection of logical forms or relations with existential subjectmatter. In Russell, if I'm right, the relation is purely external or accidental, not at all necessary from the standpoint of *either* "existence" or "logic." If you can run this down, perhaps it merits being listed as a Postulate. . . .

Likely, you are right in your understanding of the relation of non-contradiction and compatibility. But somehow I had obtained another idea; I didn't think it was a question of "substitution" with Kaufmann, but that according to him, the logical principle of non-contradiction was required in order to "warrant," or give final determining force to, what from the "empirical" standpoint is *mere* compatibility—and accordingly, perhaps no more than coincidental—I can't cite passages from Kaufmann, but I know the post-Kantian Germans. [R. H.] Lotze in his *Logic,* for

---

* On draft of "Logicians' Underlying Postulation." (Eds.)

example, took just this position. (Why Kaufmann omits "identity" I don't know.) Lotze held that it was required to give stability to empirical identifications so that they could afford a firm basis for reasoning and deduction. However, Kaufmann's "excluded middle," in conferring determinacy, performs this function; so he probably regards identity as superfluous; in fact, Aristotle has been criticized on just that score.

I think my view regarding Kaufmann can stay put now; it is a subtilized version of the old empirical-rational. Subtilized because he has mixed up the mathematical with all forms of discourse and reasoning— good, indirect evidence of the soundness of your position in firm discrimination of "symbols" from "(designatory) names."

On the whole, Russell gets beyond me. . . . Here are a few suggestions, not in the form of postulates at all, but impressions. I think he identifies "knowledge" with "Certainty"—what can't be questioned—and that is the basic motivation of his insistence on simplest entities, whether particulars (sense data) or universals, and upon immediate acquaintance with them—no chance to go wrong. Neither the common-sense world, nor that of the objects of physical science are, however, simples, but "compounds," nor are they known directly; the former (common-sense objects) are arrived at by inference and don't amount to enough anyway to demand attention—not from the standpoint of knowledge anyhow. "Physical" objects are constituted by *construction,* every step of which can be controlled, while inference is rather like a leap in the dark. Mathematics affords the rules of construction and is the only completely (certain) "Knowledge" part of physical science, though as far as construction can operate with pure sense-data simples, there is approximation to knowledge as certainty.

There is considerable "intuition of meanings" in the above. But his contempt for "a joblot, higgledy-piggledy world" is well known [*The Scientific Outlook*], and I think a passage can be found in which he definitely says that mathematics is the sole form of knowledge and that the mathematical part of mathematical-physical is all that is strictly "science," or certainty. [Cf. Russell's *The Principles of Mathematics.*]

(In *re* Cohen, I meant to ask if you had available the volume of so-called autobiographies of American philosophers [Adams and Montague, eds., *Contemporary American Philosophy*]; I have a vague memory that Cohen tells in that how he came by his logical position—a kind of combination of Kantian idealism and mathematical realism ["The Faith of a Logician"].) The [theory of] types business I never understood [fully]. Your exposition of Russell's Postulates makes it clearer to me than it ever was before. . . .

My net impression is that Russell's procedure was anticipated by the man (*Alice in Wonderland* or *Bab Ballads* or somewhere) who "painted his whiskers green and then wore so large a fan [that] they could not be seen." Obviously, he has to begin with the world we all live in, which, however, can be neglected save as translated into physical objects. Mathematics, however, gives a perfect, not partial, refuge. It consists of universals known by direct rational intuition. It is eternal and immutable. It represents the realm of possibilities, unalterably noble, over against the despicable world of actualities. By its aid, after Inference (my gosh) to uncertain entities, which, however, are certainly and directly known by direct acquaintance at the limit of analysis (how come?), those simple entities can be ordered back into the objects of physical science. Which are whiskers, which paint, and which the screening fan? It's circular, all right, but the kind of (not) merry-go-round that makes me dizzy.

I think you [are] right about Moore—give him the benefit of the doubt where there is fair ground for doing so. At least, he has a healthy regard for language. . . .

[*Dewey*]

Paoli, Indiana, August 1, 1945

Dear John:

. . . I noticed something about the propositional function the other day. By substituting "x" for a specific instance, it gets away from the complications of specific naming. But by retaining "x" as a naming (open), it aims to preserve the central vice of old procedures in a new dress. Might be said to be a half-way step toward what we have been aiming at. I took a gander at the *Logic,* but did not run across anything particular reflecting on it. I will bet, nevertheless, it is there somewhere.

. . . Unless he [Moore] can analyze sense-data, his whole project collapses. I have nowhere found any *explicit* development in this form either by himself or others. Usually they attack the sense-data issue as a special problem. But, hell, he *starts* with little propositions which *must* have sense-data for subjects. It was only after posing that problem that I began to pick up applicable material. . . . The nearest thing I have come to it is [Paul] Marhenke's discussion ["Moore's Analysis of Sense Perception"] beginning on p. 260 in Schilpp [ed., *The Philosophy of G. E. Moore*], in which he says demonstration of existence of sense-datum is fundamental [in the analysis of perceptual propositions], and p. 258, in which he says Moore does not specify his conditions and has no criteria. Marhenke, however, then goes into long, detailed arguments about a special case. (Maybe, however, he makes better points than I see. Anyway, he is the only thing I have noted on this line I am following.)

Of course, between you and me, we would brush this whole Moore business aside like a gnat. The absurdities abound. *But:* in a way his dead-center [emphasis] on simple, direct, common-sense affirmations at the start is a good forward step toward [the] natural. Incidentally, I have not read . . . [Thomas] Reid for a long time, but the old rooster had a better direct approach, and "sign" interpretation (as I recall it) than the fellows that have come after him.

[*Bentley*]

Montauk, Long Island, New York, August 4, 1945

Dear Arthur:

. . . It seems to be that in his [Moore's] case as well as in Russell's it would be well to point out that the basic assumption—if not *explicit* postulate—is that knowledge and absolute certainty are synonymous names. This assumption had a long history—Aristotle and Scholasticism —then [was] revived for modern philosophers by Descartes. It is the thing that gave Axioms as self-evident truths its long vogue; it is back of the prestige of the syllogism, and I shouldn't wonder if it had exerted an influence, without his knowing it, on Kaufmann's attachment to meanings, deduction, and intuition. One school looks to sense-data simples for ultimate certainties; the other school, to universals; then they have somehow to construct the world as known-knowings out of them. Incidentally, there is, I believe, a highly ambiguous use of "physical objects." Sometimes it is a common-sense horse or hand—or back of *the* or *my* hand—and then it is an "object (subjectmatter) of physical science." (*My* "common sense," not Moore's.)

I think I mentioned that I had an impression that somewhere Russell says that only mathematics is "knowledge" (being capable of "certainty"). In this connection, it may be significant that he denies that statements of morals, or any social statements involving desire or purpose, can be a form of even low-grade pretension to knowledge, being not even empirically factual, but just enunciations of volitional injunctions, prohibitions, etc. . . .

Yours, *Dewey*

Paoli, Indiana, August 6, 1945

Dear John:

I have searched everything I have available on Russell and the mathematical certainty, but do not have here anything I can run down to fixate him. There are indications that the most minute physical namings, which have to be mathematically established would be simples. I have touched up my footnote . . . on Russell *re* particulars—listing sense-data, point-instants, event-particles, as candidates, and adding, "And

446

sometimes mathematical-physical expressions seem the safest components of the world." About as far as I have backing to go at the moment. It is on library-search list, however.

Now as to Moore and the absolute certainty. He will claim it, but mostly he is so far from it that Susan Stebbings hurt his feelings (in the G. Moore volume [Schilpp, ed., *The Philosophy of G. E. Moore*]) when she called his pet common-sense stuff "probable knowledge" ["Moore's Influence"]. He said he held that it was *certain* that I am now sitting in this chair," etc.—[this] valuable [for us]. Altman sent a memo to the effect that Moore's argument that there are true propositions which are not known (but, I assume, known to be true), rated place in postulates for him.

I wonder if any of these items belong "in." I am not after their cosmos, or ontology, but their "logic" at this time, and for our purposes. Logic is the technical procedure. Absolute certainty and nothing less is what Moore and Russell want; still, it is not a logical essential as it looks at the moment. It is (a) a general goal, (b) something they will not stop crying for till they get it—which means never, but (c) something hardly used in their business. Moore takes the sense-data in propositional form as his only-certain-up-to-date. Russell imagines the mathematic-physical atoms to be his goal. Meantime they ride their horses up and down the road—and that is the "logic" I am trying to handle.

However, we shall see. I will work it into the setting of both sets, if not into the postulates proper. And if something new shows up, tip me off. . . .

Regards, *Bentley*

Montauk, Long Island, New York, August 8, 1945

Dear Arthur:

. . . I am quite sure from knowledge of his [Kaufmann's] German [philosophical] antecedents that his canons operate to give "empirical" findings a logical status they don't have of themselves, and since that point can be stated without reference to higher-lower, the later phraseology gives him a chance to evade the issue. What gets me is why in the world he doesn't say, "Yes, that is the difference between us," and let it go at that. . . . I've criticized that view aplenty, but I've never criticized it in him; I am afraid I'm too uncharitable to believe he [at the age of fifty] can change. He has really surrendered a good [deal] of Teutonism, but on the difference between the rational (logical) and empirical he was too firmly "conditioned." Then his identification of mathematics with reasoning as deductive affects him. It might help

447

(him) if you called his attention to your book on mathematics [*Linguistic Analysis of Mathematics*] and denial that mathematical symbols are names. . . .

Best regards, *John D.*

[New York,] August 9, 1945

[To Bentley:]

A Few Thoughts about Things in General and Nothing in Particular. . . . Moore—"The immediately present"—why the "immediately," except to narrow down commonsense? Otherwise the present [that] Moore thinks is certain is what is observed; the "what" being just what it is; deep-superficial, wide-narrow, firm-loose, etc., according to the conditions, terms, of the transaction—just as a sales contract might be for this or that, but "immediately" having nothing to do with the scope of the subjectmatter. What can commonsense name except the subjectmatter commonly observed in a given group at a given state of human culture? A colored arc in the sky can be observed as a sign from the Lord or as a refraction of light under specified physical conditions. Superstition or science—or, literally, *what have* they, we? Hebrews, Greeks, Newtonians, Einsteinians, etc.

It was almost commonsense once that the atom is what the word etymologically says—the undivided.

Now that [the] atom is a compound, and splittable, Russell's commonsense tells him that wave particles are the ultimate physical "realities." For, how else are molecules "made" of atoms, and atoms of wave particles? The only thing that can be "immediately" present to a "real" physicist is a wave particle. Atoms are constructions, etc. . . .

[*Dewey*]

Montauk, Long Island, New York, August 10, 1945

Dear Arthur:

For a change I think I am in flat disagreement with you on one point. I think in any sense in which Russell [and Moore] are occupied with Logic in their theories of knowledge, the statement that knowledge is certainty, and that only certainty is knowledge, is their fundamental premise, to which everything else has to be accommodated. Of course, one can question whether their doctrines are logic, or a mixture of psychology and ontology to which logic is related; how? but somehow.

Even so, I think with reference to a list of postulates of what they are doing, their basis premise, as [the] point of departure that controls all the rest, is as stated above. *Absolute* certainty may be *their* goal, but that is quite different from the "proposition" that only certainty is knowledge and that you have to have that at the start or else there is nothing to build on in getting knowledge—or in reducing to knowledge the subjectmatters of everyday observations and "physical objects." In other words, I "feel" that that proposition is very much on "the road" they travel on—at the start, as well as at one, the other, or last end. Or putting it slightly differently, no logical theory of knowledge is possible unless we can find something to start with that is not capable of being questioned. Maybe, of course, I don't get your point. . . .

Yours, with best regards, *John D.*

Paoli, Indiana, August 13, 1945

Dear John:

. . . About Russell, Moore, and "knowledge is certainty, and only certainty is knowledge." I am not out in the clear yet.

Your point is correct for Russell; I think it is correct for Moore (though I think Altman, who has played around with Moore some, doubts its stress). I agree that (considering Russell first) it is a presupposition, premise, and background attitude. That, however, is the kind of material to make "postulates" out of. I can't dodge on that count.

I have a memo . . . to get this in *as background.* But I just can't see at the moment how to get it in among the "postulations"—I mean not in the generalized way. Do I not have it in a sort of form in: . . . "Ultimate simples are entities that exist"? Trouble is that Russell sometimes affirms them as acquaintance. But at other times when "they are known only inferentially . . . ," how we can say he is *starting* with certainty? Once chosen, they serve as certainties, as long as [he] does not switch to something else.

In a way you have a better case with Moore. He picks sense-data and simple propositional forms for them. He asserts absolute certainty [for them]—but in a way that something about them is not [of] much "force." . . . Then when he tries to demonstrate them (the sense-data as subjects of propositions) through Analysis, he doesn't get anywhere. So while he "understands them" teetotally, he does not yet "know" them analytically and never has got it proved to himself that he so "knows" them. . . .

The question remains open for both of them whether my text meets the need you correctly set down. My answer to that is—need for what? For particularly *what* purpose? Some way I feel that if I introduced a postulation for either or for both, thus, "Fundamental is limitation of knowledge to what is certainly known, and limitation of certainty to what has become knowledge," I would, no matter what I did, be using phrasings that could be attacked—that would start arguments—that would

449

lead to mists and mistifications. What I want is bullet shots of sentences such that each, as it comes, cannot readily be gainsaid. . . .

Bentley

Montauk, New York, August 15, 1945

Dear Arthur:

. . . Moore made his first great reputation when he attacked the then ruling "Idealists" (Oxford) and started [the] Cambridge University "Realism." He held that universals, etc., were not mental, but the immediate *objects* of mind or reason or what have you. . . . (I presume Kaufmann would deny that he holds "meanings" and "concepts" to be themselves mental; they are that wonderful thing, "logical entities"— which I suppose is why he calls himself a "conceptualist"—using the word in its medieval, pre-modern "psychological" sense.) . . . I have been terribly stupid about him [Kaufmann]. I couldn't reconcile his alleged indebtedness to me with the rest of his doctrine. But it is as simple as pie. I used the word "warranted" freely. Well, the results of "empirical" inquiry—observation, by gosh—are all right in a way, but they aren't *warranted* till the logical relations of propositions enter. As he put it in his earlier letter to me . . . "I hold that observation *Implies* apprehension of meanings," and in the same letter . . . "What I deny is *Only* that factual investigation by which the empirical validity (warranted assertibility) of propositions is determined can affect the internal relations among propositions (entailment, contrariety, etc.), such relations being *Presupposed* in every judgment concerning the empirical validity of propositions." The first part of this sentence seems to contradict what I just said about being *Warranted*, but the last clause agrees. I fancy in the first part he was simply using a phrase of mine while in the last part he is telling me how come. I see you have kept comment down to a minimum. But if any comment were made, it would be that while Kaufmann has made a definite advance on Kant in holding that empirical investigation can go on its way without sense materials having to be categorized synthetically by a priori principles of the understanding, he retains the idea that it (empirical inquiry) cannot justify or warrant acceptance or rejection of conclusions it reached, without directly intuited conceptual relations being "implied" or presupposed.

(You referred in a recent letter to my having a "feeling" for his meaning; I was . . . slow in getting to it, but Kaufmann is a professionally trained philosopher and so I am, so I did have a feeling for what he *had* to be at in terms of his background.) You are right in saying that his assumptions of "meanings," "concepts," . . . [are] the root of his view— but I didn't see any way to approach him directly on that tack. His reply

450

in effect would be that meanings are meanings, not mental existences, but directly apprehended, etc., and we should continue going round in a circle. When he answers my question about "meanings" in non-mathematical discourse and in mathematical subjectmatter (which he has consistently dodged so far—I mean the topic, not just my question), I thought maybe I could approach him directly about meanings. For, I'm reasonably sure, it is mathematics he has in mind all the time as the case of pure logical relations of propositions to one another. . . .

As always when I go over your different versions I am struck practically dumb with your persistent thoroughness.

Yours with regards, John D.

Montauk, Long Island, New York, August 15, 1945

Dear Arthur:

. . . There is more similarity between Russell and Kaufmann than appears on the surface. Putting them in their historical setting, I should say they—and Moore as I wrote the other day—(i) became aware of the mistake of the philosophers who treated "conceptions, universals, and relations" as "psychological," which at that time meant, in the prevailing state of doctrine, "mental." Hence, (ii) they made a sharp division between the logical and the psychological—which was to the good as far as the latter was taken to be merely mental and subjective. But (iii) the conceptions, relations, universals weren't physical. Hence, the Logical as a realm all by itself—neither mental nor physical—but "objective" in the sense of that which is apprehended by mind. I have become convinced that this piece of history gives the clue to a lot of things in contemporary "philosophical" writings. As frequently happens in human history—not just philosophical history—one past error is detected, and its counterpart or correlate error is not detected, and the new improvement is stalled, arrested, in another mistake. The whole "realm" of the "logical"—conceptions, meanings, relations, universals—is hung up in the air—no ancestry and no posterity—save in dialectical ingenuity. I believe I have something here in the way of a clue or key to a number of things in contemporary writers that don't make sense of themselves, but which make the kind of sense that untoward historical events possess. Your clear summaries of Kaufmann and Russell have helped a lot. Before, I just couldn't make sense of these writings and so turned my back on them. I think I've got them pinned up now in the collection of historical specimens. In this context they belong, just as do some of the geological monstrosities that have appeared in the course of history called "evolution."

Regarding Moore, . . . as far as he defines "sense datum" in terms of

451

what is directly apprehended (thus reversing the usual practice of defining—specifying—direct apprehension in terms of some arbitrary prior assumption about a "sense-datum"), he is certainly moving in the direction of common sense—and in the direction of relying on "observation." . . . But his illustrations do not seem to me to live up to what he says. If they did, he would have an extended durational continuum as his original datum, and not puzzles about "my hand"—why "hand" and why "mine" taken in isolation?

I add on my own account that the situation which (as it seems to be) Moore is dealing with is what led me in some of my writings to point out an ambiguity in the use of "datum." Sometimes as used, it stands for the whole damn range of what is observed—or what one is "aware of"—good, bad, and indifferent, cognitively speaking; sometimes, it stands for a highly discriminated result of analysis which serves as a crucial check in drawing an inference. The former is the datum of observation; the latter is what is called the "sense-datum": that is, observation focused on a narrow range for the sake of obtaining a (relatively) sure evidential check on a hypothesis—like the highly specialized visual datum in observation of the eclipse of Mercury, which tested Einstein's hypothesis. (If Moore would once admit that the primary subjectmatter of observation is an eclipse of Mercury with all the scope of the best astronomical knowns to date, I think his paradoxes would disappear.) Another allied point—speaking in my own behalf, not re Moore—what keeps bothering them as a great epistemological problem is the connection of ordinary observed objects with "scientifically" observed subjectmatters. They can't see that matter serves as an extended spatially and elongated durationally observation of the same material facts. (To which I have added, in my writing [Logic, pp. 60–80], that the difference between the two versions is not that one is right and one is wrong, but that having different functions and uses, they enter into different connections—direct use and enjoyment in one case, promotion of understanding in the other —but this point isn't indispensable.) . . .

Regards, *John D.*

Paoli, Indiana, August 17, 1945

Dear John:

I am picking up Russell again. I run bang up against our little argument again.

You state that for Russell (and Moore) and "in any sense in which he is occupied with Logic, . . . knowledge is certainty and only certainty is knowledge."

I would not disagree in the slightest.

The only question is just how I should use it in the present procedure. [No, don't use it; not relevant.] *

By implication I take your suggestion to be (though you have not made it specifically in this form) that my "postulation" for Russell should present this point first.

As against this, I seem to have four arguments:

1. I do not know just how to phrase it to avoid disputation.

2. It seems to me from my present approach, it is a pretty wide generalization as to his attitude. [O.K.]

3. I have not made similar wide statements for any of the rest of you.

4. I have covered the point "concretely":

For Russell, in . . . that simples exist, and that, . . . knowledge is fixation of simples.

For Moore . . . as you indicate.

Take your own case. Should I put ahead of everything that you are maintaining the thesis that all knowings are tentative, and that your primary business is to destroy the fellow that maintains the opposite? [No.] I don't think so. You do so hold; and so do I. But your main business is not that creed. Your main business is to analyze and display the knowing-growing process. I so present you. You so present yourself in the first chapter. [You are right.]

Personally, I would say that the deeper issue still is the way all four, Cohen, Kaufmann, Russell, Moore, make procedure rest in the "decisions" of minds. You abandoned that very long ago. But in your *Logic* you did not stress it as vital. You were very careful and tentative. Thus "I doubt if any special 'thing' called 'thought' exists"—close paraphrase, though not your phrasing. If you had gone head-on along that line you would have distracted attention and probably wasted energy—though (I feel) if you had been sharper with it, then much misrepresentation of your view would have been avoided. (Practical problem.) [You are probably right. But I *might* have *sown another* crop of misrepresentations.]

It seems to me a prac*tical* issue for the *given* job.

Glad to have you more specific if I need it.

Regards, *Bentley*

New York, August 20, 1945

Dear Arthur:

. . . There is a fundamental ambiguity in Kaufmann's writings; sometimes he is talking about meanings, and sometimes about *"relation of*

* All of the bracketed material in this letter represents answers by Dewey to Bentley's questions. (Eds.)

meanings," transferring over to meanings per se the traits he attributes to relation of meanings: then he can attribute to meanings the logical status which is possessed by some relations—namely, "entailment, implication, negation," etc. Then, at other times, it is only the relation which is strictly logical or rational and is what is directly inspected. . . .

To Kaufmann the "empirical" signifies (fundamentally) disconnected particulars—and these particulars are all that can be "perceived"—till the logical or rational provides some organization—an echo of Kant's "synthesis." Kaufmann would probably deny [that] this is a fair representation of his view, and it is somewhat too bald. But I think you could, or might, get somewhere if you asked him whether (i) there is an original distinction of two kinds of observation, one of particulars, called "sense-observation," and another of certain kinds of relations or connections, such as his direct apprehension of *certain* relations of meanings—entailment, implication, negation, and (ii) if so, where do such connections as are stated in physical formulations—gravitation, interconnections of "atomic weights," etc.—come in? That is, which of the above classes do they fall in? Does he deny that connections of this sort are capable of the same kind of observability as are particular events, or, once more, what *does* he mean by "Empirical" and its difference from "Rational"? Just what limitations are set forth by "empirical" as he uses it? . . .

Yours, *John D.*

New York, August 21, 1945

Dear Arthur:

. . . I don't intend to go back to my emphasis upon the need for a correct understanding of "Experience." But Kaufmann's "empirical" is in a way a justification of my long continued harping on that subject. At least it illustrates what kept me at it—the need for an account of "Experience" which would include the relational along with the "sensible." As far as Knowings-Known are concerned, "observation" covers the ground, and while it will be misunderstood by traditionalists—not to same extent as "experience"—Kaufmann (and others) do not see that the range of connections (spatial-temporal) do all [that] they bring in "reason," etc., to do.

J. D.

Bloomington, Indiana, August 23, 1945

Dear John:

Your recent letter referred to confusion in my account of Moore. . . .

I see now, however, that my [sketch on] Moore scandalously refers to

454

propositions with sense-data-subjects, and then passes over to more complex propositions as if they too had such subjects. This is vicious, because I let something of my own approach distort and discolor Moore's, and so, also, as to blind me to what he was doing. . . .

The following . . . [passages get] rid (possibly) of some defects of statement, but are not "informative":

On the basis of such simplified common-sense-propositions having sense-data subjects, very many instances of other propositional knowledge can be evaluated through Analysis. . . .

In Analysis, propositions and propositional components are dealt with as concepts (not as words or verbal expressions). . . .

What I don't know is the sense in which [1] sense-data in propositions are conceptual, [2] sense-data become propositional, [3] sense-data propositions become conceptual (and probably other similar steps take place).

I mean, I don't know how to say (for Moore and as Moore) specifically what this atmospheric, linguistic procedure of Moore stands [for]. . . .

Best regards, *Bentley*

New York, August 25, 1945

Dear Arthur:

I have yours of the 23rd from Bloomington. I can't see why in the world you should be discouraged about your article; it's a swell job. The point I mentioned about Moore, I wouldn't call a confusion, nor did I mean to. Not having the Moore volume to consult, I thought others might find an appearance of "incompatibility," and was sure a slight verbal change or addition on your part would avert the possibility of distortion of what you are saying. I sincerely believe that what you have done is one of the best, most instructive, jobs of understanding and report that has been done. I believe it will reach some readers who won't get the point of the "Knowings-Knowns" ["A Terminology for Knowings and Knowns"] article. It is as objective, viz., fair, as it is thorough.

The point I am going to mention hasn't got anything to do with your piece, and maybe it hasn't anything to do with Moore. But I was struck in reading your analysis with his insistence that the subjectmatter of propositions, etc., consists of "concepts," and it made [me] wonder, though perhaps the wonder is crazy, whether he is moving in a groping way toward the circularity of knowings-knowns. Of course, "concepts" in the phrase "are dealt with as concepts" is open to an indefinite number of interpretations, all of them vague at best. But the expression would seem to rule out not merely "words"—or what I suppose he means by words—but also "things" in the raw. It would seem—or might be

taken to seem—to indicate realization that knowing is a kind of behavior that takes raw materials into a new and distinctive set of connections. However, it probably takes a lot of "interpreting" to make
this out of him. . . .

Yours, John

New York, September 2, 1945

Dear Arthur:

I have gone over the last versions of your paper.* It confirms my impression of a good job well done; I shouldn't wonder if it bore more
immediate fruit than the extensive papers, in considerable part just
because the paper "lets thing lie." The final portion prepares the way
for a later paper on what the symbolic approach might and should be.

Just now I have but one change to suggest. . . . You have "control
under mental clarification." I believe substituting "conceptual" or "rational" for "mental" would be an improvement for reasons indicated
earlier. I think Kaufmann thinks that he thinks that the distinctively
"logical" is a "realm" apprehended by mind, but not itself mental.
In his last . . . [essay or letter] he says he identifies mathematics with
deductive discourse as far as logic is concerned; I thought he did. He
had said earlier in effect that he got his distinctive impetus from [David]
Hilbert. . . .

Yours, John

[P.S.] "Objective." I ran across a dictionary division in which the
meaning of the word is supposed to be clarified by adding "in distinction
from that which is due to or contributed by the subject."

This struck me as a good example of the present language confusion.
There is no intimation of what would happen if the "subject" were itself
"objective"—as belonging in the same field of inquiry—as you make clear
about "nature" and "natural."

But as time goes by, I doubt if there will be need for the once projected
vocabulary paper. I think you've covered the ground pretty well. In
fact, in looking ahead, I'm wondering whether the transaction (and
cognate themes) won't about do the job.

[New York,] September 17, 1945

Dear Arthur:

. . . I haven't written lately. Get taken up with reading [Charles L.]
Stevenson's book *Ethics and Language,* a curious mixture of good and
very bad things; have written a paper for *Journal of Philosophy* ["Ethical

---

* "Logicians' Underlying Postulations."   (Eds.)

Subject-Matter and Language"] on the bad in it—especially, as he says his treatment is "not dissimilar, in broad outlines, to that found in the ethical writings of John Dewey." In one point he has followed my monograph on [*Theory of*] *Valuation Judgments* [*sic*] in the University of Chicago *Unity of Science* series—but I haven't discussed that. In reading his book, I was led to go back to Peirce as he identifies meaning, taken psychologically, with Morris's complete distortion of Peirce— I hadn't realized before either quite what a falsification Morris's account of Peirce's theory of signs and meanings is, nor yet how close Peirce's theory is to yours—ours. His use of subjective language in a non-subjective sense is the great hindrance. I've got material enough for another article on Peirce's theory of signs-meanings and incidentally nailing Morris to the cross—along the line of your earlier treatment of him, but more so—he completely inverts Peirce—and I've got some good quotations from Peirce to the effect that "psychological" material can be *known* only in non-psychological terms. . . .

Yours, John D.

Paoli, Indiana, September 19, 1945

Dear John:

What do you know about the word "identify"? What do you "feel" about it? I used it occasionally in a lousy way in earlier papers collateral to name-identification (possibly); but dropped it out on revisions; and never investigated. The question is the standard type. Would a toad "identify" a fly? or a dog "identify" his master? A man identifies by comparisons and namings. Would a man "identify" without namings? (Our general scheme would say he did not, in any proper sense and with linguistic backgrounds included.) Would tensors "identify" anything? Or even would natural numbers do any identifying purely as numbers? Answer to the last seems clearly "No"—even though, let a speculator alone, and he might have a world-scheme of tensor-identification-procedures worked out in a flash.

Only question above is [the] possibility of use of [the] word at any stage under conditions for sharp use to definitely limited ranges. "Identify" [is] apparently much the same as name "knowledge"—except it starts out with a greater accuracy—that is, with a narrower range of applications. . . .

Regards, Bentley

New York, September 20, 1945

Dear Arthur,

Here are a few suggestions for what they [are] worth *re* "specification" —perhaps more to the point than what I sent the other day.

457

I. The background—man in the world—knowing as an occurrence in world—of the nature of a transaction? (maybe, doesn't belong here—the transaction part) beginning, at least, as primitive forms of animal life; give example; signaling—signing as inclusive name. Designating-knowing-naming, that is what we discuss here—as a transactional event—men behaving in the world with names and other things in the world in and through speech-writing.

(You can make this summary review much better than above—review for readers who didn't read the earlier [paper] or who need a refresher as to the general standpoint.)

II. Names as tools—how they operate: indicating—in-forming—not just in the sense of telling something, but as giving them in sharp form *in* and *for* knowings-knowns. (Don't think we should infringe on your later paper on knowing, but I think the account of specification would be better understood with a few general remarks on what names *do—what* including *how*.) [Names function by] summing up and retaining previous knowings-knowns (the "in" part, including, for further use and extension, a settling, shaping of the known, but this does what the sharpening tools should be [doing] when shaped so as to effect revision, further development as tools in and through use) (no finalities, etc.).

We shall use characterization for the looser (unfirmed), less effective kind of tool-use—serves purpose of identification and indication, denoting, in ordinary communication—water, stone—what they do and what they *don't* do. Compare with some scientific name; H_2O for water, some formula for a rock, etc.; firmer identification and closer discrimination—breaking up fluids, rocks, etc., into sorts, kinds, species—*Specification.* What *Firming is,* that is, *does;* loose characterizations depend upon *connections* which, however, they do not name. It is in and of a system, but it is loose (vague) because it does not educe, adduce, the system in which it belongs—a scientific word does, e.g., H_2O states connections, is a name only as these connections are knowings-knowns; "water" points to traits *as if* they were exclusive, self-possessed, even though found *also* in other things—as fluidity, etc. To specify is to mark off and out within a system—the haze characteristic of characterization remains to some extent—that is, again, not final and absolute—placed in more extensive space-time system as the specifying proceeds. (This is really the gist of anything I might say.)

III. Symbols, Mathematics—signs which are not names. . . . V. Back to the case of signs-signalings—generalized statement.

If above approach doesn't appeal to you, throw it away—I was feeling for a way of approach that put the readers *en rapport.* It may be that this approach encroaches too far on discussion of language in general.

One advantage is that it prepares the ground, I believe, for an intelligible statement of propositions, terms. I think that somewhere in connection with criticism of superstitious use of these words, it is important to indicate that our point of view gives a straightforward workable account—specification in short.

Yours as ever, *John D.*

[P.S.] Don't think we have specified "firming" enough. . . .

Paoli, Indiana, September 20, 1945
[Draft of essay by Bentley for "Specification" essay for *Journal of Philosophy*]

SPECIFICATION OF TRANSACTION

I

Consider the word "knowledge." Its wandering applications cover perceptions, conditionings, instincts, habits, book-knowledge, and all sorts of linguistic knowings, aesthetic appreciations, and mathematical formulations. It is vague as to whether it belongs to a "knower" who has or does it; or whether it has some sort of "existence" apart from a knower. No wonder [that] no respectable theory . . . of "knowledge" can be found.

One thing, however, can be said: Whenever men apply the word ["knowledge"], living organisms are involved also. Since organisms not present in environments are unknown, and since the word "organism" is such that to assume one without an environment would not make sense linguistically, the environment also is implied when the word "knowledge" is used.

To get terminological firmness with respect to knowings and knowns, we must manifestly, at this stage of inquiry, limit our range of consideration. We have decided to limit ourselves to knowings-in-through-by-with-namings, and to face the inclusive organism-environment locus positively by determining for our purposes (using simple linguistic integrity as a guide) that namings and named are phases of a single process such that no named [thing is] without a naming, and no naming [is] without a named [thing].

A short inspection will make it reasonably clear that what we thus do is to confine ourselves to what is before us, thus throwing out of account things that demand consideration in their own independency, such as "independently real knowers" or "independently real knowns"; and further to broaden ourselves to observe in full process and common function what is before us, without tailoring it to some prevailing style representing other manners of speech or realms of inquiry.

We have chosen, as [we have] reported in earlier papers, the name Fact for namings-named. We have used Designations for technical namings, and Events for technical Nameds. We have discarded the word

459

"definition"—a common run-around for sundry legitimate or illegitimate purposes—from naming regions and assigned it strictly to symbolic precisions, such as those of mathematics. We have distinguished among Designations two forms with the special names "Characterizations" and "Specifications." We have allowed "Events" with respect to permanence and tests of observability at the human level to be distinguished as "Situations," "Occurrences," and "Objects" (also provisional namings). Finally, for typical forms of full functional naming-named procedure we have used the names Self-action, Interaction, and Transaction. All of this [is] definitely within the framework of Fact, which is itself in our procedure a specification of transaction.

(For these procedures and suggestion, see preceding papers ["A Terminology for Knowings and Knowns" and "Postulations" in the *Journal of Philosophy*].)

We now desire to develop more sharply Specification and Transaction, partially as namings for knowings, and partially because these two devices, Specification on the side of Naming, Transaction on the side of the Named, are the tools we propose to use in our further inquiry.

We have pre-	FACT	under	(Characterizing
sented on the	(Situation)	existential	or Specifying but
Event side	(Occurrence)	Designation	never defining)
	(Object)		

(See [Dewey's] *Logic*[: The Theory of Inquiry], p. 126.)

The above treatments describe organisms-acting-in-world (we say "naturally"). We have indicated that in the old treatments (which we call "non-natural," because they set off the knower from the known, and used many patternings on that basis) (and because "activity" was not description in durational form—was not so taken).

This whole procedure of existential designation showed types as follows: Self-Action; Interaction; Transaction. We may now note that: Self-Action, in general, stands for the non-natural "knower" made model for the [non-] natural things (spirits, fairies, ghosts, essences, principles, minds); Interaction, in general, stands for the mechanistic thing made model for everything; Transaction, in our use, is an assertion of freedom from the frozen type of actor, or of material-physical "thing" or "fact." We have argued strongly that, in the present state of knowledge, the impasse in epistemological theory suggests that the transactional view (the free-inquiry permit) should be applied to knowings and knowns.

One branch of the argument for it is that physics in all the newer inquiry . . . [relativity theory and quantum mechanics] has gone transactional as against the Newtonian interactional. (I suspect the "infinity" symbol in ordinary, common mathematics is a "transactional" intrusion.)

[Comment by John Dewey]:

1. Here we seem to be getting a dividend for having kept off the word

"exist." "Existential Designation" may be made to hold for the combined *Event and Designation* as process, since (a) it makes up Fact; (b) the context, as we have developed it, forbids extrapolations of "the existent as real"; (c) it makes the contrast with symbol and definition more vivid.

2. We seem to lack a clean statement as to the Self-Inter-Trans-[actional] status, though perhaps "Self" enters as primitive (now discarded) characterization; "inter" as a highly successful approximation in limited uses; and "trans" as a form for valid "natural" existential specification.

3. (Memo: I always ache to mention the despised Comte. His theological and metaphysical [stages] are both in our "self." His positive [stage] we analyze into "inter" and "trans.")

II

(A little more material, and a little progress in organization—but will try to hold it down to *sketch* of main points)

We have now to consider Specification as a form of Designation—i.e., of naming. We shall use Specification for the most advanced form of naming we have available. That is the form developed by science, as we have it culturally present in our age, and open to observation and study as we wish. Specification is not "a name" in detachment; nor is it a discussion either of such a name, or of what the name stands for in detachment in the way of "existing thing." We do not start out with a thing as an actual existent, and a name as a human product tied to the thing in one-to-one correspondence, and a great quantity of talk about either the thing or the name. We start out with human beings in action in a cosmos in which they are active, both as being components of it (as situations, occurrences, objects, according as viewed), and as having it [the cosmos] environmentally set over against them for many purposes of study. Thus, the naming process, that which is named, and the full import, meaning, application, of the naming are all one process.

What we have to do with every such word as Specification is (1) to see it in the full cosmic process as just set down; (2) to decide whether we shall establish its use primarily on the naming or the named side; and (3) to make sure thereafter while proceeding in the full sense of (1) not to deviate from the aspectual use as in (2) within the full sense of (1). Practically all words we use in an inquiry into knowings and knowns (or namings and named) are double-barreled in William James's sense. The word "Specification" is most familiar as used on the side of naming rather than named; though in an architect's office the "specifications" are either a document delivered, or the actual construction in view. We shall use it for our purposes as a form of naming or Designation.

We have first of all two steps to take in making the exhibit. One is to

461

distinguish "designations" from "definitions." The other is to distinguish within designations, the "characterizations" from the "specifications." The word "definition" has a broader use than any other in this field. It is so broadly and variously used that it is not of itself definite anywhere. Try to define "definition" itself. There is no consistent usage as to whether definition is done with respect to the word, or to what the word names (if it is presented as a name) or what the word is purposed to accomplish linguistically, if not presented as a name. Pass that puzzle over as far too bothersome for an initial lesson. Beyond this the word "definition" stands (1) for whatever descriptions of usages at different times and places the dictionary gives, (2) for certain logicians' goals, (3) for the best possible scientific statement, and (4) for highly precise symbolic uses for mathematical equivalence and substitution. In a preceding paper we have stated our reasons for dropping the word in the first three uses and allotting it strictly to the last. We believe that the very first requirement for advance is a firm distinction between naming and symbolizing behaviors, and that the word "definition" should be held to a single prescribed usage and not [be] allowed to drag implications from one use over into the field of another use. We propose at a later date to discuss at length the construction of knowledge in which naming and symbolizing are held as firmly apart as are, let us say, perceiving and naming today. We cannot do this now because of the space it will take and the large amount of preparatory work required. The distinction we make between naming and symbolizing, however, firm though it must be, is not to be one of the symbolic type, nor one of the quasi-symbolic logical, expressions, but instead itself a specification—a specification of uses, based on observation and analysis of the linguistic-logical scene around us.

Assume now the distinction of naming from symboling behaviors (or of Designation from Definition) in the following form. Men, having been in many contacts with their environments, . . . behaviorally have used cues, signs, earmarks, conditionings, and habitual responses [and] have "evolved" (i.e., come to symbolize) the type of sign called language, or more specifically for our purposes, naming. Their namings are active-organic environmental processes, and their nameds are under the same description. It is not the organism-as-namer over against the thing-as-named; but the organism-environment naming-activity [that is] serving behaviorally as a more highly evolved type of sign as over against the perceptional-manipulative behaviors, equally organic-environmental, equally signing activities, but in this case dealt with through a new signing specialization. We further observe that in much the same sense that word-signs developed out of perceptive signs, so a further development has evolved symbol-signs out of word-signs. The distinction here is functional. It is that while word-signs function as names (designates), symbol-signings build up symbolic systems, the boundaries of which their symbol components do not cross to produce specific namings, but which operating as system in full, through a procedure other than that of naming, give a control over events in the cosmos (an . . . [intra]-cosmic action) of much greater efficacy than the older name-controls.

The word "language" presents a problem of its own in connection with the above construction. One of the present writers [A. F. Bentley] has insisted that mathematical process be treated as a linguistic process. The other [John Dewey] has used symbol in the past to cover naming. Both are inclined now to withdraw from these positions, although the issues have no great significance in immediate workmanship, and no final decision is here suggested. The word "language" may be used to cover all the procedures of name and symbol. What we have called Designation and Definition would then appear as two divisions within language. This would tend to lessen emphasis on the distinctions between [the] name and symbol levels as of a rating correlated with that between perceiving and naming. On the other hand, to confine the word, "Language," to the sounds and markings of naming and strip it of the sounds and marking of mathematical development might likewise seem forced. The specialized use of symbol over against name in the same sense that definition is placed over against designation is strongly indicated as essential to development, in principle, whether by these particular specifications or not. The type of this development is seen in the history of natural numbers, from early uses as namings to an outcome in mathematical deduction, and all the development of arithmetic beyond.

[To] J. D. I said I was going to give an abstract or outline of development. And here are three pages of this introductory stuff. As usual, the damn typewriter does just what it wants to, and never, or rarely, what I try to tell it to do. AFB

III

LOGICAL MISCEGENATION

Given an evolutionary or developmental inspection through the use of name over against symbol, we must record a large region of apparently in-between procedures. Roughly, they include most of the procedures of logic as we have it. This is as it would be expected. Nature apparently is not seen achieving heaven by a single bound; large leaps are not evident, whatever skips and hops may seem to show themselves among quanta and genes. Various devices have been employed to separate names in language from other words—perhaps as many devices as there have been investigators. Russell, for instance, if memory serves, said names were words that applied to things in isolation, while other words had meanings only in contexts. That is short and sweet; also meaningless

463

when human behaviors are under consideration. Mill was willing to accept adjectives as names along with nouns by the device of supplying some such words as thing or object, but the rest of the syncategorematic terms he emphatically rejected as having "no title whatever to be considered as names" (*Logic*, I, ii, 2). As soon, however, as one sees namings as activities of men-in-environment, the "not" in "not a dog" has naming-validities comparable to the "dog" in plain "dog." Dewey points out that it is purely arbitrary to hold that such words as "and" and "or" do not designate what they do in fact designate, namely formal relations (*Logic*, p. 351); and he adds that "it seems to be a superstition taken over from traditional grammar that a name must designate something concrete." "In fact," he says, "every symbol names something; otherwise it is totally without meaning. . . ." (This last cannot be used, [on] account [of a] different use of "symbol." I leave it in as matter to consider.)

A simple extension of Mill's departure from the old rule of the syllogism is sufficient to produce the naming value in all words which have to do with things as subject-matter or items presented to attention, since there is no magic in a single word as a name [that makes it]. Preferable to a group of words. To have a name at all, we must in our viewpoint have a verbal value—an assertion. This is in conflict with the old treatment!—here a thing, there a name for it, then an account of it by mental logomachy—or something or other. (Development and re-study needed.) Since in our procedure the "named," designated as Event, is given appearance either as Situation, Event, or Object, the naming is not merely applied to the (fixed) object, but freely ranges the field. A class or a relation can be named under Designation without any such question arising as to whether a class or a relation corresponding to the name "exists," because existence in that arbitrary sense is not introduced under our Designation at any point. "From" and "under" as well as "this" and "cow" are all namings, none perfect, all participant, though some [are] seemingly more pronounced [when seen] as corresponding to the differentiation of "object" rather than "situation" or "occurrence." "Go and shoot" names action, in full behavioral presentation, as do the two verbs "go" and "shoot" separately. Such an issue as that of internal *vs.* external relations needs no discussion—it disappears from consideration altogether when arbitrary existential applications are dropped. What is left is not existential on either the external or the internal side in any rigidity of presentation.

The distinction between "name" and "symbol" is not based on parts of speech or on the old manner of viewing the components of a proposition and a syllogism. It is much more fully functional. It depends on how the signs and marks hold together in system. Consider behavioral name and behavioral symbol, and besides them, behavioral perception-manip-

464

ulations. As among or between manipulations (say Events in our present terminology), Dewey has used the word "connection." As running from word-name to behavioral perceptional or manipulative, his name was "reference." This leaves over the organization within symbols taken as in detachable system. Here the word "relation" was used. (Dewey, *Logic*, p. 55. This, however, was a comparatively late terminological device, not definitely used throughout the entire text.)

One point (to insert) is that in this scheme all perception is activity as much as is [the] muscular motion of organism in walking. . . . [and in] No sense opposed to action. All sensing is action. (See [Dewey,] "Naturalistic Theory of Perception.")

The word, or name, or symbol—none of them in this presentation is an "entity" [in] itself [and] set opposite some other "entity," for which it stands. The old "entity" disappears entirely, for all is process in which organism and environment are in interplay.

Here on both sides, the signing and signed, the naming and named, the knowing and known, there is activity, which means there is duration. Durations are plotted against durations, a very different business from spot-matching of entity against entity. The contrast with the [Ludwig] Wittgenstein-Russell atomic fictions is very sharp in this respect, and [also] with all logics, which have, somewhere or other, desiderata of this type.*

Let us assume the organism's smellings, touchings, seeings, etc., to become accompanied by exclamatory sounds, which become habitual and so . . . progress up toward organized language. All this is "about" something. The problem as to whether the organism does it, or the thing compels the organism, does not arise; we accept all transactionally or in interaction, interplay. As organization, the sounds get success[ful] and unsuccessful (ultimately right and wrong) effects. Even the wrong [effects] are about what's going on. It is only under a minor localized determination that the "is" and the "is not" is made dominant, decisive, absolute. Now this naming process got to naming qualities, and naming what it calls abstractions; and then it got to treating all the things-named as though they were correct namings, which in certain places and under certain limitations they were. Certain of these devices dealing with quantities, and primarily with countings (though this is not an historical account, or checked from that point of view) began to show remarkable characteristics as opposed to others. They held together; they worked; they expanded both in countings and in Euclidean geometry; they expanded into all our modern number theory and various geometries and

* (J.D. [In Section III] above from point of view of name, there was something about the in-between region between mathematical symbol and descriptive-designational naming. This needs enlargement, with some such material as the following. [A. F.] B.)

[into] much more highly specialized operational procedures. (If I went on with this, we would have the [pure] mathematics-*vs.*-existence argument [which] we cannot take up [now].) (Dewey, [*Logic*], p. 256: "Confusion arises in logical theory when propositions about kinds [in space-time that are general in the sense of *generic*] are identified with universal propositions [of non-existential import].) (Problem always is how to get enough in for illumination without going so far as to ruin whole presentation—throw it off rails.)

We have here, however, a huge region handled by existential-thing logical technique, and [we are] trying to do it with mathematical perfection, without forfeiting either the existential or the mathematical. And especially with[out] the logical trying to justify the mathematical. Here again we must make a discrimination: for the logical technical examination of the mathematical methods is always legitimate; but the logical carryover of goals, tests, and standards is something else. In this process of trying to make logic run mathematics, the logic [of Russell, Whitehead, *et al.*] has advanced (i.e., weakened itself) to the three-valued or multi-valued forms, and it has tried to make probability developments oriented to the old scheme; it has had many offshoots. (Consider hypostatizations. Consider concept as a norm around which the wording circulates. Consider pure quality assumed to be capable of mathematicised treatment.)

The point about this excursion is that in order to get a grasp of Designation, we must not only set up a separation from Definition; we must not only show that our separation is not pretentiously aping mathematical precision, but is tentative; but we must also sketch the in-between types so that designation can be kept free from misunderstanding in various minor ways.

Designation appears now not as the act of a person applying his body to a thing (i.e, a word to object), but as a development in the expanding cosmos of men in environments in which namings become more elaborate. Namings are here keys for, or clues to, or representations of descriptions, whether the descriptions have been worked out into elaborate forms or not. In fact, it is evident that an early exclamatory name is itself a description all by itself. The two, name and description, are at that stage the same.

What is it now that we have as Specification? It is naming organized with named, both as events in time and without [there being] either on the side of named, a certain fixed thing, or on the side of naming, a word of such comparable fixity. We have a continuing progress of naming toward named and vice versa. This progress is elaborated in description, in continuously more refined and more accurate namings organized together.

The outcome of such procedure would not be a perfected name perfectly applying to a perfect or perfected thing, but a process of approximations which in the end, being by men in the cosmos, components and container, would keep on going. Here is something of the asymptotic, something of the open free world, and a recognition of naming as there taking place.

We may say of this that every naming is "dated," and so also every named—that there is no need of introducing fixations—that their introduction as general standards is false—and their introduction for narrower ranges (except to simplify phrasing) loses generality just by specification of the range.

The word "term" as an illustration. It is definite in a mathematical equation. It is a matter of emphasis or formality in most logical talk. [William Stanley] Jevons said it was so obscure that he would say nothing about it. Have I taken up Specification as either stressed on naming or naming side in double-barreled usage? Yes, [above in Section II].

Russell makes a heavy distinction as to specific thing or fact. We elide this distinction, bringing thing over into the factual. Make it functional all the way.

Paoli, Indiana, September 21, 1945

Dear John:

. . . Illustrating in old style (not ours):

The "thing named." That [thing which] is out there.

The "name." That [which] is either a bodily action, or a change in environment (a product), as a writing.

The "description." The verbal elaboration of the way the name applies to the thing. (Special case of description preliminary to naming. Description of an, as yet, unnamed thing.)

(In our case there is no such "unnamed." It would have to be undesignated, and the designation may be by nod of head or flip of finger. If the word "name" is more limited, it is as specialized "cue" or "index" of the "description.")

(Point I started to make: Given an exclamatory cry as the primitive case of naming: it is both name and description. The bird says "eek" as cat starts climbing to nest. It names and describes, and can't do one without the other.)

"Characterization." Its "feel," as we use it, is more *as if* it applies to the "named."

"Specification." Here the "feel" is more *as if* applied to the "naming."

Regards, *Bentley*

467

Dear John:

. . . "Description": In your *Logic* for the use of this word, I find: 1. It connects with observation and [the] existential. 2. It runs into description of *what is not then and there* observed, by way of existential identification or characterization (p. 126). 3. It matches "Narration" as spatial against latter's temporal, but is distinguished or held separate, only aspectually (p. 220). 4. It itself involves time (p. 240). 5. Not final and complete, not judgment; but means to judgment (p. 240). 6. "A conjunction of traits or a description" (p. 241). 7. Common reference requires at least a minimum of description (p. 242). 8. No sharp separation between demonstrative and descriptive (p. 359).

In your letters . . . I find:

10-8-43: Determination of an event as fact is a description. The product is a name. Description enables an event to be identified, specified. 9-13-44: . . . Distinguish descriptive definition from old, strict definition. Descriptive Definition is a summary statement of the conclusions of knowledge (of existence) as of a given date. . . . De-scription yields determinateness, specification, and is literally a language-name. 9-20-44: Description is that what takes place, is continual improvement of specification by taking in more and more of the spatio-temporal fact.

(In these letters you have also matter about difference between ordinary and scientific forms, Characterization and Specification; and also between mathematical Definition and the type in the Universal or Category range.)

It is highly desirable that "Description" be incorporated in our work. Now is time to do it. Sorry neglected so long. Its positive constructive use in the *Logic* demands this.

In a way, "Description" and "Designation" are obverse and converse. Name and Account of Name. Layout and focus. Implement and handle. (My ordering is mixed—name, focus, and handle are "alleesamee.")

The probabilities are that what you have done by the word "Description" in the *Logic*, we are now trying to clinch down by the word "Designation." Neither description nor designation possible without being aspect of the other. In other words, we would have built just as well with "Description" as with "Designation."

"Specification," I am pretty sure of—you use it often, and even further back in your letters than our adoption of it. "Characterization," I would not be so sure of—there may be some finer points *re* your "Characteristics." It *seems* all right to me, that is all.

My next draft will put these words in their settings, so that they will show up as Characterizing Descriptions and Specifying Descriptions.

Furthermore, it may possibly (barely possibly) make some progress toward handling a name with respect both to its linguistic context and its existential reference in one transactional formulation. We have the scheme. We will do it some day—or at any rate it will be done, but it is still a tough baby for simple, popular statement.

Imperative: "General-Generic and Universal." . . . I have started to open up the territory between "Identification," [on the] one side and "Symbolic Definition" on the other. I set down various illustrations, some old, some new. One, e.g., was the "interpretation" the "Carnappers" [Carnap and his followers] use to pass from syntactics to semantics. . . .

I come to life and discover that the heaviest part of your *Logic* was development right in this region. Just look back at your "terrific" summary on pages 262–63. . . .

One minor suggestion. You oppose "Characteristic" and "Character" [to one another]. You introduce "Categories" in the latter range (but do not, so far as I note, employ the word much). Late in the book you write, "Universal propositions have instrumental and intermediate status" (p. 418—quotation not literal, I see—I wrote from memory). Universal propositions have their subject-matters provided by the operations, etc. (p. 254).

I don't like "universals" for either the mathematical kind or the instrumental-to-existential kind. It strikes me that either "categoricals" or "instrumentals" (if this word could be so narrowed) would hold the territory better. The mathematical-symbol kind could be "Universals" (despite the antique taste) or "Relationals" (following p. 55 [p. 330]). I don't know. But I sort of think mathematics is so largely "relational" that it is the stronghold of actual-relational knowledge (and maybe logic of relations will fit in)—that "Relational" would be damn good name on that end. . . .

"Possibility," as you know, does not help me out in this region. It is damn good hedge against over-done "existential"; but when we have our existential itself made transactionally "as is known," or [when the] existential is among the "possibles" and then [we are] making the predicate potential or possible as over against the subject as existential—evidence is not quite so secure.

Regards, *Bentley*

[P.S.] P. 255, you make two kinds of generals, generics and universals. P. 397, you make two types of universals, apparently to be called hypotheticals and mathematicals. Your first kind is directly intermediate and instrumental. Your second (mathematical) kind is relational in a removed degree. In a way this matches our later development. I have been steadily urging that the instrumental universal be kept with "designation" (and I would now complete it, with "description" so that sharp line would be made between generics and instrumentals, on [the] one side, and mathematical-symbol-definitional, on the other). We have tried both layouts as for [the] word "language" for set-up of terminology,

469

etc. I am keen to see how this works out as we go further. What I mean is: You have been getting pretty well to my view terminologically in this particular point, *but* you have a lot of development in between, and I have very little. That is what I want to see work out! . . .

Possibly we can state it this way. I want "quality" to always be named-event. You use "quality" in the hypothetical universal. Some sort of "existential" difference lives here. It looks as though there was here a definite blind-spot in my performances recently. I have concentrated on getting the "symbol" in shape to apply to the designation without itself designating events. I have been just taking for granted that all the designatory procedures would hold together in process without interference. I have, it is true, been perfectly well aware of the gap to be crossed, but I have assumed it would be crossed by (a) a positive symbol application, combined with (b) a general pronouncement that semantics and syntactics—to use Carnap references—were muddled and could be tossed out.

Now, however, it is clear that your distinction of "Character" from "Characteristic" (Trait) has not been faced by me—or in other words, the use of a characteristic in an instrumental proposition. . . .

I would like to know: How far would you (a, then; b, now) let "Character" run over to the mathematical abstract?

Would "hypothetical" exhaust all the "instrumental and intermediate"?

Would the mathematical abstract also be called instrumental, and just what range would "existential" take in the above? . . .

An admirable statement of the "relational" with indirect existential reference, and the "relational" without even that is at bottom of your page 271 [*Logic*]. Here your three stages are: 1. existential; 2. a non-existential relation with indirectly existential contents; 3. both the relation and the contents are non-existential even indirectly. . . . Number 2 has antecedent and consequence, but *not* existentially. Number 3 has no semblance of antecedent and consequence even logically. . . .

Concerning hypothetical universals as a separate stage, I note, p. 275 (and it in a way justifies my own holding of all this together as specification in the past), that "Generics" (at least "grounded" generics) are the products of operations [that] universals set up. This is inevitable—about same thing as saying that "named-things" do not *precede* knowings. *But* it indicates (or does it?) that number 1 and number 2 . . . are not serial as put there but a common process (designation?)—in other words I here argue for our newly published "Terminology"—tentatively. . . .

Re p. 397: the mathematical is a *type* of universal hypothetical contrasted with a *type* having "ultimate existential application." Somewhere I think I can find a passage in which you pointed out that the mathematical were not properly hypothetical. In other words the presentation in the *Logic* was not quite finished at this point. . . .

470

New York, September 24, 1945

Dear Arthur:

. . . When I got dressed this A.M. I found [the] enclosed in my pocket. I think there is something in one point; the desirability of telling what and how "firm names" are. We have said science has attained them, but not what it [firmness in names] consists in and of. Some readers are going to get the impression we just want some sort of uniformity or agreement.

I have a letter from Kaufmann in [the] morning mail; also yours of 19th and 21st. I should say toad "identifies." There was the report on newly hatched chicks pecking some years ago; [they] made a few mistakes pecking at shiny things [the] first day or two; but quickly learned to peck only food grains. I've been more or less in the habit of writing "identify-discriminate"; one is [the] same as [the] other. To work off and out is to identify [and] vice versa. It may take us back into molecular-atomic, etc. But all that would be necessary here is the particular kind of identifications-discriminations *effected in . . . naming.*

"Interplay" is a good word—covers both "inters."

Cleaning out preparatory to moving, I found an old copy of *Journal [of Philosophy]*—1922. [In it is my] "Knowledge and Speech Reaction"; am sending it to you; please return when convenient. If I had followed it up systematically, I'd have saved years. If I had only carried on observation as to what "reaction *back* into" stands for, I'd have got away from reaction and interaction into transaction a good while before I did; and there is a suggestion regarding "object" that could have been profitably developed. I never got entirely away from it, but neither did I take it seriously enough—as it is, it is left [as a] sort of "happy thought" affair.

Yours as ever, *John D.*

[P.S.] Postulates for me,* O.K.
"Specifications"—specifications for house-building contract—on side of the named; specifications of a patent application.
"Characterization"—of actor on stage—called good or poor.
Both "double-barreled," I think.
Looking up "Specify" in *Oxford Dictionary,* I found the word "specimenify" [specimenify] in good use.

Paoli, Indiana, September 26, 1945

Dear John:

. . . My first job is to get a positive (even though defective and still perhaps partly erroneous) statement of the status of *your* generic-in-

* In "Logicians' Underlying Postulations." (Eds.)

ferential "existential" as over against our present limited specification-existential. In other words, observationally, empirically, I should get these two ways of attack organized so [that] they are convertible—so we can point out how the specification, for example, has full place for the generic.

My second job is to get the mathematical-symbolic similarly laid down. Only here you have done it much more completely than I had appreciated. You have probably everything I have got except a few illustrations scattered around—the one trouble is that it is scattered around (though maybe more centered in Chapter XX [on "Mathematical Discourse" in the *Logic*] than I appreciate)—anyway, I have not checked it yet. . . .

The one region of difficulty—possible (or rather, certain) argumentation, and possible alteration—that I see is in the kind of relational that cleaves to the existence side—the hypothetical universal—as "instrumental" in a different manner than the mathematical universal is. Perhaps I should say not "instrumentally" different in the broader sense of "instrumental," but operationally *very* different—and *so very* different, that *I*, as you, of course, know very well, think there should be a split or rearrangement there in part. In other words, I shall argue in discussion with you that the "relational" fatherhood belongs on the generic side, or rather in organization with the generic, rather than on, or in organization with, the universal side. This is not what I started to write. What I started to write is that "fatherhood" seems to me closer to "father" than it does to "connectives" like "and" or to technically fully clear mathematical operational terms like "1," "multiplied by," or "square root." And I mean "closer" in terms of *kind* of technique at work.

Your set-up (in other words) runs, I take it, in terms of "propositions," something like this:

"Singulars" (including particulars and various contingents, all of directly existential assertion).
  "Generals,"
   "Generics,"
   "Universals,"
    "Hypotheticals" (instrumentals, intermediates),
    "Mathematicals" (I would want to call them "Relationals").

My set-up would want to organize the "Hypotheticals" along with the "Generics" under the "Generals," and make the "Relationals" or "Symbolics" a third group thus:

"Existentials" (direct) singulars, etc.,
"Generals" (instrumental existentials, specificatory):
  "Generics,"
  "Hypotheticals,"
"Relationals" ("Symbol" to cover mathematics and "syntactics").

A general argument would be "operational style" as above. A special argument would be: *If* you want to discuss propositions about father-hood, you should first squeeze the remaining traces of "father" out and discuss strictly the "hood"—the "hoodiness"—which if you do (just my suspicion), will reduce the procedure to what is sought by "Carnappians" (legitimately, I have thought) under their Syntactics. . . .

Put in another way, I would place "qualities" as namings on the speci-ficational side and not on the symbolic side. You boil a quality down and universalize it terminologically. (I started to write "you want to" but crossed those words out as definitely incorrect.) You positively make the distinction, but leave it unstressed. This, again, I would interpret, as a consequence upon the development of your having your eye so heavily upon the long philosophical development—you talk still mainly *in* in the old terminology, and talk still mainly *to* the old terminologists—the philosophical audience. And the facts don't quite shine through (to me)—the facts, I mean, that *you* offer.

A minor terminological note. Consider what your hypotheticals *are* and what your mathematical-relationals *are;* is there any trace of "uni-versal" about either of them? . . .

Regards, *Bentley*

New York, September 29, 1945

Dear Arthur:

. . . I am quite sure my main interest [in *Logic*] was in distinguishing "universals" as hypotheticals—if-then—from "generics," *not* in setting up universals as mathematics. But I'd have to go back and read up. . . .

Yours, *John*

New York, October 1, 1945

Dear Arthur:

You are wholly right in your revised version of my "universals." Mathe-matics should be as a distinct heading of "Relationals," not along with "Hypotheticals." I told you, as I wrote Kaufmann I think, that I hadn't got all the way over in my *Logic,* though I was well headed in your direction. I think . . . there is some confusion as to "*Non*-existential" that held me back. There is the "Non-existential" in an unqualified sense; mathematical as not names under any circumstances; then there are the "hypotheticals" in physical science which are "abstracted," pre-scinded, from any particular special existential reference, waiting around, so to speak, for such reference. I doubt if I distinguished [these] with adequate care. The use of mathematical relations, symbols, *in* scien-tific formulation of hypotheses probably was one factor in my failure to

473

make the distinction explicit. (By the way, this is a point that may need to be taken care of some time.)

As to "universal," you may be right—you *are* wholly right as to mathematics; the word has no business there. But in reading the standard logicians, I was struck by their double use of "general" and "generalization," sometimes, for what I call [1] *"generics,"* "general" statements all subject to modification in further inquiries, and [2] "hypotheticals" of the if-then type. I found a number of confusions and follies, commonly current, due to [their] failure to distinguish [1] and [2]—the same thing [reaction against this confusion] that made me distinguish relation-*ship* because of the so-called "paradoxes" that result from just the ambiguous confusion [*Logic*], pp. 400–404. Probably calling them "universals" instead of just hypotheticals was a concession to historical traditions. But when a word has got technically established, it is sometimes well to point out what it actually stands for, if anything; whether "universal" is a case of this kind, I don't know. But an if-then statement has a property that no generic one has; the latter is also always "contingent," probable. An if-then proposition is either so or not so. To change *it* is to change lot more than it.

I didn't notice that there was anything particularly new in bringing "description" in; just meant to suggest something could be said about the word along with specification—as to how specification operates. "Description" has the advantage of sharp opposition to "definition"; I can't see that any logic students have been influenced by this any more than by my distinction between "generics" and "hypotheticals." And I am not optimistic enough to think that avoiding the use of certain words—like "universals"—would modify their habits either. . . .

Yours, as ever, *Dewey*

New York, October 1, 1945

Dear Arthur:

I've been trying to read the monograph in the University of Chicago series on *Unity of Science* by L.[eonard] Bloomfield [*Linguistic Aspects of Science*]. (It's funny almost all of these attempts at unity succeed in splitting it all up.) . . . It's a queer mixture; got some good things (denial of mentalistic). The remark [p. 56] that mathematics is not a science but a skill in manipulation of speech forms is better than Russell's insistence [that] mathematics is *the* science, or model for all sciences, and better than Kaufmann's identification of mathematical constructions with deductive discourse—especially when he [Bloomfield] adds that mathematics appears as a science only as long as we believe that the mathematician is not creating speech forms and discourses but exploring an unknown realm of "concepts" or "ideas"—or of essences, or universals, or what have you. But earlier he has given, pp. 38–41, an account of the development of mathematics which flatly contradicts what he says in his summing up—or else I can't read; and p. 43, "no difference between applied and pure mathematics." *

The following is his gem of confusion—runs through, I fancy, all his others. He holds that scientific speech is of the nature of a "report" described as follows: "In the normal response to a report the hearer behaves henceforth as if his sense organs had been stimulated by the impingement of the reported situation upon the sense organs of the speaker." (p. 28.) (Not as having acquired the ability to respond in a certain way.) Scientific language is a special case of "report"—[this] taken literally, confines sciences to at best a mechanical coordination of sensory reports. But here is the prize sentence. After saying (p. 46) that "scientists . . . 'control' the forms of their technical dialect, in contrast with the world of meanings—that is, the world of events"—he goes on: "This *outside* world is reportable and predictable only to the extent that earlier acts of science have mastered it—at best imperfectly" (emphasis added). Leave out the "outside," and we have a nice statement of our circularity. But how mastery consists in responding to sense-organ stimulation, he doesn't say. Luckily for him, he doesn't try to. Going back to p. 28, . . . [one finds] the source of his trouble. He describes language [actually, English and many other, but *not* all, languages] in terms of what he calls the "actor-action construction." He gets rid of the mental, but puts an "actor" in its place. Naturally, then, he casually introduces an "outside" world which, being outside the speaker, is outside of speech, but is, nevertheless, reportable only so far as it has previously been inside speech.

He makes a good deal of the difference between speech, which to him is alone language, and writing—which isn't language or speech, but a "substitute" for it. If he had taken pains to show how written language differs from ordinary speech, he might have said something useful about how a scientific report differs from a conversational account in the kind of behavior it calls out and directs. Then he might have found out the difference between de-*scripti*on and talking about something spatially present to speaker-hearer at a particular time.

Yours, John

New York, October 2, 1945

Dear Arthur:

I'm afraid my use of "control" promoted Kaufmann's "permanent control." But I'm not sure that any other word wouldn't have occasioned

* The exact quotation is: "Within mathematical discourse there is probably no linguistic difference between applied mathematics . . . and pure mathematics. . . ." (Eds.)

some other misunderstanding. However, "systematic" might have been better—the purpose was differentiation of inquiries carried on as inquiries and incidental casual inquiries subordinated to something else. Drop out "control," no loss, some gain.

. . . [Your] interlocking of language behaviors with perceptive-manipulative behaviors is the direct and simplifying approach—gets rid of the instrumental, and so forth, including any personal-mental associations.

I think you would lose your bet on my having done the library-laboratory business; I ought to have done it, but never broke through enough to do it. Spoken language goes with the human phase of the perceptive-manipulative (?); written language with the systematic (library) interlocking. Spoken (conversation) language interlocks at short space-time range, the "scene" present to speakers, or when one reports something to another which the other has not taken part in even as spectator [differs from] the kind of scene in which the latter has taken part. Written language of which mature scientific language is a development, interlocks in extensive and continuant space-time ranges—perceptive-manipulative dips in anywhere. Laboratory [language] is manipulative-perceptional [behavior] conducted with a view to effective interlocking with language detached from immediate short-span application; the perceptual manipulative. All this is to be taken with a lot of ?'s.

If there is anything in it, it is suggested by what you say—the "logical" phase is "comparable" to the manipulative-perceptual laboratory phase; meaning that the correspondence (darn good word for a transaction) goes on in *both* phases—the language (logical) phase determining the laboratory, the laboratory testing the language-behaviors and setting new problems. It isn't just language that comes of age—it is *Logos*, the Word, logic, that come of age. We ought to have a drink to its becoming a full fledged citizen. . . .

A sergeant in the army [Emmanuel G.] Mesthene, sent me a copy of a paper ["The Ethical Dilemma of Non-Naturalism"] he was sending to the *Journal* [*of Philosophy*]—asked for comments. I made a few criticisms, including [some of] a passage in which he spoke of the "relationship between the knowing subject and known situation." I told him that phraseology went contrary to the sense of his whole treatment —which I think it did. He wrote back admitting that phrase was bad and should be changed. But he went on to ask, "Isn't the *existence* of an investigator a constant factor in every ethical (or other) investigation. . . . There is a human being present who is doing the inquiring." I wrote back, (i) as to the necessity of avoiding misinterpreting because of the currency of the old subject-object, mind-world dualism, and (ii) the need of analysis of such words as "factor," "agent," as within the

476

single factual transaction. I mention this because the question he raised is going to be the sticking point more than any other one thing—I used the eye-seeing-something analogy, and the fact that while it is legitimate enough for certain problems to study the eye, it had to be studied as one aspect of the total event, and could be studied only by means of what is already known. The other thing is that his "factor" made me think of the commercial use of that term and the legal, commercial use of agent. There ought to be some way by which this and that investigator could be treated as a deputy or representative or "agent" of the whole damn business of knowings-knowns. But our vocabulary is damned treacherous.

[Dewey]

[New York,] October 3, 1945

Dear Arthur:

. . . I think you have the relation of "Description" and "Designation" right end up. . . . Perhaps the connecting link is that no expression is a name or designation by itself or in isolation, but only in "system." *What* is described operates to select the designations, but the latter are the means, implements, by which the description is specified or taken out of the loose and vague. Each designation or name brings the description to a temporary head or focus. "De-scription" is, etymologically, *written* down, *de*-termined, *relatively* fixated—that is, for the particular description under construction, [with] designations being the operative means.

The "tough baby" you mention *is* tough. My feeling about it is that the "existential reference" is the interlocking with perceptual-manipulative behavior, and that "linguistic context" is the matter of building up that particular designation that specifies the behavior which effects or accomplishes the interlocking, completing the transaction; the latter, the interlocking, as transactional, being . . . from the beginning [to the end] in determination of linguistic context—selection and arrangement of designators. (Maybe there is something in the word "designator," just as a "name" is a "naming.") Maybe this [is] off the mark.

As to "possible," "possibility," I don't see how *future* can be brought into the existential reference without some equivalent term. Maybe the word is hopeless, but I don't seem to see it, in spite of its frequent abuse.

"Characteristics," "character." The first word [stands for] "traits" of a generic name in specification-description. Whether the word be used or not, I don't think there is any difference as to *what*. "Character"—the "nature" of a kind, generic, of a thing; it is *what* is stated or determined in a hypothetical, *if* so and so, then so and so. Words ending in "ness" and "ity"—conventionally called abstract nouns. If I have let

477

the word run over into mathematics, that is another case of the confusion I've spoken of; *if* the word "universal" is employed for the sake of indicating what the traditional word *should* be used for *if* used at all, then "universal" (hypothetical) and "character" are cognate; just as "generics" and "traits," "characteristics" as descriptive determinations, are cognate. That is what I intended in the *Logic*, as far as I recall. Give up the word "character" for *mathematical* subjectmatter.

(By the way, you once suggested "theorem" as proper for what is called a proposition in "existential reference"; maybe "formula" (?) also. As I see it now, there is no more point in calling its constituents "universals" or "characters" than there is in calling them "singulars" or "traits." Now that I have got a hold on mathematics not being designators, this goes as matter of course. Whether it is desirable to have a word for constituents of a mathematical statement, I dont know. "Operators" is as near as I have come; [it is] not very good. . . .

Sincerely yours as ever, *John Dewey*

Paoli, Indiana, October 5, 1945

[Memo by Bentley sent to Dewey]

DEWEY'S LOGIC COMPACTLY PRESENTED

The idea is to make every chapter a direct factual statement of what goes on. There should be a minimum of reference to the way things look under older approaches. A wealth of illustration is in the *Logic*, ready for use. It might even be made into a text-book which could be used with some standard logic alongside as a foil—or rather as a laboratory specimen for practical examination. I think it can be written without the use of any such words as "potentiality," "sense," "reason," "thought," "belief," "doubt"; and with nobody missing them.

The only variation from the *Logic* would be in the differentiation of "Symbol" from "Name," and the consequent separation of "Relationals" from "Hypotheticals." A new word would be needed for the "Relationals" so as to avoid calling them propositions—perhaps "formulations." "Universal" could be used if desired for "hypotheticals," but not for both "hypotheticals" and "relationals." "Relation" perhaps should be replaced as beyond salvage.

Bentley

PART I

I. The Physical World. Free subject-matter. Lacking the old fixations, Newtonian absolutes and mechanics. Wide open to techniques known as physical.

478

479

XIX. Direct Existential: Particulars and Singulars.

XX. Indirect Existential (first degree): Generics (Characteristics, Kinds).

XXI. Indirect Existential (second degree): Hypotheticals (Characters).

XXII. The Existential: as within man's contact with environment; not beyond, outside, or apart from. (*Memo.* This duplicates XVII—to be consolidated.)

XXIII. "Terms." They are Constituents of Propositions. They do not combine a previous independence to form propositions. (*Memo.* Propositions as in Systems (sets, series) not placed distinctively in above—should be.)

XXIV. "Names," as Naming-behaviors. Terms are not the "firm names"; they are specialized uses of names. Types of them.

XXV. The Next Stage of Development in Inquiry. Names strip off their naming reference to perceptive-manipulative regions, and organize, with one another in system identified solely with respect to the others in system. Symbols replace names. ("Language" or a growth beyond "language," as one wants to describe it.)

XXVI. "Connection." "Reference." "Relation."

XXVII. "Truth." Hardly mentioned. Judgment is sufficient for these men in this world. "Truth" may be that. But if it means "absolute certainty," look elsewhere.

XXVIII. Mathematical Symbolic (Relational) Formulation—with spatial-temporal relationals, including numerical serials.

XXIX. Syntactical Symbolic (Relational) Formulation—relations in the hypotheticals. (*Memo.* To take out that which in Dewey's "Abstract Universals" as Hypothetical *is* the relational as apart from the movable, substituable content of "characters.")

XXX. "Universals." Historically. Distinction first of "Generics" from "Universals" within Generals: Then of "Relationals" from "Hypotheticals" within Universals.

XXXI. The application of Mathematical Relations to Existential Namings in full system, not in named components. Illustration from Electron as Mathematical symbol or as physical name; Quanta, etc. Infinitesimals as a starter before these others.

XXXII. Symbolic Logics. Talk some simple, common sense about the history of the new logics, logic of relatives, and the later ones, including the metalanguages and the Semantics. Pragmatics and Syntactics as distinctions. Do this very simply and practically. Can be done.

480

PART III

[P.S.] I built this directly out of a first hasty jotting of titles. That is why a lot of good emphases and stresses do not show up, as I can see they should, on reading it over.

New York, October 8, 1945

Dear Arthur:

. . . As to "judgment" [in *Logic*], if I had only known then what I have now [discovered], I'd have made "judgment" the interlocking (I like the word) of the perceptual-manipulative with the linguistic; "Discourse" as sequence, series, of propositions being headed to a form of language that most readily translates into the (overt) behavioral operation which accomplishes the interlocking. ("Experiment" can be distinguished in two aspects—(i) preliminary experimen*tation* which, by preparatory manipulative-perceptual manpulations, develops that *kind* of perceptual-manipulative subjectmatter which lends itself to the operational application just mentioned—this being the other aspect; (ii) experiment as *test,* the two "conjugate" processes being so conducted, with the advance of scientific techniques, so that the test experiment is as crucial—decisive—as conditions permit. *But* the distinction is one of emphasis; there is testing in all experimentation, and there is a phase of the latter in all testing, i.e., no such thing as a decision in any unqualified sense). . . . I found a passage in Peirce [to the effect] that "individualism" and "falsity" are synonyms—he was a great guy all right! . . .

As ever yours, *John Dewey*

[New York,] October 9, 1945

Dear Arthur:

. . . If, and when, I rewrite the *Logic*, I can make my approach much more direct—your sketch ["Dewey's *Logic* Compactly Presented"] will help. I still don't believe that results can be obtained by refusing to employ words that are in use in idiomatic speech—"belief" and "doubt," for example. Beliefs are "social" facts—creeds, political platforms, isms, dogmas, scientific findings—as they actually operate in their connections

481

with other factual events. I agree that "belief" should be first identified —specified—by a direct approach. But if the word and others akin to it were dropped out entirely, it would be, in my opinion (belief), quite possible for someone to think ("believe") he accepted what is said and just lay it alongside of his old unchanged attitudes. "Believe it or not," we are engaged in a work of re-education, not in that of laying down a new layer. I don't mean, of course, that you have the latter "view," but I think carrying out the work demands statement, from the new point of view, of words that are in common, idiomatic use—as distinguished from those belonging to technical philosophic tradition. I agree that I should have much less of the latter. So as to "doubts"—unless you would also throw out "inquiry," "problem," "question," I don't see how "doubts" can be thrown out. The very fact that in philosophy these words are heavily charged with "mentalistic" features is one of the chief reasons why, in a position designed to institute firm naming, they require specification, not just omission. . . .

Sincerely yours as ever, *John D.*

[P.S.] I haven't got it worked out, but I have an idea that "Beliefs" will turn out to be as fine specimens of the transactional as can be found.

New York, October 13, 1945

Dear Arthur:

. . . Your revision rather improves my statement [in *Logic*], though I could improve on it now myself by explicit identification of "universals" with "hypotheticals," [as] "temporary abstraction" from existential reference, and in explicit differentiation from mathematical formulae having no such reference at all in their development. But, of course, it wouldn't be fair to read that in now.

Whether, *in re* pp. 44 ff. [*Logic*] about language, [it] is sufficient to insert, say, *a* statement that "terms" and "propositions" are modes of language-behavior, I don't know; it will certainly have to be explicitly brought out in any revision—as will the fact that "reasoning," "deduction," "Rational discourse," are linguistic developments—"inference" having, like "judgment," from which it can't be separated, "existential reference." However, I don't want to yield to the temptation to read in improvements made—thanks to you—since the book was written. . . .

The care with which you've formulated my postulations leads me to suggest another point—and that point bears upon the formal aspect of logic—the syntactical, but in a non-mathematical sense. Reading Morris, and the way he has missed . . . the point, has made me more sensitive on this point—and [on] the whole Carnap logistics. . . . If it appeals to you, I think . . . [you could write a statement that your work] makes possible a formal treatment (one in temporary independence of subject-

482

matter), while holding the formal logical relations in strict ultimate connection with determination of subjectmatter.

Maybe this [point] is [made by me] because I am sore at Morris for assuming that I've completely neglected the formal or syntactical. But as long as the new logistics has treated the formal as if it were [the] logical, as the essence of the mathematical, I think maybe the point demands attention on its own account.

Yours as ever, *John*

Paoli, Indiana, October 16, 1945

Dear John:

. . . *Points to sharpen.* The word "Judgment." I argued it must be linguistic. You acceded mostly. . . . But both of us have got to bring the words home to the actions. I have thus far done nothing more than to wait for the right moment and press the button to register that *This* (word) names *That* (event). In your "judgment" (in the same spirit and intent and vision) you go further than I have gone. You say "Judgment" is the living organism as the two (word and event) settle down. It is the stamp of action at the point where Habit is ready to set in and hold it. [The subject-matter of a] "Judgment" for you is Individual (p. 446 [*Logic*], as well as p. 122, *et al.*), in a sense [in] which "individual" is [a] Situation, [a unique, qualitative existential whole] settling down, and distinctive from propositions, singulars, particulars, etc. Now I suspect (without having full evidence ready) that you have gone transactional at this stage much better than I have at any point in this procedure of propositioning. I suspect this should be clinched. (It is actual *Agency* of the way we used the word—no, by doggy, your "Judgment" is more transactional than that word.)

We must picture: Situation become Indeterminate: splitting into *Questioned Object* and *Words,* coursing in two branches (hands and mouth), being named "Inquiry" throughout this course, being named "Judgment" when the two lines come together again (to roost) settled down; being named "Object" when the life goes on with this Habit (object) established. . . .

The word "Judgment" is pretty closely held in the *Logic,* but there are occasional passages where you make a kind of proposition [that refers to an ordered sequence of events] "individual" (middle of page 443—as italicized). The word "Inquiry," and the word "Object" too, are firmly (perhaps completely) set in "Behavior" as we now use it. The word "Judgment" needs touching up. The word "Existence" needs considerable adjustment (as our correspondence all along displays). In the *Logic* you always "see" existence transactionally, but you do not get it safely so used—that is, largely in its uses your reader will fall away from

483

the point. Especially our "non-existential" (again, we have discussed this often before) side-slips. I think our recent differentiation between "Name" and "Symbol" is going to handle this. Instead of "existence," as a word being used to cover all sorts of things, it is held to the status of the "named" in a construction in which the named is never "outside of" the naming (except for temporary aspectual examination); and in which no man who can "really *read*" can dodge it. Then with "existential" as "in naming," all the propositional forms you have entered as "Existential" (*Logic*, pp. 289 ff.) . . . are existential in this sense; but *also*, the hypothetical abstract (the universals you mainly saw in the *Logic* before the mathematical distinction intruded), the kind that have qualitative reflection (characters) and that "wait around" . . . to apply, are also in the Existential group. They are there because "existential" is a specification of "named," and because they have naming characteristics right in their set-up. The mathematical *and* the connectives ("and," "not," etc., and "if-then," as formed) combined run over [convey, the words that are] not connectives into a non-existential group (that would not be safe phrasing), but into a non-naming group (which, I think, *is* safe phrasing). Also the "perceptional" [is] removed thus from the shadow of existing or not existing, and just being around *as is*. . . .

"Relational" (even "relation" and "relative"). These are the devil words. I have not used them (except in some slip) for many years. You would be horrified if I showed you how many conflicting uses of that word you have. You mention some yourself. You make the analysis. But just keeping on using it at all betrays you or anybody. I am off it, more now than ever, unless we can salvage it in strict symbolic, mathematical-syntactic usage. . . .

"Subject-Predicate." You discuss [pp. 307–8, *Logic*] subjects of judgment, and have passages that [all particular] propositions [and propositions about a relation of kinds] do not have subjects (except grammatically); and that propositions themselves are subjects or predicates in Judgment. You mostly speak of subject-*matters* of propositions. But there are also passages in which subjects of propositions are spoken of (probably loosely). I can see why all the propositions from particulars on up should be denied firm subjects. Your section in which all propositions are said to be "relational" sets that up; even though the "all" assertion is not made (I think) in your exposition, but only appears in the concluding remark of the chapter (p. 310). (This is one of the conflicting uses of "relation" I had in mind.) I also understand the propositions as components of judgment. But I have found nowhere in the *Logic* that this is cleanly set down. Like to see it.

I know enough about the *Logic* to see how it grew—how various experimental inquiries were brought together, how some developments still antedate others—I mean, did when printed. I can even pick out

484

occasionally holdover alternative passages that did not drop out. I [am] all for this. It is empirical growth. It is the only way to make good. It neither retains the schematism of the past, nor does it attempt to construct schematically for the future. It has growth in it. I think this time, more than ever, that it has full interior consistency in trend and explorative orientation. The minor pick-ups I mention are the kind of things that follow along its line. . . .

[Re] Bloomfield, yours, 10-1-45. He is full of contradictions. I spent three sessions at that "seminar" at Columbia, trying to show that when a man said writing was *not* language, and then allotted linguistic work to language in excess of what speech could do, something was wrong. No effect. Bloomfield (I figure) took A. P. Weiss at an early stage (they were together at Columbus [Ohio State University, 1921–27] then), got only the Watsonian end—then made real linguistic observation—then tried to consolidate. Result, chaos.* . . .

Regards, Bentley

New York, October 17, 1945

Dear Arthur:

. . . The [Kaufmann] article ["Phenomenology and Logical Empiricism"] is largely a criticism of "logical positivism" and Carnap. I don't think he would stand by some things he said then, such as [p. 131] "The empiricist . . . bears in mind that every experience is the experience of a particular man at a particular time." As far as his criticism is a criticism of their and Russell's, . . . [*et al.*], doctrine of ultimate sense data, it's all to the good; I presume finding similar criticism by me was one thing that attracted him. Otherwise, I think—I can't be sure—that his criticism is the same as his criticism of us—they neglect certain underlying "presuppositions." The more I think of it, the more I believe that if he can [be] pinned [down] at all, it is along the line of asking him as to the source of the presupposeds—but unless you say you *don't* mean by source "temporally genetic," he will probably reply that he holds that questions of such genetics are irrelevant to questions of validity—I mean you'll have to make it clear that you are using "source" in the most general possible sense.

Kaufmann ends up his Husserl paper by saying that Husserl has "overcome the errors of idealistic doctrines while conserving their fundamental idea"—but, being a German, he means Logical idealism, not the psychological idealism of the English type. . . .

Yours as ever, J. D.

* For more, and new, light on Bloomfield's life and work, see Christine Mohrmann *et al.*, eds., *Trends in European and American Linguistics 1930–1960*, esp., pp. 196–224. (Eds.)

New York, October 18, 1945

Dear Arthur:

. . . As to "belief," in your sketch for [my] condensed *Logic* you suggested omitting the word. That was what called out what I wrote. I do not believe there is any difference between us in substance; there is, likely, some difference as to expediency in mode of approach; practically inevitable, because I came up definitely through [an] education saturated in "philosophy," and you through "sociology" primarily. All the more encouraging that our paths met—and I don't mean crossed. I am convinced that when I use such words as "belief" hereafter, I should do it in reverse—that is, specify factual subjectmatter first, and then . . . [say] such and such a word when used, should be [so used] as a name for this subjectmatter. The reason I think such a procedure is useful, and indeed necessary in some cases, is that, after all, the teachers of philosophy (and writers) do have an influence, and they can't be influenced without a re-educative process which includes telling what the words they habitually stand for actually name. Then as to the non-philosophers—the "general public"—the amount of epistemology and mentalistic philosophy they've absorbed, without knowing it, is literally enormous. The members of this so-called intelligent public are quite capable of reading radically new statements, supposing they accept them, and go right on with the old stuff, just [on] another stratum. Probably my long experience in trying to teach has made me, somewhat unduly, perhaps, aware of what a slow process re-education of attitudes and intellectual habits can be. Now all this has nothing to do with the present job we are on together. I need re-education in habits too, and I am glad to have some practice. . . .

Yours, as ever, *John Dewey*

New York, October 24, 1945

Dear Arthur:

. . . I can improve greatly my statement about "abstract" ("ity" and "ness") words, universals and characters. I wouldn't adhere today to just what I say in the *Logic*. . . . But I believe it is possible, and logically needed, to make a statement which covers the function or service of "ity" and "ness" words, abstract terms in determining selection and arrangement of kinds or generic names. Take your . . . [point] about logical equivalent and genetic descent. That method of procedure revolutionized the old traditional, Aristotelian, genera-species business. That genetic standpoint, approach, procedure, when linguistically formulated or stated, constitutes logically an abstract term. (I am inclined to think "character" might be dropped; I wanted a word to set over "characteristic," "traits," as applicative to generics; however, I haven't thought this

486

out.) "Classification," the ordering of generics in generality, isn't a matter of chance, but of a "principle." The abstract or "universal," as distinct from the generics, is a formulation of this principle. I think it can be developed in a satisfactory way.

What has just been said has a certain amount of application to the difference between us as to "conceptions." That *psychologists* have given the word mentalistic status and force is obvious; not so much so in logical writings, even of the traditional sort; not at all in idiomatic speech when idiomatic. In today's [*The New York*] *Times* I saw the following sentence in a letter by Anne O'Hare McCormick—incidentally one of the best of the foreign correspondents. Speaking of industrial conditions in Manchester and Lancashire, she writes "Old cotton men . . . admit that wage scales have to be raised and old practices and concepts discarded." I should say that "concept" here and generally in its popular usage means name for the practices in question with respect to their regulative "principle." In other words, "conception" has its proper use as giving a name to, and thereby bringing within the scope of inquiry, the behavioral attitudes, especially the more habitual ones, that tend to give direction to, or "determine," the course of behavior—they being themselves, of course, linguistically behavioral. Or leaving out any reference to any particular word, there are habitual attitudes that tend to determine "practices"; this determination as such is unreflective, affected by obstructive customs, traditions. When they are noted, named, they are brought into a new and relatively liberating context, i.e., made subject to systematic inquiry. If you can find a better name for these . . . [behavioral attitudes] than "conceptions," I'll be glad to adopt it. But there should be explicit recognition of the facts of the case, and, even if "concept" is replaced by a word less likely to misuse, it is a desirable precaution to say, if only in a footnote, that this is what "concept" stands for in its popular, non-technical use.

In the long run, we can't change the habits of others enough to get them to use firm names, in our sense, unless we tell them what the names are *of* as well as what they aren't the names of. . . .

As to "judgment," whether I made it clear or not, my attitude is that while propositions are linguistic, judgment is *overtly* behavioral, involving an organic-environmental operational transaction that gives "existential" effect to the conclusion of inquiry. It *is* "Individual" in the situational sense, though the bad, restrictive, instead of inclusive, use of "individual" is so common that my first reaction when you attributed "individual" to me was one of protest! (I don't know whether it is possible to "save" the word or not.) . . .

Yours as ever, J. D.

Dear John:

Here is another mixed-up and largely useless day, except, that while waiting around away from home, I managed to read your Peirce paper ["Peirce's Theory of Linguistic Signs, Thought, and Meaning"]. This is the answer to a maiden's prayer—me being the maiden. I have ached to see it done for several years, and it's a fine job. I am hep to most of it except the firstness, secondness, thirdness, which [I] never bothered to run down—I knew it was verbal scaffolding that was helping Peirce along—and that the [Morris]-Weiss-Hartshornes were mis-using it, but let it go at that.

There is one place [that] my manner of explaining differs from yours —but differs merely as the personal "context" differs—yours being better for your purpose. P. 14, where you connect Peirce's hold-over mentalistic language with his cosmology, panpsychism; my manner of expression has been (along with my treatment of men-minds as just social-language working at particular organic spots) (I mean only men-minds if language ranges so doing) . . . just that Peirce at his date had not enough developed psychological words and phrasings at his service to give him a better chance. . . .

Regards, *Bentley*

Paoli, Indiana, October 28, 1945

Dear John:

. . . You cite Anne O'Hare McCormick's "practices and concepts." How is the double-wording better (except rhetorically) than if she had written "procedures" or perhaps "systems"? You say that "concept" seems to *name* "practices with respect to their regulative principles"—and further in "explication" . . . you speak of "attitudes" which "give direction to" or "determine" the course of behavior. I do not think that "concept" names "practices." I think (like such words as "verb" and "noun") it names ways in which language is used about practices. But that does not make any difference—it may be a good device or not. Yours may be better.

Note I made no objection to your conceptual or ideational as naming for the predicate end—or I don't think I did. But right in your own text—in your letter—you first make "concept" name "practices with respect to their regulative 'principle'" and then in the very next sentence make it name "attitudes which direct." In other words, right in your own hands, the word "concept" starts to double-up the poor old "entities." In other words: (a) In your *Logic*, "conceptual" means something actually happening logically. (b) In your letter the very first thing it does

488

is to make it sound *as if* you were introducing a new "thing" (namely an attitude as director) when such a new "thing" is the last thing you would stand for. . . .

Regards, Bentley

New York, October 31, 1945

Dear Arthur:

. . . I wasn't sticking up for McCormick's use of "concepts" as a better word than systems or procedures—or any other; I mentioned it only as evidence of a nonmental use; my point is that the word in its common nontechnical usage is a translation into a name of what on the other behavioral mode is an attitude that orders, "determines" particulars or details of behavior, an attitude being an habitual readiness. I wrote hastily if I intimated that a concept names "practices" directly; the "with respect to" was the differential part of my sentence.

But I am not arguing that we should now use the words "concept" and "conceptual"; I am saying that to write as if "conceptual," etc., in logical writings and in its common use was meant to stand for something mental, as in most psychological writings, would give rise to needless objections and misunderstandings. In the "Terminological" paper, I *would* like a brief statement as to what the words, if used, should stand for. . . .

Yours, John D.

Paoli, Indiana, November 2, 1945

Dear John:

Two or three times you have spoken of being "behind" again. I am the one that ought to say that. For the last three months I have done nothing at all that was worth while except in the two weeks in which I changed my "knowledge about" your *Logic* into a lively sense of "what was happening." I got a big kick out of it—and it will show benefits later. . . .

Regards, Bentley

Paoli, Indiana, November 6, 1945

Dear John:

Psychological Review, September, 1944 [1945], symposium on "Operationism" . . . [Herbert] Feigl, p. 251 ["Operationism and Scientific Method"], after discussing Nominal Definition (as of Terms or Symbols), says *Real Definition* (as of things, properties, etc.) is either (a) empirical description (using old nominal definitions), or (b) characterizations for the sake of identification. Since this last (characterization) is a labeling, "it is tantamount to nominal definition. . . ." I make this note because (a) Feigl has all the distinctions mixed, yet (b) has a lot of good stuff, and (c) he uses "characterization" just where we do (maybe taking it from our use, though probably not), finally (d) it exhibits the need, and also the degree of success, or rather efficiency, we have already secured.

Query as to *Concept* (not argumentative—I just want a fingerpointing *at* something). Feigl, p. 258, end of above paper, sets down six conditions for *Defining a Concept*. Now suppose you (and I) set off to one side (a) all the formal definings of symbols via theorems, (b) all the existential characterizations and specifications via propositions (these being called "definitions" by most writers, including Feigl).

In addition to these two procedures of "defining," can you mention a type (c) on which one defines *a concept?* At this point I am not asking, as usually, a terminological question; instead I want existentials specified. I do not know any *fact* indicated by "concept," except what is in (a) and in the two forms of (b). I will swear by my uneaten hat that in Feigl's case the use of "concept" is what might be called an interlocutory pomposity, *et praeterea nihil.*

The above does not affect our layout. It is a personal underlying question. It manifestly does not affect your use of "conceptual" in the *Logic,* since "conceptual" is a phase of proposition, and proposition, or, better, "propositional," is a phase of "linguistic." So in this use, "conceptual" is linguistical, and O.K. by me.

B. F. Skinner in this same symposium writes ["The Operational Analysis of Psychological Terms"]: "'Definition' is a key term, but is not rigorously defined." Also he writes: "Modern logic, as a formalization of 'real' languages, retains and extends this dualistic theory of meaning. . . ." Good Lad. Skinner has just come from Minnesota to be head of the psychology department at Indiana. I have never met him. Bridgman in his "rejoinder" ["Rejoinders and Second Thoughts"] devotes almost all his space (3 pages) to the differentiation and organization of "public" and "private." He seems to think society is in [an] eternal conspiracy to hide the "private" from its owner.

Bentley

New York, November 10, 1945

Dear Arthur:

Got the proof [of "Postulations"] this morning. Have been over it hurriedly; am struck anew with the thorough care with which you do your job. Found practically nothing that seems to need attention. Enclosed [are] a few slight queries. I presume "ternalizations" was intended, and it is O.K. with me; didn't put question mark to question *it*, but merely [to ask] whether printer had got it wrong.

I'll go over it again more at leisure and let you know if I find anything. Doubt if it can be improved either in substance or form.

Re Kaufmann's [letter] to you, October 29. The distinction between "warranting a proposition as such" and "warranting a scientific decision regarding it" is too occult for me. But I imagine that it is the product of his difference from us, because of which he fails to take propositions *in use* in forwarding inquiries into factual subjectmatter. *If* he gives "propositions" a certain finality as logical forms, apart from what *they do* in leading to a "warranted assertion," what he says might make sense. . . . His inclusion of "recognition of observational tests" along with his rational (?), logical principles is a good illustration of his desire to cover everything without pinning himself down to anything in particular.

Feigl was (probably still is) a "logical positivist," but was sufficiently influenced to have more respect for the "logic" of actual scientific inquiry [than some others].

Your question about "concept" (yours of 11-6-45):

My answer is *No* about characterization and specification in propositions. *But,* the word [concept] as now used, when free from mentalistic reference, seems to designate a certain species of characterization, namely the grade of development in which the characterization in question specifies characterization as having (being given, or having ascribed to it) a *regulative* function with respect to a *set* of characterizations; equivalent to a "principle" when that word is specified in behavioral inquiry use, not given some outside independent standing. Once more, I am [not] making a plea that *we* use the word. But I am reasonably sure that we shall arouse needless misunderstanding unless we indicate the sense in which the word may be given a non-mentalistic inquiry-behavioral use, for it is now too extensively used as a virtually idiomatic word to be damned outright. I don't think we actually differ; I should certainly hope I don't [differ with you] as to the strictly propositional connection of the word; that would be an intolerable relapse on my part. . . .

Yours, *John D.*

Paoli, Indiana, November 14, 1945

Dear John:

At home with a light, I could see your points. O.K. The "ternalizations" was deliberate. But you raised my eye-brow, and when I looked up [its] etymology, it did not look right. My Latin dictionary is big, but too old to have decent word-histories, and neither it nor the *Century* helped with the chunk "inter," the "tern," or "ter." So I replaced the word.

I have found several cases of talk of a matching of a mathematical system to a factual system. [C. W.] Churchman, *Philosophy of Science*, last issue, p. 153 ["Probability Theory"], says it is done by "intuition." He contrasts "formal" with "image." [Guido] Beck, *ibid.*, pp. 174–78 ["Mathematical Formalism and the Physical Picture"], contrasts "picture" with "formalism," and tries to slap one on the other. I have been picking up instances lately—just as signs of effort and need—not of results. If you see any of these fumblings now and then, I would be glad to be told.

Also to notice. Churchman, p. 166, mentions "mechanical" and "vital," but apparently has no hint of our "transactional." He speaks of "mechanical" as basic, and "vital" as "added to." Historically, we show the "actor-principle"—"vital"—as primitive, "mechanical" as first try, "transactional" as later approach. Churchman refers to [Edgar A.] Singer's "solution" of the "conflict"—"logical solution." I shall look this paper ["Logico-Historical Study of Mechanisms"] up next chance I get. . . .

Later. I have finished with the proof. Sent it to Mrs. Dean. Told her you had been sent the two main changes, and they were subject to your approval. Had nothing more to change today, save possibly one or two words. It's probably full of lice, but my DDT is not good enough medicine. On the other hand, I think the main things we are after here are pretty big medicine.

Regards, *Bentley*

New York, November 14, 1945

Dear Arthur:

Don't bother to send me the missing carbons. I can make them out from previous copies, and you deserve a vacation—and several hallelujahs. You won't find the job wasted, not from the standpoint of others, and maybe in the long run you'll have got something out of it. You should at least have got additional assurance about what you are working at. . . .

Otherwise, all I have . . . [got to] say is that your paper ["Postulations"] is a classic and in the course of time will be recognized as such. You have done something that won't have to be done over again. I know how discouraging it is to have things go slow and apparently often not move at all. But your paper is more than a landmark. It's as solid and outstanding as a pyramid. It lifts discussion out of the area of pro and con "isms" into one of genuine, not fictional, "Analysis." The net effect on me is increased by getting it as a whole instead of piecemeal. . . .

Yours as ever—and more so, *John D.*

492

New York, November 15, 1945

Dear Arthur:

. . . I have just read Nagel's article ["Some Reflections on the Use of Language in the Natural Sciences"] in the last *Journal* [*of Philosophy*]. It has so many good things in it that I wish he could get a firm hold on the framework in which they belong. His special field of knowledge could be damn useful if he would venture into . . . [its] setting. I keep having the feeling that there ought to be some way of approach that would lead him to observe where he belongs.

Yours, *John D.*

[P.S.] When you get time, read Nagel's piece as sympathetically as possible with a view to telling what he needs to get the pattern.

Indianapolis, Indiana, November 21, 1945

Dear John:

As a result of my wild gyrations for ten days, I have got to a point where I am half asleep half the time when I am not sound asleep—with a day or two more of the comatose in sight. But I have looked over the preface and first chapter of your *Logic*. Instead of suggesting [that] you condense the *Logic*, I now suggest you expand the preface to about 50 volumes. And while I do not feel I know the first chapter at all, I find I have 63 annotations, of one date or another.

What I am writing about is that region where there is, not a difference, but an incomplete adjustment between us. Take "concept": I think of myself as wanting to be more *specific* than you about that word—about the *what* it has for referent. Similarly for "relation." But for "knowledge," in this first chapter you are more specific than I have ever been. You say knowledge is the close of inquiry. So also is Judgment. The two are the same, with at most this difference, that in Judgment we talk either about a single instance (or think of it as a *single*) or about the process narrowing down; whereas in Knowledge we talk of a considerable system of it. (We do not seem to have even the proper classificatory words for these distinctions.)

Now if Judgment is the stage where the word-signs, instead of being held off at arm's length and manipulated as names or terms, as sentences or propositions, plumb down into the manipulational-perceptional, still forming it, but proceeding in fusion, Knowledge is Habit; all O.K. Further *for us*, Knowledge is not Habit-owned-by-the-organism, but is the transactional habit of organism-in-environment.

To me Habit-transactional seems more "concrete" than Habit-organic because the latter traditionally requires a "subject" involved. But I suspect just when I stress Habit-transactional as Knowledge, is when I seem to have reached ultimate vagueness to many of my friends. To me

493

the Habit-transactional is additionally concrete because it has not only organism-environment locus, but also organism-organism (social communicational) locus.

Here we would have a library as intermediate-instrumental (just like your propositions and terms), a component of inquiry, not of judgment or knowledge (meaning by inquiry the unfinished, and by knowledge the provisionally finished, subject to the "probability coefficient").

Now I can set the words "relation," and "ideational" and "conceptual" as predicational-verbal, into this scheme. So also "quality." I can take "quality" and "relation" as ways of talking about phases of things (and hence with no bother as to whether they are additional to the things, the way various types of logics make them—that is out, of course). But what the hell am I going to do with "concept" from this point of view? I don't see why I should say the concept is the thing—that simply doubles names. It is not an aspect of the thing-situation—as it is held off from it subjectively. I can't see anything, but to make the concept an experimental naming, which one hopes will be the perfected naming after a while—and thus linguistic—as definitely on the linguistic-instrumental-intermediate phase of the process.

I think I'll take another nap. One hour later. I think I really got some gain about Knowledge—or me—in the above. Incidentally, your "probability coefficient" in the "Preface" is exactly our "Specification" now. . . .

Regards, *Bentley*

Paoli, Indiana, November 21, 1945

[Memo by A. F. Bentley]

DEWEY'S DEVELOPMENT

John Dewey in his *Logic*[:*The Theory of Inquiry*] identifies reflective thought with objective inquiry and investigates it not only *in,* but *as,* the latter in name and in fact. He makes this identification in a continuum of inquiry, as suggested by Peirce, i.e., as cultured behavior in the lap of biology. He obtains thus the basis for a fully empirical account of logical process—an account which, of course, as he repeatedly says, will take generations to develop. He provides under the name of instrumentalism a wider framework for both the "operational" and the "pragmatic" which, the experience of the past generation shows, tend continually to be distorted, by workers who get only fragments of their meaning, into surface statements under the ancient "mind-action" terminologies.

It is to my mind the most astonishing observation I have ever made that this development is so slightly known—I might almost say, is so

494

universally unknown. It arises at once as the direct outgrowth of Darwin's demonstration of man's development of man as place-holder in nature. The outline is well known. Wright sought a glimpse; Peirce set down the main characteristics; James made remarkable applications in special fields. Dewey has spent substantially his entire life surveying the wide ground of investigation and building up his instrumental account of logic as inquiry. Yet almost every writer who discusses Dewey—and they are legion—manages to omit the one characteristic that is critical for Dewey, and to criticize him on the basis of his having cast out or lost sight of that very particular primitive phase of casual report which Dewey has overcome. In the very *Journal [of Philosophy]* to which he has most often contributed, the editors recently accepted a leading article which set up a definition of "instrumentalism" in a way wholly alien to Dewey's use of it, though "instrumentalism" is as peculiarly his own word as any word in philosophical regions is for any individual worker, and he has taken endless pains in showing the temporal spread it involves. Nagel, brilliant interpreter of science and mathematics, uses the same background tone as Dewey, but reduces [it] to that which Dewey does not— the thing and the brain-cell using a word. Kaufmann [is] another [who] wants to improve Dewey by re-inserting all that Dewey has most painstakingly got rid of under the influence of a very vague and indescribable control of "meaning" in the Husserl heritage. Kantor, closer to Dewey in his main aim of interactional, finds Dewey something to be ignored.

Next would be Dewey's development of "term" and "proposition." Then perhaps a sketch of "generic" and "universal." Then explain through his retention of the older terminologies, his "conceptual" and "ideational," O.K. in *his* use, [but] not in his readers'.

Now when we get to the mathematical, how the next step arises. Critical point is distinction of "name" from "symbol." Name names apart from the naming-vocal-scriptorial. Symbol names only within the scriptorial. There is nothing magic about that at start. Just as "want" names only within the living protoplasmic system. But much may grow out of it. And we hold as much does grow out of this de-naming process as previously grew out of the naming.

The probability coefficient for namings.

Generally that for *all* namings. Specify. Then the certainty stuff of mathematics passes over to the symbol field just by stripping off its namings—by *de-naming* its signs. Or by letting them name only what is within the symbol-scheme.

Dewey's *Logic*, p. 52; he separated "sign-significance" from "symbol-meaning," but we need to make further differentiation.

495

Dear Arthur:

[*Re:* Bentley's 11-21-45 letter and memorandum "Dewey Develop-ment"]

. . . 1. Whatever I said or didn't say in the *Logic*—or however badly I said it, I agree now, 100%, that "habit-transactional" is proper [and] "habit-organic" improper naming. In earlier writings I had tried to make it clear that a habit always comprises environmental condition— e.g., walking the ground, etc. [*Experience and Nature*, pp. 278–80]. But the "habit" of limiting the word to the organic makes it advisable to add the word "transactional" until that view is better established.

2. I agree 100% that a "concept" is an experimental naming. I have said this before; all I have added is (i) what it is a naming of, *namely* (good word) of what is usually called "principles," that is, of attitude or habit that operates in inquiry to determine or decide other habits, as of seeing, hearing, inferring, etc., and which therefore requires es-pecial attention in processes or events of inquiry; (ii) that, while mini-mizing our own use of it because of its current ambiguities, we should, in the "Terminology" paper perhaps, tell what it names when properly used—I think that examination of its popular, "idiomatic" use, as distinct from philosophical and psychological, will show it is used in [the] sense given above.

Your statement about "Knowledge" and "Judgment" is fine; putting it down is a gain for me; even if I had implicitly assumed it before, it's a gain to have it explicit. It should, I think, help clarify the confusions about *knowledge* as distinct from knowings-knowns that you have re-peatedly called attention to—as pointing out *one* usage; firm enough to be legitimate.

I'm not stuck about or on the word "belief"; but in view of the tra-ditional and still current identification of "knowledge" with "certainty" and of the latter with "Truth"—capital T—some word seems to be needed to stand for the fact that, since knowledge is strictly connected with in-quiry, as a generalized name for conclusions reached by it (thus differ-ing, just as you say, from judgment in connection with a particular in-quiry), it is subject to revision or modification when [there is] improve-ment in inquiry-operations. Following Peirce, . . . I used the word "belief" to apply to the conclusions of inquiry as knowledge—though with reserve (*Logic*, p. 7). . . .

Yours, *John D.*

Dear Arthur:

. . . Some . . . pertinent material is incorporated [on] pp. 242–43 in [the] "Knowings-Knowns" article, so you can go now into more detail,

I should suppose, beginning with the strictly physical development. I don't know how far beyond "magic" you want to go as to the "self-moving" stage of science. But Galileo's work was definitely directed against the "science" that had been taken over from Aristotle. According to this [Aristotelian Science], there were things that so completely, inherently, and hence necessarily, possessed Being that they continued eternally in action ("movement") under their own power—not just *motion* continuing, but the *particular* movement in which they are engaged. The fixed stars with their eternal circular movement are instances—hence the commotion, among those who accepted the old astronomy, produced by Galileo.

Other things, because of Defect of Being, lost movement, and needed to be boosted from without to keep it up. All natural events, physical through psychological, were graded according to the degree of self-action retained or parted with—deprived of—till we get down to pure "matter," which is wholly passive, and "inert." I refer to this here, because it wasn't just "philosophy," but all science, astronomical, physical, psychological, and even theory of knowing in relation to Being ("Reality" in modern philosophy) [that] was systemized in detail on this basis. I should think that without going into history of change through Newton, you could state how recent science has moved over, [from the old notions of] "inertia," "matter" and "energy" for example, and how the facts involve moving from Newtonian interactionism to the transactional in observation-description—Einstein's relativity of distance-motion [space-time], "simultaneity" in particular.

Keeping the "mental," etc., out of [the] above for separate treatment, then state how "self-action" has been retained in psychology, social subjects, etc., and how, while scientific inquiry has moved away somewhat, it still operates definitely on the "interaction" basis almost entirely. Then how the transactional observation-description is urgently needed in just the latter field—as knowing-known.

(We don't want to go into ethics here, but I'll mention by way of passing illustration the extent to which "ends-in-themselves" figure—the "ends-*in-themselves*" involve complete retention of the denial of *connection* and, hence, of space-time considerations. Russell repeatedly denies that ethics can become a cognitive subject because it deals with "ends-in-themselves." In other words, with something which is never by any possibility "means"—i.e., completely isolated. My paper on valuation theory [*Theory of Valuation*] in the Chicago monograph series is an attempt, I think the first ever made, to show the complete "relativity" —connectivity—of ends and means. I could do a better job now, linking it up with the "transactional," but it wasn't bad for a pioneer effort.)

I have written the above as if the purpose was to tell the readers something they should accept. But that was to save space and time.

497

The purpose is to give *illustrations* of the names. This illustrative material is especially needed because of the newness of the transactional approach, as well as its fundamentalness. It alone demands a pretty thoroughgoing reconstruction of deep-seated current attitudes and habits. In a way, it's the key, I think, to what you have proposed, and also to the resistance it will meet.

For this reason, perhaps it would be well to introduce somewhere, illustrations from ordinary affairs where transactional features stand out —talking-hearing; writing-reading; buying-selling; supply-demand, and other cases where events can't be understood without express recognition of simultaneous two-way movement—not with reference to theoretical implications, but purely as illustrative reminders that the reader habitually uses the transactional in some matters.

In the long run, [to] the degree in which the transactional is put over, the battle is won. (I have the zeal of the convert.)

I take it the "specification" part of the paper is application of transactional treatment to a number of names fundamental in [the] theory of (linguistic) signs. . . .

Yours as ever, *John D.*

Seattle, Washington, December 2, 1945

Dear John:

Work in Progress

I. The paper [on] "The Specification of Transaction." You will be surprised (I hope). At least, I am (as is). A lot of matter is going to be capable of compact, simple statement. It is not going to take long (I hope); and I enclose a list of high-light points on the "specification" part.

Work in Prospect

II. A paper fitting the present name-symbol distinction into your *Logic*. I shall have to do this primarily (so far as present indications go) as a personal job over against, instead of in development in, your *Logic*. This is merely to sharpen the primary statement and get the values out. (I have said this wrongly. I must do it as a development out of the *Logic*, rather than as one in immediate consonance with the *Logic*.) When this build-up is prepared, then we can regard it as material, and decide how to handle it. It lies apart from our main "terminology" task, and I suspect we can best put it somewhere other than in *Journal of Philosophy*. It should do for *Philosophical Review* if you like. It *may* even be we can make the construction so sharp and plain that it will do for *Journal of Symbolic Logic*.

III. A psychological paper on "signing" as "behavioring," with the differentiation of stages as psychological subject-matter. This has been in view from away back, and no progress made except making memo of materials. Intended for *Psychological Review*. My job, I suspect.

IV. A paper on the way various terms in common use about knowings look under the treatment we have built up. You have furnished a great amount of material for this, and I have it all indexed. It has not seemed safe to me till we get the foundations in the other papers done. It should be easy and swift. For *Journal of Philosophy*. . . .

Regards, *Bentley*

New York, December 4, 1945

Dear Arthur:

. . . As I've said before, you don't need to go out of your way to conform to or bring in the terminology of my *Logic*. If I don't agree with what you say, I'll let out a yelp. But I won't yelp because you don't [use] some technical word the way I do. This applies to "character" (also to "universal"). I had need to distinguish the concrete and abstract from the standpoint of logical office-function or use in inquiry. I took "characteristics," "generics" (kinds, sorts of things), as names for the "concrete"; "character" and "universal" for the abstract. As I used "character," it is a synonym . . . [for] an "abstract" noun—scarcity, dearness, as distinct from scarce and dear; temperature as distinct from hot-cold, to cover degrees of variation in intensity. I haven't thought about it enough yet, but "descriptions," when scientific, apply to things as of a kind and also to the so-called rule, principle, law, by which kinds are determined. The legitimate office of abstract nouns, words ending usually in "ity" and "ness" ("density," "gravity," etc.), is to designate the latter. I agree with you that "rule," "principle," "law," all have associations which go contrary to what we are doing, and I wouldn't use them in the text. But I have a feeling that "specify," while a good name for one kind of description, is too closely associated with "specific" to cover the whole field. "Description" seems, feels, to me [the] more inclusive name. But I don't know a word that describes what abstract nouns do. . . .

So-called "applied" mathematics presents the development of abstract names into genuinely firm names, variations of density, gravity, etc., in terms of numerical scales. Otherwise, the words, although abstract, are given—and have been given (which is an objection to using them)—a pseudo-concreteness—they are made into a kind of thing, instead of a kind of operation, by which kinds and descriptive terms are inclusively and exclusively settled. I imagine it is historically true that reification

499

wasn't escaped from [or avoided in science and philosophy] until numerical determinations were introduced.

Whether, and how far, this brings in a transitional step in passage over to symbols and mathematics, I wouldn't know. . . .

Yours, *John D.*

[P.S.] I've looked up "Cue" in *Oxford* since writing above; the dictionary illustrations limit it to words in a way the word "signal" is not limited. Maybe cue, without the addition of "names," would serve to name the simplest kind of naming—judging from the dictionary a "cue" is definitely a word-as-signal.

Seattle, Washington, December 7, 1945

Dear John:

. . . *Re* "Stimulus." . . . My scheme would be:

In physiological discussion: "Excitation and Reaction"—the whole as a physiological transaction: the two names as differentiating organic and environmental aspects, and down with the man who calls this basically a time-sequence, with excitation preceding (as separated causal factor) the reaction. (Cf., J. Dewey ["The] Reflex Arc [Concept in Psychology].) Although practically it works out in sequential form.

In behavioral discussion: Signal level—"Stimulus and Response." Here we have perceptional representation and situational identification. Runs up through many grades.

Designation level—"Thing and Name." "Cue-name and cued-named." "Characterization and Object"—of expository definition in your *How We Think.*

"Specification and Object." . . .

I think your statement about "excitation-reaction" in the *Logic,* p. 29, can be definitely rendered in my squint that it is physiological subject-matter—i.e., that these words name situations under examination by physiology's techniques. . . .

What we do is to treat organism and object transactionally. After naming-behaviors enter, we treat the name and object-named transactionally.

In what sense do we treat the organism and the name as transactional? . . .

This [is] my standard critical pronunciamento. There is no organism apart from its actions. Or, in reverse, the organism is composed of its activity. This makes me unable to take as a serious working construction Kantor's doctrine of "products" that "interact" afresh. But also it leaves me with a difficulty of transactional statement as I attack your discussion. . . .

"Specification." You make a strong point about its being too specific

500

for our purposes. Yet there is a sense in which maximum specification is attained by, let us say, "electron." And electron, being a high-powered mathematically-fathered naming, is anything but specific in that ordinary sense of this-right-here-now. . . .

Regards, *Bentley*

[New York,] December 8, 1945

Dear Arthur:

I see I got off on [the] wrong foot about [the] next paper; I thought "transaction" was primary; see by your letter it's "specification."

Afraid my mind hasn't been running on such lines. I have [nothing] much to contribute.

1. As to "demonstrative" and "designative"—answer to your question depends on other things in development of paper. You said something lately about the wide reach of names. I should be inclined to include "demonstratives" under "designations," distinguishing between designating the short space-time span in "designating" (specify, perceptual material) and the long time-space span of organized, and organiz*ing*, connecting subjectmatter (Propositions ?). (In the sense in which specifying is particularizing in space-time, demonstratives seem to specify more than "generic" names; i.e., knowns that organize or arrange through instituting connections or telling *how* connection is to be established.) Demonstratives seem to me to be connected with specifying a problem, first roughly ("something the matter," "an interruption or break") and then through transactions with other designations, taking form conjointly with proposed resolutions. If "terms" are distinctive, then they designate specifically or differentially, the operations by means of which proposed connectives (propositions) are instituted.

2. I am not doing anything now with my "sign" paper; your comments and my further reflections showed me it needed development, and some rectifications—especially along the "specifying languaging" line.

3. You are right that after "naming" has itself been firmly named, it suffices without all the additional phrasing I threw in. The point that is relevant, if any, is to different kinds of "specifying" by names. What is called the "universal" ([I] wouldn't use that name now, save, perhaps, to say that what *had* been called "universal" was of this sort) is . . . [that] which "prescribes" a *way* of behaving, that arranges, organizes a "term" as a distinctive naming. Anyway, as I just said, I had realized before [that] my draft on "signs" was immature.

Your outline of paper [on "Specification of Transaction"] in yours of 12-2-45 strikes me as bully. [See this essay in this volume, below.] The line struck in your paragraph about naming as [the] sole "existence affirmer" is the key note; gives the opportunity to make whatever reference to previous papers is needed—in distinction made from signalings as themselves actions.

I don't know whether anything should be said about "idea" or not; probably [it] would be more confusing than helpful. But maybe in a footnote the reader could be invited to try the experiment of identifying it ["idea"] with the "representation" of your statement, and "representation," of course, as identified with name-specifying. It might help some to get the tenor of the whole business. . . .

Well, if I have anything to say now, it is along the line of specifying the different specifications made by different kinds of names—and the placing of propositions and terms.

Yours, *John D.*

Seattle, Washington, December 12, 1945

Dear John:

. . . I find that if this next paper * is to come along right, the word "term" must be pretty fairly dealt with. . . . Now "Term," we generally agree, is "Name" in its upper reaches. But it is not *just* "Name" at its best. It is "Name" in a certain process, a fixational quasi-subject in the toils of the potentially fixating conceptual and ideational predicate-namings—where all this is in operation under an agreement that Subject and Predicate proper are not established until Judgment-stage is reached.

It may be that the "Generic Proposition" has *Name-use,* and that "Character-propositions" (universals in the logic sphere) have *Term-use,* and that "Symbol-propositions" (universals in mathematical range) have Symbol-use. It may be, that is, that something like this is a usable distinction.

Boiled down, this merely says: "Term" shall be applied to such uses of names as Dewey in his *Logic* has identified as "character" instead of "characteristic." (Can't use word "universal" here.)

One little do-devil in organizing is that this (or anything we do, perhaps) is apt to drag logical-universals over into the "existential" group (*Logic,* p. 398), and thus alter the balance of classification. This, however, is not a very smart remark, since in this particular respect we have already definitely tossed out the old classification.

Regards, *Bentley*

Seattle, Washington, December 12, 1945

Dear John:

"Cues" are truncated descriptions. "Descriptions" are expanded namings.

* "Specification."

502

Seen as action, as human action in environment, as behavior, the logical distinction between name and descriptive account wholly vanishes for basic purposes. The whole procedure of hypnotizing word and thing into point-correspondence becomes absurd—as in [Ludwig] Wittgenstein and Russell. The life-long fight of Dewey against sense-elements or units (now approved by Kaufmann) generalizes. . . .

Regards, *Bentley*

Seattle, Washington, December 12, 1945

Dear John:

. . . He [Neurath] wants to get in with us—in conference at any rate—on terminology, and on things-termed. I may have told you (or maybe not) that I had a ten-page single-space letter from him. . . .

One subject was your approach in *The Quest for Certainty.* . . . Incidentally, as far as I can tell, I had never even looked into that book. He seems to have scattered his copy with exclamation points, meaning high approval, but to have been worried by many phrasings. He suspects— following the traditional idea—a surviving Hegelianism. I told him what you got out of Hegel as "system"—that you were as open to Spencer as to Hegel—and that your way of developing system was like neither of the others, and as much—or more—on its own feet. I also told him you were a master of varying your statement to your audience. . . .

Regards, *Bentley*

[New York,] December 12, 1945

Dear Arthur:

I take back what I said about equivalence of stimulus and excitation . . . excess zeal of the convert, I guess. Excitation-reaction applies in physiological knowings; in the human field as *affected* by language ("Culture"), an excitation becomes stimulus and a reaction, response; a reply that furthers—keeps up the conversation as a transaction.

I don't intend above . . . reference to language to take stimulus-response out of signaling-perception event [and] into the thing ("Object") designation-event. But would an animal not affected in any way by communication, in its broadest sense, identify situations, or "perceive"? However, I fancy my habitual use of the word "perception" has been on a "higher" level than yours—running over into observation. Terminology here is rather difficult to keep firm. "Observe" as used is distinctly, I believe, on the language-sign level. "Perceive," as it is used, applies to both. "I perceive that," like "I see that and hear that," [applies] in cases where what follows is "propositional," linguistic. In *physiological* behavior, animals certainly perceive in the sense of recognizing situations, identifying-differentiating-reacting appropriately—this must go clear down the scale, and [it] becomes highly delicate. Behavior in humans sometimes relapses, I guess, into this form—[for example, the] incredible facility of blind persons, trained to sort laundry, identifying by smell. *Sense*-perception would cover the ground, but I rather dislike the term, since it has been generally used to cover observation in which the sense-*organs* are physiologically involved to support the theory that "sensations" are involved. Well, this isn't important save as an illustration of the absence of firm names in current usage, popular and psychological. [The] above also takes back my statement that response is broader than stimulus. If excitation and stimulus are identical, as they shouldn't be, then, of course, stimulus and response are coordinate.

. . . The general line now seems to be "signal-situation," with excitation-reaction as *aspect* (not as signal); cue (word)—"event." That is, in the first case, perception, the *situation*, is identified; in the second case, the thing, "object," which touches off, acts as stimulus, is identified—cue to an actor is *in* a situation, the play, but it is a recognized, specified event that is the "cue" to what is specifically done in the situation (the play). If I had said this first, I could have omitted the foregoing.

Yours as ever, *John D.*

[New York,] December 13[?], 1945

Dear Arthur:

I have yours with inquiry about "term." Let me say first that in re-reading the pages [289–310 in *Logic*] . . . I am struck with the fact that in writing on the subject now, I could connect up the sequence of particular, singular, and generic with your point about the space-time extensive continuum of the known. There is, I hope, nothing in what I said in those pages that is incompatible [with this]; but if I had written with your point in mind, I could have tied up things in a way I haven't in the text. That [is], I could have brought [out] emphatically the cumulative interconnections in and by which the various kinds contribute to the known, carrying out better the knowledge-*system* as the product of the various *inquiries* which together form inquiry—in the singular—as a going concern. As the text stands, the locomotive isn't connected closely with the tracks, and, especially, both of them are [not] connected with the transportation system, and that with the whole system of production-distribution-consumption. Reference to *a* problem is made, but not to the problem of extensive space-time connections in a "known" as system. (The wording above is loose, but I hope it conveys my main idea.) "Term" and the *proper* use of "conception" are, I should say, synonymous. (I should, I think, if rewriting, use the word "term" where I have used the word "conception" to avoid the mentalistic interpretation

504

of the latter word—not because I think "conception" *must* mean something mental, nor that it does in present non-technical usages.)

2. Like "conception," it ["term"] stands for a word used to determine the force—significance—in inquiry to be attached to a whole set of names that are *applicable to kinds*—"operationally applicable" in the "terms" of the *Logic*—"terms" because they are employed to de-termine the proper use [of an] inclusive set of names. (The determination not being, of course, final but definitely in and with respect to the continuing course of inquiry.) A "category" is a term having unusual width of determining capacity. There is, I take it, in any given science a hierarchy of terms involved, not necessarily explicit, but growing in precision as that science advances. (Maybe this is what takes the place of taxonomic classification, but I haven't thought this out.) Maybe terms could be looked at as tools to make tools, generic names being like the tools a carpenter . . . applies to materials in actual process. A "term" is related to "generic names" as a "disposition" to an "act" (?). . . .

On page 307 [*Logic*], what is said involves confusion of mathematical subjectmatter with "characters" and "terms." . . .

Incidentally, [the] footnote on p. 299 suggests the possibility and perhaps the desirability of a technical article, pointing out the . . . lack of firmness in the symbolism used by logistic writers who claim to have reduced formal logic to mathematical accuracy. [The] footnote, p. 293, is similar. I haven't the required expertness in the logistic field, but I'd bet there are lots of cases [in point]. . . .

Yours as ever, John D.

Seattle, Washington, December 19, 1945

Dear John:

How . . . have we left this remark out: A naming of a named is no more practicable off by itself than an electric current without a circuit. . . . Bet if we could get fifty like that, maybe someone would listen. . . .

"Specification":

It states the most we have now to state—disjunction.

It connects the most fully possible with other knowns—conjunction.

It opens most fully toward the future.

It ranges all the existence we have to range through.

In other words, I am trying to jot down the make-up of "specification" for a summary statement before passing over in the paper to "Transaction." . . .

Regards, Bentley

New York, December 20, 1945

Dear Arthur,

. . . I think your piece on "Specification and Transaction" will go easily and smoothly when you get at it, judging from samples in your letters. The direct behavioral treatment with naming the behavior that develops out of physiological behavior. About the application of signalings to symbols, over 40 years ago I wrote something I re-read for the first time lately. In it I said that mathematics uses figures, diagrams, etc., which are directly perceived, same as any "objects"—no quotation marks at that time. [See *Logical Conditions of a Scientific Treatment of Morality*.] I think I got the idea from what Peirce was writing at the time about "diagrams" and "mathematics." Even pure mathematics observes its "diagrams." "Mathematical truth" is derived from observation of creatures of our own visual imagination which we may set down on paper in the form of diagrams. Of course, the signaling cue statement is much simpler and more direct, but I think Peirce here, as elsewhere, was ahead of his time. (See index references "Diagram" and "Mathematics.") [*Collected Papers*] Vol. II is probably the most complete, but [Vol. I] p. 203, sec. 383, contains a [valuable] passage. It is symptomatic of the editors that there is no cross reference between diagram and mathematics and no reference of either to "icon." P. 402, Vol. V, he [Peirce] calls them "graphs" and we proceed to observe the graph. "It is just as much an operation of *Observation* as is the observation of bees. This observation leads us to take an *experiment* upon the 'Graph.'" Another connection with behavior responsive to signalings. He links all this up definitely with "deduction"; in the Index to Vol. V, there is a cross reference [from diagram] to "Deduction."

In looking up references I found the following, Vol. V, p. 415: "The instincts conducive to assimilation of food, and to reproduction, must have involved from the beginning certain tendencies to think truly about physics." *

To go back to the muttons. What you say about negative namings should go in; it clears up at a single stroke what "logicians" have discussed endlessly without getting anywhere, save into a fog. "A cue as truncated description" goes in by all means—an illustration of the general statement that *every* naming is descriptive. All this, of course, gets under the ordinary usage of "specification," and gives the base, I think, to treatment of latter as progressive rectification of naming-knowings.

You could pretty well rewrite psychology on the line you are taking. For example, "ideas," as "suggestions-namings," "suggestions" as "cue-

---

* The exact quotation is: "In short, the instincts conducive to assimilation of food, and the instincts conducive to reproduction, must have involved from the beginning certain tendencies to think truly about physics, on the one hand, and about psychics, on the other." (Eds.)

namings," developing into what Peirce called "precepts" as rules of behavior; what earlier I called "plans of action."

On the basis of what you've written, I think you do this piece with less excursion into side fields than was necessary in the other papers. It can be, I believe, a straightforward clincher of the business. . . .

Yours with the best wishes for now and the future, *John D.*

[New York,] December 21, 1945

[To Bentley:]

Naming.

A kind of behavior; as such, it is one partner in a transaction, *that* which is named being the other partner, neither occurring without the other.

Mistakes are current due to neglect of the inclusive transaction. They take place on both sides; i.e., with reference to both naming and the named.

1. With respect to the named, making an entity of it—as in your example of a "logical entity" or "logical object" all by itself—called *subsistence* as distinct from *existence* [is common] in a lot of recent writings on the theory of knowledge. (I think it is probable that the whole theory of "essences," inherent natures, as the proper objects of "science" (knowledge) had a similar origin—common nouns, water, animal, metal, etc., named "kinds" as fixed species, "defined" in the sense of literally marking off or separation by kinds.) Physics moved steadily toward substitution of connections of space-time events, as that named. But I rather doubt if the older idea got such a shock as to be deliberately discarded until *The Origin of Species*, as entrenched in botany and zoology, brought the question clearly to the front. A large part of discussion of societal matters is still controlled by the postulate of "natures" or "essential" properties as that which is named. E.g., "society," individual," "wealth," "sovereignty"—in fact most of the "categories" that are in control of discussions in economics and politics. (See a book called *Relativity in Modern Society* [Bentley, *Relativity in Man and Society*].) When "concepts" are regarded as logical, not as "mental," they are first class examples of the postulate that the named is independent of the naming. (Of course, the whole "realistic" epistemology, according to which objects *as known* are the things which constitute The Reality that is *to be* "grasped," apprehended, etc., . . . causes all such "problems" as those [that] Russell discusses in [an] article sent [to] you: how [are] the "subjective," "empirical," "immediately known" . . . to be got into union with the "objects" of physics, which are rationally known—that is, by inference governed by logical rules. This isn't relevant to the present paper, but it is historically most instructive. It might be said, maybe, for Russell, that he

507

is aware of the locus of the problem involved in the old position more than are most of those who hold it.)

2. On the naming side. *All* views and positions which do not take naming as behavioral in its literal sense. The most obvious case, probably, is naming (language in general) as an outward manifestation or communication, "expression," of "thoughts" which are "inner" and mental.

Indirect and less obvious case is the necessity of setting up special organs and agencies (faculties) by means of which the *right* names are attached to the right "external" objects; e.g., the causal "theory of" sensations as direct effects of external things [Russell]; Kaufmann's "Intuition" (I think so in spite of his disclaimer of using it as a faculty); the various forms of epistemological "realism" ("representative" and "presentative") and "idealism." For the "idealistic" theory goes back to holding that the only possible solution is that "Things" are themselves mental, so that correct naming of the mental *is ipso facto* right naming of things.

There is quite a different line of approach *re* transactional behavioral naming: its connection with pre-naming knowings. I think what you have written covers in substance that point, as far as it can be covered without too wide an excursion into the whole languaging business, biological and societal. Connection with post-naming behavior is what, in effect, I have been [working] at for years under the caption of the "instrumental" status of knowledge. If I had made identification [of knowledge] with naming explicit, if I had been sufficiently aware of its involvement, the statement would have been tremendously simplified and saved a lot of unnecessary writing—on my side and on that of critics alike. I have pointed out that languaging-behavior involves a temporal holding aloof from other kinds of behavior, which involve greater commitments of a more irretrievable sort; and [I] have also pointed out, without adequate development, that scientific naming tends to carry this aloofness from immediate commitments to its limit, thereby extending indefinitely (by means of this emancipation) the ability to [reach] the strategic measures, by which naming-behavior (only I failed to state it that way) transacts useful business with the non-naming behaviors involving direct commitments.

The above is mostly up my alley of "philosophical" writing. But I think there is a point of application of a less remote kind—namely, to the distinction *and* the connection of demonstratives, pronouns, etc., as "here-now" namings, "general" namings, grammatically verbs, nouns, adjectives, etc.; and names which are "relational," the connectives, conjunctions, propositions, etc., grammatically. (*If* the syntactical formulists had taken this tack, they might have done something useful; "Peirce's" speculative grammar, maybe.)

Other things I shan't touch on; you've adequately covered [them] in letters. (Negative names, by the way, [are] indispensable in the process

508

of holding aloof from immediate commitments that turn out harmful "in the long run.") "Science" as firm naming can be attained in fields where now loose and confusing naming is actively at work.

J. D.

Seattle, Washington, December 23, 1945

Dear John:

. . . I recall your remark in a recent letter that I am apt to use "perceptional" more widely than you do. The difference is that you have made many studies in the sensation-perception region; I have not. I am (a) centering on the language, and (b) organizing it with the full range below, *all* of which we speak of as "signaling."

Then comes the question of little, minor descriptive extensions of "signaling." I use "perceptional," or "perceptional-manipulative." From some viewpoints these seem O.K. to you; from others, not. (Same to me.)

I think the main question is: Is there, in our sign treatment, a significant stage of differentiation between lower signalings and high-signalings (or say, between sensational and perceptional process) comparable in importance to the one between signalings and naming?

I assume the answer is No: *because* we both agree, and more and more stress, that "object" as set out, standing forth, identified existentially, requires linguistic process to produce it. . . .

The *Point* of all this is: If a better descriptive wording for the signaling range than we now have in perceptive-manipulative, or in conditioned responding (behavior), ever arises, we certainly want to nail it down. . . .

Best regards, *Bentley*

New York, December 28, 1945

Dear Arthur:

Some time ago I said there was probably a need for saying what is meant by "firm naming," and I think you agreed. Whether you did or not, you have done the job in what you say in yours of the 19th (delayed in [the] Christmas mail, I guess) about the four things specification does. They are the conditions to be met by firm naming.

Stating disjunctions is what has been called "distinction," "discrimination," "delimitation" (the discarded signification of "definition").

"Connects" is identification. And, of course, the two are strictly interdependent. We identify by distinguishing, disjoining, or unjoining (negations or ex-clusions); disjoinings are involved in identifications by means of "selected" connections—though historically, I guess, this last was the slowest to be observed. Self-enclosed essences were supposed

509

to identify and demarcate at one and the same stroke. It's election-rejection.

The last two, opening and ranging, are very (specifically) the outcomes of firm stating-connecting as seen in scientific naming; the present-science closed and fixed, nailed down.

Your previous paragraphs in bringing out how the naming-named system reacts on the alleged dualism of knowing-[known] thing . . . [need additional] statement; it *is* implied throughout, but can be made "ex-plied" in a summarizing introduction—or somewhere else.

Yours, John

[P.S.] . . . you can tell what "firms" *aren't* by what they *Don't* do—namely, open and range. It will be well, I guess, to indicate that opening and ranging involve continual rectification in and because of use.

Part V

Letters: January 4, 1946–December 29, 1946

Seattle, Washington, January 4, 1946

Dear John:

. . . I feel as if I had been in a fever ward of a hospital for the last six weeks, to the extent at least that I do not know what I have been doing, or why. I seem to have made two or three minor steps, like the express organization of names and descriptions (following your suggestions in the past as to the latter), and like the observation that "essences," "entities," and "reals" arise in the "characterization" level. But I do not seem to know how to handle them efficiently or even to appraise them properly. On the one side, we have not stressed any of our points widely enough yet, to make people see them; on the other, mere reiteration, which is about all I am doing, is just a bore to the reader.

Of course, the main point, that showed itself in drafts I and II in September, that "Specification" is needed to observe "transaction," while the transactional observation is necessary to formulate specification within proper limits as against old verbal layouts, is a good one, if sound, and if properly developed. It is sound as far as our own work goes, but it is not adequately developed, and I do not know what it will look like when it is.

Regards, *Bentley*

Seattle, Washington, January 5, 1946

Dear John:

Re your paper on Stevenson ["Ethical Subject-Matter and Language"] in *Journal* [*of*] *Philosophy.*

I read your manuscript, and ought not to be raising questions now. But this stuff is deadly hard for me to follow in finished form, and still harder in provisional draft. It is easy enough to be certain I am for all your main points, but not so easy to state sharply just what your and his basic differences are. Yet for pending work I should have this sharp.

Stevenson holds, or seems to, that men have emotions that contain no traces of cognition. Emotion ("feeling") reveals its full nature to introspection. Some signs are signs of inward states (pp. 707–708).

Dewey holds that Signs are signs only in connective developments. Dewey's position seems to negate all of Stevenson's. (I assume it is only for specialized local purposes that Dewey (pp. 709–710) speaks of non-cognitive components in a lawyer's appeal to jury—understanding here "relatively non-cognitive.")

As regards the ethical sentences (which do not interest me), Dewey's view seems to be that men are, so to speak, human, and that they can discuss their ethical sentences. Stevenson's seems to be that men have something ethically that they cannot describe, deal with cognitively, debate, or, in short—I suspect, he should add—even talk about at all.

Just to help me along: Please tell me what "basic" components I omit above for each man. And, just incidentally, does my common-man-in-the-street summary of the kernel of the issue omit anything vital to it?

Regards, *Bentley*

[Key West, Florida,] January 13, 1946

[Draft by Dewey of the essay on specification based on prior work by Bentley]

Our objective in this group of papers is to obtain a set of firm names adapted for use in investigating knowings and knowns. To understand what names accomplish when firm and to be able to use names effectively, we must have recourse to and become familiar with their most highly developed and powerful applications as exhibited in science. We must in especial, when investigating knowings-knowns, avoid taking our cue (lead) from uses that are primitive because pre-scientific. In so doing we shall steer clear from identification of firm names as dependable with rigid names. For the case of [the] sciences show that rigid names are not dependable. The only dependable names are those which are elastic enough to permit growth. For names employed in science carry forward into the future as well as sum up and retain the past. They do not merely tell; they form; they give direction. "Atom" and "electron," for example, are not mere labels for things known to and accepted by physicists as "entities." They delimit their problems in the very process of reporting the state of knowings; they serve as sign-posts to the measures that will secure further progress in which names used will obtain still firmer application.

Freedom of naming and freedom of the named are companions that in its development go hand in hand. Investigation of naming and of knowing are one and the same. Firmly named things are the things known. As far as this group of papers is concerned, namings *are* the knowings we investigate. Naming is also a tool of investigation; its use while an investigation is still in process has given rise, in connection with the view that a name is an external expression of "inner thought," to the notion that namings can be found in basic detachment from the named (and, for that matter, to the assumption that the named can be in basic detachment from the naming). But we repeat what we have said elsewhere, that we find such an assumption to be an absurdity, whichever side it is

514

made from. A naming that is a tool is not naming all by itself or in its own right, or under its own power.*

With respect to the full range of namings-named, we shall use the word "Specification" to designate the firm type. By "specification" we understand that efficient type of naming which science developed after elimination of the hampering involvements of primitive habits of knowing. "Specification," as we use the word, is employed in strict connection with what in our earlier papers we have called the transactional form of observation and report. (The remainder of this paragraph doesn't seem to me up to the level of clearness of what precedes. Perhaps, an illustration is needed; perhaps some more specific reminder about transaction. I should suppose that what has already been said about naming-named is itself an instance of transactional observation. But the rewriting which I believe is here needed can be better undertaken by you [Bentley]). . . . Then something like the following: Since we are concerned with what is inquired into (and hence is in process of knowing) and with how it can be inquired into as that which happens in the cosmos, we have no interest in any form of hypostatized underpinning. Any statement that is or can be made about a knower, self, mind, or subject must be made on the basis of and in terms of aspects of events which inquiry as itself a cosmic event finds taking place.

Within this cosmos, wherever effective adaptive transactions of organic-environmental conditions occur, and these take place all the way from amoebae to atom-splitters, the adaptations are behaviors. Anything that can be named "cognitional" or "knowings-known" is one form of such behaviors. Their distinctive process is described as sign-process.† In other words, behavioral transactions as distinctively marked by sign-processes are cases of knowings-knowns. Where human organisms (in a distinctively human sense) are the kinds of organisms in action, the special sign-process called naming occurs.‡ In the case of naming as sign-

---

* By means of insertion of a "faculty" in charge of the process, the facts can be fractured ad lib, so that it can then be claimed that the fracture exists first. This is another instance of the assumption that we, in accord with scientific practice, are endeavoring to get rid of. We have provisionally chosen "designation" as a name well-suited for use in reference to the naming *aspect* of the full process and "event" for the aspect named. Here, however, we are examining certain intimate organizations, rather than analyzing the process from a distance; we shall employ at will the words "naming" for one aspect, and "thing named" or "the named" for the other aspect. For study of special partial problems, provisional separation of the two aspects is of course legitimate, as when, from the side of naming, words are investigated philologically or grammatically. But no general theory can be arrived at save as materials separated for special study are rejoined.

† The word "knowledge" is used in such a wide and indiscriminate way as to be anything but firm and so is not here employed.

‡ The word "language" is in much the same loose state as "knowledge." (N.B. You may not care for insertion of the clause "In a distinctively human sense"; if

process behavior, life-in-environment is involved as fully and as definitively as in the pre-human sign-processes called signalings. It is this consideration which makes practicable direct inquiry into knowings-knowns.

Environments may of course be studied physically and organism physiologically. Such studies are cases of the temporary separation previously said to be legitimate. But when the necessary rejoining is instituted, it will be observed that the physical conditions in question are in fact temporarily cut out of the full organic-environmental transaction. Behaviors, including namings, occur in the case of organisms which are susceptible of physiological inquiry. But the factual, behavioral transaction does not today yield itself to technical *physiological* exposition. For while these behaviors have conditions that are subject to physiological treatment, they do not occur inside an organism's skin. They occur *across* skins in events in which organisms to environments, and environments to organisms, are in joint process. Words like "ecology" and "adaptation" bear witness. Even in the most exclusively physiological studies, air and radiations are required at every instant; water- and food-ingestion, periodically. Inquiry into knowings and knowns requires express observation of a physiologically transdermal setting. (N.B. Maybe "setting" is a little weak.) Otherwise, inquiry falls again into the relatively primitive notion that naming is a case of external manifestation of an occult, non-physiological somewhat that is somehow resident and somewhere resident within the skin.*

Taking into account the whole range of sign-behaviors in evolutionary life-development (with older types still found beneath the newer developments) (N.B. this is the point I had in mind in inserting the clause about the *distinctively* human), we have two things to do. We have to establish the place of designations among other behaviors in the total behavioral process, and we have to establish the place of specifications among designations. The aim here is to make clear the viewpoint under which our study is carried on, not to offer a new item of information. In the viewpoint adopted, the process of establishing the positions or placings just mentioned is one of conjunction-disjunction (comparison-contrast, identification-discrimination), [one] in which the manner of bring-

---

so, strike it out. I inserted it because there is so much knowing among humans of the signaling, pre-human type.)

* Failures of epistemologies to reach a coherent and generally accepted interpretation have been shown in previous writings to be due to failures to place and observe the problem of knowing as a full organic-environmental, transactional event occurring naturally in the natural cosmos. (Query: I dimly recall somewhere that James insisted that knowing is an *additive* event and that failure to see this fact accounted for the mess. Maybe express reference to it as an additive event, especially marked in the case of naming-knowings might be [of] help [to] readers.)

ing together is the very feature which makes the nature of the distinctions stand out.* (N.B. Under the transdermal sentences should you have a reference to your "Skin" article ["The Human Skin: Philosophy's Last Line of Defense"]? Where?)

If a sign-process is the distinguishing characteristic of behavior as organic-environmental transaction, we are under especial obligation to exhibit definitely its location in the natural world of events. When the sign process is of the naming type, we must specify just what is the named, including exhibition of just where it is to be found. A sign in our treatment is not a part of an organism nor is it a part of the environment. It is an event that takes place only when, and as, organism and environment are together in joint activity. Its locus is the total transactional event. Moreover, *a* sign is not an isolated event. It is a specific instance of the continued durational sign-activity of life, in which organic and environmental conditions are in joint procedure . No life-event occurs at an instant, and the life of a given organism for a day or for seventy years is but a specific instance of the indefinitely continued life process. To neglect the first condition is to revert to the condition of affairs in which a third power has to be summoned to hold together the termini that have been fractured. To neglect the second condition, is to fractionize knowings and namings so completely that the particular isolated cases which are nominally recognized are completely without traits that enable them to be distinguished and identified. (N.B. This "second" condition may be quite superfluous. Like most of my other additions, it was suggested by what you said. It also seems to lead up fairly well to what you say on your page 8.)

[*Dewey*]

[Key West, Florida,] January 16, 1946
[To Bentley:]

All naming process is positive "in inquiry as behavioral process. To say 'not-cat' is as positive as to say 'cat.' Disjunction is linked with conjunction; distinction with identification, in knowings; in namings they are present as negatives. Firm positings demand equally firm negatings."

(However, this way of stating it is not in agreement with the "minor purposes" of your further statement. Your formulation may hold good when *linguistic* procedures are emphasized as in isolation, but not, it seems to me, as far as concerns negation in *inquiry*-naming procedures.

Insert (?) "When negations are not placed within their use in inquiry-processes, there result all the puzzles and inconsistencies that are found in logical texts in connection with negative terms. The attempt to set

* Dewey: *Logic*, p. 337.

517

up a one-to-one correspondence as a standard and test also illustrates the isolation of a given knowing and naming from the extensive time-space setting in which alone it occurs and can be described." . . .

A few General Comments.

1. I miss the fourfold statement about what naming does—ending up "opens and ranges." As I said in an earlier letter, all naming, even loose characterization, does the first two things you mentioned; firm naming, as in the Sciences, does the other two also. You have something about names as indicating problems; this seems to me to convey what is intended by "opens;" in indicating problems, it gives *direction* to further inquiry. Whitehead said somewhere that a problem is not a nuisance, but an opportunity to be seized—not his wording, but his sense. "Ranging" might be amplified into a multitude of previously designated events that are at times brought ahead by an advance in a particular firm specification. Examples of what is done in physical—or in a case of physiological naming—would enforce the points.

2. I believe the paper would be strengthened by express statement, at some appropriate point, of what happens to "the named," corresponding to what is said about what naming and advance in naming consists of. You have repeated statements that "the named" *is* developed in fact, but I believe specific examples showing how, and what, are needed by the reader. . . . You have suggested the "atom" named as an indication. Perhaps that would also be the thing to develop, but I think a less far-reaching instance would also help.

3. In the early part of your paper, alert readers will not miss the point *re* firmness. But maybe it would be well to make it explicit that "firmness of naming" has to do—refers to—exclusively with *inquiry*-procedures, *not* with final acceptances, assertiveness, or "beliefs," save as the latter are noted as conclusions of inquiries at a given place and time. What you say about elasticity *vs.* rigidity covers the point, but it won't hurt to drive it in.

[Key West, Florida,] January 17, 1946

[To Bentley:]

I forget to say in mine of yesterday that the statement in your letter of 1-4-46 about Specification and Transaction is simpler and clearer to me than the one in . . . [a draft on "Specification of Transaction." See the one dated September 20, 1945 above]. It's a good start; all that's further needed is an example to show why . . . it is the case—the difference it makes. . . .

[*Dewey*]

518

Indianapolis, Indiana, January 17, 1946

Dear John:

. . . I think one of the finest pieces of writing ever done is J. Clerk Maxwell's *Matter and Motion.* . . . He used the word "transaction" for physical action and reaction, says the process must be seen as a whole (configuration); [I] say he is forecasting change from Newton to modernity—i.e., toward Einstein, *et al.* I looked at the text again at Crerar [Library] when coming through Chicago. Especially the sentence structure. If he says "pig" in one sentence, he never changes it to "porker" in the next. Always you can follow his development straight through, without fear that the shift from pig to porker hides the devil and all. Philosophy almost never does that—the minor disputants never do—they always flit from synonym to synonym. . . .

Maxwell's Preface, 1877, [1876] said: "Physical Science which up to the end of the eighteenth century had been fully occupied in forming a conception of natural phenomena as the result of forces acting between one body and another, has now fairly entered on the next stage of progress—that in which the energy of a material system is conceived as determined by the configuration and motion of that system, and in which the ideas of configuration, motion, and force are generalized to the utmost extent warranted by their physical definitions."

That, I would say, is a positive and wide parallel to what we are trying to inaugurate. I hope to use it prominently. But I will have to cut some more verbal eyeteeth before it works.

Regards, *Bentley*

Key West, Florida, January 18, 1946

[To Bentley:]

. . . *General.* It has occurred to me that in connection with naming as retention—past knowns-in-shape-for-further-knowings—something might be advantageously said about continuity as cumulative; that is, how naming thus enables knowings to meet the demands of the extensive space-time spread of events, in contrast to the more "immediate" and local events of pre-naming knowings. This isn't properly worded, but I think I have something by the tail here, if not by the head.

General. I don't know whether what I am going to say belongs in this paper, or somewhere else. But what I just said about immediate and local reminds me that the perceptual-manipulative holds over into the human naming-knowings-knowns, giving local and direct anchorage to what would otherwise be a theoretical system, in the same sense in which that word means general in the sense of remote. If it belongs here, it probably belongs by means of introduction of one topic mentioned earlier in letters and then somehow dropped out; namely, "this," "that," "now-

519

then," "here-there"—the *demonstratives* generally—"he," "me," "it," "they," pronouns which, as one able grammarian * has said, are *not* substitutes for nouns, it being more correct to say that "nouns" are extensions of pronouns. The manipulative in the general sense of *motor*, overt response, as well as sensory-perceptual clearly present in case of all demonstratives. (In scientific naming, every experimental test occurs at some spatial here and temporal now, and is involved in Warranted Assertibility. Prototype [is] in direct animal sensory-manipulative behaviors.)

. . . In various sketches, the remark that they do not merely tell, but form, is needed and can be amplified. The point is covered by reference to tools of investigation. But I don't think a sentence to the effect that the difference in knowings-knowns between savages, barbarians, and cultivated persons of today, between laymen and scientific inquirers, is [the] difference in the naming resources [of each], by means of which alone problems can be attacked and conclusions reached [and] organized for effective further use, would do . . . [any] harm.

As to phrasing—originally "telling" *told*, i.e., *counted*. Present usage much weakened. Probably, or perhaps, due to creeping up of literary use [in place] of face-to-face conversation about immediate emergencies.

In my *Logic* [p. 67], the sensory-perceptual, as found among humans, is linked to use-enjoyment as [an] objective of the cognitive aspect; in science [when perception is isolated from practical activities], knowing *as such* objective is knowing. I could improve statement now in a way that would link the two much more closely—but I think what I said was correct as far as it went—occasioned by the philosophers' writings that kept asking: does perceptual knowing or scientific knowing come nearest to "reality"?—there are things in B. Russell and in Moore that [can] hardly be understood without taking into account the historic role of this problem. . . .

[Dewey]

Indianapolis, Indiana, January 18, 1946

Dear John:

. . . I want to take up the case of the cocker spaniel. I have always recognized that right here is the crux. Our entire scheme of developing what naming is in terms of what naming does, may collapse if the cocker has too rich a personalization of John Dewey without much use of language (though it is evident [that] the better dogs react to language very widely, even if with limited utterance of their own). In other words, if a non-language-using animal acquires a sufficiently complex presentation

---

* J. H. Allen and J. B. Greenough, *New Latin Grammar*, p. 128, cited in Peirce, *Collected Papers*, II, 163 n. 1.

([of] a person) [who is] known to him by non-linguistic signs (any one of a variety of signals), so that the transfer to name-using means simply the specific naming of an already known complex, we may have to haul in our horns a long way. I fully recognize this. It is why I always want to make the construction postulational (even though it is more cumbersome).

Our technical question comes up in connection with the word "existence." It concerns the types of application. We reject the type which makes a "real" to be named by a word, or a "real" to be identified by any verbal process. We accept the *actuality* of the named within the naming-named process. We limit "existence" to this informal affirmation and construction. We know that the dog that identifies his master's car a mile away recognized an actuality through [a] signal, though it is a limited one, without benefit of gasoline-lore. We know that the cocker that has John Dewey "on his mind" after returning home, whether to say good-night to him or to make sure he has not been lost from the party, has an identification of a John-Dewey existence in the family group, but he does not have an actualization in an economic setting, for example. We know that we have to appraise the current uses of the word "existence," select one for attention, and keep it from confusion with the others. Now, if the cocker identification of John Dewey is a typical existential determination prior to linguistic development, then: 1. language in a sense identifies something beyond language; 2. this thing so identified is a "real" to the language-user as distinct from a cosmically-behaviorally-functional actuality such as we require.

Our answer to this difficulty in the end is the building up on the psychology side of a presentation of signal-word-symbol behaviors, whereby word is shown as advanced signaling. (Here is where the new insert of "cue" helps out—but also it is just a small help on the way.)

Recurring to above arrangement, we establish actuality: 1. by making naming-named transactionally functional; 2. by setting naming-named in place *in* signing behavior along with other signings, out of which it grows (signals) and which grow out of it (symbols). (Good old "Circular" back again in place.) . . .

Bentley

Indianapolis, Indiana, January 21, 1946
Dear John:
. . . Yours of the 16th got here this morning. Now I can size them all up together.

The substance of all your comments fully justifies my suspicion that I was in such rotten shape I ought not to have been doing that writing at all. I got a sort of organization, but, practically, it just reproduced organization of earlier papers. It was [the] wrong sort. Expression failed me utterly, even such as I have had before. E.g., the "four points, state, connect, open, range" are all . . . [there], but so buried in slovenly wording, you did not sense them as present. Your point that [the] first two cover all naming, and [the] last two specification, is good and must get worked in.

Your final comments, yours 1-16-46, page 2, [are] all first class. . . .

Here I have a case in which I only slowly found out what was in your expression, and another in which my expression did not carry to you what was in it. If we have this much trouble between us, then surely God help all poor sailors lost at sea. . . .

I think I shall go over your letters again for all you say on transaction, and mark it. Then take your letter 11-30-45 on transaction and check that again. Then draft the rest of transaction part of paper. Postpone all your discussion of naming and named (other than the transactional aspect) until later—as it can then be greatly condensed and only the very best parts retained.

The following is not generality or fluff. I am, as often before, appalled at the amount of significant discussion you have sent me which is not being used. I am not treating you any worse than myself. My own best developments slough off and are lost. (At least, I *hope* I am not treating you worse than myself.) Point seems to be I have accumulated beyond my ability to manipulate. The "office manager" has gone dead. . . .

Yours 11-30-45, you say "In the degree in which the transactional is put over the battle is won." One hundred per cent agreement on my part. Another reason for head-on attack in pending paper. This, indeed, is what I said [in a recent letter] to [Roy Wood] Sellars: "Accept us as postulational, rather than categorical; then see whether we have a right to the transactional treatment; then the issue will be well drawn."

. . . A "name" as expression of an inner "thought." Phrasing suggested by you: Under such treatment "name" and "thought" both tend to crystallize—to be static—to be "things." To get full activity presentation, they must fuse.

Your comment, "query," yours 1-13-46 . . . about James treating knowing as an additive event. I do not get the force of "additive." I always come back to James's use of "feeling" to cover all "mental" phenomena, both emotional and cognitive. That was in *Mind* . . . 1884, ["On Some Omissions of Introspective Psychology"], and maintained later. What I do not get in your query is the just-how of the "additive."

Yours 1-13-46 . . . on a second condition that sign is not an isolated event (the first condition having been that it has transactional status). You remark this may be superfluous. It looks to me, however, quite the contrary. An important structural plank. In short, it makes the business directly social, cultural, traditional, long-durational. Our "Postulations" paper, p. 660, does not seem to allow for this. On page 654, postulate C-6 gives a look-in to the social, but only perches there, so to speak —not fully incorporated. . . .

Regards, *Bentley*

Key West, Florida, January 22, 1946

Dear Arthur:

. . . Years ago I had a copy of Maxwell's little book [*Matter and Motion*]—I think when I was at Ann Arbor [some time in 1886–94]; I remember thinking it was the only thing on physical science principles I could understand. In the interval it has got lost. There is a wonderful passage of his, I think, in some other writing—maybe in an *Encyclopaedia Britannica* article. Foolish of me to mention it when all I can recall is that it is wonderful. Like the man who met a preacher and told him he heard him preach 25 years ago and it was a wonderful sermon—it had done him a lot of good all these years. So the preacher asked for the subject, and he said he didn't recall, but it was sure a wonderful sermon. What was the text? Similar answer. Well, don't you recall anything I said? Oh sure. You said theology wasn't religion, not by a damn sight. . . .

As to dogs, I don't think you've stuck your neck out (or your horns). On the contrary, the judiciousness of your cautionary comment suggested what I said about . . . [the] cocker. Your statement about identification and existence holds up in any case; the other matter, as to dogs, is just a question of fact not yet adequately decided by evidence, one way or another. (I recall a physicist at Columbia who was a great outdoor man. [E. L.] Thorndike, the psychologist, was saying animals couldn't think— just association of ideas. He said nothing at the time, but afterward said to me "How in hell does he think humans think?")

I note what you say about specification first. I still think a brief section on naming as transactional, together with a disjunction from the current subject-object separation—however named: self-world, organism-environment—comes first. For in any case, specification *is* the kind of naming we are dealing with—keeps the development smoother running, I'm reasonably sure, and saves repetition (in the sketches sent, you have to go backward too often) also about what we are *not* doing. A strong statement of disjunction with conjunction in connection with signing and designating at the outset (Transaction), and you can cut out later references to the topic. When you get to specification as firm naming of the kind practiced in scientific inquiry, the sentence you quote about specification and transaction in their mutuality—circularity—is O.K. in every way. Rejection of "reality" as such, or in general, or as anything but a name for cosmos under signing, [it] seems to me, comes in nicely in connection with the fact that what is named is what has been signaled—events of sensory-motor, sensory-manipulative type, which instead of ceasing with transition from pre-human organic-environmental to human organic-environmental are extended and made more deliberate—all cut—and trying as involved in even the most "scientific" experimentations, getting *new* subjectmatter to indicate new namings, i.e., improvement of old namings.

I thought your statement about existence as involving *identification* over and by means of a temporal duration was bully. How much more needs to be said about existence, I don't know as yet. . . .

With regards, yours, John D.

Indianapolis, Indiana, January 24, 1946

Dear John:

A brain is no more needed as the carrier through which thinking is conveyed than ether was needed to carry the light waves. Good illustration. Hope it gets in somewhere. . . .

Thinking is behavior, where behavior is directly described process of organism-environment at levels which cannot today be handled by physiological techniques of inquiry. "Direct description" means our best elaborated statement and naming, and this manifestly (to us) cannot be either in terms of dependence on material descriptions on the one side, or in terms of or dependence on non-material on the other side. The "material" does not cover. The "non-material" does nothing but reiterate.

I am not writing this stuff with respect to "thinking"—that happens to be only the detail. The problem is how to state the "presence of inquiry" (status, existence, localization) of the transactional. . . .

A. F. B.

Indianapolis, Indiana, January 29, 1946

Dear John:

A little useful reading. Max Wertheimer's *Productive Thinking*, especially. Some time ago I had, and used, the hunch that Newton's first law was a *trans*actional get-together as a necessary preliminary to the Newtonian third-law of *inter*action. Wertheimer has a fine account of what Galileo did, how he probably proceeded, in establishing "inertia," which Descartes then proclaimed, and Newton utilized. I think it fully bears out my hunch (although it is *not* historical, but hypothetical). Galileo faced motions assumed to be result of impressed force, he sought the *how;* he devised the inclined plane as substitute for the fall. He got aware that acceleration was the critical problem. He suggested the upward throw as reverse of the fall. This led him to negative acceleration. He then focused on the dead level between the two gradients, and

524

the two accelerations. Here he established inertia as the viewpoint, and saw that inertia was not a standing at rest, but a keeping on. In place of an older muscle applied to a weight, this produced a transaction; and on the basis of the transaction, an adequate meaningful interactional (mechanical) construction could be produced.

Nice stuff, this Wertheimer. I always did think he was well along your line, while the Koehlers, [Kurt] Koffkas and all the young men were premature systematizers. This confirms it to me still more. . . .

Regards, *Bentley*

January 30, 1946

[P.S.] The Einstein chapter is pretty good, but I suspect largely built up to show that Einstein was considering structure all the time, and so was a good sample of Gestalt psychology in action. Which would be all hunky, if the tendency was not to make "structure" a sort of "Gestalt-*an-sich*." I have a hunch that when Einstein made the velocity of light not only constant, and not only the greatest possible (maybe) velocity, but also the key to the special relativity—the controlling invariant—it may be another instance of a transaction being established. Certainly Wertheimer continually stresses how the old broken parts were re-envisaged, and re-constructed in system.

One most interesting [point:] this is how Wertheimer continually points out that the great obstacle to "thinking-through" is the old background of the imperfect statement. We say it often. And the limited extent to which Wertheimer goes, illustrates how *he* is held back. . . .

A final chapter on "[Dynamics and] Logic of Productive Thinking" has an eye on Gestalt logic to replace (I) the old syllogistic logic, (Ia) the inductive extensions, and (II) all associational treatments of the thinking process. He was probably wholly unaware of your *Logic*. . . . For instance, Wertheimer notes the failure of all the old [logics] to find out what an "object" is, is doing, and how it gets that way. Quite true in "traditional" logic—but no footnote to anything else. Beyond old-style logic, he was roughly aware of Hegel-Marx dialectics, Russell-Whitehead relational, Husserl's "phenomenological reduction," Dewey's pragmatism that stresses doing and acting along with the Wurzburg psychological school, of *Aufgabe,* and the Dewey and [W. B.] Pillsbury "naturalistic" trend, "which centers on conditions that start actual thinking in a given situation."

Key West, Florida, January 29, 1946

Dear Arthur:

1. Yours of 1-24-46. "Brain not needed as carrier . . . thinking. Better make carrier of meanings; don't know any who have said it conveyed thinking. Good sentence. . . .

2. Same letter you have something about symbols applicable to operations. I think it should go in full force. In the language I tried to develop in *Logic*, they [symbols] *refer* to *relations*, the latter being in the nature of operations-in-system, capable of application, but now developed on their own account far beyond application in the then-and-there state of inquiry. I find in my *Logic* sentences like the following: (p. 404) "mathematics proper is constituted by abstraction of the operation of *possible* transformation (transformability)." I think I recall your once making an objection to "operational" interpretations, due maybe to Bridgman's treatment rather than to the word as a name. [Eric Temple] Bell, I believe it was in one of his books, pointed out how some mathematical developments having no physical (existential) reference when they were made, later became powerful instruments of physical formulations. I think I once wrote somewhere [cf. *Logical Conditions of a Scientific Treatment of Morality*] that what is "denoted" (named) by abstract nouns can be stated from the standpoint of effectiveness in inquiry only through mathematical symbols, but I can't locate the passage, so maybe it is a later dream. But if there is anything in it, it explains the objection men of scientific habits have long had against talking in terms of "abstractions"—that is abstract nouns—though detachment from immediate circumstantial conditions is involved in common sense as well as in scientific conclusions. . . .

Regards, John

Indianapolis, Indiana, February 8, 1946

Dear John:

. . . So far as I can see, we have no difficulties ahead, except that of expression. In other words, we have all our issues in sight, and we have the meat of the answers laid out in semi-organization on the platters. There does not seem any point in which we can possibly disagree. I will qualify them in two ways—very lightly. First, if we get the pending paper laid out, not merely in a way that "will do," but so we both think we have the heart of the matter there. And second, if no bad tangle appears in the mathematical extension of the *Logic*.

About the "heart" of the matter in the present paper in progress. The changes in my way of sketching it accompany a growing feeling that the difficulty for the reader in "seeing" the transaction is almost matched by his difficulty in getting the full significance of the specification issue. The former difficulty you have stressed lately. The latter is due to the fact that hundreds of people have said a good deal of what we say in building up "specification," except that they have not *gone through* with it to the end. They limit it. It's good so and so far; it's good now and then, here and there, etc. We are proclaiming that for *basic* construc-

526

tion it is the *only* way; that the symbolic business the logical fancy-men seek as goal and control, is only an instrument. Your instrumental procedure has that. Your *Logic* has that. . . .

How about the following statement *inter nos:* "Specification" is a statement on the side of language-theory about what happens on the side of (in terms of) Inquiry in the *Logic* when *objects* appear as subject-matter "ordered in settled forms by [means of] inquiry" (p. 119 . . .).

I more or less started out five or six years ago to produce that general theory of language your preface mentioned to be a companion piece to the *Logic*. I have more or less recognized all along that the reason I worked so hard on the present job was that it was essential to the language theory, and would have to be done sometime anyway. I never got so far as to say [that] what we have been doing *is* (or, in part, is) the language theory, but preceding paragraph tends that way. . . .

Bentley

Indianapolis, Indiana, February 10, 1946

Dear John:

In your letter September 8, 1944, you make a different arrangement for transactions than I do. You have:

1. Action and Reaction—Newtonian billiard-balls
2. Interaction—Food ingestion. Reciprocal activity of food and tissues here-now.
3. Transaction—Growth. Development. Historicals.

You assume: (for 1.) that the materials *are* independent and separate; (for 2.) the tissues and grasses "may be assigned" independent status; (for 3.) no independent status may be assigned—for organism and environment.

Thus there cannot be such a thing as organism without environment or environment without organism (3). But there can be such a thing as grass without stomach or stomach without grass (2).

You continue:

All living events are transactional. All sociological events are transactional. Knowing-knowns fall wholly within the transactional. Billiard-balls studied *as a game* must be transactionally studied. There is then need of names which firmly and without ambiguity present transactional property where and as needed (understanding that actual scope of application is question of status of knowledge at the time).

Picking this up, this looked so good to me—compact and plain—that I wondered why it was not incorporated—and thought it should be—but further analysis makes me still prefer my present scheme.

You would not argue this—and I am not arguing over it. I am writing

527

as a manner of analysis to see whether there is anything in this scheme that has been missed in the other we are now using.

Probably the key is that "Interaction" must be split into several varieties:

(a) where it works mechanically, as in Newton's third law.

(b) where it is a partial statement of a phase of transaction—and I think your stomach-grass case falls here.

(c) where it is a falsification of what should be fully and transactionally approached (as per your indications). . . .

One thing I have not had straightened out is the mixed manner in which the ordinary epistemological-psychological scheme is partially self-actional (facultative) and partially interactional (causational), and defectively constructed in both respects. That is, I have not got a positive statement on this into text. Will do it.

You have recently brought in the Aristotelian substances for (1), and probably (1) should be made to include these plus the mind-selves.

Then the billiard-balls can slip over into one form of interaction, namely, the legitimate, useful, mechanics.

Your (2) is probably one legitimate provisional form of interactional with respect to a completer transactional statement. Taking the word "eating," it falls under (3), since no independent status can be assigned either to the eaten or the eater, with respect to the eating activity.

Your (3) seems to be an alternative statement of Transaction covering much same ground my various phrasings do; I have noted it. . . .

Regards, *Bentley*
February 11, 1946

[P.S.] Today I have your letter about trip to China. Grand thing. Not only the invitation, but the ability to go; all the abilities it takes. I hope it will be pleasant in every way.

I think I told you Otto Neurath spoke very strongly of Philipp Frank. And his widow mentioned him especially. You may have seen his essays *Between Physics and Philosophy,* Harvard Press, 1941. His monograph on *Foundations* [*of Physics*], I now learn, will be out end of this month. I must read the book now, and stop letting it lie around. I enclose a page of extracts. The top ones concern our "Specification" and are *musts* to quote. The bottom one is his layout of mathematics to science, defective in expression, but bully—and double-bully in tone.

February 12, 1946

[P.P.S.] . . . I have read the February 10 stuff to see what it is. There is something of a puzzle. The Newtonian billiard-balls should be brought into "Interaction," because they are not "substances," but descriptions in organization; and the Galileo-Newton advance put them there. But the case of animal-grass is not so clear. Your scheme in effect says that since cow can be found without grass and grass without cow (each thus "independent" of the other), when grass becomes eaten by cow, then the two are in *interaction*. Then you say that for the case of borrower and lender, no "loan" is possible without both, so it is *transaction*.

If, however, we say in the first case, in place of grass and cow, "food" in the general case of organism surviving by eating, you have something, namely "eating," that cannot be possible without both organism and food —just as much as loan is not possible without both buyer and lender. On the other side, if instead of "loan" you speak of *this* ten dollar bill or *this* lead pencil or *this* jackknife loaned by Bill to Tom, all these components *can* be seen [as] separate from *that* transaction.

In other words, I think both feeding, and trading or loaning *may* be studied either interactionally or transactionally, as the need may be at a particular time. The point about "knowing" is that it is vitally important at this time to introduce the *trans*actional treatment, which is totally lacking as a technical method of study in this field. Also I would say permanently the *trans*-actional is basic. But, nevertheless, one can take a reluctant boy and teach him to spell "cat" by licking him . . . and this normally takes inter-actional statement—however partial an approach it is for the wider discussion of knowings and knowns.

In the "Terminology" paper, I put the "subject-matters"—substantially as you see it in the *Logic*—at the front of the organization; and I think it governs here. . . .

Indianapolis, Indiana, February 13, 1946

Dear John:

. . . "Inter" is so regularly contrasted with "intra" in technical discussion that I think it ought to hold the place of "between two items." Of course we use "trans" in place of "intra." Even "trans" has double usage. But also I can mention that you yourself started the "trans" in your *Psychologies of 1930* paper ["Conduct and Experience"], apparently because you found "interaction" too weak and needed "transaction" to strengthen it—much as you used "integration" as a strengthener at a particular stage on the *Logic*.

There is one other remark that goes more to the heart of the matter. It is perfectly true, as you recently quoted, that Newton treated his "particles" as though God made them as is. But the mechanics did not have God in it. That remark is more on the philosophizing side as a side-up [set-up]. It is true to me, much in the same way, [that] the absolute space and absolute time were goddish [i.e., God-made]. Actually, to get the mechanics you have to have a closed system to work on. Closing the system means making the particle a phase of system— not a God-gift. Poincaré's demonstration that given one outcome solidly

529

proved in a closed mechanical system, an infinite number would be possible seems to settle matter of status of particle to me. . . .

Regards, *Bentley*

[P.S.] The above looks so vague, as I seal the letter, that I will summarize:

You are a little apt to say "re-action" and "interaction," where I say "interaction" and "transaction."

1. Terminologically: "inter" stands frequently in contrast with "intra"; and thus as "between."

2. Factually, the Newtonian mechanics *is* system, involving "inter," even though the particle (like space and sign) seems God-given. The difference here is that nobody monkeyed with the space and time till Mach and Einstein; but that each worker inserts the particular particles he wants, ad lib.

Or, so it looks to me.

Indianapolis, Indiana, February 15, 1946

Dear John:

. . . Russell's chapter [XXIV] on Analysis (in [*An*] *Inquiry* [*into Meaning and Truth*]), which I have got hold of again, is about as brilliant an example of pre-judging the case before discussing it that I know. His chapter [XXIII] just preceding about you has about as brilliant an example of quoting a man, without . . . knowing . . . what the quotation says, that I know. . . .

I think I have a somewhat fresh and useful illustration on the mathematical end. If you take a group of things (apples, say) and set them down, you can count them in both directions from a middle one, like this:

$$\ldots 2 - A, \ldots 1 - A, \ldots 1A, \ldots 2A, \ldots$$

where the $-A$ means counting in a reverse direction, or may mean just "taking away" an A. You have *names*. You have *no zero*. When the Middle Ages merchant got his figuring started, and used a "minus" he could not understand, and got a zero he could not believe in, the point was they were no longer names, but the procedure was written:

$$\ldots -2, \ldots -1, \ldots 0, \ldots 1, \ldots 2, \ldots$$

That kept the natural numbers as things, quantities, names. What they should have done was to write the right hand side as plus-one, plus-two, etc. instead of plain 1, 2, etc. Then no quantity, no names, no more bother about minus than about plus, no bother about zero.

Now I have no doubt the "plus" point has been often said, and certainly it is acted on by mathematicians. But, even a few weeks ago I read an extended lecture in *Science* by a prominent mathematician [James H. Taylor, "On the Problem of Applied Mathematics"] explaining why number-pairs were necessary to tell students about minus and zero —and that is long and complicated. I think our "Name" separated from "Symbol" will do that job, easy, quick, and sure. . . .

Bentley

Key West, Florida, February 16, 1946

Dear Arthur:

. . . I have yours [2-10-46] about mine of 9-8-44, and while I hope to get down to work tomorrow on your whole piece, I'll say a few words about that. First I don't know how important it is; that is, the action-reaction business. It doesn't seem or feel as "inter," or to have as much betweenness as "interaction," but that is quite likely because for so long a time I thought of the organism-environment affair as interaction, and thus discriminated it from action-reaction. But I certainly was far off my base if I said there could be a stomach without grass—or something to be digested. That the stomach, for the sake of a certain problem, could be temporarily investigated in detachment, we agreed. But in the full space-time setting . . . [it] would be a refinement of the stomach-edible transaction; we couldn't know enough about it unless we understood both the physical chemistry of grass—or whatever—and of the digestive organs and . . . [their] anatomical structure.

I think the notion that an organism, say, can be an organism "in itself," or apart from transactions engaged in, is [a] case of the fallacy of holding that because something can be *what* it is—as named by a general noun—without respect to this, that, and the other transaction; therefore, it can be what it is, say organism, without respect to *any* transaction. The "higher" the organism (man compared with dumb beasts, civilized man as compared with savage, civilized man in complex associations of highly differentiated functions or divisions of labor as compared with civilized man in simpler situations), the more numerous the degrees of freedom from any specifically mentioned transaction. . . .

Thus, while it would probably be seen that it is absurd to call a man a business-man if he never did any business, yet the variety of transactions into which he enters makes it easier to detach him; the same point holding with increased force when all his functions, transactions, that are *not* of a business kind are taken into account. Then he is capable of being regarded, viewed, as just *Man.* Or, if a man during his whole life engaged in but one transaction, and that with one other man, I doubt if he would ever be viewed in distinction from that transaction. The high degree of restriction of even interactions into which things were capable of entering before the rise of modern science and tech-

531

nologies certainly contributed to viewing things as having an essence that "made" them *what* they were. *Empty* space and time then was a natural enough reaction to the breaking down of the essence formulation. . . .

Yours, *John Dewey*

Paoli, Indiana, February 27, 1946

Dear John:

. . . Taking "Event" as the named, over against "Designation" as the naming, our previous paper * inspects event in the stages of "Situation," "Occurrence," and "Object" (corresponding to your *Logic*). I am now fooling with "Self-Action," "Interaction," and "Transaction." I have asked, but not carefully, considered, the question as to how these schemes fit. Little by little, maybe, we can approach an answer.

The distinction "Situation-Occasion-Object," as in your *Logic*, cannot be made except transactionally. A self-actor does not yield to development in inquiry, Newton's interaction did not "yield" itself, *qua* Event, but only as "found out by mind," and then only by making space, time, and particle "absolutes." Transaction in a way *is* just the viewing of the "named," and the "known" is capable of "transit" through Situation-Occasion-Object and on again into Situation-Occasion-Object—so that the proper formulation should be:

". . . Situation-Occasion-Object . . ." (naming and named advancing together).

Is it not clear that when in 1000 A.D. the event is seen as the action of an actor . . . [that] in the year 2000, one laughs at such an idea . . . then, that very "actor," who at the early stage was asserted to exist "out there," comes now at the later stage to be seen as a knowing-known event, not as a known-outer event? How to say it? What I mean is that "the positing of actor" and the "actor-as-posited" of the year 1000 are now in the year 2000 to be seen as a single "doing" in knowledge.

The distinction "Situation-Occasion-Object" as we make . . . [it is] transactional.

Nevertheless, the distinctions of "Self-actor" and "Interaction" at the *time they were* made, are *now known to us* to have been transactionally made. Looks to me as though it is going to take a $500,000 electromagnetic eye calculating machine to work out the statement we need.

How does this stand with reference to "Specification"? We make Specification out to be the best naming. "Specification" then couples with "Transaction" (as I have been trying to get properly said).

"Substance," "self," etc., couple with *"Cue"* at the bottom of scale.

* "A Terminology for Knowings and Knowns." (Eds.)

It does not look like it offhand, but I have half-said this before, and now can be stronger. "Cue" is the dumbest, "most brute-like" naming—in the form: this sign *is* exactly *that* thing (or in modification: *this* sign stands exactly for *that* thing). The substance, the self, are then dumb-cluck namings, both with respect to the heavy stress on the name-as-basic, and confidence on the thing as basic. (Mead, for example, never did get rid of talking as if all that he developed was *about* the Self, where[*as*] the self was actually there; while actually what he developed was replacement for the old "self" itself by way of wider and much improved description.)

As for "interaction" matching with "characterization," that does not click so well. And why should it? This is no lathe to turn out pretty pieces exactly alike. . . .

About the old "essence" in the time of transition to inter-actions, I got some nice citations from Hobbes's *De corpore:* amazingly clear and plain on independent subsistence and existence. Good to use to remind the slithery lads, who keep the same view, but don't admit it, how it ought to be frankly said, if said at all.

Regards, *Bentley*

Paoli, Indiana, March 5, 1946

Dear John:

. . . Reading your letters (beginning 1-13-46), I note your very first point is that the hitching up of "Transaction" and "Specification" "seems blind." This is the issue I have written of so many times as one that *must* be clear before [we] finish. . . . The history of it is this: In September, I started a draft of a paper on both "Transaction" and "Specification," coupled there merely for publication purposes. Before I finished the draft, I had in it a section on the two being necessary, each to the other. This has steadily developed since then, but without any assurance that I have got out of it all there is in it, or that I have an adequate statement.

Both "Transaction" and "Specification" are double-barreled words (could we call them "aspect-words"?—I mean, would that be a successful way to speak of the double-barreled ones?). We use "Transaction" mostly on the Event-side, and "Specification" mostly on the Designation-side—or, better, we use the first for the event-aspect and the second for the designation-aspect. We use each, however, deliberately and openly implying *both* aspects. That is sure.

However, if we use "Specification" implying both aspects, this means that we set *it* up transactionally, and if we use Transaction implying both aspects, this means that we do not set it up "by itself," but "as known." This is clear, but this is by no means all of the case—it is too bare a statement—rather, [more] a statement of our position than the development of it.

Under the old scheme which we reject—that of logical-defining-naming —the historical tendency has been to seek "elements." (Russell, the push-to-the-limit man in this respect—or rather the push is that of Wittgenstein, though the voice is the voice of Russell.) This is why we both are so antagonistic to him. "Over the fence is out" is the way we see him. Such elements are things, entities—logical[ly], proper names.

Now *we*, on our side, are not seeking synthesized things to be things at the far extreme from the element-things. If we were, we would not need "Specification" to get at them. We would still be saying "they are *there*—'outside'—and we are trying to name them facultatively." We are setting them as chosen envisagement and apprehension under the cultural-natural advance of "inquiry." To do this takes the reduction of the "name-absolute" to the "name-transactional" or, in its best developed form, as we call it, to "Specification."

This is to say: You cannot establish "Transaction" as we see it except through "Specification" as we use it.

On the other hand, this very "Specification" has definitely and from the start been built up by us transactionally—and that is all there [is] to it. It is not a far step from this to say that because of this "history" of it, that is the way it is—the only way it can be got. To fortify this argument we have such a case as that of Nagel, who goes all the way natural-istically, except to the point where he is (or, where *it* is) "natural." He can be 99% "naturalistic" and still astound us with his "demonstration" that knowledge entails truth—that we cannot *know* anything at all unless it is absolutely *true* to eternity.* Thus, he does *not* arrive at what we call "Specification" (the open range); and his logic has no place for "Transaction." . . .

"*Relation.*" If one takes two "things" and does not permit the use of a transactional view, then one adds a third "thing," namely a "relation." (1) You had me add a reference to "relations" as not recognized by us in this way to our statement of "Transaction." . . . (2) I have always been rabid against the use of the word "relation" as a thing. (3) Your use of "relation," p. 55, *Logic*, was hailed by me as the real McCoy—it was all on the language-side. (4) The old logics "improved" Aristotle by developing "relation"—all O.K. as a technical device—rotten as hell for a creed or basic postulate.

* Nagel's exact words in December, 1943, were: "I see no way of contesting Professor G. E. Moore's point that 'I know S' (where S is any proposition) logically entails 'S is true.' " But Nagel asserted in March, 1944: "I neither claimed nor implied that 'any empirical knowledge is irrefutable.' " "Truth and Knowledge of the Truth," quotations at pp. 177, 183, respectively, as reprinted in *Logic Without Metaphysics*. (Eds.)

534

Query: Should the relation phase be further developed in this paper? (No matter how big the paper gets. Let's put in what it "takes," and then whittle it down afterwards to fit.)

Trouble is, this "relation" phase is "off" from my present line of development. Yet it looks as though it was vital to a direct discussion of "transaction"—or, let us say, to an all-purpose discussion. . . .

Your 1-16-46. . . . The named grows with the naming. You suggest strengthening this statement, as it is dropped into background. You bet. But: is not this a *plumb good argument* for hitching up "Transaction" with "Specification"? It is—unless the only direction of growth is, as Russell sees it, to atomic bases—and we veto that. . . .

There is a passage, page 1 of yours dated 1-17, on split-distortion which should be picked up bodily and inserted. . . .

Perhaps the transition of "subject," the word, from thing to person and back (in your use) to subject-matter should be stressed along with double-barreled. Here is a cite from Hobbes on "Body":

"And lastly it is called the *subject* because it is so placed in and subjected to imaginary space that it may be understood by reason as well as perceived by us." [*English Works*, I, 102.]

What comments have you?

On that basis it looks as though what we were doing was to bring things into organization with respect to (i.e., "subjecting them to") "all of nature" (cosmos-system) instead of to "imaginary space."

There surely ought to be a way to get a statement (though not necessarily for publication—just for fun) on what we are doing with respect to Kant. He took Newtonian absolutes, added some more, made them a priori (which is big-time subjective), set them over against the world (which is big-time objective), and oriented both to small-time man with a subjective mind in an objective body. This statement is not supposed to be about Immanuel himself—wouldn't know—but just a sort of what might have happened somewhere. . . .

If I convince you of the full importance of the hitch-up of "Transaction" and "Specification," then my way is good. If not, then your way of preparing two papers is best.

If I were writing a treatise on language, I should certainly expect to follow your route of slow and full development up to the best naming, and then bring out the status with respect to "definition," "hypostatizations," "fact," etc. But an accumulation of evidence would take a book. What we have to do is to get our theses out, and then support them. One thesis is specification, another is transaction, a third is the hitch-up. We have told in previous paper what we plan for the first two, but not for the third.

I suspect that if I finish up the way I am going, it will not be at all difficult to dismember the paper and do it differently—since the main portions of each issue will be along the lines you have suggested; and only the connecting matter will have to be rearranged. I will consider this a possibility until the finish.

Regards, *Bentley*

Paoli, Indiana, March 6, 1946

Dear John:

. . . Now about your suggestion for the use of a few cases of psychological terminology as seen interactionally or transactionally; to develop the behavioral end on transaction. . . .

But one of our main objectives has been a special paper or two at the end to take up everything we can properly handle. At any rate, your suggestion that we do it in the form of a comparison of interactional and transactional (with self-actional kicked out entirely) is a new one—I don't think I got that particular point when I answered your letter. It may be the proper form in the wind-up.

Your comment . . . [in letter of 2-7-46] looks to me as not only relevant, but as making a corking good transition from the physiological to the behavioral. As the "physical" was made "fact" and stripped of essences, the "man" came to be more "essence" than ever and personified— so as to set . . . [him] over against world of objects. . . . You remark that both Berkeley and Descartes pop up with the "ego or mind," and I recall you have said in the past it was pretty mysterious how this ego-business got in so strong. Descartes was only soulful for will and emotions—he was a thoroughly mechanistic cuss with his theory of knowledge (his [La] *Dioptrique* is one of my best-loved books—the first five chapters of it). You remember you thought a straight-out sketch of the historical development of the transactional in physics would be good from me. Comparably, I think a straight-out discussion of development of this type of "ego or mind," using your present clue, would be good from you.

Here you get the self-actor into psychology. I, for my part, have mostly noted the way the inter-actor got in; which I have taken to be through a direct imitation of Newton's particles by Locke in the form of his ideas—hardly an imitation, but a development "under the strong influence of," etc.

I suspect the new physiological development which has driven the "vital-self" out of physiology may have had two effects—first to get [the] "brain" substitute for "mind" prominent; second, on other people, to push the "mind" out for inspection as over against physiology in much the way you note that physics pushed the animistic person into prominence. . . .

The development as to your "instrumental" ought to be shown—its

536

rise in pre-naming and its pointing toward post-naming. Watch that too, for I do not see a place for it yet. Still, as you say, it is not so immediately germane to this paper. I can see it strongly stressed in the paper on the growth of sign-behavior as the technically behavioral, if we ever get to it. Does it run something like this?

Peirce hit on the practical use for concept. James built a lot of stuff around it and popularized [it] (you sharpen[ed] it). Schiller made a monkey out of it in mentalist terms. You developed it instrumentally for all thought and logic—the post-linguistic outcomes.

We have now a pretty complete sign-behavior scheme, which is not operated animistically, and eliminates most of the "personalized" manner of expression, and should be free from the standard abuses in which "friends" are worse than "foes."

I badly want to salvage the word "term." I know no comfortable substitute for an occasional "in terms of." We have agreed to couple "term" with "name" and "specification." (The "term" of an equation is in disagreement, but it is in a special mathematical discipline, and can hardly interfere—it is so precisely used there.)

I find this scheme:

"Name": coupled with the entire designatory process.

"Cue": naming on the Cue level.

"Term": naming on the Specification level.

"Name": (in narrower use) applied on the Characterization level.

This probably would let us say "in terms of" without confusion. I don't think the duplicated use of "name," once in the broadest application, and again in the narrower application, does any harm.

This is not a pressing decision. Can be fixed definitely in a later paper. But [I] like to fall in line where possible now.

Regards, *Bentley*

[Key West, Florida,] March 9, 1946

Dear Arthur:

As an illustration of cueing, the following occurred to me the other day. I had in Chicago a crackerjack stenographer, a student who had earlier won a prize in one of the speed-accuracy competitions—half an hour after a dictation, he wouldn't know what it was about, much less any particular thing said. And I believe something of the kind happens when a typist copies a manuscript of mine to get a clean copy. The *sense* of what is said is of no relevancy to what [he] is doing.

The point about specification and the "open range" must be emphasized. I wonder what Nagel would say if he were asked outright, if he means to say that nothing is "knowledge" unless it is "eternally true." (I have it in mind to write later something on Validity and Truth—to the general effect that "Truth" is a moral category, not a logical (methodological) one at all, while "Validity" (the sound as opposed to the invalid—sick, ill, disabled) covers the entire latter ground—efficacy, what it does, in promoting knowings-knowns—which is a matter of date and place. "Truth"—lying, deliberate deceit, go together.)

I think (am not sure, we can talk it over) "relation" belongs later. It has to be handled—for using it where connection, spatial-temporal, should be made emphatic is, I am now persuaded, responsible for about as many ambiguous, vague, confused statements as any other thing. Something can be said in these papers as to the net effect of substituting "relation" for space-times-bonds and then giving "relation" one of a number of different senses—to "mind," to another single "object," a logical (form), *quasi* mathematical sense, etc.

Again, as [to] naming-named—if I said anything that sounded like not hitching "specification" to "transaction," I didn't intend what it sounded like—what I was concerned about was also hitching "specification" to the whole naming-named business. . . .

[*Dewey*]

[Key West, Florida, (?)] March 12, 1946
[Draft by Dewey of essay on "Specification" for *Journal of Philosophy* based on prior Bentley draft.]

Specification

1. Connection with Transaction—double-barreled and why.

2. Naming—named as case of knowing-known. Specification, a case of Naming which requires to be itself specified. It may be provisionally identified, while naming as a broader field is briefly considered, as the kind of naming that is found in and is distinctive of procedure in physics and in the biological subjects, as far as they are developed—we might say of "scientific" procedures, were it not that "science" is now so often referred to as if it named some peculiar kind of entity, while in fact it can be itself identified only as that case of naming that proceeds by specification—circular—so we here mention physics, say, in present use of atom or neutron, by way of pointing to the sort of thing to which specification is applied as its name.

Naming—a case of behavior—speech, talk, writing, printings—is transactional (listening, taking part in conversation, reading, using subsequently what is heard and read)—enters into extensive development—being guided, directed, advised, informed. Signs as distinct from signals. At present no one can tell, dogmatically, where in the animal "scale" signaling passes into using of signs—we do know that *homo sapiens* is *homo loquens*, and that mankind is the distinctive thing it is, as marked out and off by use of the kind of behavior in which certain things—bodily movements, gestures and sounds—are used to stand for, "represent," things of *direct* behavioral transactions, and in this office become names for the latter things.

[A] certain difficulty or danger [is] connected with reference to names. [It] suggests something too isolated, unit-elements. Every name, and thing named, is in *discourse*—contextual, situational—even a gesture like pointing; the pointing and thing pointed out belong to an inclusive behavioral whole and are pointings and pointed-ats only as within that transaction. Naming is in and for use—bird building nest—sequential behavior—each particular act has use—carried on and through—naming same type. Communication—a common situation—and so, when something is silently, subvocally, named there is the transitive carrying on, forward, of a situation common to all the namings in a given sequence characteristic of what is ordinarily called a transaction of communication.

A naming *does* something within the total, developing whole. . . . Identifying-marking out, distinguishing—not two processes; to do one is to do the other—we identify by discriminating, and we discriminate by identifying. Also holds on to, retains, for further use and development— as just indicated. In "telling," they form, give shape, body, substantiality —otherwise wavering wisps—as when one feels there is something all but "on the tip of the tongue," but it doesn't take body—form.

There are various degrees or grades of the doing in question—cues, characterizations, specifications—distinguished by (i) reach, narrow (local)—comprehensive (comprehension—understanding)—*some* range or degree of scope in communication, in any case, or no naming—wider, "liberal" knowing, freedom; (ii) firmness, *hold* on subjectmatter, grip, prehension—but, as just seen, not rigidity—the wider and fuller the system of connecteds, the freer—includes freedom of transfer to "other" topics, which react [so as] to liberate and broaden prior uses. Cues— reduction of name to kind of use belonging to signals. Characterization —names that develop in relatively local situations, and [their] use is to carry forward some particular job, task, piece of work, play or game. [These last are] what are often called "practical," with the result that "practice" is restricted to such cases, thus producing confusion by means of concealing (virtually denying) [the fact that] *all* naming is a matter of use (using) or of practice, and that what is needed is [a] distinction of types of practice. Specification—the kind of use and practice in which retention is most definite and complete—know what is *going on*—and in which comprehension—freedom of further development as to range—is at a maximum. Naming-knowing to promote naming-knowing, leaving it to the local situations, as they show themselves, to determine local (narrower, practical) use and application.

(Use—application—is what I was driving at, but not exactly coherent about, in discriminating "reference" along with "connection" and "rela-

539

tion" in the *Logic*. It is incoherent in that it is limited too much to a single kind of use—that of the "final" or *direct* application to space-time things, at the expense of use in development of signs in the knowing-naming affair. It looks now as if reference in the latter case were made through or by means of *relations*, and in the other case, through or by means of a connection; I haven't got this worked out, but that is the way it strikes me now.)

Term—I wrote earlier about it, but don't recall now just what I said; it looks now as if you are right in specifying term as the distinctive name in case of specifications. "Term" certainly carries with it reference to a system more openly than "name" does; a term is a term-*of*, not just in the sense in which John Smith is the name of a man, but in much more intimate sense—a condition in the given sign-development in which it is found.

I think that somewhere something should be said about demonstratives —I guess you are probably right in suggesting "common nouns" in connection with characterization; then "this-that," "here-there," "now-then" are characterizing demonstratives that name certain operations of pointing, but can hardly be said to specify—there are lots of pointings, and so lots of "heres," "theres"—not that it is needful to say this, but that I am saying it as a reason for including demonstratives along with common-nouns as belonging in the characterizing class.

It's a great pity I used "symbol" as synonymous with *sign* as representative in the *Logic*—not only for the confusing effect in mathematics, but also because if I had confined myself to signs, the point I made about their necessity for conduct of inquiry (e.g., pp. 110, 114) could have been more fundamental, and might have led me to discriminating grades of signs according to specific use in furthering the inquiry-event. I think I had something in distinguishing between "common-sense" knowing, as connected with situations of "use-enjoyment" . . . from "scientific" knowing, where the use of signs is to promote the sign-using (naming-knowing) process. But, the point could have been made better in methodological terms, as the distinction between the relatively local and the relatively extended use, and [I could have] kept the statements more firmly within the sign-range, with less danger of being supposed, by readers so inclined, to introduce some special agency of knowing.

(Incidentally—while "agent" is used in philosophy, epistemology and . . . psychology as a unit term, in every other field of use it is definitely a transactional term. It isn't just a "doer" at large, but a "doer" that is representative of, and in, some transaction.) . . .

Is it better to say that "Descriptions" are expanded namings or that "namings" are condensed, shorthand descriptions? About the only contribution I have to make that seems of importance is [to stress] the necessity of statements that will not leave the reader with the impression that

540

names are unit-elements. Statements that every name is in system are some protection but . . . development is [needed] to get [the point] . . . over. Russell's view that "ultimately" or in "reality" all names must be proper names is a logical enough development of taking names to apply to things *directly*, not through "discourse"—though I don't suppose that word can be saved—though a footnote might indicate that an inquiry-system-of-signs is the *proper* use of "discourse." . . . Incidentally, going back . . . to Kaufmann, maybe part of his difficulty was the assumption that *some* words had to be privileged to apply directly to *some* (controlling, determining) things.

I don't mean [that] there is anything new in this point as a point—only that the state of reader's habits is such, it has to be definitely labeled for him. . . .

March 21, 1946

Designations. Like signalings, designations are transactions of organism and environment. They also involve clearly differentiated accompanying transactions between and across organisms. In its earliest forms it is a signaling that is named, not as if it were in an organism, but as fully transactional. The *naming* which differentiates as running from hand or mouth of one organism to ear or eye of another organism arises and differentiates out of organic interchanges between organisms (such as those of herd life), the extent and types of which are not yet fully understood, though Jennings and others (*memo*—what others?) have made notable progress. Cue-forms, as earliest designations, begin among borderland cases in development from Signal to the more highly developed designations. Under our form of approach and observation, it is vividly clear that *what* is named through Cues is a behavioral transaction of the signaling type, not a "thing" in detachment from the organism's living. For what is "cued" is an action-requirement. Whether one of a pair of birds gives a warning-cry to its mate, or one man says "woof" to another man as sign of bear-presence or bear-trail, the designational activity is transactional. Its reference is not to "reality," ultimate or provisional, to "existence" or even [to] actuality of things (say, the bear), but strictly and exclusively to an impending behavioral event, which, of course, is inclusive of environmental conditions involving "bear," trees, rocks, or whatever. What is primarily named are sensori-manipulative-perceptional situations, the designational behavior having a comparatively narrow here-and-now locus.

When and as the designating-event develops, the locus widens. Intermediate steps of namings intervene. Some of them come temporarily into the forefront of attention, but even so are in fact members of a total inclusive transaction, and are given isolation and independence only in theories that depart from or distort factual observation. One may name a law, say the [?] Act, without putting his "finger" on it. In fact, our experts in jurisprudence talk indefinitely about a statutory or other law without being able to specify it in a way equivalent to direct "fingering." And while in this talking or writing [stage], limiting, intervening namings become temporarily the focus of direct attention; *what* is named is the "law" in its entire reach.

It is in this transition to more and more complex designations that descriptive accounts are most likely to go astray. The cry "Wolf!" is quickly settled in and by actions that yield a *Yes* or a *No*. The cry "Atomic Bomb" is evidently of a different type. It is in the cases of highly developed designations that it is most necessary so to take our clue from the simpler cases, and to be firmly and solidly aware that name cannot be identified as a process in an organism's head or "mind," and that the named cannot be identified with an "object" as an entity on its own account, that the naming-transaction has locus across and through the organisms-environments concerned in all their phases, and that it is subject to continued development of indefinite scope so that it is always in transit, never a fixture.

We are . . . [here concerned with] cue and characterization as designations merely [far] enough to lead up to presentation of Specification as the perfected (and ever perfecting) stage of naming, and so as to provide the ground for its differentiation from Symbol and Definition. It may seem strange to group the word "Cue" with the actions [doings], Characterization, and Specification, as we have done. But since all designations are designations in and of behavioral activities, the noun-form that is used does not greatly matter. We might, for example, set . . . Cue, Common Noun, Term, which are non-naming, as one naming of the series, or Interjectional Index, [with] Characterization and Specification as an alternative. Provided the behavioral transactions are taken as named with respect to development, the selection of terminology may well be left open for the present. *Symbol* and *Definition* are not discussed in the present paper, but to ensure a place for later consideration we introduce a memorandum to the effect that in our treatment they cover linguistic processes. . . . Alien as this [the attempt by Aristotelian and most modern logic to bring common namings under the control of logical rules and definitions] is from modern scientific practice, it, nevertheless, in the main, is the present basis of most linguistic and logical theory and of what is called "philosophy of science." It is at this stage that namings and the named have detachable existences assigned them by reflective or theorizing agents, their immediate users being, as a rule, protected against this abuse by the controls exercised in conversational exchange by the contextual situation directly present to those who participate in the oral transaction. Indeed, one may go so far as to doubt whether the distorted theory would have arisen if it had not been for the

542

development of written documents, with their increasing remoteness from determination by a directly observed situation. Given the influence of written, as distinct from spoken, language, it is dubious whether theoretical or philosophical formulations could have taken any form other than the one they did, [until] a high degree of development of the methods of inquiry now in use in advanced subjects [had] provided the pattern for statement in the form we have termed "Specification" as complementary with "Transaction." . . .

Specification. Specification is the type of naming that develops when inquiry gets down to hard work, concentrates experimentally and descriptively on its *own* subjectmatters—those appropriate to inquiry as inquiry—and requires flexibility to keep advance active. It is passage from conversational and other "practical" namings to namings of the research type of practice. The whale ceases to be a fish on the ground that it is identified as living in the water, swimming, etc., and is identified as a mammal on the ground of features, characteristics, that are pertinent to the work of continuing inquiry-knowing and naming. Scientific classificatory naming, as it escapes from the bonds of rigidity, illustrates the point in physiology. In physics it is illustrated by the atom, which has ceased to be a little, hard, round, or cubical "object" that no one [can] make littler, harder, or rounder (or whatever), and that has become a descriptive name, as a kind of shorthand (for the expert) for a region of carefully analyzed events. In discussing transactional development in recent physics, we also discussed, in effect, the growth of specification in its reciprocal connection with transaction. The developmental process, even in "science," is still far from complete. In biological work organism and object [are] still often present themselves as characterizations, without specification, even though much specification has occurred in the case of physiological inquiry. . . . Psychological and societal subject [matters] are even more backward.

Passage from Characterization to Specification is not in any case marked by a fixed boundary. Regions of vagueness—the "hazes" of Bridgman—remain, but they decrease, and their main implication is transformed. The earlier vagueness appeared as defects of human capacity, since the latter could not reach the infinite or the absolute. The newer vagueness, under the operation of Specification, is a source of pride. It shows that work to date is well done and carries with it the assurance of betterment in future inquiries.*

. . . A sentence or two about the attempt to give logistics a quasi-

---

* Cf. Peirce, ". . . [Although] the conclusion at any given state of the investigation may be more or less erroneous, yet [the] further application of the same *method* . . . [must] correct the error." The word "further" allowing, I take it, for indefinitely extended investigations. *Collected Works,* Vol. V, p. 90. [Dewey's emphasis.]

mathematical formulation, which then provides "rules" that are the foundation of mathematics as well as of all other knowledge, might come in here. Then another set of methodological or "semantic" rules [are required] in order that the logical and mathematical symbolic calculus can get out of the empty void and get application to existence. But probably this belongs in the next paper; certainly its development does. . . . In epistemological theories, the old "objective idealism" is perhaps too nearly obsolete to need any attention. But in its day, most of its formulations started with "absolute mind" as complete and ultimate (and primal) self-activity, and then used the *interaction* of "objects" constituted by its activity with "finite human minds" as the mechanism—the means—by which the latter became enabled to "know"; i.e., to reproduce or re-instate, to some degree, however partial, the activity of absolute mind—the "finite" becoming in knowing itself self-active through contact (interaction) with the existing manifestations of absolute self-active Mind. Out of fashion now, but might have a periodic return wave—in some ways, it is "logically," formally, the nearest coherent of any of the subject-object epistemological theories. Its dualisms are provisional, and the supreme task, duty, of man is to progressively overcome them in an asymptotic way. The theory also allowed for reproduction of the "absolute mind" taking place progressively throughout the whole historic process, so called "individual" minds adding their bit to the continuing process.

The above is just one of the historical reminiscences (of philosophical doctrines) that the text suggests to me.

[Dewey]

[Key West, Florida,] March 26, 1946
[To Bentley:]
. . . Some readers are going to say—or shout—and then sink back confirmed in previous attitudes: "Aha. How about the world before man and knowing came into existence? They deny the existence of those long, geological aeons, etc.; none of that for us." A sentence or two about the fact that these events are, by the very argument used, known and named by us, would not only obviate the retort—which will be made by some, sure as hell—but turn the point they think they're making into an evidential illustration of our position, (i) as to connection of transactional known-named with knowing-naming, and (ii) as [to] the necessity of knowings-knowns transactions being taken across in definite stretches of time-space, and (iii) as to the origin and place of man as knower in cosmos as known. I don't mean all this should go in here, and maybe there is a better place for what might go in; possibly [the] specifi-

544

cation paper, especially as to (i) and (ii) above. But there may be something worth noting somewhere. . . .

That multiplication of entities demands multiplication of relations . . . is a point which should surely go in—and the whole business as to both entitative things and relations being avoided by transactional things. (Re Russell—his "physical" events being point-moment particles, to get back to the known world he just has to have a complex apparatus of non-physical and non-psychical "relations"—hence, this wonderful "new logical" business—bastard offspring of the old classic "Reason" or *Nous*, which, at least, was supposed to be the culminating thing in the very structure of the universe—Aristotle and medievalists.) This, by way of an aside, leering at others beside Russell, who simply carries the absurdity to its limit in both directions, "existential" *and* "logical." On the whole, their "logicals" perform in a more miraculous way than the scholastics ever ascribed to the Deity. . . .

I agree about leaving out analysis, synthesis. If it goes anywhere, perhaps it [should go] in [the] third paper [where we make a] distinction between behavioral "practical" analysis-synthesis that can be named factually and alleged mental and/or logical operations. But while an important point, maybe it's *too* important to go in incidentally. A good point to be developed in an article on needed psychological reconstruction. . . .

J. D.

Paoli, Indiana, April 13, 1946

Dear John:

. . . You have frequently and very strongly said that "transaction" was the thing to put over—the key to everything. I agree with that except that I do not believe we can put this over so people concretely "get" it unless we have whittled off the extreme logic-certainty-views. Consider the illuminating cases of both Kaufmann and Nagel, whose procedures we know intimately. Can we hope to get either of them to accept "object" (in your *Logic*) (let alone the fruit of it—"transaction") until he consents to see "naming" as all there is to *that* side of the inquiry (I do not mean "all" there is; but rather "as the tangible part of"). . . .

This argument, as I make it, does *Not* mean that I think we have yet done a satisfactory job here. A shortened job *might* be more successful. Right here I rely on you pretty well up toward 100% as compared with reliance on my own judgment. . . .

Regards, *Bentley*

[To] J. D.:   [Paoli, Indiana,] April 19, 1946

Personally I do not want to do anything about the [published] criticism [of our articles]. I leave it to you as to whether, or how. But I can't help fiddling with it, to see how it works out. The following is to throw away.

With reference to the comments by C. West Churchman and T. A. Cowan on the paper "Postulations" ["A Discussion of Dewey and Bentley's 'Postulations'"], it may be remarked:

1. "Postulations" are specified in the paper as concerning "conditions required for further operations" and "for the aid that may be given research." "Moral law" is absent in both intent and in procedure.

2. Fifty-four entries of postulations grouped in eleven sets were given. It would be interesting to know which particular items are either "moral" or "law."

3. It is said that the postulates are "so definite as to reject 'all forcible applications of Newtonian space and time forms . . . to behavioral events.'" They do, indeed, oppose the "forcible" from whatever quarter, but as for the Newtonian form, their scope was much more limited. As an aid to research into knowledge, postulate H4 suggested the rejection of—

"All forcible applications of Newtonian space and time forms (or of the practical forms underlying the Newtonian) to behavioral events as frameworks or grilles of the checkerboard type, which are either (1) insisted upon as adequate for behavioral description, or (2) considered as so repugnant that behavior is divorced from them and expelled into some separate 'realm' or 'realms' of its own."

4. It was urged that in place of this form of definiteness another form of definiteness be substituted, namely, one as to the "scientific ideal." This would be very interesting and welcome if progress in interpreting knowings and knowns can be made in terms of such ideals.

5. A full postulatory analysis of the procedure with ideals would be valuable, and one may permit oneself to say, even necessary, if general understanding of the procedure is to be gained. In the present case the critics offer what they say is one of a number of equivalent ways of formulating the scientific ideal, but in which a narrowly mechanical statement of what they take to be "scientific" can be found, but nothing whatever about the "ideals" which are what they seem to be most interested in.

                                                                    [Bentley]

                                                          New York, April 23, 1946
Dear Arthur:

. . . I had great difficulty in determining just what Churchman was trying to do, beyond showing his loyalty to Singer, his old teacher.

Singer wrote, years ago, some good . . . [stuff] about a behavioral treatment of mind. But I think he also never got out from the . . . [influence] of Kant, though he re-interpreted him freely; he seemed to hold, if I can trust my rather vague memory, that there were "regulative," though not "constitutive" principles of cognitive experience, which, à la Kant, have to be "transcendental" to the knowledge (knowing) experience or knowing-behavior itself. More intelligently expressed as "ideals" than, say, [as] Kaufmann's intervening "logical meanings," but the same distrust of ability of the earth-legs transaction to carry on its own walking without outside direction.

The simplest answer to Churchman [and Cowan, "Discussion of Dewey and Bentley's 'Postulations' "] would be to say that our "ideals," directive principles, are generalizations of the most competent and successful available procedures in knowing. But, aside from the dangerous word "ideals," that seems so obvious on the face of what we have repeatedly stated that Churchman, *et al.*, wouldn't get its force. The "aid given research" involves, of course, giving specified direction to the latter, and I can't make sense of "ideal" as generalized end-in-view save as a synonym for such direction—and we state over and over where we get it from—not from an "ideal" in the sky, but from the competent practice of knowing-behaviors. In a way Churchman goes far enough to afford us some support. Your analysis of [the] Churchman paper covers the ground, but I think it is safe to let the matter lie for the present. Maybe a brief letter to him personally is desirable. For instance, I might write him for further information as how his ideals are arrived at and established. As a matter of tactics, if not strategy, we need even all the partial support we can enlist.

I agree with Altman about the Specification paper in its material; what I had in mind was getting at the central theme of Sign-behavior at closer range—it wouldn't throw out what is said before about naming, but it might bring it [in] at a later point—in connection, for example, with designating as development after signals, cues. In a way, where it is now, it anticipates quite as much as it develops. . . .

Trip to China definitely postponed; have cable now from China. . . .

Yours, *John Dewey*

Paoli, Indiana, June 10, 1946

Dear John:

I think I wrote you that [Harold T.] Davis gave a clean bill of health to the first "transaction" paper from the technical viewpoint. Now I have Ralph Lillie's reply on the physiology section of the second paper. . . . He says: "I can't think there is anything that is technically wrong in your statements of current biological fact and doctrine." He gives me two or

547

three supporting references which I had not used. He thinks "organismic," as distinct from "organic," is an acceptable word (but a slight change of phrasing will adjust to his viewpoint). . . .

With very best regards and wishes, Bentley

New York, June 21, 1946

Dear Arthur:

Yes, I think I am in shape to tackle the "Specification" paper now; send it on, and I'll go over it, and also over the previous versions I have on hand.

Well, Morris came to see me the other day, Tuesday. . . . [He said] his essay [*Foundations of the Theory of Signs*], the one my Stevenson paper ["Ethical Subject-Matter and Language"] was based on, was written in 1937, a year before my *Logic* came out, and he had made [a] mistake in using the *word* "Pragmatics" as he did, but he never meant it to cover the whole "pragmatic" movement. His next book [*Signs, Language and Behavior*] was going to deal with that. . . . He never meant to reduce behavior to the merely corporeal or physical; that was when the animal organism was given selective attention. Even Carnap didn't mean to separate the formal from the objective and environmental; that was merely a temporary abstraction for the purpose of special attention and development, etc. . . .

Yours, John D.

New York, July 7, 1946

Dear Arthur:

. . . I never answered a question in your letter of September 19, 1945—about the use of "identify." That numbers do not *identify* seems to me to follow clearly from our general position. The question as to whether toad identifies a fly, in contrast with identifications by means of language through comparisons and distinctions, is well worth discussion, it seems to me—not necessarily to insist on any particular yes or no answer but [as a way] of making a point. A toad certainly "spots" a fly, but that event doesn't bring the fly into a growing system.

Yours as ever, John D.

Paoli, Indiana, July 16, 1946

Dear John:

I have been at libraries again. I looked at [Harry L.] Hollingworth. I always thought—seemed to recollect—that he was extreme mentalist. He is not.

"Our account . . . takes flux of events as fundamental. Immediate flow of nature is neither physical nor psychical." Objects, space, subjects . . . only convenient ways of recording the immediate flow of nature. "The details" (of an object, etc.) "are what we call symbols or signs." You will know better how all this holds out? Should I mention him somewhere along our line, or does he slip off? That's all I want to know just now.

Brunswik is steadily plugging along with a development of *"gegenstand"* i.e., "property" as sign of "thing" (object—our sense). Brunswik uses cue-*gegenstand* with respect to means-object. . . . In other words, as our "signal."

It might be just on his advance that we should have switched cue to signal-place, and signal to cue-place. Too late now. But it might be [that] a footnote should be inserted as to open choice at this point. Or is it too late? If we have not as yet anywhere used "Cue" in print—and I am sure it was not used in earlier papers. But I am not clear as yet that such a switch should be made—it is just a flash. I will check to see if it *could* be [done] easily.

While we do not have "cue," we do have "signal" fixed further back in the papers, following Pavlov. Cannot afford to change. Will fix footnote to send you. Problem to leave for finish.

Taking me a whole damn day to chop over stuff from library. One ought never to go to a library.

My work is laborious, and, I think, labored. It looks to me as though it was falling off in quality. The last half of that "Transactions as Known" paper, I found clumsy reading when I went over it the other day. The Morris paper ["The New 'Semiotic'"] should, I think, cut down into good shape, but I don't know.

If I am not working right, I would any time be glad of a tip. I will lay off for a while, or permanently if necessary, except for finishing in simplest form what is outstanding.

I do not mean I will go idle. I mean I will stop fixing anything for publication.

July 17, 1946

. . . Probably what is so difficult in this business is trying to get expression without the use of a lot of typical easy-to-use words—and with other words in shifted senses. There is something there to blame in addition to myself anyways.

Regards, *Bentley*

Hubbards, Nova Scotia, July 25, 1946

Dear Arthur:

. . . I think your present statement [probably in "Specification"] states a difficult matter—difficult to understand and to state clearly in the present state of "culture." Five years from now it may appear, let us hope, unduly expanded. But considering the misunderstandings due to interpretation through use of old habits, I find the document extremely successful in putting the essentials in a way that will command attention and which may arouse dissent, but doesn't lend itself to twisting into the opposite of what it says. . . .

Yours as ever, *J. D.*

[P.S.] I hope to get your Morris paper ["The New 'Semiotic'"] back to you soon. What has delayed me is the fact that just before I left New York, The Gateway Publishing Company of Chicago wrote me about republishing my *The Public and Its Problems.* It has been out of print for some time, and Holt didn't want to reprint. I hadn't looked at it for many years—not since it came out nearly 20 years ago. So I brought a copy [here] and I was surprised to find it is pretty damn good, and also quite timely in the present situation. So I wrote a brief Introduction, 7 or 8 pages, I guess, for their reprint—my working time per day is limited and, as I hadn't been here since 1940, my cabin required a good deal of attention.

Grand Island, Nebraska, July 30, 1946

Dear John:

I have your comments on "Specification," will fix it on the train tomorrow, and forward. I think the first thing I will do is to finish the paper "Definition." I have several drafts—none ever sent you, so far as I recall. What I aim to do is, *in as short space as possible,* to state the difference between definition and specification. Or perhaps otherwise put, to show that the high-power specification we use does not answer to formal definition, and gains its virtue from this fact; to cite the [Stephen C.] Pepper paper ["The Descriptive Definition"] as giving an account of definition which is substantially our specification, and which we can almost accept as it stands; to note the other forms of definition not therein covered, and especially the symbolic-mathematical form; to illustrate by several papers . . . how involved the treatment is; to expand a little more on definition symbolically, but without yet setting up a construction for symbol applied to name.

That will be [the] first half of [the] paper. Last part (less than half) will be [a] succinct statement of [the] way specification and transaction tie in together. And if it is not *Short,* God help it. If this paper is out of [the] way, I suspect our joint job is done, except for the one thing we

550

started to do—examine technical words, and advise about them. . . .

Point of first paragraphs was: I wanted to ask your advice about the layout as above. I omitted to do it.

I have done nothing with Morris since sending you stuff. But I have re-read [Edward Chase] Tolman. Tolman has a very elaborate development of the intervening "disposition" region. I do not want to use that sort of thing. But you never fail to know what Tolman is after. . . .

Regards, *Bentley*

New York, September 7, 1946

Dear Arthur:

. . . Some years ago I met at Dartmouth a Dr. [Adelbert] Ames [, Jr.], who as a physiologist and physician had made a significant discovery in correction of a kind of eye defect that had puzzled oculists, etc. One result was the formation of an Eye Institute at Dartmouth. He has been carrying on experiments in visual observation and has some results that seem to give striking experimental confirmation of the transactional view of the factors involved. . . . He believes his experimental results show that (visual) observations involve factors through which the thing seen is rendered amenable to what needs to be done about it—which is easily translatable into denial of the short-span view of "sense perception" and into the fact that it can be understood only in the context of continuing life-behavior. . . .

As ever yours, *John D.*

Paoli, Indiana, September 11, 1946

Dear John:

. . . "Vocabulary" . . . I am starting a new folder "from now on," preparatory to writing. I have a large classified file with references all the way back. I can't get to use it for the moment. Too much else in the way. But send me anything that occurs to you. It will pop into place and by and by be sent back to you organized, some way or other. I think, as you suggest, there should be footnote references to previous papers wherever these were sharp enough. Any notes you make on such references will be stored up. My guess is that if we get fifteen or twenty of the main words and show the difference between them in our scheme and in such a scheme as Morris's, or the usual paper in the philosophical journals—any journal—it will be ample. Main principle: This stuff is not in any way known except in and through wordings. "Solar system" is not "known to" or "spotted by" an animal. Nor does it reflect on experience *qua* experience. . . .

Looking over your list, I note quite a number of words . . . [about which] we might merely say, "This is the way we have used them in our experiment." Thus "Object," "Knowledge." Other words that are, now, probably hopeless to work on like "Meaning" and maybe "experience"; others that we can definitely place; such, perhaps, as "exist" if we can in the end substitute it for event in our first temporary tabulation. If we could get a settled set-up, and get active workers to hold to it, our whole enterprise would have justified itself, I suspect.

About Dartmouth. . . . I think I recollect Ames for work on aniseikonia . . . variations on localization of "images" on the retina. Two or three people called my attention to this work, thinking it would put the snuffer on my image-procedure. I quickly recognized that the more they got down to close work, the more they wiped out the "image," no matter how they talked about it. . . .

It has been my intention when I get back to image work to go to Dartmouth, and ask them if they will let me work there, and hire one youngish man with eyes and the right ability to do my experimentation for me. . . .

Regards, *Bentley*

Paoli, Indiana, September 14, 1946

Dear John:

At some time in the future, as you know, I am going to try to do a "Behavior-Sign" paper for *Psychological Review*, [a] paper more or less ante-dating our current enterprise. Without argument, or stirring anybody up, it will be necessary to hold the whole thing within our "fact" or "cosmos." To get rid of "know" currently and philosophically, yet to keep the process as frame for the discussion, I might substitute "K" for "know." I would then get "*K-ing*" for the organic phase and "*K-thing*" for the environmental phase. Thus subjects and objects—for the particular job—held within *system*. Don't know how it will look when tried. Just thought it mentionable.

Regards, *Bentley*

New York, September 19, 1946

Dear Arthur:

. . . I had a talk with Churchman and one of his assistants yesterday. The outcome was more satisfactory than I expected as far as it went—later events may tell how far that was. They denied, and I think genuinely, not self-confusedly, any belief in fixed "ideals"; said they agreed with us [that ideals] . . . were generalizations from the actual facts of scientific inquiry, and were developed and changed with the progress of the latter. When I, naturally, inquired what then was it . . . ["Discus-

552

sion of Dewey and Bentley's 'Postulations' "] all about—in effect—I got the impression that they were writing from the standpoint of a different, but not intrinsically opposed, interest and problem. They thought we should have indicated what the present state of scientific inquiry pointed to as the generalizations which might give direction to scientific men in their further inquiries—that if the *Journal* [*of Philosophy*] hadn't cut out the first four pages of their communication, they thought maybe that would be clear. I said that our interest and problem in the articles were different and didn't call for statement on that particular point, and that I was rather skeptical about the ability of writers on the logic of scientific knowing to give much positive direction to actual workers—save in clearing up messing in border fields and immature subjects, like psychology and "social" subjects; I couldn't see any inherent conflict between the two efforts. . . .

Yours, John D.

[New York,] October 7, 1946

Dear Arthur:

. . . I have one suggestion [about "The New 'Semiotic'"] for what it is worth. On your pp. 28 and 31 you have a quotation in which *need* is given, it seems to me, the central place. I am not sure you haven't said something on this matter, but I don't recall it. If the reference is as important as those sentences seem to make it, it might be worth a brief footnote. Does the word "need" appear in the starred list? Does it receive any specific treatment anywhere? If, in fact, it is because of need that (i) something is the terminal object which (ii) starts the responsive behavior, it would seem to deserve more attention than he [Morris] gives it. . . .

Yours as ever, [Dewey]

New York, October 10, 1946

Dear Arthur:

. . . [In *re*] "clarity" and "precision"—"specification" is obviously the proper name for "clarity," and I'm not sure about "precision" for mathematical terms. (By the way "term" seems to cover both—not that all names are terms, but that *some* names are terms— . . . [those] which specify the limiting *conditions*—come to terms—to an agreement; terms of a contract; accede to terms. The original meaning is "Boundaries," not so different.) Perhaps, names are terms as far as they *determinately specify*. For specifications set forth the conditions under which inquiry proceeds. I have the feeling that something has to be added to "precision" to cover mathematical expressions. Specifications and descriptions have to be as precise as possible. For a single word, "exact" seems better than "precise." . . . *Exigere*–demand; and the first meaning given in *Oxford* [*English Dictionary*] is: perfect, consummate; "exact" as a verb has sense of imposing requirements that have to be met–and this seems to be the special qualification of a mathematical term. [It] doesn't name anything because its sense, force, meaning, is found wholly in what [it] requires–necessitates–in further developments.

However, what I'm trying to get at isn't so much a single term as something which tells what a mathematical term does–and where it does it. Specifications direct, control further inquiries, but they don't require any particular inquiry. . . .

Yours as ever, *John*

[P.S.] It would only take a sentence each to indicate the revolution in each branch of science–astronomy, from a fixed solar system moving about the earth, the sun and moon moving backward and forward in reference to the fixed earth, and the firmament (heaven) of Fixed Stars rotating above with none of the season changes found in planets, sun, and moon; physics, four elements, each fixed in essence, qualitatively different, with movements that are qualitatively unlike, earth downward to . . . [its] proper fixed place as "end"; fire upward, to its "end" . . . [in] the heavens; water, and every kind of liquid, back and forth; air, [and] every form of gas, also smoke, up, but only to the clouds or at most the moon; evaporation, steam goes up.

Biology, [with its] fixed animal and plant species–[until] Darwin, . . . *et al.* put an end . . . [to this]. I think all this could be condensed into a footnote.

New York, October 11, 1946

Dear Arthur:

I enclose some further notes. I have perhaps over-elaborated the historical reference, but I think it has a point that can be stated in condensed form.

The last paragraph probably goes unnecessarily into detail about mathematics. It depends upon whether it is important to make a statement about what differentiates subjectmatter as matter of definitions and symbols, from existential subjectmatters, physical, physiological and biopsychological, historical.

Yours, *John D.*

October 11, 1946

[Notes]

. . . Historical reference [on] Aristotle. In the (metaphysical) logic of Aristotle, all scientific knowledge took the form of Definition. This view was derived from his cosmological doctrine that scientific knowledge is always of fixed *forms, essences, or natures,* which identify and distinguish things as of *species.* To know in the scientific sense was to identify things as of certain fixed kinds or species that were de-limited by their essential natures from every other species (and included singular) that are similarly de-limited or defined. Things as singulars could not be known in the scientific sense; they fell within two lower grades of "knowledge," the lowest being sense-perception and the intermediate form being opinion, only probable in any given case, being identical with the fact that things usually, on the whole, more often than not, are thus and so. Sense-knowledge and opinion, on this basis, were inherently lower modes of knowledge dealing with particulars and with things that *change* (because of the absence of fixed forms) while scientific knowledge, because of its grasp of essential nature, was apprehension or *grasp* of the universal and eternal. The scientific revolution occurring in the fifteenth and subsequent centuries treated what had been sense perception and opinion, not as inherently separate, but as inadequate forms of knowledge, setting the task or problem of conversion into scientific form. It denied that fixed essences and species are the proper objects of science, substituting at first for such an object, *uniformities of spatial and temporal connections or "laws."* The dictionary statements, which consolidate Object and Word as the subjectmatter of definition, are a meaningless, because incoherent, mixture of the earlier and the more recent views of the proper object of science, due to change in the actual methods of procedure.

. . . I think it would be well to identify syntactics and semantics (as used by the formalists) sufficiently to show how they retain the old confusion merely attaching different names.

. . . "Equivalence" is used in connection with mathematical subjectmatter. If you think well of what I said in yesterday's letter, then it would also be well to insert a sentence to the effect that "equivalence" is not tautology, but is equality of use in the progressive construction that is going on, the second term of the equivalence translating the first into a form that carries the construction further. (My wording isn't too good, but it may convey the idea.)

[*Dewey*]

Paoli, Indiana, October 14, 1946

Dear John:

I not only "think well" of your point about "equivalence" being development onward, and not tautology. I think it is [a] main building tool. We can separate ourselves from the substitution people, and from their weaker companions, the interchangeability phrasers. I have made a strong note of this and your other remarks about "precision," "terms," etc., in my index—partly for the "Vocabulary" paper and partly for a mathematical development paper. I don't see how I can develop the equivalence point in the present paper; and discussion of special words should certainly wait a bit. There is not space here. What must be done is to get out the distinction "Specification" and "Definition" into the clear. . . . [Marvin] Farber indicates [that] the Morris paper ["The New 'Semiotic'"] will soon go to press; using your point on "need" as well as I could get it in. . . .

Best wishes, Bentley

Paoli, Indiana, October 15, 1946

Dear John:

I. "Accuracy," "Precision," "Rigor," "Exactitude," "Exactness," "Fidelity," "Mathematical precision," "Correct," "Nice," "Right." These from Roget and Webster's *Synonyms* (edition 1942).

Webster makes "Correct" the weakest. Following are the "stresses": "Accurate," greater fidelity, "Exact" emphasizes rigor of agreement, "Precise" stresses sharpness of delimitation, "Nice" implies great, often excessive delicacy of discrimination, "Right," absence of deviation. . . .

I always have had doubts. Have never stressed this. Consider "precision instruments"—they do *not* have mathematical precision.

In "Terminology" paper, *Journal of Philosophy*, 1945, p. 240, we say "The word 'definition' covers precise symbolic statements in mathematics."

I do not find "accurate" used there. Yes I do. See p. 241, line 16—"accuracy in meaning."

(I believe it would pay you to read these pp. 240–41 and the context. The pending paper ["Definition"], as I see it, elaborates what was there indicated. And, I believe, the situation needs much elaboration.)

II. The development of such a general proposition we both have (as against Kaufmann's permanence and unalterability) that "equivalence" is a growth, will take me six months to make, at the least. There is no use slapping a few idle thoughts on the subject into the present paper, and that is all I could do here, and now. . . .

We left ourselves free to change any names we started out with.

"Definition" was always a trouble.

The act of writing this pending paper develops enough difficulty to make me want now to drop the word—i.e., to relegate it to a state of "characterization" instead of elevating it to specific use.

The problem in the past has always been to find a substitute name.

In a sentence or two in recent drafts I have found myself speaking of "symbolizing" in this mathematical-syntactic region—in contrast with "designating" and "specifying" in the name-giving region.

This makes me think that it may be desirable to shift from the use of "Definition" along with "Symbols" to "Symbolization."

"Symbolization" will then be coupled with "Specification" (as top form of designating), just as "Symbol" is with "Name."

I believe I will try a draft this way, starting with an introductory note setting down the shift and its reasons.

If we don't like it, we do not need to keep it. It's a try.

Regards, *Bentley*

N.B. We have been using the word "symboling" a good deal lately—which shows the incubation of this type of change.

Paoli, Indiana, October 15, 1946

[To Dewey:]

[Notes.] Variations of "Definition."

We differentiate "Namings" from "Symbolizings," and limit "Definition" to the latter. That is, we retain the old name for one part of the job (with privilege reserved for substitute terminology).

I. I find: (1) in the dictionaries, cultural applications of words as "dictionary definition"—not concerning us; (2) cultural distinctions between "act" and "product" which we discard, and which the logics do not investigate, but the logicians assume; (3) differentiations of definitions of "word" and of "thing" *not* held apart, but consolidated in all four dictionaries examined.

In effect, the dictionaries thus regard the two forms of (3) as one problem, and nominalism and realism as theories of interpretation for the one problem (with concept and conceptualism as a third theory).

II. I start out by eliminating (1) as not germane—by asserting that (2) is fictitious, by saying then that (3) should be two separated regions of definition; and by adding to the two separated regions in (3) a third—namely *"mixtum compositum."* (I am writing this for purposes of inquiry—not by way of saying what I know in advance.)

III. My text then has three items as factually to consider in current literature: Defining names, defining things: confused, evasive treatment. The project of the paper is to kick the confusions out of the way so as to consider our own job.

IV. A first interfering item is "conceptualism" and "concept." (a) "Conceptualism" need not bother. It was an "insert" theory to handle nominalism and realism. (b) "Concept" was a pseudo-fact inserted to go with the theory of conceptualism. (c) It is necessary now to set up a comparison between "concept" and "thing" and "name" in the exposition. . . .

557

V. In our form of development, our form of distinction between "name" and "symbol" is radically different from the old form of "name" and "thing" and likewise from the form of "product" and "act." Our specifications are all phasal, aspectual, transactional, in both respects. The old forms were entitative splits. This form of differentiation entering the text of pending article [and] overlying the others was confusing. . . .

VII. *Summarizing*, we get: The Aristotelian scheme was constructive innovation. The scholastic scheme, assuming the Aristotelian fusion, tried nominalistic, realistic, and finally conceptualistic interpretations of the presumptive factual layout.

The science of the Renaissance introducing [scientific "law" might have destroyed the thing-name connection, but was not powerful enough in that direction. The many devices of relational logics, symbolic logics, and semantics have nibbled away at the difficulty, but retained its underlying source of confusion.

Mathematical symbolism has finally—to the knowledge of all men—split away from name-requirements for symbols.

We now make a fresh start (this phrase private, not for publication): recognize the split of "name" and "symbol"; build the two up into different systems with "thing"; hold "thing" frankly in system with "name" and "symbol"—not confusedly; get ready for full construction.

VIII. The above is not the kind of Summary I wanted. Instead: Aristotle studied names as showing essences. Logic since Aristotle has regarded products as different from acts; and in our special case the thing-named as theoretically severed from the naming-act, but this only by inserting a name-fact as separate in between.

Modern mathematics makes clear the presence of a type of linguistic dealing with things other than the naming-type.

The identifying of "symbolings" as different from "namings" within the linguistic-behavior-system makes possible a reorganization of the whole thing-word status transactionally.

These statements not meant in the sense of *Reasons* or *Successive Steps*, but merely efforts at factual presentation.

[*Bentley*]

New York, October 22, 1946

Dear Arthur:

I am strong for substituting "symboling" for "definition." . . .

Following are a few suggestions. . . .

(1) Symboling [is] itself a name, for there is observed subjectmatter that needs precision of specification. . . . You know a lot more about the semantic-syntactic literature that I do, but I can't escape the impression that it is a fusion-confusion, by use of new words, of two

old standpoints: (i) isolation of matter and form, which is derived (ii) from the isolation of (i.e., non-transactional treatment) "things" and "mind." If so, to hell with it, along with dropping of "definition." (*Re* dictionary definitions, which would seem to be the only legitimate usage left, when dictionary gives as one current usage a statement derived from recent scientific inquiries, i.e., H_2O for "water," it becomes a specification—generally with a lag—only a very recent lexicon would have "heavy" water specified.) *Maybe* (though I doubt it), there is a place for the word "syntactics" other than as a name usable in grammatic and philological studies as such: the connections of words as words in their respective functions as names, this being just as legitimate an object of study as any other kind of connection of observed things. But if there is any reason for linking it up with mathematical subjectmatter and symbolings, there is something I miss. I don't doubt that traditional grammar needs a lot of overhauling and that the results of overhauling would be rewarding, but only as a specific subject of observation and organization.

Your remark . . . about the dictionaries failing to take account of their own definitions is most apt. What they do do is to fail to see that their "definitions" of definition give certain historical usages, without marking them *obsolete* with respect to present day knowledge—though they could justify themselves on the ground they are not obsolete in current texts.

I never answered a question you asked some time ago about adverbs. I can't recall when or where I said what you mention about them, but I think its validity is shown in the immense superiority of "definitely" to "definition."

Yours, John D.

[P.S.] . . . The reference to "nominal" and "real." I don't know whether it is worthwhile or important, but in Aristotle, "Logic" and "Logos" (Language) were in complete one-to-one correspondence; not just etymologically—certain names were in the "realm" of language of "opinion" or current beliefs, and opinion was the kind of *knowledge* that was proper to a certain kind of things, to those which lacked stability because, owing to imperfection of Being [capable of Definition], they change so that only probable knowledge and variable *logoi* are possible. In other words, the "ancient" split mentioned represents a departure from Aristotle—technically promoted by the medieval nominalists, and getting full force when the influence of the new physics led to repudiation of "forms" as the object—objective—of science. In other words, "nominal and real" are only a pretentious verbalization of the dictionary "word" and "thing." [Alonzo] Church's ["Definition"] is, of course, simply an elaboration of the threefold dictionary treatment. All of the above might be conveniently condensed to the statement that all the philosophical dictionaries do is to make a more elaborate, seemingly more technical, statement of what is found in the dictionaries previously mentioned. Then come the quotations as evidence.

. . . In a way, in connection with language and knowns and knowings, *we* are returning logic to the Aristotelian *Logos*—on the basis of the science of the present, as his was on the basis of a science that has been outdated; as is clearly seen in all the sciences from astronomy and mathematics to biology. The transactional use of name-thing and use of "symbolings" for mathematics express our use of contemporary science.

[New York,] October 25, 1946

Dear Arthur:

. . . It looks, however, as if the "indefinables" were only another expression of what used to be called the "reference" denotation of a word as distinct from its connotation—"meaning" in the sense of what it does in "discourse." The older terms at least kept the two things in connection with another, while "indefinable" is a violent ripping-apart which makes "reference" meaningless and "meaning" without possible application—or so it seems.

The "indefinables" *might* be understood as pointing to the fact that specification, specifying, always set out from something that needs, in the interest of knowing, to be specified, and hence as it stands is (relatively) unspecified. A kind of "that" we have to convert into a "what." "Denoting," noting off, from vague to preciser specification of a subjectmatter—in what in my *Logic* I call "de-termination" as process.

Speaking of my *Logic*, it has recently occurred to me that in my pretty frequent use of "Conjugate" in it, I was feeling toward "transactional." If I had only realized that fact, I would have done a better job.

Yours, *J. D.*

Paoli, Indiana, October 25, 1946

Dear John:

. . . Yours 10-22-46 . . . on mathematics and syntactics. We all have to play hunches. Otherwise, we would never get anywhere. I can't demonstrate it, but my hunch is that a clean-cut study of "or" and "and" and "if," and "if and only if" *is* itself mathematical—it is a branch of mathematical inquiry. Call it "syntactics," O.K. as far as I am concerned. In other words, whatever is good in logic is through mathematical influence; not the other way around, as the Russells, Carnaps, *et al.*, try to make it. I *think*—I am not sure—I took this position in my *Linguistic Analysis [of Mathematics]* book, and have always held it since. Now in the manuscript you have, I have linked mathematics and

560

syntactics. One such linking in expression is O.K. But I have repeated couplings. This is not O.K., and so I began to drop them.

You speak of the connections of words *As* words being a legitimate object of study like other connections. I would suggest that when the ordinary language was considered without any *naming* effects, then a residuum is left to study. In the case of numbers, it is the start of mathematics, then in the line residua it is geometrical. . . . But, also in the "or" and "and" cases we have precision hitch-ups that *are* mathematical. That is as far as I go. It must be left for later development. . . . I suspect it is safer to give them this much recognition (them meaning the symbolic logic people), and let them prove they are worthy of more—instead of ignoring them, alienating them, and possibly being deficient in this respect in future judgment upon us. . . .

Looking up [Kurt] Gödel on Russell ["Russell's Mathematical Logic"] in [Schilpp, ed., *The Philosophy of Bertrand Russell*], page 137 and also 142—Gödel takes the view that mathematics and Logic must have *a real content*. . . . However, Gödel lacks our manner of distinction between symbol and name, so he cannot say what we would say about the manner of development there.

Regards, *Bentley*

Paoli, Indiana, October 28, 1946

Dear John:

Re your remark on "indefinables." [Robert] Adamson in Baldwin [*Dictionary of Philosophy and Psychology*] lists as indefinables, individuals at the bottom and *summa genera* at the top.

The mathematical postulation people like [Oswald] Veblen and [E. V.] Huntington [have] got to introduce them for technical reasons, to hold the fort at the start of a set of postulates. In other words, if defining means—as it does to them—specifying some existence outside, *then*, these items (point, etc.) *were* indefinable. But I—looking at it in the raw—have held all along that in mathematics the development of a system based on point actually was the *definition* of point—it told, i.e., the system told, what point was and where it could go to.

When a man like [H. H.] Dubs introduces indefinables, he is just parroting old phraseology, just as he is in his division of sense and conceptual knowledge.

The one thing I want to do is to show in a case like Dubs—without being offensive—that this is an absurdity. Dubs, as you will note in my fuller statement sent you a couple [of] days ago, wants *all* knowledge to be science, and *all* science to be strings of concepts. Thus, for him, the indefinables come in, even though definition contains indefinables itself, they are in effect bits of magic inserted to make scheme work. . . .

Almost all of these guys get the "ostensive" definition in in some sort of way. Pepper almost gets rid of it, by making it a different kind of "operation." If "ostensive" is expelled from definition at one end and "symbol" at the other, we get the three behavioral levels we are using. Or rather: We have three behavioral levels. We have previously driven symbols *upstairs* away from "designation." Now we drive the "ostensive" downstairs away from "designation"—where it corresponds to perceptive-manipulative. "Definition" (now by us called "specification" as top stage of "designation") is left to hold forth on the strictly and primarily linguistic level.

Here is another. The word "operation" covers equally ostension, designation, and symbolization. We no longer have the absurdity of understanding by operation some non-verbal operations, and thus denying that word-using is an operation. Operation thus spreads [across the] full range of behavior. . . .

Regards, *Bentley*

[P.S.] The "indefinables" in connection with "definition," as per your suggestions about their substituting for older forms, will make a good point in summarizing horrors.

I have been steadily reducing references to our program. I may be able to cut them all out except for last pages. Idea is this: When this paper started, it was designed to restate our point and illustrate the need on my collection of specimens. Now, however, the definition case seems so strong as it stands that it may show up better without any basic departure with respect to our separate manner of treatment—and our view may then come in at the end incidentally.

Paoli, Indiana October 29, 1946

Dear John:

. . . In your *Logic* you distinguished two kinds of universals. The "abstract" universal was on the mathematical side. Here you were setting up "naturally" what a lot of men have been working out "formally" or "symbolically," etc. "Syntactics" is, I take it, a standard name now (following mostly Carnap) for a development of this kind. "Semantics" is the name they use for development about "things" or "referents." But they have as yet developed no way of putting them together.

We, on the other hand, have coming along a distinction of "Name" and "Symbol," which is on the way to solution.

I can see some, and I am sure there must be many, equations worked out in Syntactics with respect to "and," "or," "if," etc., that *in their own scheme* are as fully symbolic (in our sense) as is the formulation of one-two-three.

Suppose, now, we set out our position without allowing for this. It will be defective for the people who most ought to understand us.

Among most workers of this formalist-symbolic type (and there are many varieties) the word "definition" has been set up for strict equivalence, Carnap with his (= Df), his (=), and his (≡) operates this way. So does Tarski with his requirement of "if and only if," for any definition proper. All such workers have a need for the other kind of definition. None of them have split the two procedures (name and symbol) sharply apart and made a new start toward organization. All see the organization as engineered in a personal "mind." It was this that led me to favor "definition" as name for the symbol-region. I did not appreciate how that would continue the old tangle—in short, that our fiat could not do much toward freeing the word "definition" from its other mixed implications.

Specifically then, answering the latest form of your question, I would say:

We (you and I) have name system and symbol system separate.

We have them both as behavioral, but as distinctive [in] behavioral procedures.

To make good, we *must* in the future reorganize the two systems (I have various drafts for such a paper when I can get to it).

In this reorganization we cannot (I believe) include merely the mathematical as "symbol." The evidence is overwhelming that the "or," ["if]-and-only-if" procedures are being clarified in mathematical style. . . . I felt the need of allowing for this. . . . Hence, the use of "logical." I meant by "logical" the same as "syntactical." I probably used the word "logical" here as [a] more general reference in place of "syntactical," which would be much more syntactic.

If I have not got my point of view clear yet, come again.

[*Bentley*]

[New York,] November 4, 1946

Dear Arthur:

I haven't written about the syntactics, etc., because I'm mixed up and don't know what to say; for one thing I suppose I don't like the *word* "syntactics" very well to apply [it] to what is intended; it seems too broadly—or narrowly—grammatical to convey the fact of logical formal relations. [It] covers all parts of speech, and nouns and verbs are certainly names. But to come to the genuine point, not just words. There is no doubt about words like "or," "only," and "but," that stand for formal logical relations. In my *Logic* they are expressly recognized, in Chapter

XVII on "Formal Functions and Canons" (pp. 336 ff.), [as] serving the purpose of inclusion-exclusion, making positive-negative as specific as possible. What I am stuck on is what to do with them. They aren't names of things in one sense of "things." But *inquiries* are events, and there is a difference between inquiries that are "logical" in the sense of meeting the requirements set by existing standards of competent inquiry and those which fail in that respect. "And," "or," "if," "only," etc., are expressions belonging to and fulfilling requirements of logical statement. It seems to me they make specification precise with respect to *this* property. From this point of view they seem to be names, since inquiry is an event and "logical" inquiry is one kind of inquiry. And [in] some way I seem to feel a hitch when I try to line them up with mathematics. "Precision," yes; "exactness"?

But I may be wrong about this. Perhaps, it can be held that "specification" with respect to names can't be rendered fully precise without the aid of mathematical subjectmatter; in that case "connectives" (grammatically speaking) are in line with mathematics. Damned if I know. . . .

Yours, *J. D.*

Paoli, Indiana, November 7, 1946

Dear John:

. . . You will note I am pretty well in line with you on "syntactics." I have no thought of using the name ourselves, none whatever. But the thing has a place—and it has a place in the region we are examining.

I, of course, agree with you as to your *Logic* having this field displayed. I think I remarked on this before in recent letters—in others words that I did not want to go beyond your own position in the matter. What I suspect is that the "formal" symbolic development—or whatever one or the other calls it—is bringing out sharply the organization characteristics of the connectives.

Take, for instance, the huge development for a logical base for mathematics. I regard it as mostly rot. So do you. But I also figure that when so many mathematicians recognize it favorably, there must be something to it. That something I take to be sharpened operational requirements within their own business—aids at avoiding pitfalls they had previously not recognized.

The practical point of this is that we should keep off of all references to "syntactics"—I will see to that.

However, when I say "mathematical-logical" in any sense, I involve the same question. . . .

Suppose we say that the mathematical procedure is one of equivalences *or* of substitutions. (Personally I would not [say] this latter—no matter how commonly found today.) Now logic certainly has substitutions. I do not think it has equivalences in the naive sense of an Aristotelian syllogism; and no more in the full mathematical sense. Our differentiation of "Specification" and "Symbolization" (growing out of your differentiation of the most abstract universals in mathematics from [the] less abstract forms) provides for exactly this difference.

We then take the logical connectives. If developed formulations can be made for them and successfully used in mathematics, they approach mathematical equivalences as values.

Can I then properly write "mathematical-logical" at all?

My *difficulty* in formulation is this. If I contrast "specifications" with "mathematical symbolic" alone, and no further phrase—I write so that anybody with any chance set of meanings as to "mathematics" and "science" will read his understanding into our text, and miss out, nobody knows how far, on what is being said.

That is the only issue for me at this point—[the] purely practical one of expression.

I definitely *do not mean* (as per last part of your letter [11-4-46]) that "specification" cannot be fully precise without "symbolical." . . . What we are both after is to say the symbolic aid to specification is not [in] picking out names, but in wider systematic applications.

Another matter. You use "precision" for specification and "accuracy" for mathematics. I checked uses in manuscripts back a couple years and found the reverse use has been carried on. It does not matter to me. I can drop the point out of [the] present [paper]. Probably I had better do so anyway, until we are entirely sure. . . .

Best wishes, *Bentley*

[New York,] November 8, 1946

Dear Arthur:

. . . I think it ["Definition"] is one of the best things yet and ties things together in a way that will be a decided help to all readers . . . [who are] interested, and [do] not [have] a closed mind. While it is a devastating criticism as a whole, the tone is good, and the recognition of the people, Skinner, etc., who have done anything, proves interest in the main theme, not in tearing down, save as the ground must be cleared if we are going to move ahead—or build a structure that will stand up.

I had a two hour or more interview with A. Ames[, Jr.], the Dartmouth Eye Institute man . . . not an interview with him, but a chance to see a demonstration, visually, of his net results—extraordinary. After he leaves here—he'll be here all this month, I think—the demonstration material is going to Princeton. I hope you will be able to see it. . . . I think he has experimental demonstration of the absolute soundness of the transactional treatment in the case of visual perceptions from the simplest to the most elaborate binocular forms—also of the complete futility of the optical-image theory as the basis for any theory of visual "sensation" or perception. That he completely disproves that perception is a reproduction of an "external object" is more or [less in] line with orthodox psychological treatment, but the demonstration of the transactional character is so effective as to be new—as far as I know. . . . His terminology could, I think, be improved; he talks freely about sensations, and when I said something about his demonstration of determination of the seen by "habit-attitudes," he objected in a way in which he showed that he didn't connect "habit-attitudes" and "habitual life"—purposes together—talked not only in general language about "past experience" but, seemingly while he took "purposes" concretely not reifying[ly], he didn't connect them with habitual sets or attitudes. But that didn't affect the soundness of his work.

Yours as ever, *John D.*

[New York,] November 23, 1946

[To Bentley:]

. . . Purely by the way. One of the Editors of *Fortune* sent me an article on [Elton] Mayo ["The Fruitful Errors of Elton Mayo"], the Australian labor "expert" called to Harvard, in which one of Mayo's disciples said, in effect, that it was a later discovery of Mayo's, and a surprise to him, to find that workers in factories didn't respond as much to "things" as to "the meaning of things." I wrote him, the editor, [that] the discovery stood for a fact, but it was unfortunate he hadn't said they responded to a certain kind of meanings of things better than to those of another kind ["The Meaning of a Change"]. . . . He wrote [that] he showed the letter to the author of the statement [Fritz Roethlisberger] and that he agreed with me.* (Just an instance of behavioral use—that is, "meaning" as a name for consequences of the kind of (responsive) behavior evoked. This was Peirce's original "pragmatism," taken up by James in a somewhat confused way.)

[*Dewey*]

New York, November 25, 1946

Dear Arthur:

. . . It seemed to me that you missed a point in interpreting the "indefinables" in terms of signaling behavior. It seems to me they should be looked at as referring to the activities, behaviors, involved in *spec-*

* The editors of *Fortune* quote Roethlisberger to this effect in "Fortune Letters," December, 1946, p. 38.

ifying—not that the persons who introduce them had any such idea or intention, but that is the way sense can be made of them—they are the acts of referring or applying knowledge at hand to newly observed sub-jectmatter so as to attain specification with respect to the latter. These activities in turn not only may be themselves specified, but every report of a scientific undertaking *does* specify the operations by which con-clusions were reached as an integral necessary part of his work *as* scien-tific. This is a condensed statement of what I wrote. There was a minor point about your use of "medieval" in connection with separation of names and things. That was true only of nominalism which was hetero-dox in scholastic philosophy, and which was influential only later after the subject-object, physical-mental divorce became current. . . .

Yours, *Dewey*

[P.S.] I believe something might be added to the general line indi-cated at the close of my yesterday's letter—and that is that your previous discussion bears out the original paper *for the need of firm names,* and also indicates that the great obstacle to getting them at present is the failure to bring traditional names, suitable enough in prior stages of knowledge taken to be scientific, up to date even with present practices of knowing, so that attaining of firm names is definitely a matter of names that formulate the advances made, comparatively recently, in scientific knowings-knowns.

I don't think what I wrote yesterday differs, except in one point, from what you have. The ultimates and indefinables wouldn't be of the class of primitive signalings, but of the operations by which specifications are reached in actual cases. That, as used by the writers you deal with, they are at best only signalings, I don't doubt, but they obtain sense if understood in the other way. There is nothing "ultimate" about them in their *subjectmatter,* since operations are as of date-place given. They are ultimate in *form,* in the sense . . . [that there] is no specification without performance of specified operations, and I think my remark about every responsible experimenter having to state in some detail, enough to make repetition possible, . . . the operational (including ap-paratus, etc. employed), is to the point. It isn't "definition" and it is not, immediately, specification. But it is specifying behavior in progress; it differs only from the pointing mentioned by Mill, in your quotation,* in being highly roundabout or mediated, because dependent upon a vastly more extensive previous system of already specified knowings. All this is in line with what you say about activities . . . but not with what is said about them as signalings. And I think something on above lines culminates naturally in what is said . . . about the transactional nature of specifying.

* See *Knowing and the Known,* p. 197. (Eds.)

Dear John:

. . . I have analyzed your memo on the pertinent points.

1. "Specification." When you look over the "Specification" paper that, I presume, has just appeared, and note afresh that the "Definition" paper was supposed to be coupled with it as its immediate successor, you will see why the Specification angle is not stressed. Also, I think, that there is no immediate need of stressing it heavily. I will, however, get in a strong statement about it. Perhaps, I should put such a statement at the start of the paper: namely, this new paper is a leftover from the old. The best way to get the full effect would, of course, be to have the "Definition" paper published as early as possible. Whether the *Journal* [*of Philosophy*] would be willing to advance it a little—or how much bother it would be to them—I do not know.

2. "Indefinables," "Ultimates," "Operations," "Signalings," and "Definition." (Right here I have stopped long enough to make a fresh analysis —it is the third—of all your discussions.)

One thing I can say to start with: When you say (. . . 11-25-46) that you disagree with me only on the one point that "ultimates" and "indefinables" should not be treated as "signalings," I destroy the disagreement. I agree with *you*. They are not. My phrasing . . . was not intended to list *them* in that way. It was too curt, and mis-spoke.

The main thing is that we have two lines of approach on which [we] both agree, but in this particular moment you are seeing things along one line, and I am seeing them along the other.

Suppose we are following a course in which we are differentiating "specification," as a scientific operation in linguistic embodiment, from the general ruck of "definition." We consider a statement (not the general one that there exists among forms of definition [one] that uses not words at all, but is "ostensive") but a special case of determination without words as producing ultimates or indefinables; you can properly say: here is specification going on, or rather the earlier forms of designation with rotten poor naming. There is operation; it must be specified, etc.

The line I am following, in contrast, is this. Having set up "specification" out of all the naming devices on definition and cut it apart, I started out to show how "definition" (the word) could be salvaged for mathematical equation procedure. Also to show the need of it in the confused present uses of the word "definition." I couldn't even write the paper. The word "definition" has so many messy implications that sentences could not be clearly formed by me about it. We then decided (and you promptly approved my suggestion) that we drop the word "Definition" and substitute for [it] the special use "Symbolization." Then

I could go on and describe the queer land of the definings without messing up.

Now such a description is not a negative, but positive. If you want to grow a crop on forest land, when you "clear" the land, you are at least *trying* to build, and not to destroy. It may be you are wrong; and that you destroy more value in timber than you gain in grain. But that is another story.

Now what our present paper proves (demonstrates by exhibiting in masses of instances) is that the ground *must* be cleared before men can talk understandingly to each other about these problems.

So proceeding, we get an entirely (which means, very considerably) new light on "ostensive definition." We can agree that the Specification branch, torn out of the old definition, is presented in language, and the Symbolization branch, when torn out, is at least conveyed in sounds and marks like (or so as to be) language. But now what on earth can the differentiated "definition" in an ostensive operation be? *It Cannot Be Language* by the very terms in which its proponents offer it to us. So far as definition uses language, it cannot be definition. But it comes to us asserted *To Be Definition.*

I then ask, where is it, and what? Well, my answer is that unless one inserts a direct, positive, determinable mental *Power or Faculty,* which, at will, can define by words or define by finger-pointing, and so consolidates in such facultative definition either or—and both—language and definition—unless [one does] this, one must seek to locate it in non-linguistic behaviors. But the general term we have established for all the non-linguistic under the "Sign" set-up is "Signaling."

If, now, you take both signalings and language-usings as transactional, involving organic contrasts with inorganic, you would have Ostensive process as prelinguistic or sub-linguistic, and not properly classified as "definition" (except under developed specialization as above).

(I am not arguing whether it is or isn't. I don't care about the ultimate decision. I am showing the immediate problem—in part, I hope.)

As to all the above, the problem is to get a proper phrasing in the paper. Doubtless, the reference to "Signaling" must drop out. Doubtless, I will try it several times before getting phrasings we can both approve. Also it is worth trying. . . .

One more remark on the "Ultimates-Indefinables." Everything we talk about can be talked about either on the Designating or Designated (event, existence) side. Main thing is to sort out attitudes in this way. . . .

Best regards, *Bentley*

569

New York, December 2, 1946

Dear Arthur:

I must have written very obscurely regarding "specification." The last thing I meant to do was . . . to separate it from the scientific procedure in non-mathematical subjectmatter. I didn't keep a copy and so can't tell what it was I wrote that left a different impression. I am with you also 100% in dropping "definition" as a linguistically useful name for anything, and substituting, respectively, "specification" and "symboling" as the means of escape from the hopeless confusion perpetuated in current uses of "definition." It was some purely minor verbal point I must have [had] in mind. I think I wrote you that the only point to which I attached any importance was the "signaling" matter—on which we now agree. I can't even recall what I wrote or what it was about that indicated I thought the distinction of "specification" from "symboling" was negative. Of course it is as positive and as necessary as the distinction between "existential" and "mathematical" subjectmatter. I certainly wasn't sticking up for "ostensive definition"; on the contrary, what is there is the behavioral act of reference, application, or whatever name is fitting, and as I said, that can be and is specified, itself specifically reported in any account of scientific work that has standing. . . .

Yours, *John D.*

[New York,] December 5, 1946

Dear Arthur:

. . . The paper ["Definition"] is fine. I can't see how anyone will have the nerve to use "definition" hereafter without making some effort to tell what he is talking about. . . .

What would you think of a footnote . . . to the effect that "Every report of scientific work done contains as a matter of [course] a statement of the operations undertaken in the course of the work. These operations are obviously behavioral, and the report made is a specification of them."

This gets rid of any appearance of an attempt to rescue "ostensive" definitions. It might perhaps be added that "While these operations obviously *are* a *cue,* and also a perceptive-manipulative aspect, they are much more than the latter, since the operations in question take place within a field of scientific subjectmatter that is already linguistically specified and hence is common to workers in that field."

Maybe this or something of the sort won't do. But I still don't care for "at most in the region of cue." Specifying *is* a behavioral act—to engage in a verbal repetition. And every report of a scientific experiment linguistically specifies the act. I don't see how this can merely be *reduced* to "cue" sign-behavior—to use another repetitious phrase.

570

Your statement that "That without cue values etc." . . . is O.K., of course. It does give a cue—that is, the specification of [what the] operation performed does *to other workers*. But I think the preceding sentence would weaken the statement (though probably not if it read "cue *to other workers* in the given scientific field") and [might] lend itself to misunderstanding. . . .

Yours as ever, *John Dewey*

New York, December 5, 1946

Dear Arthur:

I didn't make my point clear in my other letter, *re* "Cue." The report acts as a cue to others as to what to do and how to do it. But it does so in virtue of specifying operations performed and to be tested by other workers doing like things and seeing whether they get the results. To call it a "cue" with no further explanation didn't seem to me to cover the ground.

Yours as ever, *J. D.*

Indianapolis, Indiana, December 28, 1946

Dear John:

I have done two things:

Read [Walter] Dubislav: *Die Definition,* 160 pages, 1931, 3rd edition, very carefully.

Dubislav at one place remarks that Kant and [Jakob F.] Fries fail to note that the names they use (he is talking mostly of analytic and synthetic) bring things into close relation that by rights ought to be strongly separated. Also, more generally, that the one thing the logician should learn is not to confuse definition with ordinary word-explication and applications.

Jordan. He has a theory of the unity of the verbal elements in the whole construction of a poem—this is his aesthetics.

Now this is a fair match for our treatment of the unity of the system in mathematical development (not unity in the bad sense, but inclusiveness of a system).

Also for such a development as Jordan's, "symbol" is almost the required name. There is a large literature of symbolism in that sense.

. . . I recall that in the early drafts of papers I was allowing for an aesthetic or symbolic treatment of language (and possibly other, as yet unidentified, forms) alongside of (1) Naming and (2) Defining.

If we change from "symbol," I can easily fix it (I think—at least I can try) by saying that for the purposes of the present discussion (Definition) we put the word "Definition" in quotation marks, and discuss

571

"Definition-as-she-is" and not Definition as a clear process. I can add that the question of terminology here needs straightening out and that maybe the word "symbol" will have to be reserved for aesthetics as against our preceding use. This *might* make it necessary for us to shift "term," on which we have never taken a stand, to the mathematical side exclusively; enthroning "name" in the specification end—end so that we would get the layout: Name for specification, Term for Mathematics, Symbol for Aestheticizing.

We would have not "language" as one (in the old way), or as two (in our present way), but as three (as I have at times suspected, but have forgotten about).

Regards, *B.*

[P.S.] I forgot something.

What we have got, as I wrote Kaufmann the other day, and possibly you also, is an advance whereby the rigid play-game, frozen Hilbert [approach] is brought to life as a going process. Dubislav can say [*Die Definition*] that mathematical terms are not names (he is not quite that clear), but we can go further and add: "and yet they are alive." We transfer the Hilbert process from a third-realm mechanism to a live natural process (or, rather, I *Hope* we do).

The above is a very strong reason for looking more favorably on "Definition" in the place we previously had it.

Indianapolis, Indiana, December 29, 1946
Dear John:

Re the word "Definition" doing a double somersault:

1. I don't *mind* how much changing we do—we said we would—and it only makes it clearer that we seek no rigidities.

2. Nevertheless, I do not *want* to make changes.

3. The change in the opening paragraph of the "Definition" paper could be made in the form that: for the purposes of the present paper, and because of the difficulties of expression we shall in the present paper use the word "Definition" in a most general sense as characterizing mixed things and reserve till later a final determination. . . .

This would be more correct to events-transpiriting [*sic*] anyway.

On this basis the name of the paper might become "Definition in Current Logic" or "Logic's Use of the Word 'Definition.'"

4. If we did this, we would not have to decide finally now. What we would have to change later might be only *perhaps:*

Disconnection of the word "symbol" from the word "definition," leaving the latter where it is.

The footnote [number 4] in "Specification" paper—which could be passed off casually as a misunderstanding or something.

572

Doing this, the word "term"—if you finally like it so—can land as soul-mate to "definition."

The word "symbol" would then be free (if we disconnected it) for future poetic use.

5. Incidentally, in writing this, it occurs that the word "poetic" might not be bad. (Does it not have more deepset use than any other aesthetic word?)

The possible style might be:

Name	Designation
Term	Definition
Symbol	Poetic (Poetry. *Poesis.*)

(There must be some kind of a word around.) . . .

Best regards, *Bentley*

Part VI

Letters: March 13, 1947–December 27, 1949

Dear John:

. . . You ask about "object" and "content" from *Logic*, p. 119 and p. 520. I would say that a distinction between "content" in process and "object" as outcome is further along in technical development than we go. But also that I cannot make your particular phrasing hold very well. In other words, I am 100% for "object" being "subject-matter . . . in set- tled form," but the rest of the phrasing is difficult—or I might say repre- sents the specialized view-point you were using at the time for develop- ment. I suspect when we list "Object" in your sense, and "Subject-mat- ter," we have done all we need here.

Many things on the list I would not try to specify—merely brush away. For example:

"Context." This word is obscure without careful indication as to whether verbal or perceptive-manipulation contexts are in view at each instance of its use.

"Consciousness." This word has practically disappeared from use in research. In any substantive application (hypostatization) it is destruc- tive to epistemological discussion. (Or might say: in any such application *or* implication.)

One question: Shall we hold closely to our primary statement that we wedged a few firm names in the epistemological range, or let the list widen out?

Regards, *Bentley*

Paoli, Indiana, March 13, 1947

Dear John:

Memo on job.

This vocabulary job is not merely routine. It is interesting and opens up many little questions.

Understand throughout I have no particular interest in particular choices of words. My interest is in the terminological holes to be filled. Decisions are all up to you. I holler; you fix.

I suggest that we hold everything down close. I have the paper sketched with some 80 word-entries. Probably I will have 100 before finishing. Many of them can be handled in one line. Probably none should have over 5 or 6 lines (barring three or four "meanies").

Cross-currents in decision and selection appear:

(a) A few words are postulationally basic to selection. Such are "Fact," "Name," "Exist" as governing by postulation all specification-work such as we are aiming at.

(b) One line of selection would be words we recommend to others for daily use. But I doubt whether we care to introduce very much "thou shalt" in this matter.

(c) Another line concerns present words we have shown heaviest causes for rejecting as things now are: such as "proposition," "definition."

(d) Another line: the showing of problem-spots as to which we most heavily recommend new naming of some kind by somebody.

I merely mention these for what suggestive value they have. I think I have the postulation matter handled by a short paragraph pointing out the place such words fill in our work.

"Sensori-manipulative-perceptive." After a good deal of wavering about phrasing for this field (everything of behaviors pre- or sub-verbal, for which the verbal gives representation), we took, on your suggestion, the tripartite name in our latest papers. I doubt whether "sensori" is needed. I am entering "manipulative-perceptive," but with an idea that "per-ceptive-manipulative" might (or might not) be better. Anything that will cover the double range (and name it so that readers will understand that for our scheme perception is a form of manipulation, and all manipu-lation has perceptive value) will be the thing needed. . . .

Regards, *Bentley*

Key West, Florida, March 29, 1947

Dear Arthur:

. . . I've suggested we say something about "proposition." I doubt if it is practicable to suggest its complete ejection, though as I've said, in what I've added, I agree with you it is one of the worst abused words in the whole range of contemporary writing—the logisticists would have no capital at all if deprived of it; that is a good reason for its total ejection, but, on the whole, I believe it is better to suggest a way in which it could be used. I think its connection with proposal could be justified. It is something submitted, placed before us, for consideration; not exactly a hypothesis, but definitely hypothetical, nonetheless. And that is just what every formulation is, i.e., *does*.

I found your treatment very satisfactory, including the emphasis on a few leading terms and the emphasis upon the fact that what is said about the words in . . . ["Specification"] is by way of carrying out the general point of view rather than as specific recommendations.

I agree with you about dropping "sensori." "Manipulative-perceptive" is enough.

What I added in the case of "experience" is perhaps too much *pro domo*. But in some of my earlier writings, especially educational (explicitly in my *Education and Democracy* [*sic*]), I have used the word explicitly as name for organism-environment *in transaction,* though, of course, without use of "transaction"; probably [I] used the word "inter-action." And I've definitely said that the word covered the "experienc*ed*" as well as the "experienc*ing*." (While I haven't any occasion to go into the matter here, it has the advantage of being a more inclusive term than "knowing," covering such things as anger, fear, making war, passing laws, etc.) . . .

Best regards, *John*

Key West, Florida, April 2, 1947

Dear Arthur:

. . . "Space-time." These two axes of my thinking since I got in close contact with you are, on one side, the transaction-interaction business, and, on the other side, the importance for any theory of knowing (and the vocabulary in which it is stated) of the *Post*-Newtonian Space-time. I appreciate more and more all the time how completely the older theories of knowing—including, on the whole, logical theory—were written in terms of space-segments and time-sections. For instance, it has only just recently dawned on me how the whole logical theory of Generalization—and hence of laws—when stated as it was in terms of fixed uniformities, is dependent on the Newtonian space, time absolutes—I had got hold before, I think, of the error in the Uniformity category, but not of the way it went with the space-time limitation. Well, we've taken care of the transaction business in the "Vocabulary" paper plus the articles, but I wish there were some way of taking care of this other pivot. But I don't see how. Maybe you can present something.

Yours, *John Dewey*

Paoli, Indiana, April 5, 1947

Dear John:

. . . Trouble about "space and time" for this paper is that it has not been primarily terminological—or vocabulary. Not that there is a great difference. "Space" for us shall mean so and so. That's both. In the "Postulations" paper we stressed [in Part III] G. [Postulational Orientation] the durational spread. That's this thing. I shall try to make a short statement for space and for time—maybe send it today. I enclose reprint of a paper ["The Factual Space and Time of Behavior"] that I always thought well of, treating futures and pasts as transactionally present; and re-reading *purpose* in the transactional form. It uses the stuff everybody uses, but I thought had just enough of all-one-thing-hold-together in its presentation of a man's action from pasts into futures, and from theres to other-theres, to make it significant. I enclose it merely because a glance over it might give a hint of a phrasing you want. . . .

"Implied by"-"implication of." I have hunted often for some way to avoid the loose colloquial use of "implicated" and to leave the word free for its logical solemnity. The other day I used "import of" for a while, but it did not cover the ground. I forget other experiments. In desperation I get back to "implication." "Suggestion" sometimes is possible, etc. But nothing dependable is found. . . .

Regards, *Bentley*

Key West, Florida, April 12, 1947
Dear Arthur:

. . . I intended to add something on "Concept," but can't get it clear to my own satisfaction. I think there is one legitimate use for "conception" (not for "concept") as [a] name for the summary result of a previous generalization now accepted provisionally, of course, or *in* inquiry as a means or resource in conducting further inquiry—a kind of standpoint in outlook used to guide, direct, further observation and reports—category (not that we need say [anything] about that word) being the most inclusive of such names.

I don't see how it can be denied that [there] are such regulative names and that they perform a needed important office in conduct of inquiry. Maybe I'm just engaged in self-defence on account of my own previous use of the word in this sense. But in view of the very wide common use of the term, I am inclined to believe that we [shall] get a better hearing if we discriminate a legitimate use from the many illegitimate ones.

"Idea," "Ideal." Underlying differences of employment are so many and wide that when the words are used, it should be made clear whether they are used as behavioral names or as names of existences taken to be strictly mental.

. . . "Proposition." I am very doubtful about its being currently used as allied to proposal; I say, on the contrary, that the trouble with current usages is [that] it is *not* so used, but is taken as something complete in itself and/or a combination of two "terms" as complete in themselves— "concepts" being often used as synonyms of "terms." What . . . I intended to call attention to was that a proposition (in our usage) was never separate or complete, but was both a carrying forward of an inquiry and as such was subject to further inquiry—this isn't intended for phrasing, but to clear up what I was trying to say.

[*Dewey*]

580

Paoli, Indiana, April 15, 1947

Dear John:

. . . "Involvement." You have mentioned it tentatively once or twice, along with "implication." I do not want to see the latter go in, because that would "involve" us with a lot of recent symbolic logic, and produce unnecessary "repercussions." "Involvement," on its side, is "connection" (your p. 55 [*Logic*] . . . 5) itself directly, or it is "Inference." As you have used it, I would read it as "Connection" inspected as about to enter "Inference." As such, I do not know how to phrase it to bring out the distinction. My impression is that with "Connection," "Reference," and "Relation" sharply labeled, we have enough for the immediate present. So I have not specifically introduced it. . . .

Best regards, *Bentley*

New York, April 26, 1947

Dear Arthur:

How I missed your Space-Time article ["The Factual Space and Time of Behavior"], I don't know. *Aside* from its outstanding quality, my nose generally smells out any favorable reference to myself. Maybe I missed it because it came out in the summer when I am away and usually don't have the *Journal* [*of Philosophy*] forwarded. If evidence were needed to show how dead "psychology" is, the failure of this article to rattle the bones would prove the case.

I think the "space-time" insertion should go in in footnotes. . . .

"Operational"—I hadn't fully appreciated the difficulties—I guess [it would be best to] *drop* [it] entirely.

I think you have got it in fine shape for publication. . . .

Yours, as ever, *John D.*

[New York,] May 1, 1947

[To Bentley:]
Definition.

I passed the manuscript ["Definition"] to *Journal of Philosophy* without taking exception. But in reading the proof I had difficulty with the first paragraph. . . . I can indicate the difficulty most directly by means of suggesting it through the following revision I have ventured upon: First three and [a] half lines as is. Then after "setting forth" change to the following: "the very matter about which," etc., till you get to "namely." But while the "namely, the traditional uses" is of course O.K., the phrase "of words" seems too indefinite. Would the phrase "traditional uses of the word nominally under specification? definition?" bring the point more to a head?

Then in what follows there seems to be movement back and forth, which makes what is said rather hard to follow. At least my difficulty centers there, which may be my fault. The sentence "Two directions . . ." is, of course, O.K. But the sentence about "act" and "product" is left without explication until after that of "word and thing." I probably miss something, but it seems to me that the reader will see at once that there is something at least a little peculiar in consolidating "word" and "thing," while he will be more or less at a loss to see anything important the matter in consolidating act and product,* since that is a familiar linguistic usage. So I wonder if it wouldn't be clearer to put the word and thing business first. If the basic uncertainty and duplicity in the "word-thing" business is pointed out, then after that has been made clear —as it is in the text—there would be a background for showing how the same kind of duplicity of reference attends (as it was bound to do) the account given of *Act* and a *statement* as "product" of that act. (I've underscored "statement" because while [the] text has the word, the fact that the product consists of *words* isn't emphasized by [your] specifically calling attention to it.) The primacy of the word-thing consolidation, and yet separation, and the secondary or accompanying character of the act-product affair seems to be implied by the closing sentences in the second paragraph of the text. What I have said doesn't imply, however, that the distinction of "act-product" should be ignored, but rather that it be definitely linked to the thing-word affair by specific attention to the fact that the product is "statement," i.e., words. All the first part of the second paragraph would stand because it is in line with what is involved in the paragraph but, if I am a judge, is brought out for easy grasp by the reader. . . .

As ever yours, J. D.

New York, May 5, 1947

Dear John:

. . . Kaufmann mentions a desire for publication of the whole [set of Dewey-Bentley articles], in book form—in his note. He was pretty strong about this and, I believe, talked almost as much about it in the jive session Altman and I had with him as about his own position. . . . He wanted the thing "in growth," and he wanted it quick. Well, that is cheering. He said that, strung out as it is, people did not get the whole effect, and very few would check up and study it.

---

* As is said below, their definitions are so similar that they can hardly be told apart—which I believe is the case—which, in general, is so familiar to the reader that he won't see what is the matter with definition as both an act, and as a product of the act.

I told him we had never taken this matter up, and that I was reasonably indifferent, and would leave the whole matter to you. . . .

I believe I once suggested a possible title: "A Natural Theory of Knowings and Knowns." . . . I would want to tone that down a bit.

Regards, *B.*

New York, May 14, 1947

Dear John:

Re telephone call about publication. Suppose you tell me first of all: Do you want to publish it? How much do you want to publish?

(a) the pieces with joint signature in the magazine?

(b) those pieces plus my individually signed papers on the logicians (*Journal of Philosophy*) and on "Logicians' Underlying Postulations"?

(c) all the above plus the Morris analysis ["The New 'Semiotic' "]?

(d) part or all of the above plus any paper yet to be published by me on this line?

(e) part or all of the above plus any other paper of yours or mine previously published?

After we get that decided, then we can be specific and get after a publisher.

I have not bothered with the issue in the past.

My preference for the moment (though not a very heavy one) is to publish in the form (b)—just the papers we have had on this particular job in the last three years in *Journal of Philosophy, plus* the "Logicians' Underlying Postulations" paper from *Philosophy of Science.* This last paper has *my* analysis bringing out points in *your Logic* which the professionals thus far have overlooked; and that is why it belongs in.

Drop me a line to Paoli. As soon as we get our program right, we can show it to some publisher suggested.

Regards, *Bentley*

[New York,] May 15, 1947

Dear Arthur:

. . . As to the book, as you may judge, I've been in two minds about it. It would be mighty convenient for *us* to have the articles together; and in the long run we will probably get more attention from others, good or bad, from a book. *If* we can get good publishers, my vote is for publication.

On publication I'm for (b) anyway; and am inclined to think I might go beyond that. You may remember I once wrote a paper on Signs, or

"Representation" and Signs. It didn't come off, or rather I got off the track in one or two places; I might like to try again; I wouldn't have anything new to say, anything not [already] in articles, that is. But I think I might point up the contrast between the position we take and the mentalistic view of "ideas" (as "mental states"). It would be written more from the standpoint of past "philosophical" reports, and might on that account help reach the professors and professionals.

I'd be in favor of your Morris article, unless you think it's too technically controversial; I'd take your judgment about its going in.

Of course, the first paper, signed by you, in connection with the Introductory passage on "Firm Names" should go in. In the earlier paper ["A Terminology for Knowings and Knowns"] mentioning Definition, we could of course put in a footnote calling attention to changes in [the] article on that subject; maybe some few other additions or changes, not too many. . . .

Yours as ever, John D.

Paoli, Indiana, May 31, 1947

Dear John:

In your *Logic* you "officially"—one may say—made knowledge the end or outcome of inquiry. This left it, so far as immediate statement went, with no direct report on what it *is* (qualitatively, characteristically) so far as "end" or "object" is "beyond" (in any sense) or separate from "inquiry." In your development you went further (pp. 21, 67), but with no positive formulation—knowledge being a stage of inquiry, the latest stage, but still "by name" held apart. In some recent letter (probably within the last half year) you said directly, "Knowledge is inquiry." This made a considerable impression on me—one that is growing.

Evidently, *if* knowledge is action, instead of empyrean; and *if* inquiry, the word, is broadly enough used; and *if* no ultimates are attained, then "knowledge" most decidedly *is* inquiry.

This gives the first "localized meaning" to the word that we have had. (And, incidentally, "localized meaning" is a slight progress in expression.) Inquiry definitely is localized with respect to active human organisms. Knowledge never has been localized except by way of a "mind" constructed to possess it as a God or as an ideal.

Any time you have any remarks on possible developments in these respects, they will interest me.

Best regards, Bentley

Dear Arthur:

Your note about inquiry as knowing, in distinction from where I left off in my *Logic* "intrigues" me, if that is the proper word for it.

I'll have to give the whole matter considerable thought, before I'll be able to see just where it takes me—especially in connection with its bearing on the *Logic*. I've never done anything about a shorter version with some revisions that you once suggested, but I've carried it in mind, and your last suggestion would come in handy on the revision side.

I've wondered from time to time whether there was any way of bringing "Transactional" or "Transaction" into the proposed republication. It [is] such a central fact. But I guess it isn't possible.

I gave the two "Transaction" papers to a man with whom I had some correspondence, but hadn't seen till he came to town the other day, and today I got a fairly long letter from him, saying how much its substitution for interaction signified to him, and why it explained why he had never been able to get any help from the psychologists, and how their failure to employ it was what was keeping psychology back.

Yours as ever, *John Dewey*

New York, June 11, 1947

Dear Arthur:

As I said, I didn't see any way to get "transaction" into [the] title— just a "happy thought," stimulated probably by what [Marc E.?] Jones wrote me. I think the "transactions" will probably have the most present influence, however, on readers; the rest will come later. I think we shall find the word coming into use—usually, without any acknowledgment. I agree with you we should keep "theory" out of the title.

I suppose the briefer the title, the better, like "Knowings and Knowns" —the plural form is awkward from the standpoint of present views, but maybe its use will help readers to get used to it themselves. Maybe "Knowing and the Known" would serve—but that is only a casual suggestion.

Best regards, *John D.*

[New York,] June 25, 1947

[To Bentley:]

I have a letter from a historian of the fine arts [Alexander Dorner] who thinks our position is the only one that can make sense of its history as a movement from the static to "process." I gave him the two articles on transaction, and he says, "They walk right through our chaotic situation, show the way out and erect a clear structure, dynamic, flexible, and open to growth by its transformation." He adds that the "younger people can't help being influenced by this sort of point of view, but have a morbid tendency to withdraw as soon as there seems to be a hole through which to withdraw." He also says he [is] sending copies to [Erwin] Schrödinger —he is a German himself, not Jewish, but [was] thrown out of his job as Director of the . . . [Hannover] art museum by the Nazis . . . [before] he came over here. Has been [a] professor of Fine Arts . . . but is going to be dropped because of a book he wrote; they say they want art "taught from an evolutionary, not a revolutionary, point of view."

Yours, [*Dewey*]

New York, September 11, 1947

Dear Arthur:

. . . About "definition"—I believe the best way to handle it is to the effect that our earlier belief that a firm usage of the word might be found, was so shattered by [our] going over the literature of its present uses by reputable authorities, that we decided so and so—this is [not] intended for actual wording, but for general effect. I think some reference to the fact that the change was forced upon us by more extensive acquaintance with actual usages is the important thing.

The insertion of knowing as "goal within inquiry" is all to the good and should be employed systematically till it gets recognition. . . .

I am definitely at a loss as to how to answer your questions about Peirce. Take the sentence about Peirce's cosmic pattern ["For logical purposes there are three kinds of materials: (1) men; (2) things; (3) an intervening interpretative activity, product, or meaning—linguistic, symbolic. . . ." cf. *Knowing and the Known*, p. 3.]. . . . It seems to me that the "real" Peirce centers *within* (3), rather than in its relation to (1) and (2); that there are men and things, or things that are men and things that aren't, hardly seems doubtful. But that the various words used in (3) are all names for aspects of the intervening connecting medium, not for a lot of different things, seems to me to be what is conveyed . . . in the sentence . . . Peirce did *not* mean that minds, signs and things can be established in separation; and that *is* the real Peirce to me. (It is possible that the word "distinction" . . . might better be changed to read "separation"—for he did make a distinction while denying the separation.) Personally, I am willing to stand by the statement that [an attempt at a] departure from two orders, brought together by a third intervening order, through the effort to construct a *single* order in which, with respect to *knowing*, each has its own place and office, is what he was trying to do. Perhaps, it isn't quite right to say that he was just *stating* a problem; but that he was developing or dealing with the prob-

586

lem of how to bring the three into a single order or scheme, seems to me a fact. . . .

[Dewey]

February 21, 1948

[To Bentley:]

. . . From the point of view of Aristotle himself, the statement that definition was also the tool isn't strictly correct. *That* view is a product of the "modern" interpretation of Aristotle on the basis of *its* (the latter's) insertion of an agent—because of the rise of "individualism" culturally—in science, economics, and politics—that is, of innovators over against rule of and by custom. The "tool" in Aristotle was Nature working [through] those especially gifted intellectually—i.e., logicians—logisticists as the gifted in Logos—language. Aristotle's was the original semanticism, only there was no separation of substance and form. I don't suppose the point is worth making a correction here. But I'm sorry I didn't notice it earlier. (I doubt if anybody else does.)

This old isolation of form and content is a little ambiguous. Aristotle and the medievalists who became officially recognized (i.e. St. Thomas) had a one-to-one correspondence. It would be O.K. to change "the old" to "current," or "habitual," or something of that kind.

[Dewey]

Miami Beach, Florida, February 22, 1948

[To Bentley:]

. . . In general my comments are merely as to wordings. But I wish you *had* said something about "satisfaction." *If* a sentence *is* a *claim,* or a demand, then it [is] such that can be "satisfied" or may fail of "satisfaction"—a position that possesses positive possibilities. But it is a position that puts postulates [as] sentences *in system, not* as an entity.

The foregoing is what I wrote, and shouldn't have written, on the galley (evidently of Chapter 1 of *Knowing and the Known*). If I said it [at] all, I should have suggested it before this. The reference—in my head—was to the quotation from Tarski . . . "A sentence is true if it is satisfied by all objects." A sensible logical theory of truth can be got out of this if (i) a sentence is a claim, a demand, or pro-posal; if (ii) it is in system, not an isolate; and if (iii) "Object" is a name for the whole system of sentences in their transactional, and hence *behavioral,* use. "Satisfaction," in this case, is not a relation—except in a sense of that word too vague to be of any use—except ab-use. As a consequence, the concluding lines of the galley . . . are so condensed as to require so much knowledge of Tarski as not to be very readily grasped.

587

He certainly falls back on "objects," without telling how he gets to them. *If* he had taken sentence or assertion as one constituent of an extensive transactional system, "object" might have been understood as that designated by the system in a way that "satisfies" and is "adequate" to each member of the transaction as spatially and temporally extending, proceeding.

I think this is a good point, but as I've said, it shouldn't have been lugged in here.

Yours, *John D.*

St. Petersburg, Florida, February 26, 1948

Dear John:

. . . The most undesirable thing . . . at this stage, and for this moment, is the quantity of "must" and "should" I get into my writing. The continual stress on "postulation" is present, of course; and it would have been almost impossible to put qualifications into all sentences; but still I don't like it. However, I know nothing that can be done about it now, except in extreme cases. In other words, too much of my phrasing arouses antagonism where what we want is examination. . . .

Regards, *Bentley*

Paoli, Indiana, March 19, 1948

Dear John:

. . . A certain amount of psychoanalysis in the sense of turning up the attitudinal sod seems here needed.

You say continually I have done most of the work and should have the credit.

I am influenced by my feeling that I am bound to have a lot of faulty statements in my elaborate analyses . . . and I do not want you to get the blame.

I doubt if any of these points, or any like them, matter. Nobody in the future, if this survives, can mistake the procedure. Every sufficiently expert reader will know that you have worked the whole field and got most of the positions; and that I have been a little more explicit on some particular attitudes, and have worked to harden the formulation, and eliminate evasions. Maybe I have these statements all wrong. I don't care. Our lights are not under bushels, and they can be read, no matter what they are; and I don't care, any more than you do. We are still "alive" the way damn few of the old boys are, and almost none of the young ones; and we have never evaded the difficult problems by slick wordings. . . .

[Bentley]

Paoli, Indiana, April 1, 1948

Dear John:

. . . There is one remark I have made to myself a few dozen times, but probably never to you—that is, it never came up when I was writing. That is how very much more accurate you were in sizing up the Russian situation than I was. I counted on certain very strong natural features of the situation to straighten things out. The conveyors (human), however, could not handle the "features." Or, in more primitive language, temporarily, the devil came out on top.

Best regards, *Bentley*

Key West, Florida, April 7, 1948

Dear Arthur:

. . . *Re* Russia—I had two advantages—I was there in 1928, and was very much impressed—wrote some articles for *New Republic* ["Impressions of Soviet Russia"]—and was charged with being myself a communist, for the articles were among the first that gave the hopeful side over here. My disappointment when, under Stalin, they began to go systematically back on themselves, purging some of their best educators, party members as well as others, gave me a shock I never got over—the bitterest people I know are ex-communists—which I, of course, never was. The other thing is that I was a member of the Teachers Union in New York when a communist minority took it over—and had a first hand experience of their methods of wrecking a union—their technique is well worked out, and they must get first hand instructions [on] how to do it. I quit when the other members—who got sick of the communists spoiling . . . matters—started another union—some of the men who criticized me at the time for leaving told me afterward I was right and they wrong. . . .

Best wishes to you, *John D.*

[New York,] April 18, 1948

Dear Arthur:

. . . It struck me that if [Willard V. O.] Quine's saying that *names* weren't of any account in logic * is one of those views that identify logic

---

* "The exact words of the passage from Quine, part of which was cited in *Knowing and the Known*, p. 51, are: ". . . names generally . . . are inessential to language . . . the bound variables of quantification can be made to serve as the sole vehicle of direct objective reference. Such suppression of names is a superficial revision of language, and does not resolve the issue over universals. This issue has to do with entities, not parts of speech, and it survives the elimination of the name category." "On Universals," p. 74. For Quine's later views, see his *Word and Object*. (Eds.)

with *mathematical* subjectmatter, he should have gone further and said on that basis "names" must be completely *ruled out* of logic. At least we would know what he was at. I haven't read Quine at all, and if I had, maybe I would know *better* than to suggest this as a possibility. . . .

John

New York, April 26, 1948

Dear Arthur:

. . . In one of my earlier books, [*The*] *Quest for Certainty*, I think it was, I had a chapter entitled "The Supremacy of Method." I haven't read it for a long time, but I am pretty sure it was feeling after or moving toward the position that distinctions in subjectmatter can[not] be fully treated without bringing in attention to the *inquiry*, or knowing, involved. Church and [Arthur F.] Smullyan fell down because they neglect that fact * . . . [which] I'm beginning to think is the most widespread single failure. This Chinese student, now at Columbia, [Sing-Nan] Fen, has, I think, the most discriminating knowledge of my general position of anybody. He was here Saturday and told me his doctor's dissertation was on method; and, as I understood him, it was on this point of the necessity of linking distinctions in subjectmatter with the inquiries by means of which they are instituted. Church and Smullyan don't realize, in the first place, that logical *form*, instead of being set over against subjectmatter, is itself a distinction in subjectmatter, and in the second place, in consequence, they translate what we say over into what it would be *if they* held [it]—it is [as] if we're part of their system—a kind of criticism I've received most of my life from my professional colleagues.

As ever yours, John D.

New York, May 8, 1948

Dear Arthur:

. . . I have the habit, probably a bad one, of using it [the word "radical"] as synonym of completely, through and through, [though they have] no apparent likeness. The dictionary does give *thorough*—but aside from the tendency to give the word a political sense, the difference is not a *root* one, "common sense" being the root in this case. I think "cultural" is less likely to abuse than "social." Everyday thing is associated, and social in that sense.

* Dewey's comments pertain to Church, "Review of Four Papers by John Dewey and Arthur F. Bentley" and Smullyan, "Review of 'Definition,' by John Dewey and Arthur F. Bentley." (Eds.)

I am at work on a follow-up article [to "Common Sense and Science"] placing *philosophy* in the scheme. You may not like my using the *word* for what I have to say, but I hope you'll agree that there is a job that needs to be done, whatever name be given. And having been not only a professor, but a professor of philosophy for forty years of my life, I'd like to do something to save my face before I quit entirely. And the article . . . [I am] now writing in any case doesn't belong [in *Knowing and the Known*], as perhaps the one already published does, on account of the emphasis on transactions. I wrote something on signs once ["Concerning Signs"], but got off on the wrong foot. I've always meant to do another and do it nearer right, but I've had too many other things [to do]. And I can't do it now or in time to get it in.

By the way, the words "concern," "affair," etc., do specifically, I think, what I tried to get the word *experience* to do in a too wholesale and loose way—aside from its ambiguous philosophical usages. . . .

John D.

Paoli, Indiana, May 12, 1948

Dear John:

. . . Private *Bug*. I like to think of a laboratory, not as a place where the scientist produces, but as a place where the world passes through, with just enough channeling of its course to get better watching and observation—like the scientists sitting inside the big tube of the 200 inch telescope to modulate the happenings. I have tried to say this, never have said it right; if just as a turn of phrasing, it might fit in somewhere with your discussion of *labor*-atories on pp. 204–5 ["Common Sense and Science"]. . . .

Best regards, *Bentley*

[New York,] June 15, 1948

Dear Arthur:

. . . I hope you are using your earlier comment ["An Aid to Puzzled Critics"] upon his [Church's] charge that we are not aware of the difference between logic and psychology—I think (that is, fancy) he just can't imagine any intelligent person having any logic except the purely formalistic, symbolic [kind]. . . .

The present formalism is due (i) to retention of the old pre-scientific idea that finality, absolute certainty, is the desideratum, with recognition (ii) that it can't be had in natural science, but only [as] orders of probability, and therefore must be found in symbols, which, as mathematics proves, are not names. Peirce once said that philosophers were

591

given to aping mathematics; these people out-mathematize mathematics in their attempts to get symbols that are the foundations of mathematics— a bet that foundations for foundations will be forthcoming *ad infinitum* would be safe, I guess.

J. D.

[New York,] November 9, 1948

[To Bentley:]

Memorandum.

I got to mulling over the difficulty there seems to be in getting over to readers the organic-environmental activity as one "thing" and as in process. I concluded it was because the word *"Organism"* (especially in the *ism*) carries with it a kind of readymade hypostatization. So I resorted to my *Bible,* the *Oxford [English] Dictionary,* and as usual with a happy outcome. The original meaning was as a synonym for *organization* or anything organized. O.K. Then an organized system— a whole of dependent and interdependent parts, *compared to* a living being—underscoring of "compared" is mine. Then there is this beautiful [circa] 1770 quotation: "When an artist has finished a fiddle to give all the notes in the gamut, but not without a hand to play upon it, this is an organism"—very much O.K. . . . If I had found it in time, I'd [have] been in favor of quoting it in a footnote.

"Organism" as "an organized *body*" [Dewey's emphasis] is as late as the middle of the nineteenth century; harmless enough as a synonym for a living creature, but I'd be inclined to bet that it was through use in *anatomical* study of the living body that "organism" got so overloaded on the isolated side that even the hyphenated expression, organism-environment, fails to strike people as a name for what anyone can directly see when he opens his eyes.

I am inclined to think we should try to find and use a word that wouldn't be handicapped, as the *word* "organism" (like other Isms) has now been loaded down. I'll bet ninety readers out of a hundred wouldn't stop to think twice, coming across the expression "a dead organism." The damn "body" has got away with it. One can at least use "medium" as a synonym for "environment" when advisable. But unless one keeps saying "living being," "living creature," etc., [misunderstanding is possible]; it's too bad [that] there isn't a noun to go with biological.

The Greek *bios* is described in *Dictionary* as "life, way or course of living distinct from *zoe* (animal life)." * You hit the nail on the head in

---

* The exact quotation is: "life, course or way of living (as distinct from *zoe* 'animal life, organic life')." (Eds.)

what you've said about "biological" as covering "psychological-sociological."

But "Biology" in the *Dictionary* "is the science of physical life"—a "division of physical science"—not of *natural* science. The bible falls down.

J.D.

New York, November 12, 1948

Dear Arthur:

. . . Did you ever run across a book by N[orman] A. Cameron, of the University of Wisconsin, *The Psychology of Behavior Disorders—A Biosocial Interpretation;* which last word, as he uses it, means Treatment—and [he uses] names that are firm compared with anything on the subject I've ever read. He knows what "behavior" names—I don't think the word "mental" occurs in the book. If you already know the book, I don't need to call special attention to the extent in which he runs parallel with *Knowing and the Known,* and in [a] field that is the most bogged down in a verbal-theoretical swamp of any [field] anywhere—and to an incredible degree. When he says in the Preface that it "differs" by breaking completely with the tradition of mind-body dualism, he knows what he is saying. "We begin with what we find, a biological organism operating in and by means of a social environment.* We thus create no artificial need to solve such meaningless conundrums as," etc. Again, "It differs from classic behaviorism in rejecting reflexes, instincts and emotions as building blocks out of which human behavior was supposed to be constructed. . . . The biosocial interpretation departs entirely from traditional psychology by dispensing entirely with the concept of consciousness and the distinction between the mental and the nonmental. We can neglect them without missing them." . . .†

Yours as ever, *John D.*

Paoli, Indiana, November 20, 1948

Dear John:

. . . I recall . . . that the first time I was in Key West, I mentioned my long-standing aim at a general theory of language (your phrasing in

---

* The exact quotation is: "We begin instead with what we find, a biological organism operating in and by means of a social environment." (Eds.)

† The exact quotation is: ". . . differs from classical *behaviorism* in rejecting reflexes, instincts and emotions as building blocks out of which human behavior was supposed to be constructed. . . . The bio-social interpretation departs from traditional *psychobiology* by dispensing entirely with the concept of consciousness and the distinction between mental and non-mental. . . . We can neglect them in behavior psychology without missing them." (Eds.)

Preface to *Logic*), and you asked when? and I said five years. And you thought that was a long way in the future, which it evidently wasn't, for that time in Key West must have been eight or nine years ago. The point is that no theory of language would have come along without the coverage of the name-thing region which we have given. In a sense, this *is* the theory of language in its behavioral-environmental setting. . . .

Regards, *Bentley*

New York, November 22, 1948

Dear Arthur:

. . . I think in the future I'll forgo use of "organism" whenever possible. The adjective organic is O.K., but the noun stands too readily for a reification. I'll try "living creature" or something of that kind, which may suggest something going on which is extra-dermal. I quoted to Joe Ratner, who was in at dinner yesterday, what I wrote you about few people being stirred by seeing the expression "dead organism." He agreed and added that if one talked about a "dead ghost," they probably would react.

"Five years" wasn't such a bad guess of yours—not that the language job is complete, but quite a lot has happened since June, 1943. . . .

Yours, *John Dewey*

Key West, Florida, January 18, 1949

Dear Arthur:

. . . I have had one sad experience lately . . . from a man [Albert Balz] who took his Ph.D. at Columbia when I was still teaching [there]: a criticism of a point in my *Logic* which he takes out of the theoretical context, of which it is, for better or worse, a systematic constitutent—and he remarks quite casually in the course of his article ["A Letter to Mr. Dewey"] that if "any science *could* be dismal and un-illuminating," biology was that science; that he will concede the organism, but not the environment; and not the slightest intimation in his long paper that he was aware [that] if he was going to criticize the *Logic,* the very thing he had to center on was the matter he casually dismisses. One place in the *Logic* [p. 289] is used the word "powers" with double quotes around it—I think that is the only place in the whole book the word "powers" appears, though, of course, I haven't been through it all to check. He freely attributes "powers" to me; the word appears half a dozen times on one page when he purports to be giving my views; he even writes as if he thought I held the organic "powers" did the inquiring I write about —he does abstain from attributing them to mind or consciousness in my view. No wonder he doesn't "concede the environment." He is quite a scholar in many ways; is a professor of philosophy at the University of Virginia, and I should have ranked him above rather than below the run of the mill.

I got one thing out of his piece. He succeeded in rounding up my own view of my own views. It brought it home to me the extent how at the present time, if not always, but certainly in the *Logic,* the whole thing centers in and proceeds from life-behavior, and how specifically living is not something done by an "organism" on its own hook. You suggested once I write a condensed version of the *Logic;* I feel much more like it now than I ever did before; I always thought it a good idea, but there were other things I wanted to do first. Now I feel as if I ought to write so firmly and overtly in terms of life-behavior that at least my critics would know what to shoot at. I believe that in all probability it didn't occur to Balz that anybody could hold such an outrageous view. . . . He even began by making a correct general statement that I was agin Dualisms and held that analysis should disclose the condition under which distinctions are made which are hypostatized into existential dualities. But he ends up even that sentence by saying that distinctions are to be understood by reference to the polarities from which "they spring." I at least had the satisfaction of telling him that if the word "polarities" were used by me, it would be as a synonym for "distinctions," not as that from which they arise. His whole treatment consists in reading a backward reference instead of a forward one into everything I say. It was in this connection that Lyle [Eddy] said that *Morris* was doing to my view the same thing you expose Mackey as doing. . . . I wrote Ayres (Texas) once [asking] why didn't somebody with the knowledge of political-industrial history in the United States write an account in some detail, beginning maybe in the nineties, showing that "capitalism" wasn't an entity, but a phase of a process that at least had some fluidity *as* process. . . .

All this is by way of leading up to saying that I don't see why you red-penciled your scheme ["Logic and Logical Behavior"]. . . . And you shouldn't lean too heavily on my *Logic;* it wasn't a bad job at the time, but I could do better now; largely through association with you and getting the courage to try to see my thing through without compromise— or not so much compromise as an over-conscientious regard for "scholarship" that led me to feel that I had to work in, somehow, an account from my point of view of what the standard logics had treated from theirs. To hell with a lot of that, would be [my] present outlook, and concentrate on the main point of view, but I've got into other things. I can't think of anything more useful than your four layer scheme; "logic as is at one end, living men at the other end—and the confusions in between." I think you could show that the important confusions and incompatibilities arise because they just can't merely repeat the old; and only move far enough to introduce contradictions in it without moving through.

Korzybski, . . . [et al.], thinks he must deny Aristotle—and so what? Carnap thinks the old logic must be completely replaced, but doesn't seem to have any intimation or clue to by what. Well, you know all this new stuff, the in-between stuff, much better than I; I stuck pretty well to the standardized traditions, making excursions along the line of the Lotze, [Bernard] Bosanquet, [H. W. B.] Joseph, . . . [et al.] set. They had something, but all on the wrong foot; a good deal of the newer in-between stuff hasn't any feet at all. Or maybe I'm sore because I can't do or see it.

I think if you go ahead, you will find that you have got down to business; that is from "generalities—not so awfully wide," in any bad sense of that word—to "bird in hand" statement. Go to it; and don't feel you have to be too tender of me. As I get tougher, it includes [accepting criticisms about] certain things in my past—and I still have enough, comparatively, to be fairly cocky about. . . .

There is one thing which I am inclined to believe back of the "sense data" stuff, the feeling that we have something so "immediate," so "given," that it can't be questioned. It's the quest for certainty; they feel about the possibility of getting *scientific* statements that you have to have something that corresponds to what Axioms were once for mathematics. The more they give up first truths as mathematical premises, the more they feel lost if they can't find self-evident and self-assured existential data. . . .

Yours as ever, *John D.*

Montego Bay, Jamaica, February 13, 1949

Dear Arthur:

. . . I want to thank you for what you say about rewriting the *Logic;* I guess I've told you already that, as I look back, I fancy I was trying to compete with a lot of scholars on their own ground, and so overloaded the pages with unnecessary material; but it is also true that I didn't see the core of my own position as clearly then. Really, I am obliged to Balz for his incredible . . . remark about the biological—it brought home to me that for years I was trying to operate in biological area without being adequately aware of what I was doing—not that I am apologizing. The way I was brought up I couldn't have done anything else, so on the whole I am rather proud to have worked reasonably clear in my nine-tieth year.

I don't quite know what to say about the reply to Church and Smull-yan ["An Aid to Puzzled Critics"]. (About the latter, I wrote, and still have in manuscript, a reply to something he wrote years ago on value, published in the *Journal of Philosophy*. He was terribly and yet rather instructively mixed up—I mean by the latter word, he showed up the current state of the subject.) I think the reply should be published, and I wouldn't want the absence of my name to give the impression I didn't agree a hundred per cent. But there should be some limit to my getting credit for work you do. What would you say to a footnote saying it was written by you but that I had read it and was in complete agreement? Seems to me that would cover the ground. . . .

With my best, *J. D.*

Paoli, Indiana, February 27, 1949

Dear John:

I have had a terrible time trying to find out what kinds of Logics (as theories) stood for what kinds of logical behaviors (as human). I writ [*sic*] twenty-five sketches * last fall—none any good; and I have worked a good part of a week here—nothing any better. However, I have found out a thing or two.

One is that Kaufmann's word "rule," about which I have sought (and not received) information for about eight years, is one of the slickest double-dealers ever. Hiding behind it, he escapes dealing with all essential issues.

Another is that our "designation" or "naming" as behavior primarily, and secondarily as aspectually logical behavior, carries inside it the whole issue of correct or incorrect, right or wrong, and hence true or false; so nothing needs be done to apply such treatments from without. In other words, naming itself in any sense is a right-or-wronging process. This, of course, is involved in Peirce's 1879 paragraph on concept.† It is involved in your *Logic* as inquiry, and in your proposition as intermediate stage. It is involved in my variation of naming from the way you used name in the *Logic;* and, for all I know (I have not looked it up), in your use of name there. But a vivid statement to this effect makes "name" come alive behaviorally in a way we do not succeed in making it come alive to the other feller [*sic*] when we merely say naming is action and process under way, like all behavior.

Only point of this letter is to ask whether you have any remarks to make on possible utility of naming come alive as logicking [*sic*] in person, and no need to "Thought," "Judgment," or Thor's Hammer to make it so. . . .

Best regards, *Bentley*

* Of his essay, "Logic and Logical Behavior." (Eds.)
† Bentley probably intended to refer to Peirce's 1878 discussion in C. S. Peirce, *Collected Papers*, V, 258. (Eds.)

Dear Arthur:

. . . I've had occasion to note how frequently a statement could be simplified [by] finding and using a language phrasing, instead of one affected by philosophical or "psychological" theory. We have had occasion previously to note the superiority of adverbial expressions. "Ill" and "well," "rightly-wrongly," "correctly-incorrectly," are adverbial—and so are good and bad in *effect* when used in such expressions as good (bad) job, business, etc. It has recently dawned on me . . . that the ad-verb is closest to the active (verb) form . . . an adverb is strictly transactional: it unites *a way* of doing, [a] manner, [a] mode [of] acting, with what is done—which, I take it, is what nouns stand for when they are not hypostatic. "Well," "ill," are certainly adverbs; "right" and "wrong" look like adjectives grammatically; but in use they are adverbial in effect; "in effect" being tautological for "in use."

There was a time when I worried about "Truth-Falsity," till I came to the conclusion that in logic, they were merely synonyms for "valid-invalid"—accent the last syllable and you have an *ill* person; *valid* ought to name something that is *well done*—[e.g.] the cricketeers' "Well played." . . .

Still more lately I came to the conclusion that "truth-falsity" were originally *moral* terms: "Tell the truth, and shame the devil," as over against telling a lie. They are names for the ways of communication—using language—that are commonly—communally—approved and disapproved. Then they got used in inquiry and were carried over to inquiry-behavior—then they were turned into Nouns-substantive-hypostatized.

But we still true things up—straighten them out, and the *rect* in "*correct*" still carries that sense. I imagine "false" is related to failure; it certainly is related [to] "faulty," "de-fault," and in a sense to "*short-coming*," "delinquency."

This last paragraph simply carries what was said about "verbs-adverbs" back to the direct original use of language when people talk *together;* if there was ever a transactional term, it is "*communication.*"

Well *done*—keep it a doing.

Yours, *John D.*

Dear John:

. . . While I have spent the greater part of a year on this proof [*Knowing and the Known*], part of the work has had value in improved expression. I have also made the Index and will have that off tomorrow.

. . . It seems to me you are getting a very considerable development along a fresh line in the matter of language stresses (your letter 3-2-49 and earlier). I hope you will work them up. We have a mention of the "adverb" in footnote 8 to Chapter VII (page 200 of the text). It does not make your transactional point, and is not even in an immediate transactional connection. But it uses the comparison of "definitely" as sharp and strong in contrast with progressing weakness from its adjective "definite" to the noun "definition." I am putting a line "Adverb" in the Index.

. . . Last spring you told [Melvin] Arnold [Director of the Beacon Press] to place my name first on the title page, or so he wrote me at the time. He did not. Since then he has had three changes of book-editors, and I have had to go over every detail with each new one. I referred the present editor to that letter. Reply was this would not be done because "it is almost an unavoidable if unwritten law that the name of the senior . . . appears first as deference to his advanced age and longer scholarly career. . . . This particular protocol seems never to have been violated." Like the case of the judge, the decision may be right, but reasons are surely wrong—I mean on the "advanced age" basis—you have sounder grounds than that. I shall not answer Beacon on this matter. Honorifics are not important. There might be a little advantage to me in drawing some fire directly, which would enable me to get a little better vision into the next steps of the development, and maybe not. There might be a little less stress on my status as Amanuensis, when the chance comer thinks he has to say something, but that would be a pleasure lost rather than gained. I will leave it entirely to you to tell Arnold what to do. . . .

Best regards, *Bentley*

Paoli, Indiana, April 15, 1949

Dear John:

. . . I have only one question. [In] your . . . ["Reply to [A. G. A.] Balz's 'A Letter to Mr. Dewey'"] you stress the name Instrumentalism. You describe this as the showing of the growth of scientific subject-matter out of everyday subjectmatter, and return into it. The question arises only when a particular kind of heckler wants to know what the everyday subjectmatter "is." It is the question as to earlier debates on whether your kind of "real" *is* "real" or not. Again it is the question as to "object" in inquiry (*Logic*, p. 119); your phrasing is "things exist *as* objects [for us only as . . . outcomes of inquiry"]; the particular kind of other-fellow wants to know what sort of "existence" the "things" have otherwise than "*as* objects." It is not *I* who want to know. We have various ways of getting towards the answer, and we do not expect to climb that mountain in a day. I just sensed the possible question as I went through the paper.

Best regards, *Bentley*

Dear John:
. . . You dug up "aspect" as a verb—haven't used it yet as such. But it may come into use. How about "conspect"? in transactional observation? No such verb ancient or modern in my *Century* [*Dictionary*]. There is, however, *conspectus* and several obsolete near-noun forms. I'll have to get *Oxford* [*English Dictionary*]. Late but still usable. Can't let you have all that advantage any longer. . . .

Best wishes, *Bentley*

[P.S.] The point is I have never tried anything that I said over and over in more ways, always unsuccessfully, than the point as to "what" logic is. To differentiate between "Logic" as a Discipline, and "logic" as the subjectmatter under inquiry, is unimportant if the point of view is (1) coherent. But in this case it is not. Logic can be said to be practically a theory of proof or truth or evidence or (2) psychically a theory of decisions (as Kaufmann) . . . thought; or (3) scientifically.???

In other words, "Logic" as science gets its characterization from its subjectmatters; and its subjectmatters get their determination from Logic as inquiry into them; and the subjectmatters are just "one" with respect to the conventional logic of names—conjoined with logic of symbols. But this business of specification of names in science as distinguished from consistency of symbol in mathematics; and the business as to which is the consistency, the mathematics or the characteristic of mathematics developed by logic; etc. . . . won't let themselves be written down by me.

In your work, if recollection is correct, "logic" is at times the inquiry and at times the processes inquired into (logical behaviors)—much as physics stands to physical, but *not* as mathematics stands to mathematical. Directly you have so much unity between the two uses that nothing matters. But, nevertheless, I would bet my last peanut that if you had a developed statement as to what "logical behaviors" *are*, aspectually, phasally, or "entitatively," a considerable part of the *mis*understanding of your *Logic* would be avoided. . . .

New York, April 28, 1949

Dear Arthur:
Your two-page sketch ["What Is Logic"] has cheered me up. Someone, maybe the grumpy Carlyle, [said] that to get one intelligent per-

son's agreement was worth an army—or words to that effect. You state my position better than I have; it encouraged me to believe that I'm understandable *enough* so that others will understand me in time.

I wasn't just being polite when I said in my Balz letter that when I wrote the *Logic* book, I was overconscientious in trying to do my duty; as a matter of my own education, I had to work through that material. But now I hope I am through. And this question of its subjectmatter is primary. [Joseph] Ratner says my book has more influence than I suppose, but that it wouldn't do to mention the book in polite society; "polite" being academic, professional, in this case I take it. . . .

The present formalism is what an old friend of mine used to call "the last ditch of authority."

Yours, *J. D.*

[New York,] May 2, 1949

Dear Arthur:

. . . Joseph Ratner said he spoke to you about [Lewis S.] Feuer's terrible article ["Dialectical Materialism and Soviet Science"]. Maybe I'll write a note to Feuer and say it seems, from his article, that there was another man writing under the name of John Dewey, and could he put me in touch with him or suggest some way to clear up the confusion. . . .*

Yours, *John Dewey*

[In May, 1949, Bentley delivered a talk to one of Dr. Kaufmann's classes at The New School for Social Research in New York City on the principal conclusions of *Knowing and the Known*. Bentley sent Dewey a summary of this talk and the question period that followed. This letter comments upon some issues raised by one of the students.]

New York, June 2, 1949

Dear Arthur:

. . . There were two points in the language quoted from him [a student] that struck me. (1) He speaks of one of the two men [who] in his example, "recognized a word-pattern," though not the word itself. How come? Did the "mind" of this particular man have an intuitive understanding of word-patterns—whatever they may be? So here is my example. Four men heard some noises. Number One stopped there; he recognized that he heard a noise, and beyond that

---

* Feuer developed a more favorable attitude towards Dewey in various scholarly articles published from 1958 on, although he still maintains many views that Dewey would probably disagree with. (Eds.)

nothing in the way of "meaning." Number Two recognized the noise of the kind called clicks—and stopped there; Number Three suspected, supposed, believed, possibly "recognized" [that] they were of the kind made by instruments employed in telegraphy. Number Four tells the others what the clicks *say;* he translates them from the telegraph code into English, which they all "know." Maybe Number Three recognized a "word-pattern"—or guessed at it. Did Number Four "recognize," observe, *Four* things—or One Thing, according to Mr. W. and his like [in the class]?

(2) According to him, Bentley–Dewey hold that "word and meaning are the same." I don't "recognize" Bentley–Dewey in that statement, but I'd like to know if the "ideational contents" involved in my example (in the case of Number Four) come from four different minds in the same man. . . .

Yours, John Dewey

Paoli, Indiana, June 10, 1949

Dear John:

. . . The more I work, the more important the terminology seems. It is not a case of choosing words; it is a case of knowing what one is talking about—or rather merely of *trying to* attend to what one is talking about ("knowing" is far too strong). When ninety-nine out of every hundred—even among the cognoscenti—get you wrong, what way is left but to try to make the words walk straight. There ought to be a drunkometer for such words. . . .

Best regards, Bentley

Paoli, Indiana, June 20, 1949

Dear John:

. . . Some time ago I suggested "conspect" to go with "prospect" and "aspect." I loathe, and boycott, "concept" and "percept." I now (accidentally—when my foot slipped) note that the hated "cepts" are from "seize," "grasp," "hold,"—*capio*—while all the admired "spects" are from *specio*—observe. You see I have recently followed your course, and taken the *Oxford Dictionary* to bed.

I wish the *Oxford* would justify some sort of pre-pre-pre-historic connection of "know" with "now"—the latter in the sense of "now then" in the older sense of "now then, look here, you *know*" (or "are going to get to know if you listen"). That would make "knowledge" etymologically temporal and transitive. But it (*Oxford*) won't.

Best wishes, Bentley

Paoli, Indiana, June 26, 1949

Dear John:

. . . You have all the points in your . . . [letter] ["Communists as Teachers"] on teaching and communism—many more than I had thought of. But in the end, I am afraid each fellow will decide the way he felt like to start with. I find it very difficult to believe the country is in danger of new intolerance, despite the stink in the House committee and the small areas of Klan resurgence. Hasn't the status of the Negro (by way of its best specimens) improved more in two years—the last two— than in several cycles preceding? I hope so. I have a standard form of position. Communism as a goal is one thing. I am for free speech in excelsis. Russian enemies underground in this country, that is another thing. Mere naming them together does not make them one. I am inclined to be tough on traitors. . . . All I do is to watch for someone to make the distinction sharply.* I never hear it. Unfortunately, there is an intermediate case. How about the simon-pure home-grown who advocates Karl Marx's ultimate [goal and the] step necessary to bring it about? . . .

Best regards, *Bentley*

New York, June 29, 1949

Dear Arthur:

. . . Somehow, the net effect of the Balz episode was to sort of sour me on the word "Logos." There is one good thing about the word, though. The Greeks were as good as was possible with science and politics in the shape they were in then; they had at least an "instinct" for the relation of thought, mind, and language. The further I go on, the more I am struck with the good sense of what you wrote about the ambiguity of "knowledge." The ox knows his master's crib, the bird its nest and its young, etc. Language enables us to hold up and [examine] the conditions and members of such knowings, and that kind of knowing *makes* "all the difference . . . in the world" in knowing and what happens because of the knowing. Hurrah for "*Logos*" and damn logic, or what has been made of it.

As ever, Yours, *John D.*

Paoli, Indiana, July 7, 1949

Dear John:

. . . As to the blurb [for *Knowing and the Known*], I do not rate "philosopher," nor either of the attached modifiers, but there is apparently

* See Sidney Hook, *Heresy Yes—Conspiracy No* and *Political Power and Personal Freedom* for a position that seems very close to Bentley's on this problem. (Eds.)

603

nothing can be done about [it]. So let it ride, unless you wish a change.

Another point in the blurb (first paragraph) seems necessary to fix. That is the phrase "region of research called the science of meaning." Reasons for change: 1. In our Chapter XI, "Terminology" [actually—"A Trial Group of Names"], we say of the word meaning: "a word so confused it is best never used at all," and we say of the word science: "Our use of this word is to designate the most advanced stage of specification of our times."

To keep their phrasing is to put us in the red to begin with. I suggest for a substitute: "region of research in which knowledge is sought of the processes of knowledge itself." This will fit the space remaining open.

I do not like the word "knowledge," but it is a proper blurb-word, as it conveys knowledge where knowledge is not. Probably you can suggest a better phrasing. If so, O.K.

I am glad we have your Balz reply in the text.

Very best regards, *Bentley*

Dear Arthur:
New Alexandria, Pennsylvania, July 12, 1949

. . . It may be the passage [*Knowing and the Known*, p. 324] is still open to misconstruction, but [I] should have had to rewrite the entire eight lines to make reasonably sure it would not be [misconstrued].

The point [about the distinctions between "subject" and "object," "mind" and the "world," etc.] is that [when they were] interpreted, not ontologically, but in terms of use made, there was a needed service rendered by [this] releasing the "subject," self, individual-knower from the state of knowings-knowns *as of that* particular time—the initiation of the new physical science. The separate and independent knower gave the leverage for criticizing and sloughing off the preconceptions of the old [ancient and medieval] cosmological self in which the human knower was taken to be completely absorbed—and not by way of transacting—in the [new] cosmology which was [early modern] science. I'm afraid it's too condensed to be clear; I counted too much probably on the context— it is given as one example of the transfer of use or "function" into something ontological—*vide* previous and following paragraphs. The best I could do was to change "through" into "by means of."

As ever yours, *John Dewey*

Dear John:
Paoli, Indiana, July 17, 1949

. . . My working theory is that the spread-out languaging of men— the human behaviors seen alive—are my subjectmatter. My technique is to study them as close and hard as bug-man studies bug. Everybody alleges from time to time that [it is a] waste [of] time grubbing around. Nobody (unless it is you) gets the point when I try to tell it. I'd rather be a grub than a puff of stratospheric atmosphere. Fact (in our sphere) comes for me only when, by main force and obstinacy, the sentences are made to pour their guts out into a pot. Well, well, well—that was not what I was going to enlarge upon—but it leads to this further remark— a complete autobiography in one sentence (and an epitaph): "Here lies Obstinacy. He stood upon a wordy deck, and stood, and stood, and stood." . . .

The process of pawing over sentences in the general region of the naming and the symboling has led my pencil through half a dozen stages to say something about two different kinds of subject-object situation that are slopping around together in the material. The naming gets the named set over against it, and the knowing gets the known. But with naming and knowing-in-naming consolidated, this is just one kind (roughly) of subject-object. But mathematics has a different kind of subject-object within its operations. You do not have mathematic*ing* [*sic*] and the mathematic*ticked* (symbol*ing* and the symbol*ed*) in the sense you have naming and the named, or knowing and the known. That kind of practical differentiation does not show. Physics can be shown [to be] toward the physical fact as very much what Logic is toward the logical-behavioral fact. But mathematics (in our symbol development) does not stand in that way toward the mathematical. The mathematics *is* the mathematical in a way different from that in which physics (not *is*, but) indicates the physical. (There is a lesser distinction in the case of logic and physics, because logic is a highly developed type of logical behavior, in a sense in which we would not be able to say of physics that it itself is fully a highly developed type of physical fact.)

Now this point of two types of subject-object, both muddled in the ordinary "mind-presentation"—or rather the two not yet having become unmuddled from out of their evolutionary pathos—is not argumentative, or definitionally determinable—not in my mention of it here. The point is: I suspect a lot of types of subject-object lying mixed in the material. Too many types will kill off the old point-soul—he can't stand the differentiation—what's left of him. . . .

But the point is: What do you know about other efforts from other points of view at differentiating a variety of subject-objects?

(Senses, intellects, etc., are not to the point—they are conventional boon-doggling.) I am not thinking of developing this theme. Life-job— not for me. It just lies incidentally in the pudding. . . .

Best wishes, *Bentley*

New Alexandria, Pennsylvania, July 18, 1949

Dear Arthur:

. . . I think the ordinary person—even, or perhaps, because sufficiently out of the ordinary to have some acquaintance with [what] passes for logic—when he sees or hears the word "name" thinks of a common noun in isolation—dog, horse; and is so habituated to this extremely short sectional view that "dog" hardly *means* more to him than the isolated thing *he* calls "Fido." Not only is he accustomed to associate only so-called common nouns with names—omitting extensive and carefully qualified or conditional expressions, and omitting prepositional and conjunctive expressions—[but] in the case of *familiar* common nouns doesn't, because of their familiarity, even pause to consider *what* is named. A name to him—the reader who is habituated to ordinary grammar and logic—is simply what you *call* familiar objects *by*—as something quite independent of them—just, and merely, a word that happens to be in common use when you are talking to someone who you know uses the same words. I don't know how to handle this matter, but I am pretty [sure] that the reader needs to be made aware, somehow, of how irrelevant and misleading is the assumption with which he is accustomed to approach the matter—otherwise he will miss the point. . . .

. . . The commonest fallacy in philosophy is to take statements out of the reference to the occasion and situation in which they say something worth saying and then treat what is said as having meaning "inherently," in and of itself independently and [in] isolation. . . .

Yours as ever, *John D.*

[New Alexandria, Pennsylvania,] July 19, 1949

Dear Arthur:

. . . In connection with what you said about positions as positings, I've had an occasion lately to think a good deal about "view" as a synonym in philosophy for "position"—view held; "position taken"; view is a viewing from a selected *point* of view; that, of course, determines the outlook and what is seen, noted, observed. Plato's "*Idea*" and Aristotle's "*eidos*" are both etymologically [the] same as "View." . . . Mathematics is where viewing and viewed are identical.

Yours, *John D.*

Indianapolis, Indiana, August 11, 1949

Dear John:

Having said I couldn't, I did. I went over yours of 2nd [a letter of August 2, 1949, not printed here] carefully. Every point you make is helpful, and more than that. The big ones will be held open for action

606

till I get your feelings on later sections. Out of the situation I got a half-way thought that might work up sometime. Here you are at ninety not letting anything get by. I used to expect I would deteriorate in work before I did physiologically, but I seem to hold up here and there with pen better than with body. Now for background, we have the old mentalist, where discarded, having the physiologist as his substitute, and as a rule showing the same type of defect as the other. The half-thought is this. As against the physiological-cortical-causation, we might say: Here is a case in which weakened physiological organisms continue technical activities in a better degree than they continue physiological activities of the primary form. (Of course, for use, one would want to know whether two out of a hundred were that way or ninety-eight out of a hundred—a bit of provisional fact.) One would not want to develop this as against the physiological setting. One accepts that. But one might get to use it in support of a broad-physiological as opposed to a narrow-physiological setting; i.e., in support of an across-the-surface physiology in place of an inside-the-skin physiology; or, in other words, in support of a transactional treatment on a cultural line.

The above is just "half" stuff. However, in another connection I used the place in my last letter to Kaufmann where I turned from the upstairs theoretical statement to what happened at separate points on the pages of the book about science, methodology, and deduction, and used it as base of an argument that the mess in the book pages underneath the level of the formal presentation Kaufmann was giving, was clearly a kind of happening, not to be attributed to the Kaufmann-mind-in-action; but instead it was the past surviving directly in the Kaufmann living—and not surviving as a status caused by a "past," but as the actual, living vibration of the so-called past in the present living. Or, in other words, as I may have more lightly said it: The Kaufmann-intellect-in-action is just a slight play on the surface of action that must be seen as immensely great action-ranges, describable only in thousand and ten-thousand year units. Vibration across ages (and I would say this was good physical analogy) in place of impacts of a past billiard ball upon a present one. . . .

Your argument in the letter you sent (as separate from the memoranda) [was] that the matter could be taken up directly as a question of subjectmatter. What kind does Logic have? How locate it? Looks as though it might be right. It would put the paper at once on the field of action. It would eliminate all the expansive introductory stuff. I would have to find out just how far it would cut in before deciding. That introductory stuff was building up toward a transactional offering of Logic.* When I got to the section VII and VIII (which, as I told you,

* Of "Logic and Logical Behavior." (Eds.)

took some 50 sketches across six months, to get stated), I quickly felt that I now had a direct bit of construction. Also I felt a bit of what you indicate. But I did not stop to revalue it. I really want to get to the concluding sections, not yet in readable shape, before revaluing. However, I strongly suspect you have told me how to do it. What I need to keep is just enough to build up to section IV (the a, b, c, d, reals) which, I believe, is well stated as a working verbal tool, to section VI for transactions, and so on to "logical behavior." I will also have to face eliminations of everything possible in section V—the list of points to remember.

The next big point [of yours] is impressive. Introduction of specimens of observability. I have a little illustration I think, in addition to reiterated assertions of need. The statement [by you I note is] that observation is in descriptions, and [in] word-development accompanying. There is one crack [of yours] that it should actually be easier to see a trans-dermal transaction as an event than it is to see a "mind" in operation itself as an event. I have a good note on this and will [keep] watch [for] what to do [with it].

I think every one of the special points you raised as to phrasings should be attended to—I do not recall one that is not. The sentences you quoted from [the still unpublished] introduction to [the] new edition of *Experience and Nature* should be a footnote at least to my corresponding passage. The parallel and the deviation were both interesting. Perhaps, you will send me the precise phrasing and the page number, for eventual use.

Best regards, *Bentley*

New Alexandria, Pennsylvania, August 14, 1949

Dear Arthur:

. . . I've often wondered whether the cerebral backwardness that often seems to exist with ageing isn't a product of an unnatural loss of intellectual interests during the earlier parts of life. You and I seem to indicate it isn't inevitable. . . .

With regards, Yours, *John Dewey*

New Alexandria, Pennsylvania, August 29, 1949

Dear Arthur:

. . . You are right, of course, about the *Logic;* I was trying to let myself off, I got so disgusted, but it's very bad policy to let the others off; but speaking technically, from their standpoint, I did a pretty good job on a lot of things I didn't care much for, but wanted to show that the "inquiry" standpoint would take care of them.

About "object," I haven't the book with me. The Greeks used "subject" consistently—it was equivalent to the *topic* or *theme* under discussion, or the "cause" in a legal sense under consideration or "trial." I suppose I got my *subjectmatter* more or less from that source. Then modern epistemology turned the two right around; the "knower" became the subject, and the "Object" something out there waiting for the mind to turn its activity on—the most reasonable explanation is that it was an objec*tive* but I don't think that was it. I remember Gildersleeve, the Professor of Greek at Johns Hopkins University, writing an article in which he said the object was that which *objects*—that makes sense, and it certainly has pre-linguistic roots. I'll investigate further.

About naming—I recall agreeing with you heartily when you wrote to the effect that any part of speech could be a name—it depended upon what is named, or something like that. I've been thinking, lately, that maybe only *firm* names are names; I don't think that is at all inconsistent with the other point of view. Verbs and adverbs are more likely, on the whole, to be reasonably firm than nouns and adjectives. I was thinking of the shepherd in the fable that called "Wolf" once too often. His wolf (with an interjection after it) was not just a "common noun;" he called for help of a specific kind, and that was what he *named*. Before there was any written speech, people had to talk—except [*sic*, especially?] when they were yarning about things within the range of action of the talkers. The connection with action kept their namings fairly firm. Everything that comes in experimental science—or modern mathematics—is something . . . within the range of a specified kind of action. I have a kind of idea that if we went over the subjectmatter of the *Knowing and the Known* articles for "definition" (I haven't got them with me, either), we would find the favorite subjects for definition are things that can't be specified by any set of directions of action. The classic genus plus specific difference was certainly all inherently "ontological," à la Balz and others. It's sort of along the line of Peirce's "prescriptions." In physical science, the prescriptions end up gold . . . [or] fools's gold; in mathematics, the prescriptions are it. A letter from Joe Ratner the other day said, "Scientific language isn't like common language at all. In scientific language you have parts that can be moved around like the parts of machinery; piston rings, bolts. In H_2O and H_2SO_4, the H is the same. The complex is new, but not the parts composing the complex." The language of common sense *has* . . . to serve the purpose of doing a particular job to this and that, here and there, now and then. That's in line with what Joe says, I think; science deals exclusively with "interchangeable parts" and, hence, its greater "practicality" in the end. . . .

Sincerely yours, [*Dewey*]

Paoli, Indiana, September 4, 1949

Dear John:

. . . you are not very keen on fussing with that manuscript I sent you at present, while I, the more I think about it, am inclined to use your scheme for a changed introduction. You made a suggestion that would adapt the paper much better to my proposed place of publication.

. . . I think I have already mentioned the citation you made from one of Joe Ratner's letters: about the "H" and the "O," etc., of chemistry being "the same" in various chemical formulations built up out of them, with the "complex" new, but never the "parts." That is a very useful manner of statement which I should like to see developed. But I would still ask whether the expression "the same" is itself the same when used with respect to "one and one are two," as it is when used with respect to "H_2O." The woods are full of interesting things.

Best regards, *Bentley*

New Alexandria, Pennsylvania, September 7, 1949

Dear Arthur:

. . . In sending your material ["Logic and Logical Behavior"] back; I've only a few comments to make. Your statement . . . about Einstein's work "framing nature in man's behavioral activity as comprehensively as man in the previous generation had been framed in nature" is as near perfection as anything human can be, and should, I think, be introduced earlier as a kind of key note.

V is headed "Memoranda for Orientation" (. . . so I don't think what I am about to say will be needed). But for the *Philosophical Review* article, I think the negative statements won't need emphasis; the positive statements should absorb the attention of the reader. If they are felt to be necessary, I'd put them all, at least I'd consider doing it, at the very end in a last paragraph, as a kind of caution or warning to the reader that acceptance of the position renders it quite unnecessary to deal with such and such as issues—not, as you say several times, that you have anything against those who want to hold them—the issues—on their account, but that they just don't fit anywhere in the observed world of man-observing-nature—nature-in-human-naming-knowing. (I'm not trying to word it for you. But my feeling is that a strong positive statement, with a minimum of negative qualifications, will be the most effective form of statement with the group the *Philosophical Review* reaches. . . . In other words I am sure you have a strong hand and should lead from strength; there is no danger of its being taken for undue assurance, because it is the *position* which is so strong in itself.) . . .

About your question as to "the same" being itself the same in the two cases of chemical formula and the mathematical statement—if I get the point, I say *not;* the 2 subscript with H is affected by *H;* the 2 in "1 plus 1" is affected only by 1 plus 1. The mathematics in physical formulas seem to me much like the "figures" in a cooking recipe; take one cup of milk, two eggs, four ounces of flour, etc. Mathematical "figures" are affected only by other figurings. At least, this seems to be in line with what you said in [a] letter to me, which for me settled the matter. The old distinction between pure and applied number won't do because number *qua* number is "pure"; but that doesn't prevent its being used as part of the directions for carrying out a technique. In a letter I had written Joe Ratner, I had said techniques have the same place in scientific inquiries that technologies have in industrial operations—and as far as I can see, that holds also of the place of mathematics in both "science" and "industry."

Ever yours, *John D.*

New Alexandria, Pennsylvania, September 17, 1949

Dear Bentley:

. . . After seeing the demonstrations [on visual perception] reproduced when Ames and his assistant were in New York, I decided that they had the only sound work in experimental psychology which had been done, and that it was revolutionary compared with what passes generally as psychology and experimental work in that subject. It's almost unbelievable what they've done. . . .

Yours as ever, *John D.*

New York, September 26, 1949

Dear Arthur:

. . . Ames and [Hadley] Cantril . . . are enthusiastic about the "Transaction" articles; they had a training class of younger psychologists at the Hanover Institute [at Dartmouth College] and had them all read the articles in the *Journal [of Philosophy]*. . . . I have had some correspondence with Ames [published in 1960 in *The Morning Notes of Adelbert Ames, Jr.*] about the word "assumption"—it seems to me they don't take into account sufficiently the "how" of the results they get and consequently have a tendency to over-intellectualize the process. . . . I've been trying to get Ames to consider "habit" as the *how*, but haven't made much of any headway. . . . However, I'm confident that their endorsement of the transactional is going to be valuable. . . . They both believe that the younger psychologists are dissatisfied with what is going on in that subject and will take to transactional as getting rid of a lot of the confusion they now experience. . . .

Warm regards, *John D.*

611

Paoli, Indiana, September 28, 1949

Dear John:

Just heard a theory about why your *Logic* does not dig in faster—why, no matter how many times the book is read, the line of development is evaded. Point is: your books have been around a long time; they are classic; mostly are *required* reading for any budding philosopher; hence, budding philosophers think they have "got" you long before they get to the *Logic*. And probably, also, they think they are the front of the ages because they work in 1949 instead of 1900. Quantitative judgment by them only. . . .

Arm raised in greeting as ninety approaches on wings.

Bentley

New York, October 27, 1949

Dear Arthur:

. . . I think it is true that the work of Darwin (and Spencer through [E. L.] Youmans) created more of a ferment in this country than in Great Britain; it was more of a matter of science and religion there; aside from religion, . . . it created here the first great stir after Emerson [Ralph W.] and transcendentalism. I was . . . glad to see it put in a historical context [Philip P. Wiener, *Evolution and the Founders of Pragmatism*] . . . [as] an offset to Bertrand Russell['s] misrepresentations. . . .

Ames is the inventive and original one of the Dartmouth-Princeton group; he is a doer rather than a literary man or a professor; it's the demonstrations that count; and they *prove* perception is transactional, in the strictest sense of scientific proof. . . .*

I don't think that "social psychology" means any more than perception of *human* behavior, as distinct from that of animals . . . or inanimate things. . . .

The best of luck to you.

Yours, *John Dewey*

[Paoli, Indiana,] December 8, 1949

Dear John:

. . . Imogene [Mrs. Bentley] and I have done a great deal of work . . . assembling and sorting all the manuscripts and related memoranda on construction for *Knowing and the Known*. The idea is that some-body some time can trace the verbal at work, my attitude being that the

* Cf. Franklin P. Kilpatrick, ed., *Explorations in Transactional Psychology*. (Eds.)

work did itself and was not the output of either godlike brains or brain-like gods. There are several points that never got to clear statements, even though they had been pretty sharply set up as problems early in the work. One of them appeared under the heading "The Specification of Transaction." The point was that it took so much time to *say* what Transaction was, or alternatively to say what Specification was, that we never got to a proper presentation of the full process. . . .

Bentley

New York, December 25, 1949

Dear Arthur:

. . . I made a point [to Adelbert Ames, Jr.] [that] I don't think we have ever had occasion to take up—namely the current neglect of the connection [of] the central nervous system—cerebral sensori-motor or, with the "autonomic" [nervous] system. It's my hunch that the latter system is the biological framework of the "situations" within which and pervaded by which the central nervous system operates in making "intellectual" connections and distinctions. I have also the hunch that some time or other it will factually [be] ascertained that civilized life, the anthropologists' "enculturation," tends to twist the workings of the autonomic system away from the "normal"; hence, our human susceptibility to a lot of foolishness and mistakings [that] the "lower" vertebrate animals aren't subject to. I do not know as I told you [that] we had a milch goat this summer at Maple Lodge, and that within the limits of her life activity, I am confident she was more "intelligent" than any civilized human being. Her transactions with her life-media were so accurate as to approach infallibility—within the limits, of course, of her natural needs and her organic means for satisfying them. Anyway, I learned a lot, and I hope what I learned is so. . . .

I tend to get impatient when I realize that it is practically only within the last three or four years that I can see with reasonable clearness what I've been working at for many many years. . . .

I had a piece from Lyle Eddy, the graduate student I've referred to as [the] white hope, in which he writes as follows: "For the first time I am beginning to see (i) the transactional approach and (ii) the distinction between content—subjectmatter—[and] method (with full awareness of philosophizing as itself method) as not quite the same thing. In the development of your philosophy, the second of these came first; and if this is correct, there is something strange about [it]. For in appealing to others to give recognition to the role of method and to its recognition in and by your philosophy, an appeal to the transaction approach must be made first to warrant it and to combat the traditional 'subject-object' approach distinction that stands in the way."

There is a lot in this in explaining the difficulties I've met in getting my position understood. If I felt I needed any defense—which happily I don't—I'd say that I think it was quite a job to recognize the fact, even [though] I was late in giving its rationale. What he is saying amounts to what I have said I owe to you. I had used the word "transaction" occasionally, but I never got its full theoretical force and scope till you pointed out how free it was from the ambiguity of "interaction." Speaking of vulgarity, one professor wrote me a letter in general sympathy with my position, but regretting I found it useful to employ a word so charged with business associations! . . .

Yours, *John Dewey*

[New York,] December 27, 1949

Dear Arthur:

Just got the Einstein volume [*Albert Einstein; Philosopher–Scientist*] in the Living Philosophers series. Browsing around, I find the following. In reply to Bohr, [Max] Born, [Wolfgang] Pauli, [Walter] Heitler and [H.] Margenau, Einstein says [that] . . . a statistical quantum theory . . . "correctly describes the empirical relations between stable phenomena as they were theoretically to be expected," and "until now it is the only one [theory] which unites the corpuscular and undulatory dual character of matter in a logically satisfactory manner and that the (testable) relations which are contained in it are, within the natural limits, fixed by the indeterminacy-relation, *complete*." * (His italics.) He goes on to say: "What does not satisfy me in that theory, from the standpoint of principle, is its attitude toward that which appears to me to [be] the programmatic aim of all physics: the complete description of any (individual) real situation (as it supposedly exists irrespective of any act of observation or substantiation)." Then he discusses a radioactive atom with respect to disintegration events, saying that although the function at a chosen instant is able to determine what part of space the particle will be found at, the description is incomplete since it "does not imply any assertion *concerning the time instant of the disintegration* of the radioactive atom." (His italics.) Hence "as regards the *individual* atom (italics not now his) description by means of the [ψ-]function must be interpreted as an incomplete description."

* These quotations are from this passage: "[This theory] even now presents a system which, in its closed character, correctly describes the empirical relations between statable phenomena as they were theoretically to be expected. This theory is until now the only one which unites the corpuscular and undulatory dual character of matter in a logically satisfactory fashion; and the (testable) relations, which are contained in it, are, within the natural limits fixed by the indeterminacy-relation, *complete*." (*Op. cit.*, pp. 666–67. The brackets are in the original. Eds.)

614

He goes on then to say that what he *dislikes* in the kind of answer the quantum theorist will give is that it comes down to Berkeley's principle that "Being" is always something which is "mentally constructed by us"—a lot of exclamation points by me.

I don't know enough physics, to say nothing of knowing enough of [what] quantum physical statisticians have written and suppose they know, to suggest or assert that some different aspect of the same assumption about Being-Reality will also be found in [their] theory. But I just wonder whether they have any more understanding of knowing as transactional than Einstein shows, and whether they also don't at some point fall back on a supposed relation in knowing between a [the] knower and the known.*

Yours, J. D.

[P.S.] There seem to be indications that after lopping off a good deal in Kant as unnecessary, he [Einstein] is fundamentally a Kantian.

---

* On philosophical issues of quantum theory, cf. Herbert Feigl and Grover Maxwell, eds., *Current Issues in the Philosophy of Science*, esp., pp. 350–445; Ernest Nagel, *The Structure of Science*, pp. 144–45, 293–316. (Eds.)

Part VII

Letters: January 2, 1950–December 6, 1951

New York, January 2, 1950

Dear Arthur:

I've never read much of the interpretation of the Ames group of the demonstrations they have made. I now have read enough of their article reprint [Cantril, *et al.*, "Psychology and Scientific Research"] to see that to a considerable extent I was naively assuming that their understanding of their own work and its demonstrations would be in substance like mine—especially that of Ames'. If I had put "assuming" in quotation marks, I might have been illustrating that assumptions of a theoretical kind have themselves to be critically examined on their own standing. At all events, I see in reading the first of the four [actually three] reprints, that Ames hasn't modified at all certain points with respect to which we have carried on considerable correspondence. One of them concerns the use of "habit" as if it were on a par with stereotypes; that is, [he] accepts in effect the theory that identifies them with tendencies to repeat instead of abilities (French *habiletés*) without which we can do nothing. In my correspondence with him on this point [see *The Morning Notes of Adelbert Ames, Jr.*] I tried to show him that "assumptions" are themselves habitual predilections and aptitudes—perhaps because of the too wide or generalized scope, I got nowhere—maybe I wouldn't [have failed] if I had merely confined myself to remarks about habit as habit—though I interspersed these remarks pretty freely. Then I wrote him a fairly long letter about what was said in footnote on page 4 about the need of self-action and interaction in *psychological* inquiry. (That we provisionally accept interaction with respect to physical matters, he may or may not have noticed.) . . . Verbally, he has omitted one point, perhaps [because] of my criticisms—namely, reference of all things to "freedom of the will," as an instance of need for recognition of self-action. I pointed out the complete irrelevance of "will," and suggested that "freedom" was attained whenever transactions attained a certain "consummatory state." . . . I'm disappointed because of the naïveté of my assumptions about his assumptions. . . . If I seem to you to have [been] over-enthusiastic, it is because I was going by his experimental demonstrations on the ground of my own theoretical "interpretation." I still hold to it on *that* basis, but it is pretty depressing that they are being put before the public with assumptions that are, to some extent, just those which the demonstrations themselves are calculated to destroy. To some extent, though I hope not by any means wholly, they are undoing their own *work*. In the second article the dis-

619

tinction made between formulating a problem and the technique of investigating depends, of course, upon [their] failure to see that stating the problem is a *continuous* process and is part of [and] integral with "method of investigation." Of course what he says about "techniques" can be understood if one looks at a large part of what passes as experimental research in psychology—a kind of busy work that, scientifically, is a waste of time—and worse.

Maybe I'll get up to the point where I'll write him and point out that scientifically formulating a problem is of necessity just as much a continuous process of critical revision as he recognizes hypothesis-making to be. . . . Problem-formulation is so much a part of inquiry, that to make the distinction he makes between scientific method and scientific inquiry is out of the question.*

Yours, *John Dewey*

St. Petersburg, Florida, January 22, 1950

Dear John:

I want to draft a review of *Knowing and the Known,* . . . to show that this book (although not directly making the claim) is an advance of inquiry into "knowings" from the philosophical approach to the scientific approach. It must be in heavily condensed form—that's where the task lies. I want to ask about one word.

"Object." In your *Logic* on a famous page (125, or 121, I think [cf. pp. 119, 129]) you assert that where the situation inquired into firms itself, there is the "object." We have gone on with this by way of "transaction" to cover all knowings-knowns, as well as the specifically logical. How the question has often swallow-winged across my working page: Suppose somebody says (if anybody ever gets that deep into the subject): "Dewey did not mean by 'object' the full 'thing-known,' but only its specialized logical entry," and cites various qualifications and reservations against me. What am I going to cite in response? I do not recall any specific categorical statement that the "object" of the *Logic* (p. so-and-so) is comprehensively the *thing* involved. The only qualification I would admit is that you have deliberately offered "logic-in-growth," and how the hell can you be expected to make ultimate, dogmatically-phrased statements? I would not myself, of course, want to say: This object is all the *thing* there is, but only: This object is all that any human organic activities we know of is getting hold of. Point is: Just how would you point

* *The Morning Notes of Adelbert Ames, Jr.,* pp. 171–231, contains the direct correspondence between Dewey and Ames from December 1946 to November 1950 and helps to clarify the issues raised in the letters between Bentley and Dewey on Ames's work. (Eds.)

your index finger right now? Just how would you want to see my finger point, in double-harness?

That is all I meant to write, and I meant to do it in five lines, always remaining as I do a linguistic innocent when starting a paragraph. But along come other questions:

(a) Supposing I can get my sketch in shape, I know two younger men who might . . . re-work it . . . [for publication]. But if not these, would you have any suggestion?

(b) We throw out the word "knowledge" as hopeless. We need a noun with transactional values to replace it. But vastly more, we (or I seem to) need an adjective. A lot of words use the stem "gno-." Can any of them be adapted without false implication? ("Epistem-" is, of course, that which must be destroyed.) "Ken": Can something be made of it?

(c) More than an adjective, even, perhaps we need a name for "theory of knowing" in our sense. (Personally, and not for use now, I would prefer something of the style of "contact theory," or more expressly "behavioral contact theory"—since I make every process above the physiological "behavioral" in the sense of "contact" not physiological, but knowledge-functioning.

As usual—don't bother beyond what interests you.

Best wishes, *Bentley*

St. Petersburg, Florida, January 23, 1950

Dear John:

. . . I am het up over "Kennetic." Only to give it more distinction from physical terms, "Kennetics" would be better. Or wouldn't it?

Could such a name be introduced with a footnote: From German *kennen;* Scotch *ken;* occasional English idiom, *ken.* Or would some other form be better? Tickle *Oxford Dictionary,* and make him give me some information. When the right time comes, a lot is done with a name. "Cybernetics" by no other name would smell so much like a brainstorm. . . .

Best regards, *Bentley*

New York, January 24, 1950

Dear Arthur:

. . . I recall you asked about "object" once before; I didn't get as clear an idea of the point as I do from yours of the 22nd.

I should say that "object" [is] some existent (space-time) subject-matter that is accepted for *further* use on the ground of the inquiries, knowings that warranted taking that subjectmatter as *Known.* It does

621

not, I believe, involve any implication that the knowings that determined that particular subjectmatter as "object" are final—unalterable. It is *warranted* not in any absolute way, but for use till we know better. Whales became *objects* a long time ago, but the advance of knowings replaced the *fish*-object by a mammalian-object—and so it goes. It is a matter of logic in growth because knowings-knowns are in growth. "Object" is the full-thing *known*, but only being factual with the appropriate place-date qualifications, (i) the outcome of knowings then at command, and (ii) with reference to use in further inquiry until that further knowing puts it in question. . . .

I don't see why a properly versed critic wouldn't assume the place-date conditioning with respect to everything said; although previous training surely makes it difficult to bear in mind all the conditions involved in what is said. I think the place-date reference might be expected to be recognized. However, there is no doubt that *Knowing and the Known* is firmer on that point than the *Logic*.

The naming question raises a genuine problem. Introduction of a novel, technical phrase is likely to lose as much as it gains in accuracy; lots of readers will infer [that] the theory back of the word is equally an invention on the spot instead of a description of what goes on every day—practically every waking hour, more or less. I have just been writing something . . . ["Importance, Significance, Meaning," in which] once or twice I used "cognitive" as adjective—but I don't recommend it particularly—however "cognitive" is, I believe, the Latin equivalent of Greek *gno.* Cognostics and agnostics have pretty well ruined the Greek form. . . .

Yours, *John D.*

[New York,] January 24, 1950
Dear Arthur:
. . . Coming from others as a descriptive name of what we are doing, "Kennetics," with the footnote, isn't so bad.

The psychiatrists' discovery of the unconscious is all wet because of their having made an entity out of the abstract term "consciousness"—[in] "awareness," they make another out of the normal workings of the organism. It seems to me psychiatrists, more even than other psychologists, need to get the transactional way of seeing and telling things.

Yours, *John D.*

St. Petersburg, Florida, January 27, 1950
Dear John:
. . . Now about *Object.* My question is always the crude one. If I refer to "Dewey object" as fully included in a transaction, if some one

cracks back that I distort you—that your object is the logical (or linguistically put-forth) object, and that underlying [it], there is another Dewey "thing," "entity"—a sub-object—let us say a perceptional one, not called object here by J. D., but in common language understood to be "the" object—will he put me in any kind of hole?

This is not a matter of your view—I have found that out well enough from many readings. It is a matter of argument when someone approaches. I have to take the "someone['s]" ground. He offers Object-1 (real), Object-2 (perceptional), Object-3 (constructional in language-logic, or howsomever). He sets the conditions. He demands a show-down. (Now that I have got this fully stated, more fully, I could dig up the answer I think I need, if I were at home where my notes are.)

Maybe the answer runs like this:

You were developing logic. You established the status of object therein. You did this by putting the man and the proto-objects in a "situation." This situation includes world-contacts prior to the linguistic-logic contacts. Your construction situation extends back into the "inquiring animal" stage, even where the animal inquires merely by a whiff or glimpse. You did not expressly state (or did you?) that this sub-logical inquiry was in one long scheme with the logical. You developed this, however, to some extent along with me in *Knowing and the Known*.

There is considerable open territory, so far as development is concerned, for both of us at many stages of the inquiry-growth.

Here then is my answer. You developed logically, and forecast more. In *Knowing and the Known* we have some of that "more." If there is any passage in either your *Logic* or the *Knowing and the Known* which is "out of bounds," neither of us recalls it now.

I can therefore make a "strong" statement without much risk. Indeed, our critics-at-heart are not yet far enough along to make the point.

Best regards, *Bentley*

Key West, Florida, February 17, 1950

Dear Arthur:

. . . I always thought after reading his [Bridgman's] first book [*The Logic of Modern Physics*] that he was more promising than the other scientists who were engaged in setting forth a general theory of science. Your criticisms of his own theoretical statements of the operational point of view were justified, of course; but I felt that his illustrative treatment of topics on an operational basis provided the material for correction of his own theoretical statement about them—much as the Ames material *should* suffice to rectify some of the theoretical statements they make about their own results. . . .

Yours as ever . . . , *John D.*

Dear Arthur:

. . . It ["Importance, Significance, Meaning"] is an analysis of the form or pattern of inquiry, essentially old stuff, but trying a different phraseology: Inquiry as process of determing *importance* of subjectmatter with respect to [a] *significance* of observed conditions—location and description of problem—what they indicate as to what may be done by ways of determination of how to deal with them, [b] the subjectmatter as determining solution of problem—[c] all in terms of biological behavior, in which inquiry is deflection of primary behavior into an intermediate and mediating behavior channel—[d] that of knowings as makings out, ascertainings with a view to resumption of activity—[e] the ways of resolution as hypotheses for testing by institutions of new conditions as signs being named *Meaning*. When subjectmatter of observed (environing) conditions as determining the problem of the ways of experimental action, [and method] as determining how to deal with it, coincide—then the primary, direct, straightaway action is resolved, all in terms of [the] complementary connections of means-consequences. I've kept out the historical material. But if I had hit upon this way of approach long ago, I would [have] simplified my criticisms of (1) the subject-object split and controversy; (2) that of empirical-rational controversy, *a priori–a posteriori* disputes; (3) the phenomenal and the "real"; and (4) the difference between "common-sense" subjectmatters and those proper to scientific inquiry. This last I've treated briefly along the general line of the piece reprinted in *Knowing and the Known* ["Common Sense and Science"].

Incidentally, I think I've hit a fairly decent summary statement of the difference between the intelligent behavior of pre-human and human animals: that intentional use of artefacts—physical and language—as names making possible intentional activity on the part of those who have these two kinds of artefacts at their disposal—which humans certainly have—without the need of being dogmatic as to whether pre-human animals have them or not. The transactional behavioral statement of environing-media and organic ways of action certainly represents the simplest way out of the whole subject-object mess that can be found—not that I've hit it off as well as might be.

If I had time and strength, I'd like to write Bridgman—his paper-and-pencil work is a good example of the use of languages as names, as a development in knowing—especially scientific. His privacy business—which is only one-ended—nothing is proved for him until he sees it, but he doesn't see that it goes for what he as private sees till others see it too, etc. . . .

As ever yours, *John D.*

Key West, Florida, February 28, 1950

Dear Arthur:

Funny thing happened; I got a book of poems, *Time and the Rock*
[*Time in the Rock*] by Conrad Aiken, published [in . . . 1936], sent by a
woman I never heard of, [with] a note saying she was presumptuous
enough to send it because of its similarity in poetry with the transaction
of *Knowing and the Known*. (The Rock is Being—the immutable, a
poetical version of Process using up being to develop more being.) Here
is a sample. . . .

> The miracle said "I" and then was still,
> lost in the wing-bright sphere of its own wonder:
> as if the river paused to say a river,
> or thunder to self said thunder.
> As once the voice had spoken, now the mind
> uttered itself, and gave itself a name;
> and in the instant all was changed, the world
> two separate worlds became—
> The indivisible unalterably divided;
> the rock forever sundered from the eye;
> henceforth the lonely self, by self anointed,
> hostile to earth and sky.
> Alas, good angel, loneliest of heroes!
> pity your coward children, who become
> afraid of loneliness, and long for rock
> as sick men long for home.

Here is another:

> does the rock think of flowers in its sleep?
> Then words and flowers are only thoughts of stone
> unconscious of the joy it thinks upon;
> and we ourselves are only the rock's words
> stammered in a dark dream of men and birds.

J. D.

Key West, March 10, 1950

Dear Arthur:

. . . I suppose I've dribbled and dripped well over a hundred pages
in the article I spoke of ["Importance, Significance and Meaning"]; it's
now down to 18 typewritten pages, largely double-spaced. As far as
novelty of statement is concerned, it consists in an attempt to show that
artefacts on the side of the part taken by environmental conditions and
arts as acquired skills on the organic side do all the work that spirits,

souls, minds, consciousnesses, cerebrums, and organisms as [ex] citatives have been called upon to do, having, of course, the advantage of being as observable as are the trees and fossils that primary inquiries deal with, while being, in addition, the means through which they are subjected to inquiry.

I've made considerable of the behavior implications of observation— as involving paying heed to, taking into account, in action as distinct from merely being aware of, or *noting* as distinct from just casual noticing.

"Mark" and "re-mark" are pretty good behavioral words.

"States" of thing seem linguistic[ly] to be static; conditions are always conditions *of* something else. If I had only tried . . . a firm terminology fifteen years or so ago, I'd be much ahead of where I am. Terms as ends, limits, active boundaries, are words that *name* something in connection with determining, deciding. But that's enough of that. I expect to get my manuscript off tomorrow for retyping.

Yours with best wishes and hoping you are much better,
John Dewey

St. Petersburg, Florida, March 12, 1950
Dear John:

. . . Ames sent me a dozen printed and mimeographed papers. Some very difficult to read, with my eyes. But I have handled most of it. He has a lot of debased psychic terminology, but every now and then blooms out with a clean factual statement, 100% our way. He likes to hide himself under such a phrase as your—fine, in its place—"transaction of living," but he proceeds to talk 99% biologically and 1% transactionally. He is going to Europe May 15 to return end of June. After which I may go there (Hanover), (taking [Solomon] Weinstock along, if he can arrange time schedules). [Horace S.] Fries, Cantril, and others will be there for a while. . . .

Best wishes, *Bentley*

Key West, Florida, March 20, 1950
Dear Arthur:

Here is what E. U. Condon said [in "Contemporary Science"]: "It is doubtful speculation, most of the philosophic absorptions of modern science. One of the rare exceptions, one who has in a significant and profound way understood and used both science and the scientific method is John Dewey. He points out clearly that the growth of rational thought process may be considered a response to the biological necessity of adaptation to the environment. Its ultimate function he says is that of 'prospective control of the conditions of the environment.'" * Then he quotes a sentence in which I said the function of intelligence was that of taking account of the way in which "more effective and more profitable relations" with environing conditions may be "established in the future," not that of "copying" them. I'm glad he referred to the biological necessity of adaptation to the biological *environment*.

I got off my *Journal* article ["Importance, Significance and Meaning"] today. . . . The idea in it is not new; but I've introduced a new angle. I tried to show how use of artefacts and the arts does all that the mind, soul, etc., and brain centers have been supposed to do, and renders their introduction superfluous—to put it mildly. I presume the reaction will be that of the critic who some years ago said I was an *anthropologist*, not a psychologist or philosopher. . . . There was one sentence in Merle Lawrence's summary [*Studies in Human Behavior*(?)] that neither Ames nor Cantril seems to have attended to, about the short-span isolations and the fact that the experiments demand recognition of long-span temporal-spatial conditions. He didn't develop it, but I was struck that he, as far as I know, is the only one of the lot who has even mentioned them. Cantril criticizes the isolations of *subjectmatter* that mark current psychological theories, but, as far as I read, he showed no recognition of their *source*. . . .†

Well, I'm getting plain discouraged—partly probably because I've had the flu bug that is going 'round. . . .

Affectionately, *John D.*

Paoli, Indiana, March 25, 1950

Dear John:

. . . His [Milton Mayeroff, "The Nature of Propositions in John Dewey's *Logic:* A Reply to Miss Brodbeck"] interior development is not so satisfactory to me—nothing is, of course, without attention to your differentiation of two forms within the abstract universal. Here is one of the cases in which there ought to have been development in *Knowing and the Known* directly on this basis into symbol. But I suppose it was impracticable to bring it out in the clear then, as it is now. I hope the chance will come later. A very small speck at a time. . . .

Best regards, *Bentley*

* The quotation begins: "Yet, it is doubtful speculation which has characterized most of the philosophic absorptions of modern science." (Eds.)

† For Cantril's later grappling with this problem, see Cantril and William K. Livingston, "The Concept of Transaction in Psychology and Neurology." (Eds.)

Dear John:

. . . The stress on "Importance" [in "Importance, Significance and Meaning"] is a stroke of verbal genius. Wish we had it in the book. Take the Peirce "concept" of 1879; insert it into a full evolutional-human-being-in-action; use the word "Importance" as dominant; then you have the best expression yet. . . .

Observation. You have a distinction between "observation" and "perception." . . . Advance from noticing to noting. O.K. and fine. But I have a small suspicion we have made "Observation" stretch over perceptional regions as well [as] elaborated [it]—probably not running down to simple perception—but "running down into," anyway. This would be only slight variation of stress. . . .

Bentley

Paoli, Indiana, April 4, 1950

Dear John:

I have just read with much interest Sidney Hook's account of your position ["The Place of John Dewey in Modern Thought"] . . . in the . . . volume on French and American philosophies [Farber, ed., *Philosophic Thought in France and the United States*]. The great scope of your development, compared with the closely limited firing range of mine, always attracts me. Mrs. Kaufmann sends it to me because of Felix Kaufmann's paper "[Basic Issues in] Logical Positivism," on which he has worked long and hard. It gives a much better formulation of Kaufmann's position than there has been before. It establishes him as firmly in a transitional position as such a position could permit anyone to be established. . . .

Best regards, *Bentley*

Key West, Florida, April 10, 1950

Dear Arthur:

I have a copy of the French-American [Philosophy] book, but I hadn't read much of it and none of Sidney's [Hook, "The Place of John Dewey in Modern Thought"]. After I got your card I looked up the passage in Hook's . . . [essay] and found it right in line with what I'm trying to say in the piece I'm now working at; I thought his statement of the three influences that have shaped my position was as good as could be made—simple and clear.

I am of two minds about the idea of sending the article ["Importance, Significance and Meaning"] where it might reach a scientific public. I don't think *Science* would take it; the *Scientific Monthly* might—by the way about the first thing I ever got published was in the old *Popular Science Monthly.*[*] What Sidney says about such influence as I've had being outside the philosophers is true. . . . On the other hand, I was educated and educated myself through philosophy. If I took the first point in Hook's summary, the *historical,* I'd have to expatiate a little on what I learned from a study of the men who have had high rank in the history of philosophy. If you call the roll, they certainly don't have to take a back seat . . . in comparison with others of their respective periods who are intellectually outstanding. More or less subconsciously, I studied them on the supposition that, irrespective of any matter of agreement or disagreement, they were struggling with some genuine *human* issue, and that if I could get hold of what the problem was, I would see something that had to be taken into account in any viable intellectual position at the present time. As I have stated the gist of my position, they were actually dealing with a human-cultural issue, but they did so *under cover;* the cover or coverlet being provided by earlier traditions of an ontological-theological nature, until in our day (the other two points in Hook's statement) the cover could be thrown off. For the last fifty or sixty years, professors of philosophy have concerned themselves almost exclusively with the cover, and so I agree with you about the hopelessness of really reaching them. At the same time I think there is a need and an opportunity for something that I would call philosophy. Philosophy as itself science is a humbug and played out. But take all the science there is, and there is a question: What is its bearing on the conduct of life—not in detail, but with reference to general lines of policy forming—using the word policy to apply to the relatively more comprehensive ends by means of which activities hang together over a period of time and a fairly wide human area. I got a letter from one of the younger men I mentioned; he is teaching teachers, not "philosophers," and he wrote: "The role of the philosopher is to take all available data, especially from science, and speculate from there, on its meaning for human life; to project as well as can be from the data. The early philosophers had very little data, and thus should have been less accurate in their speculations than is possible now. Our modern philosophers have adopted rules to which they adhere. . . . So what they produce is static since the rules are static."

For a short statement, that says about what philosophy should be; I can but hope that the present dead formalism of what passes in academic circles as philosophy is a case of its being "darkest before dawn." Maybe

[*] According to Milton Halsey Thomas, *John Dewey: A Centennial Bibliography,* Dewey's first publication was in *The Journal of Speculative Philosophy,* April, 1882, and it was not until March 1886 that "Health and Sex in Higher Education" marked his first publication in *Popular Science Monthly.* In October, 1885 he published "Education and the Health of Women" in *Science.* (Eds.)

the name can't be used—but projections that use science, but are themselves too speculative, too hypothetical, to be put to *immediate* test would seem to be rather urgently indicated as needed.

The foregoing is on general principles, not about where my piece should be published. It would be a satisfaction to me to have it appear along with yours ["Kennetic Inquiry"]. . . .

Yours, John Dewey

Paoli, Indiana, April 20, 1950

Dear John:

. . . But here is a good catch on the literature side. Maybe you know him: E[milio] A[guinaldo] Lanier, Fisk University, Nashville, Professor of English. He has been doing a huge amount of work on the early American novel. Exhibits four types of "gentlemen" who appear in about 300 novels from 1774 to 1830. Classifies them in a good "social" way. [He] has sent me about 150 pages of manuscript—not yet a written text—but outlines, materials, his own projection, etc. . . . He has been acquainted with our work to some extent, runs across *Science* articles as guide to later phases, has definite orientations with respect to Korzybski in the light of *Knowing and the Known* and to many other things. Wants to know whether he can handle such new stuff "postulationally" in our sense. He really knows what he wants to know, and I have given him [an] enthusiastic "yes."

Sidney Ratner wrote a little while back—I may have told you—that Louise Rosenblatt, his wife, [professor] at New York University ([and teacher] of literary criticism), was all excited about application of *Knowing and the Known* to literature.*

I am just mentioning these things for the good of the cause. . . .

Best wishes and regards, A. F. B.

New York, May 21, 1950

Dear Arthur:

He [Albert Einstein, in *Out of My Later Years*] has an avowed *causal* theory of instincts, crasser in many ways than those you criticized in *The Process of Government*—no argument for them—just an obvious matter-of-course matter; and, of course, he never questions "psychic" states—processes with respect to knowing. When it comes to the theory of scientific knowing, he assumes as if axiomatic that the material is the totality of "sense experiences," *science* being the attempt to connect,

---

* See L. M. Rosenblatt, "The Acid Test for Literature Teaching," "Literature: The Reader's Role," and *Literature As Exploration*, pp. 265–328. (Eds.)

unify these sense experiences in a comprehensive, unified system, thereby substituting a "rational" order for that of primary "sense experiences." Well, if I knew enough science, I have a hunch that I could show that this point of view seriously affects—or infects—his actual physical theory. It seems to me that he assumed that science has a "realistic" one-to-one correspondence with "the real world." . . .*

In a word, if my impression is in the right direction, his psychology determines his theory of science, and it is wholly a non-behavioral—indeed is an anti-behavioral—psychology. His "sense" experiences have no motor links at either end. If that can be shown, it would be a home run on the transactional scoreboard.

Yours, [*Dewey*]

[New York,] May 22, 1950

Dear Arthur:

. . . Just before we went to Florida in early January I got the Einstein volume [*Albert Einstein: Philosopher and Scientist*] in the *Library of Living Philosophers*. In Bohr's contribution ["Discussion with Einstein on Epistemological Problems in Atomic Physics"] there is the following statement (page 209 of the Einstein volume) [made upon the occasion of] an International Physical Congress in 1927: "I advocated a point of view conveniently termed 'complementarity,' suited to embrace the characteristic features of individuality of quantum phenomena, and at the same time to clarify the peculiar aspects of the observational problem in this field of experience. For this purpose it is decisive to recognize that, *however far the phenomena transcend the scope of classical physical explanation, the account of all evidence must be expressed in classical terms.* The argument is simply that by the word "experiment" we refer to a situation where we can tell others what *we have done* (my italics) and what we have learned and that, therefore, the account of the *experimental arrangement* (my italics) and of the results of the observations must be expressed in unambiguous language with suitable application of the terminology of classic physics."

It seems to me that while he doesn't say so explicitly, there is here the basic contrast between dependence upon "sense impressions and upon experimentation."

Anyway, he goes on with this recognition of the transactional property of experiment (pp. 209–10): "This crucial point . . . *implies the impossibility of any sharp separation between the behaviour of atomic ob-*

---

* For Einstein's support of Poincaré's analysis of the relation of geometry and physics to the "real world," see Einstein's "Reply to Criticisms," P. A. Schilpp, ed., *Albert Einstein: Philosopher-Scientist,* esp. pp. 676–78.

jects and the interaction with the measuring instruments which serve to define the conditions under which the phenomena appear." (All in italics.)

(Page 211): "The study of the complementary phenomena demands mutually exclusive experimental arrangements. . . . Causal description is upheld in relativity theory within any given frame of reference, but in quantum theory the uncontrollable interaction between the objects and the measuring instruments forces us to a renunciation even in this respect." * I should say it is a fair inference that while Einstein is after a continuum of "rational" order, Bohr is satisfied with the extensive space-time continuity as that is attainable at a given date in the progress of physical inquiry.†

Yours, *John D.*

Paoli, Indiana, June 2, 1950

Dear John:

. . . Your comments on Bohr will be useful to me. I have not seen his paper on Einstein in the *Einstein* volume, but I have read some of his earlier essays. I think that he has broken away from the things that hinder transactional envisionment. I wonder if Danish is a better language? . . .

With best regards, *A. F. B.*

Paoli, Indiana, June 8, 1950

Dear John:

I have read several times the prefatory pages for your "Importance, [Significance and Meaning"] paper. I do not find a thing that I would suggest to change or to add. That is, if you want to give so much space to my parallel course. The parallel seems to be there, but I do not know whether it applies so much to the work you are doing in the new paper. However, one thing is certain; we work under postulatory control; we have been getting stronger in it all the time; and our postulatory points are about as closely the same as they could be, giving a growing cosmos (postulated). I have a somewhat similar statement in the "Kennetics" paper—though I have reduced it to mention of a few dates and book titles. . . .

Again with very best wishes, *A. F. B.*

---

* The last four words of this quotation are "even in such respect." (Eds.)
† For an extended exploration of this theme, see Hugo Bedau and Paul Oppenheim, "Complementarity in Quantum Mechanics: A Logical Analysis." (Eds.)

[New York,] June 8, 1950

[To Bentley:]

Here is another sentence from Bohr, writing about the [Werner] Heisenberg "uncertainty" principle: "It is not possible to separate between what we may call the independent behavior of objects and their interactions with the measuring instruments which are necessary for every definition of a phenomenon." [Condon, "Contemporary Science"]

Condon (Bureau of Standards) . . . [said] he (Bohr) pointed out that "this is important, in the broadest sense, because it reveals the intimate relationship between the phenomenon and its environment, between the particle and the measuring instruments, between the individual and his surroundings." ["Contemporary Science"]

The last phrase comes close to recognition of transactional connection of organism-environing media—maybe that's stretching it too much. . . .

Yours, *John D.*

Philadelphia—*en route* to New York—June 23, 1950

Dear Arthur:

. . . Horace Fries of Wisconsin University is at Harvard and will be there all summer. I judge [that] Ames told him that he thought *philosophers* were the ones to profit by the [Hanover] demonstrations. Fries told him [that] the philosophic statement in line with his results already existed and showed him some things in my *Human Nature and Conduct*—which seemed to surprise Ames. . . . The trouble with Ames is his background, largely Whitehead—some James. . . .

Fries is much interested in the "flash" technique which he thinks supplements Ames's experiments. . . .

Yours as ever—and the best to you, *John Dewey*

Indianapolis, Indiana, June 24, 1950

Dear John:

"Import" is a good word to cover signification and meaning. "Importance" organizes import directly to organism; also it is easily transactional to organism-environs. It struck me here was a good twist in your paper ["Importance, Significance and Meaning"].

It is probable, however, you have already got this twist in your paper, and that's where I got it by long-range bob-up. That does not hurt. . . .

With very best regards, *Bentley*

New York, July 3, 1950

Dear John:

We had an extremely interesting time at Hanover [with Adelbert Ames, Jr., and his group]. Most of the demonstrations you have seen, but I suppose not the one of the revolving window. . . .

We can take Ames's exhibits; we can take his "postulation" that perception is prognostic (why he does not say plain "pragmatic" I do not know.) We can envelop his postulation in our *Knowing-Known* postulations. We (and he) can then lay the skeleton of interpretation of subject-matters. . . .

Very best wishes, *A. F. B.*

Paoli, Indiana, August 18, 1950

Dear John:

. . . I have a paper lying around somewhere, or at least begun, on how the Knowing-Known procedure would do for basis for most general sociological construction. But I have no idea whether it would take months or years to write it. Meantime the Vision job with Weinstock seems the best bet. The problem thrown up by the way people . . . get excited over your basis (or in some fields, mine) and then are scared to death when either of us asks them to go through in plain speech with what they pretend they are representing or reflecting is a very big one. I have it on every lot of people that blow *in re Process of Government*—and there are beginning to be a good many. A professor and his graduate student . . . took quite a little of my time a couple [of] months ago. They seemed all O.K. in a moderate way, but someone seems to have told them that You (thus involving me) totally ignored the problem of epistemology. They collapsed at the horrid revelation. I should have told them [that] both of us all our lives have done nothing but try to get a factual foundation for that puff-of-wind inquiry. But I did not. A Harvard graduate student called up from Indianapolis last week. He came down. He and his boss-professor had it all figured out that he would take *Process of Government* and build it up as it should be built. That was O.K. by me (to his probable surprise), but he knows less about everything involved than you could imagine. He wanted to explain to me, for instance, how Einstein's physics grew out of his philosophy. Well, Einstein's physics did fine when he forgot the philosophy, and can be easily harmed now by traditional ghost-worship, but this lad's idea seemed to be: first get you a philosophy, then make the world work by its aid. There has not been a man-jack that has come along who is willing to stick in talk. [Bertram M.] Gross, the executive secretary of the Council of Economic Advisors in Washington, is by far the best. He has a long account ready for the September issue of the

American Political Science Review ["Review of *The Process of Govern-ment*"]—maybe a dozen pages, and is building a book on legislation along these lines. He was the one who suggested to the Washington group [that] they ask me down. Of him I have hopes. . . .

Now all this is not for itself alone, but to hitch the Ames people up in their linguistic-experimental-operational plight. . . .

Very best regards, *Bentley*

New Alexandria, Pennsylvaina, August 27, 1950

Dear Arthur:

. . . I . . . will say (i) that your article ["Kennetic Inquiry"] rings the bell, and (ii) when published in a scientific journal, [it] should do a lot in the way of bringing home in a clear-cut way the genuine issues. . . .

What you say in your letter about the withdrawals of those who begin by agreeing when they hit the epistemological snag is depressingly true. . . .

I noted Fries' use of the word "conceptualization," but in reflecting on it I decided . . . [he] was using it in its earlier sense as a logical term, equivalent to "theoretical"—earlier in that it came before concepts were taken to be "mental" existences—standing for the work done in know-ing by theoretical subjectmatter. . . .

Yours, *John D.*

Paoli, Indiana, August 29, 1950

Dear John:

For several years I have wondered in a casual manner why nobody, either in writing or in talking has (to my knowledge) faced directly the main issue of our joint work. Since I sent you the manuscript ["Ken-netic Inquiry"] a week or so ago, this has recurred to me several times. I should not be surprised if the underlying reason that I spent so long a time with the "Kennetic" paper was that I wanted to get a statement that could not easily be evaded, even though I addressed a much more limited audience. I think this situation applies to all your main work, all the way along as well as to our late joint work. I know I have often said you were the most misunderstood writer in the world. ("Misunder-stood" is not the right word—I mean, no disputant faces you straight and clean.) Take [Albert] Hofstadter. I think him exceptionally high grade. Yet, when the argument he is making ["Concerning a Certain Deweyan Conception of Metaphysics"] does not really meet the case at all, he changes *your* views into something his argument will run against. I think he has said, and I am sure others have said, that if you do not hold the views they attack, you "ought to"—that is, your general argument *ought* to come out into the form they think they can slaughter.

I have not seen Sidney Ratner's review [of *Knowing and the Known*] in *Social Research*, and . . . I doubt if I know of any review except the one by Max Black in the *Philosophical Review*, which I have not read. . . .

With very best regards, *Bentley*

New Alexandria, Pennsylvania, August 31, 1950

Dear Arthur:

Your letter [8-18-50] raises a question of *basic* import—strategically as well as tactically, to adopt the present jargon. I have been thinking about it, but not in such a specific form as you state it. The conclusion I arrived at—on the basis of the special way I had been considering it—is that the number to whom it occurs to entertain even as a hypothesis that there are those who regard Knowings-Known as facts—as existent events—of the same order as polly-wogs, meteors, geological strata, illuminating gas, etc., . . . and to be observed and reported by the same general procedures of inquiry, are very few. That statement of itself only shifts, of course, the subjectmatter content of the question—why is there such numbness, such paralysis, in respect to entertaining the idea that supposedly intelligent persons actually do hold the position which they, from their standpoint, keep presenting? I don't think that the fact that *philosophers* have promulgated the mind-world, subject-object, self-notself so long and so systematically gives the answer; without extraneous reinforcements, they simply haven't had that much influence. In fact, they only formulated what was already influential—beginning with religion, whose theme has been the alienation of man from reality; as an intellectual principle, I don't think it would have had much influence, but as a religious matter, it was emotional and imaginative. Protestantism gave it a new lease of life when the Roman Catholic version was losing out—namely, *individualism*, which is the emotional-practical *fact* back of subjectivism as an intellectual (philosophical) position. James said "consciousness" was what was left by the disappearing soul. *The* individual was what emerged from the protest against domination by external "authority" as it affected political and economic life as well as ecclesiastic institutions.

The foregoing remarks are such sweeping generalizations [that] they sound (and look) crazy. But what is meant is that the position we take so bucks the ways of looking at the world that have infiltrated from prevailing modes of culture that the phenomena of the Ames demonstrations about perception of physical events are duplicated in the currently influential observations of (beliefs about) the order of human relations.

Upon the whole, "scientists" as a group have taken over the "assumptions" of the other cultural groups instead of using the methods they employ in their professional pursuits upon what they themselves *do* in those pursuits.

Heresy may be so extreme as not to be recognized for what it is, but be treated merely as an error to be pointed out and corrected.

Yours, *John Dewey*

[P.S.] Very competent "scientists" would be shocked at the statement that science is a specific form or mode of cultural trans-acting instead of an exclusive and hence *pure* approach to Reality or Truth or some equivalent term—doing for nature what theology used to do for super-nature.

Paoli, Indiana, September 1, 1950

Dear John:

I am very glad to have your good opinion of the "Kennetic [Inquiry]" paper. . . . I have secured endorsements of my statements about Bridgman, [Ludwig von] Bertalanffy, and Ames from each of these men respectively. . . .

Bertalanffy writes quite enthusiastically. . . . He agrees that his "open system" of organism-environment is blood brother to our "transaction." He is fully set in terms of what he calls "the inadequacy of Cartesian Dualism" to become knowing-knownish. And he is all for our scientific frame in terms of "levels of description." . . .

Best regards, *Bentley*

Pauli, Indiana, September 4, 1950

Dear John:

. . . My way of handling the question in the broader form in which you put it is on a simply descriptive basis. People get to doing more things, and using more language, and results heap up, and methods of treatment and talking freeze, and new actions accumulate, including new observations, until they crack the old frameworks and maybe bust them. Einstein produced the big bust in the physical midden. . . . Maybe, some day there will be some more busts.

Your development gives fuller description, though it involves somewhat more of a causal hitch-up than I would make.

I am not surprised at the scientists who philosophize . . . [traditionally]. . . . But what I am amused to speculate upon, without getting anywhere, is why some other types or heaps of men show so little signs of change.

Best regards, *Bentley*

Dear Arthur:

Some time, two months ago or so, I wrote a sketch of a treatment of science—kenning as related to common-sense kenning, as a foreign language is related to one's native tongue—only I didn't use the term "kenning," and the sketch didn't jell enough to have a structural outline or to be specific. It grew basically out of my earlier paper on common-sense knowing and scientific knowing as having different subjectmatters, not because that of "science," in its contrast with that of everyday observations, raised the "problem" [of] which of the two stood for or represented "reality"—a standing issue of historic epistemological discussion since the rise of modern physics—but because of the different ends-in-view served respectively by the two subjectmatters; as, for example, we drink, wash with, swim, and sail on the water of everyday, or "common-sense" knowing and not with H_2O, while H_2O enters into a system [to] which water, as entering into the uses, etc., with respect to which it, as directly or "practically" used, is wholly foreign. More specifically, it grew out of an attempt I was making to rewrite my "Importance, [Significance and Meaning"] article, and in which I felt the need of saying more about language as *the* specifier of the kind of communicative behavior involved in both common-sense and scientific knowings-knowns. But it never came *out*, partly because I had the virus attack and couldn't do any work that involved hanging things together extensively and consecutively, and partly because of my weakness in scientific subjectmatter. Well, this is to say that after careful reading of your "Kennetic [Inquiry"] paper, with special attention to what you say *re* designation in human knowledge, I have the cue I needed and lacked; not that the point hadn't been clearly and definitely made before, but somehow your restatement of it in your present paper seemed to furnish the cue that brought things together in the way I was in specific need of. There is nothing unusual in treating "science" as a foreign language, that [is] as foreign to our everyday language (since the latter is adapted to ends of uses-enjoyments), but I think it fills out, completes, the common sense–science paper ["Common Sense and Science"] on one hand, and makes a proper use of the human-behavioral-designation fact, on the other hand.

And I believe that many inquirers who are competent in their own fields of inquiry are so steeped in the notion that science is superior to everyday knowing with respect to grasp on "reality," that it blocks the road to their getting the transactional point of view.

For me personally it gives the satisfaction of a much more direct and simpler way of stating what I had labeled the "instrumental" view of science—namely the fact that scientific subjectmatter has to grow out of

638

the more direct observational way—as you specifically note in your paper, e.g., p. 13 (the connection of designating with signaled subject-matter)—and tends to work back into it through inventions and technologies—while the technological arts in turn give rise to new, more effective technical procedures in scientific inquiries.

There is also a sociological aspect that is enjoyable. "Sociological" arts—politics, economics—are now seen to be capable of uses as means of *scientific* inquiry into sociological subjectmatter: they are treated as means to certain strictly "practical" ends—the split between theory and practice which, from both sides, is the source of the lack of anything like science in specifically human subjectmatters.

There is one, and but one, suggestion I have about wording . . . the distinction between factuality and actuality. It is of course O.K. when actuality is taken—as it often is in technical inquirings—as a synonym of "reality"—but, on the other hand, idiomatically the connection of "actuality" with *acting* (with doing and making) is as close as is that of factuality, what is done or made, *facere,* and it seems a pity not [to] introduce a few words to that effect while keep[ing] a reference to the schizophrenic linguistic violation. . . .

As ever yours, John D.

New Alexandria, Pennsylvania, September 9, 1950

Dear Arthur:

. . . About the causal *versus* the descriptive on my part; in chapter XXII of my *Logic,* I say explicitly and at considerable length that scientific subjectmatter, being existential, is a matter of spatial-temporal connections and that "causation" is a *practical* matter; i.e., of the relation of means to consequences. The last paragraph, headed "Conclusion," begins: "The view that the category of causation is logical, that it is a functional means of regulating existential inquiry, not ontological, and that all existential cases that can be termed causal are 'practical,' is not a view that will receive ready acceptance. But there was a time when species and essences were also conceived to be ontological." Then the same is said of *purpose* and *simplicity.* "Nothing happened save relief of inquiry from incubi when these notions were so changed that they were understood to be directive methodological principles of inquiry—logical rather than ontological. There is no risk in predicting a similar thing will happen with the conception of causation." (p. 462) *

Considering this was written in 1937, it was not bad. The chapter as a whole is over-complicated, but for another reason. At that time vir-

* The exact quotation begins: "Nothing in science happened save relief . . ." (Eds.)

tually all who questioned the necessity of causation for scientific formulation and who said it was *empirical* followed Hume and Mill in holding it was a matter of uniform sequence—and I spent some space-time in criticizing that idea. To have made the point I made in my note to you in an adequately descriptive way would have required many volumes of historical detail. I was only pointing in their direction. What I set down was by way of reasons, of whys, not of causes.

Many thanks for the copy of Bertalanffy's ["The Theory of Open Systems in Physics and Biology"]. It is too technical for my . . . scientific background, but I get the general tenor and am very glad to have it—it gives specification to the difference between the physical and the biological, and I should suppose to the behavioral, with respect to the latter.

I've forgotten whether I wrote you how much I liked your treatment of Ames in your paper ["Kennetic Inquiry"]. I would have done better if I had stuck to the cases in which Ames came out definitely for the transactional and not emphasized the case in which he deviated. He just decided that I was adding on something that was a pet idea of my own.

As ever, John Dewey

Paoli, Indiana, October 2, 1950

Dear John:

. . . I was glad to have your comments on "factuality" and "actuality." What I had been doing was using current conventional speech for the latter, while demanding for the former a full historical status (etymology, one says). Definitely I should not behave that way. That is the *trouble;* I do too much of that sort of thing. My solution was easy. I just left the phrasing out altogether. Too many words without them; and too much vagueness all over, anyhow. . . .

I am speculating a little on asking the political scientists and administrators what is wrong with [Harry S.] Truman as specific fact. I have tried that repeatedly on men infected with the current talk-habits, but not hostile to liberal advance, and I have never yet had one significant defect pointed out to me. Personally, I like to tell people that he is the finest man I have ever observed in public office, and by all means the soundest, cleanest President since Lincoln (allowing any hearer one "favorite" such as Woodrow Wilson or Cleveland, to put in first place). In other words, I do not argue the point—just make the remark and see who whoops most. Probably my eyes are now too old to observe things in Wonderful Washington from a seat in Muddy Mid-continent. . . .

Yours, A. F. B.

Dear Arthur:

I didn't say anything yesterday *re* what you said about Truman. My opinion is certainly closer to yours than to most of the negative views the experts are putting out. I have a feeling that there is something in his frankness in admitting mistakes and in his comparative freedom from glamorizing himself that is of particular value at the present time— not that they aren't always welcome in a politician, but there is so much over-elaborated pretension now, [that] they are especially refreshing. He can sit as a representative of what we like to believe the run-of-the- mill American is, in his ability to meet . . . all kinds of conditions with- out getting too excited in the process. I've been somewhat surprised a number of times at how well he came out, but now I'm inclined to bet on him regularly.

As ever, *John D.*

[New York?] October 15, 1950

Dear Arthur:

I intended to write you at once after getting yours of the 9th to say that, viewed as a symptom, the change in your wording that was enclosed is neither a parroting of the past, nor yet a decline from it. It seems to me that from its designed standpoint, greater ease in general understanding, it marks an advance. To anyone who has read your other writings, it * is well protected by what you've said about the am- biguity of just "knowledge" because of the various things, quite dif- ferent in kind, which go by that name; it doesn't contradict what you've written about the importance of the sign-*function,* beginning with the differential bearing on behavior of changes in illumination . . . up to designation by name. If another edition of *Knowing-Known* is ever called for, it probably provides the means for making a statement which for the reader makes the whole thing somewhat easier to grasp. . . .

Yours as ever, *John D.*

Indianapolis, Indiana, November 26, 1950

Dear John:

. . . Earl [C.] Kelley on Cantril and "assumption" is O.K. with its "What's the Use?", except for the fact that the values of the Ames work are put wrong-end-up by Ames-Cantril phrasings. And like you, I con- sider it a big loss. Fries is still arguing that because Ames does not "believe" in concrete assumptions, his use of the word (which leads others to believe in the belief) is not objectionable. . . .

* "Kennetic Inquiry." (Eds.)

641

On the other hand, I thought Cantril's brief display in the *Scientific American* ["Psychology"] was very useful and not noticeably objectionable in phrasing.

Fries sent me copy of his letter to you about Einstein. How he can feel that I am too realistic in hypothesizing entities such as electrons, gets me. He is a fine fellow, and I must ask him. For twenty-five years I have stressed the transformation of the electron from a "thing" to a "position taken" for "work" in a complex situation, as my basic plank in my platform. I use it in the form "we no longer have" such purported entities in physics to bolster [my attack on] their traditional use in psychology. . . .

Best regards, *Bentley*

[Paoli, Indiana,] December 14, 1950

Dear John:

. . . I cannot see how anybody who treats a duration, as I do, as a simple observable presentation with futures included in presents, should possibly be squeamish over the entry of "intent."

It is the wording that bothers me. And this must be understood strictly for the given problem in the given area. Talk today in terms of "intent" is to bring 90% of your readers (I would guess higher) into the atmosphere of the old terminologies. The "intent" will be Mind-on-the-Job to the reader's eyes. . . .

The kind of "intent" you would develop is, judged by many a past incident, certain to be a kind with which I would not quarrel. While I would not personally start in to develop in that form, I am sure that whatever I did develop would be convertible into yours. But so far as I am concerned, the current psychological terms of philosophical derivation are out. And nobody has ever shown how vicious they are more forcibly than you have.

Yours, *Bentley*

Paoli, Indiana, December 24, 1950

Dear John:

. . . Kantor's Volume II of his *Psychology and Logic* is out. . . . It is much better (I am inclined to think I will find) than his previous work. He even recognizes you to some extent. Referring to his treatment of logical forms as "products" of "systems," he writes in a footnote: "our view probably has much in common with Dewey's emphasis of [*sic*] forms accruing to subjectmatter by inquiry, but we object to things arising from inquiry out of a vague matrix called 'subject matter.'" In a later reference he slips badly. He writes: "Even Dewey agrees that

642

while this necessity does not apply to existence it does apply to the object of thought."

However, he has one passage that may throw light on the May Brodbeck distortion of "definition" in your development * ["The New Rationalism: Dewey's Theory of Induction"]. On page 178 of the book [*Knowing and the Known*] we (that is, in this case, I) have a remark that some logicians make definition minor; others make it a throbbing heart; and that we will take the latter view ". . . at Least to the Extent That When We Exhibit the Confusions . . . We Believe We Are Exhibiting . . . a Vital Disease." † [Bentley's capitalization-emphasis.]

Quite surprisingly, Kantor says, "The view of Dewey and Bentley" [is] that they "look upon definition as the throbbing heart . . . of the whole knowledge system."

He simply did not read the text [as the authors had intended it to be read]. . . .

Best wishes . . . , Bentley

Honolulu, Hawaii, January 18, 1951

Dear Arthur:

. . . I appreciate your feeling about "autonomy." Of course, I used it (as prefixed to inquiry) to indicate denial that knowings and knowns have to be subordinated to prefixed ontological and/or epistemological considerations, and considering that this subordination has marked the whole history of philosophy in what was called logic as well as "epistemology." Here is [a] necessity for emphasis on the point when the word is abandoned.

. . . I've tried to do some writing for the last two weeks for a new edition for the Beacon Press of *Experience and Nature,* changing the title as well as subjectmatter from *Nature and Experience* [*sic*] to *Nature and Culture.* I was dumb not to have seen the need for such a shift when the old text was written. I was still hopeful that the [philosophic] word "Experience" could be redeemed by [being] returned to its idiomatic usages—which was a piece of historic folly, the hope, I mean. . . .

Yours, with regards, John Dewey

* For a critique of Brodbeck, see M. Mayeroff, "The Nature of Propositions in John Dewey's 'Logic.'" (Eds.)

† The exact quotation is: ". . . at least to the extent that when we exhibit the confusions in the current treatments of definition, we believe that we are not exhibiting a minor defect but a vital disease." (Eds.)

New York, February 9, 1951

Dear Arthur:

. . . I have just had a clean copy typed of "How, What and What For in the Social Sciences"—expanded somewhat in that the introductory part points out that the recognized natural (physical and physiological) sciences made no steady or assured progress till they abandoned concern for *whats* (essences) and *whys* (what fors, "final" causes) as fixed, necessary distinctions.

[*Dewey*]

New York, February 19, 1951

Dear Arthur:

. . . The recognized natural sciences began to progress steadily when they began to drop independent "whats" (essences) and "what fors" (final causes, teleology, etc.) and devote themselves to the "how" of a temporal order . . . there is every reason to strive for a like change in dealing with "Social" (human) subjectmatters. I hope (and believe) your suggestions have helped me to point up the article more definitely than took place in the first draft.

Yours as ever, *John D.*

[P.S.] I agree with you about the significance of the Ames movement. . . .

Honolulu, Hawaii, February 21, 1951

Dear Arthur:

. . . I don't think I ever wrote you *re* yours about my Importance, Significance, Meaning paper, as I never tried to do anything with it. But I think that there is a *subjectmatter* that needs badly to be specified and be firmed by some word as name, *Pace* what was said in our paper about names.* I believe "meaning" is the best available expression. This isn't of any immediate relevance as I am not doing anything, but in going over some accumulated papers, I found your letter. To *mean* is a good idiomatic expression—to intend—and there is a fairly wide range of subjectmatters that have to be specified as of an *order* of *intentional* and/or *intended* existence—the *discriminating* specification being that they are of what is traditionally called the *ideational*. I doubt if the latter can be *specified* without reference to the function exercised, the use performed by *intentional* behavior. . . . There are words *that relate to other words,* and in such a way that it doesn't seem fitting to say they *signify* them, and yet the reference is indispensable to specification in communication. The fact in question cannot be spe-

* "Specification." (Eds.)

644

cifically designated with reference to that which intends or means it, while the latter is loose in the void til its application is definitely stated, affirmed and discriminatingly limited. . . .

This may be looked at as a small trial balloon. It needs no answer unless you are moved by the *subject.*

Affectionately, John

Paoli, Indiana, March 10, 1951

Dear John:

I have just been re-reading your letter of the 21st, February, [1951] and also going over your paper on "Importance, Significance and Meaning." I have not been accustomed to using words meaning intention in my own line of formulation. In your paper I was struck by the dominance of the word "Importance." I read the other names into it and was pleased. But if I turn around and try to specify the differentiation between "Meaning" and "Significance," I do not get so far. I recognize that the reason I do not get far is of the kind I am always calling "linguistic" or linguistic involvement and entanglement. I—I agree—am involved in a word-habit that eliminates the stress of separations in this case. I turn back convolutions of my cortex (or whatever substitute I may possess for one) and recall the page 55 of your *Logic*—the passage I most often refer to where "reference," "relation," and "connection" are distinguished. Put "signification" for the first, "meaning" for the second, and (let us risk a stab in the dark) "wave energy" for the third; there you have me on board the boat. When, however, you stress "intention" for one phase, I want to give it a lot more consideration. Here it all depends on how heavily the intent is stressed. Looking at it in another way: the perceptions (in place of energies) might hold the connective position, specification and other designations the reference region, and symbol the relation or meaning (as between words) region. But also here: The development of symbol for me as I see it, out of the prior natural-development regions, would not fit together immediately at sight with your intention-region—or rather "stress," not "region." So a first good thing for me might be a few illustrations of the "meaning" in differentiation. . . .

Very best wishes, Bentley

Paoli, Indiana, March 18, 1951

Dear John:

One more letter . . . about "intent" as you put it up. It is not the presence of "intention" as named that to me makes the trouble. It is the high probability that the reader will take this, with individuality-orientation, as stemming creatively from the "separate person." You are as

645

much against that as I am. You have been against it longer and harder than I. I don't think what I said before made the point this way. . . .

Best regards, Bentley

Dear A. F.:

I'm glad you see some point to my use of "intention." I am not stuck . . . [to the] word, but there is a kind of down-rightness about it that seems to me to belong to *signs* as distinct from the *meaning* that belongs to *symbols*. They (signs) have a *projective* carrying capacity that belongs to them as spatial-temporal to demarcate and identify them as constituting their importance as spatial-temporal, and a capacity to de-termine other existential matters in *sequence, consequence* from those that function *as signs*. If I ever get the needed strength, I want to write on *knowing* as the way of behaving in which linguistic artifacts transact business with physical artifacts, tools, implements, apparatus, both kinds being planned for the purpose and rendering *inquiry* of necessity an *experimental transaction*. . . .

John D.

Paoli, Indiana, December 6, 1951

Dear John:

I haven't heard from you for some time.* In much the same figure of speech, however, I might say that I have not heard even from myself. There is plenty to do along the line of "percept" as opened up by various of our friends, but I just am not getting anywhere. The going is hard, and when I look over the results, they just are not there.

However, I recently received a note from Ames of Dartmouth expressing very strong appreciation for the criticism you first, and I later in expanded form, gave his terminological procedure. He says that he has now got so that all the time he senses the need of great care in appraising what his leading names stand for. Several of his associates have recently sent me papers, but I can't help much.

If you feel the need of livelier action yourself, I hope you will build it up in the way you have repeatedly done in the recent years I have known you, whenever the going got rough. As for me, my Operation-Tops at present is to try a little of the same. . . .

With the best of wishes, yours, Bentley

* Dewey celebrated his ninety-second birthday on October 20, 1951. He died on June 1, 1952. During the last year of his life his strength waned, and his correspondence seems to have suffered as a result. He continued, however, to see some friends at home and even granted a newspaper interview on his ninety-second birthday. (Eds.)

Part VIII

Dewey's Essay "Means and Consequences"

[No date on essay, but note by A. F. Bentley that he received it "1-5-50"]

MEANS AND CONSEQUENCES—*HOW, WHAT, AND WHAT FOR*

The basic postulation in the following discussion is that the heart and life blood of *intelligent* behavior consists of continued and deliberate attention to the relation of things which are viewed and treated as *means* to those which are viewed and treated as consequences, it being understood that the connection in question is thoroughly *reciprocal: that* is, consequences have to be determined on the ground of what is selected and handled as means in exactly the same sense in which the converse holds and demands constant attention if activities are to be intelligently conducted, instead of in a routine or a spasmodic way.

The expression "postulation" instead of "postulate" is deliberately used in order to make it as evident as possible that postulation is itself a case of behavioral activity and hence is an integral component of the entire behavioral process; while "postulate" is often, perhaps usually, employed in another sense, namely that of a principle laid down in advance and consequently exercising a certain degree of authoritative control over the behavior that ensues.

I do not argue the case here because this entire article is an exposition of the position just set forth. But it is fitting to point out that the distinction just made is of basic, not merely casual, import. For what is at stake or issue is nothing less than the question of whether behavior is to be viewed and treated as autonomous, and hence controlling and authoritative with respect to the whole matter of activities which in being *intelligent* are specifically *human,* or whether it, being intelligent, is introduced from some source extraneous to human behavior—whether called *soul, mind, subject, intellect,* or *brain,* making little difference in as far as it is taken to be extraneous instead of a name for properties intrinsic in behavior which is specifically human.

The bearing or import of the position just stated is probably most immediate and direct in application to that centrally important way or mode of intelligent behavior which is designated meaning, and the outcome of which is institution of the subjectmatters that are said to be the knowns, whether of everyday "practical" behavior, or of that theoretical way of behavior named "science."

Postponing, for the present, consideration of the import of this position upon what is designated knowing, I begin with the bearing of the posi-

649

tion upon the process and operations constituting *knowing* when that is systematically looked upon as a mode of behavior.

Probably the most obvious consideration is the *negative,* namely, the complete ruling out of any need to introduce or refer to considerations of terms either ontological or epistemological, or that mixture of the two which has flourished so abundantly in the post-medieval systems commonly called "modern," but which in fact are heavily loaded with a heritage from Greek–medieval systems in which *Being* as synonymous with the immutable or unchanging is the all-determining authoritative fact.

The simplest way to present the significance of the statement just made is to call attention to the place occupied and the office performed in "modern" philosophy (so-called) by matters designated by the names subject, object, mind-world (no matter whether mind is viewed in terms of sense or of "rational" intellect, *nous*). In anticipation of later discussion, it may be noted at this point that it was theoretically possible ("conceivable") to view the subjectmatters involved as discriminated from and connected with one another on the basis of the service respectively and reciprocally rendered by each in the effective promotion of cognitive, intellectual behavior—that is, *knowing.* But what took place actually and historically is that the previous bias in favor of the *immutable* was so projected into the distinction and [into] the relation of the matters termed subject and object, mind and world, that they were viewed as themselves of two contrary, immutable, ontological kinds. There are few systems and/or doctrines of the post-fifteenth century, no matter whether sensationalistically empirical or rationally noetic, whether idealistic ("spiritualistic") or "materialistic-mechanistic," that can be understood without steady attention to the fact that they are operating in terms of the mental and the material, the psychical and the physical, or more generally, the inherently subjective and inherently objective, as two independently given immutable kinds of existences; the fact, that as existences they were endowed with spatial-temporal qualifications, being of immense technical importance in contrast with the prior supra-temporal-spatial value accorded to "Being," but being negligible in import with respect to consequences entailed in making it imperative to treat "knowing" as an action-reaction taking place between two independent and opposed kinds of entitative existences—[this was] the fatal heritage of Greek–medieval ontology with respect to a theory of knowing professing to be independently "epistemological," but in fact determined in every aspect and phase by the heritage introduced by the older identification of true Being with the unchanging—the "essentially" and "by nature" immutable.

650

I come now to the specific subjects constituting the title of this article, the mode of treatment consisting, as already indicated, in regarding the *how,* the *what* (or subjectmatter), and the *why* (or what for) as interconnected, transactional distinctions which it is urgently important to institute and to observe in the conduct of behavior that is intelligent in general and that in particular constitutes the way of behaving that is knowing.

It is hardly necessary to engage in elaborate argument in behalf of the proposition that there is no intelligent human behavior which does not depend on *foresight of consequences* that are likely to ensue from the course of behavior entered upon. Without going into the matter in detail, it is pertinent to refer here to my article in this *Journal* [*of Philosophy*] on Common Sense and Scientific Knowing (as synonymous with practically and theoretically instituted knowing) in which the distinction between them is based (inclusively and exclusively) upon the *range of consequences* intentionally or designedly involved. A man crossing a street in which there is two-way traffic has to note, observe, heed what is going on with respect to the consequences of the *particular* act in which he is engaged. Installation of a system of red and green lights to direct the course of traffic generally is a technological device that could not exist apart from the much more extensive purview or survey provided by . . . scientific knowing.

What is important for the purpose of the present discussion is that while anticipated, foreseen consequences constitute, or are, the *what* of that which is done, of the behavior enacted, the way in which foresight of consequences (as the what of a given behavior) serviceably operates is by means of directing deliberate search for the specific conditions by active use of which as means the consequences that are foreseen will be attained, preferably in the most economical and effectual way; a qualification which emphasizes the point already made about the comprehensive, the inclusive, foresight that distinguishes the *scientific* way of knowing. Since the more generic the foresight, the less likely is the kind of action which will be obstructive and troublesome in forming, as well as executing, future plans which will satisfy the conditions to be met in such conduct as is intelligent, rather than merely routine, on one side, and/or casually and hastily improvised, on the other side.

The *theoretical* implications of the facts just adduced may need explicit statement. In brief, they amount to the impossibility of setting up any separation or conflict within *intelligent* behavior between its *what* and its *how.* With respect to knowing, foreseen consequences as forming its what are an integral component of the how, that is, the procedure, or method, of knowing. If this were not the case, if foresight did not accomplish a distinctive use, service, office, function of this sort, there would be no difference between it and the idle daydreaming in which consequences are anticipated on the ground of their immediate agreeableness. Separation of the *what* of a course of activity from its *how*, in the sense of the continuing sequence, consecutiveness, which is the mark of any intelligent activity, results inevitably in those absurdities which bear respectively the names of *ends-in-themselves* and *means-in-themselves*—a striking instance of giving way to the ever-present philosophical fallacy of reifying, hypostatizing that which in fact is functional.

A volume could be written upon the harm that has resulted in moral-political theory by treating things, *res*, subjectmatters which function as means and consequences, as if they were such "by nature" or in their "essential" being. The inevitable outcome, logically, is setting up some things as ends-in-themselves and other things as inherently, necessarily, means-in-themselves. Look, for instance, at the sharp division that is currently accepted as gospel truth between *moral* subjectmatters and *economic* subjectmatters. The separation is now so thoroughly established as to be regarded as virtually "self-evident." In consequence it is not noted that inquiry, knowing, in both cases is tied down in advance. Instead of being free to follow where the subjectmatters involved (that is, in question) may lead, it is *pre*-committed to reaching certain conclusions. If certain matters are in and of themselves means and only means, and other things are of necessity, by nature or essence, ends and only ends, all that remains is a dialectical development of matters already asserted to be so fixedly given "by nature" or in essence as to be completely immune to investigation. They are in effect, if not in name, sacred, protected by a taboo that is not to be brought into question under any circumstances. At the very time when the moral (i.e., the human) consequences of industrial and financial arrangements are most in need of systematic, critical scrutiny, they are brought under the cover of being necessary because of the essence of the matter, while on the other side the human, or moral, principles and standards which were fixed in situations radically other than those which now prevail are given a thoroughly factitious, artificial, authoritative prestige.*

---

* The fact previously emphasized that immutability as the inherent, necessary property of any and all subjectmatters which are "scientific" was carried over and projected into the physical and the psychological objective-subjective domains of existence, is, of course, of direct and controlling import in this matter. The "revolution" actually effected in "modern" science consisted in the substitution of two immutables for the one ontological, rational immutability of Greek–medieval science. In consequence, the significance of the scientific revolution for the theory of knowings-knowns is still the central issue in contemporary philosophical thought.

III

Discussion now takes up the *what for* or *why* in its connection with the means-consequence function. It is possible, though not of course certain, that the presence of "what" in any expression has a certain "what for" import not to be found in the expression "why." At all events, the fact of its presence may be used to suggest that in its reference and bearings it is a refined amplification of the *what* as *foreseen consequences,* and it is not consequential or of moment with respect to behavior unless it is a matter of affection, in the sense of care, concern, deliberate consideration of the "why," the purpose.

Determination of *what* is required to complete apprehension of the *function* served by the *what*. Like the *what,* the *why* is subject to reification; and all so-called "normative" theory is the result of treating the "what" or "why" as something absolute, or as "in itself," instead of in the use to which it is actually put. Whatever may be said about certain subjectmatters as subjects of mere description as over against those which are said to be normative, when one fastens attention upon *method,* it is unclear that accurate and comprehensive knowledge—that kind of knowledge termed "scientific"—has coincided with elimination of reference to essences, inherent natures, and the substitution for the latter of deliberate respect for the body of spatial-temporal factualities that are involved. Until the "normative" subjects take to heart the lesson of the history of scientific inquiry, there is no hope of making any assured advance. It would be difficult to hit upon a fact for investigation that would prove more fertile or more rewarding with respect to the theory of knowings-knowns than study of the history of astronomy, physics, physiology, geology, with regard to the role played in these fields by fixed standards, principles, as determinative and hence as authoritative.

The theory involved in the historical material is not far to seek. Every such procedure, resting upon fixed standards, amounts to an automatic foreclosure of free and hence full inquiry and critical reflection. It is a mortgage against the future.

There is no sense in examining, investigating, observing—perceptual or ideational (reflective thinking)—unless these activities result in a *more* adequate grasp of the "why" or "what" of the *res,* the affair, the subjectmatter observed, examined, investigated; unless it results in a *greater, keener* appreciation and foresight of the consequentiality of the consequences. In fine, the "why" or "what for" functions in regard to intelligent behavior—(including knowing) as a part of the "how" or procedural method that has proved to be effective because not subjected to pre-established, antecedent conditions regarded as "normative" and inherently regulative. That the principle of the autonomy of knowing as inquiry, investigation, examination, search (nor just re-search) is the very life blood of all intellectual endeavor worthy of respect is demonstrable in terms both of history and theory.

In philosophy, hypostatization of functional relations "rules the roost." Philosophers have clung the more tightly to what is alleged to be "in and by" its own nature or essence, identifying the total *raison d'etre* of philosophy with unique concern with what is such and such absolutely, and not such and such because of its mere, inferior, connection with things of "merely" spatial and temporal being. Nothing can be of greater import in this connection than the fact that the natural sciences—astronomy, physics, chemistry, biology, etc.—all began their careers with this assumption of the absolute necessity of treating their subjectmatters as thus and so by essential nature; and they have all advanced in scientific knowing-knowns in the exact measure in which this assumption was negated and consideration of the connections of events as spatial-temporal affairs was substituted therefor. By a curious kink, the actual result of this historical development in the natural sciences has not been to lead to the adoption of the same method of inquiry in the human-moral subjectmatters; rather has it led to the intensification of the alleged dualism between the "normative" and the "descriptive" and the resolute, systematic identification, on the part of the human-moral studies, with what could be termed "normative itself" and "normative in authority" because based upon alleged inherent fixities and absolutes.

Part IX

Dewey's Essay "Importance, Significance and Meaning"

[No date on essay, but it seems to have been completed 1-10-50]

IMPORTANCE, SIGNIFICANCE AND MEANING

Discussion of what the words of the above caption stand for is engaged in because of the attempt that follows to re-state in outline a theory of knowing in its connection with the known and of the known in its connection with knowing which has previously been developed in detail in various writings.* The basic postulates of the view presented are (1) that knowing, as inquiry, is [a] way or distinctive form of behavior, and (2) that like all forms of behavior [it] is *transactional* in pattern in that it is constituted by the cooperation or *working together* of activities which, *when they are distinguished,* are referred respectively to an organism in one respect and to environing conditions in another regard. For no life-activity whatever, sub-human nor human, takes place in which both forms of activity do not share, participate, behave as partners. It follows, tautologically, not as inference, that the theory of knowing as inquiry is based upon, derived from, knowings which have taken place, and which, accordingly, are observable as are the materials with which the primary knowings were concerned: a point of view [which results in] rejection *in toto* of any attempt to base the theory of Knowing and the Known upon considerations antecedent to and independent of behavior in general, and in particular of behavior in the way of looking into, examining, investigating, inspecting, scrutinizing, probing (or any one of the equivalent expressions for inquiry). Considerations which were dignified in historic philosophic systems with the names ontological and epistemological are thus specifically excluded, since they are re-

* The most recent of these writings is *Knowing and the Known* (Boston, Beacon Press, 1948), by A. F. Bentley and the present writer. The book consists of a number of articles that appeared between 1943 and 1948, the larger number of them in this *Journal [of Philosophy]*. The view presented in these articles had previously been developed in articles and books by each writer separately. On the part of Bentley may be mentioned *The Process of Government* (1908) and *Behavior, Knowledge, Fact;* the present writer had published *Logic: The Theory of Inquiry* (1938), a systematic organization of material of articles and books previously published. As the modes of approach used by the two writers were different, while points of view and conclusions were closely allied, a conjoining of efforts ensued. Since the title of the joint book differs from the more usual expression "theory of knowledge" and since this difference is indicative of the difference that exists with respect to them, looseness and ambiguity of the word *knowledge* is mentioned; pp. 47 ff; 87 ff; p. 92, p. 288, and p. 306 *n.* 2.

sorted to on the assumption that something, metaphysical or mental or a mixture of both, is necessary as a "foundation" to guarantee authenticity and validity. However, the position here taken is so thoroughgoing that it meets the claim for comprehensiveness that traditionally is the distinctive work of philosophy.

I

The immediate occasion of any instance of knowing as inquiry, according to the view to be presented in what follows, is (i) the occurrence of an event in the ongoing course of life-activity which interferes in one way or another with the ongoing course of the behavior that has been proceeding smoothly, and which in consequence (ii) deflects it in the case of *human* knowings into what may properly be termed a *reflective* channel, provided "reflective" be taken literally as standing for deliberate *going over of the conditions* of direct straightaway behavior (iii) preparatory to its resumption. In terms of more specific and also more general application to inquiry behavior, animal or human, investigating, looking into, is both intermediate and mediating in the course of life-behavior which, as such, is always sequential, consecutive, in its continuity. Beginning because of an interruption, a disturbance, an unsettlement of the life-behavior going on, its work is to discover how its ongoing course may be restored by means of (a) finding out what the matter is, and of (b) finding how the immediately sequential activity may overcome or get around the obstacle that is the occasion of the "hitch" in the specific way of behavior that is in process.

It is not possible for the writer, in the present state of theory, to ignore the fact that what has been said will seem to many persons to be altogether too common and coarse, indeed a degrading view of such an undertaking as knowing. The case of higher and finer, more complex instances of human knowing will be dealt with later; but it is pertinent to say here that when knowing is treated as inquiry, and then inquiry is treated as one way of life-behavior among other ways, it is obligatory to set out with a statement of as wide, or general, application as possible. No one who has watched pre-human animals will, I suppose, deny that animals investigate their surroundings as to conditions of how to proceed. They are watchful, wary, in the presence of danger; they are ingeniously adaptive in protecting themselves and also in conducting themselves so as to catch their prey unawares. Be it remembered that what is here said is concerned with observable behavior, not with respect to some unobserved supposititious factors, mental or whatever, and it will hardly be denied that the sniffings, the cocking of ears, the poising of the body and head, the turnings and fixations of the eyes that are present in the case of wild animals with which one is familiar are temporary deflections of ongoing behavior into an intermediate route of

658

examination of conditions about them in their bearing upon *what* to do: that is, *how* to proceed in subsequent behavior. There is nothing covert in these statements; they are not made to conceal something to be sprung later upon an unsuspecting reader, but to direct attention to facts which from the *standpoint of view* to be presented in this article constitute the comprehensive pattern of knowing as inquiry even though they be systematically ignored in many traditional theories.

II

Express consideration of human inquiry as behavior may then well begin with a highly rudimentary case. Take the case of a motorist who, arriving at a crossroads and not knowing which direction to take, pauses to look at a signboard which he has espied. The existence of two roads, only one of which takes him where he has planned to go, constitutes the interruption, interference, "hitch" that occasions deflection of immediate *straightaway* proceeding on his journey into the channel or route of *inquiry*. Seeing that the hand pointing, say, in the right-hand direction has attached to it the name of the town to which he is going, he turns and proceeds in that direction. In this simple case of knowing (and of a-known as its consequence) I can hardly imagine that anyone will deny that the looking-seeing activity is as much an integral part of the journey as is the conduct of the motorist in steering his car, nor yet that while it is a constitutent of the journey, it is a temporary deflection of ongoing behavior into what was termed an *intermediate* and *mediating* way or route of behavior. There was a "hitch"; an uncertainty; a question; questioning; the answer to the latter is manifested in and is constituted by resumption of straightaway activity.

From the standpoint of a theory that regards this as an exemplary— although extremely simple—case of inquiry, it follows (i) that pausing to look served, and was undertaken so as to serve, as a *means to a consequence*, the latter consisting of obtaining direction as to how to proceed; while (ii) the instruction, information resulting from the looking *as* inquiry was had by *using* what is seen as a *sign:* a point that may seem trivial to the point of tautology in the case of looking at a *signboard*, but which is fundamental and indispensable from the standpoint of the incident in reference to the theory of inquiry as knowing. To *perceive* in the sense of *observing* is identical, positively and negatively, with observing in the sense of paying heed to what is observed as *directive or sign* in further actions. When things seen, heard, touched, smelled, and tasted are *observed* noted, heeded, they are treated as serving a specific function or office. The office in question is that serving an end-in-*view*, or purpose which is entertained; hence, it involves a need to be *tested* by its meeting or failing to fulfill the end for the sake of which it was used as a *sign;* in consequence, a fact which involves concern for additional observation, namely, the consequences actually occurring as distinct from those wanted and held in view. In the case of a signboard at a crossroads, it would be decidedly extraordinary if its dependability *as* sign had to be tested by observing what took place in consequence of employing it as a directive in behavior. But, as will appear later, while that fact affects the *adequacy* or *completeness* of it as an exemplary or typical instance with respect to theory, it does not affect it as far as it goes.

III

Before concluding, then, from what has been said that the heart and the life-blood of human knowing is that inquiry as an intermediate and mediating way of behavior is constituted, not [*sic*] by determination of subjectmatters as, on [the] one hand, means to consequences and, on the other hand, of things as *consequences* of means used (as would be the case if our motorist had to be constantly on the look-out so as to note the results of having turned in a given direction), another, more complex instance will be introduced. The instance selected is that of a physician called in to deal with a patient. It is safe to say that the physician *perceives* many things as he comes into the sick-room that are not regarded as important in signifying, telling the directive use to be made of them, in treating the patient. But as a matter of theory it holds that he has no *sure* ground of deciding in advance just which of the things that offer themselves to sight and hearing are signs and which are not. Some of them, like some of the furnishings of the room, are heeded only as directives to his locomotion; yet it *may* turn out that the position of the bed with respect to the light and air reaching it from a window has in the given case to be treated as significant with respect to the way of treatment of the patient. But what is outstanding in this case is (1) that observations undertaken in order to find out what is the trouble, the "matter," or just what sort of a "hitch" has to be dealt with are indefinitely more numerous, varied, and continuous than in the case of the suppositious motorist. It is as if the motorist, in order to find out the direction in which to move, had to study the board for hours, use various instruments to make out just what the board said or was a sign of with respect to how to proceed; and at that, had not only to call upon a store of facts previously learned and *to be* learned by consulting books, periodicals, etc., to find out what the seen fact indicated or told as a sign, and also had to come back day after day to study it, particularly with reference to noting changes that have taken place with respect to *their* signifying capacity.

(2) This, however is only half the story and with respect to theory—although not with respect to practice—the less important half. By the

660

very terms of the case as described, the motorist does not have to investigate his destination; that is settled in advance, and his only question is *how* to get there. It may be asserted that the case is the same in the matter of the physician's inquiry; his goal is also settled in advance, being the restoration of the health of his patient. The specious nature of the assumption of identity is evident, however, when it is noted that the end of restoration is the same in the case of every physician in treatment of every patient; accordingly, it provides no directive whatever to inquiry in any particular case. As ultimate destination it is as settled in advance as is destination in the case of the motorist. Hence in one case, as in the other, it does not enter in any way into *inquiry;* in one case as in the other the *what*, the subjectmatter, of inquiry is to find out *how* to arrive at the destination settled upon. When it is accomplished, restoration of health is an *end* inquiry; it is its close, its limit; its termination. Naturally every inquiry aims at arriving where it will no longer be needed in that particular case. The end in and for *inquiry* in the case of the physician, as in every other inquiry of any degree of complexity, is that of discovery of the process of restoring health: making out this, a specific way of proceeding: a *how* to act. *Practically* speaking, when the inquiry is over, the end is the end and that suffices; *during* inquiry its end is to discover what the trouble is with a view to find out how to deal with it. Assumption that a *limit* of inquiry is identical with the end-in-view *during* inquiry is a flagrant absurdity. It assumes the work inquiry has to accomplish has already been done. *What* to do in the case of inquiries under way is all one with *how* to proceed under given conditions, in which the first, the primary office of inquiry, is to ascertain what the conditions are at a specific time and place since the latter are indispensable conditions of finding out what to do as the *sine qua non* or as in attainment of the goal or destination as a settled and ended matter.

From the standpoint of facts observed or observable, what has been said is a laboring of the obvious; not so from the standpoint of traditional and still rife theories. A mechanic doing his job knows (as does the physician engaged in his special activity) that consequences which are actually reached depend upon the means employed, so that the goal or destination to be reached operates as a factor in the work that he is doing only if, when, and as it is translated into an end *held in view* as *means* (1) of selecting conditions to serve as signs, indications, of what the trouble is to be dealt with; which is itself often an exceedingly long-continued process first of making and then of revising observations (as in the case of the diagnosis of a physician), while consequences as ends-in-view are also used as means in determining what to do. Consequences are also *in process* of development or are changing as long

661

as inquiry continues, change being as proper in their case as being final and settled is proper to an end as a destination to be reached. Observation of conditions as they are at the beginning of an inquiry and as they are at various stages of inquiry-behavior as it proceeds is a matter of determination of events in their office, use, function of *means to consequences*. This fact is so evident in the case of the physician's diagnosis that it will not be dwelt upon in that case. It must, however, be expressly acknowledged as an indispensable part of observed facts in their theoretical bearing. For they prove that treating things as means to consequences and treating proposed ends-in-view as also means to a final consequence is, as was said, the life-blood of intelligent behavior in general and of inquiry as a particular phase of intelligent behavior. As a matter of record rather than as an additional matter, it is here noted that as long as inquiry proceeds, conditions observed as signs of the matter to be dealt with as a problem which is to be solved by inquiry, and ends-in-view used as means of directing activity so as to solve the problem as it is made out, are tentative, on trial; inquiry being competent in the degree in which observations made are . . . in a use that provides *improved* means with which to operate. Whatever also is to be said or left unsaid about dogmatisms and dogmas, with respect to *inquiry;* to knowing *in process,* they are fatal. To be *bound* to a given conclusion is the exact opposite of being *required* to inquire so as to find out the means of reaching a conclusion as a decision that warrants resumption of decisive behavior.

(Page 9 missing in the ms.)

and, in the case of dog chasing rabbit, as they poise tense bodies, cock ears, turn head and eyes, sniff the air as successive integral phrases of directing an inclusive ongoing process of living. The pattern of inquiry-behavior as intermediate and mediate is the same in all these cases. In each one of them inquiry as knowing maintains the transactional qualification that is so manifest when an animal, dog or man, partakes of food. Because of the greater simplicity of pre-human animal behavior it is easier to take account of lookings and seeings, listenings and hearings, as integral constituents of continually ongoing life-activity in their case. Another advantage in paying at least passing heed to the latter is that it exhibits so definitely the intrinsic absurdity of sensationalistic empiricism with its isolation first of the sensory from the motor—to which as sensory it is subordinate—and then of the motor from the ongoing course of the particular ongoing life-activity within which it takes place and operation. The facts of the case, in reference to causation, are so outstandingly obvious in the case of dog and rabbit, hen, chick, hawk, etc., etc., that it does not seem possible that they would have escaped attention in theory had not some extraneous entity been so lodged with the view taken of human activities and affairs as to blind vision.

However, this recognition of unity of pattern with reference to inquiry as intermediate and mediating form of transactional behavior is not the end of the story. On the contrary, it renders the more urgent and acute the question of determining how the differences within the unity of pattern arise and function. The issue involved is so involved with a variety of highly complicated controversial issues, that it is fortunate that the intention of this paper is to obtain understanding of a certain theoretical point of view rather than to obtain its acceptance. The latter would demand surrender of cherished traditional doctrines; those which have recourse on one side to spirit, soul, reason, intellect, mind, consciousness, as a ready-made, independent, self-active entity; and/or on the other side have recourse to reduction, via, say, special cerebral organs, or "the organism as a whole," to terms that have been found to work with a high measure of success in physical or mayhap physiological inquiries.*
The influence of one or other of these two doctrines is still so great that it probably would be over-optimistic to anticipate widespread agreement; but a certain measure of understanding may, perhaps, be hoped for.

Observed and observable facts make it evident that all distinctively human intelligent behavior is attended with use of artefacts, appliances, implements, tools, weapons, head- and foot-gears, etc., and with use of *arts*, which (as words used as names indicate) are akin to artefacts; and which are acquired, learned under, and because of, tuition of others who in turn have derived their aptitudes from parents, instructors, etc., in a succession of events going back to the first appearance of man on earth; skills, which be it noted, would *not* exist, and would be idle if they did exist, were it not for those specific artefacts which constitute language as a human concern.

That animals communicate with one another and that their communications give *de facto* direction to subsequent behavior is too obvious to need being dwelt upon. There is no evidence, however, that the activities through which pre-humans communicate differ in kind from their acts, say, in getting and eating food. That is to say, although in some animals they are marvelously developed (e.g., the chimpanzee) there is no reason to infer they are either more or less *native*, "natural," *raw*, in the sense of being independent of intentional use of artefacts.

The facts to which attention is here called are so much a matter of

---

* To one having even a rudimentary sense of irony and who is willing to indulge it, the fact that "spiritualistic" and "materialistic" interpretations and explanations are cut from the same cloth by use of one and the same logical pattern should prove amusing.

663

course, and observation of them is so inevitable and recurrent, that it is laboring the obvious to note them just as facts. Noting them, however, in their bearing on the *theory* of human action in general and human inquiry in particular lies at the other pole. To go into detail would be to engage in writing a history of civilization. It is not only physically impossible to enter upon that task here, but if there were set forth even an extensive record of only three artefacts, the wheel, fire, and conversion of "natural" seeds into articles of cultivation, there is no way in which readers can be forced into considering the facts cited in their status of evidence for a given theory. The most that can be done is to *invite* the cooperation of others; and if doctrinal pre-commitments are too strong, the invitation will be declined—without thanks. Nevertheless, it is an indispensable part of the invitation to note that the arts—and all activities akin to arts in being intentionally undertaken and involving use of *means* (including both skills and appliances)—are what they are because both *environing* and organic partakers in behavioral transactions have undergone marked transformation from their native or natural estate. It may sound strange to say that all appliances, implements, *works* of art, from a hoe to a thermometer, from a polished flint to the radar, would be wholly useless, and would *not* be instruments of action, if sounds of the human voice and marks made on paper by human beings had not also undergone transformation into names which stand for things. But the oddity, if such there seems to be, is due to the fact that the two are so actually, existentially, intimately unified in every human intelligent act that the feeling of oddity is due to the attempt to view them in separation even in imagination. The role of magic in certain stages of human culture is evidence of how names as themselves were used as effective appliances in dealing with environing conditions in lack of the material appliances by which to obtain desired consequences.

Instead, then, of accumulating cultural facts as evidence for the view that artful transformation of environing and organic conditions in their mutually complementary partnerships suffice to explain what is distinctive of human behavior, I shall point out how that is so, from the side of theory. Take the case of as simple an appliance as the hoe and an art as simple as that of the rudest gardener who has skill in using the hoe as means in consequences in cultivation of plants for food. To one who has never seen or heard of the use to which the hoe is put, the end it serves, and of the consequences following upon its use as means to consequent events, a hoe may be *perceived* as a curiously shaped thing—just as many adults have *perceived* polished stones without having had a sense of the part they have played in some age of culture. If curiosity is aroused and is satisfied as to why the thing seen or touched has the peculiar conformation it presents to view, then perception becomes *observation;* mere noticing becomes *noting.* An event in the way of specifically human behavior has come into existence. It is not just something to which pre-human animals are indifferent, but that attention, heeding, involves, brings with it, an end as a consequence *in-view.* Its being itself held in view, or heeded, as *means* for bringing something wanted into existence is all one with having the latter in view as a directive in subsequent proceedings. *De facto* processes become intentional proceedings, as *de facto* successions and subsequents are held in view. The hoe is a sign, an index, of what is still future in fact, but which *as* held *in view operates* in the present to bring future events, which would not otherwise take place, into existence.

It may not accord with customary linguistic usage to say that whatever is observed as a means-to-consequence tells something; conveys information; gives advice; operates as a warning as much as if a human stood on guard to keep others out of threatening danger. Of course the art of speech makes possible a vast extension of what the hoe has to say for itself. But this extension, say, into the habits and traditions of remote early stages of culture, could not take place were it not first for a physical grasp of a hoe as a tool in attaining an end in view, and when so used were it not followed by that apprehension which is capable of indefinitely expanded grasp, and hence of things future and past, far beyond the reach of sense-perception.

For foresight has developed, no one knows how slowly or in what roundabout ways, into that systematic intentional foresight that bears the name planning; and *planned* appliances and skills [have] indefinitely extended the range or scope of schemes of activity that look ahead into the future, and that can be carried into effect only [through] reorganization of past events. Wisdom as prudence could hardly have come into existence without a store of things to care for, which is itself, as *store,* a tie of the past to present and future. Only in recent periods of human history have there been in existence means for planning human arrangements on a large scale; that is, with respect to consequences distant in space and remote in time. Even so, we have as yet acquired so little wisdom with respect to use of the terrifically powerful new skills and new mechanical appliances suddenly and without preparation put at our disposal, that the events which result, with *physical* inevitability, from the machinery are sub-sequential, not *con*sequential; of a physical rather than of a human order. Human beings *operate,* run, the machines, but they do not *use* them. The difference between operating and using is no merely verbal matter of the kind with which what is now boomed as semantics is occupied. It involves nothing less than a problem of change in personal and institutional behavior so basic and comprehensive that it may include even the future physical existence of mankind. To operate is possible on the ground of existent habits and traditions—personal and institutional. To *use* is possible—as the entire previous discussion indicates—only on the basis of direction by ends-*in-view* systematically arrived at and framed by means of consideration of means available.

There have been periods in human history when operation of available resources on the ground of habit and precedent was reasonably pertinent. That time is no more. For the habits and precedents which now operate were developed and justified under conditions that have little in common with those which now determine what follows; what is physically sub-sequent but which one can hardly be pessimistic enough to believe are consequences of deliberate and matured intention.

The intrinsic difficulties in the way of framing ends-in-view which would work in the direction of *use* of the mechanical appliances and skills that have developed in a state of historical absentmindedness are enormous. But they are artificially reinforced and exacerbated by systematic propagation of the doctrine that "nature" suffices to do what should be done. That doctrine was outgrown ever since the day when men with adequate wit took account of how increasingly dependent is man upon works of art and the skilled workings of art which transform nature for human use and enjoyment. With the advent of world-wide operation of mechanical appliances and skills for *use* of which men were virtually completely unprepared, and the *sub*sequential events of which penetrate every remotest nook and corner of life, it is not possible to find an adjective that does justice to the enormity of the assumption that is. There is, however, no intimation in what is said that development of ends-in-view and of the kind of planning that may ensure use as distinct from operation is an easy or simple problem. It is rather credible that it will take centuries to accomplish its solution; and that it will be the main pre-occupation of mankind for long and difficult ages to come. But it is at least relevant to note that systematic acknowledgment in philosophy of the role of artefacts and arts in specifically human activity, with corresponding elimination of all the unrealities that have been depended upon to do the work that they [artefacts and arts] actually accomplish, may be the means by which philosophy would recover a position of esteem and respect.

IV

It is time, perhaps more than time, to be explicit in respect to what the words name that are used in the title of this article. It should not, however, come as a surprise to one who has followed the course of the foregoing discussion to be told that, according to the view herein presented, the distinguishing and identifying mark of human intelligently conducted activity in every one of its many varieties, knowing included, is the demand made in it and upon it, with respect to its measure as *intelligently* managed, to consider, weigh, estimate, judge or pass upon, the *importance* of what is presented, suggested, in any way entertained and held in view with how to proceed when difficulties and obstacles are incurred. According to this view, importance is the generic term; significance and meanings are the specific ways in which the issue of importance has to be dealt [with]; there being species because all behavior is transactional so that importance as a concern of knowing is twofold. It has to be determined with respect to both the *environing* and the *organic* ways of responsive, adaptive, behavior that enter into every mode of behavior.

Both of the partaking constituents of behavior have *de facto* importance; they *bear* decisively upon the activity that follows and is subsequent. Quite literally they import the following activity; that which succeeds in the sense of being successive in time, whether or not it succeeds when viewed as a mode of life-behavior. Because of the foresight and intention, that are made possible through artful products and artfully acquired skills, human beings anticipate what is to come; the *sub*sequent then becomes a consequence *to be* achieved, reached, as such it is an end-*in-view*. As a further result, importance of environing conditions and organic ways of treating them are inquired into: investigated, examined, weighed, judged in advance of being put to actual overt use in bringing about events which in any case *follow* activity engaged in. Until things are seen to have a bearing upon the consequences of activities engaged in, they may be *perceived;* they are seen, touched, or heard. It is impossible for human living creatures to avoid seeing, hearing, touching a great variety of matters to which they are indifferent until they have a reason for whether they may not be either helpful or harmful in respect to what is done. A theoretical statement has *also* to note that importance is of two distinguishable, but inseparable co-working and reciprocally complementary ways because life-behavior is transactional. When a transaction is intelligently conducted, and is intentional and deliberate, environing conditions and organic modes of responsive treatment have each of them to be weighed with respect to their importance; that is, with respect to the consequences which are to end as termination quite as much as environing conditions that are employed *as* means.

Since, as previous discussion should have made clear, environing conditions are weighed and estimated as *signs,* indices, of how to proceed, *significance* is beyond peradventure a fit or suitable word to name their distinctive mode of importance—though of course there is nothing of pre-established harmony in its use. The suitability of *meaning* as name for the importance of the contribution made by the organic partner—especially with respect to words as names—is from the standpoint of current philosophical terminology a highly questionable matter. By setting up the logical as a kind of existence which is neither physical nor mental nor yet a functional service of behavior as inquiry, [a] "domain" or realm of "essences" has been created; *meaning* has in philosophical usage become neither fowl, flesh, nor good red herring. Only one who has familiarity with the literature of the subject can even begin to be aware of how confusing, obfuscating, and boring in its multiplicity of elaborations the word "meanings" has become. But when one has recourse to the idiomatic usage of meaning: *to mean* is to intend, the suitability of *meaning* to name . . . artfully skilled ways of organized action is as evident of *significance* as [is that] name for the complementary way of being important.

Bibliographical Appendix

Adams, George P., and William P. Montague, eds., *Contemporary American Philosophy: Personal Statements*, 2 vols. (New York, 1930).

Aiken, Conrad, *Time in the Rock* (New York, 1936).

Albrecht, William A., "Discrimination in Food Selection by Animals," *Scientific Monthly*, LX (May, 1945), 347–352.

Aldrich, Virgil C., "What We See With," *Journal of Philosophy*, XXXV (May 12, 1938), 253–263.

Allen, J. H., and J. B. Greenough, *New Latin Grammar* (Boston, 1884).

Ames, Adelbert, Jr., *The Morning Notes of Adelbert Ames, Jr.*, including a Correspondence with John Dewey, Hadley Cantril, ed. (New Brunswick, 1960).

Ayres, Clarence E., *The Theory of Economic Progress* (Chapel Hill, 1944).

——, "The Ordeal of the Social Sciences," *Southwestern Social Science Quarterly*, XXV (March, 1945), 247–257.

Baldwin, James Mark, ed., *Dictionary of Philosophy and Psychology*, Vols. I, II (New York, 1901–1902).

Balz, A. G. A., "A Letter to Mr. Dewey concerning John Dewey's Doctrine of Possibility," *Journal of Philosophy*, XLVI (May 26, 1949), 313–329.

——, "Matter and Scientific Efficiency I, II," *Journal of Philosophy*, XLI (Nov. 23, Dec. 7, 1944), 645–664, 673–685.

Baron, Salo W., *et al.*, eds., *Freedom and Reason* (Glencoe, 1951).

Bartley, S. H., *Vision* (Toronto, 1941).

Beck, Guido, "Mathematical Formalism and the Physical Picture," *Philosophy of Science*, XII (July, 1945), 174–178.

Bedau, Hugo, and Paul Oppenheim, "Complementarity in Quantum Mechanics: A Logical Analysis," *Synthese*, XIII (Sept., 1961), 201–232.

Bentley, Arthur F., *Behavior, Knowledge, Fact* (Bloomington, 1935).

——, *Inquiry into Inquiries*, Sidney Ratner, ed. (Boston, 1954).

——, and John Dewey, *Knowing and the Known* (Boston, 1949).

——, *Linguistic Analysis of Mathematics* (Bloomington, 1932).

——, "Makers, Users, Masters," unpublished; ms. at Indiana University Library.

——, *The Process of Government* (Chicago, 1908).

——, *Relativity in Man and Society* (New York, 1926).

——, "An Aid to Puzzled Critics," Sidney Ratner, ed. *Inquiry into Inquiries* (Boston, 1954), pp. 320–324.

671

Bentley, Arthur F., "As Through a Glass Darkly," *Journal of Philosophy*, XXXIX (July 30, 1942), 432–439.

———, "The Concept," unpublished; ms. at Indiana University Library.

———, with John Dewey, "Concerning a Vocabulary for Inquiry into Knowledge," *Journal of Philosophy*, XLIV (July 31, 1947), 421–434; reprinted in *Knowing and the Known* (Boston, 1949) as "A Trial Group of Names," pp. 287–306.

———, "The Data of Sociology Examined with Respect to Time and Space," unpublished; ms. at Indiana University Library.

———, "Decrassifying Dewey," *Philosophy of Science*, VIII (April, 1941), 147–156.

———, with John Dewey, "Definition," *Journal of Philosophy*, XLIV (May 22, 1947), 281–306; reprinted in *Knowing and the Known* (Boston, 1949) as "The Case of Definition," pp. 170–204.

———, "Dewey's Development," printed in this volume for the first time.

———, "Dewey's Logic Compactly Presented," printed in this volume for the first time.

———, "The Factual Space and Time of Behavior," *Journal of Philosophy*, XXXVIII (Aug. 28, 1941), 477–485; reprinted in Sidney Ratner, ed., *Inquiry into Inquiries* (Boston, 1954), pp. 214–222.

———, "The Human Skin: Philosophy's Last Line of Defense," *Philosophy of Science*, VIII (Jan., 1941), 1–19; reprinted in Sidney Ratner, ed., *Inquiry into Inquiries* (Boston, 1954), pp. 195–211.

———, " 'Individual' and 'Social' in Recent American Studies," unpublished; ms. at Indiana University Library.

———, "L'individuel et le social: les termes et les faits," *Revue internationale de sociologie*, XXXVI (May–June, 1929), 243–270.

———, with John Dewey, "Interaction and Transaction," *Journal of Philosophy*, XLIII (Sept. 12, 1946), 505–517; reprinted in *Knowing and the Known* (Boston, 1949), pp. 103–118.

———, "The Jamesian Datum," *Journal of Psychology*, XVI (1943), 35–79; reprinted in Sidney Ratner, ed., *Inquiry into Inquiries* (Boston, 1954), pp. 230–267.

———, "Kennetic Inquiry," *Science*, CXII (Dec. 29, 1950), 775–783; reprinted in Sidney Ratner, ed., *Inquiry into Inquiries* (Boston, 1954), pp. 337–354.

———, "Logic and Logical Behavior," Sidney Ratner, ed., *Inquiry into Inquiries* (Boston, 1954), pp. 286–319.

———, "Logicians' Underlying Postulations," *Philosophy of Science*, XIII (Jan., 1946), 3–19; reprinted in *Knowing and the Known* (Boston, 1949) as "Logic in an Age of Science," pp. 205–232.

———, "Memoranda on a Program of Research into Language," Sidney Ratner, ed., *Inquiry into Inquiries* (Boston, 1954), pp. 223–229.

Bentley, Arthur F., "The New 'Semiotic,' " *Philosophy and Phenomenological Research*, VIII (Sept., 1947), 107–131; reprinted in *Knowing and the Known* (Boston, 1949) as "A Confused 'Semiotic,' " pp. 233–269.

————, "New Ways and Old to Talk about Men," *The Sociological Review* (London), XXVI (Oct., 1929), 300–314; reprinted in Sidney Ratner, ed., *Inquiry into Inquiries* (Boston, 1954), pp. 36–52.

————, "Observable Behaviors," *Psychological Review*, XLVII (May, 1940), 230–253; reprinted in Sidney Ratner, ed., *Inquiry into Inquiries* (Boston, 1954), pp. 175–194.

————, "On a Certain Vagueness in Logic: I, II," *Journal of Philosophy*, XLII (Jan. 4, 18, 1945), 6–27, 39–51; reprinted in *Knowing and the Known* (Boston, 1949) as "Vagueness in Logic," pp. 3–46.

————, with John Dewey, "Postulations," *Journal of Philosophy*, XLII (Nov. 22, 1945), 645–662; reprinted in *Knowing and the Known* (Boston, 1949), pp. 79–102.

————, with John Dewey, "A Search for Firm Names," *Journal of Philosophy*, XLII (Jan. 4, 1945), 5–6; reprinted in *Knowing and the Known* (Boston, 1949) as "Introduction: A Search for Firm Names," pp. xi–xiii.

————, "Situational vs. Psychological Theories of Behavior," *Journal of Philosophy*, XXXVI (March 30, June 8, July 20, 1939), 169–181, 309–323, 405–413; reprinted in Sidney Ratner, ed., *Inquiry into Inquiries* (Boston, 1954), pp. 141–174.

————, "Sociology and Mathematics I and II," *The Sociological Review*, XXIII (July, Oct., 1931), 85–107, 149–172; reprinted in Sidney Ratner, ed., *Inquiry into Inquiries* (Boston, 1954), pp. 53–100.

————, "Space, Time, Environment and Society," unpublished; ms. at Indiana University Library.

————, with John Dewey, "Specification," *Journal of Philosophy*, XLIII (Nov. 21, 1946), 645–663; reprinted in *Knowing and the Known* (Boston, 1949), pp. 144–169.

————, "Subjects and Objects," unpublished; ms. at Indiana University Library.

————, with John Dewey, "A Terminology for Knowings and Knowns," *Journal of Philosophy*, XLII (April 26, 1945), 225–247; reprinted in *Knowing and the Known* (Boston, 1949) as "The Terminological Problem," pp. 47–78.

————, "Time and the Environment in Recent Sociology," unpublished; ms. at Indiana University Library.

————, with John Dewey, "Transactions as Known and Named," *Journal of Philosophy*, XLIII (Sept. 26, 1946), 533–551; reprinted in *Knowing and the Known* (Boston, 1949), pp. 119–143.

————, "What is Logic?" published as Part VII of "Logic and Logical Behavior," Sidney Ratner, ed., *Inquiry into Inquiries* (Boston, 1954), pp. 286–319.

Bernstein, Richard J., ed., *John Dewey on Experience, Nature, and Freedom* (New York, 1960).

Bertalanffy, Ludwig von, "The Theory of Open Systems in Physics and Biology," *Science*, CXI (Jan. 13, 1950), 23–29.

Bidney, David, "On the Philosophy of Culture in the Social Sciences," *Journal of Philosophy*, XXXIX (Aug. 13, 1942), 449–457.

Black, Max, "Review of Knowing and the Known," *Philosophical Review*, LIX (April, 1950), 269–270.

Bloomfield, Leonard, *Linguistic Aspects of Science, International Encyclopedia of Unified Science*, Vol. I, *Foundations of the Unity of Science*, No. 4 (Chicago, 1939).

Bohr, Niels, "Discussion with Einstein on Epistemological Problems in Atomic Physics," in Paul A. Schilpp, ed. *Albert Einstein: Philosopher-Scientist* (Evanston, 1949), pp. 199–242.

Born, Max, "Einstein's Statistical Theories," in Paul A. Schilpp, ed., *Albert Einstein: Philosopher-Scientist* (Evanston, 1949), pp. 161–178.

Boyer, Carl B., "Quantitative Science without Measurement," *Scientific Monthly*, LX (May, 1945), 358–364.

Bridgman, Percy W., *The Logic of Modern Physics* (New York, 1927).

———, *The Nature of Physical Theory* (Princeton, 1936).

———, "Rejoinders and Second Thoughts," *Psychological Review*, LII (Sept., 1945), 281–284.

Brodbeck, May, "The New Rationalism: Dewey's Theory of Induction," *Journal of Philosophy*, XLVI (Nov. 24, 1949), 780–791.

Brotherston, Bruce W., "The Genius of Pragmatic Empiricism," *Journal of Philosophy*, XL (Jan. 7, 21, 1943), 14–21, 29–39.

Burks, Arthur W., ed., *Collected Papers of Charles Sanders Peirce*, Vols. VII, VIII (Cambridge, 1958).

Cameron, Norman A., *The Psychology of Behavior Disorders—A Biosocial Interpretation* (Boston, 1947).

Cannon, Walter B., *The Wisdom of the Body* (New York, 1932).

Cantril, Hadley, and William K. Livingston, "The Concept of Transaction in Psychology and Neurology," *Journal of Individual Psychology*, 19 (May, 1963), 3–16.

Cantril, Hadley, ed., *The Morning Notes of Adelbert Ames, Jr.*, including a Correspondence with John Dewey (New Brunswick, 1960).

———, "Psychology," *Scientific American*, CLXXXIII (Sept., 1950), 79–82, 84.

Cantril, Hadley, *et al.*, "Psychology and Scientific Research," *Science*, CX (Nov. 4, 11, 18, 1949), 461–464, 491–497, 517–522.

Carnap, Rudolf, *Introduction to Semantics* (Cambridge, 1942).

674

Cassirer, Ernst, *An Essay on Man* (New Haven, 1944).

——, "Le langage et la construction du monde des objets," *Journal de psychologie*, XXX (Jan.–April, 1933), 18–44.

Century Dictionary and Cyclopedia (Rev. and enl. ed.), 12 vols., William Dwight Whitney and Benjamin E. Smith, eds. (New York, 1911).

Chevigny, Hector, "My Eyes Have a Cold Nose," *Reader's Digest*, XLV (Oct., 1944), 46–50.

Church, Alonzo, "Definition," in Dagobert D. Runes, ed., *The Dictionary of Philosophy* (New York, 1942), pp. 74–75.

——, "Review of Four Papers by John Dewey and Arthur F. Bentley," *The Journal of Symbolic Logic*, X (Dec., 1945), 132–133.

Churchman, C. W., "Probability Theory," *Philosophy of Science*, XII (July, 1945), 147–173.

——, and T. A. Cowan, "A Discussion of Dewey and Bentley's 'Postulations,'" *Journal of Philosophy*, XLIII (April 11, 1946), 217–219.

Cohen, Morris R., *A Preface to Logic* (New York, 1944).

——, and Ernest Nagel, *An Introduction to Logic and Scientific Method* (New York, 1934).

Cohen, Morris R., "The Faith of a Logician," in George P. Adams and William P. Montague, eds., *Contemporary American Philosophy: Personal Statements* (New York, 1930), I, 221–248.

——, "Some Difficulties in Dewey's Anthropocentric Naturalism," *Philosophical Review*, XLIX (March, 1940), 196–228.

Columbia University, His Colleagues at, *Essays Philosophical and Psychological in Honor of William James* (New York, 1908).

——, Department of Philosophy, ed., *Studies in the History of Ideas*, Vol. II (New York, 1925).

Condon, E. U., "Contemporary Science," *New Republic*, CXXII (Feb. 13, 1950), 11–15.

Cunningham, G. W., "On the Linguistic Meaning-Situation," *Philosophy and Phenomenological Research*, IV (Dec., 1943), 251–266.

Darwin, Charles, *The Expression of the Emotions in Man and Animals* (London, 1873).

——, *Origin of Species* (London, 1859).

Dennes, William R., "The Categories of Naturalism," in Yervant H. Krikorian, ed., *Naturalism and the Human Spirit* (New York, 1944), pp. 270–294.

Descartes, René, *La Dioptrique* (Leyden, 1637).

Dewey, John, *Art as Experience* (New York, 1934).

——, *Characters and Events*, 2 vols., Joseph Ratner, ed. (New York, 1929).

——, *Democracy and Education* (New York, 1916).

——, *Essays in Experimental Logic* (Chicago, 1916).

Dewey, John, *Experience and Nature* (Chicago, 1925; New York, 1929).

———, *How We Think*, 1st and rev. eds. (Boston, 1910, 1933).

———, *Human Nature and Conduct* (New York, 1922).

———, *Impressions of Soviet Russia* (New York, 1929).

———, and Arthur F. Bentley, *Knowing and the Known* (Boston, 1949).

———, *Logic: The Theory of Inquiry* (New York, 1938).

———, *Logical Conditions of a Scientific Treatment of Morality* (Chicago, 1903); reprinted in *Problems of Men* (New York, 1946), pp. 211–249.

———, *Philosophy and Civilization* (New York, 1931).

———, *Problems of Men* (New York, 1946).

———, *The Public and Its Problems* (New York, 1927; Chicago, 1946).

———, *The Quest for Certainty* (New York, 1929).

———, with the Cooperation of the Members and Fellows of the Department of Philosophy [of the University of Chicago], *Studies in Logical Theory* (Chicago, 1903).

———, *Theory of Valuation, International Encyclopedia of Unified Science*, Vol. II, *Foundations of the Unity of Science*, No. 4 (Chicago, 1939).

———, "The Applicability of Logic to Existence," *Journal of Philosophy*, XXVII (March 27, 1930), 174–179.

———, "By Nature and by Art," *Journal of Philosophy*, XLI (May 25, 1944), 281–292; reprinted in *Problems of Men* (New York, 1946), pp. 286–300.

———, "Common Sense and Science," *Journal of Philosophy*, XLV (April 8, 1948), 197–208; reprinted in *Knowing and the Known* (Boston, 1949), pp. 270–286.

———, "Communists as Teachers," a letter to the editor of *The New York Times*, June 21, 1949.

———, with Arthur F. Bentley, "Concerning a Vocabulary for Inquiry into Knowledge," *Journal of Philosophy*, XLIV (July 31, 1947), 421–434; reprinted in *Knowing and the Known* (Boston, 1949) as "A Trial Group of Names," pp. 287–306.

———, "Concerning Signs," unpublished.

———, "Conduct and Experience," in Carl Murchison, ed., *Psychologies of 1930* (Worcester, 1930), pp. 409–422; reprinted in *Philosophy and Civilization* (New York, 1931), pp. 249–270, as "Conduct and Experiences in Psychology."

———, "Context and Thought," *University of California Publications in Philosophy*, XII (1931), 203–224; reprinted in Richard J. Bernstein, ed., *John Dewey on Experience, Nature, and Freedom* (New York, 1960), pp. 88–110; also published separately.

———, "The Control of Ideas by Facts," *Journal of Philosophy*, IV (April

11, May 9, June 6, 1907), 197–203, 253–259, 309–319; reprinted in *Essays in Experimental Logic* (Chicago, 1916), pp. 230–249.

Dewey, John, with Arthur F. Bentley, "Definition," *Journal of Philosophy*, XLIV (May 22, 1947), 281–306; reprinted in *Knowing and the Known* (Boston, 1949) as "The Case of Definition," pp. 170–204.

———, "The Development of American Pragmatism" in *Studies in the History of Ideas*, II, Columbia University, Department of Philosophy, ed. (New York, 1925), 353–377; reprinted in *Philosophy and Civilization* (New York, 1931), pp. 13–35, and in Dagobert D. Runes, ed., *Twentieth Century Philosophy* (New York, 1943), pp. 451–468.

———, "Does Reality Possess Practical Character?" in *Essays, Philosophical and Psychological, in Honor of William James*, by his Colleagues at Columbia University (New York, 1908), pp. 53–80; reprinted in *Philosophy and Civilization* (New York, 1931) as "The Practical Character of Reality," pp. 36–55.

———, "Education and the Health of Women," *Science*, VI (Oct. 16, 1885), 341–342.

———, "Ethical Subject-Matter and Language," *Journal of Philosophy*, XLII (Dec. 20, 1945), 701–712.

———, "Further as to Valuation as Judgment," *Journal of Philosophy*, XL (Sept. 30, 1943), 543–552; reprinted in *Problems of Men* (New York, 1946), pp. 261–272.

———, "Health and Sex in Higher Education," *Popular Science Monthly*, XXVIII (March, 1886), 606–614.

———, "How Is Mind to Be Known?" *Journal of Philosophy*, XXXIX (Jan. 15, 1942), 29–35; reprinted in *Problems of Men* (New York, 1946), pp. 301–308.

———, "How, What and What For in the Social Sciences." Ms. apparently the basis for the essay, "Means and Consequences," printed in this volume for the first time.

———, "Importance, Significance and Meaning," published for the first time in this volume.

———, "Impressions of Soviet Russia," *New Republic*, LVI (Nov. 14, 1928), 343–344; LVII (Nov. 21, 28, Dec. 5, 12, 19, 1928), 11–14, 38–42, 64–67, 91–94, 134–137; reprinted in *Impressions of Soviet Russia* (New York, 1929), pp. 3–133, and *Characters and Events* I (New York, 1929), pp. 378–431.

———, "Inquiry and Indeterminateness of Situations," *Journal of Philosophy*, XXXIX (May 21, 1942), 290–296; reprinted in *Problems of Men* (New York, 1946), pp. 322–330.

———, with Arthur F. Bentley, "Interaction and Transaction," *Journal of Philosophy*, XLIII (Sept. 12, 1946), 505–517; reprinted in *Knowing and the Known* (Boston, 1949), pp. 103–118.

Dewey, John, "Introduction," in Myrtle B. McGraw, *Growth* (New York, 1935), pp. ix–xiii.

———, "Knowledge and Speech Reaction," *Journal of Philosophy*, XIX (Oct. 12, 1922), 561–570.

———, "The Meaning of a Change," a letter to the editors of *Fortune*, December, 1946.

———, "Meaning and Existence," *Journal of Philosophy*, XXV (June 21, 1928), 345–353.

———, "Means and Consequences—*How, What,* and *What For*," published for the first time in this volume.

———, "The Metaphysical Assumptions of Materialism," *Journal of Speculative Philosophy*, XVI (April, 1882), 208–213.

———, "The Naturalistic Theory of Perception by the Senses," *Journal of Philosophy*, XXII (Oct. 22, 1925), 596–605; reprinted in *Philosophy and Civilization* (New York, 1931) as "A Naturalistic Theory of Sense Perception," pp. 188–201.

———, "Nature in Experience," *Philosophical Review*, XLIX (March, 1940), 244–258; reprinted in *Problems of Men* (New York, 1946), pp. 193–207.

———, "The Objectivism-Subjectivism of Modern Philosophy," *Journal of Philosophy*, XXXVIII (Sept. 25, 1941), 533–542; reprinted in *Problems of Men* (New York, 1946), pp. 309–321.

———, "Peirce's Theory of Linguistic Signs, Thought, and Meaning," *Journal of Philosophy*, XLIII (Feb. 14, 1946), 85–95.

———, "Persons and Things," unpublished.

———, "A Philosophy of Scientific Method," *New Republic*, LXVI (April 29, 1931), 306–307.

———, "The Philosophy of Whitehead," in Paul A. Schilpp, ed., *The Philosophy of Alfred North Whitehead* (Evanston, 1941), pp. 641–661.

——— with Arthur F. Bentley, "Postulations," *Journal of Philosophy*, XLII (Nov. 22, 1945), 645–662; reprinted in *Knowing and the Known* (Boston, 1949), pp. 79–102.

———, "Prefatory Remarks," in George Herbert Mead, *The Philosophy of the Present* (Chicago, 1932), pp. xxxvi–xl.

———, "Propositions, Warranted Assertibility, and Truth," *Journal of Philosophy*, XXXVIII (March 27, 1941), 169–186; reprinted in *Problems of Men* (New York, 1946), pp. 331–353.

———, "The Reflex Arc Concept in Psychology," *Psychological Review*, III (July, 1896), 357–370; reprinted in *Philosophy and Civilization* (New York, 1931) as "The Unit of Behavior," pp. 233–248.

———, "Reply to A. G. A. Balz's 'A Letter to Mr. Dewey . . . ,'" *Journal of Philosophy*, XLVI (May 26, 1949), 329–342; reprinted in *Know-*

ing and the Known (Boston, 1949) as "Appendix. A Letter from John Dewey," pp. 313–329.

Dewey, John, "Review of A. N. Whitehead, *Process and Reality*," New York *Sun,* Oct. 26, 1929.

———, with Arthur F. Bentley, "A Search for Firm Names," *Journal of Philosophy,* XLII (Jan. 4, 1945), 5–6; reprinted in *Knowing and the Known* (Boston, 1949) as "Introduction: A Search for Firm Names," pp. xi–xiii.

———, "Some Questions about Value," *Journal of Philosophy,* XLI (Aug. 17, 1944), 449–455; reprinted in *Problems of Men* (New York, 1946), pp. 273–281.

———, with Arthur F. Bentley, "Specification," *Journal of Philosophy,* XLIII (Nov. 21, 1946), 645–663; reprinted in *Knowing and the Known* (Boston, 1949), pp. 144–169.

———, "The Sphere of Application of the Excluded Middle," *Journal of Philosophy,* XXVI (Dec. 19, 1929), 701–705.

———, with Arthur F. Bentley, "A Terminology for Knowings and Knowns," *Journal of Philosophy,* XLII (April 26, 1945), 225–247; reprinted in *Knowing and the Known* (Boston, 1949) as "The Terminological Problem," pp. 47–78.

———, "Time and Individuality," in *Time and Its Mysteries,* Series II (New York, 1940), pp. 85–109; reprinted in Richard J. Bernstein, ed., *John Dewey on Experience, Nature, and Freedom* (New York, 1960), pp. 224–43.

———, with Arthur F. Bentley, "Transactions as Known and Named," *Journal of Philosophy,* XLIII (Sept. 26, 1946), 533–551; reprinted in *Knowing and the Known* (Boston, 1949), pp. 119–143.

———, "Unity of Science as a Social Problem," *International Encyclopedia of Unified Science,* Vol. I, *Foundations of the Unity of Science,* No. 1 (Chicago, 1938), pp. 29–38.

———, "Valuation Judgments and Immediate Quality," *Journal of Philosophy,* XL (June 10, 1943), 309–317; reprinted in *Problems of Men* (New York, 1946), pp. 250–260.

———, "The Vanishing Subject in the Psychology of James," *Journal of Philosophy,* XXXVII (Oct. 24, 1940), 589–599; reprinted in *Problems of Men* (New York, 1946), pp. 396–409.

———, "William James as Empiricist," in *In Commemoration of William James 1842–1942* (New York, 1942), pp. 48–57.

Dictionary of Philosophy and Psychology, Vols. I, II, James Mark Baldwin, ed. (New York, 1901–1902).

Dubislav, Walter, *Die Definition,* 3rd ed. (Leipzig, 1931).

Einstein, Albert, and Leopold Infeld, *The Evolution of Physics* (New York, 1938).

Einstein, Albert, and Leopold Infeld, *On the Method of Theoretical Physics* (Oxford, 1933).

———, *Out of My Later Years* (New York, 1950).

———, "Reply to Criticisms," in Paul A. Schilpp, ed., *Albert Einstein: Philosopher-Scientist* (Evanston, 1949), pp. 663–688.

Farber, Marvin, ed., *Philosophic Thought in France and the United States* (Buffalo, 1950).

———, ed., *Philosophical Essays in Memory of Edmund Husserl* (Cambridge, 1940).

Feigl, Herbert, and Grover Maxwell, eds., *Current Issues in the Philosophy of Science* (New York, 1961).

———, "Operationism and Scientific Method," *Psychological Review*, LII (Sept., 1945), 250–259.

Feuer, Lewis S., "Dialectical Materialism and Soviet Science," *Philosophy of Science*, XVI (April, 1949), 105–124.

Fortune, eds., "The Fruitful Errors of Elton Mayo," XXXIV (Nov., 1946), 180–183, 238, 241–242, 244, 247–248.

Frank, Philipp, *Between Physics and Philosophy* (Cambridge, 1941).

———, *Foundations of Physics, International Encyclopedia of Unified Science*, Vol. I, *Foundations of the Unity of Science*, No. 7 (Chicago, 1946).

Gentry, George, "Reference and Relation," *Journal of Philosophy*, XL (May 13, 1943), 253–261.

Gödel, Kurt, "Russell's Mathematical Logic," in Paul A. Schilpp, ed., *The Philosophy of Bertrand Russell* (Evanston, 1944), pp. 123–154.

Griffith, Coleman R., *Principles of Systematic Psychology* (Urbana, 1943).

Gross, Bertram M., "Review of *The Process of Government*," *American Political Science Review*, XLIV (Sept., 1950), 742–748.

Hall, Everett, "Some Meanings of Meaning in Dewey's *Experience and Nature*," *Journal of Philosophy*, XXV (March 29, 1928) 169–181.

Hartshorne, Charles, and Paul Weiss, eds., *Collected Papers of Charles Sanders Peirce*, Vols. I–VI (Cambridge, 1931–1935).

Hayek, F. A., "The Facts of the Social Sciences," *Ethics*, LIV (Oct., 1943), 1–13.

Heitler, Walter, "The Departure from Classical Thought in Modern Physics," in Paul A. Schilpp, ed., *Albert Einstein: Philosopher-Scientist* (Evanston, 1949), pp. 179–198.

Hobbes, Thomas, *De corpore* (London, 1650).

———, *The English Works of*, Vol. I, Sir William Molesworth, ed. (London, 1839).

Hocking, William E., "Dewey's Concepts of Experience and Nature," *Philosophical Review*, XLIX (March, 1940), 228–244.

Hofstadter, Albert, "Concerning a Certain Deweyan Conception of Metaphysics," in Sidney Hook, ed., *John Dewey: Philosopher of Science and Freedom* (New York, 1950), pp. 249–270.

Holt, E. B., "William James as Psychologist," in *In Commemoration of William James, 1842–1942* (New York, 1942), pp. 34–47.

Hook, Sidney, *Heresy Yes—Conspiracy No* (New York, 1953).

——, ed., *John Dewey: Philosopher of Science and Freedom* (New York, 1950).

——, *Political Power and Personal Freedom* (New York, 1962).

——, *The Quest for Being* (New York, 1961).

——, "The Place of John Dewey in Modern Thought," in Marvin Farber, ed., *Philosophic Thought in France and the United States* (Buffalo, 1950), pp. 483–503.

Hughes, Percy, "Is Whitehead's Psychology Adequate?" in Paul A. Schilpp, ed., *The Philosophy of Alfred North Whitehead* (Evanston, 1941), pp. 273–301.

Hutten, Ulrich von, *Opera*, Eduard Bocking, ed. (Leipzig, 1859).

Infeld, Leopold, and Albert Einstein, *The Evolution of Physics* (New York, 1938).

International Encyclopedia of Unified Science, Otto Neurath, editor-in-chief (Chicago, 1938—), Vols. I, II, *Foundations of the Unity of Science;* the various parts of the encyclopedia are published separately; in 1955 a combined edition was published under the editorship of Otto Neurath, Rudolf Carnap, and Charles Morris.

James, William, *Collected Essays and Reviews*, Ralph Barton Perry, ed. (New York, 1920).

——, *Essays in Radical Empiricism*, Ralph Barton Perry, ed. (New York, 1912).

——, *The Meaning of Truth* (New York, 1909).

——, *A Pluralistic Universe* (New York, 1909).

——, *The Principles of Psychology*, 2 vols. (New York, 1890).

——, *Some Problems of Philosophy* (New York, 1911).

——, *The Varieties of Religious Experience* (New York, 1902).

——, "Absolutism and Empiricism," *Mind*, IX (April, 1884), 281–286.

——, "The Chicago School," *Psychological Bulletin*, I (1904), 1–5; reprinted in *Collected Essays and Reviews* (New York, 1920), pp. 445–447.

——, "The Function of Cognition," *Mind*, X (Jan., 1885), 27–44; reprinted in *The Meaning of Truth* (New York, 1909), pp. 1–42.

——, "The Knowing of Things Together," *Psychological Review*, II (1895), 105–124; reprinted in *Collected Essays and Reviews* (New York, 1920), pp. 371–400.

——, "On Some Omissions of Introspective Psychology," *Mind*, IX (Jan., 1884), 1–26; reprinted in *Essays in Radical Empiricism* (New York, 1912), pp. 266–279.

James, William, "Philosophical Conceptions and Practical Results," *University of California Chronicle* (1898); reprinted in *Collected Essays and Reviews* (New York, 1920), pp. 406–437.

James, William, *1842–1942, In Commemoration of* (New York, 1942); the task of assembling the essays and arranging for their publication was assumed by Brand Blanshard and Herbert W. Schneider.

Jennings, H. S., "The Beginnings of Social Behavior in Unicellular Organisms," *Science,* XCII (Dec. 13, 1940), 539–546.

———, "The Transition from the Individual to the Social Level," *Science,* XCIV (Nov. 14, 1941), 449–453.

Jordan, Elijah, *Forms of Individuality* (Indianapolis, 1927).

———, *Theory of Legislation* (Indianapolis, 1930).

Kantor, J. R., *Psychology and Logic,* 2 vols. (Bloomington, 1945, 1950).

Kaufmann, Felix, *Methodology of the Social Sciences* (New York, 1944).

———, "Basic Issues in Logical Positivism," in Marvin Farber, ed., *Philosophic Thought in France and the United States* (Buffalo, 1950), pp. 565–588.

———, "On Dewey's *Logic,*" *Social Research,* VII (May, 1940), 243–246.

———, "Phenomenology and Logical Empiricism," in Marvin Farber, ed., *Philosophical Essays in Memory of Edmund Husserl* (Cambridge, 1940), pp. 124–142.

———, "Scientific Procedure and Probability," *Philosophy and Phenomenological Research,* VI (Sept., 1945), 47–66.

———, "Strata of Experience," *Philosophy and Phenomenological Research,* I (March, 1941), 313–324.

———, "The Structure of Science," *Journal of Philosophy,* XXXVIII (May 22, 1941), 281–293.

———, "Truth and Logic," *Philosophy and Phenomenological Research,* I (Sept., 1940), 59–69.

———, "Verification, Meaning and Truth," *Philosophy and Phenomenological Research,* IV (Dec., 1943), 267–284.

Kilpatrick, Franklin P., ed., *Explorations in Transactional Psychology* (New York, 1961).

Kleist, Heinrich von, *Werke,* 4 vols., E. Schmidt and R. Steig, eds. (Leipsic and Vienna, 1904).

Knight, Frank H., "Rights of Man and Natural Law," *Ethics,* LIV (Jan., 1944), 124–145.

Köhler, Wolfgang, *The Place of Value in a World of Facts* (New York, 1938).

Koestler, Arthur, *The Yogi and the Commissar* (New York, 1945).

Krikorian, Yervant H., ed., *Naturalism and the Human Spirit* (New York, 1944).

Lawrence, Merle, *Studies in Human Behavior* (Princeton, 1949).

Lewis, C. I., "The Modes of Meaning," *Philosophy and Phenomenological Research*, IV (Dec., 1943), 236–249.

Livingston, William K., and Hadley Cantril, "The Concept of Transaction in Psychology and Neurology, *Journal of Individual Psychology*, 19 (May, 1963), 3–16.

Llewellyn, Karl N., "The Constitution as an Institution," *Columbia Law Review*, XXXIV (Jan., 1934), 1–40.

Locke, John, *An Essay Concerning Human Understanding*, 2 vols. (Oxford, A. C. Fraser edition, 1894).

Lotze, Rudolf Hermann, *Logic*, 2 vols., 2nd ed., trans. Bernard Bosanquet (Oxford, 1888).

McCormick, Anne O'Hare, "Manchester Tries Comeback Despite Labor Handicaps," *The New York Times* (Oct. 24, 1945), p. 20.

McGraw, Myrtle B., *Growth* (New York, 1935).

Mackay, D. S., "What Does Mr. Dewey Mean by an 'Indeterminate Situation'?" *Journal of Philosophy*, XXXIX (March 12, 1942), 141–148.

Mannheim, Karl, *Man and Society in an Age of Reconstruction* (London, 1940).

Margenau, Henry, "Einstein's Conception of Reality," in Paul A. Schilpp, ed., *Albert Einstein: Philosopher-Scientist* (Evanston, 1949), pp. 243–268.

Marhenke, Paul, "Moore's Analysis of Sense Perception," in Paul A. Schilpp, ed., *The Philosophy of G. E. Moore* (Evanston, 1942), pp. 253–280.

Maxwell, Grover, and Herbert Feigl, eds., *Current Issues in the Philosophy of Science* (New York, 1961).

Maxwell, James Clerk, *Matter and Motion* (London, 1876).

Mayeroff, Milton, "The Nature of Propositions in John Dewey's *Logic*: A Reply to Miss Brodbeck," *Journal of Philosophy*, XLVII (June 8, 1950), 353–358.

Mead, George Herbert, *Mind, Self, and Society* (Chicago, 1934).

———, *The Philosophy of the Act* (Chicago, 1938).

———, *The Philosophy of the Present* (Chicago, 1932).

Mesthene, Emmanuel G., "The Ethical Dilemma of Non-Naturalism," *Journal of Philosophy*, XLIII (March 14, 1946), 161–162.

Meyer, Max, *The Psychology of the Other One* (Columbus, 1921).

Mill, John Stuart, *A System of Logic*, 2 vols. (London, 1843).

Mohrmann, Christine, Alf Sommerfelt, and Joshua Whatmough, eds., *Trends in European and American Linguistics 1930–1960* (Utrecht, 1961).

Molesworth, Sir William, ed., *The English Works of Thomas Hobbes*. Vol. I (London, 1839).

Montague, William P., *The Ways of Knowing or the Methods of Philosophy* (New York, 1925)

Montague, William P., and George P. Adams, eds., *Contemporary American Philosophy: Personal Statements,* 2 vols. (New York, 1930).

Moore, Addison W., *Pragmatism and Its Critics* (Chicago, 1910).

Moore, G. E., "An Autobiography," in Paul A. Schilpp, ed., *The Philosophy of G. E. Moore* (Evanston, 1942), pp. 3–39.

Morgenthau, Hans J., "Limitations of Science and the Problem of Social Planning," *Ethics,* LIV (April, 1944), 174–185.

Morris, Charles W., *Foundations of the Theory of Signs, International Encyclopedia of Unified Science,* Vol. I, *Foundations of the Unity of Science,* No. 2 (Chicago, 1938).

———, *Signs, Language and Behavior* (New York, 1946).

———, "Peirce, Mead and Pragmatism," *Philosophical Review,* XXXVII (March, 1938), 109–127.

Muirhead, J. H., ed., *Contemporary British Philosophy: Personal Statements,* First Series (London and New York, 1924).

Murchison, Carl, ed., *Psychologies of 1930* (Worcester, 1930).

Murray, Sir James A. H., Henry Bradley, W. A. Craigie, and C. T. Onions, eds., *Oxford English Dictionary,* also known as *A New English Dictionary on Historical Principles.* 10 vols. in 15 (Oxford, 1888–1928).

Nagel, Ernest, and Morris R. Cohen, *An Introduction to Logic and Scientific Method* (New York, 1934).

———, *Logic Without Metaphysics* (Glencoe, 1957).

———, *Principles of the Theory of Probability, International Encyclopedia of Unified Science,* Vol. I, *Foundations of the Unity of Science,* No. 6 (Chicago, 1939).

———, *The Structure of Science* (New York, 1961).

———, "Can Logic Be Divorced from Ontology?" *Journal of Philosophy,* XXVI (Dec. 19, 1929), 705–712.

———, "Dewey's Reconstruction of Logical Theory," in Sidney Ratner, ed., *The Philosopher of the Common Man* (New York, 1940), pp. 56–86.

———, "Fight for Clarity: Logical Empiricism," *American Scholar,* VIII (Jan., 1939), 45–59.

———, "Logic Without Ontology," in *Naturalism and the Human Spirit,* Yervant H. Krikorian, ed. (New York, 1944), pp. 210–241.

———, "Operational Analysis as an Instrument for the Critique of Linguistic Signs," *Journal of Philosophy,* XXXIX (March 26, 1942), 177–189.

———, "Review of Rudolf Carnap, *Introduction to Semantics," Journal of Philosophy,* XXXIX (Aug. 13, 1942), 468–473.

———, "Review of D. W. Hering, *et al., Time and Its Mysteries.* Series 11," *Journal of Philosophy,* XXXIX (Jan. 1, 1942), 22–24.

Nagel, Ernest, "Some Reflections on the Use of Languages in the Natural Sciences," *Journal of Philosophy*, XLII (Nov. 8, 1945), 617–630.

——, "Truth and Knowledge of the Truth," *Philosophy and Phenomenological Research*, V (Sept., 1944), 50–68.

Nathanson, Jerome, "Dewey's Vivisection of the Logical Process," *Philosophy of Science*, VI (Jan., 1939), 115–122.

Needham, Joseph, *Chemical Embryology* (Cambridge, 1931).

Neurath, Otto, *Foundations of the Social Sciences, International Encyclopedia of Unified Science*, Vol. II, *Foundations of the Unity of Science*, No. 1 (Chicago, 1944).

——, editor-in-chief, *International Encyclopedia of Unified Science* (Chicago, 1938—).

A New English Dictionary on Historical Principles, also known as Oxford *English Dictionary*, Sir James A. H. Murray, Henry Bradley, W. A. Craigie, and C. T. Onions, eds., 10 vols. in 15 (Oxford, 1888–1928).

Newton, Sir Isaac, *Mathematical Principles of Natural Philosophy*, trans. Andrew Motte, ed. Florian Cajori (Berkeley, 1934).

Ogden, C. K., and I. A. Richards, *The Meaning of Meaning* (London, 1923).

Oppenheim, Paul, and Hugo Bedau, "Complementarity in Quantum Mechanics," *Synthese*, XIII (Sept., 1961), 201–232.

Oxford English Dictionary, originally entitled *A New English Dictionary on Historical Principles*, Sir James A. H. Murray, Henry Bradley, W. A. Craigie and C. T. Onions, eds., 10 vols. in 15 (Oxford, 1888–1928).

Pauli, Wolfgang, "Einstein's Contribution to Quantum Theory," in Paul A. Schilpp, ed., *Albert Einstein: Philosopher-Scientist* (Evanston, 1949), pp. 147–160.

Peirce, Charles Sanders, *Collected Papers*, Vols. I–VI, Charles Hartshorne and Paul Weiss, eds. (Cambridge, 1931–1935); Vols. VII, VIII, Arthur W. Burks, ed. (Cambridge, 1958).

Pepper, Stephen C., "The Descriptive Definition," *Journal of Philosophy*, XLIII (Jan. 17, 1946), 29–36.

Perry, Ralph Barton, ed., *Collected Essays and Reviews* by William James (New York, 1920).

——, ed., *Essays in Radical Empiricism* by William James (New York, 1912).

Poincaré, Henri, *Les Méthodes nouvelles de la mécanique celeste*, 3 vols. (Paris, 1892–1899).

Quine, Willard V. O., *Word and Object* (New York, 1960).

——, "On Universals," *Journal of Symbolic Logic*, XII (Sept., 1947), 74–84.

Ratner, Sidney, ed., *Inquiry into Inquiries:* Essays in Social Theory by Arthur F. Bentley (Boston, 1954).

Ratner, Sidney, ed., *The Philosopher of the Common Man:* Essays in Honor of John Dewey (New York, 1940).

———, "Review of *Knowing and the Known,*" *Social Research,* XVII (June, 1950), 248–250.

Rice, Philip Blair, "'Objectivity' in Value Judgments," *Journal of Philosophy,* XL (Jan. 7, 1943), 5–14.

Richards, I. A., and C. K. Ogden, *The Meaning of Meaning* (London, 1923).

Romanes, G. J., *Mental Evolution in Man* (London, 1889).

Rosenblatt, Louise M., *Literature As Exploration* (New York, 1938).

———, "The Acid Test for Literature Teaching," *English Journal,* XLV (Feb., 1956), 66–74.

———, "Literature: The Reader's Role," *English Journal,* XLIX (May, 1960), 304–310.

Runes, Dagobert D., ed., *The Dictionary of Philosophy* (New York, 1942).

———, ed., *Twentieth Century Philosophy* (New York, 1943).

Russell, Bertrand, *The Analysis of Matter* (New York, 1927).

———, *The Analysis of Mind* (London, 1921).

———, *An Inquiry into Meaning and Truth* (New York, 1940).

———, *The Principles of Mathematics* (Cambridge, 1903).

———, *The Scientific Outlook* (New York, 1931).

———, "Logical Atomism," in J. H. Muirhead, ed., *Contemporary British Philosophy: Personal Statements,* First Series (London, 1924), pp. 357–383.

———, "The Philosophy of Logical Atomism," *Monist,* XXVIII (Oct., 1918), 495–527; reprinted in J. H. Muirhead, ed., *Contemporary British Philosophy: Personal Statements,* First Series (London, 1924), as a part of "Logical Atomism," pp. 357–383.

———, "The Philosophy of Logical Atomism to July, 1919," *Monist,* XXIX (Jan., April, July, 1919), 32–63, 190–222, 345–380.

Santayana, George, "Dewey's Naturalistic Metaphysics," *Journal of Philosophy,* XXII (Dec. 3, 1925), 673–688.

Schilpp, Paul A., ed., *The Philosophy of John Dewey* (Evanston, 1939).

———, ed., *Albert Einstein: Philosopher-Scientist* (Evanston, 1949).

———, ed., *The Philosophy of G. E. Moore* (Evanston, 1942).

———, ed., *The Philosophy of Bertrand Russell* (Evanston, 1944).

———, ed., *The Philosophy of Alfred North Whitehead* (Evanston, 1941).

Schumacher, G. A., "Uniformity of the Pain Threshold in Man," *Science,* XCII (Aug. 2, 1940), 110–112.

Singer, Edgar A., Jr., "Logico-Historical Study of Mechanisms," *Studies in the History of Science,* University of Pennsylvania Bicentennial Conference (Philadelphia, 1941).

Sisson, E. O., "Relation in Reality and Symbolism," *Philosophy of Science,* VII (July, 1940), 342–354.

Skinner, B. F., "The Operational Analysis of Psychological Terms," *Psychological Review,* LII (Sept., 1945), 270–277.

Smith, Benjamin E., and William Dwight Whitney, eds., *Century Dictionary and Cyclopedia* (Rev. and enl. ed.), 12 vols. (New York, 1911).

Smullyan, Arthur F., "Review of 'Definition,' by John Dewey and Arthur F. Bentley," *Journal of Symbolic Logic,* XII (Sept., 1947), 99.

Smullyan, Raymond M., *Theory of Formal Systems* (Princeton, 1961).

Spencer, Herbert, *Principles of Psychology* (New York, 1872).

Stebbing, L. Susan, "Moore's Influence," in Paul A. Schilpp, ed., *The Philosophy of G. E. Moore* (Evanston, 1942), pp. 515–532.

Stevenson, Charles L., *Ethics and Language* (New Haven, 1944).

Tarski, Alfred, "The Semantic Conception of Truth," *Philosophy and Phenomenological Research,* IV (March, 1944), 341–376.

Taylor, James H., "On the Problem of Applied Mathematics," *Science,* CII (Sept. 28, 1945), 315–320.

Thomas, Milton H., *John Dewey: A Centennial Bibliography* (Chicago, 1962).

Titchener, Edward B., *Systematic Psychology: Prolegomena,* H. P. Wald, ed. (New York, 1929).

Valtin, Jan, *Out of the Night* (New York, 1941).

Vigotsky, L. S., "Thought and Speech," *Psychiatry,* II (Feb., 1939), 29–54.

Vivas, Eliseo, "A Natural History of the Aesthetic Transaction," in Yervant H. Krikorian, ed., *Naturalism and the Human Spirit* (New York, 1944), pp. 96–120.

Walker, Charles R., "American Productivity," *Fortune,* Vol. XXXIII (Jan., 1946).

Weiss, Paul, and Charles Hartshorne, eds., *Collected Papers of Charles Sanders Peirce,* Vols. I–VI (Cambridge, 1931–1935).

———, "An Effective Logic," *New Republic,* LXXXXVII (Nov. 23, 1938), 79–80.

———, "Logic of Semantics," *Journal of Philosophy,* XXXIX (March 26, 1942), 169–177.

Wertheimer, Max, *Productive Thinking* (New York, 1945).

White, Morton G., *The Origin of Dewey's Instrumentalism* (New York, 1943).

Whitehead, Alfred North, *Adventures of Ideas* (New York, 1933).

———, *Modes of Thought* (New York, 1938).

Whitehead, Alfred North, *Nature and Life* (Chicago, 1934); reprinted in *Modes of Thought* (New York, 1938).

——, *Process and Reality* (Cambridge, 1929).

Wiener, Philip P., *Evolution and the Founders of Pragmatism* (Cambridge, 1949).

Whitney, William Dwight, and Benjamin E. Smith, eds., *Century Dictionary and Cyclopedia* (Rev. and enl. ed.), 12 vols. (New York, 1911).

Williams, Elgin, "The Morality of the Machine," *Scientific Monthly*, LXX (Feb., 1950), 90–96.

Woodbridge, Frederick J. E., "The Problem of Consciousness," *Studies in Philosophy and Psychology:* The Garman Commemorative Volume (Boston, 1906), pp. 139–66, reprinted in *Nature and Mind* (New York, 1937), pp. 321–45.

——, "The Problem of Consciousness Again," *Journal of Philosophy*, XXXIII (Oct. 8, 1936), 561–568.

Biographical Appendix

Adamson, Robert (1852–1902), a Scottish scholar, is identified with the tradition of Neo-Kantian critical realism. He wrote *On the Philosophy of Kant* (1879) and *A Short History of Logic* (1911).

Aiken, Conrad [Potter] (1889–   ), author of *Time in the Rock* (1936), is an American poet, novelist and critic. His early writings include *Earth Triumphant* (1914), *Punch, the Immortal Liar* (1921), and *Selin* (1925). Other important works of Aiken's are *The Blue Voyage* (1927), *Great Circle* (1933), and *The House of Dust* (1920).

Albrecht, William Albert (1888–   ) was Professor of Soils at the University of Missouri from 1930 to 1959.

Aldrich, Virgil [Charles] (1903–   ), born in India, Ph.D., University of California, is Professor and Head of the Department of Philosophy at Kenyon College. His philosophical writings range from essays on Descartes and Hume to analyses of logical positivism, Dewey's use of language, and English "ordinary language" philosophy.

Allen, Joseph Henry (1820–1898) was an American classical scholar. He lectured on church history at Harvard University, 1878–82, and was editor of the *Unitarian Review*, 1887–97.

Altman, Julius (1914–   ) studied philosophy at New York University and the Graduate School of the New School for Social Research. He worked closely with Arthur F. Bentley on various philosophical problems for many years and aided him in seeing through the press *Knowing and the Known* (1949) and *Inquiry into Inquiries* (1954). He is a field examiner with the National Labor Relations Board.

Ames, Adelbert, Jr. (1880–1955) is known for his highly original work in the psychology of visual perception. Educated at Harvard, he practiced law, studied art, and painted before he went to Clark University as a research fellow in 1914 and became Research Professor of Physiological Optics at Dartmouth in 1919. From 1953 to 1955 he was Research Consultant Psychologist at Princeton. His experimental work was admired by Dewey and Bentley. Ames' theories were discussed in his correspondence with Dewey in *The Morning Notes of Adelbert Ames, Jr.* (1960). Ames was the founder of the "transactional psychology" that Hadley Cantril and his associates have developed in various directions.

Ayres, Clarence E[dwin] (1891–   ) taught philosophy at Amherst and Reed Colleges before he became Professor of Economics at the University of Texas in 1930. Dewey regarded him as a friend and sympathetic coworker. His *Science—the False Messiah* (1927), *Theory of*

Economic Progress (1944) and *The Divine Right of Capital* (1946) are among his better known works. Ayres has systematically criticized the "obsession" of classical economists with price theory. He has also attacked the tendency of scholars to allow an outmoded psychology and philosophy to define their problems.

Baldwin, James Mark (1861–1934) was a psychologist and philosopher who developed a highly technical system of evolutionary social psychology in the 1890's and early 1900's. His best work was a three-volume treatise, *Thought and Things or Genetic Logic* (1906–11). He regarded himself as a pragmatist along the lines of C. S. Peirce but not of James or Dewey. In his *Genetic Theory of Reality* (1915) he affirmed the primacy of the aesthetic consciousness. He taught at Princeton, 1893–1903, at Johns Hopkins, 1903–09, and at the National University of Mexico, 1909–13.

Balz, Albert G[eorge] A[dam] (1887–1957) took his Ph.D. at Columbia in 1916, during Dewey's tenure there. He taught for many years at the University of Virginia, becoming Corcoran Professor of Philosophy in 1938. An expert on Descartes, Spinoza, and Hobbes, his chief interests were social philosophy and the history of ideas.

Bartley, S[amuel] H[oward] (1901–   ) is Professor of Psychology at Michigan State University. He was at Dartmouth from 1942 to 1947. Interested in physiological psychology, he stresses the study of perception as an area for psychological inquiry. His *Vision: A Study of Its Basis* appeared in 1941, his *Principles of Perception*, in 1958.

Beck, Guido is a mathematical physicist who was connected with the Astronomical Observatory at Cordoba, Argentina, in 1944.

Bedau, Hugo (1926–   ) is Associate Professor of Philosophy at Reed College.

Bell, Eric T[emple] (1883–1960) was Professor of Mathematics at the California Institute of Technology from 1927 to 1953, when he became Professor Emeritus. He has been most widely known for his books, *Men of Mathematics* (1937) and *The Development of Mathematics* (1940). He was also an original mathematician of distinction and won several important prizes for his contributions to mathematics.

Bentley, Imogene Shaw (1876–   ), the widow of Arthur F. Bentley, was born in Cleveland, Ohio, the third of three children. She was graduated from the Indianapolis High School in 1895. Although she had no further formal schooling, she acquired more than the equivalent of a college education through wide and discriminating reading. She earned her own living from 1896 to 1946 when she retired as an officer from the real estate and insurance firm in which she had worked since 1897. When she married Arthur F. Bentley on May 18, 1946, she was almost seventy, and he was almost seventy-seven. She acquired knowledge and insight into the problems Bentley dealt with, and undoubtedly was a source of inspiration and encouragement to him. She has done much to make his work available to the scholarly world.

Bergson, Henri [Louis] (1859–1941), French philosopher, expounded brilliantly his theories concerning free will, "lived time" or duration, "creative" evolution, and the superiority of "intuition" to intellect. He attacked the spatialization of time, the "logic of identity," and deterministic materialism. In 1927 he won the Nobel Prize for Literature. In 1940 he protested against the anti-Jewish legislation of the Vichy government. His most influential book is *Creative Evolution* (1907).

Bernard, Claude (1813–1878), a distinguished French physiologist, is the author of the classic *An Introduction to the Study of Experimental Medicine* (1865). Bernard held that medicine could be a science and helped to establish physiology on a strict scientific basis.

Bertalanffy, Ludwig von (1901–   ), Professor of Biology at the University of Ottawa and formerly Professor at the University of Vienna, is noted for his contribution to "organismic" biology. In contrast to mechanists and vitalists, he stresses *organization* as fundamental. He contrasts the closed systems of classical physics with the open systems of contemporary physics and biology. He regards his theory of open systems as allied to Bentley and Dewey's "transaction" approach. His *Modern Theories of Development* (1933) and *Problems of Life* (1952) have had considerable influence.

Bidney, David (1908–   ), Professor of Philosophy and Anthropology at University of Indiana, is author of *Theoretical Anthropology* (1953).

Black, Max (1909–   ), born in Russia, educated in England, Professor of Philosophy at Cornell, is an empiricist and linguistic analyst. His major fields of interest are the foundations of logic and mathematics, the theory of knowledge, and the philosophies of language and science. His books include *The Nature of Mathematics* (1933) and *Problems of Analysis* (1954).

Bloomfield, Leonard (1887–1949) was Sterling Professor of Linguistics at Yale University 1940–49. His best known work is *Language* (1933), and his *Linguistic Aspects of Science* (1939) has been influential. A leader in the movement to make linguistics a science, he was regarded as a "mechanistic" behaviorist by some because he insisted upon strictly scientific descriptive statements without mentalistic verbiage. He helped to create "structural linguistics" through his emphasis upon discovering the regularities in the speech of a community.

Bohr, Niels (1885–1962), the distinguished Danish physicist and Nobel Prize winner in 1922, was Professor of Physics, 1916–62, and director of the Institute of Theoretical Physics at Copenhagen, 1920–62. In 1913 he developed a quantum theory of the atom and showed how it could be used to explain the spectra emitted by atoms in excitation. In the 1930's and 40's he did important work on nuclear fission and worked out a liquid-drop model of the nucleus. He was a pioneer in justifying the principle of complementarity in quantum mechanics and other areas of knowledge (increase of precise knowledge on one phase of a problem leads to decrease of such precision on another phase of the problem). He also upheld the validity of statistical laws in modern physics as against the strict deterministic laws of classical physics.

Boole, George (1815–1864) was a founder of modern mathematical or symbolic logic. He also contributed to the theory of probability. His most influential works are *The Mathematical Analysis of Logic* (1847) and *An Investigation of the Laws of Thought* (1854).

Born, Max (1882–   ), a German physicist and Nobel Prize winner in 1954, was Professor at Berlin and other German Universities until dismissed by Hitler in 1933. He was Tait Professor of Natural Philosophy at Edinburgh from 1936 until 1953. He is noted for his work in quantum mechanics.

Bosanquet, Bernard (1848–1923), British Neo-Hegelian philosopher, developed a system of philosophy that ranged from aesthetics and logic to political theory. He was opposed to formal logic. His *Logic* (1888) stressed his concern with "the conditions of logical stability." He admitted every method of inquiry, however informal, to the field of logic.

Boyer, Carl B[enjamin] (1906–   ), Professor of Mathematics at Brooklyn College, is the author of *Concepts of the Calculus* (1939). His field is the history of science and mathematics.

Brentano, Franz Clemens (1838–1917), an Austrian priest, psychologist, and philosopher, advocated psychology as the fundamental science. He held that our knowledge of psychical phenomena is direct and certain. While we do not *observe* mental acts, we can *perceive* them. Each mental phenomenon is not an idea, but an "act" that "points towards an object" and "relates to a content." His *Psychology from an Empirical Standpoint* (1874) and other writings influenced Husserl and other German philosophers.

Bridgman, P[ercy] W[illiams] (1882–1961) was an authority on high-pressure physics, thermodynamics, and the foundations of physics; Hollis Professor of Mathematics and Natural Philosophy, 1926–50; Higgins University Professor, at Harvard, 1950–54; emeritus, 1954–61. He won the Nobel Prize for Physics in 1946. In the field of philosophy, he is known for his "operationalism," the doctrine that "the concept is synonymous with the corresponding set of operations." His philosophy is expounded in *The Logic of Modern Physics* (1927), *The Nature of Physical Theory* (1936), *Reflections of a Physicist* (1950), *The Way Things Are* (1958).

694

Brodbeck, May (1917–   ), is Professor of Philosophy at the University of Minnesota. She has written a number of essays on Dewey's logic and on the philosophy of science. She is, with Herbert Feigl, editor of and a contributor to *Readings in the Philosophy of Science* (1953).

Brotherston, Bruce Wallace (1877–1947) was Professor of Philosophy at Tufts. He wrote on ethics, religion, empiricism, and process philosophy.

Brunswik, Egon (1903–1955) was Professor of Psychology at the University of California. His major works are *The Conceptual Framework of Psychology* (1952) and *Systematic and Representative Design of Psychological Experiments* (1947).

Cameron, Norman A[lexander] (1896–   ) has been Professor of Psychiatry and Associate Psychiatrist of the Psychiatric Institute at Yale University since 1953. He is author of *Psychology of Behavior Disorders* (1947); co-author, and associate editor, *American Handbook of Psychiatry*, 2 vols. (1959).

Cannon, Walter B[radford] (1871–1945) was George Higginson Professor of Physiology in Harvard University from 1906 until 1942. He was celebrated for his work on the effects of emotions on bodily processes and the autonomic nervous system. He developed the concept of homeostasis—the tendency of the body to maintain a constant state of equilibrium. Perhaps his best known book is *The Wisdom of the Body* (1932).

Cantor, Georg [Ferdinand Ludwig Philipp] (1845–1918) is distinguished for his contributions to number theory and the theory of sets, and for his "positive theory of the infinite." He was Professor of Mathematics at the University of Halle.

Cantril, [Albert] Hadley (1906–   ), formerly Professor of Psychology at Princeton University, is Research Associate in Psychology at Princeton and Senior Counsellor and Chairman of the Board of the Institute for International Social Research. He worked very closely for many years with Adelbert Ames, Jr., at Hanover and edited Ames' notes and the Dewey-Ames letters. Cantril is a leading exponent of transactional psychology and is the author of a number of books, among which is *The Why of Man's Experience* (1950).

Carnap, Rudolf (1891–   ), Emeritus Professor of Philosophy at the University of California at Los Angeles, is the outstanding exponent of logical positivism or empiricism, a movement that grew out of the famous Vienna Circle of the 1920's and 30's. He has contributed many highly technical analyses and controversial theories to the theory of knowledge, mathematical logic, the philosophy of science, and the foundations of induction and probability. His name is associated with the "verifiability theory of meaning," in a strict and liberal version; the laws of logic and mathematics as linguistic structures following conventionally adopted syntactical rules; philosophy as first the logical syntax of the language of science, then as embracing an analysis of the syntax, semantics, and pragmatics of science. He has regarded aesthetics, ethics, and metaphysics as asserting "emotive," nonempirical, nonanalytic statements, outside the realm of science. Some of his key works are *The Logical Syntax of Language* (1934), *Introduction to Semantics* (1942), *Meaning and Necessity* (1947), and *Logical Foundations of Probability* (1950).

Cassirer, Ernst (1874–1945), German Neo-Kantian philosopher, made important contributions to the history of modern philosophy, the philosophy of science, and the theory of language. He taught at the University of Berlin and of Hamburg before Hitler came to power, then at Oxford, Göteborg, Yale, and Columbia. His major works include *Substance and Function* (1910), *Einstein's Theory of Relativity* (1921), *The Problem of Knowledge in Modern Times*, 4 vols. (1906–50), *Philosophy of Symbolic Forms*, 3 vols. (1921–29), *An Essay on Man* (1944), and *The Myth of the State* (1946). He agreed with Kant that human thinking was conditioned by categories or forms of thought by which phenomena were organized and made intelligible. But Cassirer maintained that the Kantian categories for scientific thought were preceded and supplemented by categories or forms of mythical, historical, and everyday practical thinking. He threw light on these forms of nonscientific thought by examining the forms of expression in different languages.

Chevigny, Hector (1904–   ) is the author of *Lost Empire* (1937) and *Lord of Alaska* (1942), among other works, and is co-author of *The Adjustment of the Blind* (1950).

Church, Alonzo (1903–   ), American symbolic logician, is Professor of Mathematics at Princeton University, and one of the chief editors of the *Journal of Symbolic Logic*. He is the author of an *Introduction to Mathematical Logic* (1956) and is known for the thesis that every effectively calculable function is recursive, and for his proof of the impossibility of a universal decision procedure for general logic. He is a strong champion of the Platonic reality of mathematical entities and of Frege's distinction between "reference" and "sense" in the theory of meaning.

Churchman, C[harles] W[est] (1913–   ) has published studies on the general problems of methodology, measurement, and the philosophy of science. He taught philosophy at the University of Pennsylvania and Wayne University and is now Professor of Business Administration at the University of California at Berkeley.

Cohen, Morris Raphael (1880–1947), American philosopher and logician, was Professor of Philosophy at the College of the City of New York for many years, then at the University of Chicago. He was a vigorous champion of naturalism and liberalism and a stern critic of *a priori* rationalisms, Leibnitzian, Kantian, and Hegelian; of sensationalistic empiricism; and of positivism, from Comte to Carnap. He was opposed to the Jamesian and Deweyean forms of pragmatism, but sympathetic to Peirce's version. He was an exponent of logical realism: that logical truths represent the absolute invariants exhibited by all possible objects. His chief works are *Reason and Nature* (1931), *Law and the Social Order* (1933), and *The Meaning of History* (1944). His and Ernest Nagel's textbook, *An Introduction to Logic and Scientific Method* (1934), is one of the best and most widely–used modern logic texts.

Commons, John R[ogers] (1862–1945), Professor of Economics at the University of Wisconsin, 1904–32, was an expert on labor, labor unions, industrial relations, and immigration. Among his works are the *Legal Foundations of Capitalism* (1924) and *Institutional Economics* (1934).

Condon, Edward U[hler] (1902–   ), American physicist, has taught at Columbia, Princeton, Minnesota, and Washington University at St. Louis. He was director of the U. S. National Bureau of Standards, 1945–51. He is co-author of *Quantum Mechanics* (1929) and *The Theory of Atomic Spectra* (1935).

Cowan, T[homas] A[nthony] (1904–   ) is Professor of Law at Rutgers, The State University. He taught philosophy at the University of Pennsylvania for some years. His major interest is the relation of law to science, especially decision theory in law, science, and philosophy.

Croce, Benedetto (1866–1952), Italian philosopher, critic, historian, and statesman, developed an impressive Idealistic philosophical system based on the thesis that reality, the object of our thinking, is spirit, the physical a construction of the mind, and the history of human experience the history of the spirit. His phenomenology of the mind, expounded in his *Philosophy of the Spirit*, 4 vols. (1909–21), distinguished four principal activities of the mind, two theoretic and two practical: aesthetics (knowledge of the individual), philosophy (knowledge of the universal), economics (action for individual aims), and ethics (action for universal aims). Unlike Hegel, he asserted that these activities do not oppose, but complement each other. History is the description of these four activities of the human spirit; philosophy is the systematic account of the methodology of history. He rejected metaphysics and the tenets of positivism and formal logic. He exalted the role of active intuition and regarded natural science not as knowledge, but as action. Minister of Education in Italian governments before Mussolini and after the Second World War, Croce was the leading critic of Fascism during the Mussolini regime.

Cunningham, G[ustavus] W[atts] (1881–   ) taught at Cornell University and at the University of Texas. He is best known for his work on Hegel and Bergson and as a historian of idealistic doctrine.

Darwin, Charles [Robert] (1809–1882), English naturalist, whose *Origin of Species* (1859) and *The Descent of Man* (1871) had a profound influence upon the development of Dewey and Bentley's naturalism and theory of the knowing and the known.

Davis, Harold T[hayer] (1892–), formerly Professor of Mathematics at the University of Wisconsin and at Northwestern University, is now teaching at Trinity University, San Antonio, Texas. He was a close friend of A. F. Bentley's and is known for his contributions to mathematics, mathematical physics, and econometrics, as well as to the history of mathematics and the philosophy of modern science.

Dedekind, [Julius Wilhelm] Richard (1831–1916), German mathematician, is one of the pioneers, with Weierstrass, of modern mathematical analysis with its stress on logical precision. His interest in problems of continuity, the ordinal theory of number, and the nature of irrationals resulted in work of the highest originality in those fields.

Dennes, William R[ay] (1898–), Professor of Philosophy at the University of California at Berkeley, has written on naturalistic ethics and value theory. The naturalism he espouses stresses "events," "qualities," and "relations" as against the older naturalistic stress on a single substance, matter, space-time, or mind-stuff. His latest work is *Some Dilemmas of Naturalism* (1960).

Dorner, Alexander (1893–), art historian, Professor of Art at Bennington College, was Professor of Art at Hannover and Director of the Hannover Museum of Art, Germany, before he came to the United States. He is the author of *The Way Beyond Art* (1947).

Dubislav, Walter (1895–), one of the Berlin group of logical empiricists, is the author of *Die Definition* (1931).

Dubs, Homer H[asenflug] (1892–), Professor Emeritus of Chinese at Oxford University, is known for his work in ethics, philosophy of religion and Chinese philosophy and scholarship. His works include *Hsuntze, the Moulder of Ancient Confucianism* (1927) and *Rational Induction: An Analysis of Method in Philosophy and Science* (1930).

Ducasse, C[urt] J[ohn] (1881–) has taught philosophy at Brown University. Born in France, educated in England and the United States, he is known as an aesthetician, ethical theorist, and scientific methodologist. He is relativist in aesthetics, a defender of causality as a relation between single individual events, and an "ontological liberal." He believes that the "real" is ultimately a value term, a function of taste and interest. He is the author of *The Philosophy of Art* (1930), *Philosophy as a Science* (1941), *Nature, Mind, and Death* (1951), and *A Philosophical Scrutiny of Religion* (1953).

Eddy, Lyle Krenzien (1917–   ) is Assistant Professor of Education and Philosophy at the University of Nebraska. His major interest is philosophy of education.

Edman, Irwin (1896–1954) was Johnsonian Professor of Philosophy at Columbia University, 1950–54, an authority on aesthetics and Santayana, and author, among other works, of *Philosopher's Holiday* (1938), *Candle in the Dark* (1939), and *The Mind of St. Paul* (1935).

Einstein, Albert (1879–1955), mathematical physicist and philosopher, won world fame with his special (1905) and general (1916) theories of relativity. His merger of the traditionally absolute space and time into a new space-time continuum led to the creation of a new system of mechanics. The special theory allowed the laws of nature to be written in the same mathematical form whether we suppose the observer to be at rest or in uniform motion. The general theory allowed the laws of nature to be the same whether we suppose the observer to be at rest or in any kind of motion, accelerated or rotary. Einstein did not accept the complementarity principle in quantum mechanics and attempted by his unified field theory (1950) to establish a merger between his general theory of relativity and quantum mechanics. He hoped to bring subatomic and large-scale physical phenomena under one set of determinate laws. In philosophy he adhered to one form of Neo-Kantianism. He played a crucial role in the development of the atomic bomb in World War II and in the movement for international control of atomic warfare after 1945. He came to the United States at the height of the Nazi fanaticism, renounced his German citizenship, and became a United States citizen in 1940. From 1934 until his death, he was a member of the Institute for Advanced Study, Princeton.

Faraday, Michael (1791–1867), English chemist and natural philosopher, laid the foundations for research in electrochemistry, electromagnetic induction, and electromagnetic waves. His insistence on the importance of the electromagnetic field of force was the historical starting point for the electrical side of modern theories of field physics.

Farber, Marvin (1901–   ), Professor of Philosophy at the University of Pennsylvania, has been prominent in the phenomenological movement. Among his books are *The Foundation of Phenomenology* (1943), *Husserl* (1956), and *Naturalism and Subjectivism* (1959).

Feigl, Herbert (1902–   ), Professor of Philosophy at the University of Minnesota, was a member of the Vienna Circle. He has been an active exponent of logical positivism or empiricism. He has published essays on the philosophy of science and has edited with others various studies in scientific philosophy.

Fen, Sing-Nan (1916–   ) is Professor of Education at Portland State College, Oregon. After studying in China, he came to the United

States to study American education under the provisions of the Boxer Indemnity fund. He has published essays bearing on Dewey and Bentley's most recent work.

Feuer, Lewis S[amuel] (1912–   ), Professor of Philosophy at the University of California, is the author of *Psychoanalysis and Ethics* (1955) and *Spinoza and the Rise of Liberalism* (1958). He has also written essays on Marxism, Dewey's philosophic career, and the origins of modern science.

Frank, Philipp G. (1884–   ) Austrian physicist-philosopher, taught at Prague, 1912–38, was a member of the Vienna Circle and a Lecturer in Mathematics and Physics at Harvard University, 1941–   . He was the author, among other books, of *Modern Science and Its Philosophy* (1949).

Frege, Gottlob (1848–1925), German logician and philosopher, advanced the thesis that mathematics is an extension of logic in a path-breaking treatise, *Begriffschrift* ("Concept-script") (1879). He expounded his theory without symbolism in *The Foundations of Arithmetic* (1884). Here he also set forth some profound insights on the theory of meaning, e.g., a word has meaning only in the context of a sentence. In 1893 and 1903 he published his great work, *Fundamental Laws of Arithmetic*, 2 vols. This set forth his derivation of arithmetic from logic in a rigorous and difficult logical symbolism. Russell pointed out to Frege that his theory contained a contradiction when it was extended to the class of all classes. Although Russell attempted to get around this antimony with his Theory of Types, Frege at the end of his life is reported to have concluded that his logistic thesis was an error. Frege developed a distinction between the "sense" and the "reference" of a proposition that contemporary logicians like Carnap and Alonzo Church regard as crucially important.

Fries, Horace S[nyder] (1902–1951) was Professor of Philosophy at the University of Wisconsin. He was interested in Ames' work on perception and the logical relation of science to values. He was in Hanover with Bentley on one occasion.

Fries, Jakob Friedrich (1773–1843), a German philosopher in the Neo-Kantian tradition, called his system "'philosophical anthropology'" and made self-knowledge the basis of all other forms of knowledge. He took the *a priori* to mark the final limits of our human knowledge, the limits being essential human restrictions. His most important book is *New Critique of Reason* (1807).

Gentry, George [Vincent] (1903–   ), Professor of Philosophy at the University of Texas, is known for his work on Whitehead and Peirce and for his interest in concept formation, experimental psychology, and the theory of meaning.

Gildersleeve, Basil [Lanneau] (1831–1924) was a distinguished American classicist and philologist. He took his Ph.D. at Goettingen, taught Greek at the University of Virginia from 1856 to 1876, and went to Johns Hopkins University as Professor of Greek when it opened. He taught there for thirty-nine years; John Dewey was one of his admirers.

Gödel, Kurt (1906–   ), noted Czech-Austrian mathematical logician, demonstrated in 1930 that there are sentences in logico-mathematical systems like Whitehead and Russell's *Principia Mathematica* that are formally undecidable; one cannot prove in the systems that they are either true or false. In 1931 Gödel showed that any system of mathematics as a whole was incomplete and incompletable. He achieved the arithmetization of logical syntax by correlating each of his primitive signs with a natural number. A member of the Vienna Circle, he came to the United States in 1940 to be first a member, and then a professor of the Institute for Advanced Study at Princeton. He has continued to do major work in the realm of mathematical logic, as well as in relativity theory and the philosophy of Leibniz.

Greenough, James Bradstreet (1833–1901) was Professor of Latin at Harvard University, 1874–1901.

Griffith, Coleman R[oberts] (1893–   ) was Professor of Education and Psychology and Director of the Bureau of Institutional Research at the University of Illinois before becoming Emeritus Professor in 1953. He has written a number of books on systematic psychology and applied psychology.

Gross, Bertram M[yron] (1912–   ) is Professor of Administration at Syracuse University. He has been a fellow in the Center for Advanced Research in the Behavioral Sciences at Stanford University, and has held many administrative and advisory positions in government, foundations, and business. His *The Legislative Struggle* (1953) is based on Bentley's prior work in this field. Gross contributed to *Life, Language, Law: Essays in Honor of Arthur F. Bentley* (1957).

Grote, John (1813–1866) was Professor of Moral Philosophy in the University of Cambridge. He was a critic of the claims of Phenomenalism or Positivism outside the natural sciences and advocated some sort of objective or metaphysical idealism. His distinction between "knowledge by acquaintance" and "knowledge about" was taken up by William James and Bertrand Russell. His *Exploratio Philosophica*, I and II (1865, 1900), contains most of the central themes of his philosophy.

Gumplowicz, Ludwig (1838–1909), a Polish sociologist, was Professor of Law at the University of Graz from 1875 until his suicide in 1909. His almost exclusive interest was in groups and their relations. He saw the dynamic of civilization as a conflict between, first, racially distinct groups, then between states founded by stronger groups who had conquered and subjected to themselves the weaker ones, and ultimately between classes in these states. He is regarded as one of the founders of sociology in that he sought to set it up as a discipline subject to the same objective inquiry as the physical sciences.

Harris, William T[orrey] (1835–1909), was the founder of the *Journal of Speculative Philosophy,* a leader in the St. Louis school of German idealism, and a critic of agnosticism and empiricism. He encouraged Dewey to pursue a philosophical career. He was also administrator of the St. Louis, Missouri, public schools and was United States Commissioner of Education from 1899 to 1906.

Hartshorne, Charles (1897–   ) has taught philosophy at the University of Chicago and Emory University, and is now at the University of Texas. He edited with Paul Weiss the first six volumes of the *Collected Papers of Charles Sanders Peirce* (1931–35). He is the author, among other works, of *The Divine Relativity* (1948) and *Reality as a Social Process* (1953).

Hayek, Friedrich [August von] (1899–   ), Austrian economist and philosopher, was born in Vienna but became a naturalized British citizen. He has taught at the University of London, and since 1950 at the University of Chicago. His works include *The Pure Theory of Capital* (1950) and *The Counter-Revolution of Science* (1952).

Heisenberg, Werner [Karl] (1901–   ), German physicist, is Director of the Max Planck Institute for Physics and Astrophysics, Munich, and Professor at the University of Munich. His famous paper setting forth the uncertainty principle in quantum mechanics was published in 1927. He was awarded the Nobel Prize for Physics in 1932. In 1958 he announced the formulation of a unified field theory which has not yet been established.

Heitler, Walter (1904–   ) is Professor of Theoretical Physics at the University of Zürich. He is known for his (and F. London's) *Theory of the Chemical Bond* (1927) and his *Quantum Theory of Radiation* (1936).

Hilbert, David (1862–1943) was Professor of Mathematics at the University of Göttingen. He made important contributions to the theory of numbers, the theory of invariants, and mathematical physics. He attempted to avoid various paradoxes by introducing or strengthening rigor in the formulation of axioms or postulates for different branches of mathematics. In contrast to the logistic school of Whitehead and Russell and the intuitionist school of Brouwer, he developed a formalism or metamathematics that was designed to save mathematics from contradictions by interpreting it as the study of symbols and their interrelations.

Hocking, William Ernest (1873–   ) is Emeritus Professor of Philosophy in Harvard University. He has been an ardent champion of the kind of philosophic idealism advocated by Josiah Royce and a severe critic of various aspects of Dewey's philosophy. His best known books are *The Meaning of God in Human Experience* (1912) and *Human Nature and Its Remaking* (1918).

Hofstadter, Albert (1910–   ), Professor of Philosophy at Columbia University, is known for his writings on Locke, the logic of imperatives, aesthetics, and a naturalistic metaphysics.

Holt, Edwin B[issell] (1873–1951) taught psychology at Harvard and at Princeton. He was a brilliant disciple of William James and a vigorous champion of the New Realism and behaviorism. He defined consciousness as a special kind of sensorimotor adjustment to an object and characterized the "meaning" of a word as nothing but a conditioned response to that word. His major works were *The Concept of Consciousness* (1914), *The Freudian Wish* (1915), and *Animal Drive and the Learning Process* (1931).

Hollingworth, Harry L[evi] (1880–1956) was Professor of Psychology at Columbia University and became Emeritus Professor in 1946. He wrote on abnormal, educational, and experimental psychology and carried on research into the effect of drugs on behavior. In his *Psychology of Thought* (1926) he attacked the association of ideas doctrine by emphasizing in his theory of "redintegration" total experience and the way in which an element in thought *functions for* the whole situation of which it once was a part; the part acts for the whole.

Hook, Sidney (1902–   ) is Professor Emeritus of Philosophy at New York University. He is a noted champion of experimental naturalism, democracy, and economic reform. He has written extensively on Marxism and is known for his penetrating analyses of social and political issues. He has been unusually close to Dewey as student, coworker, and exponent of Dewey's philosophy. Among Hook's works are *The Metaphysics of Pragmatism* (1927), *The Hero in History* (1943), *Education for Modern Man* (1946, rev. ed. 1963), and *Heresy, Yes–Conspiracy, No* (1953).

Hughes, Percy (1872–1952) was Professor of Philosophy at Lehigh University from 1931 to 1942. He wrote on the underlying theory of psychology, the concept of action, and education.

Hull, Clark L[eonard] (1884–1952), American psychologist in the behavioristic tradition, taught at the University of Wisconsin and at Yale where he was Sterling Professor of Psychology from 1947 until his death. He made important contributions to the scientific study of human behavior by stressing measurement of both stimulation and response, and formulating in a rigorous mathematical way their interrelations. He set up postulates concerning the events that go on inside an organism between the stimulation and the response, and sought to test conclusions based on these postulates by critical experiments. His *Principles of Behavior* (1943), *Behavioral Systems* (1952), and *Mathematico-Deductive Theory of Rote Learning* (1940) are widely known.

Hunter, Walter S[amuel] (1889–1954) was Professor of Psychology at Brown University from 1936 to 1954. He worked in the fields of animal behavior and learning theory. He defended behaviorism in psychology on the ground that an adequate account could be given of psychological problems without referring to the terms consciousness and introspection. Probably his best known book was *Human Behavior* (1938).

Huntington, Edward V[ermilye] (1874–1952) was Professor of Mechanics in the Harvard University Department of Mathematics from 1919 to 1941, when he became Emeritus Professor. He made important contributions to mathematical logic.

Husserl, Edmund [Gustav Albrecht] (1859–1938), Austro-German philosopher, is noted for his "transcendental phenomenology." He believed that philosophy has a special method of its own. Briefly, this method consists of a series of "reductions" from the phenomena presented to us in consciousness. These reductions increasingly permit us to forget the object and concentrate on our *experience* of the object. Husserl calls this process "bracketing"; it is a form of suspension of belief or judgment. Perhaps *Ideas for a Pure Phenomenology*, Book I (1913), Books II, III (1952–54), and *Logical Investigations* (1900–01, rev. ed. 1913–21) are his most significant works.

Hutten, Ulrich von (1488–1523), German humanist, was educated for a career in the church, but he became a roving scholar interested in turning humanistic learning to social and political purposes. He especially hoped to free Germany from foreign and papal domination.

Infeld, Leopold (1898–   ), a Polish physicist, is Professor at the University of Warsaw. He wrote (with Einstein) *The Evolution of Physics* (1938), a biography, *Albert Einstein* (1950), and *Motion and Relativity* (1960).

James, William (1842–1910), American psychologist and philosopher, in his *Principles of Psychology* (1890) firmly placed psychology upon a physiological basis and at the same time explored "the stream of consciousness" on an introspectionist basis. In *Pragmatism* (1907) he extended to the term "truth" Peirce's notion that the meaning of a term is completely exhausted by the practical effects the term might have. James treated all ideas in terms of their function. He stressed the relatedness of ideas as elements in experience to future experiences that explicate or fulfill their meaning in his *Essays in Radical Empiricism* (1912). In metaphysics he was a thorough-going pluralist and advocate of free will against the claims of universal mechanistic deter-

704

minism. He also espoused a version of realism he called "neutral monism": mind and matter are different organizations of the "neutral" stuff of which the world is made. His "will to believe" stressed "the right" to champion a hypothesis when the available evidence was not conclusively against it.

Jennings, H[erbert] S[pencer] (1868–1947), American biologist and philosopher, specialized in research on the physiology of microorganisms, animal behavior, and genetics. Two important books of his are *The Behavior of Lower Organisms* (1906) and *The Biological Basis of Human Nature* (1930).

Jevons, William Stanley (1835–1882), English economist and logician, is known for his *Pure Logic* (1864), in which he made some notational improvements upon Boole's work and his *Principles of Science* (1874), in which he stressed the importance of framing and testing hypotheses in inductive reasoning.

Jordan, E[lijah] (1875–1953) is, perhaps, best known for his *The Good Life* (1949). He was Professor of Philosophy at Butler University until his retirement in 1945. He also wrote *Forms of Individuality* (1927) and *The Aesthetic Object* (1937).

Joseph, H[orace] W[illiam] B[rindley] (1867–1943) was an English logician and a Fellow of New College, Oxford University. In *Logic: The Theory of Inquiry*, Dewey referred to Joseph's *An Introduction to Logic* (1906), contrasting his own view with the Aristotelian logic presented by Joseph. The latter held that logic must be anchored in metaphysics and developed a philosophy in the direction of Platonic Idealism. His books include *The Concept of Evolution* (1924) and *Some Problems of Ethics* (1931).

Kantor, J[acob] R[obert] (1888–   ), Professor of Psychology, Indiana University (Emeritus since 1960), developed an "interactional," organismic psychology, in which the interdependence and formal unity of all organic responses are noted, but with an emphasis upon objectivism. His work in this field and in the psychology of language were praised by Bentley as moving in the direction of Bentley and Dewey's positions in *Knowing and the Known*. Kantor's *Psychology and Logic*, 2 vols. (1945, 1950), is perhaps his most ambitious work.

Kaufmann, Felix (1895–1949), Austrian philosopher, was Professor of Philosophy, Logic, and Methodology at the New School for Social Research in New York. An active member of the Vienna Circle, he came to the United States in 1938. He, Dewey, and Bentley carried on a vigorous correspondence. Perhaps Kaufmann's best known work is *The Methodology of the Social Sciences* (1944).

Kelley, Earl C[larence] (1895–   ) is Professor of Education at Wayne State University. His *Education for What is Real* (1947, with a foreword by Dewey) is a report on some aspects of Ames' work in visual perception that are important to educators.

Kilpatrick, Franklin P. (1920–   ) taught psychology at Princeton University and is now at the Brookings Institution. He was associated with Ames and Cantril and edited *Explorations in Transactional Psychology* (1961).

Kleist, Heinrich von (1777–1811), German dramatist, poet, and short-story writer, regarded by critics as an *avant-garde* writer of great distinction and power.

Klüver, Heinrich (1897–   ), Gestalt psychologist, born in Germany, came to the United States in 1923. He has written on experimental psychology, animal behavior, and the development of methods in comparative psychology. He has been Sewell L. Avery Distinguished Service Professor at the University of Chicago since 1957.

Knight, Frank H[yneman] (1885–   ), American economist and philosopher, is Hull Distinguished Service Emeritus Professor of Social Science at the University of Chicago. He has written on risk, uncertainty, and profit; the economic order and religion, freedom and reform.

Koestler, Arthur (1905–   ), Hungarian-born author and journalist, wrote *Darkness at Noon* (1941), *The Yogi and the Commissar* (1945), and *The Sleepwalkers* (1959). He is known as a humanist and as a critic of communism.

Koffka, Kurt (1886–1941), German psychologist, was one of the founders of Gestalt psychology. After holding posts in German universities, he became William Allen Neilson professor of experimental and educational psychology at Smith College in 1927. He was interested in problems of perception and optics and contributed to value theory. His writings include *The Growth of the Mind* (1924) and *Principles of Gestalt Psychology* (1935).

Köhler, Wolfgang (1887–   ), German psychologist, born in Esthonia, was one of the founders of Gestalt psychology. He was Professor of Psychology at Swarthmore, 1935–55, and was a member of the Institute for Advanced Study in 1956. Among his works are *The Mentality of Apes* (1917; English ed. 1925) and *The Place of Value in a World of Fact* (1938).

Korzybski, Alfred [Habdank Skarbek] (1879–1950), Polish semanticist, the founder and director of the Institute of General Semantics in Chicago, 1938–50, was the author of *Science and Sanity* (1933). He and Bentley corresponded on problems of mathematical logic in the late 1920's and early 1930's.

Krikorian, Y[ervant] H. (1892–   ) is Emeritus Professor of Philosophy at the College of the City of New York. Born in Turkey, he

706

took his Ph.D. degree at Harvard in 1933. He is oriented philosophically toward naturalism and was editor and contributor to *Naturalism and The Human Spirit* (1944).

Lanier, Emilio Aguinaldo (1900–　　) is Professor of English at Fisk University, Nashville, Tennessee.

Lashley, Karl S[pencer] (1890–1958), Director of the Yerkes Laboratory of Primate Biology and Research Professor in Neuropsychology at Harvard University until 1955, was a behavioristic, experimental psychologist who emphasized the importance of viewing the organism as a system which in some sense functions as a whole. He demonstrated the futility of punctiform localizations in the brain as clues to specific learning processes. His major work was *Brain Mechanisms and Intelligence* (1929).

Lawrence, Merle (1915–　　) is Professor of Physiology at the University of Michigan.

Lewes, George Henry (1817–1878), English philosopher, psychologist, and scholar, was a positivist in most of his scientific and philosophic views. But at the end of his life he made room for the study of empirical metaphysics. He had some insights on emergent evolution but never developed them adequately. His *Biographical History of Philosophy* first appeared in 1845–46. His major philosophical work is *Problems of Life and Mind* (1873–1879).

Lewin, Kurt (1890–1947), German psychologist, is best known for his "topological" psychology. After coming to the United States in 1932, he taught at the University of Iowa, 1935–44, and at Massachusetts Institute of Technology, 1944–47. He developed a view of psychological activity occurring within a "life space," and saw psychological needs as tension systems. He did important work on child behavior and group dynamics. His major books are *A Dynamic Theory of Personality* (1935) and *Principles of Topological Psychology* (1936).

Lewis, C[larence] I[rving] (1883–1964), American logician and philosopher, was Edgar Pierce Professor of Philosophy at Harvard University and until 1964 Professor Emeritus. He had made basic contributions to mathematical logic and the theory of knowledge and of value. He worked out a logic of "strict implication," one of the first successful symbolic systems of "modal" logic as an alternative to Russell's system of "material implication" and its paradoxes. Lewis recognized the possibility of a large number of self-consistent, but distinct logics, none intrinsically superior to the others. He held that the sole criterion of choice among them is the pragmatic one of greater convenience in organizing our intellectual experiences that may result from adopting one system rather than another. He developed in *Mind and the World Order* (1929) a special pragmatic theory

707

of the *a priori* as a definition or postulate that we can maintain in the face of all experience. In his *An Analysis of Knowledge and Valuation* (1946) he linked empirical propositions and valuations and contended that ethics is the "cap-stone" of epistemology and the theory of meaning.

Lillie, Ralph S[tayner] (1875–1952) was Professor of Physiology at the University of Chicago. He specialized in research on the fundamental properties of living substance and the physiology of growth. In his *General Biology and Philosophy of Organism* (1945) he expounded an "organismic" theory of biology stressing the role of mind and goals in evolution.

Llewellyn, Karl N[ickerson] (1893–1962), American legal scholar who taught at Yale, Columbia, and the University of Chicago, is well known as a "realist" in the field of law. Jerome Frank referred to him as a "legal Deweyite." His major field of interest was the law of contracts. He is the author of *Jurisprudence: Realism in Theory and Practice* (1962).

Lotze, Rudolf Hermann (1817–1881), German Idealist philosopher, resisted the tendency, strong among neo-Kantians, to abandon metaphysics for epistemology. He held that things happen in a manner determined by material conditions, but that there is a plan, or ideal purpose, controlling events. He had an important influence, positive and negative, on English and American philosophers. James, Dewey, and Santayana referred to Lotze's ideas in their early writings. His major works were *Logic* (1843), *Microcosmus* (1856–64), and *Metaphysics* (1879).

Mach, Ernst (1838–1916), Austrian physicist and philosopher, in his *Science of Mechanics* (1883), demolished the view that mechanics was the main basis of physics. A vigorous exponent of positivism in the philosophy of science, he attacked all metaphysics and denied the "reality" of atoms, absolute space, absolute time, and causality. His writings laid the foundations of logical positivism. They influenced Einstein in his youth, but Einstein later took issue with several of Mach's positions.

Mackay, Donald S[age] (1892–1951) was Professor of Philosophy at the University of California. He published essays on knowledge and society and on Plato and the history of science. He criticized Dewey's use of the phrase "indeterminate situation."

Mannheim, Karl (1893–1947) is best known for his work in the "sociology of knowledge." A refugee from Nazi persecution, he lectured in the London School of Economics and Political Science until his death. His *Ideology and Utopia* (1929), subtitled *An Introduction to the Sociology of Knowledge,* found a large audience among scholars and laymen.

Margenau, Henry (1901–   ), born in Germany, educated in the United States, is Eugene Higgins Professor of Physics and Natural Philosophy at Yale. He is the author (with R. B. Lindsay) of *The Foundations of Physics* (1936) and *The Nature of Physical Reality* (1950).

Marhenke, Paul (1899–1952), born in Germany, educated in America, was Professor of Philosophy at the University of California. He wrote on the theory of knowledge, the relation of logic to language, and the criterion of significance.

Maxwell, James Clerk (1831–1879), Scottish physicist, wrote a classic *Treatise on Electricity and Magnetism* (1873). This gave a mathematical formulation to Faraday's theory of electrical and magnetic forces and led to the discovery of electro-magnetic waves by Hertz in 1886. His scientific papers on analogy, experimentation, and theory formation are still illuminating.

Mayeroff, Milton (1925–   ), Assistant Professor of Philosophy at State University College, Cortland, N. Y., has defended Dewey's *Logic* against certain criticisms and written on the self and its unity.

Mayo, [George] Elton (1880–1949), an Australian-born industrial relations expert, was Professor of Industrial Research at the Harvard Graduate School of Business. He revolutionized the study of industrial relations by carrying out experiments that demonstrated that individual efficiency was greatly affected by the harmony or disharmony of each working group within an organization. His volume, *The Human Problems of an Industrial Civilization* (1933), has had an influence on industrial sociology and economics.

McCormick, Anne O'Hare (1882–1954), writer and for over fifteen years a member of the editorial board of *The New York Times,* won the Pulitzer Prize for distinguished foreign reporting in 1937.

McGraw, Myrtle B[yram] (1899–   ), teacher of psychology at Briarcliff College, wrote *Growth* (1935), with an introduction by Dewey, and *Maturation of the Human Infant* (1963).

Mead, George H[erbert] (1863–1931), American philosopher and social psychologist, was an original mind of a high order. He developed a social psychology based upon a behavioristic theory of signs. Mind he held to be a part of the natural process of emergence, reducible "without residue" to language. He analyzed the social factors resulting in the formation of the "self," especially through each human organism learning to play different roles. He stressed the temporal present as the ultimate locus of existence and the world as "a world of events." He attempted to overcome the Newtonian "bifurcation of nature" and the realists' abstractions from experience by constructing a new metaphysics. A thoroughgoing relativist and pluralist, he held

709

that each situation is equally real with every other and that all have novel aspects that require a reconstruction of customary perspectives. His chief works are *Mind, Self and Society* (1934), *The Philosophy of the Act* (1938), and *The Philosophy of the Present* (1932).

Mesthene, Emmanuel G. (1920–   ) has been a research analyst with the Rand Coroporation.

Meyer, Adolf (1866–1950), psychiatrist, neurologist, born in Switzerland, came to the United States in 1892. He was Professor of Psychiatry at Johns Hopkins University and director, Henry Phipps Psychiatric Clinic, Johns Hopkins Hospital, 1910–41; Professor Emeritus, 1941–50. He interpreted mental disorders as inadequate habits of dealing with the difficulties of life. Independently of Freud, he emphasized the explanatory importance in dementia praecox of symbolic operations by the person as against the physiological activity of his neurones. He defined mind not as a form of mind stuff, but as a "sufficiently organized living being in action," with stress on the adaptation and adjustment of the individual as a whole to the social setting of which he was a part.

Meyer, Max Frederick (1873–   ), born and educated in Germany, was Professor of Experimental Psychology at the University of Missouri until he retired in 1932. He developed a behavioristic psychology in *The Fundamental Laws of Human Behavior* (1911) and in *Abnormal Psychology* (1927). He presented certain insights in *The Psychology of the Other One* (1921) that Dewey appreciated.

Mill, James (1773–1836), English economist and Utilitarian philosopher, was the father of John Stuart Mill. James Mill's *Analysis of the Phenomena of the Human Mind* (1829) is a classic statement of associationist psychology.

Montague, William Pepperell (1873–1953), Johnsonian Professor of Philosophy, Columbia University, and colleague of John Dewey, was distinguished as an originator of neo-Realism and the formulator of a panschistic cosmology. He attempted a synthesis of realism, subjectivism, and critical realism. His challenging positions in the philosophy of science, ethics, and religion were expounded in *The Ways of Knowing* (1925), *Belief Unbounded* (1930), and *The Ways of Things* (1940).

Moore, Addison W[ebster] (1866–1930), Professor of Philosophy at the University of Chicago, contributed to *Studies in Logical Theory* and was a member of the Chicago school of pragmatists. His *Pragmatism and Its Critics* (1910) was an important defense and development of Dewey's and his own ideas.

Moore, G[eorge] E[dward] (1873–1958), English analytic philosopher, was a pioneer in the New Realist movement and in recent "ordinary

710

language" philosophy. He stubbornly defended our common-sense beliefs, holding that we really know the meaning of such words as good, know, real, etc. His ethical system rested on the thesis that the meaning of good is a simple, nonnatural quality, known to us but unanalyzable. His prose is greatly admired both for its grace and its lucidity. Among his many works are "A Defence of Common Sense" in *Contemporary British Philosophy,* Vol. 1 (1925) and *Principia Ethica* (1903).

Morgan, [Conway] Lloyd (1852–1936), English biologist and philosopher, developed the doctrine of "emergent evolution"—the belief that the "higher life processes" evolve out of physico-chemical processes and are continuous with, but not reducible to, them. In *Emergent Evolution* (1923) and *Life, Mind and Spirit* (1926), he rejected vitalism as a scientific hypothesis.

Morgenthau, Hans J[oachim] (1904–   ), Professor of Political Science at the University of Chicago, has written on foreign and domestic politics and political theory in *Politics in the Twentieth Century,* 3 vols. (1962).

Morris, Charles W[illiam] (1901–   ), American philosopher, tried to synthesize the behavioristic pragmatism of George H. Mead and the logical empiricism of the Vienna Circle. He has taught philosophy at the University of Chicago, the New School for Social Research, and the University of Florida. His book on semiotics (the general theory of signs), *Signs, Language and Behavior* (1946), won approval from most logical empiricists, but sharp criticism from Dewey and Bentley.

Nagel, Ernest (1901–   ) is John Dewey Professor of Philosophy at Columbia University. Born in Czechoslovakia, he migrated to the United States in 1911, and studied with Morris R. Cohen and Dewey, who regarded Nagel's technical command of logic so highly that he sought his criticism of much of *Logic: The Theory of Inquiry* while it was in preparation. Nagel shares Dewey's contextualistic naturalism but dissents from Dewey on some characteristic pragmatic doctrines. Nagel wrote, with Cohen, an outstanding textbook on logic. In his *The Structure of Science* (1961), Nagel made a notable contribution to the philosophy of science.

Nathanson, Jerome (1908–   ) is Leader in the New York State Society for Ethical Culture and Chairman of the Fraternity of Leaders of the American Ethical Union. A historian and philosopher, he is the author of *John Dewey: The Reconstruction of the Democratic Life* (1951). He was close to Dewey in Dewey's latter years.

Needham, [Noël] Joseph [Terrence] (1900–   ), Reader in Biochemistry at Cambridge University, has written on the biology and the

711

philosophy of biology in *Order and Life* (1935), *Chemical Embryology*, 3 vols. (1931), and *Biochemistry and Morphogenesis* (1942).

Neurath, Otto (1882–1945), Austrian sociologist and philosopher, was one of the "physicalist" group of the Vienna Circle. He held that all the sciences depend ultimately on protocol sentences stated in terms of physical objects and processes. Hence, all empirical sentences can be stated in the language of physics. This was the theoretical foundation for his "unity of science" movement. He was editor-in-chief of the *Encyclopedia of Unified Science* at the time of his death.

Nicholas of Cusa (1401–1464), Roman Catholic Cardinal, reformer, and scholar, developed a neo-Platonic philosophy that served as a bridge between a waning Thomism and the Renaissance. He denounced perverted scholasticism in his *Of Learned Ignorance* (1440), and anticipated modern scientific advances on several basic questions, such as the movement of the earth around the sun.

Ogden, C[harles] K[ay] (1889–1957), English philosopher and linguistic reformer, is best known, perhaps, for his *The Meaning of Meaning* (1923, with I. A. Richards) and for his work in the Basic English movement.

Oppenheim, Paul (1885–   ), German-born philosopher, came to the United States in 1939. He has contributed, with his collaborators, valuable essays on the logic of explanation and on the philosophy of science. He has been closely allied with the Logical Empiricists.

Pauli, Wolfgang (1900–1958), Austrian-Swiss physicist and a professor at the University of Zürich, wrote *Meson Theory of Nuclear Forces* (1947) and *The Interpretation of Nature and the Psyche* (1955). He won the Nobel Prize in Physics in 1945.

Pavlov, Ivan [Petrovich] (1849–1936), Russian physiologist, author of *Lectures on Conditioned Reflexes* (first English edition, 1928), is known for his work on "conditioned" or acquired reflexes and for having put experimental psychology on a "behavioristic," natural-science basis.

Peirce, Charles [Santiago] Sanders (1839–1914), American logician and pragmatist, developed the logic of relatives, a frequency theory of probability, and important analyses of the logic of scientific method. His theory of signs became the basis for modern developments. His "pragmaticism" was a method for clarifying ideas in terms of their experimental consequences. He exalted logical generalization and rational habits of action as against James' stress on the individual's perception and personal experience. Peirce worked out a cosmology and metaphysics of great speculative brilliance and power, if not complete consistency. He attacked mechanism and determinism as universal principles of explanation and defended the reality of absolute chance. He pictured the universe as evolving from a chaotic state and acquiring laws, regularities, or "habits of mind." He influenced James, Royce, and Dewey in divergent ways. His major writings were published in his *Collected Papers*, 8 vols. (1931–58).

Pepper, Stephen C[oburn] (1891–   ) was Professor of Philosophy at the University of California, 1930–1958. He is a naturalist and pragmatist who has developed his own system, building on the work of Dewey and R. B. Perry. Pepper has stressed the relationship of cognition to ethical choices and aesthetic appreciations. He recognizes the diversity of possible world views, but emphasizes the historical and social context of each qualitatively unique event, object, and individual. His main works are *World Hypotheses* (1942), *The Work of Art* (1955), and *The Sources of Value* (1958).

Perry, Ralph Barton (1876–1957), Professor of Philosophy at Harvard University, was co-author of an attack upon Idealism called *The New Realism* (1912). He stressed the independence of the existence of known objects from the knower and asserted the empirical or naturalistic thesis: to have value is to be an object of interest to some human being. His main works are *General Theory of Value* (1926) and *Realms of Value* (1954). He also wrote a notable biography, *The Thought and Character of William James,* 2 vols. (1935), which needs, however, to be supplemented by the writings of Horace M. Kallen on James.

Pillsbury, Walter B[owers] (1872–1960) was Professor of Psychology at the University of Michigan from 1910 until 1942. He contributed to studies in physiological psychology and problems in reading and wrote an influential *History of Psychology* (1929).

Poincaré, [Jules] Henri (1854–1912), French mathematician and physicist, contributed to mathematics, physics, and astronomy. He held that there were many alternative geometries and that many divergent scientific theories might be built on any finite set of observations. His *Science and Hypothesis* (1903) and *Science and Method* (1908) were highly influential books.

Proust, Marcel (1871–1922), French novelist, wrote *Remembrance of Things Past,* an eleven-volume work which profoundly influenced the development of the psychological novel.

Quine, Willard V[an] O[rman] (1908–   ), American mathematical logician, is Edgar Pierce Professor of Philosophy at Harvard. He contends that formal logic cannot be ontologically neutral, since he believes any system of logic commits us to accept the existence of some distinctive kinds of entities. Ontology, he argues, is not determined by the proper names in a statement, but by the types of variables in it for which substitutions must be made. He has attacked the distinction between synthetic (roughly, empirical) and analytic (or necessary) statements. He also holds that isolated statements cannot be tested by themselves. His chief philosophical works are *From a Logical Point of View* (1953) and *Word and Object* (1960).

Randall, John Herman, Jr. (1899–   ) is F. J. E. Woodbridge Professor of Philosophy at Columbia University. He has written notable books in the history of philosophy, e.g., *Aristotle* (1960) and *The Career of Philosophy* (1962). His *Making of the Modern Mind* (1926) blazed a trail in intellectual history for several generations of college students. He has developed a naturalistic metaphysics and a philosophy of history and religion. A student and colleague of Dewey's, he has written incisively on Dewey's ideas and place in philosophy.

Ratner, Joseph (1901–   ) has taught philosophy at Columbia, the City College of New York, and New York University. He was a student and colleague of Dewey's at Columbia and edited several important selections of Dewey's writings, e.g., *Characters and Events*, 2 vols. (1929), *Intelligence in the Modern World: John Dewey's Philosophy* (1939). His introduction to the latter book is excellent. He gave highly valued suggestions to Dewey on such works as *Experience and Nature, Logic: The Theory of Inquiry,* and *Knowing and the Known.*

Ratner, Sidney (1908–   ) is Professor of History at Rutgers—The State University. He has published in economic history a standard work, *American Taxation: Its History as a Social Force in Democracy* (1942). He has also contributed essays on the history of ideas and the philosophy of history, e.g., "History as Inquiry," in S. Hook, ed., *Philosophy and History* (1962). He edited *The Philosopher of the Common Man: Essays in Honor of John Dewey* (1940), *Inquiry into Inquiries: Essays in Social Theory,* by Arthur F. Bentley (1954), and *Vision & Action: Essays in Honor of Horace M. Kallen* (1953). In 1956–57 he was a member of the Institute for Advanced Study at Princeton. In 1959–60 he was the chairman of the executive committee of the International John Dewey Centennial Committee.

Reid, Thomas (1710–1796), originator of the Scottish common-sense philosophy, attacked the skepticism of Hume in his *Inquiry into the Human Mind* (1764). Reid asserted that there were certain instinctive, unquestionable presuppositions at the basis of all knowledge, implanted in us by God. These principles of common sense include a belief in the external world, our own thoughts and existence, and causality. He held that men have an intuitive grasp of right and wrong and that to know the good is to desire it. Reid inspired C. S. Peirce's "critical common-sense" and anticipated much in G. E. Moore's "Defence of Common Sense."

Richards, I[vor] A[rmstrong] (1893–   ), English semanticist, literary critic, and poet, is the author, with C. K. Ogden, of the pathbreaking work, *The Meaning of Meaning* (1923). In this book he and Ogden fused Peirce's theory of signs with a behavioristic psychology. Among his important works are *Principles of Literary Criticism* (1924), *Practical Criticism* (1929), and *Speculative Instruments* (1955). He has been University Professor at Harvard University since 1944.

Rice, Philip Blair (1904–56), Professor of Philosophy at Kenyon College, 1944–56, was an exponent of ethical naturalism. His major work was *On the Knowledge of Good and Evil* (1955).

Roethlisberger, Fritz Jules (1898–   ) has been Donham Professor of Human Relations at Harvard University since 1950. His field is management and worker relations and worker motivation.

Romanes, G[eorge] J[ohn] (1848–1894), British naturalist, pioneered in the study of intelligence in animals. He was interested also in the development of the faculty of reason in humans. An ardent Darwinian, he sought to understand the development of mind in Darwin's categories.

Rosenblatt, Louise Michelle (1904–   ) taught English at Barnard and Brooklyn College and is Professor of English, School of Education, New York University. She has written on the art for art's sake movement, the theory of literature, and the teaching of English. She is author of, among other works, *Literature as Exploration* (1938).

Royce, Josiah (1855–1916) was the most distinguished Absolute Idealist in America, a brilliant defender of the Christian view of the world with dialectical arguments that professed a complete acceptance of modern science. From 1882 to 1915 he was Professor of Philosophy at Harvard University. His Idealism meant that the universe is not alien at bottom to human thought and effort and that its true inner nature is revealed in the process of our thinking. All things find their condition and meaning in the totality to which they belong. Yet he recognized that there is an irrational element in the world and that there is constant frustration of our wills and ideals. This he justified on the ground that life is a struggle between good and evil, and the struggle for the good life cannot be unless evil exists. In his later writings the unity of the World Mind or Logos became replaced by the unity of a community, indeed the unity of a federal republic, in which the parts have their own spheres of supremacy. He contributed to pragmatism by his stress on the practical aspect of ideas and to neo-Realism by his writing on logic as the most general science of objective order. His two major books were *The Spirit of Modern Philosophy* (1892) and *The World and the Individual,* 2 vols. (1901).

Runes, Dagobert D[avid] (1902–   ) is president and editor of the Philosophical Library, a New York publishing firm.

Russell, Bertrand [Arthur William], third Earl Russell (1872–   ), distinguished English philosopher-logician-mathematician, developed a variety of philosophic positions over his long life, yet he propounded many influential theses and has held to some of them persistently. At Cambridge he first became converted to Hegelian Idealism through the writings of F. H. Bradley, but was won over to neo-Realism by G. E. Moore, largely because Moore's assertion of the independence of the known object from the knower seemed to preserve the objective validity of mathematics. To achieve a full guarantee of mathematical truth, he attempted to reduce mathematics to logic, first in his *Principles of Mathematics* (1903), and then in *Principia Mathematica* with A. N. Whitehead, 3 vols. (1910–13). Certain paradoxes that developed he tried to dissolve through his controversial theory of types. In his epistemology Russell distinguished between knowledge by acquaintance and knowledge by description; the first type giving greater security than the second. In his metaphysics he was a pluralist and a believer in the thesis that mind and matter are logical constructions out of sense-data which themselves are neither physical nor mental. Through Wittgenstein he came to hold the doctrine of Logical Atomism, viz., the world consists of atomic facts characterized by their directly corresponding to elementary propositions. In the 1930's he praised the Logical Empiricists and gave up his platonic views of the reality of mathematical entities. But he has come to stress the limits of empiricism and to feel the necessity for developing postulates that will justify induction and other nondeductive phases of science. He has always criticized Dewey's theory of truth and his theory of logic as inquiry. But he and Dewey are at one in espousing liberalism and one form or another of naturalism. Russell's latest important works are *An Inquiry into Meaning and Truth* (1940) and *Human Knowledge: Its Scope and Limits* (1948).

Santayana, George (1863–1952) was born in Spain and educated in America. He taught philosophy at Harvard University with James and Royce until he could retire to Europe in 1912 to devote himself exclusively to his meditations and writing. He was the most distinguished representative in America of a rationalistic naturalism based upon the Hellenic ideal of the good life. For him "everything ideal has a natural basis and everything natural has an ideal development." He rejected supernaturalism in metaphysics and morals and saw mind as an outgrowth and function of the body. He taught that the existence of ideals and values depended upon matter in motion, but not their validity. His book, *The Life of Reason*, 5 vols. (1904–05), is a magnificent study of the ways in which human effort and intelligence have achieved or may achieve satisfaction in ideal forms in the areas of common sense, society, art, religion, and science. To him, reason was a harmony of diverse impulses, truth, and fate. Dewey praised this work as a great contribution to moral philosophy, but most American philosophers have disliked Santayana's atheistic catholicism, antipuritanical aristocracy, and relativistic aesthetics and ethics. His later writings replaced his earlier stress upon naturalism with an emphasis upon the life of spirituality and the contemplation of essences and eternity as against the world and all existences. His doctrine of essences separated universals from existence and held that all beliefs about existence are acts of irrational "animal faith." His main later works are *Scepticism and Animal Faith* (1923) and *Realms of Being*, 4 vols. (1927–40).

Schiller, F[erdinand] C[anning] S[cott] (1864–1937), the "English pragmatist," was born in Germany, educated in England, and taught philosophy at Cornell, Oxford, and the University of Southern California. He discovered the basic principles of pragmatism on his own early in 1891, but did not proclaim himself a pragmatist until 1902 in a brilliant essay, "Axioms as Postulates." In *Humanism* (1903) he declared that truth and reality are man-made. He espoused a subjective Idealism that neither James nor Dewey accepted. Schiller at first called his philosophy humanism ("man is the measure of all things"), but later he preferred the term voluntarism. His basic tenet was that all human thinking and action are molded by human purposes and are intelligible only by reference to them. Truth is what gives satisfaction in the cognitive realm. Peirce criticized his initial vagueness on what he meant by "satisfaction." Schiller tried to correct this failure in his later writings and won partial approval from Dewey. Schiller persented in his *Logic for Use* (1929) an account of reasoning with a stress on hypothesis, verification, and approximation that anticipated some recent accounts of scientific procedures.

Schilpp, Paul A[rthur] (1897–   ), born in Germany, educated in the United States, is Professor of Philosophy at Northwestern University. He is the originator and editor of the *Library of Living Philosophers*, the first volume of which is on Dewey. His special field is Kantian ethics and the philosophy of religion.

Schneider, Herbert W[allace] (1892–   ) has been Director of the Blaisdell Institute at Claremont, California since 1959. Previously he was Professor of Philosophy and Religion at Columbia University. He belongs generally to the naturalistic, pragmatic tradition and has made important contributions to ethics, the philosophy of religion, and the history of ideas. Among his writings are *A History of American Philosophy* (1946, 2nd ed., 1963), *Three Dimensions of Public Morality* (1956), and *Ways of Being* (1962).

Schröder, [Friedrich Wilhelm] Ernst (1841–1902), a German logician, extended the Boolean algebra of logic to what is called the Boole-

Schröder algebra of logic, which he set forth in his *Lectures on the Algebra of Logic* (1891–1905). He was much influenced by C. S. Peirce, and their work became a basis for Whitehead and Russell's *Principia Mathematica*, 3 vols. (1910–13).

Schrödinger, Erwin (1887–1961), Austrian physicist, was Senior Professor of Physics, Institute for Advanced Studies, Dublin. He won the Nobel Prize in 1933 for his work in wave mechanics. Among his philosophical books are *Science and the Human Temperament* (1935) and *What is Life?* (1944).

Sellars, Roy Wood (1880–   ) was Professor of Philosophy at the University of Michigan from 1923 until his retirement. In epistemology he is a Critical Realist, an exponent of the doctrine that perception is an event involving three terms: the existent, the perceived datum, and the percipient. To him knowing is a "descriptive interpretation" of objects. In metaphysics he is an evolutionary naturalist, but differs from Dewey in stressing as his starting point, not human experience, but the physical object. In *A Philosophy of Physical Realism* (1932) he argued that "everything which exists is spatial and temporal and is either a physical system or is existentially inseparable from one." He was co-author of *Essays in Critical Realism* (1920).

Simmel, Georg (1858–1918), a German philosopher and sociologist, was important for stressing the individual as the basis of all groups and of society. To him the true essence of society or a group was in a sufficiently harmonious interworking of individuals to create a semblance of real unity. In his major work, *Sociology* (1909), he defined the prime subject matter of sociology as the study of social form, the characteristic, general modes of human relationships, e.g., subjection, contract, and competition. In his specific studies of social phenomena he showed himself to be a very discerning analyst of empirical data. Simmel made contributions to the philosophy of history and the social basis of economics. He maintained that the main determinants of an economic system, as well as of intellectual activities, are the general peculiarities of people's ways of thinking and standards of living.

Singer, E[dgar] A[rthur], Jr. (1873–1955) was, until his retirement in 1944, Adam Seybert Professor of Philosophy at the University of Pennsylvania. He developed an experimental and objective theory of life and mind as forms of behavior compatible with, but not reducible to the laws of mechanics. He was opposed to the assumption of superempirical entelechies or vital forces in biology on the ground that "a question not answerable by experiment is meaningless." His postulates for a philosophy of experimental science were an independent formulation of the logic of pragmatism. At the same time he

718

attempted to reconcile naturalism and idealism through his view of Nature as an "ideal reality," the limiting conception that makes scientific progress possible. Among his works is *Mind as Behavior* (1924).

Sisson, E[dward] O[ctavius] (1869–1949) was Professor of Philosophy at Reed College, 1921–39. His major interests were moral philosophy, education, and the philosophy of language.

Skinner, B[urrhus] F[rederic] (1904–   ), Professor of Psychology at Harvard, is a "re-inforcement" psychologist who has developed the theoretical assumptions and experimental techniques necessary for clarifying and quantitatively studying those types of learning which, while not of the classical Pavlovian type, exemplify reward for successful learning. He is an exponent of operational logic, an advocate of a behavior-centered psychology, and strongly opposed to introspectionism. Two of his major works are *The Behavior of Organisms* (1938) and *Verbal Behavior* (1957).

Smullyan, Arthur Francis (1912–   ) is Professor of Philosophy and Chairman of the Department of Philosophy at the University of Washington. His major interests are logic and epistemology.

Smullyan, Raymond M[errill] (1919–   ), Assistant Professor in the Graduate School of Science at Yeshiva University in New York City, is the author of *Theory of Formal Systems* (1961).

Stebbing, L[izzie] Susan (1886–1943), Professor of Philosophy at Bedford College in the University of London, 1933–43, was an exponent of mathematical logic who did justice to the merits of Aristotelian logic and even on some points to the empirical logic of J. S. Mill. But she was a strong opponent of all metaphysical and pragmatic logic. She also did important work in analytic or linguistic philosophy, e.g., *Philosophy and the Physicists* (1937). Her main work is *A Modern Introduction to Logic* (1930, 2nd ed., 1933).

Stevens, S[tanley] S[mith] (1906–   ) is Professor of Psychology and Director of the Psycho-Acoustic Laboratory at Harvard. He is co-author of *The Varieties of Human Physique* with W. H. Sheldon and W. B. Tucker (1940), and *The Varieties of Temperament* with W. H. Sheldon (1942).

Stevenson, Charles L[eslie] (1908–   ) is Professor of Philosophy at the University of Michigan. In *Ethics and Language* (1944), he set forth his famous "emotivist" theory of ethical terms: to say something is good is to state that one approves of it and seeks to evoke the same attitude in one's hearer.

Tanner, Amy Eliza (1870–   ) took a Ph.D. degree in philosophy at the University of Chicago in 1898. She was a research associate in psychology, Clark University, 1907–18.

Tarski, Alfred (1902–   ), Polish logician, Research Professor of Mathematics since 1958 at the University of California, is noted for his distinction between logic and metalogic and his "semantic" definition of truth. His work on semantics has influenced Carnap to shift his emphasis from the logical syntax of language to semantics. Tarski's major work is *Logic, Semantics, Metamathematics* (1956).

Taylor, James H[enry] (1893–   ), Emeritus Professor of Mathematics at George Washington University.

Thorndike, Edward Lee (1874–1949) was Professor of Educational Psychology in Teachers College, Columbia University from 1904 to 1940, when he became Emeritus Professor. A reinforcement psychologist, he is famous for his work in the theory of learning and for his attack on the doctrine of "formal discipline." Among his better known books are *The Measurement of Intelligence* (1926), *The Fundamentals of Learning* (1932), and *Human Nature and the Social Order* (1940).

Titchener, Edward B[radford] (1867–1927), born in England, Ph.D. in Germany, Professor of Psychology at Cornell, 1910–27, was considered the leader of the German mentalistic school of psychology in the United States. He helped to establish psychology as an experimental science, and he developed a systematic view of psychology as a science of conscious phenomena. As a leader of the conservative wing of American psychology he opposed the functionalism of James and Dewey with a "structuralism," and the behaviorism of Watson with an "introspectionism." He was critical of animal psychology, psychoanalysis, mental tests, and applied psychology. His most influential works perhaps were a *Textbook of Psychology,* 2 vols. (1909–10) and *Systematic Psychology* (1929).

Tolman, Edward C[hace] (1886–1959), was Professor of Psychology at the University of California from 1928 until 1954. He developed an original behavior-centered psychology that takes into account human purposes and goals in the light of certain insights of Gestalt psychology, especially the work of Kurt Lewin. To Tolman, organisms are constantly responding to *sign-Gestalts.* A sign-Gestalt "consists of a sign object, a signified object, and a signified means-end-relation." He is the author of *Purposive Behavior in Animals and Men* (1932) and co-author, with Talcott Parsons et al., of *Towards a Theory of Action* (1951).

Valtin, Jan [pseudonym for Richard Julius Herman Krebs] (1905–1951), a German-born writer, came to the United States illegally, served in the Second World War, and became a United States citizen with a full pardon.

Veblen, Oswald (1880–1960) was Professor of Mathematics at the Institute for Advanced Study from 1932 to 1950. One of the world's great geometers, he was the author of many classic studies in his field.

Vigotsky, L[ev] S[emenovich] (1896–1934) was Professor of Psychology at the Second Moscow University. He worked mainly in genetic psychology and in the higher psychological functions. His *Thought and Language* (English translation, 1962) is a powerful, original work, with affinities to that of G. H. Mead and Jean Piaget.

Vivas, Eliseo (1901–   ), born in Colombia, Ph.D. at Wisconsin, is Evans Professor of Moral and Intellectual Philosophy at Northwestern University. His major interest is ethics and aesthetics. He is author of *The Moral Life and the Ethical Life* (1950) and *Creation and Discovery* (1955).

Watson, John B[roadus] (1878–   ), American behaviorist psychologist, was Professor of Experimental and Comparative Psychology at Johns Hopkins University from 1908 to 1920 and is now vice-president of an advertising firm in New York City. One widely-read book of his is *Behaviorism* (1925).

Weinstock, Solomon (1925–   ), Assistant Professor of Psychology at Brooklyn College, was associated for a short while with A. F. Bentley on some research in the psychology of perception.

Weismann, August (1834–1914), German biologist and Professor at the University of Freiburg, formulated the germ-plasm theory of heredity, which denied the transmission of acquired characteristics. Darwin wrote an introduction to the English edition of his *Studies in the Theory of Descent* (1882).

Weiss, Albert P[aul] (1879–1931), was Professor of Psychology at Ohio State University 1918–31, and the author of *A Theoretical Basis of Human Behavior* (1925), an important contribution to behaviorism.

Weiss, Paul (1901–   ) is Professor of Philosophy at Yale University. Inspired by A. N. Whitehead, he has developed his own philosophical system. Perhaps his best known books are *Man's Freedom* (1950), *Nature and Man* (1947), and *Modes of Being* (1958). He was editor, with Charles Hartshorne, of the first six volumes of C. S. Peirce's *Collected Works* (1931–35).

Wertheimer, Max (1880–1943), German psychologist, the primary founder of Gestalt psychology, insisted that a proper understanding of structured wholes can be achieved only by relating the component parts to the system as a whole in which they are functioning. He threw new light on the psychology of perception, learning, and creative thinking. His *Productive Thinking* (1945) won praise from Dewey and Bentley. From 1933 until his death he was Professor of Psychology in the Graduate Faculty of the New School for Social Research in New York City.

White, Morton [Gabriel] (1917–   ) is Professor of Philosophy in Harvard University. He has contributed to the theory of logic, epistemology, and the philosophy of history. He has been both a critic and historian of American pragmatism and other recent currents of thought. His major books are *Social Thought in America* (1949) and *Toward Reunion in Philosophy* (1956).

Whitehead, Alfred North (1861–1947), the distinguished British-American philosopher and mathematician, wrote with Russell the classic attempt to derive mathematics from logic, *Principia Mathematica*, 3 vols. (1910–13). After 1914 he broke with Russell's neo-Realism and developed in *The Principles of Natural Knowledge* (1919) and *The Concept of Nature* (1920) a new philosophy of physical science in which he stressed the study of continua as against discrete sense data and the primacy of organic sensation over visual. He also expounded a Platonism based on the distinction between events and eternal "objects," the permanent features of Nature, and fought the "bifurcation of Nature" between the qualitative world of immediate experience and the purely quantitative world of scientific entities. After he was appointed Professor of Philosophy at Harvard in 1924, he elaborated an impressive system of metaphysics in his *Process and Reality* (1929), with a philosophy of organism applicable to all phases of nature. To Dewey, M. R. Cohen, G. E. Moore, and others in the empirical, analytic schools, this philosophy has seemed a brilliant, original, but vulnerable version of Hegelian Idealism. To others, e.g., Paul Weiss, Victor Lowe, Mason W. Gross, and F. S. C. Northrop, Whitehead's *Process and Reality* has represented a constructive and basically sound metaphysics.

Wiener, Philip Paul (1905–   ) is Professor of Philosophy at the College of the City of New York. He has written on the philosophy and history of science and is the author of *Evolution and the Founders of Pragmatism* (1949), with a foreword by Dewey.

Wittgenstein, Ludwig [Josef Johann] (1889–1951), Austrian philosopher, was Professor of Philosophy at Cambridge University, 1939–47. His *Tractatus Logico-Philosophicus* (1922), greatly influenced the philosophers of the Vienna Circle. He presented a metaphysics according to which the world consists of simple facts, none dependent upon any other. Language, he held, has as its primary aim the picturing of facts and has a structure similar to what it describes. Language may also legitimately state the tautologies of logic and mathematics. Any attempt to use language to state ethical and metaphysical doctrines will result in non-sense, pseudo-propositions. He distinguished between "saying" and "showing." Much of philosophy, he thought, was an effort to say what can only be shown. By 1933 he repudiated this early philosophy and developed the revolutionary linguistic philosophy set forth most systematically in his posthumously published *Philosophical Investigations*

(1953). He emphasized a pluralistic approach to language. Each distinct way of using language he called a "language game." He regarded philosophical problems as arising out of philosophers misunderstanding the proper functioning of our conceptual tools. The key to the meaning of a term is in its use.

Woodbridge, Frederick J[ames] E[ugene] (1867–1940), American naturalistic philosopher and Johnsonian Professor of Philosophy at Columbia University, 1904–39, maintained that metaphysics is a descriptive analysis of the fundamental characters presented in experience and not a normative study of *a priori* principles. He was allied with the New Realists. Yet he called the objective order or logical structure in nature which thought discovers the "realm of mind" in order to distinguish it from the subsistent essences of the New Realists. He stressed the importance of time as against eternity in philosophy and developed a pluralistic philosophy of history. His influence on Dewey's philosophical development is seen in Dewey's *Experience and Nature* (1925). Two important books of Woodbridge's are *Nature and Mind* (1937) and *An Essay on Nature* (1940).

Woodger, J[oseph] H[enry] (1894–   ), English biologist, Emeritus Professor of Biology at the University of London, is noted for his efforts to formalize biology on a mathematical basis. His works include *Axiomatic Method in Biology* (1937) and *Biology and Language* (1952).

Wright, Chauncey (1830–1875), American philosopher, was a great exponent of Darwinian evolution and one of the founders of pragmatism. He developed an original and important philosophy of science and influenced in many ways James, Peirce, and Justice Oliver Wendell Holmes. Wright was a strong advocate of positivism and empiricism and an opponent of metaphysics and teleology. In his *Philosophical Discussions* (published posthumously in 1877), he worked out a theory of cosmic weather, of functional psychology, and of the role of signs in experience.

Youmans, Edward Livingston (1821–1887) is best known for his efforts to bring science to the general public. He edited *Popular Science Monthly* for many years and brought the *International Scientific Series* into being. He was influential in arousing interest in Darwin's and Spencer's theories of evolution.

723

References to the joint publications of Dewey and Bentley are listed only under Dewey. General ideas of an author are listed under his name. Variations in grammatical and semantic forms of entries are not listed separately. (*Prepared by Jules Altman*)

726

Brouwer, L. E., 33
Brunswik, Egon, 148, 549
Bryan, William, 14

Caird, Edward, 6
Caird, John, 6
Cameron, Norman, 593
Cannon, Walter, 147, 431
Cantor, Georg, 72
Cantril, Hadley, 44, 611, 619, 626, 627, 641, 642
Carnap, Rudolf, 3, 64, 69, 71, 73, 86, 183, 257, 266–267, 268, 281, 283, 285, 287, 288, 290, 291, 292, 294, 295, 311, 312, 316, 325, 330, 333, 334, 336, 337, 342, 343, 344, 347, 380, 469, 470, 473, 482, 485, 548, 560, 562, 563, 596
Carlyle, Thomas, 600
case, 427
Cassirer, Ernst, 108–109, 119, 139, 340, 342
causation, 249, 639, 640
certainty, 446, 447, 496, 545, 596
characterization, 311–312, 379, 392, 458, 467, 468, 491, 513, 533
characters, 429, 469, 470, 477, 486, 499, 502, 505
Chevigny, Hector, 319
Chipman, Alice, 7, 10
Chipman, Susan, 29
Church, Alonzo, 17, 34, 559, 590, 591, 596
Churchman, Charles, 492, 546, 547, 552–553
circularity, 205, 353, 391, 422, 434, 440, 455, 521
Clark, John, 24, 26
class, 426, 427, 464
Cleveland, Grover, 640
cognitive, 256, 318–319, 322, 324, 325, 331, 381, 383, 385, 387, 515, 622
Cohen, Morris, 3, 12, 18, 29, 36, 42, 64, 267, 286, 289, 290, 292, 293, 396, 433, 439, 440, 443, 444, 453
common sense, 228, 234, 341, 391, 400, 609, 624, 638, 651
Commons, John, 16, 67, 68
communication, 89, 137, 139, 250, 302, 318, 321, 325, 327, 335, 598, 663
communism, 14–15, 603
compatibility, 440, 443

Comte, August, 5, 20, 232, 461
concept, 61, 62, 63, 65, 75, 80, 81, 202, 216, 344, 399, 401, 405, 406, 407, 410, 412, 416, 430, 432, 434, 435, 436, 437, 438, 442, 487, 488, 490, 491, 493, 494, 495, 496, 504, 505, 507, 557, 580
concrete, 401
Condon, Edward, 626, 633
connection, 145, 158, 159, 162, 164, 166, 167, 173–174, 175, 277, 308, 360, 442, 454, 465, 497, 509, 539, 560, 561, 581
connectives, 339, 343, 472, 484, 562, 563, 564, 565
consciousness, 245, 247, 577, 622, 626
consequences, see means-ends
consistency, 99, 100, 334, 440
content, 577
context, 93, 144, 219, 321, 322, 577, 606
continuity, 162
control, 118
convention, 394
correspondence, 476
cosmos, 157, 167, 216, 261, 275, 350, 351
Cowan, Thomas, 546, 547
Croce, Benedetto, 342
cross-section, 213, 232, 384, 385, 411, 412
cue, 502, 533, 537, 541, 549, 571
Cunningham, Gustavus, 227, 230
Curry, Haskell, 41

Darwin, Charles, 5, 7, 8, 41, 82, 113, 210, 323, 341, 495, 507, 554, 612
data, 160
datum, 113, 115, 116, 120, 124, 126, 137, 140, 147, 155, 156, 165, 190, 218, 219, 246, 277, 315, 320, 348, 375, 452
Davis, Harold, 547
Dean, Iris, 492
Debs, Eugene, 28
Dedekind, Richard, 72
definition, 141, 172, 180, 304, 311–312, 323, 328, 354, 390, 392, 395, 416, 418, 426, 427, 460, 462, 463, 466, 490, 550, 561, 562, 563, 569, 570, 571, 572, 584, 586, 587, 609, 643
dictionary, 390, 392, 395, 417, 559
degeneration, 233
delimitation, 390, 391, 392, 509

727

728

Dorner, Alexander, 585
double-barreled, 250, 253–254, 265, 366, 461, 533
doubt, 482
dualism, 6, 215, 595, 654
Dubislav, Walter, 571, 572
Dubs, Homer, 561
Ducasse, Curt, 254, 257
durational, *see* space-time
Durkheim, Emile, 27

economics, 53
Eddy, Lyle, 595, 613
Edison, Thomas, 94
Edman, Irwin, 11
education, 8, 9, 10, 13, 14, 127, 579
Einstein, Albert, 32, 94, 191, 228, 305, 306, 307, 309, 316, 345, 354, 384, 411, 452, 497, 519, 525, 530, 610, 614, 615, 630, 631, 632, 634, 637, 642
Ely, Richard, 24
emergence, 403, 404, 407, 426, 427
Emerson, Ralph, 612
empirical, *see* observation
ends, *see* means-ends
energy, 124, 126, 127
enjoyment, *see* having-knowing
entail, 425, 428
entity, 314, 334, 335, 366, 465, 513, 545, 642
environment, 77, 78, 86, 122, 138, 189, 207, 216, 219, 244, 431, 459, 516, 592, 657
epistemology, 234, 238, 243, 246, 251, 278, 296, 303, 314, 347, 350, 354, 364, 366, 419, 440, 507, 508, 516, 528, 544, 609, 634, 638, 650
equivalence, 555, 556, 563, 564
error, 69, 71, 72, 318, 428
ethics, 12, 13, 497, 598, 629, 652, 653, 654
Euclid, 41, 166, 170, 390, 465
event, 75, 139, 141, 143, 155, 159, 160, 164, 171, 174, 176, 178, 180, 182, 186–187, 200, 201, 202, 204, 206, 210, 214, 223, 231, 297, 351–352, 380, 381
evidence, 169, 173
evolution, 21, 121
exact, 554

excitation-reaction, 148, 149, 152, 153, 156, 193, 226, 298, 303, 305–306, 471, 500, 503, 531
existence, 19, 64, 174, 187–188, 191, 205, 223, 231, 314, 326, 327, 352, 374, 393, 442, 464, 477, 484, 521, 524
existent, 323, 327, 331
experience, 21–22, 56–57, 101, 121, 123, 124, 126, 127, 128, 138, 142–143, 145, 147, 148, 155, 156, 162, 179, 189, 214–215, 218, 222, 246, 248, 252–254, 315, 316, 323, 331, 348, 387, 404, 411, 424, 434, 454, 579, 591, 643
experiment, 481, 631
expression, 323, 325, 332, 341
extensive-intensive, 147

fact, 137, 138, 140, 149, 155, 159, 160, 161, 164, 165, 168, 169, 171, 173, 177–178, 180, 191, 195, 200, 203, 204, 205–206, 208, 210, 223, 238–239, 255, 274, 277, 292, 296–298, 313, 316, 323, 326, 327, 328, 333, 338, 348–349, 351, 358, 365–368, 369, 374, 402, 459, 605
factant, 326, 328
Faraday, Michael, 217
Farber, Marvin, 556, 628
Farrell, James, 42
feelings, 29, 105, 107–108, 111, 120, 179, 219, 241, 337, 341, 344, 383
Feigl, Herbert, 489, 490, 491, 615
Fen, Sing, 590
Feuer, Lewis, 601
field, 141, 188, 319, 345, 431, 668
firm, 471, 509, 510, 514, 518, 567, 609
focusing, 144, 145, 157, 191, 411
Ford, Franklin, 9
Frank, Jerome, 16
Frank, Philipp, 528
Frege, Gottlob, 439
Freud, Sigmund, 41
Fries, Horace, 626, 633, 635, 641
Fries, Jakob, 571
functional, 147, 148, 169, 176, 264, 286, 303, 317, 326, 462, 464, 467, 604, 652

Galileo, 301, 305, 306, 310, 385, 400, 497, 524, 528
Gauss, Karl, 41

733

Nagel, Ernest, 3, 11, 39, 64, 68, 88, 89, 106, 198, 149, 257, 267, 268, 286, 287, 289, 290, 292, 293, 316, 317, 318, 334, 396, 403, 425, 493, 495, 534, 537, 545, 615

name-naming, 149, 158, 159, 160, 161, 167, 169, 182, 183, 184, 185, 187, 191–192, 195, 202, 203, 221, 247, 248, 260, 262, 272, 279, 311–312, 313, 320, 332, 339, 346–358, 360, 362–368, 377, 378, 380, 400, 416, 417, 420, 457, 458, 459, 463, 464, 467, 484, 502, 507, 508, 514, 518, 519, 520, 530, 538, 540, 589, 597, 606, 609, 624, 664, 668

Nathanson, Jerome, 82, 83

naturalism, 79, 87, 125, 158, 240, 269, 314, 346, 358, 375

nature, 20, 21, 244–245, 434

Needham, Joseph, 426

negatives, 508

Neumann, John von, 40–41

Neurath, Otto, 338, 339, 341, 342, 344, 503, 528

neutral, see datum

Newton, Isaac, 32, 41, 80, 86, 94, 102, 103, 176, 204, 217, 218, 222, 223, 235, 298, 300, 301, 302, 305–306, 307, 308, 309, 310, 320, 345, 354, 384, 392, 400, 401, 411, 422, 460, 478, 497, 519, 524, 527, 528, 530, 532, 535, 536, 546, 579

Nicholas of Cusa, 413

normative, see ethics

nouns, 101–102, 141, 145, 158, 520, 598

number, 611

object, 19, 92–93, 94–95, 97, 109, 116, 141, 176, 212, 232, 287, 288, 296, 297, 298, 313, 314, 320, 361, 362, 366, 368, 379, 394, 402, 471, 504, 522, 545, 577, 585, 599, 604, 605, 609, 620, 622, 624

objective, 456

observation, 56, 58, 59, 65, 68, 76, 90, 190, 194, 195, 213, 222, 252, 259, 266, 271, 278, 333, 346–348, 349–351, 359, 362, 364–365, 366–367, 375, 404, 408–409, 415, 418, 426, 441, 442, 454, 551, 608, 626, 628, 639, 658, 665

occasion, 522

occur, 427

Ogden, Charles, 52, 152, 324

Oppenheim, Paul, 632

operating-using, 665, 666

operations, 151, 166, 174, 304, 329, 374, 382, 433, 472, 494, 526, 562, 567, 581, 623

organic-organism, 86, 116, 122, 150, 155, 156, 163, 189, 207, 304, 376, 459, 465, 516, 531, 543, 592, 657, 663

organization, 330, 341, 426, 431, 465

pain, 84, 107, 111, 337, 341, 343

Parker, Francis, 10

Patten, Simon, 24, 26–27, 31

Pauli, Wolfgang, 614

Pavlov, Ivan, 61, 62, 65, 67, 109, 168, 191, 353, 549

Peirce, Charles, 6, 10, 16, 20, 21, 24, 46, 71, 72–73, 76, 77, 82, 91, 96, 100, 111, 113, 115, 121, 123, 131, 184, 212, 247, 252–253, 267, 280, 283, 285, 286, 287, 289–290, 320, 322, 324, 348, 377, 387, 424, 428, 439, 443, 457, 481, 488, 494, 495, 496, 506, 507, 508, 520, 537, 543, 566, 586, 591, 597, 609, 628

Pepper, Stephen, 550, 562

perception, manipulative-perceptual, 55, 57, 96, 104, 106, 116–117, 128, 191, 192, 194, 222, 329, 333–334, 352, 361, 408, 425, 429, 430, 435, 441, 465, 476, 477, 484, 503, 504, 509, 519, 520, 551, 566, 578, 628, 665, 667

Perry, Ralph, 12, 17, 130

person, 80, 81, 84, 92, 94, 111, 112, 113–114, 399

phase, 218, 224, 332

phenomenon, 314, 327

philosophy-philosophers, 345, 386, 419, 430, 440, 441, 451, 473, 482, 486, 508, 520, 591, 598, 606, 629, 636, 654, 658, 666

physics, 20, 21, 74, 75, 151, 176, 217, 247, 296, 301, 305–306, 307–308, 355, 405, 415, 419, 543, 605

physiological, 148, 151, 158, 163, 176, 204, 209, 215, 301, 305, 337, 355, 405, 428, 500, 516, 536, 607

Pillsbury, Walter, 525

placing, see localization

Plato, 4, 394, 606

367, 368, 422, 428, 496, 537, 587, 597, 598, 637
Tufts, James, 4, 7, 10, 12, 28
Tugwell, Rexford, 15

universals, 472, 473, 474, 478, 482, 484, 487, 499, 501, 502, 562, 627
unnamed, 248, 250, 255–256
use, *see* application

validity, 537, 598
Valtin, Jan, 85
Veblen, Oswald, 561
Veblen, Thorstein, 10
verbs, 158, 178, 609
Vico, Giambattista, 9
Vierkandt, Alfred, 32
view, 606
Vigotsky, Lev, 340
vision, *see* image
Vivas, Eliseo, 291

Wagner, Adolf, 25
Ward, Lester, 27
warranted assertion, 327, 338, 350, 358, 421, 450, 491, 520, 620
Watson, John, 35, 72, 153, 220, 389, 485
Weinstock, Solomon, 626, 634
Weismann, August, 308
Weiss, Albert, 485
Weiss, Paul, 39, 68, 98, 488

Wells, Harry, 15
Wertheimer, Max, 524, 525
Weyl, Hermann, 41
what, 315, 335, 349, 365, 651, 652, 653, 661
White, Morton, 13n, 46, 328, 439
Whitehead, Alfred, 4–5, 13, 20, 33, 72, 97–98, 100–101, 102, 103, 340, 341–342, 344, 439, 466, 518, 525, 633
Whitman, Walt, 29, 85
why, 653
Wiener, Philip, 612
Wiese, Leopold von, 32
Wilson, Woodrow, 640
Wittgenstein, Ludwig, 34, 46, 465, 503, 534
Woodbridge, Frederick, 5, 11, 62, 65, 66–67, 89
Woodger, Joseph, 426
word, 62, 63, 154, 161, 211, 213, 221, 226, 229, 285, 332, 335, 344, 347, 364, 394, 463, 521, 557, 601, 602
word-clusters, 327, 414
word-meaning, 109, 117, 184, 188, 203, 275, 278, 326, 432, 436, 602
Wright, Chauncey, 82, 495

Yarros, Victor, 29
Youmans, Edward, 612
Young, Ella, 10